"WORTHY PARTNER"

Pair of Miniatures. First Subject: Martha Dandridge Custis Washington, age 65. Artist: James Peale, 1796. Medium: Watercolor on ivory. *Credit*: Mount Vernon Ladies' Association. Second Subject: George Washington, age 44. Artist: Charles Willson Peale, 1776. Medium: Watercolor on ivory. *Credit*: Mount Vernon Ladies' Association.

"WORTHY PARTNER"

The Papers of Martha Washington

Compiled by
Joseph E. Fields

with an introduction by
Ellen McCallister Clark

Contributions in American History, Number 155
Jon L. Wakelyn, Series Editor

Greenwood Press
Westport, Connecticut • London

Library of Congress Cataloging-in-Publication Data

Worthy partner : the papers of Martha Washington / compiled by Joseph
   E. Fields ; with an introduction by Ellen McCallister Clark.
      p.   cm. — (Contributions in American history, ISSN 0084-9219
; no. 155)
   Includes bibliographical references and index.
   ISBN 0-313-28024-X (alk. paper)
   1. Washington, Martha, 1731-1802—Manuscripts. 2. Washington,
George, 1732-1799. 3. Presidents' spouses—United States—
Manuscripts.   I. Fields, Joseph E. II. Series.
E312.19.W34W67 1994
973.4'1'092—dc20   93-35842
  [B]

British Library Cataloguing in Publication Data is available.

Library of Congress Catalog Card Number: 93-35842
ISBN: 0-313-28024-X
ISSN: 0084-9219

First published in 1994

Greenwood Press, 88 Post Road West, Westport, CT 06881
An imprint of Greenwood Publishing Group, Inc.

Printed in the United States of America

The paper used in this book complies with the
Permanent Paper Standard issued by the National
Information Standards Organization (Z39.48-1984).

10 9 8 7 6 5 4 3 2 1

To Irma, The Best Loved,
Without whose encouragement,
unselfish devotion, help,
and perseverence, this work
would never have been possible.

Contents

Editorial Method

Transcription of the letters and documents has been retained as closely as possible to the original. Capitalization, punctuation, spelling and paragraphing have been preserved as they appear in the original text. Mrs. Washington's habit of using dashes for punctuation persisted throughout her life; they have been retained. Misspellings of places and proper names have been preserved as written. Should any misinterpretation or doubt be encountered, an explanatory note is provided. All superscripts have been lowered. Round brackets have been used to denote missing, mutilated, and illegible words. Datelines have been placed as they appear in the original. When dates have been omitted, an approximation, as close as possible, has been made and placed in brackets at the head of the document. In several instances obviously incorrect dates have been used. They have been noted and the correct date inserted. Document symbols are those recently recommended by the Manuscript Society's *Criteria for Describing Manuscripts and Documents* (1990).

In preparing the manuscript, the editor was presented with the same question as that faced by Washington's great biographer, Douglas Southall Freeman: By what name shall Mrs. Washington be called? The solution was somewhat easier than Freeman's. Before her first marriage she is referred to as Martha Dandridge. Following her first marriage she is referred to as Martha Dandridge Custis; in the footnotes of this period it is abbreviated to MDC. Following her marriage to George Washington, she is called Martha Washington or Mrs. Washington, and in the footnotes as MW. George Washington is referred to as Colonel, General, President, or former President, as best fits the time. In footnotes he is designated GW.

Symbols Designating Documents

AD   Autograph Document

ADS   Autograph Document
        Signed

ADf   Autograph Draft

ADfS   Autograph Signed

AL   Autograph Letter

ALS   Autograph Letter
        Signed

D   Document

DS   Document Signed

Df   Draft

Dfs   Draft Signed

L   Letter

LS   Letter Signed

LB   Letter Book Copy

[S]   Signature clipped

Repository Symbols

AUB-R	Reynolds Historical Library, University of Alabama, Birmingham, Ala.
CBhM	Joseph Maddalena, Profiles in History, Beverly Hills, Cal.
CPcO	Dr. Walter Ostromecki, Panorama City, Cal.
C-S	California State Library, Sutro Branch, San Francisco, Cal.
CSmH	Henry E. Huntington Library, San Marino, Cal.
CtY	Yale University, New Haven, Conn.
DLC	Library of Congress
DLC:GW	George Washington Papers, Library of Congress
DTP	Tudor Place Foundation, Washington, D.C.
ICHi	Chicago Historical Society, Chicago, Ill.
MB	Boston Public Library, Boston, Mass.
MdAN	United States Naval Academy, Annapolis, Md.
MeHi	Maine Historical Society, Portland, Me.
MHH	Houghton Library, Harvard University, Cambridge, Mass.
MHi	Massachusetts Historical Society, Boston, Mass.
MiU-C	Clements Library, University of Michigan, Ann Arbor, Mich.
MWi:W-C	Chapin Library, Williams College, Williamstown, Mass.
NhD	Dartmouth College Library, Hanover, N.H.
NjMoNP	Washington Headquarters Library, Department of the Interior, Morristown, N.J.
NN	New York Public Library, New York, N.Y.
NNHi	New York Historical Society, New York, N.Y.
NNPM	Pierpont Morgan Library, New York, N.Y.
PHC	Haverford College, Haverford, Pa.
PHi	Historical Society of Pennsylvania, Philadelphia, Pa.
PPamP	American Philosophical Society, Philadelphia, Pa.
PPRF	Rosenbach Museum and Library, Philadelphia, Pa.
RHi	Rhode Island Historical Society, Providence, R.I.
ViHi	Virginia Historical Society, Richmond, Va.
ViMtV	Mount Vernon Ladies' Association of the Union, Mount Vernon, Va.
ViMtV-W	Woodlawn Plantation, Mount Vernon, Va.
ViWF	J. E. Fields, Williamsburg, Va.

Introduction

The Life of Martha Washington

In many ways, Martha Washington was the ideal woman for the new American republic. She was not born of the aristocracy, but she gained the admiration and respect of all classes of people. She was devoted to family and home, but she readily made personal sacrifices to join her husband in his public duties. During the Revolution, which she referred to as "our cause," she gave up the comforts of Mount Vernon to travel every year to Washington's winter quarters. During the presidency, she was called both dignified and democratic as she forged the role of the president's wife that would be followed for generations to come. She neither sought nor relished her public positions, but carried out the duties that were thrust upon her with enormous consideration and care. Her simple appearance bespoke quality rather than ostentation, and after the Revolution she set a patriotic example by wearing American-made clothes. She was aware that her presence helped "humanize" her often preoccupied husband. Abigail Adams, who was never too free with compliments, wrote in a letter, "Mrs. Washington is one of those unassuming characters which create Love and Esteem," and admitted when in her presence, she found herself "much more deeply impressed than I ever did before their Majesties of Britain."[1] Years later a former Mount Vernon slave is quoted as having said, "The General was only a man, but Mrs. Washington was 'perfect.' "[2]

A family Bible records the birth of Martha Washington on June 2, 1731 between 12 and one o'clock. She was the oldest child of John Dandridge, a first-generation Virginian, and Frances Jones, of New Kent County, Virginia. The Dandridges were a respectable, but by no means wealthy family, who belonged to what Washington biographer Douglas Southall Freeman called the "second tier" of planters in Virginia society of the time. Little is known of Martha's childhood, but it is fair to assume that her education was typical of her peers - receiving an education emphasizing domestic arts, religion, music and dancing. This was knowledge imparted by the women in her household and by the itinerant tutors who traveled from plantation to plantation.

By all accounts, Martha Dandridge grew up to be a sensible and pretty young woman, and her contemporaries often remarked on her "amiable nature." Still, it must have seemed her very good fortune when at the age of eighteen, she married Daniel Parke Custis, a man twenty years her senior, who belonged to two of the wealthiest and most notorious families in the Virginia colony. They settled on his estate, White House, on the Pamunkey River. It was there that their four children were born. The first two, Daniel Parke Custis and Frances Parke Custis, died in early childhood. Their two surviving children were John Parke Custis (b. 1754) and Martha Parke Custis (b. 1756), called Jacky and Patsy.

After seven years of marriage, Daniel Parke Custis, at the age of forty-five, died suddenly, probably of a heart attack. Leaving no will, his vast estate which included almost 17,500 acres of land, was divided among his 26-year-old widow and their two young children. The earliest known letters of Martha Custis date from this period, written to the London merchants with whom her husband did business. "I take the Oppertunity to inform you of the great misfortune I have met with in the loss of my late Husband," she wrote to John Hanbury and Company on August 20, 1757. "As I now have the Administration of his Estate and the management of his Affairs of all sorts(,) I shall be glad to continue the correspondence which Mr. Custis carried on with you..."[3] On the same day she also wrote to Robert Cary and Company: "I shall yearly ship a considerable part of Tobacco I make to you which I shall take care to have as good as possible and hope you will do your endeavour to get me a good price."[4]

But Mrs. Custis would not have to manage her affairs alone for long. Less than a year after her husband's death, she began a courtship with a tall young colonel named George Washington. There is no contemporary account of their first meeting, though it is likely that they would have at least known of each other in the close society of Williamsburg. Martha's grandson, George Washington Parke Custis, in his memoirs, gives a wonderfully romantic account of love at first sight when the two were introduced at the home of mutual friends, the Chamberlaynes, in early 1758.[5]

Whatever the circumstances, Washington's account ledger shows two visits to Mrs. Custis in March of 1758, when he tipped her servants.[6] The exact date of their engagement is not known, but there may be a clue in Washington's April order to his London factor, "By the first Ship bound to any part of Virginia...as much of the best superfine Blue Cotton Velvet as will make a coat, waistcoat and breeches for a tall man..."[7] It was probably at about the same time that Mrs. Custis also sent out her order to have her favorite nightgown dyed a fashionable color, and to have a seamstress make "one Genteel suite of cloths for myself to be grave but not Extravagant (and) not to be mourning."[8]

George Washington married Martha Dandridge Custis on Twelfth Night, January 6, 1759, at White House. It was not until April of that year, however, that Washington brought his bride and young family to his estate up on the Potomac River to Mount Vernon. Washington had become proprietor of this family property in 1754, when at the age of 22, he first leased about 2,500 acres, including a simple story-and-a-half cottage from the widow of his elder half brother, Lawrence Washington. Even before he gained full ownership of the estate in 1761, he began the expansion and improvement of the house. By the time Martha first saw her new home, the original house had already been raised to two and a half stories, although it still lacked the north and south wings of the mansion house that exists today. The first floor had been much embellished with fine paneling and other architectural details, and the exterior siding had been rusticated to give the appearance of stone. Although at this point, Mount Vernon was still a far cry from the elegance the former Mrs. Custis had known in New Kent County, she seems to have moved happily into the nucleus of what would evolve over the next thirty years to be one of the finest homes in America.

The first fifteen years of Washington's marriage has been called the golden years at Mount Vernon. In the year of his marriage, Washington wrote to an English friend, "I am now I believe fixd at this Seat with an agreeable Consort for life and hope to find more happiness in retirement than I ever experienced amid a wide and bustling World."[9] He surely had no idea how impermanent this "retirement" would be, but he devoted himself to his family and farm. Mrs. Washington became an expert at her role as mistress of a busy and expanding plantation. Though she and Washington never had any children of their own, he accepted her children fully and affectionately.

Her domain was the mansion house, the kitchen, the spinning house, and the wash house, and those she seems to have run with care and efficiency. One of her specialties was the hanging and curing of meat in the smoke house. "Virginia Ladies value themselves on the goodness of their bacon," Washington once explained to Lafayette.[10] Lund Washington, who managed Mount Vernon during the Revolution, noted that "Mrs. Washington's charitable disposition increases in the same proportion as her meat house."[11] As time went on there were increasing numbers of relatives and guests at Mount Vernon, all to be ultimately looked after by Martha Washington herself.

Her immediate family took her greatest attention, however, and she can only be described as a doting mother. She worried over her children's many illnesses and was miserable at any separation. In 1762, she wrote to her sister of a trip she took to Westmoreland County: "I carried my little Pat with me and left Jacky at home for a trial to see how well I could stay without him though we were gon but (a) fortnight I was impatient to get home. If I at any time heard the doggs barke or a noise out, I thought thair was a person sent for me. I often fancied he was sick or some accident happened to him so that I think it is impossible for me to leave him..."[12]

Patsy Custis was, like her mother, dark-haired and pretty, and well accomplished in music and needlework, but her health was always frail, and from the age of about six she suffered from epileptic seizures that came with greater and greater frequency as she grew into adolescence. She was treated by many doctors, was made to wear an iron ring, and was taken to Berkeley Springs in search of a cure, but her ailment was beyond the help of 18th century medicine. In June of 1773, when she was seventeen, she was seized with one of her fits and died at Mount Vernon,-- a blow, that in Washington's words, "reduced my poor wife to the lowest ebb of misery."[13]

Mrs. Washington's sadness was deepened by the fact that her only other living child was away at King's College at the time of Patsy's death. Jacky Custis was always healthy and good natured, if somewhat unenergetic, probably a victim of handsome inheritance and his mother's indulgences. But even when consumed with Patsy's problems, Mrs. Washington worried over her son as well. Not only could she not bear their separation, but when Jacky was to be innoculated for smallpox, it was arranged for his mother to be spared of all knowledge of it until the deed was performed and he had fully recovered. Jacky was never much of a scholar, though Washington sought the best education for him. He was much more interested in gentlemanly recreations and what Washington called "Dress and equipage."[14] The Washingtons must have been both offended and embarrassed when Jacky's tutor, the Rev. Jonathan Boucher, wrote to them, "I must confess to you that I never in my Life know a Youth so exceedingly Indolent or so surprizingly voluptuous; one wd suppose Nature had intended him for some Asiatic Prince."[15] But Jacky loved the easy life, and was a good son and a great comfort to his mother. A few months after his sister's death, he left college to return home. In the spring of 1774, he married Eleanor Calvert of Maryland, and finally settled down at Abingdon, his estate up the river from Mount Vernon.

Family life at Mount Vernon was soon to be drastically altered. In May of 1775, George Washington rode away from Mount Vernon to attend the Second Continental Congress in Philadelphia. The next month,

Congress appointed him Commander-in-Chief of the Continental Army, to lead the colonies in the fight for their rights. Only three letters of George to Martha survive, but it seems more than coincidental that two were written on this momentous occasion that changed their lives, as well as the lives of others, forever. On June 18, 1775, he wrote to break the news of his appointment, in words he could only express to his wife: "It has been determined in Congress that the whole Army raised for the defence of the American Cause shall be put in my care, and that it is necessary for me to proceed immediately to Boston to take upon me the command of it. You may believe me my dear Patsy, when I assure you, in the most solemn manner, that, so far from seeking this appointment I have used every endeavour in my power to avoid it, not only from my unwillingness to part with you and the Family, but from the consciousness of its being a trust too great for my Capacity and that I should enjoy more happiness and felicity in one month with you, at home, than I have the most distant prospect of reaping abroad, if my stay were to be Seven times Seven years."[16]

Martha Washington's devotion and behind-the-scenes support of her husband in all of his pursuits characterized her entire married life; however, it is during this period that she emerges as a selfless, courageous and patriotic American. Beginning in December of 1775, she traveled every year to winter quarters with her husband. How far away the peace and tranquility of Mount Vernon must have seemed! That first winter in Cambridge, she wrote to a friend: "I have waited some days to collect something to tell, but allass thare nothing but what you will find in the papers -- every person seems to be chearfull and happy hear -- some days we have a number of cannon and shells from Boston and Bunkers Hill, but it does not seem to surprise any one but me; I confess I shuder every time I hear the sound of a gun -- I just took a look at pore Boston & Charles town from Prospect Hill Charles town has only a few chimneys standing in it, there seems to be a number of very fine Buildings in Boston but god knows how long they will stand; they are pulling up all the wharfs for firewood -- to me that has never seen anything of war, the preparations are very terrible indeed, but I endeavor to keep my fears to myself as well as I can."[17]

Winter after winter, conditions became increasingly rough and Mrs. Washington became indispensable as a nurse and comfort to Washington and his men. A soldier, James Thacher, noted candidly in his diary: "Mrs Washington combines in an uncommon degree great dignity of manner with the most pleasing affability, but possesses no striking marks of beauty.."[18] But though surrounded by those who loved and needed her, she missed her real family terribly. In a letter to her son and daughter-in-law, written from Middlebrook in March 1778, she wonders if everyone has forgotten her and begs them to write, threatening in desperation, "if you do not write I will not write to you again."[19] Returning home each spring must have soothed her, for she never let her husband down.

Martha Washington impressed all who met her. An aide to Baron Steuben wrote: "She reminded me of the Roman matrons of whom I had read so much, I thought that she well deserved to be the companion and friend of the greatest man of the age."[20]

Washington refused a salary for his services of commander-in-chief, but applied to Congress for his expenses only. One of the treasures of the Mount Vernon collection is the document in which he carefully kept account of Mrs. Washington's traveling expenses to and from winter quarters, year after year. Listing round-trip expenses from Mount Vernon to Cambridge, New York, Morristown, Valley Forge, Philadelphia, Middlebrook, New Windsor, and Newburgh, the document provides a succinct chronology of the war as well as a testimonial to the devotion and fortitude of Martha Washington.

It was not until Christmas eve of 1783 that General Washington returned home, having resigned his commission in Annapolis. Together he and his wife set about the work of putting their home and farm back in order after eight years of war. Although Jacky Custis had never enlisted, he went along with his stepfather to see the action at Yorktown in 1781. It was there that he contracted camp fever and died, leaving his young widow with four small children. To ease her burden, the Washingtons took the two youngest, Eleanor Parke Custis and George Washington Parke Custis, into their home, and so a second generation, a girl and a boy, grew up at Mount Vernon.

For Mrs. Washington, the presence of Nelly, as Eleanor was called, in the household, undoubtedly filled the void that Patsy's death had left ten years before. From all accounts her doting grandmother now guided with a firmer hand, and Nelly grew up with a sophistication and confidence an earlier generation would never have known.

George Washington Parke Custis was called Washy, or Tub, as a child. The youngest and only grandson, his health and well being were always under careful scrutiny. He inherited some of his father's indolent and engaging manner and was something of a trial to his grandpapa, General Washington. Like Jacky, he knew how to keep his grandmother on his side.

Life at Mount Vernon in the mid-1780s was busy and happy for the Washingtons. George Washington was overseeing the finishing touches on his Mansion and the layout of his formal grounds. Once again there were always extra guests and relatives in the house. The family dining room routinely accommodated any number of visiting nephews and nieces, old acquaintances, well wishers and those whom Washington suspected of having come out of curiosity. Once he had a note that "unless someone pops in unexpectedly, Mrs. Washington and I will do what has not been (done) by us in nearly 20 years -- that is set down to dinner by ourselves."[21]

But their domestic contentment was interrupted once again. Although Washington treasured his life as a private citizen, he continued to maintain a keen interest in public affairs as the new nation tested its foundation. It was with some reluctance that Washington consented to preside over the Constitutional Convention that opened in Philadelphia in May of 1787. As the structure of the new federal government was hammered out in the debates, it became obvious that Washington was the only choice for its highest office. When formal notification of his election to the presidency arrived at Mount Vernon in April of 1789, Washington dutifully answered the call of his country and immediately embarked on his journey to New York. His inauguration took place on April 30, but it was not until a few weeks later that Mrs. Washington, Nelly and Wash left Mount Vernon to join him. A nephew, Robert Lewis, who accompanied the family on their journey, left a poignant account of Mrs. Washington's reluctant departure. His diary describes confusion and excitement at Mount Vernon, the children and servants in tears, and the packing of trunks and boxes as overwhelming. "After an early dinner and making all the necessary arrangements...it brought us to 3 o'clock in the afternoon when we left Mount Vernon," he wrote. "The servants of the house and a number of the field Negroes made their appearance to take leave of their mistress. Numbers of these wretches were most affected and my aunt equally so."[22]

Like her husband before her, Mrs. Washington was greeted with great fanfare at each of the stops as her party made its way northward. The President joined her in New Jersey to escort her on what can only be described as a triumphal entry into New York, centering the role of the president's wife as a national figure.

There was an interesting debate over what the wife of the president should be called in the new nation (the term, "first lady," would not gain currency for another century). While the pro-Federalist Gazette of the United States suggested "Marquise" or "Lady," Mrs. Washington remained "Mrs. Washington," setting the precedent for every president's wife thereafter.[23]

Among other precedents established by the Washingtons were their official weekly receptions. The President held a "levee" every Tuesday afternoon, a very formal occasion to which only men were invited. To complement this, Mrs. Washington hosted a Friday evening reception called a "drawing room," a kind of open house that included both politicians and men and women of prominent social standing. The first of these drawing rooms was held just two days after her arrival in New York and was described as being "thick" with people. The protocol of these occasions was carefully worked out to offer gracious hospitality that did not appear ostentatious. The President made a point of always being present and would appear without his hat or sword, as an indication of the informal nature of the affair. Mrs. Washington remained seated as she received her guests, while Washington freely mingled with the company. It was said that he spent most of his time talking with the ladies, claiming it was his only opportunity for this particular pleasure amidst his busy schedule. Refreshments included tea, coffee, and cakes, and on at least one occasion, ice cream and lemonade. The story is told that to close the party, Mrs. Washington would stand and announce: "The General always retires at nine, and I usually precede him."[24]

Despite their careful planning to make the entertainments both dignified and democratic, the Washingtons were denounced in the anti-Federalist press as creating the trappings of an American court. Already a reluctant public figure, Mrs. Washington was no doubt deeply hurt by these attacks, but she carried on with dignity. Rather than entering any political debate, she scrupulously honored all her state obligations and won scores of admirers.

In her private letters to family back home, Mrs. Washington revealed some of her true feelings. After less than a year in New York, she wrote to her niece, Fanny Bassett Washington, "I live a very dull life hear and know nothing that passes in the town -- I never goe to any publik place, indeed I think I am more like a state prisioner than anything else, there is certain bounds set for me which I must not depart from -- and as I can not doe as I like I am obstinate and stay at home a great deal."[25]

The accounts of her contemporaries present quite a different picture. Abigail Adams, the Vice President's wife, had written only a short time before: "I took the earliest opportunity...to go and pay my respects to Mrs. Washington... she received me with great ease and politness. She is plain in her dress, but that plainess is the best of every article. Her Hair is white, her Teeth beautiful, her person rather short than otherways..Her manners are modest and unassuming, dignified and femenine, not a tincture of ha'ture about her."[26]

In 1790, the seat of government was moved from New York to Philadelphia and Mrs. Washington had to oversee the move and readjustment of her family in a new city. She also quickly established herself in Philadelphia society, which remembered her earlier visits during the dark days of the Revolution when, to quote the Pennsylvania Packet, "She contributed to relieve the cares of our beloved chief, and to soothe the anxious moments of his military concern." But even with the attention of strangers and the kindness of friends, Mrs. Washington confided in a letter to Mercy Warren that she had grown too old for the "innocent gaieties of life" in New York and Philadelphia and "has long since placed all the prospects of my future worldly happiness in the still enjoyments of the fireside at Mount Vernon."[27]

In March of 1797, George Washington stepped down from public life for the third and final time. For the two-and-one-half years that remained to him, the Washingtons were able to enjoy a degree of tranquility and togetherness that they had so long desired.

When her husband died in their bed at Mount Vernon on December 14, 1799, Mrs. Washington is reported to have said, "Tis well, I have no more trials to pass through, I shall soon follow." Virginia law entitled her to only one third, but in his will Washington bequeathed her "the use and benefit" of his entire estate for the rest of her life.

Following an old custom, Mrs. Washington closed off the bedroom she had shared with her husband and moved to a small chamber on the third floor. Her grandchildren, Wash and Nelly remained in residence, along with Nelly's husband, Lawrence Lewis, and their infant daughter, Parke.

It is clear that Mrs. Washington would have preferred obscurity in her last years, but Mount Vernon had already become a mecca for Americans who came to pay tribute to the father of their country. With the help of her grandchildren, Mrs. Washington continued to receive visitors with the gracious hospitality that characterized her earlier years. Her loss had left its mark, however. Chief Justice Marshall, after a visit, wrote to his wife that Mrs. Washington "appears cheerful, but not to possess the sort of cheerfulness as formerly." Another visitor was the Rev. Manasseh Cutler of Massachusetts, who called on her in January of 1802. In his diary he wrote: "Mrs. Washington appears much older than when I saw her last in Philadelphia, but her countenance is very little wrinkled and remarkably fair for a person of her years. She conversed with great ease and familiarity and appeared as much rejoiced at receiving our visit as if we had been her nearest connection...We were all federalists, which evidently gave her particular pleasure. Her remarks were frequently pointed and sometimes very sarcastic on the new order of things and present administration ...she frequently spoke of the General with great affection, viewing herself as left alone, her life protracted, until she had become a stranger in the world. She repeatedly remarked the distinguished mercies heaven still bestowed upon her, for which she daily had cause for gratitude, but she longed for the time to follow her departed friend."[28]

Martha Washington died on May 22, 1802, at the age of 70 and was entombed beside her husband in the family vault at Mount Vernon. A line for her obituary in an Alexandria newspaper underscores the essential role she played in her life: "She was the worthy partner of the worthiest of men."[29]

Alexandria, Virginia   Ellen McCallister Clark

The Correspondence and Papers
of Martha Washington

Martha Washington has been the subject of several popular biographies.[30] While her husband's voluminous papers have been published in numerous editions,[31] her writings, scattered into private hands, archives, and repositories, have never been collected and published. Through the diligence of her grandson, George Washington Parke Custis, his daughter, Mrs. Robert E. Lee, and other members of the Lee family, many of her papers have survived the ravages of time. The largest portion of her papers are located at the Virginia Historical Society, and in the collections at Mount Vernon. Smaller collections exist at Washington and Lee University, the Library of Congress, the Etting Collection at The Pennsylvania Historical Society, and at the Henry E. Huntington Library. This edition has attempted to compile all the known Martha Washington papers from every possible source.

The bulk of Martha's correspondence relates to key periods in her life: her first widowhood, the Revolutionary War, Washington's presidency, and the period after Washington's death. No scrap of her handwriting is know to exist prior to the sudden death of her first husband, Daniel Parke Custis in August 1757. Almost immediately the twenty-six year old widow, as executrix of her husband's intestate estate, found it necessary to conduct the affairs of her huge inheritance. There were over 17,500 far flung acres, managers, overseers, tenants, indentured servants and slaves to manage. Fortunately she had a capable manager, Joseph Valentine, as well as several attorney friends in high places, such as John Robinson, Speaker of the House of Burgesses, and Robert Carter Nicholas, Treasurer of the Colony, who could be relied upon for advice. No sooner had Daniel Parke Custis been interred at Queens Creek Plantation, than she began corresponding with her English and Scottish factors. She shipped and sold her tobacco, ordered household and plantation supplies, and personal items for herself and her two small children. She promptly paid her personal debts as well as those of her deceased husband, loaned out large sums of money at interest and collected her just debts. There was little time for withdrawal to her room for prolonged mourning. She immediately became deeply involved in the commercial affairs and legal entanglements of the Parkes and Custises, just as Daniel had been. Certainly there were many other women who had been thrust into similar circumstances, but few whose affairs have been so well documented.

Almost immediately following her marriage to George Washington, letters and documents in Mrs. Washington's handwriting, concerning estate affairs, cease. From 1759 until 1774, the first fifteen years of her second marriage, her correspondence consists of relatively small numbers of commercial letters, and short letters to relatives, friends, and neighbors. Twenty-two have survived from this period. Few incoming letters exist, perhaps indicating many others were not preserved.

Much of the existing correspondence composed during the Revolutionary era consists of letters to family, friends, and newly made wartime acquaintances. They are especially revealing for their references to military affairs, experiences at the various encampments, as well as for their personal and family affairs. Again there are few incoming letters that have been preserved. Of thirty-three letters from this period, only eleven incoming letters are known. During the years from 1784 until 1789, the interval between retirement to Mount Vernon after the war, and the onset of the presidential years, nine letters have been found, only one of which was an incoming letter.

The largest portion of Mrs. Washington's correspondence was produced during the presidential years, 1789-1797. Her most frequent correspondent was her niece, Francis Bassett Washington, usually called Fanny. She was the beautiful and demure young daughter of Martha's sister, Anna Maria Dandridge Bassett and her husband, Burwell Bassett, of "Eltham," New Kent County. Fanny's mother had died suddenly in 1777. In 1784, at the age of fifteen, she came to Mount Vernon to make her home. At approximately the same time, Major George Augustine Washington, the General's twenty-one year old nephew came to Mount Vernon to assume the management of his uncle's farms. During the war he had served with distinction as an aide to General Lafayette. What could be more natural than that the young couple, members of the same household, would fall in love? Shortly after their marriage, George Augustine developed "the family disease," tuberculosis. After a prolonged, debilitating and tragic illness, he died in April 1793, leaving Fanny and three children.[32]

During the presidential years, Fanny Washington remained at Mount Vernon caring for her three small children, nursing her desperately ill husband, maintaining the mansion house in respectable order, acting as hostess, preparing the house for company at short notice, and overseeing the household slaves. Fanny and her aunt exchanged letters on an average of every two weeks. Approximately forty letters from Mrs. Washington to Fanny Washington are known, although there is documentary evidence that more were written and received. Unfortunately, they have not survived or have not become evident. Of Fanny's replies to Mrs. Washington, only a few partial drafts are known, written on the verso of letters from her aunt.

After the death of her husband, Fanny fell in love with another Mount Vernon non-resident, Tobias Lear, the President's secretary and himself a recent widower. They married in August, 1795. Unfortunately, the marriage was a brief one. Fanny, already ill at the time of her marriage, died of tuberculosis in March, 1796.[33] Thus the long and revealing correspondence between the two women, that told so much of the life at Mount Vernon, New York, and Philadelphia came to an end.

Following Fanny Washington Lear's death, a closer relationship sprang up between Mrs. Washington and another niece, Frances Henley, daughter of Mrs. Washington's youngest sister, Elizabeth Dandridge Henley. This second Fanny, although she became a frequent visitor at Mount Vernon and spent several months there, never took the place of Fanny Washington in the affections of the Washingtons. Fanny Henley also became enamored with Lear, as had her cousin before her. They were married in June, 1803.[34]

Fanny Bassett Washington Lear's correspondence, together with Lear's correspondence with General Washington, was kept by Lear. Following his death by suicide in 1816,[35] his papers became the property of his widow, Fanny Henley Lear. In 1854, Mrs. Lear packed up her long dead husband's papers. A "trunk load" was given to George Washington Storer, a nephew of her husband, and "a lot more" to members of the Henley family. A portion of the letters from Martha Washington to Fanny Bassett Washington (Lear), that had passed to George Washington Storer, were inherited by his descendants, the Stephen Decatur family. Those given to the Henley family have apparently been dispersed over the years.

The 1790s also produced a revealing correspondence between Mrs. Washington and Elizabeth Wiling Powel. She was the wife of Samuel Powel, a prominent Philadelphian and former mayor of the city. Their friendship with the Washingtons dated from the Revolution and continued until the President's death. The correspondence casts considerable light on the personal, social and political life of the Washingtons during their years in Philadelphia and in the twilight years at Mount Vernon.[36]

What of the enigma posed by the almost complete lack of correspondence between the Washingtons themselves? We have documentary evidence of the many letters exchanged between them during their frequent periods of separation, for in his voluminous correspondence the General mentions sending and receiving letters from his wife. One episode serves to illustrate: at the time of his retirement to Mount Vernon in 1797, a portion of their excess furniture was put up for sale, including the President's desk. The purchaser was Mrs. Powel, who, after taking possession, discovered "a large bundle" of letters written by George Washington to Mrs. Washington. He inadvertently left them in one of the desk drawers. Mrs. Powel discreetly attempted to return them, unopened of course, by way of Tobias Lear. Lear refused to accept the responsibility, whereupon Mrs. Powel sent them directly to the former President, who had shortly arrived at Mount Vernon. Mrs. Powel, who enjoyed indulging in good natured humor and banter with him, referred to them as "love letters to a lady."[37] In a humorous reply he denied they were "enamoured love" but of "friendship," and that had they been of love they would have been consigned to the flames.[38]

Of the hundreds of letters they must have exchanged during a marriage of forty years, only four exist.[39] Two are of consequence. One of these, dated June 18, 1775, conveyed the news of his appointment as commander-in-chief of the Continental Army, expressed his concern for his absence from her and reassured his affection for her. The second letter, written five days later, informed her of his departure for the camp at Cambridge and again reaffirmed his affection for her. Following Mrs. Washington's death, the letters were discovered in her little writing desk by one of her granddaughters, Martha Parke Custis Peter.

What of the remainder? We can only conjecture a possible answer. Family tradition once held that Martha had been seen burning her personal correspondence following the death of the General - not an uncommon practice. Washington's close friend and kinsman, Lund Washington, had instructed his wife to destroy a portion of his correspondence. It is possible that the Washingtons had a similar understanding - that the survivor would destroy their correspondence. Of the many thousands of letters in his files, it would have been virtually impossible for Mrs. Washington to have had sufficient time or opportunity to separate out their correspondence. Nor would she have entrusted the task to anyone else, including family members. Thus it seems likely there might have been a prior separation, preparatory to destruction, and possibly even by the General himself. The "large bundle of letters" found by Mrs. Powel would seem to bear this out. Since very few, if any, letters passed between them following their return to Mount Vernon in March, 1797, it would have been an easy task for her to consign the "large bundle" to the flames of the library fireplace at a propitious moment.

It seems plausible Mrs. Washington may have also disposed of other portions of her correspondence as they were received: letters from Fanny, Abigail Adams, Mercy Otis Warren, Mary Stilson Lear, Elizabeth Schuyler Hamilton, her sisters, brothers, grandchildren and other Potomac neighbors and friends.

Early on it became evident a number of Martha Washington's letters were drafted by her husband and then copied by her before being dispatched. Letters to Mrs. Powel, Mercy Otis Warren, and certain others of a commercial nature are examples. This was not surprising, considering her dislike of letter writing, for she was self-conscious of her erratic rhetorical habits. Different styles of spelling and diction easily distinguish the letters drafted by George Washington from those drafted by Martha. Several examples were found in which the draft copy in the hand of her husband co-exists with the recipient's copy in the hand of Mrs. Washington.[40]

Following the death of George Washington, letters of condolence, together with copies of orations and eulogies poured into Mount Vernon. Etiquette required that each be acknowledged. Mrs. Washington, who never relished letter writing found herself inundated with an insurmountable task. Burdened with grief and loneliness she turned to her husband's military secretary and friend, Tobias Lear, still living at Mount Vernon. Letters and packages had arrived in such profusion that Congress, when informed of the situation, passed an act granting her franking privilege. Lear took on the task, drafting acknowledgments and sending them out in Mrs. Washington's name, under his own signature or in the third person. Being a capable secretary, he kept draft copies. Most of the condolence correspondence is in the archives at Mount Vernon and at Tudor Place Foundation in Washington, D.C. Thirty-nine additional condolence letters are in the possession of the Peter family in Washington D.C., the texts of which have not been released for publication. The condolence correspondence is mostly of a routine and stereotyped nature, its primary importance being indicative of the national outpouring of grief by the citizens over the loss of their beloved leader.

After surveying the correspondence, at what conclusions may we arrive? There was an amazing metamorphosis from the somewhat shy and retiring provincial girl of rural Virginia into a woman of prominence in the world. She began as the eighteen year old bride of one of the wealthiest men in the colony. Yet she became increasingly certain of herself during her widowhood and following her marriage to George Washington. There was a resiliency and an ability to adapt to circumstances beyond her control, viz: her removal from the scenes of her childhood and young married life, into a second marriage; taking up residence in a new locality and gradually taking on the duties of wife and hostess in a highly charged social and political world.

Several themes recur throughout the papers, illuminating more clearly the shadowy figure of the woman most often seen at George Washington's side. First, Martha continually expressed apprehension over the health of her family, friends and neighbors. Living in an era when death and disease struck often and suddenly, there is a small wonder her personality was conditioned by the succession of tragedies to which she was subjected. Within four years, death had claimed her first husband, two children, her father and a younger sister. By 1775 five brothers and a sister were dead, and within a ten day period, in 1785, death came to her mother and last surviving brother. Her attachment to her sister, Anna Maria Bassett, and her daughter Fanny, was a particularly close one. Their deaths had a profound effect. Likewise, she was prostrated with grief when her only surviving daughter, Martha Parke Custis died in 1773. Devastating grief again descended upon her when her last surviving son, John Parke Custis, died in October 1781, a week after her husband's victory at Yorktown. Her only surviving sister, Elizabeth, died twelve days prior to the death of George Washington. Thus she was the last of her father's large family. In addition she grieved over the plight of the soldiers and their families. Reflecting these personal tragedies, she often became over-solicitous about the welfare of her family. Concern about the slightest cold or fever pervaded her correspondence and on several occasions she expressed the opinion that never again did she expect to be a well woman. Her greatest apprehensions were for her husband's health and safety, especially during his two serious illnesses in the first eighteen months of his presidency, and her correspondence is replete with references to the state of his health.

Great concern was frequently expressed for those who were less fortunate or bereaved. During the war, she frequently opened her larder to those who found themselves short of food. In wartime she cared for the sick and wounded during several of the catastrophic winter encampments. Her letters are filled with expressions of love for children and young people, and her generosity toward them was manifested by frequent purchases of gifts. She seemed always to crave the company of children and young people about her and was happiest in their presence. Frequent invitations were extended to nieces, nephews and young friends to spend time at Mount Vernon and their departure was always regretted.

At times, Martha Washington appeared overmeticulous, exacting and autocratic. She was kind, but usually adamant with the younger members of her family, particularly where behavior, courtesy, and decorum were concerned. However, she invariably displayed an over-indulgence toward her son and his four orphaned children. She was aware of this weakness, but seemed powerless to control it. Her letters reveal a God-fearing woman of deep religious convictions, with a strong belief in the hereafter, and a faith that her God was always doing what was best. Her faith in her husband was likewise unwavering. Her letters shout out her love for privacy, for she shared with her husband the one great desire, that they spend their life together, "under their own vine and fig tree."[41]

Nearly as important as the correspondence with her husband was the close contact she maintained with her women friends and relatives. Fanny Bassett Washington, Anna Maria Bassett, and Elizabeth Wiling Powel all provided a network of friendship and intimacy for Martha at critical stages in her life. They not only shared with her the typical womanly concerns of the day - childrearing, housekeeping, and the vagaries of social life in the new republic - but also helped relieve the loneliness she felt.[42] For much of her life, Martha was isolated from those she loved the best: the absence of her husband during the Revolution; during the difficult years of the presidency; during her widowhood. The unfortunate consequence of her husband's success was to set Martha apart from the women around her. Her correspondence with previous acquaintances helped alleviate the burdens of her position.

In only one surviving letter does Martha complain of her lot as wife of the president of the United States. She called herself a "state prisioner" who was not free to move about as she chose.[43] For the most part, however, Martha accepted her fate uncomplainingly. As a good eighteenth-century wife, she saw her role primarily in terms of the support she could provide for her husband.[44] Her virtue and constancy would sustain his resolve in the face of the immense personal sacrifice he must make to serve the republic. But even more than other "republican wives,"[45] Martha Washington directly helped shape the future of the young nation. What were her greatest attributes? - loyalty, selflessness, constancy, and compassion for others.

Acknowledgment of the generosity and courtesy of librarians, archivists, historians, and friends, who have aided and cooperated in so many ways is a gratifying experience. Without the encouragement and generosity of the Regents and Vice-Regents of the Mount Vernon Ladies' Association of the Union, this book would not have been possible. The same can be said of the entire Mount Vernon staff: Mrs. Ellen McCallister Clark, emeritus librarian, and Miss Barbara McMillan, librarian, have been untiring in their efforts. John Riley, Mount Vernon's archivist, has always responded when an archival quandry arose. Miss Christine Meadows, long time curator of collections, could always be relied upon to share her tremendous store of knowledge and sage advice. Charles C. Wall, emeritus resident manager, Neil Horstman, director, and James C. Rees, associate director, have constantly given encouragement, assistance and cooperation whenever called upon. I also wish to express my gratitude to the late Frank Morse, librarian and curator emeritus, for much "down to earth" advice and encouragement, always given in his own inimitable way.

I am exceedingly grateful to the late Stephen Decatur, Jr., for the informative correspondence he shared with me, and for permission to use the texts of the Martha Washington letters contained in his book, *The Private Affairs of George Washington, From the Accounts of Tobias Lear*.

I have threefold indebtedness to the late Dr. Malcolm Harris, of West Point, Virginia: for his encouragement; for his two volume work, *Old New Kent County, Some Account of the Planters, Plantations, and Places in New Kent County*, without which it is doubtful this work would have ever been completed; for the frequent journeys we made, visiting the many sites and places in New Kent, King William and King and Queen Counties, associated with the lives of George and Martha Washington.

My appreciation must be expressed to Osborne P. Mackie and the Tudor Place Foundation, for making available the texts of the large number of condolence letters sent to Mrs. Washington following the death of the General. I am of course indebted to the Virginia Historical Society, its emeritus director, John Jennings, and its former archivist, Hewson Cole, for their generosity in making the Custis Papers available to me. Dorothy Eaton, retired custodian of the George Washington Papers at the Library of Congress, answered many questions and furnished information on hitherto unknown Martha Washington letters. My gratitude also goes to the late Dr. David Mearns, formerly Chief of the Division of Manuscripts and Assistant Librarian of Congress, who always kept a watchful eye for Martha Washington correspondence. Dr. William W. Abbot, editor of *The Papers of George Washington*, repeatedly urged the writer to put the papers and correspondence of our first first lady into print, and offered much good and frequent advice. To the staff of the Swem Library of the College of William and Mary, for their assistance in guiding me through the reading room and stacks, I give my thanks. I am indebted to Dr. John Haskell, Assistant Librarian of The Swem Library, who did much "biblio-sleuthing" for me. Mrs. Elizabeth Taylor of "Eltham," New Kent County, graciously extended her hospitality, and pointed out the various historical sites on her property that are so intimately associated with the lives of the Bassetts and the Washingtons.

My appreciation is extended to my friends and neighbors, Thomas Mills and James Dunn, for researching, arranging, and guiding me to the site of the "lost" Queens Creek plantation of John Custis, IV, now on Camp Peary property. My thanks also go to Dr. Rosemarie Zagarri, Associate Professor of History at the Catholic University of America, for her editorial assistance and reassurance, and to my editor, Ms. Cynthia Harris, of the Greenwood Press Group, for her encouragement, support, and patience. I am thankful also to the private and institutional custodians of Martha Washington correspondence for their cooperation and generosity. The technical assistance rendered by Ann and Bruce Brownson and Robert McNeil of Staff Directories, Ltd., at a critical period, is greatly appreciated. Lastly, I extend my apologies to all those who have aided me but have not been mentioned. It was not through lack of appreciation, but inadvertance on my part.

The research, composition, and word processing has been solely the work of the editor. All errors are his alone. Many pleasant associations and friendships were made along the way, and for these, I am grateful.

"Chantilly"
Queens Lake
Williamsburg, Virginia

Notes to the Introduction

1. Stewart Mitchell, ed., *New Letters of Abigail Adams, 1788-1801* (Boston: Houghton Mifflin Co., 1947), p. 15.

2. Manuscript journal of Eleanor Agnes Lee, entry for March 23, 1856, collection of the Virginia Historical Society. Cited in Mary P. Coulling, *The Lee Girls* (Winston-Salem, N.C.: John F. Blair, 1987), p. 57.

3. Martha Custis to John Hanbury & Co., August 20, 1757. ViHi.

4. Martha Custis to Robert Cary & Co., August 20, 1757. ViHi.

5. George Washington Parke Custis, *Recollections and Private Memoirs of Washington* (New York: Derby & Jackson, 1860), 499-501.

6. George Washington's account book, Ledger A, folio 38, March 16 and 25, 1758. Washington Papers, Library of Congress.

7. George Washington to Richard Washington, April 5, 1758. William Abbot and Dorothy Twohig, eds., *The Papers of George Washington*, Colonial Series (Charlottesville, Virginia; University Press of Virginia), vol. 5, 112.

8. Custis Papers, Virginia Historical Society. Reproduced in Douglas Southall Freeman, *George Washington: A Biography* (Charles Scribner's Sons: 1948-57), v. 2, between 299-300.

9. George Washington to Richard Washington, September 20, 1759. *Papers*, Colonial Series, v. 6, 359.

10. George Washington to Marie Joseph P.Y.R.G. Du Motier Lafayette, June 10, 1786. John C. Fitzpatrick, *The Writings of George Washington* (Washington, D.C.: U.S. Government Printing Office, 1931-1944), v. 28, p. 457.

11. Lund Washington to George Washington, January 17, 1776. Collection of the Mount Vernon Ladies' Association of the Union.

12. Martha Washington to Anna Maria Bassett, August 28, 1762, Original at MHi.

13. George Washington to Burwell Bassett, June 20, 1773. *Writings*, v. 3, 138.

14. George Washington to Reverend Jonathan Boucher, December 16, 1770. *Writings*, v. 3, 35.

15. Reverend Jonathan Boucher to George Washington, December 18, 1770. Stanislaus Murray Hamilton, ed. *Letters to Washington* (Boston and New York: Houghton Mifflin Co., 1898-1902), v. 4, 42.

16. George Washington to Martha Washington, June 18, 1775. DTp.

17. Martha Washington to Elizabeth Ramsay, December 30, 1775. Originial at NNPM.

18. James Thacher, *Military Journal of the American Revolution* (Hartford: Hurlbut, Williams & Co., 1862), 160-61.

19. Martha Washington to John Parke Custis and Eleanor Calvert Custis, March 19, 1779. ViMtV.

20. Pierre Etienne Du Ponceau, letter. *Pennsylvania Magazine of History and Biography*, v. 63 (July, 1939), 313.

21. George Washington to Tobias Lear, July 31, 1797. Tobias Lear, *Letters and Recollections of George Washington* (New York: Doubleday, Doran & Co., Inc., 1932), 120.

22. Journal of Robert Lewis, May 13-20, 1789. Collection of the Mount Vernon Ladies' Association.

23. *Gazette of the United States*, May 30, 1789. Cited in Betty Boyd Caroli, *First Ladies* (New York and Oxford, 1987), 4, 281.

24. Anne Hollingsworth Wharton, *Martha Washington* (New York, 1897), 197. Also in Stephen Decatur, Jr., *Private Affairs of George Washington* (Boston, 1933), 44.

25. Martha Washington to Frances Bassett Washington, October 23, 1789. PHi.

26. Stewart Mitchell, ed., op.cit., 13.

27. Martha Washington to Mercy Otis Warren, December 26, 1789. MeHi.

28. Typescript of article by William E. Curtis written for *The Star and the Chicago Record-Herald*. ViMtV. "Early Descriptions Notebook," January 2, 1902.

29. *Alexandria Advertiser and Commercial Intelligencer*, May 25, 1802.

30. See, Margaret Cockburn Conkling, *Memoirs of the Mother and Wife of Washington* (Auburn, N.Y.: Derby, Miller and Company, 1853); Custis, *Recollections and Private Memoirs of Washington*; Alice Curtis Desmond, *Martha Washington* (New York: Dodd, Mead and Co., 1951); Benson J. Lossing, *Mary and Martha, the Mother and Wife of George Washington* (New York: Harper and Brothers, 1886); Elswythe Thane, *Washington's Lady* (New York: Dodd Mead, 1860); James Walter, *Memorials of Washington and of Mary His Mother, and Martha, His Wife* (New York: Scribner's, 1887); Anne Hollingsworth Wharton, *Martha Washington* (New York: Scribner's, 1897).

31. The earliest edition of George Washington's works was Jared Sparks, ed., *The Writings of George Washington...*(Boston: American Stationer's Co., 1834-1837). The standard edition has long been regarded as John C. Fitzpatrick, ed., *The Writings of George Washington from the Original Manuscript Sources, 1745-1799*, 39 vols. (Washington, D.C., U.S. Government Printing Office, 1931-1944). This is being superseded by a new edition in progress. W.W. Abbot, ed., *The Papers of George Washington* (Charlottesville: University Press of Virginia, 1983-).

32. For George Augustine Washington's military service, see Fitzpatrick, ed., *The Writings of Washington*, hereafter referred to as *Writings*, v. 16, 392 n. For his illness, see GW to GAW, Newburgh, November 14, 1782, *Writings*, v. 25, 342; GW to Lafayette, Newburgh, December 15, 1782, *Writings*, v. 25, 435; GW to Lafayette, Newburgh, March 23, 1783, *Writings*, v. 26, 255; GW to David Parry, Governor of the Barbadoes, Mount Vernon, April 25, 1784, *Writings*, v. 27, 393; GW to Governor George Clinton, Mount Vernon, November 25, 1784, *Writings*, v. 27, 502-3; MW to Fanny Bassett Washington, Philadelphia, July 1, 1792, IKB; MW to FBW, December 3, 1792, MWiW-C; MW to FBW, February 3, 1793, ViMtV. For his marriage to Fanny Bassett, see GW to Burwell Bassett, Mount Vernon, May 23, 1785, *Writings*, v. 28, 151; GW to George William Fairfax, June 30, 1785, *Writings*, v. 28, 183. For his funeral obsequies, see GW to Reverend Bryan Fairfax and Dr. James Craik, Mount Vernon, April 9, 1793, *Writings*, v. 32, 413-14. His surviving children were: Anna Maria (1788-1814), George Fayette (1790-1867), Charles Augustine (1791-?). See *The Diaries of George Washington*, ed. Twohig and Jackson, Charlottesville, 1979, 5: 131; 6: 252, 288.

33. GW to Tobias Lear, Mount Vernon, October 1, 1792, *Writings*, v. 32, 173; March 27, 1796, v. 34, 506; v. 35, 1, 5, 6, 27.

34. Brighton, Ray, *The Checkered Career of Tobias Lear* (Portsmouth N.H., 1985), 199. The exact date of the marriage is not known.

35. Tobias Lear committed suicide in Washington, D.C., October 11, 1816. The most likely cause of his self destruction was mental depression. See Brighton, supra, 329.

36. The correspondence between the Washingtons and the Powels extended from 1786 until after GW's death. Samuel Powel (1739-1793), long-time mayor of Philadelphia, was a strong supporter of the Revolution and an avid agriculturalist. See *Diaries*, v. 4, 210. His wife, Elizabeth Wiling Powel, carried on an extensive correspondence with GW and MW. See *Index to the George Washington Papers* (Washington, D.C.: U.S. Government Printing Office, 1964), 214. A large portion of this correspondence is at ViMtV.

37. Elizabeth Wiling Powel to GW, Philadelphia, March 11, 1797. ViMtV.

38. GW to Elizabeth Wiling Powel, Mount Vernon, March 26, 1797, ViMtV.

39. The third known letter written by GW was dated, Verplanck's Point, October 1, 1782. The letter, introducing John Brown to MW, was never delivered. The original is at RHi. A fourth letter is known to have existed, written by MW to GW, Mount Vernon, March 30, 1767. It concerned weather conditions at Mount Vernon and regrets his absence in Williamsburg, where he was attending the session of the House of Burgesses. Its location is unknown.

40. For example, see letters by MW to Elizabeth Powel, dated May 1, 20, and December 18, 1797, which co-exist with draft copies in the handwriting of GW.

41. GW to Marquise de Lafayette, February 1, 1784, *Writings*, v. 27, 317; GW to Landon Carter, October 17, 1796, *Writings*, v. 35, 246; GW to George Clinton, February 28, 1797, *Writings*, v. 35, 407; GW to John Quincy Adams, June 25, 1797, *Writings*, v. 35, 476.

42. For a comparison with other networks among women emerging at this time, see Nancy F. Cott, *The Bonds of Womanhood: "Woman's Sphere" in New England, 1780-1835* (New Haven: Yale University Press, 1977), esp. 160-196.

43. MW to Fanny Bassett Washington, New York, October 23, 1789. Original in PHi.

44. MW to Mercy Otis Warren, New York, December 26, 1789. Original in MeHi.

45. Jan Lewis, "The Republic Wife: Virtue and Seduction in the Early Republic," *The William and Mary Quarterly*, 3rd. ser., XLIV (1987), 697-721.

I

The Young Widow Custis,
1757–1759

Subjects: John Parke Custis and Martha Parke Custis. Artist: John Wollaston, 1757. *Credit*: Washington/Custis/Lee Collection, Washington and Lee University, Lexington, VA.

From Robert Carter Nicholas

Madam: Williamsburg, 7th August, 1757

It gave me no small pleasure to hear with how great Christian patience and resignation you submitted to your late misfortune; the example is rare, though a duty incumbent upon us all; and therefore I can not help esteeming it a peculiar happiness when I meet with it. My late worthy friend,[1] from a very short acquaintance with him, had gained a great share of my esteem, which would naturally continue towards his family, had I been an utter stranger to them. How greatly this is increased by the pleasure of even a slight acquaintance with you, I shall leave it to time to evince, as it might savor of flattery were I to attempt the expression of it. When your brother[2] was with me, I was indisposed, and therefore could not conveniently comply with your request, in writing my opinion upon the several matters he proposed. As it will be absolutely necessary that some person should administer upon the estate and no appear so proper as yourself, I would recommend it to you, and that so soon as it may be done with convenience, I dare say your friends will endeavour to ease you of as much trouble as they can; and since you seem to place some confidence in me, I do sincerely profess myself to be of that number. I imagine you will find it necessary to employ a trusty steward; and as the estate is large and very extensive, it is Mr. Waller's[3] and my own opinion, that you had better not engage with any but a very able man, though he should require large wages, nothing appears to us very material to be done immediately, except what relates to your tobacco; if it is not already done, it will be necessary that letters should be wrote for insurance and that we, or some other of your friends should be acquainted with the quantities of tobacco put on board each ship that we may get the proper bills of lading. If you desire it, we will cheerfully go up to assist in sorting your papers, forwarding invoices, etc., and in any other instance that you think I can serve you, I beg that you will freely and without any reserve command me. I congratulate you upon your little boy's[4] late recovery, and am madam your hearty well-wisher and obedient humble servant,

Robert Carter Nicholas[5]

Original not found. Text taken from G.W.P. Custis, *Recollections and Private Memoirs of Washington*, New York, 1860, p. 497-98.

1. Daniel Parke Custis (1711-57) was the son of John Parke Custis IV (1678-1749) and Frances Parke (1687-1715). Frances Parke Custis was the daughter of Colonel Daniel Parke II and Jane Ludwell. Freeman and all others give the date of marriage between Daniel Parke Custis and Martha Dandridge as 1749. The Washington-Lee family Bible states they were married by the Rev. Chichley Gordon Thacker on Tuesday May 15, 1750. Their principal residence was White House, New Kent County. He died intestate, July 8, 1757.

2. Bartholomew Dandridge (1737-85) was the eldest and younger brother of Martha Dandridge Custis. He was an attorney and later Judge of the State Supreme Court.

3. Benjamin Waller (1710-86) was one of Virginia's leading attorneys, member of the House of Burgesses, Clerk of the General Court, and Judge of the Court of Admiralty.

4. John Parke Custis (1755-81) was the third child of Daniel Parke and Martha Custis. They had four children, in order: Daniel Parke II (1751-54), Frances Parke (1753-57), John Parke (1755-81), Martha Parke (1756-73). See Earl Gregg Swem, *Brothers of the Spade*, Barrie, 1957, p. 117-123. (Cited hereafter as *Swem*).

5. Robert Carter Nicholas (1728-80), attorney, Burgess for York County, and treasurer of the colony.

From Epaphroditus Howle

(August 12, 1757)

Recd August the 12 pf Mrs Martha Custis the sum of twenty one pounds one shiling and three pence in full of accounts Recd by me

his
Dite X Howl[1]
mark

DS, Custis Papers, ViHi.

1. Epaphroditus Howle was an overseer on one of the Custis plantations. The Papers of George Washington, Colonial Series, Charlottesville, 1988; 6:252, 266, 376. Hereafter cited as *PGWC*.

From John Roan

(August 12, 1757)

Recd of Mrs Martha Custis foure poun three and four pence in full of accounts Recd by me

his

John R Rone[1]

mark

John Roan

£4. 3. 4. in full

D. S., Custis Papers, ViHi.

1. John Roan was the overseer at the Custis plantation, "Claibornes," on the Pamunkey River, King William County. *PGWC*, 5:219.

To Robert Cary and Company

Gentlemen   Virginia Aug 20, 1757

I imagine before this you will hear of the great misfortune I have met with in the Colony my late Husband Mr Custis your Correspondent, by which all his Affairs fall under my management, I believe to both your satisfaction correspondence with you and I now having admon of his Estate I hope I shall continue the Correspondence and that it will be lasting and agreable to us both. I shall yearly ship a considerable part of the Tobacco I make to you which I shall take care to have made as good as possible and hope you will do your endeavor to get me a good Price, Yours by Capt. Coxen of the 10th of March, & by John Hanbury Captn Talman[1] of the 17 & 21st & the Goods you sent came safe to Mr. Custis's hands before his Death.

I wrote you sometime ago insurance on 34 Hhds of Tobo which I informed you would come in Capt. Coxen which I hope you have put 2 more Hhds on board which I have not insured, the whole Shiped to you by him is now 36 Hhds which I have inclosed a Bill of Lading for, I have reason to believe they are as good as they can well be and hope you will get me a Price suitable to them. I shall want some Goods this Year for my Family which I have inclosed an Invoice of and hope you will take care they are well bot and sent me by your first Ship to this river. If Mr Custis in his lifetime has wrote to you for 2 *(illegible)* please to send them & omit sending them in my Invoice, otherwise send them as my Invoice according to the instructions there set down. As soon as you have sold all the Toba. shipped to you by Mr Custis last year, please to make out an Account Current and send it to me by the first Oppertunity. As Mr Custis died

Without Will and left but two Children his Estate will be kept together some time and I think it will be proper to continue this Account with you in the same manner as if he was living, as most of the goods I shall send for will be for the use of the Family, I am Gentlemen Your most hble Servt.

Martha Custis

To Robt Cary Esq. & Co.[2]
Merchts in London

Df, Custis Papers, ViHi.

1. Captains Coxen and Henry Talman were captains of two of the Cary's ships in the York River trade. *PGWC* 6:269, 376.

2. Three generations of the London based Cary family sold tobacco for Virginia planters. Robert Cary (1730-77) was the third generation of the family. After his death the business was carried on under the name of Wakelin Welch & Co. See *Swem*, 153, n.

To John Hanbury and Company

Gent.   Virginia 20th August 1757
    I take this Oppertunity to inform you of the great misfortune I have met with in the loss of my late Husband Mr Custis, your Correspondent
    As I have now the Administration of his Estate & management of his Affairs of all sorts, I shall be glad to continue the Correspondence which Mr Custis carried on with you.
    Yours of the 16th of March Mr Custis rec'd before his Death with his Account Current inclosed wch I believe is right; and he had put on board the Ship King of Prussia Capt. Necks[1] 28 Hhds of Tobacco and wrote to you for Insurance for it, I now inclose the bill of Lading for the Tobacco which I hope will get safe to your hands, and as I have reason to believe it is extremely good. I hope you will sell it at a good Price, Mr Custis's Estate will be kept together for some time and I think it will be proper to continue his Account in the same manner as if he was living. Please to send an Account Current when the Tobacco is sold I am Gentlemen Your very hble Servt

Martha Custis

To Mr John Hanbury & Co[2]
Merchts in London

Df, Custis Papers, ViHi.

1. Robert Necks, acted as master of several of the vessels that came into the York River. In 1759 he was master of the *Adventure*. *PGWC* 6:376.

2. John Hanbury and Company was one of the most important mercantile firms in England. They were regarded as the foremost tobacco merchants of their day and represented many of the leading planters, acting as purchasing agents and bankers for them. John Hanbury, a Quaker, was the senior member of the firm. He was a member of the Ohio Company. It was through his influence that the King in Council granted authority to the Ohio Company to acquire 500,000 acres in the western part of the colony. *Swem*, p. 146.

From Benjamin Waller

Madam, August 30, 1757

I am at a loss in drawing your power of attorney for receiving the interest or dividends of your bank stock.[1] I had formerly a printed form which I am pretty sure I gave to Mr Power,[2] to draw one by for the late Colonel. Mr Lyons[3] says he remembers it, and that he believes Mr Power gave it to the Colonel; and so amongst us it is lost. I send you a general power of attorney, which you may execute before some person going to Great Britain, and send it by this fleet; it may possibly be of service till they send you a letter. It will be proper for you to get letters of administration from your clerk, send them here for the governors name and seal of the colony (all of which you may have for the fees already charged you), and to send them with the power to Messrs Cary and Co.; and desire them to send you, in proper forms and directions, what to do concerning the bank stock another year. I return the letters relating to Dunbar's appeal, which very probably received a determination before the Colonel's death.[4] I know not what further you can do than advise Mr Cary and Mr Hanbury of the time he died, to desire them to continue their case in that affair, and to instruct you what your solicitor thinks needful for you to do. In all these cases they will preserve their own forms and methods. My wife[5] tenders you her best respects and I am, madam,

Your most obedient servant
Ben Waller[6]

Williamsburg, August 30th 1757

Custis, *Recollections*, p 498-99.

1. The Custis estate owned stock shares in the Bank of England to the amount of £1650. *PGWC* 6:276, 451-52.

2. James Power was a prominent attorney of New Kent and King William Counties and served both in the House of Burgesses. He is believed to have been a native of Ireland and attended the Wakefield School in Yorkshire. He was a close friend of John Custis IV and Daniel Parke Custis and was godfather to Daniel Parke Custis II. He was instrumental in persuading John Custis to look favorably upon the engagement of Daniel Parke Custis to Martha Dandridge. Freeman, *George Washington*, New York, 1948, 2:293-95. Hereafter cited as *Freeman*.

3. Peter Lyons (1734/35-1809). He was persuaded to immigrate from Ireland to Virginia by his uncle, James Power. He studied law under Power and was licensed to practice in 1756. After his uncle's death he succeeded to his law practice. He was plaintiff's attorney in the celebrated "Parson's Cause," and later was judge of the General Court and president of the Court of Appeals.

4. Charles Dunbar, surveyor-general of the Leeward Islands, brought suit against John Custis IV, as executor of the estate of his brother, Thomas Dunbar. The latter had married Lucy Chester, the natural daughter of Colonel Daniel Parke. John Custis IV had married the legitimate daughter of Colonel Parke. Parke had been aide to John Churchill, Duke of Marlborough, at the Battle of Blenheim and had carried the news of the victory to Queen Anne. Appointed Governor-general of the Leeward Islands, he was killed in a riot in 1709. His will left his Leeward Island property to Lucy Chester and directed his legitimate heirs

in Virginia to assume all his debts. Dunbar brought suit against the Custis family to require them to reimburse the insular heirs for the Parke debts they had satisfied. The suit was a thorn in the side of the Custises for many years. To a lesser extent it later involved Washington. The best and most concise presentation of this complicated case can be found in *Freeman*, 2:276-302.

5. Martha Hall Waller, wife of Benjamin Waller.

6. Benjamin Waller (1710-86). See supra, Robert Carter Nicholas to MDC, August 7, 1757, n. 3.

From Elizabeth Vaughan

(August 31, 1757)

1757	Daniel Parke Custis Decst. Dr	£
July 7	to Altering of one Gown for your wife	0 . 3 . 0
9	to Mkg of Two Gowns @ 6/6	0 . 13 . 0
August 18	to Mkg of a pair of Sleaves	0 . 2 . 0

August 31 1757 Then Rec'd of Mrs Custis the sum of Eighteen Shillings By me

Elizth Vaughan[1]
E Vaughan Rect
Mrs Vaughan
July 18/18 Aug 1757[2]

D.S. Custis Papers, ViHi.

1. Daniel Parke Custis died July 8, 1757 following a short illness. Elizabeth Vaughan was a neighborhood seamstress, called in to hurriedly alter gowns and sew mourning clothes for Martha. *Swem*, p. 118; *PGWC* 6:264, 328-29.

2. The docketing is in the hand of GW.

Power of Attorney

September 1757

Know all men by these Presents that I Martha Custis of the County of New Kent in the Colony of Virginia Widow Administrix of all and singular The Goods and Chattels Rights and Credits of Daniel Parke Custis late of the same Place Gent. deceased Have made ordained constituted and appointed and by these Presents Do ordain constitute and Appoint Robert Cary John Moorey and Wakelin Welch[1] of the city of London Merchants jointly and severally my true and lawful Attornies & Attorney for me and in my Name and to my Use to ask demand sue for recover and receive of and from all and every Persons and Person whatsoever all such Sums of Money and other Effects whatsoever as now are, or hereafter may be due and oweing to me from any Person of Persons whatsoever within the Kingdom of Great Britain and more especially from the Governor and Directors of the Bank of England all such Dividends and Paiments which are or shall be due and oweing to me or the Estate of the said Daniel Parke Custis from Time to Time and in Default of Paiment thereof to have use and take all Lawful Ways and means in my name or otherwise for the Recovery thereof and to compound and agree for the same and on Receipt thereof Acquainttances or other sufficient Discharges for the same for me and in my Name from time to time to make Seal and deliver and to do all Lawful Acts and things whatsoever concerning the Premisses as fully in every respect as I myself might or could do if I was personally present and an Attorney or Attornies under them for the Purposes aforesaid to make and at their Pleasure to revoke I hereby ratifying allowing and confirming all and whatsoever my said attornies shall Lawfully do or cause to be done in and about the Premisses by Virtue of the Presents in Witness whereof I have hereunto set my Hand and Seal the   Day of September in the thirty first year of the Reign of King George the Second and in the Year of our Lord One Thousand Seven hundred and fifty seven.

> Sealed and Delivered
> In the Presence of

Df, Custis Papers, ViHi.
  1. Wakelin Welch and Robert Moorey were partners in the Cary firm. *PGWC* 6:451-52.

From George Brett

(September 8, 1757)

The Estate of Daniel Parke Custis, esq. deceased, to George Brett[1]

1757		£ Sh d
July 16th	To Building a Schooner the first agreement	14 -
	To additional work done more than was agreed for at first viz: building the vessel 2 feet in length, & 6 inches in depth, working upon getting the Frame, wch his People was to do	6 -
		20

King William Co This day came before me, Peter Robinson,[2] Gent; one of His Majestys Justices of the Peace for the County of King William, George Brett, Carpenter, and made Oath to the above Accot, and that the said sum of Twenty Pounds Current money is justly due to him from The Estate of Daniel Parke Custis Esqr. Dec d and that he never received any Satisfaction for the same. Given under my hand this 8th day of Septr 1757

> Peter Robinson

Sepr 8th 1757 Recd of Mrs Martha Custis Twenty Pounds Current Money in full for the Above Accot.

> George Brett

ADS, Custis Papers, ViHi.

1. George Brett was a local carpenter and shipbuilder. The schooner was used for commercial fishing in the York and Pamunkey Rivers. See *PGWC*, 6:252.

2. Peter Robinson (1718-65) was the youngest son of Colonel Christopher Robinson. He matriculated at Oriel College, Oxford, in 1737, resided in St. John's Parish, and represented King William County in the House of Burgesses (1758-61).

The Estate of Daniel Parke Custis

(September 15, 1757)

At a Court held for New Kent County on Thursday the 11th of August 1757 - Ordered that Benjamin Eggleston, John Blair Junr,[1] John Prentis[2] & Peter Scott[3] (or any three of them) appraise in Current Money the Personal Estate of Daniel Parke Custis Esqr. dec d in James City County Returning such Appraisment to this Court.

Will: Clayton[4]

Septr 15, 1757 John Blair Junr John Prentis & Peter Scott were sworn before me.

John Randolph[5]

ADS, PHi.

1. John Blair, Jr. (1732-1800) attorney, Burgess for the College of William and Mary, Clerk of the Council, member of the Privy Council of the Commonwealth, Chief Justice of the Supreme Court of Virginia, delegate to the Federal Constitutional Convention, and Associate Justice of the United States Supreme Court.

2. John Prentis was a Williamsburg merchant.

3. Peter Scott, also rented property from the Custis estate. *PGWC* 6:252, 253, 273.

4. William Clayton was the son of John Clayton, the botanist. He was deputy clerk of the New Kent County Court under Colonel John Dandridge, the father of Martha Custis. When Colonel Dandridge died in 1756, Clayton became clerk and served until his death. He was a member of the House of Burgesses, the General Assembly of 1776 and 1788, the New Kent County Committee of 1774, Justice of the County Court, member of the Committee of Correspondence, Colonel of the New Kent County militia, and vestryman of St. Peter's Parish. See, Harris, M.H., *Old New Kent County, Some Account of the Planters, Plantations, and Places in New Kent County,* 1:159-64; West Point, Virginia, 1977. Hereafter cited as *Harris*.

5. John Randolph (Ca. 1727-84), attorney, clerk of the House of Burgesses, Burgess for the College of William and Mary, Attorney General for the Crown. Later he was known as "John Randolph the Tory," to distinguish him from others of the same name and because of his Tory sympathies during the Revolution.

From Richard Littlepage

October 8, 1757

The Estate of Coll Danl Parke Custis Esqr.

1757	To Stepn Furn Hoomes[1]	
June 21st	To 208 lb of Bar Iron @ 3d P lb	£ 2 : 12
	this day came before me Stephen Furneau	
	Hoomes & made Oath to ye above Acct. Given	
	under my Hand this 8th Day of Octbr 1757	

Richard Littlepage[2]

ADS, Custis Papers, ViHi.

1. Stephen Furneau Hoomes, a merchant and resident of New Kent County. He sold Daniel Parke Custis iron and other plantation supplies. He died at Cumberland Plantation, New Kent County, in 1771. *Harris*, 1:88-89.

2. Richard Littlepage III, of Cumberland Plantation, New Kent County. Heavily in debt, he drew up a deed conveying 1000 acres of Cumberland Plantation to Stephen Furneau Hoomes in 1750. Cumberland Plantation was on the south side of the Pamunkey River and was close to the ferry that crossed to the land of Thomas Claiborne in King William County. It lay on the direct route between King William Courthouse and New Kent County Courthouse. It was later known as Smith's Ferry. At the time of his death in 1767 Littlepage had lost all of his extensive lands along the Pamunkey River except 175 acres. *Harris*, 1:87-89.

From John Wollaston

(October 21, 1757)

Recd Oct 21st. 1757 of Mrs Custis the sum of fifty six pistoles for three pictures being in full of all demands.

John Wollaston[1]

ADS, Custis Papers, ViHi.

1. John Wollaston was an itinerant English portrait painter who arrived in America about 1749 and spent a number of years painting portraits in the middle colonies. He painted the gentry of Maryland and Virginia from about 1755 until 1758. Later he appeared in the southern colonies and in the Caribbean. He left about 300 portraits, characterized by large heavy lidded slant eyes. The three portraits he painted for the Custises were of Daniel Parke Custis, Martha Dandridge Custis, and the double portrait of John Parke Custis and his sister, Martha Parke Custis. The originals are at Washington and Lee University, Lexington, Va.

From Burbidge & Armistead

(November 1, 1757)

Mrs Martha Custis	To Burbidge[1] & Armistead	D
1757		
Augt 6	To 1 No 8	1 -- . --
31	To 1 Kegs Vinegar	-- . 6
	Ball. of Col Custis Acct	1 -- . 6

Nov 1, 1757 Rec'd of the Revd Mr. Mossom[2] the Above Acct

John Armistead[3]

ADS, Custis Papers, ViHi.

1. Julius King Burbidge of Pamocra, New Kent County, was Collector of Revenue for St. Peter's Parish and justice for New Kent County and James City County. John Armistead was his partner in the mercantile business. His daughter married Bartholomew Dandridge, eldest brother of Martha Dandridge Custis.

2. Reverend David Mossom (1690-1767) was born in London and came to America about 1718. He first settled in Marblehead, Massachusetts, where he was missionary for the Society

for the Propogation of the Gospel. He came to Virginia in 1762 and was directed to the Vestry by Acting-governor Robert Carter. He served St. Peter's until his death in 1767. He was the minister who officiated at the wedding of Martha Dandridge Custis and George Washington. *Harris*, 1: 92-95; Meade, Bishop William, *Old Churches, Ministers and Families of Virginia*, Phila., 1852, 1:386. Hereafter cited as *Meade*.

   3. John Armistead resided in St. Peter's Parish. He was a member of the Committee of Safety in 1775. *Harris* 1:41-42.

From Richard Chamberlayne

(November 2, 1757)

1751	Dr. Daniel Parke Custis to Richard Chamberlayne[1] Cr	
	To Sawing 2000 foot of 2 . 1/4	
	By Cash Recd	£ 11 . 0 . 0
	Inch Plank & finding Timber at £ 7.10 pM	15 . 0 . 0
	Balle Due RC	4 . 0 . 0
		15 . 0 . 0

   Capt Richard Chamberlayne came before me and made oath that the above ballance of four pounds was Justly due to him from Colo Daniel Parke Custis dcd & that he had never Recd any Satisfaction for the Same Certified Under my hand this 19th day of October 1757

Edmund Bacon[2]

by grace of
November 2d 1757
Received of Mrs Martha Custis the Just sum of four pounds in full of all accounts
Rd Chamberlayne
(Docketed)
R Chamberlayne
Recd £ 4-0-0
2 Novr. 1757

ADS. Custis Papers, ViHi.
   1. Richard Chamberlayne lived at Poplar Grove, along the south shore of the Pamunkey River, New Kent County. He was the son of William Chamberlayne who came to Virginia in 1722. While on a trip to Williamsburg in 1758, GW stopped at Poplar Grove and was induced by Chamberlayne to remain and dine. According to G.W.P Custis, Martha's grandson, GW met Martha at that time. See Appendix II, p. _____. *Harris*, 1:127-28.
   2. Edmund Bacon (1722-?1767) was Justice for New Kent County. He spent his entire life in St. Peter's Parish, where he was a vestryman. *Harris*, 1:173-76.

From Robert Cary and Company

Madm　　　　　　　　　　　　　　London 26 Novr 1757
　　　Your favr of the 25th. July & 20th. August, We duly recd, and the loss
of our good friend has been no little Concern to Us. Whatever Services lay
in our Power to Oblige you, We beg you may always Command us, as it
will give Us a particular pleasure to have an Oppertunity of being in the
least serviceable to you and family - Agreable to your Ordr of the 25th.
July We Inclose you the Charge of £400 - insd on Coxen wch Charge £53,
4, 6 is placed to the Estates Debit, and when your 36 hhds by Coxen are
landed shall do the best for your Intst. - By the several Letters which we
have wrote - and have likewise sent from Mr Sharpe, your Solcr on the
Affair of Dunbars you will Perceive that the matter is deferr'd to another
hearing, wch now must be a work of time, and there is no knowing when
it will be determin'd, for our own parts you may rely on our own Care
that nothing shall be neglected in it - We have wrote to Messrs. Oswald
of Glasgow who will send the Stockings & Carpet by the first Vessel that
goes for York River - in Feby Convoy will be Appointed out at home for
our Virginia Ships, by Coxen who we shall then send, shall send your
goods with the Tomb,[1] and against whose Arrival hope as Usual You'll
favor Us in reserving your Tobco - Not having an Oppertunity before of
transmitting the last Years Sales we have now sent them - the proceed Viz:

D P C	10 hhds	P Johnson	£ 200
xx			
	16	do	256

　　　Both which are to the Estates Cr. and which believe are such as
Virginia had before, and therefore rest satisfyed that they'll meet your
Approbation. We likewise Inclose the Estates Acct currt to the 22d August
last, wch leaves a Ballce in our hands of £3697 : 10 : 8 which believe you'll
find in Conformity to Mr Custis's Books, as we ev'ry half year receive from
the Bank the Intst of £1650 Bank Stock, it will be necessary for sending Us
over the Copy of Lrs of Administratn as also a fresh power of Attorney
from You to us to Receive the said Dividend otherwise We cannot,
therefor the sooner this is done ye better, We respectfully are

　　　　　　　　　　　　Madm
　　　　　　　　　　　　Your most hble Servt
　　　　　　　　　　　　Robert Cary & Co.
　　　　　　　　　　　　(Originall p Turner)

Copy
Mrs Marta. Custis
(Address)
To

Mrs Martha Custis
New Kent County
York River
Virginia
p th Supply
Capn Denins
(Docket)
Cary & Company Lettr

ALS, Custis Papers, ViHi.

1. Martha presumably had ordered a tombstone for her husband. In the invoice book of DPC, located in the Library of Congress, page 40, there is a notation, "One handsome tombstone of the best durable marble to cost about £100 with the following inscription and the arms sent in a piece of paper on it to wit: 'Here lies the body of Daniel Parke Custis, Esquire who was born the 15th day of October, 1711 and departed this life the 8th day of July, 1757. Aged 45 years.' " He was interred in the family burial plot at the Queens Creek plantation, York County. The tombstone was later removed to the churchyard of Bruton Parish Church, Williamsburg. *Swem*, p. 131-32.

From John Hanbury and Company

Esteemed Friend   London Novr, 1757

We wrote thee p. the Rialto via Bristol Inclosing a duplicate of ours p. the Montgomerie. Thyne of the 20 of Augt is come safe to hand & we are heartily sorry for the loss of our Friend - The King of Prussia is safe arrived at Portsmouth & is Daily expect'd up with Convoy. no endeavours of ours shall be wanting to make the most of the 20 hhds Tobacco, thereby to merit a continuance of thy Consignments. As we wrote fully p. the Montgomerie relative to yr affair with Dunbar, have now only to say that we will strictly watch their proceedings & from time to time advise thee thereof as also of anything thy Solliciter may see necessary for thee to do & all the satisfaction that we shall desire is a continuance of a least a part of the Estates Tobacco & if we render as good Sales as the other Merchants do we hope thee (& whoever else may be concerned in the management of the Estate) will favor us with a considerable part of the Estates Tobacco, & that by ye Baltimore we shall partake of the Consignments We are with Esteem

Thy Assured Friends
J Hanbury & Co

To Martha Custis York River
(Address)
To Martha Custis
York River Virginia
p the Beaver

(Docketed by GW[1])
21 Nov 1757 John Hanbury & Co

ALS, Custis Papers, ViHi.
    1. Following his marriage to MDC in 1759, GW meticulously examined the Custis account, made notes upon them and often made copies. He took over the settlement of the estate of DPC as well as the residual settlement of the estate of John Custis, uncompleted by DPC. According to Virginia law, Martha's one-third share of the Custis estate passed to George Washington when they were married. He was required to make annual reports to the General-Court on this portion as well as the remaining two-thirds belonging to her two children, ample reason for him to peruse and examine the correspondence and accounts.

From Dr. James Carter

(November 28, 1757)

The Estate of Colo Danl Parke Custis Dr to James Carter[1]

June 12	To a purge of Rhubarb &c Mastr Johnny		: 2:
	To Chamonile Flowers		: 1:
July 5	To lbi Cordial astringent Mixture Colo C		: 7: 6
	To lbi almonds 1.3.1 Hartshorn prepar's 4		: 5: 3
	To 6 oxs Balsam - astringent & Electuary		: 7: 6
6	To 1/2 ozs Rhubarb 4 1/2 Cinnamon Waters 4		: 8: —
	To a pot Diascordium 1.6 Syrup Poppies 2/2		: 3: 8
7	To Visit Colo Custis	3: 4: 6	
	To 2 days attendance Do	2: 3: —	
	To 10 ozs Cordial Mixture Do		: 5:
	To 4 ozs Diascordium (illegible)		: 2: 8
	To 10 ozs Cordial Astringest mixture (illegible)		: 5: —
	To Prepared burnt Hartshorn		: 4: —
	To 10 ozs Cordial astringent Mixture expect Do		: 5: —
	To 2 ozs chamomile Flowers .s 1 Barley 1.3		: 1:11
	To 3 ozs Pot Venice Treacle		: 2: 1
	To Visitg Son 3.4.6 3 Days Attendance 3.4.6	6: 9: —	
25	To 12 Papers Cordial Powders Do		: 6: —
	To 1/2 ozs Oil Aniseed 1.4 i oz Laudanum 2./		: 3: 4
Augst 1	To 10 ozs Cordial astringent mixture Visiting Negro Wom:		: 5: —
10	To 4 ozs Powderd Ipecacuanna & vial		:10: 2
13	To preparing 2 & 1/2 Hartshorn		: 3: 9
14	To Visit Mrs Custis 3.4.6. 3 Days Attendance	5: 6: 9	
	(illegible) Hartshorn 2 : 6 : 22d Tamarinds&pots 10/6		:13: —
1757		£ 23: 7: 4	
	To Account brought over	£ 23: 7: 4	
Nov 26	To 2 ozs Elixr Proprietalis		: 2: 6

		£ 23 : 9 : 10
Octor		
13	Cr by 10 Doz : 15	1 : 11
	6 Doz (illegible) pots 6	
		£ 22 : 8 : 10
Novr 4	To Cash pd Dr Amson[2]	8 : 12 : 0
	To Cash pd You by Mr Barthw Dandrige	45 : 0 : 0
28	To Cash pd Mr Valentine[3]	£ 53 : 10 : 2
		£ 130 : 0 : 0

Cr. By a Bill of Exchg on Cary   (illegible)

(Docketed)
Dr Carter's Audt
Novr 28th 1757

AD, Custis Papers, ViHi.

1. Dr. James Carter set up an apothecary shop and practiced medicine and surgery at "The Unicorn's Horn," in Williamsburg, as early as 1751. He served in the militia during the Revolution. He continued to practice until his death, about 1800. Blanton, W., *Medicine in Virginia in the Eighteenth Century*, Richmond, 1931, p. 35, 323. Hereafter cited as *Blanton*.

2. Dr. John Amson practiced medicine in Williamsburg as early as 1751. During his protracted illness on the frontier in 1757-58, GW rode to Williamsburg and consulted Amson on March 15, 1758. His treatment and advice must have been effective, for he was back at his command and fully recovered on April 5, 1758. See Fitzpatrick, John C. (ed), *The Writings of Washington*, Washington, 1931, 2:167. (Cited hereafter as *Writings*).

3. Joseph Valentine was manager of the Custis estates on the York River. He later managed Washington's dower lands and GW found him competent and reliable. *Writings*, 2:330. *Freeman*, 3:2, 23, 46, 286.

From George Taylor

Hanover County to Wit.   (November 9, 1757)
        George Taylor[2] Made Oath before me that the above Ballance of One Pound three Shillings and Ten & one half penny is justly due and that he Never Received any Sattisfaction for the Same Given Under my hand this 9 Day of November 1757

                                                              J Syme

(Docketed)
29th Novr 1757G Taylor
£ 1 . 3 . 10 1/2

ADS, Custis Papers, ViHi.

1. George Taylor was one of three appraisers of the Custis Estate in Hanover County. *PGWC* 6:231, 252.

From James Gildart

Madam   Leverpoole Decem 6th 1757

I was truly Sorry to hear of the Death of my good Friend your
Consort Collo Custis & do Sincerely Console with you for so great a loss
but to the Almightys will we must Submitt. I wrote him of the 21 June wch
no doubt came to your hand and to whch refer. This Serves to inclose you
Invoice p Goods p The Gildart to order as So on acc of Mr Jos Valentine.
both sums to the Debt of Mr Custis acc agreeable to order which I wish
may be delivered safe & to content by the Hare. I have held five hhds Tobo
You were pleased to Consign me but not any letter which I impute to the
Affliction you must be under. Please to be assured nothing in my Power
shall be wanting for your most advantage for the Sale. & if you are pleased
to Honr me with a Continuance of your Friendship you shall ever find me
ready to render you the best Services in my Power. We had a brisk demand
for Tobo before the Fleet Arrived In which I sold most of the Gildarts Cargo
but as Its not quite finished must defer sending the Accounts till the
Spring. When I intend a vessell for York River the Price for Tobo are from
2d p to 3 1/4 p & hope wont be lower. This will be delivered you by Capt
Mulloy[1] toward whoes dispatch your kind assistance will much Oblige.

> Madam Yr Most Obt Hum.
> Sert.
> Jam Gildart[2]

Mr Custis Acct Currt shall
be sent with the Sales
(Docketed)
Mr. Gildart Dec 1757

ALS, Custis Papers, ViHi.

1. John Mulloy was master of the *Gildart*, one of the firm's ships. *PGWC* 6:325-26.

2. James Gildart, of Liverpool, was the head of the mercantile firm bearing his name and
served as an agent for the Custis estate. Later GW continued to avail himself of their services,
but frequently expressed dissatisfaction with their methods. He eventually severed business
connections with them. *Writings*, 2:326, 358, 443, 481, 494.

From James Gildart

(December 6, 1759)

Invoice of Sundries Shipt By James Gildart on Board the Gildart Capt. John Mulloy for Virginia on the Propper Account of Daniel Parke Custis Esqr. in Virginia.

D P C a Cask No 1

x x

Est	1 piece white Sheeting q 39 yards	@21d. 3.. 8.. 3
Do	2 pieces Irish Linen No 19 q 50 yards	@ 3/4. 8.. 6.. 8
Do	2 pieces Do No 7 q 50 yards	@ 2/8. 6..13.. 4
Do	1 piece Do N 22 q 25 yards	@17d3/4. 1..16..11
Do	1 piece Do No 1 q 26 yards	@15d.. 1..12.. 6
Do	1 piece Strong Doulas q 55 yards	@12d.. 2..13.. 0
Est	2 pieces Fearnaught No No 5	@23/.. 2.. 6.. 0
Do	2 pieces Do No 6	@37/.. 3..14.. 0
MC	1 piece Fine thick Camberick	@..... 3..13.. 0
Do	8 yards Best Superfine Mininel Lace	@ 9/6. 2..17.. 6
( )	Pieces New Fashioned yd wide Silk Stuffs 30 yd wide each	at 81d 8.. 2.. 0
( )	6 Best Long Round Silk Laces	@ 7d.. 0.. 3.. 6
( )	8 Strong Cart halters	@3/6.. 1.. 8.. 0
( )	20 lb Browne thread	@1/6.. 1..10.. 0
Do	2 lb whited Browwne Do	@2/8.. 0.. 5.. 4
MC	1 Brass hand Bell	@..... 0.. 2.. 9
( )	1 doz Monmouth Caps	@..... 0.. 3.. 2
Do	4 ounce thread	@6d... 0.. 2.. 0
Do	4 ounce Do	@8d... 0.. 2.. 0
Do	4 ounce Do	@12d.. 0.. 4.. 0
Do	4 ounce Nuns Fine Thred	@5/6.. 1.. 2.. 0
( )	1 Best Large Mounted Saddle	@..... 1.. 2.. 0
Do	1 Furniture Bridle Silver Buckles	@..... 0.. 8.. 6
	Cask 5/ Primage	2/6.. 0.. 7.. 6
	No 2 atruss	52.. 6.. 1 3/4
Est	4 pieces Dutch Blanketts No 7 q 30 yards Each	@75s/.15.. 0.. 0
Do	1 piece Blue Duffell No 8 q 17 yards	@..... 1.. 8.. 0
Do	12 Ruggs N 9	@ 5/.. 3.. 0.. 0
Do	6 Ruggs N 10	@ 6/.. 1..16.. 0
MC	2 Mattresses	@ 21/. 2.. 2.. 0
Est	3 pieces Kendall Cotton RR13	@ 23/. 3.. 9.. 0
	Canvas and Cord 5/Prim 5s/	0..10.. 0
	No 3 a Cask	27.. 5.. 0
Do	8 thousand 20d ney Nails	@ 6/ . 2.. 8.. 0
Do	8 thousand 10d ney Do	@ 4/ . 1..12.. 0
Do	8 thousand 8d ney Do	@ 3/ . 0..15.. 0
Do	4 thousand 6d ney Nails	@ 2/6. 0..22.. 8

Cask 1/2 Primage _____ 5.. 7.. 8

Carried Forward   £ 84..18.. 9 3/4

Invoice Continued and Brought Forward _____£ 84..18.. 9 3/4

--No 4 a Cask--

Est	3 doz Narrow howes	N_____	@ 18/ --- 2..14.. 0
Do	2 doz Do	N_____	@ 20/ --- 2.. 0.. 0
Do	1 doz Do	N_____	@ 24/ --- 1.. 4.. 0
Do	1 1/2 doz Broad howes	N_____	@ 24/ --- 1..16.. 0
Do	2 Doz Do	N_____	@ 27/ --- 2..14.. 0
Do	1/2 doz Do	N_____	@ 29/ --- 0..14.. 6
Do	6 plate Stock Locks _____		@ 2/3 --- 0..13.. 6
Do	6 Narrow Axes q 31 1/4 lb_____		@ (?) --- 0..14.. 3 3/4
	(illegible)_____		@ 8d --- 0.. 4.. 0
Est	3 thousand 8d ney Nails _____		@ 3/ --- 0.. 9.. 0
Do	4 thousand 6d ney Do _____		@ 2/6 --- 0..10.. 0

white Rope for 4 Long Bed
Cords q 15 lb _____ @ 6d --- 0.. 7.. 6

Cask 3/6 Prim 2/   --- 0.. 5.. 6

--No 3 a Cask --/4/0/6

Do	6 Double Loaves Sugar 0 . 1. 19_____	@ 11 1/2-	2.. 4.. 3/4
Do	8 Single Do _____ 0 . 2. 20 _____	@ 78/ ---	2..12..11 1/4

Cask 3/ Primage 2/--------------------

0.. 5.. 5

---Loose--------------------------------------   5.. 2.. 0

Do	1 Sack Clover seed q 1.0.0 at 56/Sack 2/2 prim 6d_____	2..18.. 8
Est	2 Sacks of Oats q 10 Bushells at 2/2 is 26/Sacks 5/Prim 1/ _____	1..12.. 0
Do	25 Baggs Salt at 5/Primage 6/_____	6..17.. 6

-- a Cask --   11.. 8.. 2

Est	10 7/8 Gallons old nants Brandy _____ @ 9/ 4..17..10 1/2	
	Cask 3/6 Prim 1/_____ 0.. 4.. 6	5.. 2.. 4
MC	1 Barrell F Gunpowder 6..5..0 Prim 1/_____ 6..6..0	

Carrage of Goods Packing Carting & porters _____   0..15.. 0

Commission 2/2 PC _____   3.. 4.. 0

£ 131.. 2.. 8

Deduct Debenture on Linnen Sugar & lether   1.. 3.. 7

£ 129..19..11

Insurance on £ 130 at 15Gs Pct 20.9.6

Com. 2 1/2 PC   0.10.3   20..19.. 3

£ 150..18.. 4

From James Gildart

Liverpoole Decemr 6th 1757

Invoice of Sundries Shipt By James Gildart on Board the Gildart Capt. John Mulloy for Virginia on the Acct of Daniel Pake (sic) Custis Esqr. for Mr Joseph Valentine

---IV a Cask---

1 piece Kendall RR 10	@	1.. 1.. 0
1 piece Ozenbuggs q 83 yards	@ 76	2..11..10
1 piece Irish Linnen N 17 q 24 yards	@ 2/	2.. 8.. 0
1 piece Do No 11q 25 yards	@ 1/	1.. 5.. 0
1 piece yd wide Cotton Check 35 for 34 1/2	@ 1/d	1..17.. 4 1/2
1 piece fine Drab Jerman Serge 29 1.2 yards	@ 3/6	5.. 3.. 3
1 piece Brown holland Lineing 35 yards	@	
3/ oz Silk and Twist _____	@ 2/4d	0.. 8.. 2
4 yards Buckram _____	@ 1/	0.. 4.. 0
5 1/2 Doz Coat Buttons 4/8 6 1/2 doz Vest Do _____	2/2	0.. 6..10
( ) yards colloured Fustian _____		0.. 4.. 0
( ) lb Thred _____		0.. 1.. 2
( ) lb whited Browne Thred _____		0.. 1.. 4
( ) Browne thred _____		0.. 1.. 8
1 Boys Castor _____		0.. 4.. 0
2 Mens Do 12/Box 6 _____		0..12.. 6
2 Broad howes　No _____	@ 20/	0.. 5.. 0
3 Do　　　　　No _____	@ 24/	0.. 6.. 0
2 Narrow Axes of 8 11/4 lb _____	@ 5 1/2-	0.. 3.. 9 1/4
Cask 3/ Primage 2/		0.. 5.. 0

--Loose---------------------------------------　19.. 3..11 1/2

1 Large Brass Kettle in Weight 37 1/2 lb	@ 16d	2..11.. 0	
Primage		0.. 1.. 0	2..11.. 0
Carriage of Goods Packing Carting and Porters			0.. 2.. 6
Commission　　2 1/2 PC			0..10..10 1/2
			£ 22.. 8.. 3 3/4
Deduct Debenture on Linnen			0..13.. 6
			£ 21..14.. 9 3/4
Insurance on £ 22 at 15 Gs PCt 3.9.4　}			3..11.. 0
Commission on 2 1/2 PCt 1..8　}			
Liverpoole Decemr. 6. 1757			£ 25.. 5.. 9 3/4
25 PCt			6.. 6.. 5 1/4
			31..12.. 3

Excepted
Jam Gildart

To
Mrs Custis
York River
Virginia
P the Gildart
Capt Mulloy

DS, Custis Papers, ViHi.

To John Hanbury & Company

Gentlemen   Virga Dec. 20. 1757

I received yours of the 16th of July last inclosing a Lre from Mr Sharp wth the Order of Council and printed Cause, and am obliged to you for the care you have taken in that Affair,[1] I was surprised to find the determination of that if there was no mismanagement the Cause against me and am advised by my lawyers here that Mr Custis was very unfortunate in losing so good a Cause, it is needless for me to mention their reasons for it, for as the Cause is to be sent here and I suppose to you again, I shall have time enough to *(illegible)* mention and what is the necessity, to you anything that is necessary relating to it the only thing I have now to desire of you relating to that is, to pay off all the charges attending it and then send me a particular Accot of it them the first oppeertunity, I am obliged to you for your good intention in applying to Dunbar's Son to accomodate the matter, and if he was ever so willing to do it, it is not now in my power,and not withstanding what Mr Sharpe says, make no doubt the matter will turn out in my Favour.

I have shiped you by Capt. Crookshanks for which I have enclosed a Bill of Ladg. Hhds of Tobo which I hope will turn out very good and that you will do your endeavour to sell them for a good Price.

I beg you will by no means omit sending me an Account Sales of the Tobo. I ship you, as soon as it is sold, and that you will send me one immediately to the time of Mr Custis's Death including the charges of the Lawsuit. Mr Cary has the letters of administration of Mr Custis's Est. under the Seal of the Colony & which you may refer to if occasion requires, I am

Your very hble Servt
Martha Custis

To Messrs John Hanbury & Co.
Merchants in London
Baltimore

P The Osgood Capt. Crookshank
& Capt. Baker

Df, Custis Papers, ViHi.
   1. See supra, Benjamin Waller to MW, August 30, 1757, n. 4.

From William Macon

December 21, 1757

(illegible) 55	Dr. Daniel Park Custis Esqr	
	To Willm Macon Senr[1]	
Septr	To bills of Exchange on Messrs Ledderdale & Co.	£ 40. 0. 0
	Merchants in Bristol	
(illegible)	Colo. Custis gave me (illegible) orders on John	
	Hanbury & Co. Merchants in London	
	(illegible) forty pounds Sterling in discharge	
	of the above acct which orders (illegible)	
	the Ship Molly July 1756 but (illegible) being	
	taken by the French the (illegible) order did	
	not git to hand	

                                        Willm Macon Sr

King Wm County to Wit
William Macon Senr made Oath that the above
recd of Forty pounds Sterling in full and
(illegible) he hath received no Satisfaction
for the (illegible)

                    Sworn before me this 21t day
                    of December 1757
                    Petr Robinson[2]

DS, Custis Papers, ViHi.
   1. William Macon, Sr. was the son of Gideon Macon of "The Island," New Kent County. He was a Colonel of militia, Justice of the Court, and member of the House of Burgesses from 1735-43. He was an uncle to Martha Custis's mother. See *Harris*, 1:132-138.
   2. Peter Robinson (1718-1765) of St. John's Parish, King William County, *William and Mary Quarterly*, Series 1, 18:186. In accordance with the method used by E. G. Swem in his *Virginia Historical Index*, this publication will be designated by the initial *W*; the volume number will precede the initial; the series will follow the initial, and this will be followed by the page numbers. See *supra*, George Brett to MW, September 8, 1757, n. 2.

From William Macon

Madam   Decr 21, 1757
    Be pleased to pay the within Sum of Forty Pounds Sterling to
Bartholomew Dandridge and his Receipt shall be a sufficient discharge for
the same agt,

Yr hble Servt
Willm Macon

To Mrs. Martha Custis

Custis Papers, ViHi.

From Robert Clopton

December 23, 1757
    Receiv'd of Mrs. Marthy Custis, Twenty Shillings current money in
full of all demands I say recivd December 23, 1757

(illegible) Robt Clopton[1]

Clopton's Rect
20/
23 Decr 1757

Custis Papers, ViHi.
    1. Robert Clopton was one of the numerous Cloptons of New Kent County. The estate
was indebted to him for £ 1, for assisting Charles Crump for making and lining Daniel Parke
Custis's coffin. *PGWC* 6:252.

From George Heath

December 1757

1756	Colo Daniel Parke Custis Dr	£	s	d
	To Makeing a Black full Trim'd Cloath Suit	11..	6..	6
	To Makeing a Black Cloath Jackett Full trim'd	0..	7..	6
	To yr Boy Wilem a pr off Shagg breeches	0..	3..	0
June	To yr Self a pr off Black Cloath breeches	0..	4..	0
Octor	To Frank Dandriges Blew Cloath Coat & breeches	0..	11..	0
	To finding 2 Sticks of twist at 6 d each	0..	1..	0
Do	To Yr Boy (illegible) Cloath Coat (Illegible)			
	Jacket p each (illegible)	0..	14..	0
	To Yr Man	0..	2..	6

Do	To Makeing a (illegible) and (illegible) Coat	0..10.. 0
Nov	To a Blew Duffel Great Coat	0.. 8.. 0
1757		
June	To Makeing yr Son a Coat & breeches (illegible)	0.. 5.. 0
	To Ditto Yr (illegible)	(illegible)
July	to Do yr Virginal Cloth (illegible)	0.. 8.. 0
7	To Do yr Boy Brechey (illegible)	(illegible)
8	To altering yr 2 Velvett	0.. 8.. 0
9	To Do yr Coat off (illegible)	0.. 1.. 0
1757 13	To Makeing yr Man a suit of Mourning	0..14.. 0
	To Do yr Boy (illegible) Suit	0..13.. 0
	To Do yr Boy Billeys Suit	0..12.. 0
Augst 4	To Do Yr Son a Coat & bree s off Mourning	0.. 5.. 0
7	To Do yr Son a Black Wastcoat & Bree s	0.. 4.. 0
	To do Another Black Wastcoat & bree s	0.. 4.. 0
	To Do Yr Man Anthoney a Double Breasted Wastcoat	0.. 4.. 0
	To Do Yr Boy (illegible) a (illegible)	0.. 3.. 6
	To Do Brechey (illegible)	0.. 4.. 0
	To Do a Black Wast coat & bree s	0.. 7.. 0
Decr 23	To Do yr Son a (illegible) Coat & (illegible) Scarlett Wastcoat	0.. 9.. 0
	To Do yr Son John Virginia Cloath	0.. 4.. 0
Feb	To Do yr Son John Virginia (Cloath)	0.. 3.. 0
	To Do yr Boy John a Suit of Mourning	0..11.. 0
May 20	To Do yr Son makeing Another Coat & bree s	(illegible)
	To Do a Black Wast coat & bree s	(illegible)
June	To Do Yr Son Scaret camblet Bree s	0.. 2.. 0
July 4	To Do a Scarlett Cam(blet) Coat	0..12.. 0
22	To Do 2 (illegible)	0..11.. 0
	To Do yr boy Coat & bree s	0.. 5.. 0
	To Do 1 Frock	0.. 2.. 0
Sept 6	To Do a Coat of Silk & Scarlet Wastcoat & bree s for your Son	0.. 9.. 0
20	To Cutting 20 Negro suits at 2 d pr suits	0.. 3.. 0
Octo	To Do 20 Ditto	0.. 3.. 0
	To do 20 Ditto ·	0.. 3.. 0
Novr 18	To making yr Son Cloath Coat & bree s & wast coat	0..10.. 0
Decr	To makeing Yr Son Crimson Velvet bree s	0.. 2.. 0
	carried over	1..10.. 6
		14..10.. 6
	Ditto To Makeing Jacks Livery Suit	0.. 9.. 0
	To Makeing Brecheys Do	0.. 9.. 0
	To Makeing Georges Do	0.. 7.. 0
	To Makeing Julius Do	0.. 7.. 0
Jan 29	To Makeing yr Sons Cloath bree s	0.. 2.. 0
	To Ditto yr Man's Georges Great coat	0.. 6.. 0

	To Ditto yr Man's Brecheys Coat	0..10.. 0
Feb 3rd	To (illegible)	0.. 6.. 8
	Errors Excepted By Me Geo Heath	17.. 8.. 2
	(illegible)	12.. 1.. 9
	(illegible)	5.. 6.. 5
		17.. 8.. 2

Rec d the above account in full of all demands
against the Estate of Colo. Danl Parke Cutis (sic)
his
George G X Heath[1] 39
marke

DS, Custis Papers, ViHi.
    1. George Heath was a tailor who was often employed by MW to make clothes for her son and the male servants. He may be the George Heath who, as a fourteen year old orphan, was bound to Thomas Bearcroft on July 13, 1748. *PGWC* 6:263, 267, 328-29.

To Bartholomew Dandridge

1757	Mrs Custis Dr. To B Dandridge[1]		
	To Cash		£ 21 . __ . __
	Col Macon's[2] Order Ster £ 40		58 . __ . __
	45 PCt Excha	18	
			79 . __ . __
	Cr		
1757	By Cash		£ 5 . 7 . 6
	By pd Doctor Carter[3]		44 . 14 . 9
	By Mr Dandridge's Order		10 . __ . __
	By 1 pc Lutestring[4] sterl		
	75 p ct, advance		

AD, Custis Papers, ViHi.
    1. See Robert Carter Nicholas to MW, August 7, 1757, n. 2.
    2. See William Macon to MW, December 21, 1757, n. 1.
    3. See Dr. James Carter to MW, November 28, 1757, n. 1.
    4. Lutestring or lustring was "a type of glossy silk fabric - a dress or ribbon of this fabric." *(Oxford English Dictionary)*

To Robert Cary and Company

1758

    An invoice to Mr Cary & Company for the year 1758 on a suite of cloths for myself.
    One Genteel suite of cloths for my self to be grave but not Extravagent nor to be mourning. I have sent a night gown to be dide of

and fashanable couler fitt for me to ware and beg you wont have it dide
better than that I sent Last year but was very badly done. This gown is
of a good Lenght for me one pr Taby stays for myself. I have sent a measure
and beg they may be well shaped and of stiff Bones that will keep there
shape. I wont have my gown made to my stays as I had a hoop Last year.
I have no ocation for one now. The man to make can tell the size to make
my cloths by also. Too of gowns to be made the Best Indien one Dark
(illegible) one of white Callaco gound to be made of very fine
Cala. one hansome suite of Drisdon worked head cloth
2 Drisdon worked hankerchief one (illegible) of plain lavender
4 Indian worked hankerchiefs to cost 10 shillings apeice
one peice of fine plain Lawn (illegible) half Doz (illegible) and   (illegible)
one peice of fine Cambrick (missing) most
2 Cambrick frocks to fitt a girl of three years old
2 pr (illegible) Do to be Covered with Red (illegible)
        and a (illegible) to them a hansome fillitt Ruffes and Tuckes
2 pr silk shoes for Do to be Laced
4 pr Callamanco for Do 4 pr Leather for Do
2 fans for Do 2 necklaces for Do   (2 fans 2 fillits)
12 yeards of Ribbon for Do   self (for a girl of 8 years)
6 pr white kid mittens for Do   (and 4 pr gloves for Do)
4 pr silver shoe Buckles for Do
4 pr fine thread stockings for Do
One cap for a child of one year old
half a dozen pr kid gloves for myself
half a Doz pr kid mittens for Do
4 pr of silk hose of the small 5s fashonod and of the Best silk and very
        (illegible) if shapes are none I woud have 2 pr Pound
6 pr Callamanco Do
4 pr fine thread stockings for Do
8 pr shoes for to fitt a boy of five years old
4 pr thread stockings for Do
4 (illegible) for Do
4 pr worstead stocking for myself
1 Fan to cost 20 shilling
1 Do to cost 10 shillings
2 neck Laces for Do very handsome
a very handsome pr of Gold Shoe Buckles for Do & Gold Girdle   Buckle
(illegible) hatt andd feather for a boy of five years of age
2 plain hatts for Do
one Black satten Bonnett for a Woman
2 Blew satten Bonnetts for a child of 3 years old
3 (illegible) to put in (illegible)
3 (illegible) hankerchiefs

8 pound of starch
too pound of powderd Blew
3 pound Do figg
2 pound of Best indego
half a peice of fine Long Lace
6 thousand Large pins
6 Do of short white Do
6 Do (illegible)
5 hundered of the Best White Chappel sorted neadles none Large
5 hundred Large nedles to sew corse work
2 fine Ivory combes fine tooth
2 large Tortis shell combs fine teeth
2 horn combs
one Rose (illegible)
2 pound of Best Whited Brown thread
4 ounces of 12 peny Do
4 Do 2 shilling Do
4 Do 3 shilling Do
4 ounce of 8 p Do
4 Best Comb Brushes
2 (illegible) to cost 3 shillings a pease
20 Yards of Scarlett Flanning
6 peices of fine (illegible) Tape
3 peices of Narrow Do
3 peices of filliting Do
2 pounds of fine perfumed powdr for the hair
one silver chain & Ring and 2 pin cushions
one handsome neadle
one silver thimble (illegible) for a child of 4 years old
one silver nutmeg grinder
       for the negroes
N 6 Dozen Broad hose
S 4 hansom Chaffen disheses to warm plates on
N 8 peices ozen Biggs
N 20 peirs of Brown (illegible)
N 6 peices of (illegible)
N 10 peices of Best (illegible) cotten
S 4 handsome mahogney (illegible) of Different sizes
S one fine (illegible)
one fine heir sifter
S 20 pound of Reisons
30 do of Currents in Large stone pots
S 6 Mops 6 Clamps
S 3 Brushes to Rub (illegible) with

S 4 to clean silver (illegible) with
S one pound of nutmeggs
S half pound of clover
S half pound of mace
S 3 ounces of Canded nutmegs
S 3 pound of Comfills
S 6 pound of white sugar candy
S 8 pound of almonds
S a Case of Best pickels of all sorts
S a hansome Buroe Dressing Tabe and Glass mahogney
S 4 gallons of Best Salled oil
S one Grose hoghead of Best portter
S one Best Copper preserving Pan
S one Box of Genger (illegible) the Best sort
S half a Reem of (illegible) paper

Df, Custis Papers, ViHi.

From Margaret Carlton

1758	Mrs Margaret Carlton		
	1 Black Sattin Bonnett	£ 0:	5
	1 pr Ticken Stays with Tabby Stomacher	1:	12
	2 yds fine clear Lawn @ 8/0	:	16
	1 pr laced Shoes	(?)	
		3:	4
	50 pc adva	(?)	
		£ 4:	10
	By 5 months & half Service at 8 £ p Ann	3:	14
	By Cash	1:	2
		£ 4 : 16 :	0

(Docketed)
CCG Carlton   Mrs. M: Carlton[1]
Margaret Carlton   Acct 4:10
                              1758

AD, Custis Papers, ViHi.

1. This would indicate Margaret Carlton dealt in clothing and dry goods and that she was employed by MW. She was probably the wife of one of the numerous small land-holding Carltons of King William County. *Harris*, 1:531, 554.

From John Mercer

Madam (January 4, 1758)

I am sorry I put you to the trouble of a Journey to Williamsburg about my Account, as I understand it is only like to produce a Reference, in which I am sure to be the Sufferer. When your Brother acquainted me that you desired a Copy of my Account,[1] I made no manner of doubt that the late Colo. Custis had either left particular Directions about it, or that you had been well acquainted with his Intentions upon that head, more especially as he had desired me not long before to draw off his Father's[2] & his own Accounts from the beginning & to give Credit for everything I had ever received from either of them. This I accordingly had drawn off before I saw him, for the last time, but as I then little imagined that would be the Case & he did not particularly enquire for it, I did not choose to deliver it to him (tho I was persuaded so to do) for this very good reason, that the Appeal was not then decided & as he, as well as his Father always made the Success of the Cause the measure of the Satisfaction I was to expect, & I was always sanguine enough to believe that Determination would be in his favor, I thought it would be more to my Advantage to wait that Event & I left the Account with several others in the hands of Mr Lyon.[3]

I understand by my son Mr Waller reckons the Interest on my bond amounts to something considerable: It is an Article I little expected to have heard mentioned except my demand was likewise to bear Interest the great number of years I was employed in that Cause. I should never have taken that money from old Colo. Custis, but as part of my fee, for tho he often promised he would liberally reward me if the Cause was determined in his Favour, a friend of mine who knew he had given Sir John Randolph[4] a piece of Land as part of his fee in the same Cause & whose death before it was finished, made the old Gentleman cautious of advancing, advised me to secure something in hand which I might do under pretense of borrowing & not wait till the Determination of the suit which was like to last many years. This last put me upon asking him to lend me an hundred pounds, which he readily agreed to on my own giving a Bond for it, which I did not think fit to scruple as it must have shewn that I mistrusted his Generosity. What he might have done had he lived till the Trial I can't tell, but his Professions were always such that I was persuaded they were sincere; Mr Waller told my wife he had left me a Legacy in his will, what it was or how it came to be altered I never heard but I am sure no Behaviour of mine occasioned it.

The late Colo Custis always promised that if he gained the Cause he would satisfy me to my utmost Expectation; He was so far from looking on my Bond as a Debt that when he came up to my House he said he had intended to have brought it up & delivered it to me, and I don't doubt but he may have mentioned the same thing to some of his Acquaintances, but if not, it can hardly be presumed that he would have paid me so much money as he did, if he had esteemed me his Debtor. At the time he paid me the forty nine pounds credited in my Account he told me it was all the money he then had, but again repeated his Promise that he would make me ample satisfaction, & when it is considered that this was before I had drawn that long state of the case to send to England, I could not persuade myself that was not only the last money I was to receive, but that my Bond would afterwards be set up against me: That Colo. Custis looked upon himself to be in my Debt, I presume will very plainly appear from the last Letter I received from him, a Copy of which is annexed.

Mr Waller, I dare say, is as proper a Judge of my Fees as any man in Virginia but he cannot know what trouble I was at during the sixteen years I was concerned in the Cause. I can't even give an Account of it myself but from the several items mentioned in my Books, which were never set down but on Occasion of some very extraordinary trouble; but surely it would seem very odd if I was not allowed for all the Trouble I have been at as much the Secretary[5] has long since received out of the Cause for his Clerks copying the Papers, which as yet I dare say I fall far short of. What Col. Custis intended me had he lived & the Cause been determined in his favor I can't tell. I own I expected five hundred Pounds & my Reason was that he offered me so much to go to England & sollicit it.

I am told Mr Waller seems to be of Opinion that the Matter will in the End be determined against you, but recommends putting out your money at Interest & not letting it lie dead till the Determination. Tho he is certainly right in the last part of his Advice I can't help differing with him as to the first Point or I should not have made such an Offer as I did in my letter to Mr Power[6] to indemnify you against that claim on having the Use of the Principal Sum demanded till your Children come of age, & which to Prove the Sincerity of my Opinion I would still stand to & give the most Unexceptional Security can be desired. But should you not think proper to accept that Offer I should be obliged to you to let me have four thousand pounds at Interest for four or five years in which time you could not want to call it in, which I am always in doubt may be the Speaker's Case,[6] who is only obliged to give me Six months Notice which might in the presnt Scarcity of money in the Countrey put me to very great Inconvenience. The Security I am sure you will have no Objection to, being Colo. Tayloe,[7] Colo. Presley Thornton[8] & Colo. Champe,[9] all or any of them. I flatter myself that you would give me the Preference as the late Colo. Custis promised he would do, if he got clear of Dunbar's demand. I shall be glad to receive an Answer as soon as it will suit your Convenience & I am with very great Regard [10]

Madam
Your most obedt & humble
Servt
J Mercer[11]

Jan 4th 1758

Copy of Colo. Custis's Letter to me.

Dear Sir

Your by your I received & am sorry to hear that you are so involved as you say you. I thought or at least hoped that I had satisfied you that I had not near the quantity of money as you & some others imagined, I am sure I have not increased my flock much since, & I have the same Complaint to make as you have having a great Sum of money out & cannot get any in. There are several Gentlemen that have very lately applied to me for Money one of which is of the Council,[12] which made me make a very solemn Declaration that I never would meddle with one farthing I have in England until my Law suit there was over, which if should go against me, all that I have in the whole World wou'd scarce do: It is very true that you have all along gave me the greatest Assurances that cou'd be, that I could not be hurt, but you nor no one here cannot tell what the Opinion of the Judges in England will be. As to the Complaint which you make against your Client not paying you, I do not know whether you mean me as one that will not pay you, neither will I say you do: I presume you have kept an Account of what I have already paid you on Account of Dunbar's Suit, & if you will let me know what it is I still remain in your debt which I suppose will not be out of Reason, I will readily pay it. I am

Dr Sir
Your most obedient humble
Servant
Dan Parke Custis

(Docket)
4 Jany 1758

ALS, Custis Papers, ViHi.

1. In auditing the estate accounts attention was focused on bonds (loans) held by the estate against John Mercer, as well as unpaid legal fees due Mercer by the Custises. Mercer had acted as attorney for the Custises in the Dunbar suit. Martha, apparently acting on the advice of her brother, Bartholomew Dandridge, communicated a desire to obtain an accounting from Mercer. She was concerned enough to make a special trip from White House to Williamsburg to inquire into the matter.

2. John Custis IV (1678-1749), father of Daniel Parke Custis, married Frances Parke, daughter of Colonel Daniel Parke, in 1705. He possessed about 15,000 acres in Northampton, York, New Kent, and King William Counties. He was one of the wealthiest and the most eccentric Virginians of his time. For upwards of twenty years he was embroiled with the heirs of his father-in-law, Daniel Parke's natural daughter, Lucy Chester Dunbar. See supra, MDC to John Hanbury, December 20, 1757, n. 1.

3. See supra, Benjamin Waller to MDC, August 30, 1757, n. 2; *Dictionary of American Biography*, N.Y., 1943, 11:536, hereafter cited as *D.A.B.*

4. Sir John Randolph I, of Turkey Island. He possessed the outstanding legal mind in Virginia, was a skilled diplomat, and the only Virginian knighted during the colonial period. In 1734 he was elected Speaker of the House of Burgesses and Treasurer of the Colony. See *D.A.B.*, 11:360-61.

5. Thomas Nelson (1715-1787), often designated "Secretary Nelson." He was Secretary of the Colony from 1744 until 1776. He served as a member of the Council and as its President. See 10 W (1) 167; Evans, *Thomas Nelson of Yorktown*, Williamsburg, 1975, p. 10-11.

6. James Power, attorney of New Kent and King William Counties. He served both counties in the House of Burgesses and served on committees that were concerned with military affairs during the late war. He was a close friend, confidante, and legal advisor of Daniel Parke Custis. See supra, Benjamin Waller to MDC, August 30, 1757, n. 1.

7. Colonel John Tayloe (1721-1779) of Mount Airy, Richmond County. Member of the Council from ca 1757. He became a staunch friend of GW.

8. Colonel Presley Thornton (1721-1769) of Northumberland County. Member of the House of Burgesses from 1748-1760, and then a member of the Council. GW described him as "a man of great worth."

9. Colonel John Champe of Lambs Creek, King George County. His daughter married Samuel Washington, GW's younger brother. (See *Genealogies of Virginia Families*, 1:722-729).

10. Her answer has not been found. During the sixteen years Mercer had acted as attorney in the Dunbar case, what little payment received from the Custises was recorded, but never presented to them in full account for services rendered, preferring to wait until the case was settled. It was Mercer's understanding they would take ample care of him for his efforts. Both parties were hopeful it would be decided in their favor. Others, such as Colonel Benjamin Waller, were not as optimistic. In addition Mercer had borrowed money from old Colonel Custis, steadfastly maintaining it was to be used to offset his legal fees when the case came to a conclusion. Later Mercer made a large loan from MDC. It was not until 1760 that he received full payment from GW for his services in the Dunbar case. *PGWC* 6:211 (n), 272, 274 n. 4.

11. John Mercer (1704-1768) immigrated from Ireland in 1720. He settled at "Marlborough," Stafford County, and acquired considerable wealth as a successful lawyer and businessman. He was Secretary of the Ohio Compay. His aggressive tactics in the courtroom resulted in his disbarrment for a time in 1734. He then turned to legal scholarship and spent the next two years in writing *An Exact Abridgement of all the Public Acts of the Assembly of Virginia in Force and Use*, Williamsburg, 1737. All county justices were advised to possess a copy. Later he became a justice for Stafford County. His advice was widely sought and GW consulted him on a number of occasions. (See, *The Diaries of George Washington*, Jackson, et. al., (ed) Charlottesville, 1976, 1:9, 247 (hereafter cited as *Diaries*).

12. Both John Blair, Esquire and Burwell Bassett were members of the Council and had bonds due. *PGWC* 6:254, 256.

From Robert Crawford

(January 10, 1758)

Shipped by the Grace of God, in good Order and well Conditioned, By Richd & Alex. Oswald & Compy, Merchts in Glasgow in and upon the good Ship Called the -Tryal- wherof is Master, under God, for this present Voyage, Robert Crawford and, by God's Grace, Bound for York River in Virginia.

One Bundle Merchandize On the proper Accot & risque of Mrs Martha Custis being Marked and Numbred as in the Margin, and are to be Delivered In the like good Order, and well Conditioned, at the aforesaid Port of York River in Virginia (the Danger of the Seas only Excepted) unto said Mrs. Martha Custis or to her Assigns, he or they paying Freight for the said Goods already pay'd with Primage & Average accustomed, In Witness whereof, the Master or Purser of the said Ship hath affirmed to three Bills of Lading, all of this Tenor and Date; the one of which three Bills being accomplished, the other two to stand Void. And so God send the good Ship to her desired Port in Safety, Amen. Dated in Port Glasgow 10th Jany 1758

Robert Crawford

(docketed)

M 4 C

x x

1758

DS Custis Papers, ViHi.

From George Gordon

January 12, 1758

Then Recd of Mrs Custis the Sume of thirteen pounds fourteen Shils being in full for one hog d of mollases & one hund limes.[1]

pr Geo Gordon

(Docketed)

Gordon's Rect.

£ 13 - 14

12th Jany. '58

DS Custis Papers, ViHi.
 1. The document is in the handwriting of MDC.

From Nath. Woodroof

January 17, 1758

Mrs. (sic) Cary

D P C Bot of Nath. Woodroofe Hosier at the Unicorn near the Corner of Friday Street, Cheapside

4 p. girls fine white thread hose	20	0. 6. 8
4 p. boys do	do 21	0. 8. 0
6 p. wom 4d Super fine Cotton	6/6	1.19. 0
		2.13. 8

A.D., Custis Papers, ViHi.From Stephen Fourneau Hoomes
January 18, 1758

The Estate of Coll: Danl Parke Custis Esqr To Stephen Furnea (sic) Hoomes[1]
1758 June 21st To 208 lb of Barr Iron @ 3d p lb £ 2 : 12 This Day come before me Stephen Furnea Hoomes & made Oath to ye above Acct. Given under my Hand this 8th Day of Octobr 1757. Recd Jan 18, 1758 The Contents.
Rich. Littlepage[2]
(docketed) Mrs. Custis's Acct
Hoomes Rect
£ 2. 12
18 Jany 1758

A.D.S., Custis Papers, ViHi.
    1. See Supra, from Richard Littlepage, October 8, 1757, n. 1.
    2. See Supra, from Richard Littlepage, October 8, 1757, n. 2.

From Bartholomew Dandridge

February 21, 1758

1757	Mrs Custis Dr to B Dandridge		
	To Cash		£ 21
	Col Macon's[1] Order Shw	£ 40.._.__	
	45 p Cr. Excha	18.._.__	58 _____
			79.._.__
1757	Cr.		
	By Cash		£ 5.. 7.. 6
	By pd Doctor Carter[2]		44..14.. 9
	By Mr Dandridges Order		10.._.. 0
	By 1 ps Lutestring		
	By Cash		
	75 pct advance		

      Recd of Mrs Custis the sum of eight Pounds Seven Shilings, nine pence Paid in full of all Demands
B Dandridge
(docketed)
21 Feby 1758
Mrs Custis
Accot with
B Dandridge
£ 8.7.9

A.D.S., Custis Papers, ViHi.
    1. See supra, from William Macon, December 21, 1757, n. 1.
    2. See supra, from Dr. James Carter, November 28, 1757, n. 1.

From George Brett

February 23, 1758

Received of Mrs Martha Custis three Pounds ten Shillings ct money For Building too Fishing (illegible)

(docketed)

Bretts Rect[1]

£ 3 - 10

23 Feby 1758

DS. Custis Papers, ViHi.

1. George Brett was a local carpenter who built fishing boats. See supra, from George Brett, September 8, 1757, n. 1.

From Robert Cary and Company

Madam   London 1 March 1758

Having disposed of your Tobacco received p Coxen inclosed recd Transmit the Sale

21 Hhds TC	Nett Proceeds	£ 330/5
15 Do D P C	do	216

both wch are to your Credit & as included the best for your Interest we hope theyll give Content

By this Conveyance we have sent all the Goods wch you were pleased to Order, We wish them safe & hope they'l meet your Approbation. The Charge £ 458 - 4 - 10 is here Inclosed

The Bearer Capn Coxenns Usual we Recommend to you in the Dispatch p his Ship & whatever Freight you may please to command he will gladly Accomodate you

We Truly are

> Madam
> Your Most Hble Servt
> Robert Cary & Co

Copy[1]

The Original p Coxen

(Docket)

Sales of 36 Hhds by Cary

L.S., Custis Papers, ViHi.

1. There are two almost identical copies in the Custis Papers, the second of which was probably Captain Adam Coxen's copy.

From Robert Cary and Company

London, March 1, 1758

"Estate of Colonel D.P. Custis; charges on Fifteen Hogsheads of Tobacco received p the Hazard, Adam Coxen, Virginia."

14704 pounds of tobacco were sold by Robert Carey and Company to four buyers for £ 642.. 3.. 5. Expenses incurred: subsidies, imposts, duties, freight, primage, cooperage, cartage, warehouse room, brokerage, postage, entry inwards, bond, bill money, commission, and petty charges. The expenses totalled £ 426.. 3.. 5. The net proceeds amounted to £ 216 and was applied to the estate's indebtedness to the Cary Company.

Five hogsheads were sold to John Burdon and five hogsheads to Kirby & Co. Two were sold to William Featherstone and three to Lardner & Co.[1]

D.S., Custis Papers, ViHi.

1. The document has been summarized. The original is on an oversized ledger sheet, creating difficulties in reproduction.

From Robert Cary and Company

Madam   London 2 March 1758

We have already wrote you by this Conveyance but as the ships are not gone down it gives us an opportunity of Acknowledging the rec t of yours by Crookshanks of the 20 December covering Letters of your Administration, as also Power of Attorney to receive the Dividends on the Bank stock all wch are quite Necessary -- Your Goods now Ordered are putt on Board the Hazard & enclosed them in your general Invoice; we received the Order but 2 days before the Convoy was to sail so that is they are not so Compleat as we could wish we hope you'l excuse it.

It is always our Maxim in Trade to furnish our Correspondants with the Sales of this Goods as also Acct. Curt. Annually (missing) be not only Satisfactory but really Necessary -- We believe you may thank us for the Sale of your Tobacco at Mr. H house they were partly sold at 10/2 but on our disposing of our's at 11 s they gott as we have hear'd of our Friend the same Price.
We Remain

> Mad m Your Most Hble
> Servt
> Robert Cary & Co.

Copy
the Original P. Coxen

ALS on the verso of supra, from Robert Cary and Company, March 1, 1758. Custis Papers, ViHi.

From Charles Crump

March 6, 1758

Dr.

The Estate of Collo: Custis Deceasd	£ 2 - 3
to a black Walnut Coffin	
to my Coming to line to line (sid) ye Coffin	
Mar: 6 1758	1 - 1 - 6
	3 - 4 - 6

(docketed)
Chas Crump[1]
Recd 3 - 4 - 6

A.D., Custis Papers, VIi Hi.
   1. Probably Charles Crump of New Kent County. He was a captain in a Virginia regiment in 1758. See, 9 W (2) 66; *Henning's Statutes*, 7:228; PGWV 6:252

To Robert Stephenson

March 8, 1758

Madam Custus	To Robert Stephenson	
	March the 8 1758	
	To one Bottle Clarrett	5. 0
	To one Hund Limes	5. 0
	To 2 Grose of Best Corks	6. 0
		£ 8.16. 0

Recd the above of Mr Vallentine in full
Rob:t Stephenson[1](docketed by G.W.)
M C Vo 16
Stephenson Rect
to
Vallentine

A.D.S., Custis Papers, ViHi.
   1. A payment was allowed Robert Stephenson for "Sundries for Mourning." PGWC 6:253.

To John Case

March 20, 1758
   Recvd of Mrs Martha Custis twelve Shillings and six pence for mending and (illegible) two Saines
March 20th 1758
p Mr Jno Case[1]
(docketed by G. W.)
Jno Case for

Mending 2 Saines
12/6
20 March 1758

ADS. Custis Papers, ViHi.
    1. John Case was also allowed £2.7.6 for mending seines. *PGWC* 6:252.

From Charles Whitlock

Mrs Custis to Chals Whitlock	Dr.
34 barrels Corn @ 7/	£ 11 - 18
34 lb feathers @ 1/4	2 - 5 - 4
2 1/2 yds lining @ 2/6	- 6 - 3
	2 - 11 - 7
	9 - 6 - 5

Recd April 5, 1758
of Mrs Custis Nine pounds six shilings & five pence in full of all accounts pr me
Charles Whitlock[1]
Chs Whitlock
Acct in full
9-6-5 Apl 1758

A.D.S., Custis Papers, ViHi.
    1. Charles Whitlock is listed as an overseer on one of the Custis plantations. The document
is docketed by GW.

From Lain Jones

Recd of Mrs Martha Custis the Tax on 63 Tithes a 4 The Tax on 6264
Acres of Land at 2/3 1 chariott & chais due for the year 1757.
Lain Jones DSh[1]
Lain Jones Shr of
New Kent Rect
1758

A.D.S., Custis Papers, ViHi.
    1. Lain Jones, deputy sheriff of New Kent County, was a cousin of MDC. *PGWC* 6:252,
256, 258.

From William Poindexter

April 11, 1758

Recd of Mrs Martha Custis fore Pounds it Being for Inspection pr Wm Poindexter[1]

11 Apl 1758

Inspectors Rect £ 4

A.D.S. Custis Papers, ViHi.
1. William Poindexter (1721-?) of Cedar Lane, New Kent County. The charge against the estate was for inspection of Tobacco. The docket is in the handwriting of GW.

From Richard Usrey

April 24, 1758

Recd April 24, 1758 of Mrs. Custis twelve Shillings & six pence for Potatoe Seed in full of all demands.

Richard Usrey[1]

(docketed by G.W.)

Richd Usrey

12/6, 21st April 1758

A.D.S., Custis Papers, ViHi.
1. *PGWC* 6:252.

From John Mercer

Dear Madam   April 24, 1758

I have yet heard nothing mentioned of Dunbar or his Cause which I imagine I should have done had he come to a Resolution to have gone on with it. He may proceed not withstanding, but it is very plain he is not so sanguine as Mr Hanbury represents in his Pursuit. Had he been so, he might have sent in the original Order of the King in Council, as soon as Mr Hanbury could have sent you the Copy of it. Should he proceed I am of Opinion that your Resolution of having a Guardian appointed for your Son is a very prudent one, but much will depend upon the Choice of a proper one. It must not only be a Man of Fortune and Character but a Man of Interest & Reputation in England. Few Men would answer your Expectations that way better or do more for your Son's Interest than the Speaker[26] if he would undertake it & I am persuaded from the Knowledge I have of his general Benevolence that he would hardly refuse it, if applied to. I spoke to him about my account which he said he would undertake to settle if you would signify your Consent to him before which I thought it would be improper to lay the Papers before him.

The Principal Reason however of this Trouble is to know, Madam, whether you have yet come to a Resolution what sum of money you will supply me with. Whether Sterling or currency and when I may have it. The sooner it could be the more Service it would be to me & if it could be during this General Court. Colo Tayloe & Col Thornton are & will continue in Town, so that it would save me a good deal of trouble. Your answer will very much oblige[2]

Dear Madam

> Your Most Obedient
> Humble servant
> J. Mercer
> April 24, 1758

(Docket by GW)
Mr. Mercer
24 April 1758

A.L.S., Custis Papers, ViHi.
  1. John Robinson. See Supra. John Mercer to MDC, January 4, 1758, no. 7.
  2. The estate made loans on May 12 and November 4, 1758, totaling £2100 current money (£1500 Sterling) *PGWC* 6:256, 261, n. 29.

From John Blair

May 8, 1758

Received May 8th of Joseph Valentine Twenty Two Pounds Ten Shillings & five pence Curt Gold as the Quitrents of 17438 acres belonging the Estate of Col. Daniel Parke Custis Decd for the year 1757. in the Several County just he paid it for 1756. wch I promise to pay to the Several Sheriffs as usual

John Blair[1]

(Docket by GW)
The President's rect for Quitrents
17,438 acres pd 8th May 1758

A.D.S., Custis Papers, ViHi.
  1. John Blair, President of the Council, and at this time Acting-governor. As President of the Council he assumed the office of Governor due to the departure of Governor Robert Dinwiddie for England. Dinwiddie asked to be relieved of his duties because of ill health. Blair served until Governor Francis Fauquier arrived in June, 1758. (Morton, R. L., *Colonial Virginia*, 2:605, n. 3, 714).

From Epaphroditus Howle

May 12, 1758

Recd May 12th 1758 of Mrs Martha Custis pounds twelve in full for my Shear of Corn made in the year 1757[1]

        his

Recd by me Dite x Howl

        mark

(Docketed by G.W.)

£ 12. 12

D. Howls Acct in full for his

Corn - 1757

May 12, 1758

D.S., Custis Papers, ViHi.
    1. *PGWC* 6:252, 266

From James Gildart

Liverpool 20 May 1758

Sales of 5 hhds of Tobacco p. the Hare Daniel Darcy from Virginia on Acct of the late Daniel Parke Custis Esqr.[1]

D P C No. 2. 9. 3

A.D. Custis Papers, ViHi.
    1. *PGWC* 6:325.

From James Gildart

Liverpool May 1758

Sales of 16 hhds of Tobacco rec d p. the Gildart John Mulloy from Virginia on Acct of the late Daniel Parke Custis Esqr.[1]

D P C No 3. 9. 12

A.D., Custis Papers, ViHi.
    1. *PGWC* 6:325.

From Robert Cary and Company

May 29, 1758

To Martha Custis: Charges on Twenty Hogsheads of Tobacco, received per the King of Prussia, Robert Neks, at Virginia.

19461 pounds of tobacco were tallied at London on March 1, 1758. The tobacco was sold on May 29, 1758 to a single buyer, John Burton, for

£ 816.. 2.. 6. The net proceeds amounted to £ 230.. 3.. 3 and was applied to the estate's indebtedness to the Cary company.[1]

A.D., Custis Papers, ViHi.
    1. Due to the large size of the document it has been summarized.

From James Gildart

Sales   Liverpool, May 31, 1758
    Of 16 hhds Tobacco recd P Gildart John Mulloy from Virginia for Acct of Daniel Park Custis Esqr[1]

D P C No 3	9.. 1..26				
x x 5	9.. 0.. 5				
14	9.. 1.. 5				
1	8.. 1.. 9				
25	9.. 1..26				
9	9.. 1..23				
	55.. 0..10	Suttle	6570		
			430		
6 p cent 370	Draft			5740 @ 3 1/2	84..14.. 2
No 13	9.. 1..12				
6	9.. 0.. 2				
12	9.. 2.. 9				
11	9.. 3..26				
4	9.. 3..16				
10	9.. 1..16				
2	7.. 3.. 5				
7	9.. 3..22				
3	8.. 2.. 2				
	81.. 1..26	Suttle	9126		
6 p Cent 5488	Draft 90		638	3488 @ 3/4	114..18..10
					206..15.. 0
Freight 56	Impost 32	Mark 1/		Primage 8/	
	Town & Trade duty 8/		commission 40		62.. 6.. 0
					144.. 6.. 0

E Excepd May 31, 1758
James Gildart

ADS. Custis Papers, ViHi.
    1. See supra, from James Gildart, May (31), 1758.

From James Gildart

Sales   May 31, 1758

Of 5 hhds Tobacco recd p Hare Daniel Darcy from York River for Acc of Daniel Park Custis Esqr[1]

SD P C
  X X

No 2.	9.. 3.. 8	cutt 26				
1.	8.. 1..24	cutt 73				
4.	9.. 2..13			99 _____@ 1/2		0.. 4.. 1
	27.. 3..17	Suttle	3125			
6 p Cent	188 Draft	30	218	2907	@ 2d	(?)
No 5.	9.. 3.. 0					
3.	9.. 0..16	Cutt	87			
	188.. 3..16	Suttle	(?)			
6 p Cent	127 draft		147	1969	@ 2d	21..10.. 8 1/2
						52.. 4.. 1

Freight £ 17..10   Impost 10/Mark 11
Primage 2/6d
Town & Trade duty 2/6d Commission 25   19..11.. 0

£ 32..13.. 1

May 31st 1758
Jan Gildart
A.D.S., Custis Papers, ViHi.

1. See supra, from James Gildart, May (31), 1758.

To Robert Cary & Company

Gent   Virginia, June 1, 1758

I wrote to you the 30th of April last by the Anna Capt. Eastern to which I refer you. I have only now to acquaint you that besides the Bills of Exchange there mentioned viz. one Set of Bills for £ 600-three Sets for £ 200 each, one Set for £ 107.10--one Set £ 100 --& one Set for £ 92.10 - dated the 28th of April payable to Col Burwell Bassett, I have since drawn on you 1 Set of Bills for £ 500 --& 1 set for £ 250 payable to Col Thomas Moore dated May 16th. One set of Bills for $ 100 -- One Set for £ 200, One Set for £300 --, and one Set for 400 -- dated May 12th payable to Mr John Mercer & one Set payable to Mr. Bartho. Dandridge for £200 dated May 18th which I as I am obligated to make use of all the Money due to Mr

Custis's Estate I hope these Bills will all meet-with due Honor, & am Gentlemen[1] Your most hble Servt

M C

To Robt Cary Esq & Comapny
Merchts in London
Cary & Co June 1, 1758

Df., Custis Papers, ViHi.
1. The bills of exchange were for money owed by the estate.

To John Hanbury & Company

Gentn.   Virginia. June 1st 1758
I wrote to you the 30th of April last by the Anna Capt. Eastern to which I refer, by him I sent you 17 Hhds of Tobo, which I hope will prove very fine and as Tobo is now very scarce & it is certain very little will be made the ensuing Crop, I hope I shall get an uncommon Price for this Tobacco, inclosed is a Bill of Lading for it, I wrote to you for Insurance which I dont doubt but you have made.
Besides the Bills of Exchange mentioned in my Letter by Eastern drawn on you viz 4 Sets for £ 250 cash payable to Colo. Bernard Moore, dated April 18th, 2 Sets payable to Mr. Philip Whitehead Claiborne, for £ 100 each dated the same Day, & One Set for £ 200 -- two Sets for £ 50 -- each payable to Mr. William Dandridge dated the 29th of April, I have drawn 1 Set of Bills for £ 250 -dated May 16th payable to Col. Thomas Moore. One Set for £ 500 -- payable to Mr. John Mercer dated May 8th and two sets for £ 100 each payable to Mr. Bartholomew Dandridge, one dated May 20th & the other May 18th being obliged to make use of all the money due to Mr. Custis's Estate. I hope these Bills will all meet with due Honor, & am[1]

Gent n
Your mo. hble Servt
M C

To Messrs John Hanbury
& Company Merchts in
London

Df, Custis Papers, ViHi.
1. See supra, to Robert Cary and Company, June 1, 1758.

From John Wheldon

(June 5, 1758)

Shipped by the Grace of God, in good Order and well Conditioned by Mrs Martha Custis in and upon the good Ship, called the Prince Fredrick of London whereof is Master, under God, for this present Voyage, John Wheldon of London and now riding at Anchor in York River and by Gods Grace bound for London so say Fifteen Hogs Heads of Tobacco. being Marked and Numbered as in the Margent, and are to be delivered in the like good Order, and well Conditioned, at the aforesaid Port of London (the Danger of the Seas only excepted) unto Mr. Robt Cary Marchant of London - or to his Assigns, he or they paying Freight for the said goods at Fourteen Pounds Sterling p. Tun - with Primage Overage accustomed. In Witness whereof, the Master or Purser of the said Ship, both affirmed to three Bills of Lading, all of this Tenor and Date; the one of which three Bills being accomplished, the other two to stand void. and so God send the Good Ship to her desired Port in Safety. Amen. Dated in Virginia, the 5th of June 1758

John Wheldon[1]

TC No A:B:C:D:E:F
No 1:2:3:4:5:6
DPC No 7:8:N
Impost & Cocket not pay'd
(Docket)
15 Hhds p the Prince Fredrick
London 5th June 1758

A.D.S., Custis Papers, ViHi.

1. John Wheldon was a shipmaster, sailing for the Hanbury firm. On September 29, 1759 GW complained to Hanbury concerning Wheldon's premature sale of tobacco.

From James Wheldon

June 6, 1758

Reced of Mrs Custis fifteen shills for on Jars of Raissens
pr Jas Wheldon
(Docket by GW)
Jas Wheldons
Rect 15/
6th June 1758

A.D.S., Custis Papers, ViHi.

From Capel Hanbury

Esteemed Friend   London June 23, 1758
     It is with very great Concern that I am to acquaint thee that yesterday morning my dear Relation & Partner J Hanbury died at his house in Essex; his Son & myself will carry on ye business & hope for a Continuance of thy Consignments & friendship & shall be extremely oblig'd to thee to recommend us to any of thy friends, we will endevour to conduct business so as to meet with the approbation of all our friends. We hope our not enlarging at present will be excusd as it is owing to ye great affliction we are under, shall do it in a very short time & advise all occurrances relative to affairs now under our care.[1]
I am with great regard

                                             Thy Assurd Friends
                                             Capel Hanbury

To Mrs. Martha Custis
New Kent County
Virginia

A.L.S., Custis Papers, ViHi.
     1. See, GW to Capel Hanbury, June 12, 1759. *PGWC* 6:322, 323.

From John Mercer

                                                       June 14, 1758

1758	April 18	Drew on Hanbury[1] in Favr	Bernd Moore	£ 1000 at 40	
		Do	Ph W Claiborne	200	
	28	Cary	Burwell Bassett	1500	40
	29	Hanbury	Wm Dandridge	300	
	May 16	Do	Tho Moore	250	
		Cary	Do	750	
	12	Do	Jno Mercer	1500	
	18	Do	Bartho Dandridge	200	
		Hanbury	Do	100	
		Gildart	Do	200	
	20	Hanbury	Do	100	
	June 14	Cary	Phil Johnson	50	

A.D., Custis Papers, ViHi.
     1. The accounts represent funds drawn on the three English mercantile firms and deposited to the accounts of the individuals listed in the right hand column.

From Capel and Osgood Hanbury

Esteemed Friend   London 6 July 1758
    Our C Hanbury has wrote Thee by sundry opportunitie's advising the Death of our dear Relation & Partner J Hanbury, that we continue the Business and hope for Continuance of thy Friendship and Consignments. Inclos'd we have sent the Sales of thy hhds Tobo p the King of Prussia, hope they will meet with thy approbation. We were assured by sundry Persons that the Tobo sent to Cary was better than that Sent us. Herewith comes thy Books wch wish Safe & to thy satisfaction. Dunbar has not said anything to us about the Law affair, nor have we anything to Communicate relative thereto, when we have shall embrace the first opportunity to advise thereof. We are very sorry to inform our Friends that the Anna was taken the 13th Ulto by a Bayone Privateer of 18 guns and 142 men and after being in her possession 7 days was luckily retaken by 3 Privateers Belonging to Bristol and Carried into Falmouth.[1] We are taking the necessary Steps to adjust the Salvage and get the ship and Cargo into our own Possession that no Care may be wanting to make the most of our Friends Tobo. We have no Letters by the Anna owing to the Privateers People all papers and everything Else out of the Cabbin whether they are destroy'd or not we cannot yet learn, as soon as the Salvage is adjusted shall advise Thee, as also The State of the Insurance. We hope for a continuance of thy Friendship and Consignments and we assure Thee That no endeavours Shall be wanting to Conduct Business so as to meet wth approbation.

                                        We are with Esteem
                                        Thy assurd Friends
                                        Capel Hanbury
                                        Osgood Hanbury

To
Martha Custis
York River
Virginia
p Capt Danmer
(Docket)
Hanbury 6. July 1758

ALS. Custis Papers, ViHi.
    1. *PGWC* 6:268-70; GW to Capel and Osgood Hanbury, June 12, 1758, 324, n. 4.

From Robert Cary and Company

Madm   London 17 July 1758

To our's already wrote you by this Conveyance we Referr, since which your Favour of the 30th April is now before us & your several Drafts to the Amount of £ 1500 we have already Accepted & when we shall punctually be paid

As the Accot sales & Accot. Currt. sent p Turner have in all probability miscarried we have now sent the Copy's

Inclosed is the Charge of Obtaining Letters of Administring to the Receiving the Dividend on the £ 1650 Bank Stock which Charge £ 7..7 is to thy Estates Debit - the Bank Directors have as yet not Entered your Power of Adm. in their Books till they do tho we hope it won't be long we cannot receive the Interest - Mr John Hanbury departed this Life the 23d Ulto. & while he lived we coud not ask for the Enlargement of your Consignments but now as things are Differently cicumstanced we may safely do it & as such we hope (in) the future to receive all your Crops, for it is Evident the less hands Tobacco goes in the greater Probability there is of keeping up a living Price & therefore must naturally be productive of our Friend's Interest-.

Are sorry to hear the Crops are so short & we hope the Prices will Compensate (illegible) little matter for the Difference.

> We are Madm
> Your most Hum. Servt
> Robert Cary & Co.

Copy
Mrs. Martha Custis
To
Mrs Martha Custis
New Kent Co. Virginia
p the Dispatch
(illegible)
(Docket)
Letter 17th July --- 1759 (sic)
Cary - 17th July - 1759 (sic)

A.L.S., Custis Papers, ViHi.

From John Hazelgrove

July 21, 1758

Received of Mrs. Custis July 21, 1758 one pound in all for 2 spinning wheals[1]

John Hazelgrove[2]

(Docketed by GW).
John Hazelgrove
£ 1 - 0 - 0
21st July 1758

D.S., Custis Papers, ViHi.
    1. In the handwriting of MDC.
    2. *PGWC* 6:253.

From Sarah Ragland

July 22d 1758

received of Ms Custis on pound 12/ in full of all Demands to this Day I say Received by me

her
Sa X Ragland[1]
mark

(Docketed)
Sarah Ragland
Rect £ 1 . 12 . 6
22d July 1758

DS. Custis Papers, ViHi.
    1. The receipt is in the handwriting of MDC. The payment was for weaving Virginia cloth on four occasions. *PGWC* 6:253.

From William Clayton

At a Court held for New Kent County
the 10th of August 1758

On the Motion of Anthony Waddy a witness for Francis Foster at the Suit of John Parke Custis an infant by Martha Custis his next Freind It is ordered That the said Foster pay him Four hundred and Ten pounds of Tobacco for Two Daies attendance and Travelling Sixty Miles twice and returning according to Law.[1]

Wm Clayton

A.D.S., Custis Papers, ViHi.
    1. *PGWC* 6:263, 264 n.5.

From Joseph Pond

August the 10 1758
Received of Mrs Custis ten shillings in full of all Demands to this day

I say Receivd by me
his
Joseph X Pond[1]
mark

(Docketed by GW)
Jos: Pond Acct
10: 10th Augt 1758

D.S., Custis Papers, ViHi
1. Joseph Pond was a brickmason who did "brickwork at the graveyard and and Monument." *PGWC* 6:252. Receipt in the handwriting of MDC.

From Epaphroditus Howle

August 12, 1758
Rec.d August ye 12 of Mrs Martha Custis the sum of twenty one pounds one shilling and three pence in full of accounts.

Recd by me
his
Dite X Howl[1]
marks

(Docket)
D Howles Ret
£ 21 - 1 - 3 in full
Aug 12

D.S., Custis Papers, ViHi.
1. *PGWC* 6:252, 266.

From John Richmond

August 19, 1758

1756 The Estate of Colo Daniel Park Custis to John Richmond Debt

January 6	To 9 hanks Raven gray Sewing Silk 9	6. 9
	To 2 dozn Black Breast Buttons	1. 6
	To 2 ozs Black thread	1. 3
	To 4 yds. bla Mantua for puffs	1.10 1/2
	To 2 pr Bla Sil Knee bands	5. -------
	To Hair Clo Covering and Wadding for a Suit of bla Cloth	7. -------
1758 May 7	To 3 yds Scarlet Camblet[1] @ 9/6	1. 8. 6
	To 1/2 yds do Blue	3
	To 6 1/2 yds do Silver Chain @ 3/9	1. 4. 4 1/2
	To 1 oz Silver thread & (illegible)	18
	To 2 1/2 doz Coat & 1 dos breast Buttons	6
	To 1 Stick Scarlet Twist	6
	To 3/8 Ell Garlex Linnen[2] to line ye Coat Sleeves	9
	To 7/16 yds Velvet	2
	To 3 Hanks Scarlet & White Silk 10	2.11
	To 1/2 oz thread	11 1/2
		£ 5.10. 4 1/2

Augt 19 1758

Then reced of Madam Custis ye full contents of ye above Accot Being in (sic) full of all demands.

John Richmond[3]
August 19, 1758

(Docket)
John Richmond
Acct & Rect
5.10.41/2
19 Augt 1758

A.D.S., Custis Papers, ViHi.

1. Camlet was a cloth material made of a mixture of wool and cotton or linen.
2. Garlex was a linen from Germany.
3. John Richmond was a tailor. *PGWC* 6:252, 263.

From Andrew Marr

August 26, 1758

Received 26 August 1758 of Mrs. Custis Thirty three shillings & four pence for Dely of a Pipe of Wine
Rec's (illegible) for mr. Wm. Meridith (illegible)

p Andrew Marr[1]

(docketed by G.W.)
£ 1.13.4
26th Augt 1758

DS, Custis Papers, ViHi.
   1. The receipt is in the handwriting of MDC. *PGWC* 6:252.

From Adam Coxen

Aug 28, 1758

Shipped by the Grace of God, in good Order, and well Condition'd by Mrs Martha Custis in and upon the good Ship called the Hazard Adam Coxen whereof is Master, under God, for this present Voyage, and now Riding at Anchor in the York River and by God's Grace bound for London to say, Twenty Hhds of Tob being mark'd and number'd as in the Margent, and are to be delivered in the like good Order, and well Condition'd, at the aforesaid Port of London (the Danger of the Seas only excepted) unto Robt Cary Esqr & Compy Merchts. in London or to their assigns, he or they paying Freight for the said Goods as per the Rate of Fourteen pounds Sterling p ton with Primage - Average accustom'd. In witness whereof the Master or Purser of the said Ship hath affirm'd to three Bills of Lading, all of this Tenor and Date; they one of which Bills being accomplish'd, the other two to stand void; and so God send the good Ship to her desired Port in Safety. Amen Dated in

Virginia August y 28 1758
Adam Coxen

(Docket)
20 Hhds p Coxen
1758

ADS, Custis Papers, ViHi.

To Thomas Horner

Mrs Martha Custis   September 6, 1758
To Thomas Horner

1758

Feby 24th	To 2 horse Collers	11/6	£ .11. 6
April 19	To 1 Powder	2/6	. 2. 6
Sepr 6	To 6 Tin Pans	13/6	.13. 6
	To 2 pr H L Hinges	6/	. 6. –
			£ 1.13. 6

AD Custis Papers, ViHi.

From Capel and Osgood Hanbury

Esteemed Friend   September 12, 1758
      Wee wrote Thee p the Packet & Capt Downes to which Referr. Thy
Bills have duly Hon d, as they Appear d for the future must Request Thee
not to draw more Setts then One, to the same Person, of the same Date
& Sum, & Same time fr Payment, without some pticular mark or
Distinction, as otherwise the first Second & third of the Same Sett, is liable
to be paid if Presented here at Different times. Wee have not heard
anything of the affair with Dunbar since Our last. Wee are Inform'd that
Thee has been told by some Person in the Country, that something (what
Wee Can't Learn) might have been done by us, that was not done. Wee
shall be glad to know if you had any Such Information, & what it was, that
thereby Wee may have an Oppty to Convince Thee, That that Person
knew Nothing of the Matter, or else didn't with a Veiw to prejudice us
in Thy Esteem. Wee can truly Say no Endeavours was Wanting in that
affair, & very Thoughtfully & Anxiously attended it, and will Continue to
Render the Family in this or any other affair all the Services in our Power.
It gives us no small Concern that Wee cannot Inform Thee that the Salvage
of the Anna is adjusted having to Doe wth the owners of three Privateers,
Occasioned Some Perplexity. Wee Act under the best Advice, & are not
without hopes to Settle it Soon in an Amicable Way. The Baltimore Capt
Crookshanks is Comeing wth Troops to Virga, & Wee hope Our Friends
will Forward Her dispatch, so as to Return with the Convoy She goes Out
with. Thy kind Assistance Wee shall Acknowledge as a very Pticular
Favour & with great regard --

Thy Assured Friends
Capel & Osgood Hanbury
September 12, 1758

(Address)
To Martha Custis
York River
Virginia

A.L.S., Custis Papers, ViHi.

From John Mercer

Dear Madam   October 21, 1758

I am to inform you that yesterday a Copy of the Order of his Majesty in Council in relation to Dunbar's Cause was produced in Court & in Consequence thereof the last Decree of the General Court was reversed & The Causen as sent back to the office for the Plts to make such Parties therein as they think proper.[1]

I imagine as I heard of it before I came to Town the Report can hardly have escaped you. however I am in hopes you will not suffer it to give you any the least Uneasiness for as far as I am a Judge I assure you in the most solemn manner that I verily hope & believe the Plts will never be able to recover a single Shilling. On the contrary was it my own Case I would immediately bring a Suit for the Island Estate which would not cost much & might be determined before this present suit is like to be tried. I would venture all I am worth in the World: & think I might my Life too upon the Success of it. However as you seemed determined in Case The suit should be renewed to have some Gent of Reputation & Fortune appointed your Son's Guardian I enquired in a round about manner of the Speaker[2] if such a thing had ever been proposed to him, he said not, but added, that it would be to no manner of purpose as he would not upon any Account undertake it, as it would be attended with so much trouble as must necessarily accompany the management of so large an Estate (as your Son was intitled to) & at such a distance from him. As I observed that I apprehended you would be satisfied with his being appointed his Guardian for the management of his Law suits. in which his Advice and Character might be of great benefit to the young Gentleman & that his Estate might be continued under the same management as at present. he said upon that Condition if you desired, he would very readily undertake the matter & do your Son all the Service he could either by his Advice or Interest. This Madam I Thought proper to advise you of, as you may thereby be better enabled to form your Resolution on that head.

You will be pleased by some safe hand this Court to forward all the Papers you have relating to this troublesome Affair in which you may assure yourself of my utmost Care & diligence for your & your Son's Care of it.

My Son informed me that you chose to have a Bond for Currt. Money at forty per Cent rather than Sterling. I have not seen Colo. Tayloe & Thornton since I came to Town (as they left it the Week before) or I would have got them to have joined in such a Bond. however the thing will be the same--it may be done at any time & till tis you may depend I shall pay the Interest punctually as it becomes due in that manner,but if you should have an Opportunity of sending the old Bond to be lodged in Mr. Waller's hands as both the Colo. Tayloe & Thornton are expected in Town before the Court breaks up. We may have an Opportunity of compleating the thing before I go up.[3]

> I am with great regard
> Dear Madam
> Your most obedt Servt
> J Mercer
> Oct 21, 1758

(Address leaf)
Sent by Mad (missing) hble servt
To Mrs Custis
New Kent
Sir
As this Lre is of consequest Mrs Custis no doubt
will be oblige to you to forward it by a special messenger
To Captn Dansie P.L.[4]
(Docketed by GW)
Mr Mercer Oct 11th 1758

A.L.S., Custis Papers, ViHi.

1. The Virginia General Court first heard the case in April, 1754, where it was dismissed. The plaintifs (Dunbars) then appealed to the Privy Council in England in July, 1757, where the Virginia decision was overturned. It was remanded to the Virginia General Court for retrial.

2. John Robinson, then Speaker of the House of Burgesses and Treasurer of the colony.

3. Loan bonds made to John Mercer, John Tayloe, and Presley Thornton by MDC, for £ 2100 Sterling. *PGWC* 6:256.

4. Peter Lyon.

From Joseph Pond

October 17, 1758

Received of Mrs Custis Ealeaven sillings current money I say Received by me

> his
> Joseph X Pond[1]
> mark

(Docket)
Ponds Rect
11/ 17th Octr 1758

D.S., Custis Papers, ViHi.

1. The receipt is in the handwriting of MDC. The payment was probably for additional brickwork. *PGWC* 6:252.

From John Mercer

Dear Madam   November 2, 1758

I received all the Papers together with your Letter and should have waited on the Speaker[1] in two or three days after but I heard he was gone for a few days out of Town. On Saturday last I applied to him & he promised to be in Court that day but something prevented. however this Day he came to Court, and was admitted not only by your Son's but your Daughter's Guardian to defend & prosecute, such Suits as may be for their Interest, for it seems that not only your Son but Yourself & Daughter will be sd Parties to the Suit of Dunbar here The Speaker has had the Papers and State of the Case with my Argument lying before him this whole Court & says he has not yet come to any Resolution about bringing a Suit for the Island Estate, though he seems to think it would be much the best & most expeditious as well as the cheapest way of determining them after I expect however to have his Result before I leave Town.

Mr Waller tells he has not yet got my Bond, however as I expect Colo. Thornton will be Brought to Town by the meeting of the Assembly Colo. Tayloe & I will execute a Bond for Current money at forty per Cent & leave it in Mr. Waller's hands in order for Colo. Thornton to execute it when he comes to Town, therefore be pleased to send the other Bond to him by the first good Opportunity.

I shall from time to time advise you of the Steps taken in the Cause in which you may depend upon my utmost Care for you & your Childrens Interest. & should have done myself the pleasure of waiting upon you in my way home. but the Loss of one of my Sons & the pressing Insistances of my wife to return with the utmost Expedition engages me to make the best of my way. I am with great Regard. Dear

                                        Madam
                                        Your most obedt Servt
                                        J Mercer

(Docketed by GW)
Mr Mercer 2 Novr 1758

A.L.S., Custis Papers, ViHi.

1. See supra, John Mercer to MDC, January 4, 1758, n. 7.

From Robert Cary & Company

Mad m   (November 30, 1758)
      We are favoured with yours & are particularly thankfull for your
kind Assistance to him when your 20 hhds are landed (illegible) Safe those
by Wheldon are all sold at 11/2 & hope soon they will be all delivered when
shall Transport the Sales--your drafts are nearly all paid when the other
appear they shall punctually be discharged -- By your Acc at Currt now
in (illegible) you'l perceive that to the 29 August last the Balance which
believe you'l find right was (illegible) & £ 1138 Curt of which 546:15 is
included for the procuring of the last Years Tobacco which at present we
are not in (illegible) for neither shall we (illegible) next March so that with
this the Bills Paid since the 22 August entirely discharges your Accot leaves
us no money to pay th Discounts of your present Tobacco thought it
necessary to mention this in Order to spare any disappointments
hereafter.---Are sorry your Goods did mot meet your Approbation the
additional endeavour (illegible) but took all the Care we cou'd (illegible)
for the Glass China & Tea say they thought (illegible) had the Best
however shall be more particular with them (illegible) stockings we have
directed from Glasgow by the first ship that goes from York River Messrs
Oswald will send them to you for Jany or Feby. We suppose a Convoy will
be appointed for the (illegible) what few Virginia ships that may go by
them you may depend on having your Goods & as the shortness of the
Crops are likely to be so bad we shall send only one ship to Accomodate
our Friends with Freight by the time This reaches you we suppose she may
be there she is called the Cary Capt Talman will have the Management
of her & hope what Tobacco you have you will favour us in putting on
Board him[1] Interim We remain

                                        Dr Mad m Your most
                                        Humble Servt
                                        Robert Cary & C.

Copy
Original by Capt. Walker[2]
Mrs. Martha Custis
To Mrs. Martha Custis
in Williamsburg, Virginia
(Docket)
Cary & Co 30 Nov. 1758

A.L.S., Custis Papers, ViHi.
    1. *PGWC* 6:269, 351 n. 8.
    2. *PGWC* 6:411, 477.

From Charles Whitlock

December ye 2nd 1758

Recd of Mrs Martha Custis Seven pounds two shillings & 6 pence
Current money in full for my share of Wheat made in the year 1758

pr me
Charles Whitlock [1]

(Docketed by GW)
Chs Whitlock
£ 7/2/6 in full
2 Decr 1758

D.S., Custis Papers, ViHi.
   1. The Receipt is in the handwriting of MDC. *PGWC* 6:252, 266.

From Robert Bowis

December 12, 1758

1758 Mrs Martha Custis dr

Nov 24	To (illegible) Dark Ground Chence	3.10
Nov 21	To Trunk 10/3 3 Groce Corkes 9/	− .19
		£ 4. 9

Recd December 12 1758. the above
Contents of Lewis Smith

Robt Bowis[1]

(Docket)
Recd £ 4.9
2 Decr 1758

D.S., Custis Papers, ViHi.
   1. Robert Bowis was a New Kent County merchant. He was one of a group of New Kent
citizens appointed by the Governor to act in relieving persons injured by the destruction
of the New Kent County records by an arsonous fire. See *Harris*, 1, 97-99.

From Burbidge & Armistead

(December 16, 1758)

Decem 12	In accot wth Burbidge & Armistead	
1758	To 1 chair	-10
Feby 2d	To large Stone Jugg	5
Mar 10	To 3 pr Kid Gloves & China	10
		1- 5

Sept 26   to 2 Pair Fare Tongs & 1 pr Kid Gloves 4/
                 2 yds Kitt 2/6 1 Silk (illegible) 5/
                 1 pr Yarn Shoes 2/9/ Scisors 2/   2-14- 1
                 Cork (illegible) 1/ Silk lace 18d Grater 10d
                 Mil'd (illegible) 5/ Jugg 18d18d Grater 10d
                 1 Yds (illegible 5/6 Iron Candle stand
                 Errors Exd   3

                 Dec 16, 1758   4- 2-11

                                             John Armistead

Recd the Contents
J Armistead
(Docket)
(illegible)
£ 4.2.11
16 Decr 1758

A.D.S., Custis Papers, ViHi.

From Joseph Pond

(December 16, 1758)
Received of Mrs Custis 15 shillings of all demands by me The saide
Joseph Pond is finish my ditching for the same money that I pay now

                              his
                              Joseph X Pond[1]
                              mark

(Docketed by GW)
s. Pond rect
15/
16th Decr 1758
D.S., Custis Papers, ViHi.

1. The receipt is in the handwriting of MDC. *PGWC* 6:252.

From Capel and Osgood Hanbury

Esteem'd Friend   London Decr 26, 1758
     We have wrote Thee p the Packet & sundry other opportunity's,
one of wch was p the Supply Capt Downs who was so unlucky after
sailing wth Convoy as to be seperated therefrom & to be taken, was
afterwards retaken and carried into Bristol[1] & instead of our Letter to

thee geting to hand in due course, it was sent us a few Days agow & comes inclos'd. the Law Books were also sent p that Ship value £ 17.10.2; as soone as the Affair can be setled, the Estate shall have Credit, for the moiety of the net amount of the Sale thereof, as all the Goods are to be sold at Publick Sale. We bespoke other Books to replace them & wch intend to find p the Dispatch in a short time if a suitable Convoy offers as it seems likely that the Virginia Fleet will not sail untill late Spring. The Anna is now safe in this River & delivering her Cargo. No endeavours of Ours shall be wanting to make the most of the 17 hhds DPC by her, and as soone as will get the Accounts relating to the Salvage finally setled & communicate the same (illegible). Thy favour of the 1st of Sepr is now before us. We shall find our Friends Account Currt in a short time. We have wrote to Hill of Madeira for a Pipe of good old Wine & a Box of Citron for thee, his Bills for it shall be duly honoured as has been all the Bills thee Drew upon us that have appeared; we request thee not to draw (illegible) sets of Bills of the same date to the same Persons for the same sum as it is liable to create great errors by paying two Bills of the same set. We are very sorry that We have no Tobacco from thee by the Dispatch, nor by any other Ship in the Fleet, we hope it is not owing to our having incurred thy displeasure & continuance of the Consignment, of the Estates Tobacco will give us no small pleasure, & no endeavour of ours shall be wanting to make the most of it & to transact every Affair the entrust to our care so as to merit thy approbation. We are wth great Esteem
December 26, 1758
Thy Assurd Friends
Capel & Osgood Hanbury
To
Martha Custis
York River
Virginia

A.L.S., Custis Papers, ViHi.
　1. *PGWC* 6:269, 270 n. 17, 447, 453, 454 n. 5.

From Capel & Osgood Hanbury

Esteem Friend　　　　　　　　　　　　　　　　London Jany 9,1759
　　　We wrote Thee ye 26 Ulto to wch refer and as nothing material has since occurrd, have now only to inclose Invoice (missing) for thy Goods, wch comes herewith & wch we wish safe to hand and to thy satisfaction. We shall at all times be glad to hear of thy welfare, & by all opportunitys

(but more especially by our own Ships) to partake of thy Consignments & are with great Esteem

> Thy Assurd Friend
> Capel & Osgood Hanbury

To Martha Custis
York River
(Address)
To Martha Custis
York River
Virginia
(Docket)
Hanbury 9th Jany 1759

A.L.S., Custis Papers, ViHi.

Complete Inventory, by Counties, of the Estate

The Appraisment of the Estate of Danl Parke Custis According to the Returns made to the County Court of New Kent by Sworn appraisers whose Names are hereunto annex'd

A Negro man named Anthony £20
Ditto Shomberg 45
Ditto Squirre 50
Ditto Morris 60
Ditto Jack Palmer 50
Ditto Jemmy 12
Ditto Ned 50
Ditto Michael 60
Ditto Joe 60
Ditto Sampson 1
A Negroe Woman Jenny 45
Ditto Moll 45
Ditto Doll 40
Ditto Betty & child Austin 60
Child Hue 15
Girl Nanny 40
Ditto Sall 35
Boy Davy 35
Ditto Julius 30
Ditto Emanuel (?)
Woman Leck (?)
Girl Fanny 20
Ditto Queene (?)
Ditto Grace 15

Ditto Joe 20
Ditto John 15
Ditto Peter 20
Girl Christian 15
Ditto Jemima 35
Ditto Alce 12
Ditto Lucy 25
Ditto Doll 30
Boy George 40
Ditto Sampson 25
Woman Alce (?)
Boy Tom 40
Ditto John 42
Ditto Billy (?)
Woman Esther & Chd Phil 50
Girl Eve (?)
Ditto Hannah (?)
Ditto Betty 25
Boy Toby 17
Woman Kate 15
Ditto Moll 35
Girl Arbor 10
Boy John 20
Woman Betty 35

Ditto Alce & Chd Phebe 40
Boy Bob 20
Ditto George 14
Woman Abbeey 40
Boy Pompey 30
Girl Amy 30
Ditto Patt 15
Girl Nell 15
Boy Perry 25
Ditto Sam 30
Ditto Tom 30
Woman Hannah 15
Man Charles Baker 20
Ditto Brunswick 40
Woman Arbor (?)
Man S(?) 40
Ditto Gooding
ditto Abram 45
ditto Jacob 35
ditto Goliah 35
ditto Roger 50
Woman Dinah 40
Boy Dickey 25
ditto Peter 30
Woman Sarah 40
Girl Peggy 20
Boy Godfrey 15
Woman Elizabeth 35
boy (?) 20
Ditto Paul 25
Woman & chd (?) 50
Girl Abby 20
Woman Molly 50
ditto Venus (?)
girl Beck 45
Woman Nanny 10
Girl Rose 30
ditto Nanny 15
ditto Cosiah 10
ditto Nanny 30
Boy Daniel 25
Woman Phillis 50
girl Sarah 30
Ditto Nell 35
Woman Esther 30
Man Sam 20ge 14
ditto Pompey 10

Boy George 20
Woman Nan 40
Girl Sal 16
Ditto Phebe 30
Boy Stephen 35
Man Jack 60 30
Ditto Mingo 60
ditto Ned Hall 50
ditto Stephen 50
Boy Shomberg 30
Girl Rachel 30 50
Man Will Harlow 50
Woman Patcy 30
Boy Tom 20
Ditto Harry 25
Man Joe 45
Boy Davy 35
ditto Billy 40
Man Duke 40
Ditto Bristol 35
Ditto Charles 40
Ditto Breechy 50
ditto Peter 15
boy Billy 40
Man Northampton 6d
Ditto Isar (?) 50
ditto Bob 40
ditto Tom 40
boy Bat 40
Man Bob 40
ditto Tom 40
ditto Prince 10
ditto Jemmy 40
woman Jenny 40
ditto Bella & Chd Milly 55
ditto Kitty 15
ditto Betty 20
Man Paul 30
ditto Martin 30
boy George (?)
Man Will 40
ditto Dick 45
ditto Jerry 15
ditto Joe 45
ditto Moses 15
ditto Hercules 40
ditto Narcissus (?)

Woman Eve & child Dick 55   ditto Nanny & Chd Nanny 50
boy Harry 35   Girl Sal 20
ditto Crafish 25   ditto Frank 15

Amt of Negroes in N. Kent £4769. 1. 6

1.	25 HHd Flat with Cable and Anchor	25.
2.	1 Horse Boat, 1 large Canoe	6.10
3.	1 Ox Cart, Yokes, Chain &ca	1.10
4.	2 Old Iron Pots	.12
5.	a parcel old Hoes, Axes, grubp axes, boxes, hoops & ca	4.
6.	2 Work Horses	12.
7.	100 head Nett Cattle	105.
8.	40 head Hogs	20.
9.	80 Barrls of Corn at 4/	16.
10.	1 Iron Chain, 1 Grindstone, & 1 Hide	1. 5
11.	16 Good Casks, & sevl old Casks & ca	10.
12.	1 Ox Cart, Wheels, Chains and Yokes	3.
	1 Bed and Furniture	6.
	80 lb. Sheet Lead	.13. 4
13.	200 Barrels of Corn at 4/	4.
15.	304 head Hogs	91.
15.	284 head neat Cattle	360.
16.	1 Ox Cart, Chain, and Yokes	2.10
17.	25 old hoes and axes, and 1 Grindstone	1. 4
18.	61 narrow hoes	9.
19.	476 lb. Lead	3.19.
	1 Charriot and Harness for 6 Horses	80.
20.	1 two wheeld Chair	20.
	1 Iron Mortar, 1 old still and 2 pestles	1.
21.	25 Head Hogs	4.10
	4 brass Tenders, and 1 wire rat Trap	1.
22.	1 old Chair and Harness & old Bedstead & ca	2.
23.	6 whipsaws and two xcut saws	4.
24.	3 hides 5 old Hhds 4 brass Sieves & Iron do & Lumbr	1.10
25.	2 pr Hand Mill Stones	4.10
26.	1 new Sein	7.
27.	2 Casks old Seins	4.
28.	A parcel hhds Casks & ca	1.10
	1 schooner with (?)ing & ca	50.
29.	1 Small Boat	1. 5
30.	1 large table	2.
	2 large Sorrel horses at 25 £ each	50.
	2 large bay ditto at 16 £ each	32.
31	2 Small bay ditto at 8 £ each	16.
31	3 Mares and 3 Colts	36.
	1 old Roan horse	8.

	1 young Stallion	25.
33.	2 horses and two mares	24.
34.	2 old Work horses	12.
	2 young mares	16.
	1 young Sorrel horse	18.
	1 ditto bay ditto	12.
35.	1 ditto bay Mare	6.
36.	1 Silver Coffee Pot, 4 Candle Sticks, 1 Tea Pot, 1 milk pot, 2 Salvers 4 Salts and Shovels, 1 Sugar dish, 2 beakers 2 Sauce Boats, 1 punch Ladle, 1 Strainr 1 cross, 12 Teaspoons, 1 pr Sugar Tongs 1 Strainer 1 lar. Spoon, 1 Rim & Castor Wt 23lb. @ 6/6 pr Oz.	119.
37.	1 large Silver Tankard, 1 small Tankd 2 porringers 2 Candle sticks & Snuffers 12 Table Spoons 1 Shovel 7 Tea spoons 1 pepper box 1 Sugar Caster 1 Can and 2 Small Dishes wt 16 3/4 lb @ 4/7 pr oz.	60.
	30 Wine and Beer Glasses @ 6d	.15
	2 Tumblers 2 Jelly Glasses 1 cruet, 11 Salt, & 1 Mustard pot	. 3
	7 Sweetmeat glasses @ 1/3	. 8. 9
	1 Sett gilt China and Coffee Mill	4.
	3 two quart Muggs, 3/9 4 Slider's 3/	. 6. 9
	a parcel of Earthen ware	1. 5
	4 dozn & 8 China Plates & 15 dishes of China	10.
	a parcel China Tea Cups, Saucers, Tea Pot Milk Pot Bowles and Canisters	5.
38.	An assortment of Medicines & ca	8.
	8 Razors case 1 hone and Strop	1. 1
39.	1 Sword and pr of Pistols	3.
40	1 Gun	1. 5
41.	a parcel of old and new Books & ca	4.
	2 pr money Scales and Weights	3.
	1 Mahogany Desk	4.
42.	12 Mahogany Chairs	10.
43.	2 Corner Chairs	2.
43.	2 Large Mahogany Tables	6.
	1 Marble Table	3.
	1 large looking glass	4.
44.	1 leather Couch, 2 pictures, & 3 Maps	1.14
45.	1 Walnut Table	.10
46.	10 Leather Chairs	2.
47.	1 large easy Chair	3.
48.	1 old Chest of Drawers (15 s.) & 1 old Cabinet (£ 1)	1.15
49.	2 Trunks and 1 Walnut Table	1.10
50.	1 looking Glass and 1 dressing glass	2. 6
51.	1 Corner Cupboard	1.
	2 Shagreen knife cases wt 12 K: & forks in each	3.10
52.	2 Tin Sugar Boxes, 16 canisters (?) gratn & (?)	.12

	2 Box Irons and 2 Stands & 7 Smoothing Irons	1.14
	2 Bed Bolsters, 1 Rug, 2 pr Sheets, 2 Counterpains 2 Bedsteads and Cords	10.
53.	4 brass Candlesticks 1 pr Snuffr & old Knives & Forks	.18
	20 pr Sheets	8.12
	41 Table Cloaths	14.
	99 Napkins and Towels	7. 8
	24 Pillow Cases and Towells	2. 5
	2 Pieces of Callico	4.
	10 Counterpins and bed Quilts	12.10
	2 Bed Bolsters 4 Pillows 2 pr Blankets 1 Suit old Curtains and Cords Bedsteads	10.
	2 pr Blankets	2. 5
	2 Beauro dressing Tables	. 6.
	2 dressing Glasses	3.
54.	5 old Chairs 1 Trunk and 1 Chest	.17. 6
55.	1 Table 1 Trunk and 5 Chairs	1.15
	2 Beds and Furniture	12.
56.	2 pr of Handirons	. 7. 6
	A Quantity of Wine of several sorts Bottles Juggs & ca	40.
57.	1 man's Saddle and bridle, 3 pr handirons 1 Cooler Treacle, Juggs and old Lumber	10.
58.	18 pr Cotton wool, and Clothiers Cards	1.10
	2 Bell mettle Skillets, & Patty Pans	2.
	1 Brass Plate Warmer 2 pr Tongs & Shovels	1. 0
	a parcel Salt Petre	2.13
	6 Potts and Jarrs with Raisons	1.
59.	a parcel of old Trunks, boxes and Lumber	1.
60.	12 pr Mens Shoes and Slippers	5.
61.	30 Mens hats	3.16
62.	1 Ditto ditto	1.15
63.	3 yds Serge dinem, & Remts Tammy 2.5 2 ps. Check and part ps. of ditto	4.
	25 Quire of Paper	1.
64.	2 pr Stilliards	.12
	2 plate Baskets, 1 Bread ditto, and a bag Corks	1.
65.	2 Housing and 16 girths	9.
66.	9 Cinches and Clamps 1 curry Comb & 1 Belt	.13
	22 loaves dble & single refind Sugar	12.
	2 Jockey Cap	.10
67.	5 Whipthongs, 1 Search 1 sifter, 1 handsaw 1 brass Cock and 1 dark lanthorn	.14
	1 Tea Chest and 4 old China Cups	. 2
68.	4 M small Nails, and a Paper brass nails	.19
69.	1 Saw Rest and 4 brass Runners	. 9. 3
	4 dozn Whetstones & a papr Sadler's Tacks	. 8
70.	21 Chisels, 6 pr Sheep shears, & 12 Gimblets	1. 8

71.	11 plain Irons & 2 dozn whipsaw Files	1. 4
72.	5 dozn & 8 file of sevel Sorts	2.
73.	10 Iron Screws 2 hatchets, 4 Taper bits 2 pr Nippers & 1pr Markg Irons	.12
74.	33 hasps and staples and 16 whet Stones	. 9
	9 Plain Irons, 1 gouge, and 2 Augers	. 9
75.	2 plain Irons, 3 Center bitts 14 Files 1 xcut Saw Rests, 1 gouge and 1 pr of Irons	. 8
76.	9 Hats and 8 Dutch Blankets	4. 3
	22 Staples 1 currying knife & 2 fleshg do	1.13
77.	13 Sides of Leather	2. 5
	1 Crate Earthen Ware & 2 Baskets Corks	.14
	1 Barrl of sugar & part of Barrl of ditto	7.
78.	36 Yards of Virginia cloth	1.16
	28 yards of Duck	1.15
79.	75 lb. Gunpowder and 1 G 3Q o lb. of Shott	8.18
80.	1 piece of plains qty about 75 yds	10.
81.	2 ps. Kersey qty 50 yds	
82.	15 1/2 yds dufle & 7 1/2 yds Kersey	
83.	510 yds Cotton at 2/	
84.	3 ps. dutch Blanketting 23 glasses and 1 ps. of Ropep	
85.	39 pieces of Rolls	
86.	9 ps. qtty about 900 Ells Bro. Linn	
	4 ps. Sale Duck	
87.	177 pair plad Hose, & 1 pr Shoes	
88.	Powder Shott, Chests, Boxes, Vials Casks old Iron & ca 1 pr Standard Weights and Scales	
89.	8 Barrels of Nails	
90.	1 coarse Sifters	
91.	2 frying Pans and 1 pott	
92.	202 Sides, and 46 skins of upper Leather	
93.	a parcel of Salt	
94.	a parcel of Rope and Earthenware	
95.	Sain Corks, Iron, Lead & ca	
96.	1 Casks narrow Axes & 8 broad Axes	
97.	8 Cooper's Axes 5 narrow Axes, 6 brubg axes Mill Pecks Augers &ca	
98.	11 Spades 1 dozn Sickles & 6 dozn xgarnet Hinges	
99.	24 narrow Hoes, and 21 broad hoes	
100.	6 Grass Scythes and Furniture	£ 2.
101.	Iron ware, old iron, Curry Combs Stock Locks Rope Lumber &ca	30.
102.	2 large Sains and Ropes	20.
103.	17 lb Sain Twine	.17.
104.	50 3/4 lb Bro: & colored thread & 1 lb. whitd bron Thread	7.
	141 yds Irish Linnen	24. 8. 6
	5 diaper Table Cloths	3.15

	1 ps. Sagathy Shalloon Buttons & Twist	6.10.
	1 silk pattern for Breeches	2.
	2 1/2 pieces of Nankeen	1.10.
105.	11 pair Mens Stockings	2.17. 6
106.	1 Rug 20/. 5 pr Mens gloves 10/	1.10.
107.	1 ps. brown holland	3.
108.	a remnant of Ticking and a Pillow	1.
109.	a parcel of Shoe thread	1.
	1 Shaving pot and Bason	. 1.
	1 groc horn Buttons	1.
110.	1 Slate and Pencils	. 2.
111.	14 pr Stirrup Leathers and 1 Crupper	. 7. 6
112.	350 Ells brown Linnen	21.17. 6
113.	1 ps. Rolls & several ps wrappers	3.
114.	1 pr Stirrups & 1 Charriot Whip	. 7.
115.	39 pair Negroes Shoes	6.16. 6
116.	1 desk 4 Trunks and Lumber	6.10.
117.	1 cutting Sword	2.10.
118.	140 lb. washd wool	7.
	5 3/4 dozn Pewter Plates	5.10.
	41 Pewter dishes and 4 Basons	11.10.
	1 Bed Pan and 8 Pattipans	. 7. 6
	1 Pestle and Mortar, and 3 Spits	1. 5.
119.	2 old Skillett and 2 Tea Kettles	1. 5.
120.	4 Iron Potts and Hooks & 1 pr Andirons	7.
	1 dripg Pan, Flesh fork, Ladle Shovel & Tongs	1.
	1 Stew pan, 1 frying pan, 4 pot Racks & lumbr	2. 1.
121.	2 Copper Kettles	8.
	1 Fish Kettle 1 copper Pot 3 Coffeepots 1 Chocalate pot, 1 Tureen, & 2 Tin Kettles	5.
122.	4 Jarrs, 2 Safes 1 apple Mill & ca	2. 1.
123.	82 Milk pans	1.13. 6
124.	A parcel Carpenters (?) er's, Cooper's Smith (?) Awls & Lasts	10.
125.	154 (?) of (?) cattle	154.
126.	12 (?) sheep	24. 4.
127.	hogs	30.
128.	5 (?) Chairs, & 1 Desk and Bookcase	3. 5
129.	1 Looking Glass and 1 dressing Glass	1.
130.	1 large Copper Kettle & 1 Iron Pot	10.
	1 dozn Wine Glasses	. 7. 6
	8 Carboys and 1 Jug with Rum and Brandy in them 3 buttr Potts empty Bottls	7.10.
	1 Jar quantity abt 14 gals. Train Oil	3.
	1 Tierce qty abt 60 gals. Rum	12.
	3 Small Barrl Paint	3. 5.
131.	A parcel of Tar Barls and Tar	.15.

132.	1 ps qty yds white flannel	8. 3. 4
	1 womans Sadle and Furniture	2.
133.	2 drawing Knives	. 4.
134.	5 Staples, 4 hasps, 1 rasp, brass Cocks & ca	. 5.
135.	2 Bricklayers Trowells	. 4.
	4 M 3d Nails	. 8.
	5 paint Brushes	. 2.
	3 Locks 1 bung borer and 1 Belt	. 5.
136.	137 Awl blades	. 3.
137.	1 pr Negro Shoes	. 3.

Total Amt   £ 7268. 6. 5

Edmond Bacon }
Lewis Webb   }   Apprs
Frans Foster }
　20th Octr 1757

Estate in King Wm

Wench Dyner 45
ditto Patt 50
ditto Kitt 35
ditto Sarah 30
ditto Guy 50
ditto Sam 40
ditto
. Marlborough 45

ditto Rachel 35
ditto Lucy 20
ditto Nan 12
ditto Milly 15
ditto Solomon 65
ditto Hector 40
ditto David 60

man Frank 10
ditto George 20
ditto (?) 55
ditto Parros 65
ditto Will 45
ditto Sue 45

		£ 832.
138.	10 Oxen	30.
	21 Steers	52.10.
	101 Cows and Steers	131.10.
	24 Small ditto	24.
	40 Calves	(?).
139.	67 Sheep	20.
140.	4 Work Horses	20.
141.	30 Shoats	8.
	11 Sows & 66 Pigs	6. 1.
	38 Hogs	23.22.
	9 Small Sows and 25 Pigs	3. 7. 6
	6 Shoats	15.
	3 ditto	15.
142.	A Cart &ca	2.
143.	A parcel of old Tobacco Hogshead 2 Corn Barrls & Corn Crib	1. 3.
144.	2 Cow hides	. 2. 6

145.	100 Barrels of Corn @ 5/	25.
146.	5 old Wedges 7/6. a parcel of old Iron	.19. 6
147.	13 hoes 26/. 6 Axes 18/. 4 ditto 3/	2. 5.
148.	A Parcel of Butter Pots 28/. ditto Milk pans 18/	2. 4.
149.	A parcel of Tubs, Piggens, and Pails	.10.
150.	1 pr Steelyards	.15.
151.	1 ppr Scales & ca	.10.
152.	1 pr hand Mill Stones & ca	1.
	Whole amount	£ 1219.11. 6

Wm Dandridge }
ThomasnFox } Appraisors
James Richeson }
3d Feby 1758

Inventory of the James City Estate

In the left hand Room up Stairs

153.	2 Tables 15/. Trunk 2/. 1 dressg box 2/	.19.
154.	1 Bed and Furniture £ 7 4 Maps & 4 Prints 8/	7. 8.
155.	4 Cain bottom Chair	1.
156.	1 brass Fender, shovel & old dogs	. 5.

In the Right hand Room

157.	8 Cain and 3 leather bottom Chairs	2.15.
158.	5 prints & 3 Maps 8/. 2 dressg glasses 10/	.18.
159.	2 Trunks and 1 Cloaths Chest	.12.
	1 Bed and Furniture £ 4. 8 Table Cloths 40/	6.
	4 pr Cotton Sheets 1 pillow case 60/	3.
	27 Towels 27/. 3 Fenders 9/	1.16
160.	an old Trussel Bed	. 3.

In the Passage & Staircase

161.	2 maps 2/. 5 glass prints 10/	.12
162.	12 Caesars 30/. 24 painted Pictures £ 10	11.10.
163.	5 prints of Alexanders Battles	.13.
164.	6 pictures painted on Wood	1.
165.	5 Chairs 25/. 2 old Tables 4/	1. 9.
166.	Warming pan and 1 Broom	.10.

In the Chamber

167.	an old Desk 20/. 1 Escrutore 60/	4.
168.	9 Chairs 27/. 1 Bed and Curtains £ 9	10. 7.
169.	5 prints 5/. 32 glass prints 64/	3. 9.
170.	13 painted pictures	6.10.
	1 looking Glass	1.

In the Closet

171.	12 pewter plates 15/. 8 old ditto 5/	1.

	8 old dishes, 3 old Pie plates, 1 Bason and 1 Cullinder	1.10.
172.	Scollop Shells 1/ 1 pr Stilyards 3/	. 4.
173.	2 Candlesticks 6/. 2 pr Snuffers 1/. p (?) hol (?)	. 9.
174.	1 old Tea Chest, 1 Cannister, 1 buttr Pot 1 Decanter, 1 Basket	. 4.
176.	1 pr Bellows	. 2.

In the Library

177.	A parcel of Books	25.
178.	A parcel of Pictures	1.
179.	s Short Barrel Gun & 1 Sword	.15.
180.	An old Desk & some few odd trifles	.10.

In the Hall

	a sett of Fruit pieces	5.
	a sett of Flower pieces	5.
181.	21 glass prints 25/. 1 looking glass 60/	4. 5.
182.	2 painted pictures 25/. 12 Chairs 60/	4. 5.
	8 Small China Bowles, 29 Saucers, 25 Cups	1.10.
183.	1 pair Pumps, and 2 Cloaths Brushes	.12.
184.	1 Couch 10/ 1 writing Desk 20/	1. 1.
185.	1 large Table 30/. 1 marble Slabb £ 4	5.10.
186.	an old Dutch plate case	2.10.
187.	1 Square Table with a picture in it	.15.

In the Closet next the Garden

	a parcell of glass ware	1. 2.
	a parcell of China and Earthen ware	1.10.
	12 pewter plates and 1 gill pot	.15.
	1 Marble Mortar	7.
188.	12 knives and 12 forks	.12.
189.	2 old Chafing dishes, 2 pr old Bellows and 1 Tea board	. 6.

In the Right hand Closet

| 190. | 1 Tinn Cannister a small parcel of bottles a few knives & Sundry triffling Articles | .15. |
| 191. | 26 oz. 15 dwt Silver plate @ 6/oz. | 8. 0. 6 |

In the Apothecaries Shop

| 192. | A parcel of old drugs and some old odd Trifles | 2. |

In the Cellars

193.	10 dozn Wine £ 15. 1 gallon Pot 2/	15. 2.
	1 gross bottles 26/. 5 Jugs 10/	1.16.
194.	6 Jars with some Oil and Soap	8.
195.	2 Pewter measures 1 Tawier (tarrier), 1 Cock	. 4.
	a little Brandy and some old Cyder	1.
196.	A cistern to Cool Meat and 1 Jarr	.10.

| 197. | 1 pr of old Tongs, 1 pr of old Dogs and 1 old Water pot | . 8. |
| 198. | 1 Mouse Trap, 1 old Lanthorn 2 old Casks & 1 old Safe | 2. |

In the Kitchen

199.	2 Bell Mettle Skillets	.12
200.	2 Chocolate Potts, 1 Grid Iron 1 Ladle 1 Pestle and Mortar branding Iron 1 frying Pan, 2 flesh Forks 2 Spits, 1 pr of Scales	1.
201.	1 pair of Kitchen Dogs	.15.
202.	4 pots and two pr pot hooks 30/. old Kettle 12/	2. 2.
203.	Some old Iron	. 3.
204.	1 butter pot, one Search, 3 Chamber pots, one Mouse Trap	. 6.
205.	2 old pails, one old Piggins 2 old Tubs	. 2.
	An old Negro Woman Cornelia	30.
	Ditto girl Beck	30.

In the Grainery

	Aout 50 Bushls Oats @ 9 1/2d.	1.19. 7.
206.	8 Chests 40/. a Still £ 6	8.
207.	2 Shovels, 2 Riddles 2 Measures	1. 5.
208.	17 Hilling Hoes and 1 Coopers Ax	2.16.
	6 Sides of Sole leather	1. 7.
	6 Sides of upper leather skins	1.
209.	A parcel of Nails	5.
210.	A Fender two Water pots 1 Small hoe	.10.
211.	A Table and a small Quantity of Red Lead	.10.

Up Stairs

| 212. | 10 Chests, two Shovels and one old Bedstead | 2.10. |

In the Salt House

| 213. | a Small quantity of Large Salt | . 8. |

In the Coach House

| 214. | 1 Grind Stone and Iron handle | . 4. |

In the store loft

215.	1 Cloathes chest	15.
	4 old chests	6.
216.	a parcel of old Pictures	. 6.
217.	An old Gun, a few small Barrls Lampblack, a parcel of old Window glass 2 close stools pans & 2 Bell glasses	.13.
218.	about 40 lb. of mixed Shott	.10.
219.	2 yds of hair Cloth and 2 Tin Cherry pots	. 3.
220.	16 Scyth Stones, 3 rubbers and 1 pair of Canhooks	. 6.

221.	1 leather Russell Couch	.10.
222.	12 pains large glass	.15.
	1 garden pot	. 2.
223.	2 Dog Collars and one Cowpers Compass	. 3.
224.	1 Screw Jack and an old Anchor	1. 5.
225.	Some old Casements and a piece of hollow brass	. 6.

whole amt   £ 268. 2. 1

John Blair   }
Peter Scott   }   Apprairs
John Prentis }

York

226.	2 Sows and two Barrows 36/ 20 Shoats and Pigs 60/	4.16.
227.	6 Calves 48/. 15 Steers £ 30	32. 8.
228.	24 Cows £ 30.12. 1 Bull 20/. 15 young Cattle £ 12	52.12.
229.	2 Sows and 5 Shoats 31/. 15 Steers £ 30	31.11.
230.	21 Cows £ 33.12 2 Bulls 40/. 23 young Cattle £ 20	55.12.
231.	12 Steers £ 24. 19 Cows £ 30.8s.	54. 8.
232.	13 young Cattle £ 9.15s. 2 Bulls 40/	11.15
233.	40 Calves £ 15. 10 draught Steers $ 20	35.
234.	13 Steers £ 26 30 young Cattle £ 19.110.	45.10.
235.	25 Cows £ 41.5. 1 Bull 20/. 8 Steers £ 16	58. 5.
236.	13 young Catttle 10.8. 46 Cows & Steers £ 73.12	84.
237.	1 Bull 20/. 8 Steers £ 16. 19 Cows & Steers £ 30.8	47. 8.
238.	2 Bulls 40/. 4 young Cattle $ 3.12.	5.12.
239.	1 Cart & Furniture £ 11. 1 large grindste 12/	11.12.
240.	A parcel of old Iron & Harrows 40/. 9 large Hogs	13.14.
241.	4 Sows, 1 boar £ 4. 20 houng hogs £ 10	14.
242.	10 Shoats 50/. 12 Pigs 12/	3. 2.
243.	1 Cart harness & 3 horses £ 15. 1 horse £ 7	22.
244.	1 young bay horse £ 20. 1 pr Stilliards 6/	20. 6.
245.	3 Currying Knives 20/. 3 butter pots 9/	1. 9.
246.	7 Cyder Hhds 20/. 300 Barls Corn @ 6/ £ 90	91.
247.	2 doz. Milk pans 15/. 1 mill spindle & horns 20/	1.15.
248.	a parcel of Carpenters Toos £ 7.10. Irn Wedgs 12	8. 2.
249.	A Sett of Cart wheel hoops 12/. 2 brd hoes 6/	. 8.
250.	24 M 6d Nails £ 4.16. a parcel old Nails 15/	5.11.

£ 712. 6.

Old Johny £ 15
Ockney 40
Joe 60
Cupid 50
young Ned 50
Crispin 40
Peter 40
Danl Twine 10
Ned 50
Old Captain 15
Isaac 50
Old Jager 15
Eugene 45
Mill Betty 50
Frank & Chd Judith 50
Jack 35
Ockney 23
Moll & Chd Brunswk 50
Fanny 40
Dinah & Chd Jenny 50
Beck 50
Cornelia 40
Arber 15
Patt 15
John Blair Junr　}
Matthew Shields　}　Appraisers
William Graves　}

Evelin 15
Sall 16
Moll 50
Pegg 50
Caesar 25
Lucy 15
Amey 10
Roger 25
Arlington 35
Grace 40
Old Chance 20
Orange 40
Miller Jemmy 60
Jupiter 50
Tobey 40
Sam 50
York 50
Muccon 50
Peter 70
Will 50
Bachus 40
Be (?) 50
Ph (?) 40
Arlington 5

Alice 40
Hannah 40
Tom 20
Lydia 26
Grace & Chd 50
Old Nanny 25
Betty 40
Eulin & Chd Phil 50
Acre 40
Hannah 25
Sukey 25
Doll 15
Alice 16
Daphne & Chd Jemy 55
Pegg 25
Danl 20
Nelly 15
George 30
Betty 35
Daphne 25
Fabbey 45
Ned 35

Negroes £ 2501.
(Total £ 3213.6)

Northampton

Caesar £ 10
Simon 30
Gurshire 40
Susannah 30
Gurshire 35
Simon 15
Caesar 10
Doll 20

Perry 25
1 young Fellow 35
Judith 30
1 old Wench 30
George 30
Daniel 15
Perry 7
Polly 15

Negroes　　　　　£ 377.

Stock of Cattle at Arlington

251.	2 Bulls 40/. 16 Cows £ 116	18.
252.	3 young Steers 70/. 14 Calves 70/	7.

Stock of Cattle at Smiths Isld

253.	6 Cows and Calves at 25/	7.10.
254.	4 four year old Steer's at 25/	5.
255.	6 two year old Ditto @ 12/	3.12.
256.	6 one year old ditto @ 7/6	2. 5.
257.	Abt 80 or 90 wild Cattle @ 12/6	53. 2. 6

Stock of Cattle at Mockon Isld

258.	4 large Steers @ 45/. 1 Steer 25/	10. 5.
259.	19 Cows £ 19. 2 Heifers 40/	21.
260.	21 Year olds $ 7.17.6. five Calves 25/ 1 Bull 17/6	10.
261.	3 young Horses @ 70/	10.10.
262.	2 old Ditto	6.
263.	1 Ditto	(?)
264.	(?) old Mare (?) Colt	(?).10.
265.	50 Sheep @ 5/	12.10.
266.	old axes and one broad Ax 2/	.12.
268.	7 New broad hoes @ 3/4	1. 3. 4.
269.	4 narrow ditto @ 3/. 4 old ditto 2 6d	.14.
270.	8 0ld broad ditto @ 20 d 9 Wedges	1.11. 4
271.	4 old plows @ 3/6	.14.
272.	1 Cart and Wheels	1.17. 6
273.	1 old Cart	. 5.
274.	7 Bushels of Salt @ 2/6	.17. 6
275.	1 old Spade 1/. 1 handsaw 7/6	. 8. 6
276.	1 Hatchet 1/8. 2 weir Sie es @ 3/6	. 8. 8
277.	1 hand Mill 20/. 1 Ditto 13/6	1.13. 6
278.	1 old Grindstone 3/. 1 Augur 2/	. 5.
	(3) new Narrow Axes @ 4/	.12.
279.	1 Iron Pot and pothooks	.10.
280.	500 gals Cyder @ 3d.	6. 5.
	whole amt	563.16.10

Littleton Eyre   }
John Kendal   }   Appraisors
John Wilkins   }

Hanover

281.	1 old Bay horse £ 5, ditto £ 5	10.
282.	5 Hogs 50 16 Shoats £ 4. 4 Sows and 24 pigs	8.10.
283.	1 Ox Cart & Wheels with 2 Yokes & Chains	3.
284.	4 Working Steers	8.
285.	6 Cows £ 6 4 Heifers £ 4	10.
286.	11 young Cattle $ 8.5 1 Bull 20/. 3 Calves	10.
287.	1 new narrow hoe	. 3. 6

288.	18 old hoes 32 Axes, & some other old Iron	1. 5.
289.	1 Collar and Haims & 1 old Auger	. 1. 6
290.	1 pr hand Millstones and Peck	.12. 6
291.	1 old half Bushel & old Barrls	. 2.
292.	15 Barrls of Corn at 4/6	3. 7. 6
293.	3 Iron Wedges & Reap hooks 1 old curry Comb & 1 pr of Iron Spancels	.10.
294.	1 grind Stone	. 2. 6
295.	1 Wheat Sieve	. 3.

Matt £ 45	John 20	Sam 45	Paul 23
Sarah 30	Patrick 15	Moll 35	Davy 12
Jenny 40	William 6	Kitt 40	Hannah 25
Morris 25	Alice 25	Bob 25	Jenny 8
			Negroes

£ 419.
_____

474.17. 6

Willm Taylor   }
George Taylor   }
Elisha Meridith   }

New Kent	4769. 1. 6	£ 2499. 4.11	7268. 6. 5
King William	832.	387.11. 6	1219.11. 6
James City	60.	208. 2. 1	268. 2. 1
York	2501.	712. 6.	3213. 6.
Northampton	377.	186.16.10	563.16.10
Hanover	419.	55.17. 6	474.17. 6
Totals	8958. 1. 6	4049.18.10	13008. 0. 4

D,ViLxW: Washington's Account Book. Following the death of Daniel Parke Custis in August, 1757, three appraisers were appointed in the six counties in which Custis had owned land and personal property. The appraisals and inventories were made in 1757 and 1758. They were then returned to the New Kent County court, since that was his principal abode. Apparently John Mercer, the attorney for the estate, made a combined county inventory, deriving the material from the separate county inventories. GW then took Mercer's copy and transcribed it into his account book. It appears this is the only copy extant. Water staining of the pages has rendered much of it undecipherable, however it has been possible to reconstruct the material from the other portions of the inventories. This editor is grateful to the editors of *The Papers of George Washington, Colonial Series,* for their diligent and almost super-human accomplishment to successfully bring order out of chaos by putting the estate papers in an understandable and functional form.

The books from the library of Daniel Parke Custis were, for the most part, derived from his father, John Custis, IV. Most were kept at the latter's home in Williamsburg, although a lesser portion were at White House, New Kent County, At the death of Daniel Parke Custis his library consisted of "nearly three hundred volumes." See *PGWC,* 6:284; also entries 41 and 177 in the Combined County Inventory for their appraised value. Since the inventory of the library is given in consummate detail in *PGWC*, 6:283-300, and is not pertinent to this work, it is not being included in the recapitulation of the estate. The reader is referred to the above reference for a complete list of titles. Suffice it to say, three lists were made: GW made the first in 1761 and another in 1763-64. A third was made by Lund Washington for the inventory of John Parke Custis's estate in 1782. *PGWC*, 6:283.

II

Young Mrs. Washington,
1759–1774

Letter, Martha Washington to Margaret Green, 26 June 1761. *Credit*: Mount Vernon Ladies' Association.

From James Gildart

Madam   Leverpoole Feby 21st 1759

   I have before me both your esteemed Favours of 6th June that you
had been pleased to favour me wth. The Consignment of Sixteen hhds.
Tabo p the Gildart wch Am much oblighed to you & please to be Assured
no Pain shall be Spaired in Selling them for your most advantage. as yet
there is only 4 of them sold. At 3 p 3 3/4 & 4 P. I am sorry to tell you they
are not near of so fine a Quallity as formerly. the many factors that has
ever had them knew I had the Honr of being Aployed by the Family would
not this year take them unless I would let him pick Wch I refused which
was luckey as they have since Advanced and are now from 3 1/2 to 4 1/2
p. you have Inclosed Invoice of Goods to your Order wch hope will be
delivered you Safe & to your Satisfaction as every thing is of the best and
on the most reasonable terms. Your Bill In favour of Mr. Barthow
Dandridge for two hundred Pounds has (illegible) & is to your Debt.
   Capt Mulloy has Persuaded me not to send him till the Fall. therefore
that I may not loose such of my Friends favours on York River that are
inclineable to Ship have ordered Capt. Gaweth of my ship the Johnson
to Waite on them. I hope by him to Receive a Share of your favours, which
I shall greatly esteem. & am

                                  Madam
                                  Yr most Obliged Hum Sert
                                  Jam Gildart

(Docket)
J Gildart
Feb.21.1759

ALS, Custis Papers, ViHi.

From Hill, Lamar and Hill

Mrs Martha Custis   Madera 29th March 1759
    Inclosed we have a Bill of loading for a pipe of wine & box of Citron
which Messrs Capel & Osgood Hanbury directed us to ship for your own
use; & should you not have occasion to use the wine till the latter end of
this year we doubt not its proving Satisfactory altho few or none of the
new wines appear to us so good as usual. We should have shipped you
old wine had there been any of the better sorts to be bought & if we were
favored with an order to send you a pipe yearly you might depend on
being supplied with the best.
    We shall value for the cost on the above Gent. as noted at bottom
& are sorry it is so extravagantly dear, but a scanty vintage & the
unreasonable Portugese who flatter themselves with a continuance of the
great demand, here has lately been for their wines leave us no remedy

                              We are respectfully Madam
                              your most obliged Friend
                              Hill Lamar & Hill[1]

No MCSI

a pipe of wine	£ 26.10. 0
10 pc Virga	2.13. 0

                                                      £ 29. 3. 0
do 2 a box of citron   .16. 6
                                                      £ 29.19. 6

(Address leaf)
Mrs Martha Custis
In Virginia
P Capt Blake.
ALS, Custis Papers, ViHi.

    1. Hill, Lamar & Hill also sent GW a bill of lading for a pipe of wine on March 28, 1760.
PGWC 6:404-05.

To Bartholomew Dandridge

(1756-1759)

1757 Mrs Martha Custis Dr.		To Batholomew Dandridge Cr.	
To Cash	£ 21	1757 By Cash _____	£ 5. 7. 6
Col. Macon's Order(?) £10	58	By pd Doctor Carter _____	£ 44.14. 9
15 pct S. exctd			
	79	By Mr. Dandridge's Order____	10. _. _
		Bot 1 ps Lutestring_____	10.10. _
		By (illegible) _____	8. 7. 9
			79. _. _

1758 To Cash paid you	£ 40. 9. 5	1758 By Cash of Major Gaines _____	44. 0. 2
To my last year's accot agst you C of Custis for Lawyers Fees	3. 2. 6	By Cash of Gill Armstead for	7.10. _
To Francis Foster & Fox	1.11. 3	Ex Pennington	
To Pd. Geo. Webb	1. 7.(?)	By 1 Saddle & Bridle	2. 5. 9
To Order on Chs Whitlock	1. 2. 6	By 4 Steers at 40/	8. .
To Pd. Francis Foster	2. . _		61.15.11
To Ballance due to Mrs. Custis	49.16. 2		
	£ 11.19. 9	By Ballance	£ 11.19. 9
	61.15.11	1759 Apr 23 By Interest on my Bond £ 28. 3. 9	39.12. _
		(illegible) 11. 6. 3	51.11. 9
		(illegible)	

- -

(Verso)

1756	Colo Custis Dr.	
Fees	Gaines	15.__.__
	Pennington	15.__.__
	Tax on (illegible)	2. 6.__
1757	Mrs. Custis Dr.	
Fees	Pennington	15.__.__
	Gaines	15.__.__
		£ 3. 2. 6

B. Dandrige
(?) Mrs. Custis

ADS. ViHi, Custis Papers

George Washington's Queries to John Mercer and Mercer's Answers

Sir   Williamsburg 20 April 1759

Be pleased on the other side to answer the following queries in a full and ample manner and oblige very much, Yr most Obedt Servt.[1]

G°: W(ashington)

First Does the Law require that all the Personal Estate & (Negroes only excepted) of the late Colo Custis be sold, in order to lay off his widows dower and daughters part.-or can it be done by the Inventory & appraisment - or lastly by dividing the Estate as it stands at this present - Which of these three is the Right Method? - & had Mrs. Washington a claim to one third of the Chattels of every kind whatsoever?

To the first

All such Goods as may be liable to perish or be the worse for keeping are by Law directed to be sold by public auction as soon as conveniently may be after the Debts paid - Yet I am of Opinion a Division may be made of the personal as well as the real Estate by the method hereafter mentioned - Mrs Washington has a clear right to one third of the Chattels of every kind whatsoever.

Second - What steps are necessary to Effect this in either Case? & how is the Money and Bonded Debt to be divided?

To the Second of (illegible) & best method to have Mrs Washington's Dower assigned (illegible) Estate divided will be by a Bill in Chancery to be brought in your & Mrs Washingtons names against the Children upon which Commissioners will be appointed not only to set apart her Dower in the Lands but to divide the money & bonded Debts & every other part of the Estate, one third thereof which belongs to Mrs Washington - and as I am satisfied your chief motive is to have the Children's Shares set apart & ascertained, so that fair & regular Accounts may be kept of the Profits & all Disputes that might be occasioned by a joynt Occupation, avoided, so I am assured the Speaker who is appointed Guardian to prosecute & defend for the Children will agree to any Division that may be for the Ease & advantage of all Persons concerned: and such a Division I am confident (will) readily be established by the Court.

Third - Has Mrs Washington a Right to take any part of the Furniture or Personal Estate (negroes excepted as before) at the Appraisment price? - or is she under a necessity or taking the whole or none?

To the third. As it would be very inconvenient either to part with the furniture of the House or expose it to Sale in order to purchase it I make no doubt but the Commissioners will assign you any part of the household furniture you desire at the appraised value & the remainder may be sold.

Fourth - Whether if the Law does not require the whole Personal Estate to be sold, I have notwithstanding a power, or can obtain one (& by what means) to sell such part as I (consider) to be for the Estate Interest?

To the fourth. The Cattle must be kept on the Heirs Lands for his benefit & at his Risque. Except they are too numerous in which Case part of them may be sold. One third of the Cattle belongs to Mrs Washington & the Heir will be answerable to his Sister for one Half of the appraised value of (the oth)er two thirds. The (real) & the personal Estate that will not (be for) the benefit of the Estate to keep (missing) may be sold.

Fifth - Is Mrs Washington obligated to render (an acco)unt of every thing Inventoried & appraised? I mean Household goods that perhaps are broke or worn out, - Plantation Utensils that are lost or used - Liquors &ca that may have been Drank - and if she is, what sort of an acc't is required by Law? - and whether that account shoud be previous to a Division of the Estate?

To the fifth Mrs Washington is accountable for everything inventoried and appraised but ought to have Credit for such things as have been used or worn out about the Plantation: an account of which will be properly made us before the Commissioners.

Sixth - Has she not a Right to have her Expenses of every kind borne, as well those which may Relate to her particular self, as Housekeeping &ca in general? Does that Right still continue till a Division be made, or does it cease upon her Marriage?

To the sixth I also am of Opinion that she must be at the whole Expense of housekeeping since the Appraisment, but as she accounts for the Profits of her Children's Estates she is entitled to a liberal Allowance for their Maintanance.

Seventh Whether it is necessary to get appointed guardian, and Manager of (the) Estate & (of the) Children - or do I become so as Husband (illegible) obtaind the administration? But (missing) that some (one other than myself) shoud be choose Guardian till a Division (of) the Estate & a Settlement be made.

To the seventh Mrs Washington is by Law entitled to the Guardianship of her Children till they attain fourteen years of age, when they may choose their own Guardians but it is by all means advisable that a Division & Settlement be made before you undertake the Guardianship in her right. When that is done you must undertake it, or some other Guardian, must be appointed, as the Speaker will have nothing to do with their Estates.[2]

Eighth -If Dunbar obtains his Suit at Law against Colo Custis's Estate how far will Mrs Washington's Dower be liable?

To the eighth. As Dunbar's Claim is against Genl Parke's Estate that alone is liable, consequently no other Part of mrs Washington's Dower than what she holds of that Estate can be affected by Dunbar's Recovery.[3]

Ninth - If the Money and Chattels which in any other case woud have become my absolute property, should be made liable - am I accountable for the Principal & Interest, of what I may now receive - or the Principal Only?

To the ninth. So none of the money or Chattels you receive can be liable Should the Court adjudge Parke's Lands & Negroes to be so. I am of Opinion they will adjudge that Mrs. Washington's Dower of that Estate should contribute in proportion to her Interest therein which is only for Life.[4]

J Mercer

ADS, Custis Papers, ViHi.

1. John Mercer (1704-1768), a resident of Stafford County, was one of the ablest and most learned lawyers in the colony. He had been retained by John Custis (1678-1749) and by his son, Daniel Parke Custis (1711-1757) to represent them in the Dunbar controversies. After Daniel's death he continued to advise and represent Martha Dandridge Custis and her children. After her marriage to GW he served as GW's attorney in the settlement of the estate. In the original document, Washington's nine queries are stated, followed by Mercer's reply to each question, as a separate document. To aid the reader, the editor has taken the liberty of inserting Mercer's answers to each of GW's queries. The queries are in the hand of GW. The replies are in the hand of John Mercer.

2. See supra, John Mercer to MDC, October 21, 1758; John Mercer to MDC, November 2, 1758.

3. Should Dunbar's suit prevail, Mrs. Custis's liability, as a result of her portion of the dowery derived from the Parke estate, might have been considerable. It would certainly have involved almost the whole of the Queens Creek Plantation that John Custis had derived from the Parke estate by virtue of his marriage to Frances Parke, the daughter of Col. Daniel Parke. The properties in the counties of New Kent, King William, Hanover, James City, and those on the Eastern Shore were derived from John Custis and the Custis inheritances, and thus, not a liability. See, *Freeman*, 2:281.

4. See supra, Benjamin Waller to MDC, August 30, 1757, n. 4. For the best account of the Parke-Custis-Dunbar legal entanglement, see *Freeman*, 2:276-312.. See also, Helen Hill Miller, *Colonel Parke of Virginia, The Greatest Hector in the Town*, Chapel Hill, 1989.

From James Biggs to George Washington

Sir   May 10th 1759

According to your Command (I have) sent you as near as I am able (mutilated) accot of the nigros and stocks (mutilated) Rest of the (Estate) of Colo. Custis on this Shore[1] Except (in) Smith's Island[2] which I omited on accot of its being Rented out - but if meteral may be seen by a leas that Mr Vollentime has in his pirsession heare is som corn which is sold tho not delivered yet and will be about 1000 Bushells

(illegible) am at Command your humble sevt.

James Biggs

ALS, Custis Papers. ViHi.

1. James Biggs was the overseer of the Custis plantation in Northampton County on the

Eastern Shore. The slaves on the Eastern Shore were appraised at £377. See, Combined County Inventory.

2. Smith's Island belonged to the Custis Estate. It was located off the Virginia coast at the entrance to Chesapeake Bay. It remained in the Custis-Lee family until about 1915, when it was sold.

From Lain Jones

(26 June 1759)

Mrs Martha Custis[2]	Dr.	Dr.
To 63 Levies at 49 1/2	3118 1/2	
To (?) K.W.	36	
To surcharge fee	578	
To W Clayton	505	
To the Publick	140	
To Majr. Armistead's Order	590	
	4967 1/2	
By ye Order on Mr. Mossom	4829 1/2	
	138	

1. 7. 7

(Docket)

138 lb Tobo 1. 7. 7
26th June 1759
1. 7. 7
12.10
2. 0. 5

26 June 1759
Recd the Balance
of 138 lb Tobo a 20/pc
Lain Jones[1]

AD, Custis Papers, ViHi.

1. As sheriff of New Kent County, Lain Jones was responsible for collecting all levies on tobacco. "Levies, taxes &ca pd Lain Jones by 2 Rects & Clks fees 23.15.11 1/2 & 4967 1/2." (pounds of tobacco). *PGWC* 6:252,258, n. 4.

From Robert Cary & Company

Madm   London the 17 July 1759

To our's already wrote you by this Conveyance we Referr, since which your Favour of the 30th April is now before us & your several Drafts to the amount of £1500 we have already Accepted & when due shall punctually be paid-

As the Accot sales & Accot Currt sent p Turner have in all probability miscarried we have now sent the Copy's-

Inclosed is the Charge of Obtaining Letters of Administring to the Receiving the Dividend on the £1650 Bank Stock which Charge £7.7 is to thy Estates Debit - The Bank Directors have as yet not Entered your Power of Atty in their books till they do tho we hope it wont be long we cannot receive the Interest - Mr John Hanbury departed this life the 23d Ulto & while he lived we coud not ask for the Enlargement of your Consignments but now as things are Differently circumstanced we may safely do it & as such we hope in the future to receive all your crops. for it is Evidend the less hands Tobacco goes in the greater Probability there is of keeping up a Living Price & therefore must naturally be productive of our Friends Interest

Are sorry to hear the Crops are so short we hope the Prices will Compensate since little matter for the Difference - We are

> Madm
> Your most Hum Servt
> Copy Robert Cary & Co
> Mrs. Martha Custis

(Docket)
Letter
Cary - 17th July - 1759

ALS, Custis Papers, ViHi.

Sundry Goods for a Bride

Invoice of Sundry Goods to be Shipped by Robert Cary Esqr. & Company for the Use of George Washington

A Light Summer suit made of Duroy or by the inclosed measure

4 peices best India Nankeen[1]

2 best beaver Hats plain each to cost a Guinea

1 ps of Irish Linnen @ 4/

1 ps of black E Sattin Ribbon

1 Sword-belt of Red morocco leather or buff. N.B.. no buckles or rings.

4 lb. Ivory blacking

2 best (?) bladed knives

1 pair good horse Scissars

A Sammon coloured Tabby[2] of the inclosed pattern with Sattan flowers to be made in a Sack or Coat.

1 Cap handkerchief, Tucker[3] and Ruffles to be made of Brussels Lace or point proper to wear wt ye above Negligie[4] to cost £10.

1 ps bag holland[5] to cost 6s

2 flowered Lawn[6] Aprons.

2 stole handkerchiefs

2 pr Womans white silk hose

6 pr. ditto fine Cotton Do

4 pr B thread Do

1 pr. black & 1 pr. White Sattan Shoes of the Smallest Sizes.

4 pr. Callamanca[7] Do

6 pr Woman's best kid gloves

6 pr. Do. Mitts

1 fashionable hat or Bonnet

1/2 dozn.knots & breast knots.

1 dozn Silk Laces

1 black Mask

1 dozn. most fashionable Cambrick pocket handkerchiefs

2 pr. neat small scissars

1 lb sewing Silk Shaded.

1/4 lb Do cloth - coloured Do

4 ps.binding Tape

6 M Miniken pins[8]

6 M short Whites

6 M Corking pins[9]

1 M hair pins

6 lb perfumed powder

3 lb best scotchsnuff

3 lb best violet Strasburg[10]

2 lb powdered blew

2 oz. Coventry thread 1 of wh. to be very fine[11]

1 ps White Sattin ribbon pearl edge.

1 Case of pickles to consist of Anchovies Capers Olives Salid Oil & 1 bottle India Mangoes.

1 large Cheshire Cheese

4 lb green tea

10 Groce best Corks

25 lb best Jar Raisins

25 lb Almonds in the Shell

1 hogshead best Porter

10 Loaves of dble & 10 of Single refined Sugar

6 strong halters hempen reins

3 best Snaffle bridles

9 best Girths

25 lb brown soap[12]

12 lb best Mustard

2 dozn packs playing Cards

2 Sacks best English Oats

1 dozn painters brushes

11 bushl tares[13]

12 best hand padlocks

18 bell Glasses for Garden

2 more chair bottoms such as were wrote for in a former invoice

1 more Window Curtain & Cornish

8 Busts &ca according to the following directions & measures of Copper Enamel or Glazed. viz.

1 of Alexander the Great - 1 of Julius Caesar 1 of Charles ye 12 of Sweden & another of the King of Prussia these all to be of the same size in order to fill up broken pediments over doors, & not to exceed 15 inches in height nor 10 inches in width.

2 Furious Wild Beasts of any kind, not to exceed 18 inches in length & 12 in higth but as near that size as may be drawn as if approaching each other & eager to engage at the distance of about 4 feet. to be the same Colour as those above.

Prince Eugene & the Duke of Marlborough of somewhat smaller size than the above to stand on each end of a pediment wch is carved in this manner

Sundry Small ornaments for a Chimney piece that is 6 feet long and 8 inches wide

100 lb White Bisquet

2 Lanthorns

3 Gallns Rhenish in pint bottles.

25 Yds broad cloth of the inclose Colour to cost about 7/6

15 Yds Course thick Duffle of ye same Colour

6 Yds Do. to cost 8/6

30 Yds red Shaloon

20 dozn white washed Coat buttons

12 dozen waist coat do.

Twist, thread, Silk &c sufficient to make up the above cloth.

40 Yds Course Jeans or fustians for Summer frocks for Negro Servants.

1 pc Irish Linnen 2 1/3

1 pc Dowlas[14] a 10d

1/2 dozen pr course strong thread hose fit for Negro Servants.

6 Caster[15] hats a about 5/

1 dozn pr Course Shoe & knee buckles fit for Do.

2 Postillion Caps[16]

450 Ells Oznaburgs

4 ps brown Rolls

350 Yds Kendal Cotton[17]

100 Yds Dutch Blankets

2 ps fearnought[18]

8 dozn pr plaid hose Sorted

4 dozn Monmouth[19] Caps

20 lb bro thread

15 lb best Shoe Makers do

20 Sacks Salt

2 Casks 3d Nails
2 Do 10d Do
10 M 20d Do
20 M 4d Nails
20 M 6d Do
6 Spades
200 lb German Steel
2 dozn best Staples[20]
6 best Whites handsaws
6 best broad axes
6 House Adzes
2 dozn box Gimblets
6 pr Steel Compasses
1 dozn Augers sorted from 2 inches to 1/2 Do
1 Cowper's Taper bitt[21]
1 Do Croe[22]
1 Do Dowling bitt
1 Do Vice
1 Do pr large Compasses
1 Do Adze
1 do Round Shave[23]
1 Do Howell
1 Wheel Wright's Buz
1 Do large Gouge
1 Do Anter Bitt
2 Dozn pair H's hinges
Joiner's Tools
1 jointer
2 long plains
2 Jack Do
4 Smoothing Do
10 pr hollows & rounds
6 ogees
4 two Square Astricles
3 pr Grooving plains
1 Snipes bill
4 quarter rounds
4 Sash plains
3 beed plains
6 ovalos
1 plow & irons
1 Moving philister
1 Screw Rabbit plain
1 Square Do

3 raising Do

1 Spring Brace & bit compleat

1 Turkey oil-stone[24]

1 handsaw

1 pannel Do

1 tenant Do[25]

1 Compass Do[26]

1 Sash Do

1 dozn firmers

1 Do Gouges

1 morticing Chizzels

1 Adze

1 drawing knife

2 pr Compasses

2 Rules

2 Chalk lines

1 small hatchet

2 punches

2 Saw Setts

2 dozn Gimblets

2 dozn plain Irons

6 Rasps 2 of a Sort

2 dozn handsaw fills

2 of Tennant Do

25 lb Glew

2 vent saws

12 inch Chizzles

6 Bottles Turlington Balsam[27]

8 Oz Spirit of Lavender[28]

1/2 lb. Ipca:powdered[29]

1/2 lb. Jalap powdered[30]

12 Oz Venus Treacle[31]

4 Oz best Rhubarb[32]

12 Oz Diascordium[33]

4 Oz pearl barley[34]

4 lb. Sago[35]

4 Oz balsam Capivi[36]

5 Oz liquid Laudanum[37]

5 Oz Spirits Sal Ammoniac[38]

5 Oz Spirits Hartshorn[39]

4 Oz Spanish flies[40]

3 lb Bird lyme[41]

6 lb Oil of Turpentine

2 lb. Spirits Do

5 lb White Sugar Candy

10 lb. Bo Do.

1 lb barley Sugar

2 lb. linseed Oil Cold drawn

4 lb. Allum[42]

1 lb Spirma Citi

4 Oz tincture of Myrrh

4 Oz. balsam Sulphur[44]

4 Oz pulvus Basilii[45]

2 Oz. Mer Dulcis[46]

4 Oz. Sal Volatile[47]

10 lb. hartshorn Shavings[48]

2 Quarts strong Cinnamon Water[49]

2 Quarts Weak Do.
   N.B. all liquids to come in double flint bottles.

40 S. worth of Medicines proper for Horses - Among wh let there be

4 lb. flower of brimstone[50]

4 lb. Annis seeds[51]

4 lb. Carthamums[52]

5 lb. Syrup of Coltsfoot[53]

5 lb. black Soap

4 lb. Cummin seeds[54]

4 lb. Fenngreek [55]

2 lb. juice of Liquorice[56]

3 lb. long pepper[57]

2 lb. Diapente[58]
   & such other as are most proper

G°: Washington
20th Sepr 1759

From a copy in an unknown hand and furnished through the courtesy of ViMtV.

1. A type of corduroy.
2. A fabric of plain or taffeta weave.
3. A small piece of fabric used to fill in a low decolletage.
4. A woman's loose gown.
5. Imported linen.
6. Sheer linen.
7. A sized linen material.
8. Small common pins.
9. Large common pins.
10. A sweet scented snuff, often used by women.
11. Blue yarn used for embroidery.
12. In GW's letter book copy at DLC:GW, it appears as "Crown soap." An herb used for skin eruptions.
13. Vetch seed.
14. Coarse linen.

15. Long haired felt.

16. A beaver hat, with tall crown and narrow brim.

17. Green colored cotton.

18. Heavy woolen fabric.

19. A flat round military cap.

20. The letter book copy reads, "sickles."

21. A wood-boring bit.

22. Crowbar.

23. A rounded draw-knife used to round out the inside surface of barrel staves.

24. Whetstone.

25. A tenon saw.

26. A scroll saw.

27. Tincture of benzoin was used for treating wounds and abrasions.

28. Used to relieve menstrual discomfort.

29. Powdered ipecac was made from the root of a West Indian plant. When combined with powdered opium it was effective in the treatment of diarrhea.

30. Made from the root of the wild Jalap, it was used as a cathartic.

31. Used as a perspirant and opiate.

32. When dried or in syrup form it was used as a purgative and astringent.

33. A syrup, made from an herb, used as a diuretic and perspirant.

34. An antipyretic.

35. Sago jelly, made from the Sago palm, was mixed with milk and used as a dietary supplement.

36. Made from the Copaiva tree, it was used as a diuretic and cathartic.

37. Laudanum was 10% opium in water. When combined with alcohol, it was called tincture of opium. It was used to alleviate pain.

38. Used as a stimulant and tonic.

39. Ammonium dissolved in water and used as smelling salts.

40. Finely ground Spanish Flies, used as an aphrodisiac.

41. An antacid and astringent, derived from a plant.

42. An astringent, used to control bleeding from wounds.

43. Used for intestinal colic.

44. A concoction of sulfur and olive oil, used for various complaints.

45. Used for catarrhal infections.

46. "Sweet mercury," a circulatory stimulant.

47. Used to revive those who had fainted.

48. Shavings from the horn of a hart or deer. It was a source of ammonia.

49. A suspension of cinnamon, used as an astringent.

50. A laxative and cleansing agent.

51. Used to treat gastro-intestinal disorders.

52. A member of the thistle family, used as a cathartic.

53. A syrup made from an herb, used in the treatment of respiratory ailments.

54. Used for poulticing infected wounds.

55. The seed were used for making poultices.

56. Used for respiratory diseases and as a purgative.

57. Used to promote flatus and thereby relieve colic.

58. A mixture of myrrh, laurel berries, Sentian root, ivory shavings, and bathwort, used to purge horses.

From Capel & Osgood Hanbury

Esteemed Friend.   London Ocr 1:1759

We are favored with Thine of June 12th, informing Us of Thy Marriage with our friend Martha Custis, upon which circumstances we heartily congratulate you both, & wish you a great d(ea)l of happyness, - We observe Thy directions in regard to our addressing our Letters in relation to Coll. Custis's Estate, which we shall do accordingly-

We are sorry the Sales of the 28 Hhds Tobacco P the King of Prussia was not satisfactory, assure Thee that considering the Quality, we thought we sold Them very well, and was told by the Buyer that they were not near so good as those sent (mutilated) indeed it was with no small difficulty, that we ob(mutilated)e price we did; please to observe that many of them were light, which Hhds paying the same charges as heavier, reduces the produce consideraby, & we are sorry to say the Quality of those P the Anna were far from what we could wish, owing to their being put up in too high case, and that Crop of Tobacco in General as but ordinary - inclosed comes Acct. Sales for Them wch (mutilated) these are too light, indeed much lighter than we could wish'd, No. 2 was exceeding bad, & it gave us a good deal of trouble to get the price it sold for, the Buyers informs us that they were put up in too high a case, which we mention again for Thy government - It will give Us great pleasure to receive Thy Consignments P the Fleet & we (mutilated) our endeavours shall not be wanting (mutilated) entrusted to Our care, This now forwards Acct Current (mutilated) hope will be found right, if otherwise please to note it, & the Error shall be carefully examin'd into, - Thee cannot well imagine what trouble we have had in the settlement of the Salvage of the Anna, she being retook by Three privateers, each of which had its manag(mutilated) but we look upon it, that considering the time she was in Possession of the French, we (adjusted it as) well as could be, and indeed had the concern been all our own, we could not have done better - the chief News at present, or what is mostly talked of, is the intended invasion from the French, to be sure they have assembled a large Body of Troops together, to embark on board Transports, but when they really think of attempting it, is very uncertain, N(o) doubt but any probability of Their landing on our (mutilated) will put us here in great confusion, all the necess(ary means) for preventing it hath been & are taken, which they must certainly be acquainted with it, & which we hope weill make them laid the plan aside - Concludes with regard

                 Thy Assured Friends
                 Capel & Osgood Hanbury

To Geo: Washington, Esqr.

ALS, Custis Papers, ViHi. For GW's announcement of his marriage to MDC and his dissatisfaction concerning the sale of the Tobacco shipped in the King of Prussia and the capture of the Anna, see GW to C & O. Hanbury, June 12, 1759. *PGWC* 6:322.

An Account of the Sail of the Estate of Col Custis Decst In Wms Burg

Estate of Col Custis Dec^st In Wms Burg

October 25, 1759

	£	S	D
2 Pewter Dishes and 6 Plates	104 Cash paid	1	2	6
4 Pewter Dishes	105 To George Chaplain		12	6
9 High Leather Chears	106 To Thos. Wilkins	2	5	6
1 Tin Basket & other Lumber	107 To John Greenhow		11	
1 Jarr one pr Scales & weights	108 To Wm Graves		15	6
1 Ladle 2 Candle Sticks & snuffers	109 To John Bartley		10	
1 Brass Gun & Close Stool Chear	110 To John Greenhow		14	6
15 Paines Large Glass	111 To John Greenhow	1	11	
1 Warming pan	112 To Thos. Craig		8	3
1 Case & Bottles & mose Trap	113 To John Greenhow		8	
A parcel of Shot and Gun Flints	114 To Wm Graves		5	3
1 Table and Dressing Glass	115 To Thos. Craig		19	
3 Picturs	116 To John Greenhow		14	
12 Picturs	117 To Mr Frank	1		6
5 Picturs	118 To John Greenhow		10	6
12 Small picturs	119 To Mr Frank	1		
A parcel of oald Iron	120 To Wm Graves		7	
A pair of oald Dogs & Tongs & shovel & funnel	121 To George Chaplain		7	6
1 Spice Mortar and pessel	122 To Col.Bernard Moore		7	
7 Picturs	123 To Thos. Craig	1	1	
15 Picturs & a Bull Dog	124 To John Greenhow	1	11	
3 Picturs	125 To Mr Frank		7	9
2 Bell mettle Skillets 4 wheat stones 2 sullinges	126 To John Greenhow	2		
1 Chocolate pot	127 To Mary Rise		7	8
1 Chocolate pot	128 To Wm Graves		7	3
1 Jarr	129 To John Buston		8	6
1 Small Jarr	130 To Mary Rise		3	
1 oald Safe	131 To George Chaplain		9	
1 oald Chest	132 Cash paid		5	
1 oald Bead stead	133 To John Grainger		15	
1 Large Looking Glass	134 To Thos. Craig	4	10	
1 oald Desk	135 To Mr Frank	1	8	
1 Small Glass picture	136 Cash Paid	5		
1 Large Looking Glass	137 To Mr Frank	1	4	6
1 Book Case & Draws	138 To Patr Connelly	3	13	
8 Low Leather Chears	139 To Jos. Vallentine	1	6	

6 Glass Decanters	140 To Cash paid	11
1 Small Dressing Glass	141 To John Grainger	7 9
1 Small Table	142 To Patr. Connelly	11 6
1 Leather Couch	143 To Mr Frank	7
A parcel of oald broken picturs	144 To Mr Frank	3 6
7 picturs	145 To John Greenhow	12
18 Small picturs	146 To Mr Frank	2 13
5 Woodin Immageis	147 To John Greenhow	15
A parcel of Brimstone	148 Cash paid	1 11
1 Large Ovel Table	149 To Patrick Connelly	1 15
1 Parge Press	150 To John Greenhow	2 12
A Teaster of a Bead	151 To Mr Frank	5
A pair old Garden Tiers & Iron Fender	152 To Mr Frank	5
1 Cain Trussel	153 To Emanal Taylor	1 4
A pair of old scales and weights	154 Cash paid	2
2 Oald Earthen pots	155 To James Yeats	1 6
A parcel of oald Galley pots & Lumber	156 To Thos Cobbs	8 2
2 Pewter dishes	157 To Wm Richardson	10 2
1 oald pewter Bason 6 plates	158 To Eadward Cummins	4 6
1 oald Iron pot & hooks	159 Cash paid	5
A parcel of small pictures	160 To Thos Craig	6 6
1 oald Table	161 Cash paid	1 3
A parcel of read Lead	162 To Wm Smith	4 1
1 Iron pot	163 To John Ormiston	5 9
1 oald Beadstead	164 Mr Frank	3
1 oald Iron pot & Duch oven & pan	165 George Chaplain	13 6
1 Writing Table	166 Wm Hobt	16 9
8 Large oald picturs	167 Mr Frank	5
3 picturs	168 Cash paid	5 2
2 Maps	169 Cash paid	9 1
9 Pictures	170 Cash paid	3 4
6 Pictures	171 To Thos Craig	7 7
1 Large Picture	172 To Mr Frank	3 1
9 picturs	173 To John Ormiston	11 4
3 maps	174 To Jos Vallentine	6 10
3 picturs	175 Cash paid	3 3
1 pictur of an horse	176 To Thos Craig	10 3
3 picturs	177 To Mr Frank	4
1 Dish and 6 plates	178 To John Ormiston	17 6
5 Pictures	179 To John Grainger	4 6
5 Pictures	180 Cash paid	5
1 pair oald Doggs	181 To Thos pait	8 1
1 Stone Judge	182 To Wm Smith	3 1
1 Trunk and spit	183 Cash paid	6 6

1 Chest & Bottles	184 To Wm Smith	4	1
1 Chest & Bottles	185 To Wm Smith	4	6
1 Oald Table	186 To Thos Wilkins	6	
1 Chest	187 Cash paid	4	
1 Chest	188 Cash paid	1	3
210 pounds oald Iron	189 To Thos Pait	17	6
		58	7	7

58 7 7
3 5 6
19 2 5
36 1 5

Errors Excepted

58 9 2

(Docket)
Sale of the Estates Goods
in Williamsburg for
Jos Valentine

AD, ViHi. The document is in the handwriting of estate manager, Joseph Valentine.

The Inventory of the Estate of Daniel Parke Custis

1757

The Estate of Daniel Parke Custis Esqr deceased Dr.[1]

To Mrs. Martha Custis for Sundrys paid on Acct of the Estate viz. for Funeral Expenses. to Charles Crump for makg & ling a Coffin 3-4-6; Robt. Clopton assisting about Ditto £1 the Reverend Mr. Mossom for a Funerl Sermn 3-4-6

£ 7- 9

Debts due from Colo. Custis in his lifetime[2] Viz to
Thomas Dixon for two Cheeses 1-1-4
George Brett for building a Shooner £20
John Wollaston for 3 Pictures £60-4
Richd Chamberlayne for Plank £4
Doctr. Amson for Attendance £8-12
George Taylor for Ballance of his acct provd 1-3-10 1/2
Stephen F. Hoomes for Iron £2-12
Colo. Wm Macon for a Bill of £40 Sterl. £58
Barthw. Dandridge for Attorneys Fees 1-12-6
Thos. Pasley for Schoolg 2 Children of Ann Smiths £2
John Richmond. Taylor for work done 1-3-4 1/2
Smiths £2
John Richmond. Taylor for work done 1-3-4 1/2
Andrew Marr for the duty of a Pipe of wine £1-13
James Darnforth for Smiths work 13-18-9

Lyde & Cooper of Bristol for a bale due them 5-0-4   181- 1- 2
Overseer's Shares. to Jno Roan as by his Rect 4-3-4
Chs Whitlock as by his four Receipts 41-1-8
Epaphroditus Howle as pr his four Receipts 36-7-3
Roger Tandy as by his Receipt £40
William Hatton as by ditto 4-3-4
Edward Valentine for his share of Butter 2-0-7 1/2   127-16- 2 1/2
Sundries for the Use of the Estate viz.
Brick work done by Joseph Pond as by his 3 Rects £1-16
Crops pd Richd Usrey for Potatoe Seed 12-6
Col Macon for Wheat to sow 4-13-9
Doctors. Dr Scott curg a Negroe Woman's Finger £2-3
Dr McKenzie visitg ye Coachn 1-1-6
Fishing. Geo: Brett for a Boat 35/
Jno Case mendg Saines 2-7-6
Inspection. pd Wm Poindexter £5-3. Do £4.
Jas Clarkson 2-10
Wm Graves £3
Law Charges. Barth: Dandridge Attr Fees 3-1-3
John Mercer & Mr Nicholas for retainrs £10-15
Levie, Taxes &c pd Lain Jones by 2 Rects &
Clks fees 23-15-11 1/2 & 4967 1/2; Negroes cloaths
vizt Stockings of Burbidge &c 7s 9d; pd Sarah
& Molly Cook for makg them £3-4; Eliza Langston for
Do £2-4; Ann Smith for Do £1; Quitrents pd Mr Blair by
Rect 22-10-5; Repairs of a house pd Jno Wheatley by
rect £4-9; Shoe thread bot of Thos Frame 19s; Smiths
work paid James Darnforth pr Rect 7-17-2; Spinning &
weaving pd Jno Hazlegrove for 2 Wheels £1; pd Sarah
Ragland for weavg Virga Cloth 4 times 10-6-2 1/2   118-17
To Joseph Valentine for Sundries paid by him on acct
of ye Estate allowd by Mrs Custis on passing his acct
Viz. Mourning for the family. of Mr Prentis £53-10 1/2;
Mr. Stephenson £14-6d; Mr Franks £7-4-6; Mr Tarpley
5-2-4 1/2; Mr John Carter 1-14-7; Mr Nelson £1-8-6
Jno. Bartley making 20 s.; Mrs Carlos do 32/; Mrs
McKenzie do 24/5; Nichs Syme 17/8; Cash paid for 2 pr
black Stockings 17/; 1 pr black gloves 5/.   89- 3- 5
Debts due from Colo. Custis in his Life time. to Jno.
Carter by acct provd £3-14-6; Mr. Peter Lyons £1-2-6;
Jas Bigs 9-1 1/2; Jno. Greenhow 7-10 1/2   5-14
Overseers. a years wages to himself £80; to Richd Croshire
Graves a years ditto £25; James Biggs overseer on the
Eastern Shore by Rect £10-16-6   115-16- 6
Sundries for ye use of the Estate. Viz. punch at ye
Appraisment 2-6; Brickwork abt the Graveyard and Monument
£16-4; Smiths acct 18/9; Doctors Accts paid Dr Carter
£24-2-3; Dr Hay £2-3; Inspection 22 Hhds £5-10, 15 at
Littlepages £3-15, 1 at Newcastle 5/; Law charges Writs
Sowell 3-6, Peter Lyons Attrs fees 2-17-6, Benj Waller
Clks fees 6-10-11, Thos Penman Prison fees &c 3-14-10;
Levies Taxes &c pd the Sherif of hanover 2-6-3, Jas

City 12/. King William £6-5, York £11-13-2 1/2., paid for 1690 lb Tobo £14-1-8; Sheep, paid forr 35/. from the Eastern Shore & their freight £10-5; Tar, paid for a Barrel 15/ & for 3 Horse Collars 15/	130- 4-10 1/2
	£776- 2- 2
Note of the above Tobo 4967 1/2 lbs. there was paid in Tobo left in the house by Colo Custis at his death 4829 1/2 and for the Balle. there was paid to the Sherif 20/prct 138	1- 7- 7
	£777- 9- 9

	Sterling	Current money
To the ballance to be divided. one third to Colo. Washington & his Wife	£ 1617-18- 0 5/12	£ 7618- 7-11 1/2
one third part to Jno Parke Custis	£ 1617-18- 0 5/12	£ 7618- 7-11 1/2
& one third to Martha Parke Custis	£ 1617-18- 0 5/12	£ 7618- 7-11 1/2
	£ 4853-14- 1 1/4	£ 23632-13- 7 1/2

Each of them to be Chargeable with one third part of any demands against the Estate and to be entitled to one third part of all Credits to the Estate not containd in this Acct.[3]

1757 Contra	Cr Sterling money	Current money
By the Inventories of the Estate taken in the several Counties of New Kent in which the Slaves were appraisd to $4769- 1- 6		£ 7268- 6- 5
King William 832		1219-11- 6
James City 60		268- 2- 1
York 2501		3213- 6
Northampton 377		563-16-10
By Bank Stock in England	£ 1650	
By Goods recd of Robert Cary Esqr & Compa in 1758	458- 4-10	
of Ditto 1759	346- 2- 8	
of ditto by Messrs Oswald in two parcels	23-11-11	
of James Gildart Esqr. in 1758	150-18- 4	
of ditto in 1759	102-14- 8 3/4	
of ditto for Jos. Valentine £25-5-9 3/4 wch Mr Custis agreed for at		31-12- 3
By Cash in the House at his death £1081-1-6 let out at Interest except		284-17- 6
By Bonds due John Custis Esqr. Viz from Benja. Hubbard & Jno Robinson Esqr		350
Interest receivd in full to May 4th 1759		47- 0- 7

John Robinson Esqr. for £150 Ster:
Intt in full £89-3-4 Excha: at
35 pr Ct 83-14-2 paid of in full   322-17- 6

Nathl. Edwards Jas. Wray and Clmt
Read the balle of which due Octr
21st 1749 appears from the receipts
endorsed to be   28-

John Blair Esqr. and Jno Blair Junr   300

Intt. receivd in full to April 23d 1759   51- 4

Henry Armistead and William Armistead
assigned by Carter Burwell the Bale of wch
due Dec 1. 1753 appears from
the Receipts endorsed to be   132- 1- 8

To the ballance to be divided John Mercer
(who says it is paid) & Benja. Hubbard datd.
Novr. 6th 1749   100

By bonds Edmon Pendleton and
Bernard Moore   200

Interest recd. in full to May 8 1759   28- 6- 2

Joseph Moreton and Presley Thornton
assigned by John Randolph   300

Intt. Recd. in full to Mar. 20th 1759   54- 3- 4

The Reverend David Mossum dated
April 9th 1756   17- 6- 8

By protested Bills for Wm Bowler's
Excha on Jas Gildart Esqr dated
July 11th 1754 & protested April
8th 1755, endorsd D.P. Custis
besides Intt. charge of Protest   90

By Promissary Notes payable to D P
Custis on Demand Viz: Abner Clopton's
dated Jany. 8th 1756   3- 4

Edward Pye Chamberlayne's dated
June 28 1756   12-

By Mortgages for Francis Foster's
dated Novr. 1757 for so much money
then lent him on Intt. by Mrs.
Martha Custis out of ye money in
ye house   500

Intt. recd. in full till Novr. 1758   25-

By Bonds payable to Mrs. Martha Custis
for money lent by her at intt.[4]
Joanna McKenzie Jno. Palmer & Jas.
Carter for money in the House
Valentine   216-

Intt. Recd. in full to April 23. 1759   10- 6

Thos. Dansie and Nathl. West Dandridge dated Octr.8 1/58 for money
in House   100-

Bernard Moore & Jno Robinson Esqr. dated
Apl. 12th 1758 for so much drawn for   1000-

Philip Whitehead Claiborne and Bernard Moore Do. £200 sterg.		280-
Intt. recd in full to April 25 1759		14- 5- 9
Burwell Bassett and Presley Thornton Do £1500 Sterg		2100-
Intt. recd. in full to April 23rd 1759		102-16- 3
William Dandridge Carter Braxton & P.W. Claiborne for 20.9. Cash & Do £300 sterl.		440- 9
Intt. recd. in full till April 29th 1759		22- - 5
Thos. Moore Carter Braxton P.W. Claiborne & Ber: Moore Do £1000 St.		
Intt. recd in full till May 2 1759		70-
John Mercer Jno Tayloe & P Thornton payd. May 12th dad. Nov 4th 1758 £1500 Ster.		2100-
Bartho. Dandridge P.W. Claiborne & Wm. Dandridge Do £600 ster.	600	
Interest recd in full till April 23rd 1759		39-12
Philip Johnson & Ber: Moore for £141 B: due Jno Custis Esqr. & Do £50 ster.		211-13
Intt. recd. in full till April 23d 1759		9- 2- 5
By Profits received by Mrs. Custis vizt for Fish. by transfer Notes pd Lain Jones £28-6-11; Jos Ferguson 12-6 besides sundries paid & recd. for the Estates use for which no acct was kept		28-19- 5
Flat hire of Captn John Thomas £2-4-8 & Captn Crawford £2		4- 4- 8
Butter of Edward Valentine Overseer		5-13-10
Sundries of John Roan Overseer		18- 5
Horses running in the Marsh of Mr Allan		6-
Salt of Dyer Bristow		- 6
4 Steers sold to Mr. Bartho. Dandridge		8-
By Ditto Receivd by Mrs. Custis of Joseph Valentine ye Ests Steward as by his Book Profits unaccounted for in Colo. Custis's Life time		70- 9- 8
Butter sold Sundries 561 lb.		20-19- 3
Brandy 82 Gallons		12- 6
Cattle 3 Cows 16 Beeves and 666 lib Beef		56-18- 4
Corn 570 1/2 Barrels		214-17- 6
Pork 19725 lib		136-14-10
Wheat 1091 1/2 bushels		185- 3- 9
Weathers 8 and Lambs 7		7- 2
Sundries sold to the College		32- 5

Rents..of Abra. Coles £4; Emery Hughes £8;
Geo Jones £5-3-9; Wm Keen £10; Michl
Mcarty £11; Geo Powel £16; Ship Landg £5;
Peter Scott £8; (John) Warrington
£20; Jno Wheatley £19-11   116-14- 9

By Debts recd. of Jas. Carter £107-121-2; Majr
Gaines 344-2d;Thos: Ivy £1-1-3;
Colo Macon £1-2; Pennington £7-10; Ben.
Powel £(15); Colo. Syme 5/; Jno. Wheat £10   186- 9- 7
                                                    _____   _____
                                        £ 4853-14- 1 1/4   £ 23632-13- 7

(Docketed)

an

Inventory --by

Mercer Esqr

AD ViHi. *In GW's handwriting. s.n.b.*

1. At the time of his death Daniel Parke Custis had no bonded indebtedness. Whatever debts owed were for current expenses, medical care, funeral expenses and other short term obligations incurred shortly before his death. The only exception to this general statement might be the sum claimed for legal fees by John Mercer against John Custis and Daniel Parke Custis for his efforts in the Dunbar suits that extended over a period of many years. However, this indebtedness is open to question. See supra, John Mercer to MW, January 4, 1758. DPC carried on his father's abhorrence of debt and passed on large liquid assets and debt free lands, just as his father had done.

2. Most of the current obligations listed here are noted in MW's receipted documents, given in the text.

3. See *PGWC* 6:258, n. 7. This notation does not appear in GW's copy in the Custis Papers, ViHi, but does appear in the Washington Account Book copy at ViLxW.

4. At Daniel Parke Custis's death there was £1081 1. 6 Sterling, in the house. See entries below for MW's loans to neighbors and relatives from this amount.

Things reserved for the Use of the Estate and not sold.

No.		
1.	An Anchor	£ 1. 2.
5.	An Applemill	1. 8.
4	4 Pots & Pothooks	2.
6	Augers Coopers & other Axes Millpicks &	5.
7	1 Do & Collar & harness	. 1. 6.
8	76 Awl blades	. 1. 8.
9.	16 Axes & hoes	19.
17	2 Barrels 1 Corn Crib & old hhds	1. 3.
18	Old Do & a half bushel	. 2.
27	A large Flat with Anchor &c	25.
28	A horse Boat & Canoe	6.10.
29	a small Boat	1. 5.
30	Colo Custis's books (18/6)	4.

31	His Fathers books	25.
33	Boxes & old Trunks	1.
42&c	Butter pots 1 Search & Spinning wheel	2. 3.
53&c	Carts yokes & Chains	25. 2. 6
61&c	Cyder Casks 7 1/2 yds Kersey &c	12.12.
66	3 Center bits 14 files 1 Gouge 1 pr marking Irons &c	8.
82	1 pr Can Hooks & 19 Whetstones	6.
88&c	Chests & Trunks	2. 4. 2
91	21 Chisels 12 Gimlets 6 pr sheepshears	1. 8.
93	A Cistern for meat & a Jarr	.10.
98	A large Copper kettle & 1 Ironpot	.12.
99	An old copper (kettle)	51.
105	510 yds Cotton; 115 2 Currying knives & 1 fleshing knife	1.20.
112	1 Currycomb 1 pr Iron Spancels 3 Wedges	1.10.
127&c	2 Dog collars 1 Coopers Compass & 2 drawing knives	. 7.
132	15 1/2 yds Duffel & 7 1/2 yds Kersey	4.19. 6
133	8 Dutch blankets & 9 hats	4. 3.
134	3 pr Dutch blanketting	18.
135	Earthenware & a parcel of Rope	6.
139	24 whipsaw files & 11 plane Irons	1. 4.
140	68 files of different Sorts	2.
143	49 yds of flannel	4. 1. 8
147	5 Grind stones	2.16. 6
163	75 lbs Gunpowder & 1 C 3 qrs Shot	8.18.
169	A handmill	1.
170	33 hasps & Staples & 16 Whetstones	7. 4
172.3	3 hatchets 10 Iron screws 2 pr nippers 4 taper bits	10. 3
174	30 mens hats	3.16.
178.9	5 hides 5 hhds 5 sieves & Lumber	1.12. 6
180	6 pr garnets 1 doz Sickles 11 Spades	4.
181&c	145 Hoes	21. 6. 2
197	a set of hoops for Cart wheels	12.
210	4 Iron Pots & 2 pr hooks	1.10.
215	50 yds Kersey	8. 7. 6
217	396 lbs Lead	3. 5. 8
219.20	215 Sides & 46 Skins of Leather	51. 9
238.40	1 gallon pot 2 measures 2 Riddles 2 Shovels	1. 7
242.3	Medicines	10.
245.6.7	4 pr hand millstones & 1 pick	6. 2. 6
248&c	106 milkpans & a parcel	3. 4. 6
253.4.5	Nails & barrels &c	80.11.
257	Old hoes Axes boxes hoops &c	4.

261	A parcel of old Iron & old harrows	2.
262.3	9 ps of 350 Ells Ozenbrigs	74. 7. 6
265.6	Pails Piggins & Tubs	.12.
275	177 pr plaid hose & 1 pr shoes	11. 4. 3
276	75 yds Plains	10.
280	Plate	187. . 6
284	4 Plows	.14.
287.3	40 ps of Rolls & wrappers	55.10.
293.4.5	Saines	31.
297.9	4 whipsaws 2 x cut 1 handsaws	3. 7. 6
300	1 Sawrest	. 1. 3.
301.2.3	Salt	11. 5. 6
306	6 Scythes & furniture	2.
310	52 pr Shoes & Pumps	11.19. 6
314	a parcel of Shoe thread	1.
324	21 corn Sifters	1. 6. 3
326.7	2 wire Seives & 1 wheat Do	10.
334	1 old Spade	1.
339	22 Staples	3.
341.2.3.4	4 pr Stillyards	1.16.
364	Tar & Tarbarrels	15.
369	Thread	7.
	Carried over	£ 870. 3. 7
372.4	Tradesman & Carpenters Tools	17.10.
375	2 Trowels	. 4.
384	17 lb Twine	.17.
386	36 yds Virginia Cloth	1.16.
390&c	20 Wedges	1.17.
		£ 892. 8. 1
	Charge the Estate with	370. 4. 3
	young Mr Custis with the Balla	522. 3.10
	Plate already charged	187. . 6
	to be yet charged	£ 335. 3. 4

AD in the hand of John Mercer. Custis Papers, ViHi.

Account of Land and Acreage, Estate of Daniel Parke Custis

In the County of

York	3074 Acres
New Kent	6264
Northampton	4650

Hanover	911
King William	2880
	17779 Acres[1]

Sign'd John Blair

AD, ViLxW. In GW's handwriting.

1. No mention was made of the Custis lots in Jamestown and Williamsburg.

Rental Accounts in the Estate

In Williamsburg	John Warrington	£ 20
	Peter Scott	10
	Thomas Weathers	10
	George Chaplain	10
	Andrew Lindsey	5
	James Yates[1]	5
		£ 60
In York County	Emery Hughs	8
	Abram Co(les)	4
	George Jo(nes)	3
	Jno A(shwell)	5
	Tobo 630 lbs	
		20
In Northampton (?)	Smiths Isld	12
	(?) ra Co(?)	1.10
		£ 13.10
Total Amt[2]	630 lbs	£ 93.10

There are besides, belon(ging) (sev)eral unimproved Lotts in James Town (and Williamsburg 3 Mills viz: 1 in New Kent 1 in Yo(rk) (Co)un(ty) & 1 (in (Ja)mes Cit)y calld the Paper Mill

AD, ViLxW. In GW's handwriting.

1. At least some of the above were probably inhabitants of the Custis tenement on Duke of Gloucester Street.

2. No mention is made of the rentals in King William, New Kent, and Hanover Counties.

The Dower Share of Martha Dandridge Custis Washington

(ca. October 1759)

All the Lands in King William County   2880 acres[1]

N.B. the Marsh adjoing this Land is to furnish the other parts of the Estate with Hay (they being at the Expence and trouble of getting it) and this Land to receive necessary Timber from the Estate upon the same Conditions.[2]

Bridge Quarter Land is supposed to be about 700 acres

Ship Landing Quarter and to make up the above 700 acres[3]   1000

A Mill in York County[4]

Dwelling House, Gardens, and Appurtanances in Williamsburg[5]

One third of the Lotts in James Town[6]

Negroes pr Appraisment

House Servants			
	Breechy	£50	
	Doll	40	
	Betty & Chd Austin	60	
	Beck	50	
	Jenny	45	
	Sally	35	£280

Tradesmen			
	Morris	60	
	Michael	60	
	Tom	50	
	Scomberg	45	
	Mulatto Jack Jobber	60	£275

In New Kent			
	Anthony £20		
	Wife Betty £25	55	
	Will	40	
	George	40	
	Doll Dolls	30	
	Lucy Children	25	
	Peter	20	
	Alce	12	
	(illegible)	15	
	Phillis	50	
	Duke	40	
	Scomberg	30	
	Prince	10	£367

£922

In York

Bacchus	£ 40
Ben	50
Crispin	40
Ned	50
Old Captain	50
Young Ned	50
Jupiter	50
Cupid	50
Old Daphne	25
Moll	50
Pegg	60
Young Daphne	25
Child Je(my) (illegible)	
Young B (illegible)	(50)
Frank & C(hild) Judith	(50)
Brunsw(ick)	(50)
Arling(ton)	(35)
Caesar	(25)
Geor(ge)	(30)
Doll	(15)
Lydia	2(6)
Suckey	25
Hannah	25
	(illegible)

In K. William

George	2(0)
Stephen	6(illegible)
David	60
Guy	50
Marlborough	45
Sam	40
Parros	65
Hector	50
Solomon	65
Will	45
Sarah	30
Sew	45
Patt	50
Rachel	35
Crayger	25
Kitt a girl	35
George	35
Bi(l)	25
(Frank)	10
Nan	15

		15	
			£ 845

In Hanover

Matt	45	
Sam	45	
Sarah	30	
Moll	35	
Jenny	40	
Morris	25	
Bob	25	
John	20	
Paul	23	
Patrick	15	
Davy	12	
Alce	25	
Jenny	8	
Kitt	40	£ 388
In all		£ 2986[7]

Signed as before

Stock[8]

	Cattle	(illegible)	Sheep	Hogs
At Claibornes K:William	161	35	78	195
Hanover	31	3		30
Bridge Quarter (York	68	12		
Ship Landing	32	4		
To get from Rocahock	32			
from the Eastn Shore			19	
In all	324	54	97	225

NB The Estate to be charged with £100 for 80 head of Neat Cattle delivd Short of one T(hir)d[9]

1. The tract, known as *Claibornes*, was part of the original grant of 5000 acres, made to William Claiborne I, in 1653. Through inheritance it became the property of his great grandson, Philip Whitehead Claiborne. It was purchased from him by Daniel Parke Custis about 1752. Operated as a quarter, the overseer was John Roan. See supra, John Roan to MDC, August 12, 1757. *Harris,* 2:587-88.

2. A considerable amount of Claibornes was, and still is, marshland along the north bank of the Pamunkey River.

3. Bridge Quarter and Ship Landing Quarter were located on Queens Creek, north of Williamsburg along Capitol Landing Road. The former was located near the north end of the bridge that crossed Queens Creek. Ship Landing Quarter was probably contiguous. See, *Carte des Environs de Williamsburg en Virginie,* drawn under the direction of Col. Desandrouin, Chief of Engineers in General Rochambeau's army in 1782. Reproduced from the original in the Library of Congress.

4. The Custis mill was located about one and one-quarter miles southwest of the Queens Creek Plantation and about three quarters of a mile northwest of the Bridge Quarter tract. It is marked on the Desandrouin map, as is the Queens Creek Plantation.

5. The Williamsburg home and gardens of the Custis family was located on Francis Street. It was later referred to as "Six Chimney House." It disappeared early in the nineteenth century.

6. The 3880 acres was out of a total of 17779 acres in the Custis estate. See, *Account of Land and Acreages, Estate of Daniel Parke Custis.*

7. This amount represents one-third of the total value of the slaves in the six counties. Those not assigned to MDC were to become the property of John Parke Custis.

8. In the delivery of the cattle, GW, who under the law became the owner of his wife's share of the estate, received eighty head less than he was entitled to. His full third was compensated for by deducting £100 from John Parke Custis's account.

An Account of Items used Before the Division of the Estate

(1759)

An Account of Sundries used before the Estate was Divided

No.		£ s. d
19.	478 lb. Lead	3.19.
24.	3 hides 5 old Hhds 4 brass Sieves & Iron do	1.10.
38.	An assortment of Medicines &ca	8.
60.	12 pr Mens Shoes and Slippers	5.
61.	30 Mens Hatts	3.16
76.	9 Hatts and 8 Dutch blanketts	4. 3.
77.	13 Sides of Leather	2. 5.
78.	36 yds Virga cloth	1.16.
79.	75 lb. Gunpowder & 1 C 3 Q Shott	8.18.
80.	1 piece plains qty abt 75 yds	10.
81.	2 pieces Kersey qty abt 50 Yds	8. 7. 6
82.	15 1/2 yds duffle & 1/2 yds Kersey	4.19. 6
83.	510 yds Cotton at 2/	51.
84.	3 pieces dutch Blanketting	18.
85.	39 pieces of Rolls	52.10.
86.	9 pieces qty abt 900 ells Bro: Linn	52.10.
87.	177 pr plaid hose and 1 pr Shoes	11. 4. 3
92.	202 Sides & 46 Skins of uppr Leathr	49. 4.
93.	a parcel of Salt	10.
104.	50 3/4 bro: & colored thrd & 1 lb. whtd bro: do	7.
109.	a parcel of Shoe thread	1.
112.	350 Ells brown Linnen	21.17. 6
113.	1ps of Rolls, and sevl ps of Wrappers	3.
115.	39 pr of Negro's Shoes	6.16. 6
118.	140 lb. Washed Wool	5.[1]
132.	49 yds white Flannel	4. 1. 8
137.	1 pr Negroes Shoes	. 3.
144.	2 Cow Hides	. 2. 6
192.	a parl of old Drugs & some old odd Trifles	2.

196.	1 Cistern to Cool Meat & 1 Jarr	10.
213.	1 Sml qty of large Salt	8.
223.	2 Dog Collars & Coopers Compass	3.
274.	7 Bushels of Salt & 2/6	17. 6
280.	500 Gallns Cyder & 3d	6. 5.
13.	&ca Corn	174. 7. 6
		£ 540.14. 5

D, ViLxW. Washington's Account Book. The numbers in this account are identical with those in the Combined Inventory. The three heirs, MW, JPC, and MPC, were to receive one third of the total appraised value, given above.

1. Item 118: The appraised value in the Combined Inventory is given as £7. See, *PGWC*, 6:236.

Account of Sundrys taken and used by Mrs. Custis out of the Inventories[1]

(October 1759)

New Kent

A Bed and Furniture	6.	
80 Lib sheat lead	.18. 4	
A Chariot and Harness	80.	
1 Iron Mortar still and pestles	1.	
4 brass fenders	1.	
2 Whipsaws	1.	
2 Sorrel horses	50.	
2 Bay Ditto	32.	
1 old Roan Ditto	8.	
1 Young Stallion	25.	204.13. 4
1 Young sorrel horse	18.	
1 young bay Ditto	12.	
30 wine and beer glasses	.15.	
2 Tumblers &c	. 3	
7 Sweetmeat glasses	. 8. 9	
1 Set gilt China &c	4.	
2 Muggs &c	. 6. 9	
Earthen ware	1. 5	
China Plates & Dishes	10.	
Tea cups &c	5.	51.18. 6
8 Razors &c	1.10	
2 pair Money Scales	3.	
1 Mahogany desk	4.	
1 Table	3.	
1 looking Glass	4.	

1 old Cabinet	1.	
2 Cases Knives & forks	3.10	
2 Box Irons	1. 4	
2 Beds &c	10.	34. 4
20 pair Sheets	8.12	
41 Table cloths	14.	
99 Napkins & Towels	7. 8	
24 Pillow Cases & Towels	2. 5	
2 Pc Callico	4.	
10 Counterpanes &c	12.10	
2 Beds &c	10.	
2 pair blankets	2. 5	
2 dressing Glasses	3.	70
2 beds and furniture	12.	
Wine	40.	
A Cooler & treacle & 2 pr Andirons	3.10	
2 Skillets &c	2.	
1 brass plate warmer &c	1.10	
6 Pots and Jarrs with Raisins	1.	
2 Pc Cheese &c	4.	
Salt Petre	2.13	
25 Quire Paper	.16	
2 plate Baskets &c	1.	67.19
22 loaves Sugar	12.	
2 Jockey Caps	.10	
1 Tea Chest &c	. 2	
4 Brass Runners	. 8	
4 doz Whetstones &c	. 8	
2 pair Sheep sheers & 2 gimblets	. 2. 2	
1 hatchet 2 taper bits 1 Marking Iron	. 3.	
7 hasps & 4 whetstones	. 2. 2	
9 Plane Irons &c	. 9.	
1 currying & 1 fleshing Knife	1.	15. 4. 4
1 Crate Earthenware &c	.14.	
Sugar	7.	
23 Glasses	.11. 6	
1 pair weights & Scales	5.	
4 Coopers Axes	.14	
141 Yrds Irish Linnen	24. 8. 6	
5 diaper Table cloaths	3.15.	42. 3
		£ 486. 2.
Brought up		£ 486. 2.
1 Ps Sagathy	6.10	
1 Pattern for Breeches	2.	
2 1/2 Ps Nankeen	1.10	

1 Shaving pot and Bason	. 1	
4 groce horn buttons	1.	
5 3/4 doz pewter plates	5.10	
41 Dishes &c	11.10	
1 Bedpan &c	. 7. 6	
1 pestle Mortar &c	1. 5	
2 Iron Potts & hooks	2.10.	32. 3. 6
1 dripping pan &c	1.	
1 Stew pan &c	2. 1	
1 Copper Kettle	4.	
1 Fish Kettle &c	5.	
1 doz Wine Glasses	. 2. 6	
8 Carboys &c	7.10	
1 Jar Oil	3.	
1 Tearce Rum	12.	
3 Barrels Paint	3. 5	
1 Womans Saddle &c	2.	
4 M 3d Nails	. 8	
5 Paint brushes	. 2. 6	
1 bung borer	. 1	
60 Arol blades	1. 5	40.16
		559. 2
A mare and Colt	12.	
2 brass cocks	.2. 6	
10 chalk lines	. 1	
20 Clouts for Chariot & tacks	.5	
2 Cornice plane Irons	. 2	
1 Rabbet Do	. 1	
4 Whet stones	. . 4	
4 M small nails & a (illeg) brass Do	.19	
4 Screws for hanging hats	. 1	
1 hand screw	. 3	
1 broad axe	. 7. 6	
2 Cornice Stocks	. 5	
1 brass Socket	. 6	
6 Sickles	. 7. 6	
1 Mill Spindle	1.	
4 Mill Picks	. 2	
1 pair large hinges	. 5	
19 Yards flannel	4. 1. 8	
6 Pair Cotton wool & clothiers cards	10.	20.19. 6
		£ 580. 1. 7

James City

A Bed and Furniture	7.
1 Do 8 Table Clothes	6.
4 pair Sheets 1 pillow case	3.

27 Towels 3 Fenders	1.16
1 Bed and Curtains	9.
20 Plates	1.
8 Dishes & 30/ 2 Scollop Shells 2/	1.11
A set fruit peices 5/ a set of flower peices 5/	10.
8 China Bowls &c	1.10
1 Marble Slab	4.
Glass ware	1. 2
China and Earthenware	1.10
22 plates and 2 Jell pots	.15
1 Marble Mortar	. 7
10 doz wine	15.16
1 groce Bottles & 5 Juggs	1.16
Brandy & Cyder 20/ 3 Pots Butter 36/	2.16.
3 Chamber Pots	. 3
Oats	1.19. 7
2 Chests and a Still	6.10
6 sides Sole 6 sides upper leather & 7 skins	2. 7. 0
1 Garden Pot	. 2

		79. 4. 7
		£ 659. 6. 2
Brought over		£ 659. 6. 2
King William		
a Work horse	5.	
York		
a young Horse	20.	

Goods Mrs Custis had out of those Shipped by Cary & Company

2 doz Scythe Stones	1. 8
4 plate Stock Locks	10.
7 hand saw files	1. 2
2 doz pit saw Ditto	12. 6
3 half round Rasps	.10. 1/2
3 strong grass Scythes & furniture	13. 6
1 pair Garden Shears	4. 6
2 hand saws	16.
6 Scribing Chissels	2. 9
1 broad Do	7.
Sugar Spice &c from Newnham Shapley & Co	9. 9.10
1 doz printed Handkerchiefs	1.16
1/2 ps fine Gulix Holland	7.10
- ps demy Cambrick	3. 7

- ps British Ozenbrigs	6.10
- ps crocus	. 8. 6
- best bro Rolls	1.15
- Iron wire Seive	.15. 9
- brass wire Do & pint charger	. 6. 9
Silk from Palmer & Son & Fleetwood	25. 1. 6
Mantua maker John Schersberg	11. 2. 9
2 pair good horse Sissors	. 2
6 pair white Tabby Stays	2. 5
6 pair black everlasting shoes	1.19
Rings and buttons of J Payne	8.15. 6
6 pair woms black kid gloves	.10. 6
Tea of Carteny and Son	6.16. 6
8 groce corks	.16. 6
6 Strong halters	.15
2 Bridles	. 4. 6
1 Wilton carpet	4.15.10
Buckles &c of Passavant	3.13
Millinery of Jane Backhouse	8.15. 9
Mops Brush &c of Thoma Johnson	.17. 9
Castle Soap Capers & Olives	1. 5.
Cheshire Cheese	1. 8. 8
Snuff Box	10.15
A Tea Chest and board	.18
1 doz knifes and forks	.15
A Cardinal & Bonnet	2. 7. 6
6 pair kid Mittens	.10. 6
1 Pair Neken Stays and Tabby Stomacher	1.18
A Box for Bread	. 4. 6
2 Yards clear Lawn	.16
5 pair womens shoes	1. 3
21 lb.wt. Besket	. 7. 6
Glassware & China of Richard Farrar & Co	10. 2. 8 1/2

	148. 1. 2	
Insurance & Charges at 12 1/2 pct	18.10. 1 1/2	£ 166.11. 3 1/2
6 pair Cotton hose	1.19	
A Gown died	. 7	
Silk of Palmer Son and Fleetwood	24. 5	
Fans &c of Passavant	8.17	
3 Gause handkerchiefs & a Bonnet	1. 1. 6	
Millinery of Jane Backhouse	14. 1. 1	
Mantuamaker John Scherberg	26. 8. 8	
Shoes of Λ Greshan	5.15. 6	

Gold Shoebuckles &c of J Payne	21. 3. 3	
	£ 103.17. 4	
carried up		
Brot up	£ 103.17. 4	£ 166.11. 3 1/2
Haberdashery of Lardner & Barnaby	4.13. 9	
Turlingtons Balsam & Sps Lavender	.13. 2	
Tea from Cartoney & Son	7.19. 2	
2 pair Stays	4.10	
Gilt Paper & Book	. 8. 6	
6 curry Combs & Brushes	.12.	
1 doz Gloves and mittens	1.	
Snuff	.14. 6	
Ginger bread	1. 6.	
4 Chaffing dishes & preserving pan	1. 7.	
22 Yards fine Scarlet Bays	3.17.	
1 pair packthread stays	1. 1.	
3 doz blunt handsaw files	5. 3	
6 Whipsaw Do	2. 9	
1 doz Cop Gimlets	.10	
1 doz X Garnets	10.	
6 pairs HL's	6.	
6 drawing knives	6. 6	
6 claw Hammers	4.	
3 lathing Do	3.	
3 pair steel compasses	. 9	
6 two foot Rules	. 4. 6	
2 Cop Irons heaters & stands	.18	
2 pair Steel Dogs brass heads	5.	
2 Sets Shovels & tongs for Do	1.10	
2 M 3d Nails	. 2. 8	
1/2 ps long Lawn	3.	
1 broad Kenting	1.15	
1 Demy Cambrick	3. 8	
1 Superfine clear Lawn	4. 5	
A Cheshire Cheese	3. 9. 7	
Mops clamps &c Thos Johnson	1. 3. 3	
Mahogany Beuroe &c of Philip Bell	5. 2	
1 Case of Pickles	4.17. 3	
Fruit Spice &c of Newnham & Shapley	7.17. 5	
1 Groce of Porter	3.15	
	£ 182. 6. 2	
11 per cent charged &c	20. 1. 1	
		£ 202. 7. 3

Goods from Gildart

39 Yrds white Sheeting 21/d	3. 8. 3	
50 Yds Irish Linnen 3/4d	8. 6. 8	
50 Yds Do 2/8d	6.13. 4	
25 Yds Do 1/5 3/4d	1.16.11 3/4	
26 Yds Do 1/3 d	1.12. 6	
55 Yds Do (illeg.) 1/	2.15	
1 pc Cambrick	3.13	
6 yds lace	2.17	
6 Silk Laces	. 3. 6	
8 Strong halters	1. 8	
1 hand bell	. 2. 9	
16 Ozs thread	.10. 8	
2 Matresses	2. 2	
6 doz Sail Needles	. 4	
6 loaves double sugar	2. 4. 3/4	
8 single Do & Cask	2.17.11 1/4	
1 Sack Clover seed	2.13. 3	
10 7/8 Gallons Brandy	5. 2. 4 1/2	
1 Barrel Gunpowder	6. 6	
	£ 55. 2. 8 1/4	
21 percent Insurance & charges	11.11. 6 3/4	£ 66.14. 3
A Cask Tin Ware & doz kid Mittens	6. 1.10	
3 ps Kendall Cotton	3. 7. 6	
1 ps Indian Blanketting No 1	3.15	
1 Cask Linnens	25. 1. 7 1/4	
1 Cask of Loaf Sugar	8.11. 5	
1 Cask of Malt	2. 8. 6	
4 Mahogany hand boards & box	1. 6	
2 Baggs of Salt	.19	
	£ 51.10.10 1/4	
3.7.6 P cent for charges	1.14. 9 1/4	£ 53. 5. 7 1/4
1 doz knifes and forks	£ 53. 5. 7 1/4	
Carried over	488.18. 5	

Goods from Oswalds

2 doz mens plaid hose	1. 1	
1 doz Womens----	8. 6	
10 Lib brown thread	15. 3	
10 Lib shoe threads	10.	
	2.14. 9	
10 percent for Charges	5. 5 3/4	£ 3. 0. 2 3/4
Sterling		491.18. 7 3/4

Goods for Miss Patty

	£	
1 pair pack thread Stays	. 7	
4 pair kid Mittens	. 4	
2 pair Silk pumps	.10	
2 Lawn frocks	1.18. 6	
a cap & Egret	. 6	
Toys	1. 9	
Books	4. 1	
a cardinal & Bonnet	1.15	
	£ 6.13. 7	
12 1/2 percent	16. 8	£ 7.10. 3
4 pair thread hose	6. 8	
a Baby	5	
2 Cambrick frocks & a Bonnet	2.11	
a Cap fm Jane Backhouse	2. 2. 9 1/4	
4 pr worsted & 4 pr thread hose	(.17. 4)	
1 pr Silver Buckles & Thimble	(.13. 1)	
10 pair of Shoes	1.10	
10 pair gloves & Mittens	6. 8	
1 pair pack thread stays	1. 1	
Toys	11. 1	
	9.17. 8 1/4	
11 P cent	1. 1. 9	10.19. 5
Sterling		£ 18. 9. 8 1/4

For Mr Jackey

4 pair of Gloves	2. 8	
Silver laced hat	12. 9 1/2	
Hat	18. 6	
Toys	1. 9	
Books	. 4. 1	
2 hats	.13. 6	
	£ 4. 1. 6 1/2	
12 1/2 P cent	.10. 1/2	£ 4.10. 7
4 pair thread hose	8.	
A Rose & Bag	2. 6	
4 pair thread stockings & hats	2. 4.10	
2 Lib perfumed powder	2.	
8 pair Shoes	17. 6	
A Suit of Cloaths	2. 7. 3	
Toys	11. 1	
2 pr Andirons	6.13. 2	

11 P cent	14. 8	7. 7.10
Sterling		£ 11.18. 5

Goods out of the Inventory omitted

3 Work horses in King William	£ 15.	
2 pr Andirons	2.10	
1 pr Bellows	. 2	
1 ps brown holland	3.	
2 doz Cane Chairs	6.	
2 yds hair cloth 3/ cloaths brushes &c 2/	.15	
6 (illeg.) &c 13/ 5 pr gloves 10/	1. 3	
1 Rug 20/ 1 slate 2/ 2 pr snuffers 6/	1. 3	
11 pr stockings 57/6 a table 20/	3.17. 6	
1 pr stirrups & a wh 7/ a hat 35/	2. 2	
Brought forward	684. 6. 2	£ 719.18. 8
2 Bureau dressing tables	6	£ 719.18. 8

The Account of Martha Washington's Share of the Estate of Daniel Parke Custis

George Washington Esqr Dr[1]	Sterling	Currency	Contra Cr	Sterling	Currency
To Mrs. Washington in the Negroes appraisd[1]		£ 2986	By Mrs. Washingtons Dower	£ 1617.18	£ 7618.7.11
To Sundries as by ye several Inventories[2]		1232.6.2			
To Sundries out of the	£ 491.18.				
Goods Imported from G: Britain[3]	7 3/4				
To 1/3 of £ 540.14. 5 made as of for the Estate before ye Divin.		180.4.9 1/2			
	£ 419.18.7 3/4	£ 4398.10.11 1/2			

Contra Cr	Sterling	Currency
By Mrs Washington's dower	£ 1617.18	£ 7618.7.11 1/2

D, Custis Papers, ViHi. An identical copy is in the Washington Account Book at ViLxW. Both copies are in GW's handwriting.

Colo George Washington

Dr.				Cr.
		Sterl		Currt
To Dower Negroes allotted Apprd to £2986 by Mrs. Washingtons Dower		£ 1617.18		£ 7618. 7.11
To Cattle delivered £100 short of 3d		£ 421.13.10		
To Goods taken & used horses included		£ 491.18. 7		£ 684. 6. 2
To 1/3 of the Hogs delivered				£ 77. 7. 2
To 1/3 of the Sheep delivered				£ 18.18. 8
		£491.18. 7		£ 4188. 3.10
To J P Custis for 3 horses chgd him				15
To goods omitted				20.12. 6
To 1/3 of 370. 4. 3 expended for Plantation Use				123. 8. 1

D, Custis Papers, ViHi. This is an earlier draft of the preceding document, using different categories as well as figures. It was written by John Mercer.

    1. Refer to assignment of Dower of Martha Washington.

    2. See, The General Account of the Estate of Daniel Parke Custis.

    3. Refer to General Account, Supra, Goods rec'd of Robert Cary Esqr, Oswald, Gildart; also, Account of British goods charged to MDC, John Parke Custis, and Martha Parke Custis.

The Account of John Parke Custis's Share of the Estate of Daniel Parke Custis

Mr John Parke Custis Dr	Sterling	Currency
To 2/3 of the Negroes appraisd at[1]		£ 5972. 1. 6
To sundries as by the several Inventories[2]		2026.17. 9
To Sundries out of the Goods Importd[3]	£ 571. 4. 1 1/2	
To 1.3 of £540.14.5 made use of for the Estate before Division[4]		180. 4. 9 1/2
To Jno Richmond Taylor		4. 6.11 1/2
To Witnesses attend in a Suit re Foster[5]	435	
To Lewis Webb for 7 dozen buttons		. 7. 9
To Jas Darnforth mendg Buckles		. 2
To George Heath makg Cloaths		.12. 9
To Jno Jas Hulet for his part of the Mill		50.
To Jno Palmer for drawg the Deed		1. 1. 6
Tobo 435	£ 571. 4. 1 1/2	£ 8235.15.

Contra　　　　　　　　Cr	Sterling	Currency
By his third of the Estate	£ 1617.18.	£ 7618. 7.11 1/2

D, Custis Papers, ViHi. Copy also in Washington Account Book, ViLxW. Both are in GW's handwriting.

John Parke Custis

To Two thirds of the Negroes			£ 5972. 1. 6
To 2/3 of the Cattle			1043.10. 8
To Cattle short Delivered Colo Washington			100.
To 35 Horses Mares & Colts			161.
To 2/3 of the Hogs			154.14. 4
To 2/3 of the Sheep			37.17. 4
To all the Plate			187. . 6
To Goods from England		11.18. 5	
To Jno Richmond for Cloathes and makeing			4. 6.11 1/2
To Witnesses Attend in Suit Foster	435		
To Lewis Webb for 7 doz buttons			7. 9
To Jas Danforth for mending buckles			2.
To George Heath for making cloaths			12. 9
To John James Hulet for Part of the Mill			60.
To John Palmer for drawing the Deed			1. 1.16
	435	£ 11.18. 5	£ 7675.15. 3 1/2
To Goods for your Plantations		559. 5. 8 1/4 &	
To 1/3 of £370. 4. 3 used for Do			335. 3. 4
To maintanance			123. 2. 1
			Cr
		Strlg	Currt
By his third of the Estate		£ 1617.18 5/12	£ 7618. 7.11 1/2
~~By Col Washington for 3 horses~~			~~45~~

D, Custis Papers, ViHi. This is an earlier version, in the handwriting of John Mercer.

1. See General Account of the Estate of Daniel Parke Custis.

2. See Disposition of Goods in the Estate of Daniel Parke Custis.

3. See Account of British Goods charged to MDC, John Parke Custis and Martha Parke Custis, as well as to the General Account.

4. See supra, August 10, 1758, re the suit of John Parke Custis vs. Francis Foster, for payment of withness fees. The number, 435, refers to the pounds of tobacco awarded Custis.

5. See, Account of Items Used Before the Division of the Estate of Daniel Parke Custis.

The General Account of the Estate, 1758-1759

VIRGINIA At a General Court held at the Capitol the Twenty first day of October One thousand Seven hundred and sixty one (illegible) George Washington (illegible) Guardian to John Parke Custis and Martha Parke Custis Infant Orphans of Daniel Parke Custis Esq. deceasd and thereupon he together with (illegible) Securities entered into and acknowledged Bond in the penalty of Twenty Thousand pounds for securing the Estates of the said Orphans (illegible) The Estate of Daniel Parke Custis Esq dec'd

Dr

	Currt Mony			Sterling		
	£	s.	d.	£	s.	d.
To Joseph Valentine the Estates Steward for Sundry's paid by him on the Estates Account and allowed him upon his Settlement Viz: Overseers & Servants -his own Wages £160- Henry Richardsons share of Corn £5.9 Charles Whitlock's £1.1.3 Henry Richardsons share of Tobo £1.15 John Roans £1.5 and £28.5.71/2 Dite Howle's share of Corn & Tobo £41.1 Lewis Smiths £17.6.6 Roger Tandys Wages £38.12.6 William Jacksons £12.10 John Valentine £12.10 Benja Piggots £8 Bigges Ferriage over the bay £1.10 Valentines Ferriage in1758 £1.5 and in 1759 £1.5	332.	5.10 1/2				
Levies & Taxes both years in York £65.13.11 New Kent $76.1.7 3/4 James City £1.4.1 Hanover £7.18.4 King William £17.9.7	168.	7.	6 3/4			
Quit Rents both years	7.	5		&	30.	
Negroes Expences Rice,Sugar,Rum Shoe thread Oil and Shoemakers Tools £2.11.6 Doctr Carters acct £27.8.9 the midwife 15/	30.15.	3				
Tobacco-Inspection 15 hhds 1758 £3.15 95 hhds 1759 £23.15. bringing 3 hhds over the Bay £1.2.6. Nails 6/	28.18.	6				
Atts Fees Armistead 7/6	8.	9				

Plantation Expences for Leading
Lines, Sheep Sheers, horse Collars,
Cart Saddles Tobacco knives, and
a padlock £1.4.6 Rum & Meat for
Reapings 2.14 Mending Sein 20s A
trenail head 15s. trimming the
Flats £1.18.6 Mending a watch 15s.
Expences at the Sale of the Goods
£2.16.9 underpinning the Dairy 2s.
carrying Timber to the Eastern
Shore £2.0.0 bringing Sheep from
thence £1.11.3   15.18. 0

Accounts-paid to Tarpley and
Knox[1] £4.19.9 W(illegible)
Langston £1.13.9 George
Heath,Taylor, £5.6.5 Thomas Pate
£2.8.0 1/2   14. 7.11 1/2

To George Washington for
Sund(ry illegible)

To Littleton Eyre for Freight of 615
Bush(ls illegible) of Wheat   6. 4. 7 1/2

James Hunter for Freight &
Charg(es illegible) Shipped in the
Fair American   7.10

John Mercer for the Balle of his
Ac(illegible) his Bond for £100 for
which the Estate has Credit
(illegible)[2]   183. 5

Peyton Randolph Esqr. for the
Balle (illegible)   19.14

Revd David Mossom for the Balle
(illegible)   20. 3. 1

Naval officer for a Certificate of
(illegible)   6. 3

To James Gildart Esqr. for the Balle
of (illegible) 1759   23. 9.11 1/2

To Hanbury Esqr. &Co for the Balle
(illegible) 1759   11.13. 6

To Ditto for a Bill Payable to Thos
More (illegible) Interrest   250.

To Ditto for Insurance on 20 hhds[3]
Tobo (illegible)   22. 2. 6

To Robt Cary Esqr & Co. for
Insurance by the (illegible)[4]   100.19. 6
                                               _____   _____
                                               £ 835. 6. 1 1/5   £ 438. 5. 5 1/2

To John Parke Custis for one third
of the Balle of this Account   92. 6. 9 5/12 &   563. 4. 0 11/12

To Martha Parke Custis for
another third part thereof   92. 6. 9 5/12 &   563. 4. 0 11/12

To George Washington & Martha
his Wife for the other third   92. 6. 9 5/12 &   563. 4. 0 11/12
                                               _____   _____
                                               £ 1112. 6. 5 1/2 &   £ 2127.17. 8 1/4

Contra

	Curren Mony	Sterling
Cr	£ s. d.	£ s. d.
1758 and 1759		
By Joseph Valentine for Sundrys he accounted for as disposed of for the Estates Acct Vizt		
Corn 790 1/2 Barrls	£ 408. 9. 7	
Wheat 752 1/2 Bushls	170. 1. 3	
Pork 20021 lb.	172.11. 1	
Butter 332 lb.	16.12.	
Beef 669lb.& a barren Cow & Veal	11. 5. 7 1/2	
Pease 87 1/2 bushls	8.14. 6	
Fodder	1.	
Pasturage of Horses in the Marsh	3. 7. 6	
Balle of James Bigges the Eastn Shore Oversr Acct	11.19. 5	804. .11 1/2
Cash recd by him of John Blair Esqr. for Interest		30.
William Hallop for his note of hand & (illegible)hing	7. 8	
Phillip Johnson	1.	
By George Washington for Sundrys recd by him Viz: from Littleton Eyre for 900 Bushels of Corn	90.	
John Mercer for Interest	183. 5.	
Abner Clopton for his Note of hand	3. 0. 4	
By ditto for 567 Bushels of Oats @ 10d	23.12. 6	
By James Gildart Esqr. for 1 hhd Tobacco by the Everton	8. 4. 1 1/4	
By Hanbury & Co. for 17 hhds Tobacco Insured upon the Anna	251. 8. 8	
ditto for Goods in the Supply taken retaken & sold at Bristol for[6]	5. 8. 7	
By Robt Cary Esqr. & Co. for the Balle of their Acct Currt dated Augt 22 1759	987. 4. 2	
ditto for the proceeds of 15 hhds Tobo by the Fair American [7]		267.15.
ditto for 50 hhds Tobo shipped upon the Cary, Henry Talman		577.17. 2
	£ 1112. 6. 5 1/2	£ 2127.17. 8 1/4

Note. there is in the hands of -Master (illegible hhds of) Tobo shipd by the Deliverance - Russia Mercht - Gildart (illegible) not yet Accounted for which in order to (illegible) carried to the Account of Jno. Parke Custis (illegible) and George Washington and Martha his wife one third each

AD, ViLxW, Washington's Account Book. This document is an updated revision of the estate. It lists the proceeds from tobacco shipments that were not yet included in the earlier 1759 account. This account was probably part of the report of the estate commissioners to the General Court.

1. Tarpley and Knox were merchants in Williamsburg.

2. This may be a repayment of John Mercer's loan of £100 in the settlement of his legal fees. See, John Mercer to MW, January 4, 1759.

3. Shipped in the Deliverance. See, GW to C & O Hanbury, November 25, 1759, *PGWC* 6:373.

4. Insurance for 50 hhds of Tobacco, shipped in The Cary, November, 1759. See, GW to Robert Cary, November 25, 1759. *PGWC* 6:373.

5. See, Capel & Osgood to MW, July 6, 1758, supra; *PGWC* 6:324, n. 2.

6. See, *PGWC* 6:270, n. 17; GW to Capel & Osgood Hanbury, August 10, 1760, *PGWC* 6:447, n. 2.

7. See, GW to Robert Cary and Co., September 20, 1759, *PGWC* 6:348, 350, n. 1.

Account of Items in the Estate Sold

(1759)

Sale of the Estate

Sundries	Appraised at			Sold for		
	£	s.	d.	£	s.	d.
2 pair Andirons		. 7.	6		.15	
3 pr Ditto Saddle Bridle &ca	10.			6.14.	7	
1 pr ditto and 4 pots and Pot hooks	7.			2.		
1 Basket Butter pot Cannister &ca		. 4.			.13.	6
(?) old Trustle Bed Tea Chest	4.13.			2. 7.	5	

D, ViLxW. Washington Account Book. In his account book, GW lists these accounts as, "Account of Items in the Estate Sold." This is an incomplete list, GW having ceased with the last entry.

From Dr. James Carter

1758

The Estate of Daniel P: Custis deceas'd Dr. To James Carter & c Cd

Decr

1.	To a Visit James at ye Qters 10/ and Visit Do in Town 5/	15/
2.	To bleedg Do 2/6: a Purge Do 4/: emollt Ingredient Do 1/6	6/
	To Pearl Barly Do 1/4 3d Visit Do 5/ 4th Visit Do 5	11/ 4
4.	To 12 Papers (illegible) Powders 6/. a Purge Do 2/0	8/
	To Mercurial ointmt 2 Do 5/ 5th a Visit Do 5/0	7/
6.	To a Purge Do 2/ 7th a Visit Do 5/. a Merc Vomit Do 1/6	8/ 6
11.	To a Cordl Draught Do. 1/6 9th a Visit Do 5/ a purge Do 2/1	8/ 6
11.	To a Visit 5/. 12th a Visit 6/. a Purge Do 2/	7/

14.	To Do 5/. 2 Mercl Purges 4/. 4 oz Mercl Ointment 2/.	11/
16.	To Visit Do 5/. a Purge Do 2/. 18th a Visit Do 5	12/
18.	To 3 Doses Mercurial Pills Do.	4/ 6
20.	To Visit Do 0/ 22d a Visit Do 5/. a Purge Do 2/.	7/
23.	To 13 oz Balsamic Electary Do 9/9 a Desct Plaster Do 1/6	11/ 3

1759

Feby		
25.	To a Visit Jacob in N Kent & dress his Head with Dressg	3/ 4/ 6
Mar		
13.	To a Visit Miss Betsy 1/6. 5 oz Cordl Mixture Do 2/6	4/
19.	To 12 (illegible) Powders Jas. at Town Quters 6/	6/
	To 5 oz Cordl Mixture Do 5/ 21st 1 lb Honey 9d	5/ 9
27.	To 8 oz Pectoral Infus Jack 6/. 1 Cordl Mixture Do 7/6	13/ 6
	To Visit James at Valuntines 5/. an Annod Mixture Do 2/	7/
28.	To 9 oz Cordl Mixture 4/6. 31st. 6 oz Strength; q ElectaD 4/6	9/
Apl		
2.	To 8 oz Pectoral Linctus repted Jack 6/. Electary repted	4/ 6
	James	10/ 6
18.	To Dress Jacobs Head from 25th Feb to this date	3/
		4/ 6
28.	To 8 oz Electary Pectoral Minor 8/. 11 Cordl Mixture 7/6	15/ 6
May		
3.	To 1 oz Spirits of Ammoniac. 9 6oz Balsam Electary 4/	5/ 3
11.	To (illegible) Bleeding Do 2/6 (illegible)	9/ 6
16.	To 2 oz Rattle Snake Root 8. 24 Visit Jacob N. Kent 2.3.0	2/11/ 0
24.	To (illegible) Mixture Do 7/6 12 Papers (illegible)	13/ 6
	To (illegible) his side 2/6 (iilegible)	3/ /6
June		
1.	To Visit Master Johnny Custis N Kent 3/4/6 (iilegible)	4/ 6/ 0
21.	To Visit Jacob (illegible) 10/ 21st a Purge (illegible)	12/
23.	To Visit Master Jacky at Eltham	2/ 3/
July		
10.	To (illegible) Balsamich Pectoral Electic Tonic	8/
24.	To (illegible) 2/6 Novr 3 2oz (illegible)	4/ 6
Novr.		
16.	To (illegible) Purges (illegible)	2/ 6
		27/ 8/ 9

Received of Mr Joseph Valentine[1]
the sum of twenty seven Pounds
eight shills & nine pence in full
of the above account
James Carter[2]

ADS, Custis Papers, ViHi.
1. See supra, November 28, 1757, n. 1, 3.

Account of Martha Parke Custis's Share of the Estate of Daniel Parke Custis

Dr

Miss Martha Parke Custis	Sterling	Currency
To Sundries out of the Goods Impord[1]	£ 18. 9. 8 1/2	
To 1/3 of £540.14.5 made use of for the Estate before Division[2]		£ 180. 4. 9 1/2
To Doctor Amsons Acct		9. 1. 6
To Eliz: Vaughan makg Cloaths		.19. 3
To 5 Yds printed Linen		1.
To Toys & altering her Stays		4. 6
	£ 18. 9. 8 1/2	£ 191.10. 1/2

Contra	Cr		
		Sterling	Currency
By her third of the Estate		£ 1617.18	£ 7618. 7. 1/2

AD, Custis Papers, ViHi.; AD. GW's Account Book, ViLxW. Both copies are in GW's handwriting and are almost identical.

Miss Martha Parke Custis

	Sterlg	Currt
To Goods from England	£ 18. 9. 8 1/4	
To Pd Dr Amson's Acct		9. 1. 6
To Eliza Vaughan for making Cloathes		19. 3
To 5 Yds printed Linnen		1.
To Toys & altering her Stays		4. 6
To 1/3 of £370.4.3 expended for Plantations		123. 8. 1

	Cr	Sterlg	Currt
By her third of the Estate		1617.11 5/12	£ 7618. 7.11 1/2

AD. Custis Papers, ViHi.: an early draft in the handwriting of John Mercer.

1. See Account of British Goods Charged to Martha Dandridge Custis, John Parke Custis and Martha Parke Custis.

2. See Account of Items Used Before the Division of the Estate of Daniel Parke Custis.

The Estate of Daniel Parke Custis

Tradesmen belonging to ye Estate.   (c. 1759)

Names	Age	Occupation
Anthony[1]	55	Carpenter's
Peter	39	"
Ned	48	"
Morrice	29 W[2]	"
Ned	32	"
Jack Palmer	28	"
Isaac	28 W	"
Mike	28	"
Tom	30 W	"
Jack a boy	15	"
Squire	21	"
Scomberg	42 W	Shirtmaker's
Crispin	50	"
Macon[1]	30	Tanner's[3]

Servants in & Abt ye House

Names	Age	Business
W Breechy	24	Waiter
W Mulatto Jack	41	Waiter
Julius	10	Waits on Jacky Custis .
Moll	19	Waits on Ditto & Miss Patcy Sews &ca for them
W Doll	38	Cook
W Beck	23	Scullion
Mima	36	Ironer
W Jenny	39	Washer
W Sally	15	Mrs. Washington's maid
Rose	12	Miss Patcy's Maid
Phillis	25	Spinner W
W Betty	21	Seamstress

AD, in GW's handwriting, ViHi.

1. Anthony and Macon were crossed out.

2. GW indicated the dower slaves by the letter "W". The eleven slaves, so designated, probably came to Mount Vernon from the lower counties in 1759.

Report of the Commissioners
Appointed by the General Court
to Settle the Estate of Daniel Parke Custis

In Obedience to the Order of this Honable Court made the 28th of Apl in the present Year[1] We have stated a General Account of the Estate of the said Danl Parke Custis Esqr[2] deceasd from the several Inventories thereof & having compared the same with the Sales of the Estate as carefully as we were able it being impossible to do the same with Exactness by reason of the many Lumping Articles in the said Inventories We discovered several Errors on both sides the Account but the same being equal within 50 s which is to the prejudice of George Washington Esqr. We with his Consent to prevent stating the whole account over again have agreed to report the Account marked hereto annexed as the General Account of the said Estate. We have also with the Schedule hereunto annexed marked C Stated the separate accounts[3] of the said George Washington in right of himself & of John & Martha the two Children of the said Daniel Parke Custis according to the Division of the Estate made between them which in or Opinion is the fairest & most equal Division thereof that could be made as the Accounts have been so itemized that it would be impossible to distinguish the several Articles with any Certainty

In obedience to the Order of the Genl Court made the 28th of April in the year 1759 we have allotted & assigned to Mrs Martha Washington her dower in the land and Slaves of her late husbd D.P.C. as will appear by a schedule hereunto annexed & marked As has been also stated.[5]

AD, Custis Papers, ViHi. Copy in the handwriting of John Mercer. Another copy in GW's handwriting is in the Washington Account Book, ViLxW.

1. At this point, in the Washington Account Book copy, there is inserted the following phrase: "we have allotted and Assigned Mrs Martha Washington her Dower in the Lands and Slaves of her late Husband Daniel Parke Custis Esqr. deceased as will appear by a Schedule hereunto annexed."

2. See, Inventory of the Estate of Daniel Parke Custis.

3. The separate accounts are: (1) The Account of Martha Washington's Share of the Estate of Daniel Parke Custis; (2) The Account of John Parke Custis's Share of the Estate of Daniel Parke Custis; (3) The Account of Martha Parke Custis's share of the Estate of Daniel Parke Custis.

4. In the Washington Account Book copy, the signatories were to be Peyton Randolph, Bernard Moore, Burwell Bassett, and Philip Whitehead Claiborne. At this time Peyton Randolph was attorney general of the colony. Bernard Moore and Burwell Bassett were New Kent County planters. Bassett was also MW's brother-in-law, having married MW's sister, Anna Marie Dandridge. Claiborne was a King William County planter. Moore, Claiborne, and Bassett were indebted to MW for large loans she had made them. See, Inventory of the Estate of Daniel Parke Custis.

5. The above addendum is written in a different and unknown hand. Neither is its purpose known.

From Capel & Osgood Hanbury

London, March 1759
To Martha Custis; To charges on seventeen Hogsheads of Tobacco received p The (missing) Colony of Virginia.
(Summary)
13701 Pounds of tobacco were sold to five buyers for £7113..4..6. Expenses of subsidies, freight, duties, primage and petty charges, entry inwards, bond bill money, lander's fee, cooperage, cartage and warehouse room, brokerage, shipping charges, porterages, wharfage, lighterage, postage of letters, and commission totaled £251:8:8. The Net proceeds were £461:2:8.[1]

DS, Custis Papers, ViHi.
   1. Oversized ledger sheet necessitates summarizing the accounts.

From Capel & Osgood Hanbury

Esteemed Friend   London Apl 4. 1760
   We hope our P Capt Walker got to hand of wch please to (mutilated) Inclosed are the sales of thy 17 Hhds DPC P (the Anna) to assure thee that We have taken every method that We could think of to make the most of them & had they not been out of Condition we should have got a much better price for them.[1] hope the next We have will be of a fine sent (sic) & quality & that We shall have the pleasure of some JP & P all opportunitys thy Consignments will be very acceptable. The Insurance upon the Deliverance is made at £200 upon 20 Hhds at Gs P cent premm. the Ship is lost in the Bay of Biscay as soone as the Papers comes to hand & the loss can be adjusted thy Accots shall have Credit - Since thy Acct Current was sent Thy Bill to T. Moore is paid £250[2] - We wish Thee and they Wife Health & Happiness & are with great Esteem Thy Assurd Friends

C & O Hanbury

To George Washington Esq
York
Virginia

P the George
Capt Chew

ALS, Custis Papers, ViHi.
   1. The Anna was captured by a French privateer on June 13, 1755, and was recaptured by the British seven days later. See supra, Capel & Osgood Hanbury to MDC, July 6, 1758.
   2. MDC drew a bill of £250 on Capel & Osgood Hanbury for a loan made to Thomas Moore. See infra, General Account of the Estate.

To Mrs. Burwell Bassett

Dear sister[1]   June 1st 1760 (Mount Vernon)

I have had the pleasure of receiving your very welcome and affect Letters of the 10th of may intended to come by Jack[2] and the 23d by Mr Bassett[3] who I must acknowledge myself greatly obliged to for the favour of his last visit - I shoud not have suffered him to go without a letter to you had I not known of the oppertunity that now offers and hear I must do myself the pleasure of congratulating you very sincerely on your happy deliverence of I wish I could say boy as I know how much one of that sex was diesired by you all - I am very sorry to hear my mammas complaints of ill helth and I feel the same uneasiness on the account that you doe but hope Mr (illegible)[4] perscriptions will have the desired effect - The children are now very well and I think myself in a better state of helth than I have been in for a long time and dont dout but I shall present you a fine healthy girl again[5] when I come down in the Fall which is as soon as Mr W-ns business will suffer him to leave home I am very much pleased to hear Betsy[6] continues to grow a fine hearty child and (missing) Soon will make you happiest in that desirable blessing I also hope you are out of all fear of sore Breasts before this time

Mr Bassett will inform you of the mirth and gaiety that he has seen so I hope I have no occasion to enlarge upon that head in order to induce you to Try Fairfax in a pleasanter season than you did last time I shall now conclude but not till I have desired you to present my Best good wishes to Mrs Dawson and Judy[7] in which Mr Washington desires to join me also beg you will give our Blessing to the dear little children and Each of them half a Dozen kisses and hope you will not imagin that yourself and Mr Bassett is forgot by dear nancy your sincere and Loving sister

                                        Martha Washington

To Mrs Bassett

ALS, Dreer Collection, PHi.

1. Anna Maria Dandridge Bassett (1739-1777) was the younger sister of MW. She married Burwell Bassett of Eltham, May 7, 1757. *Harris*, 1:47, 82.

2. This might be John Augustine Washington, younger brother of GW. It is more likely to be a servant.

3. Burwell Bassett (1734-1793) of Eltham, Blissland Parish, New Kent County. He was the son of William Bassett, III and his wife, Elizabeth Churchill. *Harris*, 1:45.

4. Unidentified. Probably a local apothecary or physician.

5. Refers to herself and hardly to be construed that she was pregnant.

6. Eldest child of Burwell and Anna Maria Bassett. *Harris*, 1:46.

7. Elizabeth Dawson was the second wife of William Bassett, III. After his death she married Reverend William Dawson, President of the College of William and Mary, Commissary of the Bishop of London, and Member of the Council. Following the death of Commisary Dawson she ran a successful boarding house in Williamsburg. The Washingtons often were guests. Judith was the daughter of Burwell and Anna Maria Bassett. In 1773 she married Peter Lyon, later a Supreme Court Justice. *Harris*, 1:45, 48.

Account of the Custis Estate in Ledger A

Contra[1]   (1759-1760)

1759	By Casy at Sundry times as pr acct		£ 1397.14.10
Augt	By a Sett of Excha: drawn by Jas Corbet		54.12. 2
	on Mesrs James & Robt Berrie Merchs.		
	Glasgow for Sterling	£ 40. 9	
	35 prCt Excha	£ 14. 3. 2	
	Cury	£ 54.12. 2	
	By a sett of Excha: of my drawing on Messrs Capel and Osgood Hanbury for £99.00. Sterlg payable to Messrs Champe & Hunter Virga & dated 10th Septr 1759		
	By another sett of Excha. drawn by me on the same Merchants payable to R Washington £50 Sterlg dated 20th Septr 1759		
	By 567 Bushels of Oats ffrom the Eastn Shore		
Novr 8	By Intt on Francis Foster's Bond		25. 0. 0
	By Benja Hubbard & Jno Robinson Esqrs. Bd £350		
	By 6 Months Intt on Ditto 8.15		£ 358.15. 0
Novr 27[2]	To Cash of the Estate - by ye hands of Mr Valene		£ 110. 0. 0
Decr 2	To Cash of the Estate - recd of Mr Holt for Linnen damag'd by Captn Hooper		15.11. 7 1/2
1760			
Apr 25	By Cash of Colo Eyres pr Accts for Corn		76.13. 7 1/2
26	By Captn Joseph Moreton's Bond taken in		300. 0. 0
	Intt thereon to the date		16.11. 3
	By Interest of Mrs McKenzies Bond one Year		10.16. 0
	By Cash of Josh Valentine (being amt of the Sales in Williamsburg after deducting 20/ for cryer		57. 9. 2
28	By Mr B. Pendleton's Bond & Interest		209.14. 5
	By Intt of Mr Claibornes Bond one Year		14. 0. 0
	By one Years Interest on Colo Bassetts Bond		105. 0. 0
May 30	By one Years Interest of William Dandridges do		22. 0. 5
	By Balle of the Revd Mr Mossoms Acct		0. 2. 6
Oct 2	By a Sett of Excha. drawn by me on Robt Cary Esqr. & Company in favr of Mr G Brent for £200 Sterg.		

The Estate of Danl P. Custis Esqr. decd.

1759 To my Wife's full third part of all his Personal Estate.
Decr 5. To Cash paid Mr James Hunter for Freight & Charges on 15 Hhd
Tobo shipd pr the Fair American 7.10.3[3]

March[4]	To Cash of Colo Custis's Estate	£	2.15. 0
Apr 20	To Cash of Colo Custis's Estate		96. .0. 0
Apr 25	To Cash of Colo Custis's Estate		14. 5. 9
Apr 26	To Cash of Colo Custis's Estate		19. 0. 0
	To Ditto of Ditto		10. 0. 0
May 4	To Ditto of Ditto		400. 0. 0
	To Ditto of Ditto		3.10. 0
	To Ditto of Ditto		60. 0. 0
May 11	To Cash of Colo Custis's Estate[5]		46. 7. 6
June 13	To Ditto of Ditto		154
9	To Ditto of Ditto		20
	To Ditto of Ditto		77
	To Ditto of Ditto		12.15
	To Ditto of Ditto		6.12
July 5	To Ditto of Ditto		3. 7. 6
July 10	To Ditto of Ditto		15. 0. 0
	To Ditto of ye Estate		4. 1. 3
	To Ditto of Ditto		8.10
	To Ditto of ye Estate		311.18. 4

AD, DLC:GW.

1. Ledger Book A, page 57.
2. Ledger Book A, page 62.
3. This entry is contained on the opposite page, page 57, Ledger Book A.
4. Ledger Book A, page 55.
5. Ledger Book A, page 56.

To Mrs. Margaret Green[1]

(September 29, 1760)
_____ I have the pleasure to tell you my dear little girl[2] is much
better she has lost her fitts & fevours both and seems to be getting well
very fast[3] we carried her out yesterday in the charriot and the change of
air refressed her very much _____

ALS, location unknown. Complete text not available. The original was sold in the Gribbel
Sale, Part I; Parke Bernet Sale No. 223, October 30, 31, November 1, 1940, item 788.

1. Mrs. Green was the wife of Reverend Charles Green (c. 1710-1765), rector of Truro
Parish and later of Pohick Church, Fairfax County. He had practiced medicine in the area.
In 1735, on the recommendation of Augustine Washington, he returned to England and was
ordained by the Bishop of London. Returning to Virginia in 1736, he took up his ministry

but still continued to prescribe for his parishioners. He was frequently consulted by the Washingtons and the families often exchanged visits. Two years after the death of her husband Mrs. Green married Dr. Thomas Savage of Dumfries. At insistence she returned to her home in Dublin and died there. For an explanation of her tangled financial affairs, which was a thorn in GW's side for a number of years, see *Diaries*, 2:181-82. For a full account of the peculiar relationship between the Green and Washington families see, P. R. Henriques, *Major Lawrence Washington Versus the Reverend Charles Green: A Case Study of the Squire and the Parson*, V.M.H.B., 100:233, no. 2.

2. Martha Parke Custis (1756-1773). Swem states her year of birth is unknown; *Swem*, p. 18. Freeman states she was born in 1756; *Freeman*, 2:298. MW, in a letter to Mrs. Thorpe, July 15, 1772, states she was sixteen. This verifies Freeman's date. See also, *Writings*, 3:88; *Diaries*, 1:211. For MW's letter to Mrs. Thorpe, see infra, July 15, 1772.

3. This may be the first mention of the epileptic seizures that were to plague her the remainder of her life. In the end one of them proved fatal.

4. For a full account of the peculiar relationship between the Green and Washington families see, P.R. Henriques, *Major Lawrence Washington Versus the Reverend Charles Green: A Case Study of the Squire and the Parson*; VMHB, 100:233, n. 2.

To Dr. James Carter

The Estate of Daniel Parke Custis   Dr
    To James Carter & Co[1]

March 29th	To Worm Purges. Boy Anthony	4
	To an Astringent Mixture Do	4
April 1	To 10 oz Cord Mixture Roger	5
		13

    Nov 10th 1760 Recd. the above
for Partner & Self

                       W Carter

ADS, Custis Papers, ViHi.

1. Dr. James Carter (before 1732-ca 1800) and his brother, Dr. William Carter (1751-1799) were the sons of John Carter, the public gaoler in Williamsburg, and his wife, Thomasine. They practiced as partners for a number of years in Williamsburg. They both served as surgeons during the Revolution. *Blanton*, p. 323, 403.

The Dower Slaves

A List of Working Dower Negroes, where settled, & under whose care, 1760.

At Claibornes John Roan[1]

George	A Man	1 Share
Stephen	Ditto	1 Ditto
Parros	Ditto	1 ditto
Argyle	Ditto	1 ditto
Solomon	Ditto	1 ditto

Marlbrough	Ditto	1 ditto
Sam	Ditto	1 ditto
David	Ditto	1 ditto
Hector	Ditto	1 ditto
Will	Ditto	1 ditto
Sam	Ditto	1 ditto
Sarah	A Woman	1 ditto
Sew	Ditto	1 ditto
Patt	Ditto	1 ditto
Rachel	Ditto	1 ditto
Jenny	Ditto	1 ditto
Citt	Ditto	1 ditto
Citt	A Girl	1/2 ditto
George	A Boy	1/2 ditto
		18 shares
	John Roan	2 shares

At Moncock Hill[2] Isaac Osling

Matt	A Man	1 Share
Will	Ditto	1 ditto
Moll	A Woman	1 ditto
Sarah	Ditto	1 ditto
		4
	Overseer	1
		5 In all

At Bridge Quarter - York

Bachus	A Man	1 Share
Ben	Ditto	1 ditto
Young Ned	Ditto	1 ditto
Cupid	Ditto	1 ditto
Old Daphne	A Woman	1 ditto
Young Daphne	Ditto	1 ditto
Moll	Ditto	1 ditto
Frank	Ditto	1 ditto
Arlington	a Boy	1/2 ditto
Caesar	Ditto	1/2 ditto
George	Ditto	1/2 ditto
Suckey	a Girl	1/2 ditto
		10 ditto

At the Ship Landing

Crispin	A Man	1 Share
Ned Holt	Ditto	1 ditto

Old Captain	Ditto	1 ditto
Jupiter	Ditto	1 ditto
Brunswick	Do	1 ditto
Moll	A Woman	1 ditto
Betty	Ditto	1 ditto
		7 ditto

AD, DLC:GW.[3]

1. John Roan was the overseer at the Claiborne tract, King William County. See, John Roan to MDC, August 12, 1757.

2. Unidentified.

3. The list is in the handwriting of GW and is entered on blank pages in the forward part of his copy of *The Virginia Almanac....1760*, printed by William Hunter, Williamsburg.

To Anna Maria Dandridge Bassett

My Dear Sister   April 18 1761

With great concern I bore this disappointment of not coming to you as I promised you, I have pleased myself with coming and would be very happy with you and family but the hooping coughs has put an end to all hopes for some time I have had it so bad that I could not go out of the house this four weeks past, the children are getting well but did not care to carry them so long a jurney and to houses where the coughs had not been and carrying children with so troublesome a disorder is of no pleasure in winter and I considered your dear little girl had not had it, I pray give my love to Mr. Bassett & Betsy and accept the same from dear Nancy, your most

affectionate & loving sister
Martha Washington

Jackey[1] would fain come with Mr. W-n to see Betsy[2] he often talks of her he and Patty[3] gives their duty to their uncle and ant & love to their cousin I hope to hear by Mr. W-n you have a nice Boy[4]

ALS. Feinstone Collection, David Library of the American Revolution, Washington Crossing, Pennsylvania. On loan to the American Philosophical Society, Philadelphia, PA.

1. John Parke Custis (1754-1781).

2. Elizabeth (Betsy) Bassett. See supra, June 1, 1760, n. 6.

3. Martha Parke Custis was also called Patsy (Patcy) by the family. This was also GW's "pet name" for MW.

4. Anna Maria Bassett (Nancy) was expecting her second child at this time. Their desire for a boy, notwithstanding, she delivered a girl, Anna Maria Bassett. *Harris*, 1:46.

From Richard Adams

(April 9, 1761)

Dr. Mrs. Martha Custis in Acct. Richard Adams
To 1 pr Callimanco Shoes[1]
1758
May 2d
April 9th 1761 Recd of Mr Jos Valentine the above amt of Eight Shillings

Richd. Adams

ADS, Custis Papers, ViHi.

1. A woolen material manufactured in Flanders. It was woven with a satin twill, which gave it a checkered appearance on one side.

To Mrs. Margaret Green

Dear Madam   June 26, 1761

Julious comes for Betty[1] - I hardly know in what manner to return suitable thanks to you and Mr Green for the troble you have taken upon this occasion - it was a near mistake her being Left but as I am persuaded apologies of this nature are altogether unnecessary to the person I am addressing I shall cease to make more.

Mrs Colvill and niece[2] with Doctr Laurie[3] dind hear yesterday and in the evening Mr W-n took his vomit - but it did not worke him well today he has begun with the Barke[4] & and continues it till an ounce is taken.

I gave Patsy the mercury last night it has worked her twice. Our ears are mending very fast.[5]

Our compliments are offered to Mr Green Miss Bolan and am Dr Madam

Your most Obed
Martha Washington

Please to send your Ear rings
if you so resolved not to have
yours now

ALS, ViMtV.

1. Julious was possibly a servant. Betty might be Elizabeth Dandridge, daughter of John and Francis Jones Dandridge, and therefore a younger sister of MW. She was born at Chestnut Grove, New Kent County, May 25, 1749. *Harris*, 1:82 (Dandridge family Bible).

2. Mrs. Thomas Colvill, of Cleesh. Her niece was Catherine, the natural daughter of Colonel John Colvill, brother of Thomas Colvill. She later married John West, Jr. See, Stetson, *Washington and His Neighbors*, p. 129-31, Richmond, 1956. Hereafter referred to as *Stetson*.

3. Dr. James Laurie was an Alexandria physician GW had contracted with to care for his slaves. GW occasionally used his services for himself and was a frequent visitor at Mount Vernon. On April 8, 1760 he appeared at Mount Vernon, drunk, stayed all night, and "blooded" MW the following day. See, *Diaries*, 1:265.

4. Jesuits, Peruvian, or Cinchona bark was widely used for the treatment of malaria, then called "ague and fever." GW had frequent attacks and took the bark on these occasions. Dr. James Craik was of the opinion GW suffered from a chronic form of malaria. See, *Blanton,* p. 309.

5. Apparently some of the ladies had their ears pierced.

Report of the Estate Commissioners to the General Court

(November 5, 1761)

We the Subscribers have pursuant to the Order of the Honble the General Court examined the Accounts of George Washington Esqr. against the Estate of Daniel Parke Custis Esqr. deceased and his infant children John Parke Custis and Martha Parke Custis[1] to whom the said George Washington is Guardian[2] and find the same fairly and justly stated and prooved by proper Vouchers and have therefore Settled the Ballances as due April last according to the Several Accounts annexed. Given under Our hands this 5th day of November 1761.

(Signed)
Peyton Randolph[3]
Ro. C. Nicholas[4]
Thos Everard[5]

D, ViLxW.

1. The commissioners were probably appointed by the General Court during its spring session, 1761. See, *PGWC,* 6:265, n. 1.

2. The General Court appointed GW guardian of the Custis children on October 21, 1761. See, *PGWC,* 6:259, n. 6.

3. Peyton Randolph (1721-1775) was the eldest son of Sir John Randolph and a graduate of William and Mary College. He was elected to the House of Burgesses and was King's Attorney for the Colony. He was later elected Speaker of the House of Burgesses and in 1774 became the first President of the Continental Congress.

4. Robert Carter Nicholas. See his letter to MDC, August 7, 1757, n. 5.

5. Thomas Everard (1704?-1784) was and attorney, Clerk of York County from 1745 until 1784, Clerk of the General Court, Auditor of Accounts for Virginia, and mayor of Williamsburg. 9 W (1) 123; 16 W (1) 37, 42.

From Jane Hamilton

Mdm Washington Dr. to Jane Hamilton
To Knitting a pair Silk Stockings for Miss

0 . 4s . 0

Receivd the Contents in full of all Demands

Jane Hamilton
Decemr 12, 1761

DS, ViHi.

To Mrs. Margaret Green

Dear Madam   Decr 18th 1761
    I fear it will not be in my power to be at Mr Wests [1] as Mr W-n intends to send his man to Williamsburgh this week but shall be extreemly glad to see you and Mr Green at Mount Vernon in your way thare & at your return, if you have any Commands to Williamsburg shall be very glad to oblige you Our Compliments to your self Mr Green & Miss Bolan I am much obliged to you for your kind wishes
and am Dear Madam your

> most sincear & Hble servant
> Martha Washington

ALS, ViMtV. See, *Annual Report, Mount Vernon Ladies' Association of the Union*, 1969, p. 48. Hereafter referred to as *A.R.*

    1. John West, Jr. His home, West's Grove, was situated on the north branch of Little Hunting Creek. He was assistant surveyor of Fairfax County, aided in laying out the town of Alexandria, and was a member of the 1776 Virginia Assembly.

Inventory of the Estate of Daniel Parke Custis

	Inventory			appraised		sold for	
1.	Anchor & a Jack 224			1. 5			
2.	Andirons 2 pr		56	34	7. 6		.15
3.	Do 3 pr	214.292.	57	Do	10.	GW 2 pr 50/	
4.	Do 1 pr & 4 Pots & hooks	120		Do	7.		
5.	Applemill & 4 Jars & 2 Safes		122	Do	2.10	P	
6.	Augurs &c	·10.	224	97	5.		
7.	1 old &c Collars & hammer			289	. 1. 6		
8.	Awl blades		76	136	.18	GW 1. 4	
9.	Axes & hoes 25 1 grind stone			17	1. 4		
10.	8 Coopers 5 narro 6 grub			6			
11.	8 broad 1 Cask narro			96	11.	P	
12.	7			147	1. 1		
13.	1 Coopers & 17 hoes			208	2.16		
14.	1 broad 5 narrow			266	.12		
15.	3 narrow			267	.12		
16.	2 & 18 hoes & old Iron			288	1. 5		
17.	Barrels 2 &c	104.196		143	1. 3		
18.	&c & 1 half bushel			291	. 2		
19.	Basket 1 &c	43.49.151.367		175	. 4	No 107	.11
20.	Bed 1 old Trussel			160	. 3	No 164	. 3
21.	Beds steads &c		69	22	2.	No 32 99. 4	.11. 5
22.	1 old &c 10 chests 2 shovels			212	2.10	11.5 8. 15 27. 5	
23.	Bellows 1 pr			176	. 2	GW	
24.	2 pr &c	67.366		189	. 6		
25.	Belt 1 &c	40.94.110		66	.13		
26.	2 & a bung borer & 3 Locks			136	. 5		

27.	Boats 1 flat anchor &c		1	25.		P
28.	1 Horse Do &c	51	2	6.10		P
29.	1 small		29	1. 5		P
30.	Books a parcel		41	4.	3.	P
31.	A parcel		177	25.		P
31.	Book Case Desk & 5 Chairs		128	3. 5	No. 8 4. 5	
32.	Bottles &c	50.213	190	15	3.	
33.	Boxes & old Trunks		59	1.		
34.	&c 63,86,164,258,318,385		88	10.	No. 88 2/6	
35.	Brand iron &c 92.144.146. 387.157.214.304		200	1.	No. 108	15. 6
36.	Brass Cock 1 &c 118.298.323.396		67	.14	GW 1 1.3	
37.	1 &c 171.285.340		134	. 5	Do 1, .1.3	
38.	1 &c a Tarnier &2 measures		195	. 4		
39.	Brown Holland 1 pc		107	3.	GW	
40.	Brushes 9 &c		25			
41.	Broom 1 & Warming panarel		166	.10	No 87 .9.6	
42.	Butter pots 1 parcel		148	1. 8	P	
43.	1 &c		19			
44.	1 &c 252.325.336		204	. 6	P	
45.	3		245	. 9	P	
46.	Candlesticks 4 &c 217.331		53	.18	No 109 .10	
47.	2 &c		173	. 9	No 68 .7.2	
48.	Cannisters 16 &c 155.204.348		52	.12	No 77 4.1.3	
49.	1 &c		19			
50.	1 &c		32			
51.	Canoe 1 & c		28		P	
52.	Cards Cotton wool 18 pcs		58	1.10	No 72 6.3.4	
53.	Carts 1 ox yoke & Chain		3	1.10	P	
54.	1 Do Chain & yoke		12	3.	P	
55.	2 Do &c		16	2.10	P	
56.	1		142	2.	P	
57.	1 & furniture		239	11.	P	
58.	1 & Wheels		272	1.17. 6	P	
59.	1 old cart		273	. 5	P	
60.	1 ox 2 yokes & chain		283	3.	P	
61.	Casks 16 good & sevl old		11	10.	P	
62.	a parcel of Do & hhds		28	1.10	P	
63.	&c	34				
64.	2 &c 216.251		198	. 2	P	
65.	7 Cyder hhds		246	1.	P	
66.	Center bits 3 &c 141.154. 236.278.300		75	. 8	P	
67.	Chafing dishes 2 &c	24				
68.	Chair 2 wheels & harness		20	20.	No 38	17.
69.	1 old &c	21				
70.	Chairs 12 Mahogany		42	10.	No 6	11. 0. 6
71.	2 corner Do		43	2.		
72.	10 leather		46	2.	No 79.16	2. 2
73.	1 easy Do		47	3.	No 7	6.
74.	Chairs 5 old &c 85.337		54	.17. 6		
75.	5 & a table & a Trunk		55	1.15		
76.	5 leather &c	31				
77.	4 cane bottom		155	1.		
78.	8 Do & 3 Leather		157	2.15	No 139	1.6
79.	5		165	1. 5		
80.	9		168	1. 7	No 106	2. 5. 6

81. 12	182	3.	No 31	4. 5
82. Canhooks 1 pr &19 whetstones	220	. 6	
83. Cherrypots 1 & 2 yds hair cloth	219	. 3 GW	
84. Chest of Drawers	48	.15 No 10,	2.14. 6
85. Chests 1	74	. 5 No 132	. 5
86. &c	34	No 184	. 4. 1
87. 1 & 2 Trunks	159	.12 No 185,	. 4. 6
88. 6	206	1.10 No 187,8,2 .	. 5. 3
89. 10 &c 22			
90. 1 pr cloaths 15/4 old 6/	215	1. 1	
91. Chisells 21 &c 147.309	70	1. 8 P	
92. Chocolate pots 2 &c 35			.14.11
93. Cistern for meat & 1 jar	196	.10	
94. Clamps 9 &c 25			
95. Cloaths brushes 2 1 pr pumps	183	.12 GW	
96. Close stooll pans 2 &c 149.	217	.13 GW	
152.167.215			
97. Copper kettle 1	121	4. No 39,	4.10.
98. 1 large Do & Iron pot	130	10. P	
99. 1 old Do	202	.12 P	
100. Cocks for same Iron Lead &c	95	3.	
101. Corner Cupboard 1	51	1. No 100	1.15
102. Corn 695 barrells		174. 7. 6 £90	
103. Cattle 1354		1565. 4. 6	
104. Corn crib 17			
105. Cotton 510 yds	83	51.	
106. couch 1 2 Pictures 3 Maps	44	1.14 No 9, No 4	2.12. 6
107. 1	184	.10 No 143	. 7
108. 1	221	.10 No 153	1. 4
109. Crupper 1 & 4 pr Stirrups leather	111	. 7. 6	
110. Currycombs 1 &c	25		
111. &c 213.221.			
258.290	101	30.	
112. 1 &c 321.335.393	293	.10	
113. Casement & a Socket	225	. 6 GW socket	. 6
114. Collar & harness 7			
115. Currying knives 3	245	1.	
116. fleshing Do	77	.10	
117. Cyder 500 gals	280	6. 5	
118. Dark lanthorn 36			
119. Desks 3 4 trunks & lumber	116	6.10 No 64 2	
120. 1 31		No 63,3, No 66	1.15. 6
121. 1 old Do	167	1. No 135 1.8	
122. 1 old Do & matrisses	180	.10	
123. 1 writing	184	1.	
124. Dog 1 pr old & 1 brass fender			
hood	156	. 5 No 121 . 7. 6	
125. 1 Do 1 pr tongs & water pot	198	. 8 No 181 . 8. 1	
126. 1 pr kitchen Do	201	.15 No 33, 2.11	
127. Dog collars 2 4 Coopers Compass	223	.3	
128. Drawing knives 2	133	.4	
129. Dressing box 1	153	.2	
130. Duck 28 yds	78	1.15 Greenhow	1.13. 9
131. 4ps	87	10.	14. 7.10
132. Duffcell 15 1/2 yds & 7 1/2 Kersey	82	4.19. 6	
133. Dutch blankets 8&9 hats	76	4. 3	
134. 3 pcs	84	18.	

135.	Earthenware & 1 parcel Rope		94	6.	
136.	Escritoire 1		167	3.	No 138 3.13
137.	Fender & brass	124			
138.	1 hoe & 2 water pots		210	.10 No 152 . 5	
139.	Files 2 doz whipsaws &c	277	71	1. 4	
140.	68 of several sorts		72	2.	
141.	14 &c	66			
142.	Fire shovel	124			
143.	Flannel 98 yrds		132	8. 3. 4 GW	£ 4. 1. 8
144.	Flesh forks 2	35			
145.	Frying pans 1 & 1 Pott		91	.12. 6 P No 95,4s, No 163 .5.9	
146.	1	35	75	P 4.6	
147.	Gimlette 12		91		
148.	Girths 16 & 2 Housings		65	3.	No 67,17s.6d No 43,44, 2.8
149.	Glass a parcel old windows	96			
150.	12 panes large Do		222	.15 No 111, 1.11	
151.	Decanter	19			
152.	2 Bell Glasses	96			
155.	2 old earthen pots				
156.	a parcel old gally pots & lumber			8. 2	
157.	2 pewter dishes			10. 2	
158.	1 old pewter bason 6 plates			4. 6	
178.	1 Dish & 6 plates			17. 6	
30.	30 books sold for 18.6				
44.	1 (illegible)	1.3			
155.	2 old earthen pots	1.6			
	yd plains	1.6			
61.	Maps & Prints				
228.	Alexanders battles 5		163	.13	
229.	Cesars 12		162	1. 1	
230.	3 v 106			No 47, 5.	
231.	4 Mapps & 4 prints		154	. 8 No 116 to 119, 32	
232.	3 Do & 5 Do		158	. 8	
233.	2 Do 5 glass Do		161	.12 No 123 to 125, 25	2.19. 9
234.	5 prints 32 glass Do	64	169	3. 9 No 136 .5	
235.	21 glass prints		181	1. 5 No 144, 5, 6&7 30 odd pictures	
236.	Marking irons 1 pr	66		No 37 .2	4. 3. 6
237.	Measures a pint pot	47		No 69	
238.	a gallon pot	193		.2	
239.	2 pewter	38			
240.	2 & 2 Riddles & 2 shovels		207	1. 5	
241.	1 old half bushel	18			
242.	Medicines		38	3.	
243.	a parcel & some trifles		192	2.	
244.	Millpacks	6			
245.	Millstones 2 pr hand Do		25	4. 1 P	
246.	1 pr		152	1. P	
247.	1 pr & a peck		290	.12. 6 P	
248.	Milk pans 82		123	1.13. 6	
249.	a parcel		148	.16	
250.	2 doz		247	.15	
251.	Mousetraps	64			

252.	1 Do	44			
253.	Nails 8 barrels		89	70.	
254.	a parcel		209	5.	
255.	24 M 6d a parcel old		250	5.11	
256.	Nippers	192	73		
257.	Old hoes axes Boxes Hoops		5	4.	
258.	Old Iron	34.100.111.16		No 120	. 7
259.	a parcel		146	.12 No 189	17. 6
260.	some		203	. 3	
261.	a parcel & old Harrows		240	2.	
262.	Ozenbrigs 9 ps		86	52.10	
263.	350 Ells		112	21.17. 6	
264.	Paint some red lead & 1 table		211	.10 No 162	. 4. 7.
265.	Sails Piggins & Tubs		149	.10	
266.	2 old 1 Piggin 2 Tubs		205	. 2 ·	
267.	Pictures 2	106			
268.	24 painted		162	10.	
269.	6 painted on wood		164	1.	
270.	13 painted		170	6.10	
271.	a parcel		178	1. No 160 .6.6	
272.	2 painted		182	1. 6 No 167 .5	
273.	parcel old ones		216	. 6 No 168-178	
				40 pictures	3. 3.11
274.	Pillow 1 & a remnant of ticking		108	1. No 179,10, 9.6	
				No 90. .15	
275.	Plaid hose 177 pr & 1 pr shoes		87	15.	
276.	Plains 75		80	10. No 61 1/6	
277.	Planer irons 11	139			
278.	Do	66			
279.	Pistols a pr & 1 sword		39	3. No 45 15.	
280.	Plate 23 lib		36	119.19 JC £ 119	
281.	16 3/4 lib		37	60 Do 60.	
282.	26 oz 15d		191	8. 0. 6 Do 8. .6	
283.	Plate case 1		186	2.10 No 150 2.12	
284.	Plows 4		271	.14 P	
285.	Rasp 1	37			
286.	Riddles 2	240			
287.	Rolls 39 ps		85	52. 1	
288.	1 ps & sevl wrappers		113	3.	
289.	Rope 1 ps		84	. 6 Greenhow	9.12. 1
290.	a parcel	135.111			
291.	Rug 1		106	1. GW	
				No 92 1.0.6	
292.	Saddles & bridle 1	3			
293.	Sains a new one		26	7.	
294.	2 Casks old	100	27	4.	
295.	2 large ones & Rope		102	20	
296.	Safes 2 V 5, 64			No 131 .9.0	
297.	Saws 6 whipsaws & 2 x cut		23	4 GW 2w 1.	
298.	1 handsaw	36			
299.	1 handsaw		275	. 7. 6	
300.	Saw rests 1	66	69	. 1. 3	
301.	Salt a parcel		93	10.	
302.	a small quantity of large		213	. 8	
303.	7 bushels		274	.17. 6	
304.	scales 1 pr	35	151	1.	1.16. 2
305.	Schooner		25	50. Greenhow 50.	
306.	Scythes & furniture 6		100	2.	

307.	Serge Denim 3 yds & 2 Brown Tammy		63	2. 5 E Bacon 2.2.6
308.	Sheep 238			56.16
309.	Sheepshears 6	91		
310.	Shoes 12 pr mens Do & slippers		60	5.
311.	39 pr Negro Do		115	6.16. 6
312.	1 pr Do		137	. 3
313.	1 pr Pumps	95		
314.	Shoe thread a parcel		109	1. 5. 3
315.	Shovels 2		240	
316.	2 Do	22		
317.	Shot	163		
318.	&c			
319.	abot 40 lib mixed		218	.10
320.	Sickles 1 doz	180		
321.	6	112		
322.	Sieves 4 brass 1 Iron		178	
323.	1 search & 1 sifter		36	
324.	21 course sifters	32	90	1. 6. 3
325.	1 search	44		
326.	2 wire seives		276	. 7
327.	1 wheat seive		295	. 3
328.	skellets 2 old & 2 Tea kettles		119	1. 5 2. . 3
329.	2 bell mettle Do		199	.12 No 56 1.1
330.	Slate 1 & pencils		110	. 2 GW
331.	Snuffers & ps	46		
332.	2 pr	47	143	. 1 GW
333.	Spades 11	180		
334.	1 old Do		215	. 1
335.	Spancels 1 pr Iron	112		
336.	Spinning wheel	44		
337.	Spits 2	35		
338.	Staples 33	170		6.6
339.	22		76	. 3
340.	5	37		
341.	Stillyards pr		64	.12
342.	1 pr		150	.15
343.	1 pr		172	. 3
344.	1 pr		244	. 6
345.	Stockings 11 pr mens	275	105	2.17. 6 GW
346.	Stirrup 1 pr 1 chariot whip		114	. 7 GW
347.	Stirrup leathers 4 pr	109		
348.	Sugar boxes 2 tin	48		.9
349.	Swords	279		No 40 2.10
350.	1 cutting		117	2.10
351.	1 sword	166		.8
352.	Tables 1 large Walnut Do		30	2. No 4 1.15
353.	2 large Mahogany Do		43	6. GW No 2, 3.10
354.	1 Walnut Do		45	.10
355.	1 Do & 2 Trunks		49	1.10 No 149 1.15
356.	1 table	75		
357.	2 Do		153	.15 No 27,28 1.5.6
358.	2 old		165	. 4 No 161 1.3
359.	1 large Do		185	1.10 No 166 16.9
360.	1 square Do wth a picture in it		187	.15 GW .1
361.	1 table Mahogany	264		No 142 11.6
362.	Tammy 2 Remnants	307		No 59 1.10.6 102. .13

363.	Taper bitts 4	172			
364.	Tar & tar barrels		131	.15. 0	
365.	Tarrier 1	38			
366.	Teaboard 1	24		No 101	.10.6
367.	Tea chest one old	19		No 76	.2.6
368.	Tea kettles 2	328			
369.	Thread 50 3/4 lib bro & colld & 1 lib bro		104	1.	
370.	Tickin & Remnant	274			
371.	Tongs 1 pr old	125			
372.	Tools for sundry Tradesmen		124	10.	
373.	a Coopers compass	127			
374.	a parcel of Carpenters		248	7. 1	
375.	Trowells 2		135	. 4	
376.	Trunks 2	355		No 82	2. 1. 6
377.	1 Do	74		No 80	.14. 6
378.	1 Do	75		No 81	.14
379.	a parcel old Do	33			
380.	4 Do	199			
381.	1 Do		153	. 2	
382.	2 Do	87			
383.	Tubs	265.266			
384.	Twin 17lib		103	.17	
385.	Vials	34			
386.	Virginia Cloth 36 yds		78	1.16	
387.	Warming Pan 1	41		No 87,	.9.6
				No 112,	.8.3

Articles appraised under Lumber &ca so as not to admit of any certainty

(No)
3.	1.0
11.	10.
22.	2.
24.	1.10
28.	1.10
38.	8.
41.	4.
56.	40.
57.	10.
59.	1.
88.	10.
95.	3.
97.	5.
101.	30.
116.	6.10
122.	2.10
130.	2.10
134.	.5
180.	.10
190.	.15
192.	2.
388. Water pot 1 old	125
389. 2 Do	138

390. Wedges 5 old		146	. 7. 6	
391. 6 Do		248	.12	
392. 9 Do		270	.18	
393. 3 Do	112			
394. Whet or Ragstones 16	170			
395. 19 Do	82			
396. Whipthongs 5	V 36			
397. Chariot whip	346			
398. Wool 140 lib		118	7.	40 lib .40
399. Wrappers	288			

New Kent Estate ends	No 137
King William	152
James City	255
York	250
Northampton	280
Hanover	295

153. Gloves 5 pr mens		106	.10 GW
154. gouge 1	66		
155. grater 1	48		
156. Grid Iron	35		No 74, . 5. 6
157. Grindstones 1.a hide & Chain		10	1.15 P
158. 1 &c	9		
159. 1 & Iron handle		214	. 4 P
160. 1 large Do		239	.12 P
161. 1 old Do		278	. 3 P
162. 1 Do		294	. 2. 6 P
163. Gunpowder 75 lib & 1 o 3d shot		79	8.18
164. & 6	34		
165. Guns 1		40	1.5 No 62, .16
166. 1 short barrel Do & 1 sword		179	No 110 .14. 6 No 41, 1.8
167. 1 old Do	96		
168. Hair cloth 2 yds	83		
169. Handmill 1 & staples		277	1. P
170. Hasps & staples 33&16 whetstones		74	. 9. 6 GW 7& 4 . 2. 2. 2
171. 4 &c	37		
172. Hatchets 2 &c 212.256.363		73	.12 GW part 3.
173. 1		276	. 1. 8
174. Hats 30 mens		61	3.16
175. 1 Do		62	1.15
176. 9 Do	V 133		
177. Hides 1	V 157		
178. 3,5 hhds 5 Sieves & Lumber		24	1.10
179. 2		144	2. 6
180. Hinges 6 pr garnet &c	320.333	98	4. 0
181. Hoes 25	9		
182. 61 narrow		18	9.
183. 24 Do & 21 broad		99	8.
184. 13		147	1. 6
185. 17 narrow	13		
186. 1 small	138		
187. 2 broad		249	. 6
188. 7 Do		268	1. 3. 4
189. 4 narrow 12/ 4 old 2/		269	.14
190. 8 old broad		270	.13. 4
191. 1 narrow		287	3. 6

192. 18 old   16
193. 756 Hogs   232. 1. 6
194. Hogsheads 5   178
195. a parcel   62
196. a parcel   17
197. Hoops for Cart Wheels a Sett   249   .12
198. Horses 45   306.
199. Housings 2V   148
200. Jack 1 Screw Do V1   1. 0
201. Jarrs 4   36   .13
202. 6 wth some Oil & Soap   194   8.   No 129 .30, .11.6
203. 1   93
204. Ink Stand 1   48   No 93,   .6.6
205. Iron chain   1.157
206. Iron pots 2 old   4   .12   No 165, .13.6
207. 1 Do   145
208. 4 Do & hooks   4
209. 1 Do   V 98   No 159, 1 &
                                           hooks .5
210. 4 Do & 2 pr Hooks   202   1. 1 P 5 pr hooks & 3
                                           Pots
211. 1 Do & Hooks   279   . 5   No 83   1. 1. 2
212. Iron screws 10   172
213. Iron ware &c   111
214. Juggs   3   182   . 3. 1
215. Kersey 50 yds   85 82 8. 7. 6
216. 7 1/2 yds   132
217. Knives & forks   V 46
212. 12 Do   188   .12 GW
213. a few   32
214. Ladle 1 V 35 V 109 sales
215. Lamp black a few barrels   96
216. Lanthorn 1 old   64
217. Lead 476 lib   19   3.19 GW 80, 13.4
218. &c 100
219. Leather 13 sides   77   2.5
220. 202 sides & 46 skins of upper   92   49. 4
221. Stocklocks &c   V 111
222. 3   V 26
223. Looking glasses 1 & a
     dressing Do   50   2. 6   No 137 1. 4. 6
224. I Do   129   1.   No 29   1. 3. 6
225. 2 Dressing   158   .10   No 115 .19
226. 1   171   1.   No 134 4.10
227. 1   181   3.   No 1   1.18. 6 No 141 .7.9
No 2 a Large Mahogany table   4. 1   7. 9 (maps&prints)
    5 a Tea table   1. 6
    11 Stoneware   1. 6. 6
    12.13.14.15.16.17.18.19.20.21.22
        23.24.25.26. China & Glassware   10.15. 6
    30 a silver watch   6.
    42 A horn   . 5. 6
    46 A ps of Stuff   4.
    48 Do   3. 3
        49.50.51.52.53.54.55 Pewter   10.10. 6
    60 2 yds black bcloth   .18
    86 1 Funnell   . 1. 6

94	3 Portmanteaus	. 5
95	1 pr Garden shears	. 3. 7
104	105 Pewter	1.15
122	1 Mortar & pestle	. 7
140	6 Decanters	.11
148	Brimstones	1.11
151	a Bed teaster	. 5

AD, Custis Papers ViHi. The inventory is in the hand of John Mercer. It was derived from the combined county inventory and from the table of the disposition of goods. He arranged the inventory in five columns. The first is the number of the entry; second, the name of the item; third, the number of the entry in the combined county inventory and in the table of the disposition of goods; fourth, the appraised value; fifth, a partial identification of the purchaser and the sale price.

To Anna Maria Dandridge Bassett

Dear Sister   Mount Vernon April 6, 1762

Your kind Letter by the man that brought the syder round I received the 4th of ult which gave me great conscern to hear of Mr Bassett being so unwell but as you inform me he has lost his fevour makes no doubt but he is recovered long before this time it was a very great disappointment to me your not comeing as we had so long expected you but a visit from you will yett be most acceptable to me, as we may sertainly hope for fine weather now after so much bad as we have had. I have had the pleasure of hearing of you by several that has come from below but had no opportunity to write or would not neglect it as it is the only pleasure absence can afford me - I have had a very dark time since I came home. I believe it was owing to the severe weather we have had. I think I never knew such a winter as it has been the only comfort was that Mr Washington and my children have had their health very well. I think Patsy has been hardier than Ever she was till lately they have boath had colds and fevers - I just heard of this opportunity by Capt Posey,[1] if my good man shoud be come a way you may send a line to me by him as he lives close by

I am very sorry to hear my mamma[2] is still complaining and her staying at home so much as she doze I believe is a great hurt to her I hope she is happier at home than she seemed to be when I was down I never think of her but with consern as she appears always to be uneasy I shoud be glad you woud take care of Betsy[3] and keep her in proper order she has her own way so much at home I am affraide she will be quite spoild - It is with the greates pleasure I hear the well fair of you and your little babys - pray give my duty to my Mamma and love to Brothers and sisters and except the same from Dear Nancy your most Affectionate

Martha Washington

till Mamma I was in great hast
or wood have wrote to her[4]

ALS, ViMtV.

1. John Posey, a close neighbor of GW, lived at "Rover's Delight," immediately southwest of Mount Vernon on Dogue Run. His farm, consisting of about 400 acres, was called Ferry Farm. Posey also operated a ferry that crossed the Potomac from that point to Marshall Hall, Charles County, Maryland. A portion of his land had been purchased from GW's younger brother, Charles. It was later purchased by GW and incorporated into the Mount Vernon farms. Since 1755 Posey was continually in debt to GW, and the latter seems never to have been able to say "no" to Posey's repeated applications for loans or favors. Posey had served as a captain in the 2nd Virginia Regiment in 1755, under Colonel William Byrd III. He was a frequent visitor at Mount Vernon and for many years his daughter, Amelia (Millie) was a great favorite at Mount Vernon.

2. Frances Jones Dandridge (1710-1765) was the daughter of Orlando Jones and his wife Martha Macon. She married John Dandridge, July 22, 1730. After the death of her husband in 1756 she continued to live at Chestnut Grove, New Kent County. Later she lived with her son, Bartholomew Dandridge, at *Pamocra*, New Kent County. *Harris*, 1:81-83, 138.

3. See supra, MW to Margaret Green, June 26, 1761, n. 1.

4. There is no extant correspondence between MW and her mother.

To Anna Maria Dandridge Bassett

My Dear Nancy   Mount Vernon August 28, 1762
    I had the pleasure to receive your kind letter of the 26 of July just as I was setting out on a visit to Mrs Washingtons[1] in Westmoreland where I spent a weak agreably I carred my little patt with me and left Jackey at home for a trial to see how well I coud stay without him though we ware gon but wone fortnight I was quite impatiant to get home if I at any time heard the doggs barke or a noise out I thought thair was a person sent for me I often fansied he was sick or some accident had happened to him so that I think it is impossable for me to leave him as long as Mr Washington must stay when he comes down - if nothing happens I promise myself the pleasure of comeing down in the spring as it will be a healthy time of the year I am very much obliged to you for your kind invitation and assure yourself nothing but my childrens intrest shoud prevent me the sattisfaction of seeing you and my good Friends I am always thinking of and wish it was possable for me to spend more of my time amongst
    It gave me great sattisfaction to hear of your dear billys[2] recovry which I hope will be a lasting wone you mention in your letter that Col More[3] intended here but we have seen nothing of him we heard at Fredericksburg that he and my Brother[4] had been thaire but no higher I shoud be very glad to seen them heare
    We all injoy very good health at preasent I think patty seems to be quite well now Jackey[5] is very thin but in good health and learn thaire

books very fast I am sorry to hear you are unwell but hope your complaint is slight I have no news worth telling you

We are daly Expect the kind laydes of Maryland to visit us - I must begg you will not lett the fright you had given you prevent your comeing to see me again if I coud leave my children in as good care as you can I woud never lett Mr W-n come down without me please to give my love to Miss Judy and your little babys and make my best complments to Mr Bassett and Mrs Dawson

I am with sincear regard Dear sister your most affectionate

Martha Washington

ALS, MHi.

1. Hannah Bushrod Washington, wife of John Augustine Washington, younger brother of GW. They lived at "Bushfield," Westmoreland County.

2. William Bassett (1760-1775), eldest son of Burwell and Anna Maria Dandridge Bassett.

3. Bernard Moore, of "Chelsea," (d. 1775) *Diaries*, 2:54. He was a colonel and Burgess for King William County. *Diaries*, 1:274.

4. Bartholomew Dandridge (1737-1785). *Diaries*, 6:274.

5. John Parke Custis, then eight years old.

To Mrs. Shelbury

To - Mrs. Shelbury - Milliner Dean Street Soho. London

Madam   August - 1764

In an Invoice to Mr Cary I have directed all the goods for Miss Custis's use to be got from you as I approvd of your last years choice - Such things as Misses of her age usually wear here I have sent for; but if you can get those which may be more genteel and proper for her, I shall have no objections to it, provided it is done with frugality, for as she is only nine years old a superfluity, or expence in dress would be altogether unnecessary - you will please to observe that all her things is to be charged separate from mine altho both accounts will be paid you by Robt. Cary Esq & Co.[1]

I have also ordered a few things for my own use together with a pair of stays which I beg may be very good, easy made, and very thin, - The Ruffles you sent last year I have kept myself and desired Mr Cary to pay you for them - Mr Washington wrote Mr Cary in February last to purchase of you a french necklace & earings for me - if they are not already sent, I woud rather choose a blew Turkey stone Necklace and Earings sent in their place if the price does not exceed two Guineas -

I am Madam
Yr very Hble Servt
Martha Washington

Mount Vernon
10th August 1764

LB, In the handwriting of GW, DLC:GW.

1. MW's expenses were paid by GW. Her children's expenses were paid out of the income derived from their Custis inheritance.

To George Washington

My Dearest   March 30, 1767
    It was with very great pleasure I see in your letter that you got safely down. We are all very well at this time but it still is rainney and wett. I am sorry you will not be at home soon as I expected you.[1] I had reather my sister[2] woud not come up so soon as May woud be much plasenter time than April. We wrote you last post as I have nothing new to tell you I must conclude myself

Your most Affectionate
Martha Washington[3]

ALS, Location unknown.

1. In mid-March, 1767 GW journeyed to Williamsburg to attend the session of the House of Burgesses. The session ended April 11. From Williamsburg he went south, across the James River, to visit the Dismal Swamp area. From there he returned to Mount Vernon. *Journal of the House of Burgesses of Colonial Virginia*, p. 131; *The Papers of George Washington Ledger A*, DLC:GW; *Freeman*, 3:180-81.

2. Anna Maria Bassett of Eltham.

3. Formerly in the collection of Forest H. Sweet, Battle Creek, Michigan, this is the only known letter of MW to GW.

To Hector Ross

Sir[1]   October the 8th 1770
    As Mr Washington is from home, and I do not Expect him so soon as Mr Christian[2] will be going down. I shall be much obliged to you to pay his account against the children and this shall be a reacept

I am Sir your Hble Servant
Martha Washington

November 10th 1770. Received from Hector Ross the Sum of Ten Pounds Current Money by order of Mrs George Washington

F Christian

(Address leaf)
To Mr Ross

in
Colchester
By favour of
Mr Christian

(Docket)
Oct 8 1770
Mrs Washington order to
Christian with her
Receipt

ALS, ViHi.
    1. Hector Ross, a merchant of Colchester, Fairfax County, purchased corn and tobacco from GW. His firm was a source of supply for clothing and other necessities. He was a frequent visitor at Mount Vernon.
    2. Francis Christian was a dancing master from Richmond County. He conducted dancing classes for the young people of the Mount Vernon neighborhood. They were held at Mount Vernon, Gunston Hall and other nearby great houses. *Diaries*, 2:219, 219 n., 221, 229 n., 235-36.

From John Johnson

Madam   Annapolis 21 March 1772
    The very bad Weather which prevented almost any Communication and my Expectation that the Means left with Miss Custis[1] are not yet expended occasioned my not sending any more so soon as I designed - I now send by the Post a small Phial to be frequently smelt to as Hartshorne or other Drops commonly used to prevent faitiness and a small Bottle of Ointmt to be applied as before directed - the Decoction I left must be taken if Occasion requires it tho' I hope Nature will perform her Office without. I imagine it will be unnecessary to assure Miss Custis that I have the greatest Hopes her Happiness will be much promoted by regular moderate Exercise, temperate living which she may think Abstemiousness and her being attentive to keep her Body cool and open which last may I hope be effectually done and agreeably to herself by the Use of Barley Water and light cooling Food - Frumenty made of Barley or even of wheat wou'd I think be very proper Food is agreeable to many and perhaps might be so at Times to Miss Custis - I hear that Master Custis said in Annapolis she was better I have great Pleasure in it and should be glad to hear more particularly of her State

                I am Madam
                Your most obedient Servant
                John Johnson[2]

ALS, DLC:GW.

1. Martha Parke Custis (1756-1773). It is likely she had her first seizure June 15, 1768, although there are earlier hints, as mentioned in MW's letter to Margaret Green, September 29, 1760. See supra. The frequency and severity of the seizures increased in spite of numerous medical consultations and remedies. She expired suddenly after a violent seizure on Sunday June 19, 1773. *Freeman*, 3:204, 325 n.

2. Dr. John Johnson (b. 1745) of Frederick, Maryland, was the brother of Thomas Johnson, close friend of GW, Member of the Continental Congress, Governor of Maryland, and Associate Justice of the United States Supreme Court. During 1771-72 Dr. Johnson sent various herbal remedies to prevent the epileptic seizures, but his medicines and advice were as ineffectual as all the others.

To Mrs. S. Thorpe

(July 15, 1772)

To - Mrs S Thorpe   Milliner in London

I cannt. help writing to you in behalf of my daughter, Miss Custis, who together with myself, Imported some very hard bargains from you last year. Messrs Cary & Co. was wrote to for a handse Suit of Brussels Lace to cost £20, in cons of wch., she recd. from you a pr of tripple Ruffles, a Tucker[1] & Ruff[2] set on plain joing. Nett (such as can be bought in ye Milliners Shops here at 3/6 pr yd) When, if you had ever sent a Tippet[3] & Cap w. ye othr. things I shd still have thot them Dr.- These things have been shewn to sevl. Ladies who are accustomd to such kind of Importns, & all agree, that they are most extravagantly high chargd.

I now sd for a suit at ye price of £40; w. Lappels & ca but if you cant afford to sell a much better bargn. in these, that yo. did in ye last I shd hope yt Mr. Cary will try elsewhere, as I thy her last add. to my own is worth a little pains- and ye. othr. things sent last yr. for myself &ca were 5 gauze Caps. w. Blond Lace bordrs. at a Ga. each, when ye same kd. might have been bot. in ye Country at a much less price.- I have now sent for 2 Caps for M. Custis, & 2 for myself of Mint. lace & wd have ym gentl but not expens. hers to suit a Person of 16 yrs old mine one of 40 & I cant. help addg. that I thk it neccesy that ye last yrs Suit (wch ought to be retd. if she cd. do witht in ye meanwhile) shd be compld w. a Tippet & Cap, as it is Scae more yn 1/3 a (?).

I am Madm yr Hble Servt
Martha Washington

July 15 - 1772

LB, (Handwriting of GW), DLC:GW.

1. A frill of lace worn around the neck or bodice.

2. A circular out-standing frill on a sleeve or collar.

3. A garment of fur or wool, covering the neck or shoulders. With hanging ends, it would resemble our present day scarf or stole.

From John Parke Custis

My Dear Mama,   Kings-College[1] July 5th (1773)
I have at length the Pleasure of informing you that I am settled in every respect according to my Satisfaction.[2] There has Nothing been omitted by the Professors, which could be in any means condusive to my Happiness, & contentment during my residence at this place, and I believe I may say without vanity that I am looked upon in a particular Light by Them all, there is as much distinction made between me & the other students as can be expected. I dine with them (a liberty that is not allow'd any but myself) associate & pertake of all their recreations, their Attention to my Education keeps pace with their other good offices, and from their Words as well as Actions. I have reason to form the most pleasing Hope of Pleasure & Satisfaction entertainment in the pursit of my Studies. It does not become me to Speak much in praise of my own attendance but I assure you that I have done as much or more in 2 months than in the eight Months before, and I flatter myself you will never hear anything but what is agreable from Doctor Cooper[3] or any other of the Professors. It is now time to give you short plan of my apartments, and of my way of living. I have a large parlour with two Studyes or closets, each large enough to contain a bed, trunk and couple of chairs, one I sleep in, & the other Joe[4] calls his, my chamber and parlour are paper'd with a cheap tho very pretty Paper, the other is painted; my furniture consists of Six chairs, 2 Tables, with a few paultry Pictures; I have an excellent Bed, and in short every thing very convenient & clever. I generally get up about Six or a little after, dress myself & go to chappel, by the time that Prayers are over Joe has me a little Breakfast to which I sit down very contented after eating heartyly. I thank God, and go to my Studys, with which I am employed till twelve than I take a walk and return about one dine with the professors, & after dinner study till Six at which time the Bell always rings for Prayers they being over college is broak up, and then we take what Amusement we please.

Things My dear Mother were going on in this agreable Manner, till last Thursday, the day I receiv'd Pappa's melancholy Letter,[5] giveing an account of my dear & only Sister's Death. I myself met the Post, & brought the sad Epistle to Doctor Cooper who I beg'd to open his Letter immediately, the Direction I did not know, but the Seal[6] I knew too well to be deceived. My confusion & uneasiness on this occasion is better conceiv'd that expresst. Her case is more to be envied than pitied, for if we mortals can distinguish between those who are deserveing of grace & who are not, I am confident she enjoys that Bliss prepar'd only for the good & virtuous, let these considerations, My dear Mother have their due weight with you and comfort yourself with reflecting that she now enjoys in substance what we in this world enjoy in imagination & that there is no real Happiness on this side of the grave. I must allow that to sustain a shock of this kind requires more Philosophy than we in general are (possest) off, my Nature could not bear the shock. (illegible) sunk under the load of oppression, and hindered me from administring any consolation to my dear and nearest relation, this Letter is the first thing I've done since I received the malancholy News, & could I think my Presence wou'd be condusive to the Restoration of your Tranquillity neither the distance nor the Fatigue of traveling could detain me a moment here. I put myself & Joe into deep Mourning & shall do (all) Honour in my power to the Memory of a deceas'd & well belov'd Sister, I will no longer detain you on a subject which is painful to us both but conclude with beging you to remember you are a Christian and that we ought to submit with Patience to the divine Will and that to render you happy shall be the constant care of your effectionate and dutiful son

John Parke Custis[7]

Mrs Washington
New- York
July 5th 1773

ALS, DLC:GW.

1. The college was established by Royal Charter in 1754, as the College of the Province of New York. It was always referred to as King's College. It was re-chartered in 1784 as Columbia College.

2. On May 8th John Parke Custis set out for Mount Airy, the country seat of Benedict Calvert in Maryland. He had become secretly engaged to Eleanor, Calvert's second daughter. *Diaries*, 3:178. GW left Mount Vernon on May 10th and arrived at Mount Airy later that day. He and Jackie then set out for New York on the 13th. Considerable time was spent in and around Philadelphia. They arrived in New York on the 26th. After JPC matriculated at the college, GW departed from New York on May 31, and arrived at Mount Vernon on June 8th. *Diaries*, 3:178-86.

3. Upon his arrival in New York, GW discussed Jackie's financial arrangements with Cooper. Myles Cooper (1737-1785) was named the second president of King's College in 1763. He became an ardent Loyalist, fled to England in 1775, and never returned to America. *Writings*, 3:134.

4. The slave servant of JPC.

5. GW's letter has not survived. Martha Parke Custis died suddenly on Sunday afternoon, June 19, 1773. *Diaries*, 3:188.

6. Probably a black seal, bearing the Washington coat of arms or cypher.

7. JPC arrived at Mount Vernon on December 10, 1773, and never returned to King's College. In a letter to President Cooper, December 15th, GW stated JPC's college career was at an end. He married Eleanor Calvert on February 3, 1774. *Diaries*, 3:231 and n.

Mrs. Washington is alleged to have written a sentimental letter to Eleanor Calvert Custis. The text of the letter first appeared in Lossing, *Mary and Martha, the Mother and the Wife of George Washington*, p. 126, New York 1886. The text as given by Lossing is as follows:
"My dear Nelly: God took from me a Daughter when June Roses were blooming. He has now given me another daughter about her age when winter winds are blowing, to warm my heart again. I am as happy as one so afflicted and blest can be. Pray recive my benediction

and a wish that you may long live the loving wife of my happy son and a loving daughter of your affectionate mother, M Washington." MW did not attend the marriage ceremony, since she was in mourning and did not wish to detract from the gaiety of the occasion. Lossing states GW was instructed to present the letter to the bride immediately after the ceremony. The original letter was supposedly preserved at Arlington by the family of G.W.P. Custis and copied by Lossing about 1860. It is also printed in *Freeman*, 3:344, n. Freeman was of the opinion the letter was a forgery, since "the style and diction" does not resemble her other letters. Neither does it resemble that of GW, who on a number of occasions drafted letters for his wife. Freeman suggests it was written by the same person who wrote the letter of GW to MW, July 20, 1758. *Freeman*, 2:319 n., 405-06. Similarly, this letter was first printed in Lossing's *Mary and Martha*, p. 99. Lossing again states he copied the text from the original at Arlington. It is interesting to note Lossing was the source of two childhood letters exchanged between Richard Henry Lee (of Stratford) and George Washington. Supposedly they were written when both boys were nine years old. Lossing states the texts were supplied by a son of Richard Henry Lee. The letters would indicate the boys were exceedingly precocious, for the diction and style is not that of nine year old boys. Furthermore the historiography is inaccurate, since GW left the Northern Neck neighborhood at the age of three. Lossing, *Mount Vernon and Its Associations*, p. 23, 41, New York 1859. The editor concurs with the conclusions of Freeman, with regard to the letters of GW, Lee, and MW.

To Elizabeth Ramsay

Dear Miss[1]   January the 14th 1774
    I shall be very much obliged to you to enquire in town if there is black & white (illegible) lustring[2] - and a handsom plain black satten cloak I had reather not have a lace on it if one with a (illegible) or gimp[3] is to be had - I shoud have been very glad to have seen you hear this christmas if you coud have spared so much time out of town My compliments to Mr & Mrs Ramsay[4] and all the little Folks

> I am Dr. Miss
> your most affetionate
> Friend
> Martha Washington

Your answer a few days
hence will be as well today

ALS. CSmH.

    1. Elizabeth (Betsy) Ramsay, eldest daughter of William Ramsay and Ann McCarty.

    2. A glossy silk fabric (*OED*).

    3. A neckerchief or stomacher (*OED*).

    4. William Ramsay (1716-1785) and his wife Ann McCarty Ramsay (c. 1730-1785) had two sons and five daughters. Ramsay, a close friend of GW, was the first mayor of Alexandria and served as postmaster.

To Robert Cary and Company

A copy Of the Inventory, Refer'd To in Letter to Robert Cary & Co.
Dated June 1, 1774[1]

An Inventory of the Estate of Danl. Parke Custis, Esqr, which came to my hands or the hands of my Attorney under the general Letters of Administration of the said Decedents Estate Granted by the Arch Bishop of Canterbury in the year 1774 Inventories of the Virginia Estate having been returned to the Court in that Colony where Administration was granted to me and the money due from the Merchants in England to that Estate having been also Accounted for to the General Court of Virginia. One Thousand Six hundred and Fifty Pounds in the Bank of England.

(signed)
Martha Washington

LB, (In the handwriting of GW), DLC:GW.

1. In a letter of March 5, 1774, the Cary firm dunned GW for payment due them for purchases. He replied on June 1, 1774, requesting payment be made from his Bank of England stock. The stock had been purchased by John Custis. He bequeathed it to his son, Daniel Parke Custis. At his demise it became the property of his daughter, Martha Parke Custis. At her death half became the property of MW and the other half reverted to her brother, John Parke. By law, MW's share became the property of GW. There being nothing unadministered from the estate except the bank stock, GW requested the Cary debt be retired with his share of the stock. MW is therefore substantiating the proper administration of the settlement of the Custis estate. The Cary letter of March 5, 1774 has not been located. See, *Writings*, 219-221.

III

The Revolutionary Period, 1775–1783

Subject: Eleanor Parke Custis, age 17. Artist: James Sharples, 1796. Medium: Pastel on paper. *Credit*: Mount Vernon Ladies' Association.

From George Washington

My Dearest   Philadelphia June 18, 1775

I am now set down to write you on a subject which fills me with inexpressible concern - and this concern is greatly aggravated and Increased, when I reflect upon the uneasiness I know it will give you - It has been determined in Congress that the whole Army raised for the defence of the American Cause shall be put under my care, and that it is necessary for me to proceed immediately to Boston to take upon me the command of it. You may believe me my dear Patcy, when I assure you, in the most solemn manner, that, so far from seeking this appointment I have used every endeavour in my power to avoid it, not only from my unwillingness to part with you and the Family, but from a consciousness of its being a trust too great for my Capacity and that I should enjoy more real happiness and felicity in one month with you, at home, than I have the most distant prospect of reaping abroad, if my stay were to be Seven times Seven years. But, as it has been a kind of destiny that has thrown me upon this Service, I shall hope that my undertaking of it, is designed to answer some good purpose - You might, and I suppose did perceive, from the Tenor of my letters, that I was apprehensive I could not avoid this appointment, as I did not even pretend (t)o intimate when I should return - that was the case - it was utterly out of my power to refuse this appointment without exposing my Character to such censures as would have reflected dishonour upon myself, and given pain to my friends - this, I am sure could not, and ought not be pleasing to you, & must have lessend me considerably in my own esteem. I shall rely therefore, confidently, on that Providence which has heretofore preservd, & been bountiful to me, not doubting but that I shall return safe to you in the fall - I shall feel no pain from the Toil, or the danger of the Campaign - My unhappiness will flow, from the uneasiness I know you will feel at being left alone - I beg of you to summon your whole fortitude Resolution, and pass your time as agreeably as possible - nothing will give me so much sincere satisfaction as to hear this, and to hear it from your own pen.[1]

If it should be your desire to remove to Alexandria (as you once mentioned upon an occasion of this sort) I am quite pleased that you should put it into practice, & Lund Washington may be directed, by you, to build a Kitchen and other Houses there proper for your reception[2] - if on the other hand you should rather Incline to spend a good part of your time among your Friends below, I wish you to do so.[3] - In short, my earnest, & ardent desire is, that you would pursue any Plan that is most likely to produce content, and a tolerable degree of Tranquility as it must add greatly to my uneasy feelings to hear that you are dissatisfied, and complaining at what I really could not avoid.

As Life is always uncertain, and common prudence dictates to every Man the necessity of settling his temporal Concerns whilst it is in his power - and while the Mind is calm and undisturbed, I have, since I came to this place (for I had not time to do it before I left home) got Colo Pendleton to Draft a Will for me by the directions which I gave him which will I now Inclose[4] - The Provision made for you, in cas(e) of my death will, I hope, be agreeable; I Included the money for which I sold my own land (to Doctr Mercer) in the Sum Given you, as also all other Debts.[5] What I owe myself is very trifling - Cary's Debt excepted, and that would not have been much if the Bank stock had been applied without such difficulties as he made in the Transference.[6]

I shall add nothing more at present as I have several Letters to write, but to desire you will remember me to Milly[7] & all Friends, and to assure you that I am with the most unfeigned regard,

> My dear
> Patcy Yr Affecte
> G°: Washington

P.S. Since writing the above I have receivd your Letter of the 15th and have got two suits of what I was told wa(s) the prettiest Muslin. I wish it may please you - it cost 50/ a suit that is 20/. a yard.[8]

ALS, DTP.

1. This is the earliest known surviving letter of GW to MW. Their correspondence indicates many letters passed between them. All except three letters from GW to MW were destroyed by MW shortly before her death in 1802. Only one letter of MW to GW is known. See supra, March 30, 1767; Appendix III.

2. MW did not take up residence in the Alexandria house, preferring to remain at Mount Vernon.

3. In late October she visited her sister, Anna Maria Bassett, at Eltham, New Kent County. The other members of her immediate family lived close by.

4. This will has not been found and was probably destroyed by GW at some later and propitious time. Edmund Pendleton (1721-1803) was a prominent jurist and a man of great legal talent. He was a member of the Committee of Correspondence in 1773, a member of all the Virginia revolutionary conventions, president of the Committee of Safety, a delegate to the First and Second Continental Congress, and first speaker of the Virginia House of Delegates. Pendleton drew up the resolves, instructing the Virginia delegates to propose independence. Together with Wythe and Jefferson he revised the laws of Virginia. He had a long standing friendship with GW and served as a legal advisor. However, they did not always agree on foreign and fiscal policies in government.

5. Dr. Hugh Mercer (c. 1725-1777) was a native of Aberdeenshire, Scotland, studied medicine, and was surgeon's mate at the Battle of Culloden. Sometime thereafter he immigrated to America and at the outbreak of the French and Indian War joined the provincial forces. It was at this time he became acquainted with GW. After the war he settled in Fredericksburg, where he opened an apothecary shop and practiced medicine. At the outbreak of the Revolution he again volunteered and was commissioned a Brigadier-general in July of 1776. He was killed at the Battle of Princeton, January 3, 1777. Washington sold his boyhood home, Ferry Farm, to Mercer in 1774. Mercer was still in arrears for the purchase.

6. Amelia (Milly) Posey was the daughter of John Posey by his first wife, Martha Price Posey. She was a childhood companion of Patsy Custis and is frequently mentioned in GW's diaries and correspondence. She was a frequent visitor at Mount Vernon. The Washington's interest in her did not wane after the death of Patsy, for she spent most of the war years at Mount Vernon. The last mention of her is in a letter of GW to Lund Washington, March 18, 1781, in which the Washingtons send her their best wishes.

7. GW requested the Bank of England stock be sold and the proceeds used to pay off his indebtedness to the Cary firm. MW executed the request, since the stock was part of the Custis estate, having been purchased by John Custis many years before. The bank directors refused to honor the request, requiring additional documentation. The matter was not settled until after the Revolution.

8. This letter, like all others, has not been found.

From George Washington

My dearest,   Phila. June 23d. 1775

As I am within a few minutes of leaving this City, I could not think of departing from it without dropping you a line, especially as I do not know whether it may be in my power to write you again till I get to the Camp at Boston - I go fully trusting in that Providence, which has been more bountiful to me than I deserve, & in full confidence of a happy Meeting with you sometime in the Fall - I have no time to add more, as I am surrounded with Company to take leave of me - I retain an unalterable affection for you, which neither time or distance can change. My best love to Jack & Nelly[1] and regard for the rest of the Family concludes me with the utmost truth & sincerity,

Yr entire
G°: Washington[2]

(Address)
To
Mrs Washington
at
M Vernon

(Docket by MW)
June the 23
1775

ALS, ViMtV.

1. John Parke Custis and his wife, Eleanor Parke Custis.

2. From Monday June 19th until Friday, June 23rd, GW was occupied by conferences with Congress and making preparations for his departure for Boston. He and his official military family, together with Generals Charles Lee and Philip Schuyler, were ready to depart on the morning of the 23rd. Just prior to leaving he wrote the above letter to MW. A note on the verso of the address leaf is as follows: "This letter was secured and repaired by Edmund Law Rogers Great Great Grandson of Mrs Washington for his great Aunt Mr Martha Peter having first taken a facsimile Edmund Law Rogers Tudor Place Georgetown Feb 1st 1841." The folds have been taped with paper.

From Christian Scott Blackburn

(September 26, 1775)

Dear Madam   Westwood

I send the Bearer to inquire after Mrs. Custis's Health, who I hope is long before this recovered, & am sincerely sorry to hear of the loss she has sustained in the Death of her Daughter.[1]

I flatter myself that you have enjoyed a perfect state of health since I had the pleasure to see you last. I shall be glad to know when you heard from the General last, who I hope was then very well.

I have been confined here, upwards of 3 weeks with a Fever, of which I have got the better so far as to be able to ride out; & shall I hope be able to return home in about a fortnight, when I hope I shall have the pleasure of seeing yourself, Colo. Bassit & Lady, your Nieces, & Mr Custis at Rippon Lodge in your way down the Country.[2]

> Believe me to be
> Dear Madam
> Your respectful humble
> Servt
> C. Blackburn[3]

26th Septr
1775
To Mrs. Washington

ALS, DLC:GW.

1. Eleanor Calvert Custis apparently delivered a female infant shortly before this date. See infra, John Parke Custis to MW, June 9, 1776. No other reference to this occurence has been found.

2. MW, together with the Bassetts and John Parke Custis, was preparing to leave Mount Vernon and visit with the Bassetts and the other members of her family along the Pamunkey River in New Kent County.

3. Christian Scott Blackburn (b. 1745), daughter of Rev. James Scott, rector of Quantico Church. She was the wife of Col. Thomas Blackburn of Rippon Lodge. Their daughter, Julia Ann, married Bushrod Washington, nephew and heir of GW.

From George Gilpin

Madam   Alexandria Virginia Octr 8, 1775

I should have waited on you agreeable to promise but was prevented by the Rain on Friday & Saturday last. I shall set out to morrow morning on my way for New York if you have any Commands - I will Serve you the best in my Power please to Send me a Memorandum of what you would have done & I will Comply with it.[1] I am Madam your most Obedient Humble Servt

Geo Gilpin[2]

ALS, DLC:GW.

1. MW had not departed from Mount Vernon for New Kent County as of this date. She was at Eltham on November 2nd. See infra, MW to Mr Devenport (sic), November 2nd.

2. George Gilpin (1740-1813), a native of Maryland, had settled in Alexandria before the Revolution. During the Revolution he was a colonel of the Fairfax County militia and a member of the Committee of Safety. Gilpin was a close associate of George Washington in the affairs of the Potomac Company.

To Mr. Devenport

Mr Devenport[1]   Eltham[2] November 5th 1775

I desire you will lett Mrs Bayly, that lives at west point have corn or wheat as she may want it, while her husband is ill and unable to provide for her, you may let her have a barrel of corn and half a barrel of wheat as sends for it and give her a fat hog

I am sir your Hbl
Martha Washington

ALS, PHi.

1. Mr. Devenport (sic) is unidentified. He may have been an overseer of one of the Custis plantations. He might also have been a local merchant.

2. By early October the Bassett family had apparently returned to Eltham. For some reason not known to us, MW delayed setting out for her visit to Eltham. Most likely household responsibilities were the cause. She left Mount Vernon on October 17th, accompanied by Jackie and Nelly Custis, and intending to spend a few days in Fredricksburg, See, *Lund Washington to GW*, October 22, 1775, PGWR 2:219. Even before her departure, GW had requested her to join him at the camp at Cambridge, See, *GW to John Augustine Washington*, October 13, 1775, PGWR 2:162. Allowing six days for travel and visiting, she probably arrived at Eltham about October 24th. Just when she received her husband's invitation to join him is not known. We do know she tarried after receiving it. In a letter of November 5, 1776 to GW, Lund Washington states, "The Inclose'd I expect will inform you that Mrs Washington Intends to come to you - she informs me she will leave Colo. Bassetts tomorrow & lose no time in getg home where she will Stay but a few days, before she sets out for the Camp - I think her stay in New Kent so long after she had your invitation to come to you, was rather ill judge'd, & will I fear occasion her haveg a very desagreeable journey - I suppose one way or other she will make it near the 20th before she will set off - I will do all I can to get her off sooner if Possible," PGWR 2:304. Lund's chief concern for her comfort and safety was the coming of severe weather. Her stay at Eltham and vicinity was probably no longer than thirteen days.

To Elizabeth Ramsay

Dear Miss   Cambridge December the 30th 1775

I now sit down to tell you that I arrived hear safe,[1] and our party all well - we were fortunate in our time of setting out as the weather proved fine all the time we were on the road - I did not reach Philad till the tuesday after I left home, we were so attended and the gentlemen so kind, that I am lade under obligations to them that I shall not for get soon. I dont doubt but you have see the Figuer our arrival made in the Philadelphia paper - and I left it in as great pomp as if I had been a very great somebody

I have waited some days to collect something to tell, but allas there is nothing but what you will find in the papers - every person seems to be cheerfull and happy hear, - some days we have a number of cannon and shells from Boston and Bunkers Hill, but it does not seem to surprise any one but me; I confess I shudder every time I hear the sound of a gun - I have been to dinner with two of the Generals, Lee[2] and Putnam[3] and I just took a look at pore Boston & Charlstown - from prospect Hill Charlestown has only a few chimneys standing in it, thare seems to be a number of very fine Buildings in Boston but god knows how long they will stand; they are pulling up all the warfs for firewood - to me that never see any thing of war, the preparations, are very terable indeed, but I endever to keep my fears to myself as well as I can.

Your Friends Mr Harrison[4] & Henly[5] are boath very well and I think they are fatter than they were when they came to the Camp - and Capt Baylor[6] is as lusty man to what he was when you see him - the girls may rest sattisfied on Mr Harrisons account for he seems two fond of his country to give his heart to any but one of his virginia Friends, thare are but two young Laides in Cambridge, and a very great number of Gentlemen so you may gess how much is made of them - but neither of them is pretty I think,

This is a beautyfull country, and we had a very plasant journey through New england, and had the plasure to find the General very well we came within the month from home to the Camp

I see your Brother[7] at Princeton he was very well but did not talk of comeing home soon

Please to give my love and good wishes to your Mamma[8] & grandmamma,[9] Mr Ramsay and Family, my compliments to all enquiring Freinds, the good gentlemen that came with me up to Baltimore, and Mrs. Herbert[10] - in which the General and Mr & Mrs Custis' joins, please to remember me to Mr & Mrs McCarty[11] and Family

I am Dear Miss your most
affectionate

Friend and Servt

Martha Washington

(Address)

To

Miss Ramsay

In Alexandria

ALS, NNPM.

1. MW arrived in Philadelphia on November 21. To have arrived on that date she must have departed from Mount Vernon about November 16 or 17. After being extensively entertained, she departed from Philadelphia on November 28. She arrived at Cambridge on December 11. While in Cambridge she resided with GW at his headquarters in the former house of John Vassal, a Tory. It later became the home of Henry Wadsworth Longfellow.

2. Major-general Charles Lee (1731-1782) was a former British Army officer on half-pay. He had been commissioned the second major-general in the Continental Army on June 17, 1775. Throughout his adult life he was an eccentric and a controversial character. See, biographical sketch by Randolph Adams in DAB, 11:98-100.

3. Major-general Israel Putnam (1718-1790) of Connecticut. He took an active part in the Battle of Bunker Hill during the seige of Boston. He was a legendary figure and a popular leader.

4. Robert Hanson Harrison (1745-1790) was a native of Charles County, Maryland. He was an Alexandria lawyer who had done considerable legal work for GW. Harrison was given the rank of lieutenant-colonel and appointed aide-de-camp to GW on November 6, 1775. He acted as private secretary to the General from 1775 until 1781.

5. Unidentified.

6. George Baylor (1752-1784) was appointed Aide to the General in July 1775, on the recommendation of Edmund Pendleton, although his family was well known to Washington. He was sent by Washington to escort Mrs. Washington from Philadelphia to Cambridge. See, *Writings*, 4:123; *Freeman*, 3:522, 581.

7. William Ramsay, Jr., eldest son of William Ramsay. Washington paid £ 39 -9d to Dr. John Witherspoon, president of The College of New Jersey, for the schooling of young Ramsay. See, supra January 14, 1774, n. 4; Ledger B, folio 47, *The Papers of George Washington*, DLC:GW

8. Ann McCarty Ramsay, daughter of Dennis McCarty of "Cedar Grove," Fairfax County, and his wife, Sarah Ball. See, *Diaries*, 2:46 n.

9. Sarah Ball McCarty was distantly related to Washington through his mother, Mary Ball Washington. See *Diaries*, 2:166 n.

10. Sarah Carlyle Herbert, daughter of John Carlyle and his wife, Sarah Fairfax Carlyle. She married William Herbert, an Alexandria merchant. See, 3 *Diaries*, 3:154.

11. Daniel McCarty and his wife, Sarah Ball McCarty. Their residence, "Mount Air," was in the Pohick Creek area of Prince William County. They were close friends of the Washingtons and frequently visited and dined together. Both men were vestrymen of Truro Parish. They were also fox-hunting comrades. Washington was distantly related to both Daniel McCarty and his wife through the Ball family.

To Mercy Otis Warren

Cambridge, January the 8th 1776

Mrs. Washington presents her respectfull compliments to Mrs Warren,[1] and thanks her most cordially for her polite enquire, and exceeding kind offer - If the Exigency of affairs in this camp should make it necessary for her to remove, she cannot but esteem it a happiness to have so friendly an Invitation as Mrs Warren has given.[2] In the meanwhile, Mrs Washington cannot help wishing for an oppertunity of shewing every civility in her power to Mrs Warren, at Head Quarters in Cambridge -

The General begs that his best regards may be presented to Mrs Warren, accompanied with his sincear thanks for her favourable wishes for his honour and success; and joins in wishing Mrs Warren - the speaker[3] - and thair Family, every happiness that is, or can be derived from a speedy, and honourable peace

(address leaf)
To Mrs. Warren
at
Plymouth
(Docket)
Mrs Washington
Cambridge 8th Jany
1776

ALS (3rd person) MHi.

1. Mercy Otis Warren (1728-1814) was the wife of James Warren (see infra) and sister of the patriot-orator, James Otis. She was an historian, playwrite, poetess, and feminist. One of her most notable works was a history of the American Revolution. She carried on an extensive correspondence with many of the literary and political figures of her day.

2. The unsettled affairs at the Camp, occasioned by the formation of a new army to replace the one decimated by the expiration of enlistments, and the threat of British attack, prompted Mrs. Warren to invite Mrs. Washington to her home where she would be farther removed from danger.

3. James Warren (1726-1808) was a member of the Massachusetts Provincial Congress, and after the death of Dr. Joseph Warren at Bunker Hill, its President. Later he served as Speaker of the Massachusetts House of Representatives. During the Revolution he was paymaster of the Continental Army from 1776 until 1781.

To Anna Maria Bassett

My Dear Sister   Cambridge January the 31, 1776

I have wrote to you several times in hopes that would put you in mind of me but I find it has not had its intended affect and I am really very uneasy at not hearing from you and have made all the excuses for you that I can think of but it will not doe much longer if I doe not get a letter by this nights post I shall think myself quite forgot by all my Freinds The distance is long yet the post comes in very regularly every week --

The General myself and Jack are very well Nelly Custis is I hope getting well again, and I beleive is with child, I hope noe accident will happen to her in going back[1] I have not thought much about it yet god knows whare we shall be I suppose thare will be a change soon but how I cannot pretend to say - A few days a goe Gen. Clinton, with several companyes Sailed out of Boston Harbor to what place distant for, we cannot find out. some think it is to Virginia he is gon, others to New York[2] -they have been keept in Boston so long that I suppose they will be glad for a place where they may have more room as they cannot get out anyway here but by water - our navey has been very successful in taking thair vessels two was taken last week loded with coles and potatoes wines & several other articles for the use of the troops - If General Clinton is gon to New York, - General Lee is there before him and I hope will give him a very warm reception, - he was sent thare some time a goe to have matters put in proper order in case any disturbance should happen,[3] as thare are many Tories in that part of the world or at least many are susspected thare to be unfreindly to our cause at this time - winter hear has been so remarkable mild the Rivers has never been frozen hard enough to walk upon the Ice since I came heer, My Dear sister be so good as to remember me to all enquireing friends - give my Duty to my mam(ma) and love to my brothers and sisters Mr Bassett your Dear Children and self - in which the General Jack and Nelly joins me.

> I am my Dear Nancy
> your ever effectionate sister
> Martha Washington

(Address)
To Mrs. Bassett
at
Eltham
to ye care of
Randolph Esq
Feb 24, 1776
Recd last night
and (missing)

ALS, NjMoNP.

1. John Parke Custis and his wife, Eleanor, were preparing to leave Cambridge and return to Virginia. Eleanor was indeed pregnant.

2. Sir Henry Clinton was detached from Sir William Howe's force at Boston and sent south to open a campaign against the rebellion in the Carolinas. General Washington first became aware of Clinton's departure from Boston about January 20, 1776. See, *Writings*, 4:289; *PGWR* 3:171, n. 8.

3. Major-general Charles Lee was dispatched from the camp at Cambridge to New York in mid-January, 1776. *PGWR* 3:53.

To Mercy Otis Warren

Madam   Cambridge April the 2nd 1776
You may be assured that nothing would give the General, or me greater pleasure than to wait upon you at dinner this day, - but his time is so totally engrossed by applications from one department and another and (missing) - part in which last I am also concerned and busy - as indeed all the Family are - that it is not in any of our powers to accept your polite and friendly Invitation,[1] nor will it be in my power I am perswaded to thank you personally for the polite attention, you have shewn me since I came into this province, I must tharefore beg your acceptance of them in this way and at this time and that you will be assurd that I shall hold them in greatfull remembrance - I am desired by the General to offer you his sincear thanks for your kind wishes and present his Compliments along with Mr & Mrs Custis and my own to you and Colo Warren - with every Sentiment of esteem I am and shall remane to be

> Your much obliged Friend
> and Hble servant
> Martha Washington

To Mrs Warren
at
Watertown
Docket:
Mrs Washington
April 2d 1776

ALS, MHi.
1. Mrs. Washington was preparing to leave Cambridge for New York, following the evacuation of Boston by the British. General Washington arrived in New York on April 13, 1776. Mrs. Washington joined him on April 17th, having been delayed by the illness of John Parke Custis. In New York they occupied the house of Abraham Motier, paymaster of the British army. It was located at what is now the corner of Varick and Charlton Streets. See, *Freeman*, 4:89, 635; *New York Gazette and Weekly Mercury*, April 16 and April 22, 1776.

From John Parke Custis

My dear Mamma   Mount Airy June 9th. 1776
The receipt of your kind Letter by Mr Ross, and the Generals by Post, gave Me the sincerest pleasure to hear You were in so fair a Way of getting faverably through the Smalpox:[1] - the smal Danger attending that Disorder by Innoculation when the patients follow the Directions of their Phycian, has releived Me from much Anxiety, which I doubt less should have felt on the Innoculation of so dear a Mother: - I do with the truest affection congratulate you on and thank God for your recovery - I should

have wrote by Mr Nelson[2] but the Want of Time, and Gile's[3] returning so soon prevented Me, I could only have told you we well had I wrote, which he promised to inform you off - I propose leaving this Place for Williamsburg next Tuesday. I shall stay a Day at Mt Vernon and return as soon as I finish my Business, to be present at a certain Occasion which I beleive is not far distant, as soon as the Lady recovers I shall carry Her to Virginia, as the Family here is rather too Large for ye House, and I beleive the Province of Maryd. will shortly be in a State of the greatest Confusion; the People being much discontented with their convention; and Mr. Calvert[4] takes a Part which I fear will involve Him in many Troubles - Govr Eden[5] sails for England in a few Days, or goes on board a man of War, there are many Tories who would go with Him most willingly, but I hear He has absolutely refused to carry them with Him - It will always give me the greatest Pleasure to hear from you, as I shall Neglect no Opportunity of Writeing you

> I am dr Mamma yr. mst
> affecte. Son
> John Parke Custis

Paper is very scarce

To Mrs Washington
To
Mrs Washington
at Mr. Randolphs[6]
Philadelphia

ALS, ViMtV.

1. In a letter to John Augustine Washington, April 28, 1776, General Washington stated Mrs. Washington was considering being innoculated for small-pox, but doubted her "resolution." *Writings*, 4:529. According to Freeman, Mrs. Washington accompanied her husband on his visit to Philadelphia from May 21st until June 4th. He arrived in Philadelphia on the afternoon of May 23rd. This would indicate she did not travel with him, but separately. It would seem unlikely he would allow her to travel without him, at a time almost identical to his. Freeman may seem equivocal in this, since he states she arrived not later than May 18th, May 31st being the thirteenth day of her successful innoculation. *Writings*, 5:93. Their living quarters in Philadelphia is not known. After consultations with Congress, the General left the city on June 4th and arrived in New York on June 6th. *Writings*, 5:103. Freeman states Mrs. Washington recovered completely from her innoculation and had returned to New York, probably during the week of June 16th. *Freeman*, 4:129 n. He later doubted she ever returned to New York. *Freeman*, 4:635. Joseph Reed stated in a letter to Mrs. Reed, "Mrs. Washington and the other ladies are gone from here, (Reed Papers, N-Y HS), *Writings*, 5:327. In a letter to John Augustine Washington, July 22, 1776, General Washington stated Mrs. Washington was at Philadelphia and has "thoughts of returning to Virginia as there is little or no prospects of her being with me any part of the summer." *Writings*, 5:327. Mrs. Washington, however, was still in Philadelphia on August 28. See, infra, letter to Anna Maria Bassett on that date.

2. Thomas Nelson, Jr. (1738-1789), member of the Virginia House of Burgesses, of the Council. Nelson introduced the motion for independence in the Virginia Convention of

1776, and signed the Declaration of Independence. Ill health forced him to return to Virginia early in 1777. Later he became a brigadier-general of the militia and Governor of Virginia.

3. Giles was a slave belonging to the Washingtons. He served as a messenger, as well as coachman and postilion.

4. Benedict Calvert (c. 1724-1788) also known as Benedict Swingate, was the natural son of Charles Calvert, fifth Lord Baltimore. After being acknowledged by Lord Baltimore, he took the Calvert name. His wife was Elizabeth Calvert a distant relative. Their daughter, Eleanor, married John Parke Custis.

5. Governor Robert Eden (1741-1784), colonial governor of Maryland. His wife was Caroline Calvert, sister of Lord Baltimore, Proprietor of Maryland. He made efforts to ameliorate the difficulties between the province and the crown, but was unsuccessful. Forced to leave Maryland in June, 1776, he returned to England.

6. Randolph operated a tavern on Chestnut Street, Philadelphia.

From John Parke Custis

My dearest Mamma   Mount Airy August 21st. 1776

I have the extreme Happiness at last to inform you, that Nelly was safely delivered this Morning about five oClock of a fine Daughter; [1] and It affords Me much Pleasure that I have an Opportunity of transmitting this agreable News so early, I make not the least Doubt but you will heartily join us in the Pleasure We feel on this Happy Event; I wish you were present. You would be much more pleased, if you were to see the strapping Huzze. The other little One was a mere Dwarf to this, Her Cloths are already too smal for Her. She is in short as fine a Healthy, fat Baby as ever was born;[2]

Poor Nelly had a very indefferent Time, her Pains were two Hours long & very severe. She is now thank God as well as can be expected and the Pleasure her Daughter gives Her. compensates for the Pain She has suffered. She has been fortunate in the Weather. It is now very fine, for ten Days last past We have had nothing but Rainy close Weather, - I cannot pretend to say who the child is like, It is as much like Doctor Rumney[3] as any Body else. She has a double Chinn something like His, in Point of Fatness with fine black Hair, & Eyes, upon the whole I think It is as pretty & fine a Baba as ever I saw. This not my opinion alone, but the Opinion of all who have seen Her - I hope she will be preserv'd as a Comfort, and Happiness to us all.

I have been for some Time past in the state of the greatest Anxiety for the Fate of New York, I confess It has engaged my Thoughts so much, that I have not been able to do Anything, my first Wish was to see Nelly safely delivered, my second (has always been) that the General may obtain a compleat Victory over his Enemys, which I sincerely pray God may be the Case. - I am kept in the cruelest State of Uncertainty. I have scarcely had a Letter from New York, the Gen has been much kinder than I expected, but the others have very seldom wrote, - I must beg of you to write me everything you can collect relative to the Army at New York & in Canada, and all other News, by every Post - You may get much Intelligence from Colo. Nelson[4] - I am sorry I have Nothing to inform you off, Every Thing being quiet (which is I think the best News) since Dunmore[5] left Us - Mr. Calvert's John is just return'd from Annapolis. It is reported & sworn to by Two Deserters, that Dunmore is dead of the Flux (I wish it may be true.)[16] I wrote to the General the last two Posts. I shall write you again next Post, and ask Him to stand with yourself for my little Lady. My Love to Him in which Nelly joins Me. Nelly, the little Lady & Myself write in Love to you

> and am dear Mamma your
> most affectionate Son
> John Parke Custis

The Family send their
Comp to Nelly's & mine
to Mr. Nelson & Lady & Mr Pleion.[6]
For Mrs Washington
in Philadelphia
Upper Marlbo Augt 23d

ALS, ViMtV.

1. Elizabeth Parke Custis (1776-1832), was born August 21, 1776.

2. A child previously born to the couple in September, 1775, had died shortly after birth. See supra, Christian Scott Blackburn to Martha Washington, September 26, 1775, n. 1.

3. Dr. William Rumney was a native of England and had served with the British army during the French and Indian War. He remained in America and settled in Alexandria in 1763. He treated various members of the Mount Vernon family over a period of years. *Diaries*, 2:31.

4. Governor John Dunmore and his family boarded the British warship, Fowey, at Yorktown, June 1, 1775. His British military forces were defeated at Great Bridge in December 1775, again forcing him to retire to a warship. Once again Dunmore's assault was repulsed at Gwynne's Island, Virginia in July, 1776. Several attempts to land a military force on St. George's Island, Maryland were repulsed by the local militia, and he then sailed for England. Rumors of his death were unfounded. In the summer of 1775 a belief persisted that he intended to sail up the Potomac and capture Mrs. Washington, but nothing came of it. Despite his early popularity in Virginia, he turned out to be cruel, vindictive, and dangerous. Eckenrode, *The Revolution in Virginia*, Boston, 1916, p. 54, 95. Selby, *The Revolution in Virginia, 1775-1783*, Williamsburg, p. 55-80, 1988.

5. Emanuel de Plearne, a merchant of Nantes. Together with Pierre Penet, they were the first to furnish supplies for the American army from abroad. See: *Writings*, 4:159 n.

To Anna Maria Dandridge Bassett

My dear Sister   Philadelphia August the 28th 1776
    I am still in this town and Noe prospects at present of my leveing it, - the General is at new york he is very well and wrote to me yesterday and informed me that Lord Dunmore with part of his fleet was come to General Howe at Staten Island, that another devision of the Hessians is expected before they think, the regulars will begen thare attack or as, some hear begen to think thare will be noe Battle after all - Last week our boats made another atempt on the ships up the north river - and had grapp a fire ship with the Phoenix ten muniets but she got clear of her; and is come down the river on satterday last. Our people burnt one of the tenders.[1]
    I thank god we shant want men - the army at New York is very large and numbers of men are still going there is at this time in the city, four thousand on their march to the camp and virginia is daily Expected[2] - I doe my Dear sister most releigiously wish thare was an End to the matter that we might have the pleasure of meeting again -
    My Duty to my Dear mamma - and tell her I am very well - I dont hear from you so often as I used to doe at Cambridge - I had the pleasure to hear by Colo Aylett[3] that you and all Friends were well and should been glad to have had a line from you by him - I hope Mr Bassett has got the better of his cough long agoe - please to present love to him my Brother and sisters my dear Fanny and the Boy[4] & Except the same yourself

> I am my dear Nancy your
> ever affectionate sister
> Martha Washington

ALS, NN.

1. On July 12th the British ships, Phoenix of 40 guns, the Rose of 20 guns, and three tenders, were sent up the Hudson River to cut off supplies coming down the river for the Continental Army in New York City. General George Clinton was ordered to form a chain of craft at The Narrows at Fort Constitution, to serve as fire boats. The British ships proceeded up river forty miles to Haverstraw Bay. There a landing was attempted but was repulsed. Nevertheless, all water connections with Albany were cut, the British ships being too far out in the river to sustain serious damage from shore batteries. On July 26th they dropped down river eight or ten miles. On August 3rd they were attacked by Connecticut and Rhode Island galleys and moderate damage was inflicted. On August 16th two fire vessels succeeded in burning one of the British tenders. Another was grappled to the Phoenix for about ten minutes but was cut free. *Writings*, 4:446. On August 18th the Phoenix and Rose rejoined the main British fleet off Staten Island. *Writings*, 4:452.

2. Sir William Howe had about 20,000 effective rank and file available for the attack on New York. On August 7th Washington declared he had 10,514 men fit for duty. *Writings*, 5:390. By August 19th enough militia had arrived to bring his force to about 23,000 men. *Writings*, 5:457.

3. William Aylett (1743-1781) was deputy commissary for the Continental Army. He died of "camp fever" at Yorktown. A brother, John, was the first husband of Mrs. Washington's younger sister, Elizabeth. *Diaries*, 2:108.

4. Frances Bassett (1767-1796), and John Bassett (1765-1822).

To Lund Washington

Sir October the 23d 1776
Please to give to Milly Posey, the sum of five pounds Virginia money

I am your most Hble Sert
Martha Washington

To Mr Lund Washington[1]
Recd. the above sum
Amelia Posey

ALS Location unknown. From a facsimile in Thomas Birch Sons catalogue, No. 663, item 139.

1. Lund Washington (1732-1796) was a great grandson of Lawrence Washington. Lawrence's brother, John, was the great grandfather of the General. Lund Washington was manager of Mount Vernon during the General's absence during the Revolution and for several years thereafter.

To Joseph Reed

Sir[1] Morristown Ju(ne)
The very polite and obliging invitation to lodge with you, contained in your favor of the 12th inst - came to my hands yesterday - I beg you to be perswaded sir that I should accept it with much pleasure did I not conceive myself under an engagement to Mr Petit,[2] who was pleased when he was here to request me to make use of his house while I stayed in Phila which will not exceed 3 or 4 days - and for which place I shall leve this tomorrow

It gives me much plasure to hear of Mrs Reeds recovery and that she is in a (situa)tion to receive company down (missing) my greatful thanks and best wishes attend her and you (missing)

I am sir
Your most obedt and
obliged
Martha Washington

(Docket)
Morristown 1777
Mrs Washington to
Mr Reed.
Morristown

ALS Location unknown. Formerly in the collection of the editor.

1. Joseph Reed (1741-1785) was a native of Trenton, N.J. He studied law under Richard Stockton and at the Middle Temple. Reed served as President of the 2nd Provincial Congress in Philadelphia. He was an intimate friend of General Washington, served as his military secretary and adjutant. He was present at the battles of Brandywine, Germantown, and

Monmouth. From 1778 until 1781 he was President of the Supreme Executive Council of Pennsylvania.

2. Charles Pettit (1736-1806) was a Philadelphia merchant. He was assistant quartermaster-general of the Continental Army from 1778 until 1781, and a member of the Continental Congress. He was a brother-in-law of Joseph Reed. See, supra, n. 1.

To Anna Maria Dandridge Bassett

My Dear Sister   November the 18th 1777
    I have the very great pleasure of returning, - you your Boys[1] as well as they were when I brought them from Eltham - They have had the small pox exeeding light and have been perfectly well this fortnight past- Mr. Claiborne[2] came up with us and had the small as light as they had, he has been here ever since I came up - his going down determined me to send your sons with him as I think he will be a guide to them on the road and better than they should goe so far by themselves, they have been exeeding good Boys indeed and I shall hope you will lett them come to see me when ever they can spare so much time from school - they have been such good Boy that I shall love them a great deal more than I ever did - I have paid the Doctors £ 9 for them. - and £ 8 for two Hatts (?) which could not be got for less (?) 9/9
    I have given to Mr. Claiborne to bare thare expens down - and five seven Dollar Bills I inclose in this letter which is all that is owed - the Doctor's charge is very high but I did not say a word - as he carred the children so well through the small pox -
    The last letter I had from the General was dated the 7th of this month - he says he says nothing hath happend since the unsuccessful attack upon our forts on the Dalaware, - the Boys bring the last papers down with them -
    Nelly Custis has be over the river this three week - Jack is just come over, he tells me that little Bet is grown as fat as a pigg - Nelly is not well her self -
    I was glad to hear that you had got the horse and hope you have before this found great benefet from riding everyday - I have often wished for my dear sister and Fanny, as the small pox was so trifleing with the Boys - believed that it would have been as slight with them I have had all thare cloths washed and rinsed several days - and do veryly believe that they can bring no infection home with them - if you are afraide lett some one who has had the small pox put out thare cloths to air for a day or two in the sun - an Thomas has also been washed and his cloths changed - his cap & shoes he did not ware, when he was sick - I shall be glad you will let me know how the Boys gett down - by Peter who set off today with Jacks mares & colts to carry them down to his quarter in New Kent -

Jack joins me in love to Mr. Bassett your self Dear Fanny and all Friends - I am my Dear sister your sincearly affectionate

Martha Washington

I was sorry to find that I had given away all the Blew satin but this piece Please do give the piece of muslin to Mrs Dangerfield[3] with my Compliments - my compliments and good wishes to Mrs Davis[4] & Mrs Newman[5] - I hope John Davis has got well of his indisposition - all the Boys Cloths are sent

ALS, ViMtV.

1. Burwell Bassett, Jr. (1764-1841) and John Bassett (1766-1826).

2. One of the numerous Claibornes who lived in the vicinity of Eltham.

3. Probably Hannah Daingerfield of New Kent County. See, *Harris*, 1:59.

4. Elizabeth Davies, wife of Pryce Davies, rector of Blissland Parish, New Kent County, from 1763 until 1786. She was first married to Rev. Chickley Corbin Thacker, rector of Warreneye Church, Blissland Parish, who officiated at the marriage of Martha and Daniel Parke Custis. *Harris*, 1:26, 86.

5. A Mrs. Newman was an occasional visitor at Mount Vernon. *Diaries*, 3:297-98, 303.

To Burwell Bassett

My Dear Sir   Mount Vernon December 22d 1777

I doe most sincerely lement and condole with you, on the loss of our dear departed Friend[1] she has I hope made a happy exchange - and only gon a little before us the time draws near when I hope we shall meet never more to part - if to meet our departed Friends and know them was scertain we could have very little reason to desire to stay in this world where if we are at ease one hour we are in affliction days

Lett me beg of you my Dear Brother to consider your one indisposition and indevor to be a comfort to your friends that are now about you - nothing in this world do I wish for more sincerly than to be with, but alass I am so situated at this time that I cannot leve home - my dear sister in her life time often mentioned my taking my dear Fanny[2] if she should be taken away before she grew up - If you will lett her come to live with me, I will with the greatest plasure take her and be a parent and mother to her as long as I live - and will come down for her as soon as I come from the northward, - the General has wrote to me that he cannot come home this winter but as soon as the army under his command goes into winter quarter he will send for me, if he does I must go, if he does not, I will come down as soon as Nelly Custis gets well she is hear and Expect every day to be brought to bed[3] - is the reason I cannot come down at this time - my Dear sister for the last three or four years of her life could have but very little pleasure her health was such that must render her life a misere to herself and a very great affliction to her friends

- which I hope will in some measure reconcile you to your very great loss of her, - I must one to you that she was the greatest favorite I had in the world - it will always give me the greatest pleasure, if I could be usefull to you or the children in any thing - be pleased to let me know - I have often wished that fortune had plased us nearer to each other - and particularly at this time when I should have it in my power to take care of the Dear children - I hope Mrs Stith[4] or Mrs Aylett[5] will stay with you for that purpose at least for a sort time - I sincearly wish your recovery and pray god to enable you to support yourself under your great affliction - and bless your children - I am with love to them and all inquiring Friends

> My Dear Brother your ever
> affectionate
> Martha Washington

ALS, PPRF.

1. Anna Maria Dandridge Bassett, Mrs. Washington's sister, died at Eltham, December 17, 1777.

2. Nelly Custis was far advanced in her pregnancy. She delivered her third daughter, Martha Parke Custis on December 31, 1777. Her first daughter died shortly after her birth.

3. Frances (Fanny) Bassett (1767-1796) came to live at Mount Vernon in 1784. There she met a widower, Major George Augustine Washington, nephew of General Washington and acting as manager of the estates. They were married on October 15, 1785. After his death in 1793 she married Tobias Lear, secretary to the General, during as well as after the presidential years. They were married early in August, 1795. Fanny died in late March, 1796. Most of Mrs. Washington's surviving correspondence was with Fanny Bassett Washington Lear.

4. Probably Joanna Stith, sister of Burwell Bassett, Sr. *Harris*, 1:45.

5. Mary Macon Aylett, wife of Col. William Aylett of Fairfield.

To -

I had nothing but kindness everywhere on my journey. The travelling was pretty rough. I found snow in crossing Delaware, and at an inn on Brandywine Creek, at a ford, where I lodged, the snow was so deep in the roads in some places, that I had to leave the chariot with the innkeeper and hire a farm sleigh to bring me here. The General is well, but much worn with fatique and anxiety. I never knew him to be so anxious as now, for the poor soldiers are without sufficient clothing and food, and many of them are barefooted. Oh how my heart pains for them.[1]

Text taken from Lossing's *Mary and Martha*, p. 165.

1. Lossing states the letter was written shortly after Mrs. Washington's arrival at headquarters at Whitemarsh, and after the British raid on December 7, 1777. He cites G.W.P. Custis as his authority. There is no evidence that Mrs. Washington was ever at the Whitemarsh headquarters. In December, 1777 she was still in Virginia and did not arrive at Valley Forge until February 2nd or 3rd, 1778. See infra, letter of MW to Mercy Otis Warren, March 7, 1778. In a letter from GW to John Parke Custis, February 1, 1778 he states Mrs. Washington left Mount Vernon January 26, 1778; *Writings*, 10:414 and n. If this is an authentic

letter, then it has been extensively edited. If based on an authentic letter it may have been written from Valley Forge.

To -

The general's head-quarters have been made more tolerable by the addition of a log-cabin to the house, built to dine in. The apartment for business is only about sixteen feet square, and has a large fireplace. The house is built of stone. The walls are very thick, and below a deep east window, out of which the general can look upon the encampment, he had a box made, which appears as a part of the casement, with a blind trap door at top, in which he keeps his valuable papers.[1]

Text taken from Lossing's *Mary and Martha*, p. 171-72.

1. Lossing states the letter was addressed to Mrs. Lund Washington, but nowhere gives his authority. The statement is inaccurate, since Lund Washington did not marry until 1782. In view of the risk of capture of the mail and the close proximity of British patrols it is unlikely Mrs. Washington would put this information on a piece of paper. If the letter is authentic, it has again been extensively edited. See, *Virginia Magazine of History and Biography*, 33:160. Hereafter cited as VMHB. *Writings*, 27:187.

To Mercy Otis Warren

Dear Madam   Valley forge March the 7th 1778
    I am now to thank you for the two very kind Letters which you have been pleased to favor me with. - the one written some time Last summer, and the other by Mr Bowdoin.[1] It gave me a peculiar pleasure to hear by the gentleman that you and Genl Warren enjoyd good health - and this pleasure was not a little increased by hearing from yourself that you are so very happy in your state - noe traces of the enemy being left; but on the other hand, plenty of every thing usefull and necessary to be percured - indeed I think providence was very bountifull in her goodness to your state: even when the enemy was in it, we found then every article in plenty, and full sufficient for the use of the army - in virginia we have no British troops since the cruel Dunmore left us - but how soon we shall, is not at this time known; I hope, and trust, that all the states will make a vigorous push early this spring, if every thing can be prepard for it, and thereby putting a stop to British cruelties - and afford us that peace liberty and happyness which we have so long contended for -
    It has given me unspeakable pleasure to hear that Genl Burgoyne and his army air in safe quarters in your state[2] -would bountifull providence aim a like stroke at Genl Howe,[3] the measure of my happyness would be compleat
    I came to this place about the first of February whare I found the General very well - I left my Children at our House - Mrs Custis has lately

had a fine girl,[4] which makes the second since she left Cambridge; she is so much confined with her children, that she stays altogather with them

I left Mr Bowdoin in Alexandria he was a good deal distressed on account of Mr Blairne[5] a french gentleman his partener - who was by accident drowned crossing the Potomack river; his Body was not found when I left home; his behavour and agreeable manners, rendered him a favourite with all that know him, and caused his death to be much lamented

The General is in camped in what is called the great Valley on the Banks of the Schuykill officers and men are cheifly in Hutts, which they say is tolarable comfortable; the army are as healthy as can well be expected in general - the Generals appartment is very small he has had a log cabben built to dine in which has made our quarter much more tolarable than they were at first.

It would give me plasure to deliver your compliments to Mrs. Gates,[6] but she lives at so great a distance from me that I have not seen her since we parted at Newport two years agoe; the General joins me in offering our respectfull compliments to Genl Warren and yourself. -

> I am Dr Madam with esteem
> your affectionate Friend and
> very Hble servt
> Martha Washington

ALS, MHi.

1. James Bowdoin (1726-1792) was a wealthy merchant of Boston. He was influential in the establishment of constitutional government and served as governor from 1785-1787.

2. Major-general John Burgoyne (1722-1792) had an illustrious career in the British Army. He arrived in Boston on May 25, 1775, with Generals Sir William Howe and Sir Henry Clinton. Following his defeat at the Battle of Saratoga in 1777, he and his army were held prisoner in western Massachusetts while awaiting exchange. He was also author, playwrite, and Member of Parliament.

3. Sir William Howe was appointed Major-general in 1772 and became Commander-in-Chief of the British Army in America in April 1776.

4. Martha Parke Custis, born December 31, 1777.

5. Emanuel de Pliarne was drowned while attempting to cross the Potomac River near Georgetown, Maryland. See supra, August 21, 1776; *Writings*, 3:159 n.

6. Elizabeth Phillips Gates (? - 1784), the first wife of General Horatio Gates.

From John Parke Custis

Hond. Madam   Mt Airy[1] April 3d, 78

My Long Letter last Post has left me very little to say this Post. I have however the Pleasure to inform you that we continue well. poor little Pat[2] has been innoculated three Times, and has not taken the Infection.[3] this leaves Us in a very disagreable Suspence, as We shall be very uneasy lest She should get the Disorder in the natural Way, the Doctor is much at a loss how to account for her not taking the Infection, unless Nelly[4] was with child when she was innoculated, and this can hardly be the Case. I shall wait some Time before I try a fourth time. I sincerely hope no Accident will happen to the dear Child. She has grown the finest Girl I ever saw and the most Good natured Quiet little Creature in the World. You took the advantage of Me to ask for her just after my Disappointment. I do not know how to comply for I could not have loved It better if It had been a Boy. Ms Bet[5] has grown very much, and is very saucy and entertaining. She can say any Word but Washington.

I left Mt Vernon last Tuesday all the Family were well. the only news I heard were the Deaths of Nancy Whiteing[6] & Miss Sally Fairfax[7]. the Former died in childbed - I should have sett off this Day Eltham but the Wind blows so hard I can't cross the River. The Election comes the ninth which oblidged me to make all the Haste in my Power, you must remember to set cross leg'd that Day for me.[8] - I must beg of you to write Me every Week, and be sure to send Me all the news while you stay at Camp, if you are too much ingaged, see that Gibbs[9] and Mead[10], I know they are generally idle - write you can now and then inclose a newspaper when there is any thing Particular in them, you will please to take Care of Doctor Craiks[11] Letter. I was at a Loss where to direct to him. My Affecte Regards to the General. I would have Wrote to Him, but the Want of some thing Agreable to communicate prevented me. I will do myself the Pleasure to write him from Belop[12] and inform him of all the News there. I return Him many Thanks for his Letter of the 1st of which got to my Hands on Tuesday last.[13] My Compts to the Gentlemen - Nelly joins in Love to the Genl and Self and in wishing for your every Happiness

> I am Hon'd Madam Yr. most
> Affecte Son
> J.P.Custis

Mrs Washington

ALS, DTP.

1. Mount Airy, Prince George's County, Maryland, was the home of Benedict Calvert (1742-1788), the father of Eleanor Calvert Custis.

2. Martha Parke Custis (1777-1854), second daughter of John Parke Custis and his wife, Eleanor Calvert Custis. She later married Thomas Peter.

3. Custis here refers to the child's inability to contract the cow-pox following innoculation, which would render her immune to small-pox, a far deadlier disease. Apparently the child had a natural immunity.

4. "Nelly," refers to Eleanor Calvert Custis, the baby's mother.

5. Elizabeth (Eliza) Parke Custis (1776-1832) was the eldest child of John Parke Custis and Eleanor Parke Custis. She later married Thomas Law.

6. Ann (Nancy) Whiting (1761-1778), daughter of Col. John Carlyle and his first wife, Sarah Fairfax Carlyle. She wed Henry Whiting, son of Francis Whiting. She died with the birth of her first child, Carlyle Fairfax Whiting.

7. Sally Cary Fairfax was the eldest child of Bryan Fairfax (1732-1802) and his first wife, Elizabeth Cary Fairfax (1738-1788). She died unmarried.

8. John Parke Custis was elected as a delegate from Fairfax County to the Virginia General Assembly. His fellow delegate was George Mason. The sessions were from May 4 - June 1, 1778, and from October 5 - December 19, 1788. See, *The General Assembly of Virginia, 1619-1978. A Bicentennial Register of Members*, Virginia State Library, Richmond, 1978., p. 129.

9. Caleb Gibbs (1748-1818) served as adjutant of the 21st and 14th regiments of the Continental Infantry. He was appointed captain in command of General Washington's guard, March 12, 1776 and aide and secretary to the General on May 16, 1776. Obviously Custis met him while staying at headquarters in Cambridge during the winter of 1775-76.

10. Richard Kidder Meade (1746-1805), a native of Nansemond County, Virginia, joined the patriot cause at the very beginning of the conflict. He served with the General throughout all his campaigns and was appointed aide on January 12, 1777. He may have known Custis in Virginia. He was the father of Bishop William Meade, third Episcopal bishop of Virginia.

11. Dr. James Craik (1730-1814), a native of Scotland, served with the General at the Great Meadows in 1754 and at Braddock's defeat in 1755. He served throughout the Revolution in various medical capacities. When war with France was threatened in 1798 General Washington insisted Craik be appointed Physician-general. He was a long-time intimate friend and companion in arms of the General. It is the editor's opinion that no one except Mrs. Washington knew him better. Craik was one of the physicians who attended GW during his final illness.

12. Unidentified.

13. The letter has not survived.

To Bartholomew Dandridge

Dear Brother   November the 2d 1778[1]

I received your kind favor by Mr. Posey[2] and should have wrote to you long before this but have everyday expected everyday Jack would be ready to set out, I am very sorry to hear that my Mamma has been so unwell and thank god that she has recovered again -- I wish I was near enough to come to see you and her.[4] I am very uneasy at this time - I have some reason to expect that I shall take another trip to the northward.[4] The pore General is not likely to come to see us from what I can hear - I expect to hear seertainly by the next post - if I doe I shall write to you to inform you and my friends-if I am so happy to stay at home. I shall hope to see you with my sister hear as soon as you are at leasure. Please to give little Patty a Kiss for me I have sent her a pair of shoes-there was not a Doll to be got in the city of Philadelphia or I would have sent her one (the shoes are in a bundle for my mama).

I am very glad to hear that you and your family are well - Jack can tell you more news than I can. I have had no letter since he came from the camp - by some (illegible) of the postmasters my letters doe (not) come regularly to hand.

I am with my Duty to my mamma my Love to my sister Aylett[5] my sister[6] and Family my Dear Brother

Your ever affectionate
Martha Washington

ALS, ViMtV.

1. On this date Mrs. Washington was at Mount Vernon.

2. John Price Posey, overseer of the Pamunkey River estates of the Custis family. He was the son of John Posey and brother of Milly Posey. He later became a notorious character. For his tragic ending that still has modern-day repercussions, See, *Harris,* 1:97. Also see, Posey, "The Improvident Ferryman of Mount Vernon," *Virginia Cavalcade,* 39:36.

3. Frances Dandridge was living with her son, Bartholomew, at "Pamocra," New Kent County. *Harris,* 1:83.

4. Mrs. Washington left Mount Vernon early in November, 1778. There was considerable apprehension concerning the journey, because of the poor roads, bad weather, and an indifferent coach. On December 17th the General wrote Lund Washington from Middlebrook, New Jersey, that he had learned of her safe arrival in Philadelphia. He later informed John Parke Custis that his mother was well and with him in Philadelphia. They left Philadelphia on February 2, 1779, and reached Middlebrook on February 5th. She remained at Middlebrook until early in June, when she returned to Virginia. The General broke camp and left for the Highlands of the Hudson on June 4, 1779. See, *Writings,* 13:407, 478; 14:68 n.; 15:225, 315.

5. Elizabeth (Betcy) Dandridge. She married, (1) John Aylett in 1773; (2) Leonard Henley in 1779.

6. Mary Burbidge Dandridge.

To John Parke and Eleanor Custis

My Dear Children   Middle Brook March the 19th 1778 (sic)[1]
    Not having received any letter from you, the two last posts - I have only to tell you, that the general & my self are well, all is quiet in this quarters; It is from the south ward that we expect to hear news, - we are very anxious to know how our affairs are going in that quarters Colo Harrison[2] is not yet arrived at camp we have heard that he is in Philad several days ago -
    I hear so very seldom from you, that I dont know where you are or weather you intend to come to Alexandria to live this spring or when[3] - The last letter from Nelly she now says Boath the children have been very ill, they were she hoped getting better - if you doe not write to me - I will not write to you again or till I get letters from you - Let me know how all friends below are they have for got to write me I believe
    Remember me to all inquireing friends give the dear little girls a kiss for me, and tell Beth[4] I have got a pritty new doll for her - the general joins me in love to you Boath - and begs to be remembered to all our friends that enquire after us

> I am with sincear love
> your truly affectionate
> mother
> Martha Washington

ALS, ViMtV.

1. Mrs. Washington erred on the date. She spent the winter of 1778 at Valley Forge. On

this date in 1779 she was with the General at Middlebrook. See, *Writings*, 11:63; 14:221.

2. Robert Hanson Harrison, secretary and aide to General Washington. See supra, December 30, 1775, n. 4.

3. In 1778 John Parke Custis purchased "Abingdon," along with 900 acres of land, from Robert Alexander. It was situated on the west bank of the Potomac River, north of Four Mile Run (Washington National Airport presently occupies the site). The Custises lived there in proximity to Mount Airy and Mount Vernon. After JPC's death in 1781, his widow, Eleanor, continued to live there until her marriage to Dr. David Stuart. For the disposition of the property, see, *Diaries*, 4:101; 5:291; *Writings*, 12:266-269; 27:60. The house is no longer standing.

4. Elizabeth Parke Custis, Mrs. Washington's eldest grandchild.

To Mrs. John Parke Custis

(Middlebrook, May 15, 1779)

Yesterday I saw the funniest, at the same time the most ridiculous review of the troops I ever heard of. Nearly all the troops were drawn up in order, and Mrs Knox,[1] Mrs Greene,[2] and myself saw the whole performance from a carriage. The General and Billy,[3] followed by a lot of mounted savages, rode along the line. Some of the Indians were fairly fine-looking, but most of them appeared worse than Falstaff's gang. And such horses and trappings! The General says it was done to keep the Indians friendly toward us. They appeared like cutthroats all.[4]

Location of original unknown.

1. Lucy Flucker Knox (c.1754-1824), wife of General Henry Knox.

2. Catherine Littlefield Greene (1755-1814), wife of General Nathanael Greene.

3. Billy Lee was the General's mulatto body servant. The General purchased him from Mrs. Mary Lee in 1768 for £ 61/15 s. He had assumed the surname, Lee. He accompanied the General throughout the war. By the terms of the General's will he was manumitted, given an annuity, food and clothing for life. See, *Diaries*, 2:278; Prussing, *The Estate of George Washington Deceased*, p. 45; Boston, 1927.

4. From Lossing, *Mary and Martha*, p. 85. The letter, if authentic, has undergone editing. The Delaware Chiefs, on their way to Philadelphia, stopped at Middlebrook on May 12, 1779, and were recipients of a speech by General Washington. *Writings*, 15:53; Thacher, *Military Journal*, p. 163, Hartford, 1862.

To Elizabeth Schuyler

(Morristown 1780)

Mrs Washington presents her best respects to Miss Schuyler.[1] She sends her some nice powder, which she hopes will be acceptable to her. She is much obliged to Miss Schuyler for her cuffs and thinks them very pretty.[2]

A.L. (3rd person) Unlocated.

1. Elizabeth Schuyler, second daughter of General Philip Schuyler. She married Colonel Alexander Hamilton in December, 1780.

2. The note was offered for sale by the Walter R. Benjamin Company. The text is taken

from *The Collector*, 56:149, n. 10. Accompanying the note was a letter dated April 20, 1880, from George L. Schuyler to Mrs. Martin Van Buren, in which he identifies the letter and states it had been written to his aunt by Mrs. Washington.

To Colonel Samuel Blatchley Webb

Morristown May 1780

Mrs Washington presents her compliments to Colo Webb[1] and thanks him for his polite invitation; but She will not have it in her power to wait upon him.[2]

To
Colo Webb
(Docket)
Mrs Washingtons Billet
Morristown May 1780

An (3rd person) CtY.

1. Samuel Blatchley Webb (1753-1807), a stepson of Silas Deane, was appointed Lieutenant-colonel and secretary to General Washington. He participated in the battle for Long Island, White Plains, Trenton, and Princeton. In 1783 Webb was breveted a brigadier-general.

2. The note is in the hand of a secretary, but the address leaf is in the handwriting of Mrs. Washington.

To Burwell Bassett

Dear Sir   Mount Vernon July the 18th 1780

When yours and my dear Fannys[1] letters came to my hands - I was in expectation of leving Camp every week - I left the General about the Middle of June - the last I heard from him he was going up the North river - I got home on Fryday and find myself so much fatique with my ride that I shall not be able to come down to see you this summer and must request you to bring Fanny up - as soon as you can - I suffered so much last winter by going late that I have determined to go early in the fall before the Frost set in - if Fanny does not come soon she will have but a short time to stay with me - we were sorry that we did not see you at the Camp - there was not much pleasure thar the distress of the army and other difficultys th'o I did not know the cause, the pore General was so unhappy that it distressed me exceedingly

I shall hope to see you soon after the assembly rises, with Fanny - please to give my love to her and the Boys who I should be very glad to see with you - my compliments to Mrs Dangerfield Mr & Mrs Davis[2] and all Friends - I am dr Sir your affectionate friend & hmble sert

Martha Washington

ALS, NjMoNP.

1. Frances Bassett Washington (1767-1796), only daughter of Burwell Bassett and Anna Maria (Nancy) Dandridge Bassett.

2. This might be the Reverend and Mrs. Price Davies. He was rector of Warreneye Church, Blissland Parish. Eltham was located close to this church.

To Arthur Lee

Dear Sir[1]   September 15th 1780
I have been honored with your polite letter of the eighth[2] and the present of the elegant piece of china[3] for which and the flattering sentiments accompanying it I pray you to accept the thanks and best wishes of

Your most obedient and
obliging
humble servant
Martha Washington

ALS, DLC.

1. Dr. Arthur Lee (1740-1792), brother of Richard Henry, Francis Lightfoot, William, and Phillip Ludwell Lee. Together with Benjamin Franklin and Silas Deane, he served as one of the American commissioners to the Court of Versailles.

2. The letter has not survived.

3. "The elegant piece of china" remains unidentified.

To Mrs. Elizabeth Powel

Mrs Washington present her compliments to Mrs Powel,[1] - and sends the piece of Nett that was left in her care by Mrs Fitzhugh,[2] - Mr Lee[3] has promised, to be carefull of it, and to deliver it himself, -

Mrs Washington begs the favor of Mrs Powel to present her compliments to Mr Powel -

Mount Vernon september the 20th 1780

ALS (third person, Powel Collection) ViMtV.

1. Elizabeth Willing Powel, wife of Samuel Powel, mayor of Philadelphia. They were intimate friends of the Washingtons during the war and the presidential years.

2. Anne Randolph Fitzhugh, wife of William Fitzhugh of "Chatham." Their daughter, Mary Lee Fitzhugh, was to marry Mrs. Washington's only grandson, George Washington Parke Custis.

3. Probably Arthur Lee; see supra, September 15, 1780, n. 1.

To Charles Willson Peale

Sir   New Windsor December the 26th 1780
      I send my miniature pictures to you and request the favor of you to
get them set for me - I would have them for Braceletts to wear round the
wrists - the picture already set I beg you to have cut the same size as the
other two and set as I may make a pair of either of the three pictures - the
dimonds may be set in a pin for the hair - I would have the three pictures
set exactly alike - and all the same size - if you have no crystals your self
if they can be had in the city I beg you to get them for me - I would like
to have them set neat and plain - and will be much obliged to you to hurry
the person that undertakes the doing of them as I am very anxious to get
them soon -[1]

> I am Sir your most obd
> and Hble ser
> Martha Washington

in the Box three
pictures - 2 half Joes, 2 small pieces of
gold

ALS, PHC.
      1. During the latter part of May, 1772, Peale came to Mount Vernon and painted
miniatures of Mrs. Washington, John Parke Custis, Martha Parke Custis (Patsy). While in
Philadelphia in 1776 he executed a second miniature of Mrs. Washington. The miniature of
the two children and the 1776 miniature are the ones mentioned in this letter. See, Johnson,
Original Portraits of Washington, p. 17, Boston, 1892; *Mount Vernon Annual Report*: 1956,
frontispiece, p. 20; *Ibid*, 1960, p. 20-22.

From Charles Willson Peale

Philada January 16, 1781
      Dr. Madam,- The Jeweller promises me to have the bracelets done
in a few days. I have begged him to take the utmost pains to set them
neatly...As no foreign glasses were to be had, I have moulded some of the
best glass I could find and got a Lapidary to polish them; which, I hope
will not be inferior to those made abroad. I have cut the Pictures to one
size, and mean to go a little further than you are pleased to direct - That
is to have spare loopholes for occasional use as a Locket, and the additional
expense in inconsiderable.

> Respectfully yours
> C.W. Peale[1]
> Mrs Martha Washington

Location unknown
      1. Text taken from Johnson, *Original Portraits*, p. 18. See, *A. R.*, 1960, p. 20-22.

To -

Mrs Washington will be glad to know if the cotton for the counter pins was wove and whitend, - how many yards was there of it, how many counter pins will it make - she desired Milly Posey to have the fine peice of linning made white how is Betty has she been spinning all winter - is Charlot done the worke I left for her to do[1]

ALS, (Third person) MiU-C.

   1. The letter was found in the papers of Sir Henry Clinton together with letters from General Washington to General Lafayette, John Parke Custis, and Lund Washington. They were all dated May 31, 1781. The 3rd person note was probably intended for Lund Washington. The four letters were intercepted by the British and turned over to Sir Henry Clinton.

From Mrs. Martha Mortier

Mrs Mortier[1] presents her Compliments to Mrs Washington has been Informed that some Intercepted Letters mention her being Indisposed[2] and that she finds a difficulty in procuring some Necessary Articles for her recovery. Mrs M: has taken the liberty to send her such as this place affords, by means of a flag of truce, which she had procured for that purpose,[3] & begs leave to offer Mrs W: any other Assistance her situation may require -

New York 15th June 1781[4]

ALS (3rd person) DLC:GW.

   1. Mrs. Martha Mortier was the widow of a paymaster of the British army. It is possible she was a confidante of General Sir Henry Clinton.

   2. Mrs. Washington's illness was mentioned in letters the General wrote to John Parke Custis and Lund Washington, dated New Windsor, May 31, 1781. On the same day a military letter was sent to General Lafayette. Accompanying the three letters was a short note by Mrs. Washington, thought to be intended for Lund Washington, concerning household affairs at Mount Vernon. The four letters were sent by the usual carrier of the mail, but were intercepted by the British, June 3rd. They were promptly turned over to Sir Henry Clinton. (Fitzpatrick, *Writings*, 22:142-45; Freeman, *George Washington*, 5:292). Mrs. Washington's illness began about May 21st, while the General was in conference with General Rochambeau at Wethersfield, Connecticut. (Fitzpatrick, *Writings*, 22:142, 145). The illness was manifested by abdominal pain, billiousness, and jaundice. Undoubtedly she was suffering from gall-bladder disease, complicated by a stone obstructing the common bile duct. Her illness lasted about five weeks. She was sufficiently improved to enable her to leave New Windsor, on her way to Virginia, June 26th. (Fitzpatrick, *Writings*, 22:266.)

   3. The articles sent included: a box of lemons, a box of oranges, four boxes of sweetmeats, one keg of tarmarinds (medicinal seed from tamarindus indica), 200 limes, two dozen capillaire (to prepare a syrup from maiden hair fern), two dozen orgeat (used to prepare a syrup made from barley, almonds, or orange flower water), two dozen pineapples, and two pounds of Hyson tea. (Fitzpatrick, *Writings*, 22:250.)

   4. Mrs. Mortier's letter was received at New Windsor on June 21st. The General immediately and emphatically instructed Major General Robert Howe to allow nothing to be landed under the flag of truce; the flag was to depart immediately; no detachment of the flag was to be allowed to set foot on shore; reiterrated that nothing should be landed; a billet addressed to Mrs. Mortier be transmitted to her by the flag. (Fitzpatrick, *Writings*,

22:240.) His letter is as follows: "Headqrs., June 21, 1781. General Washington presents his compliments to Mrs. Mortier and thanks her for her very polite attention to Mrs. Washington, who has so perfectly recovered as to be able to set out for Virginia in a day or two. This being the case, General Washington hopes Mrs. Mortier will excuse his returning the several articles which she in so kind a manner sent up by the Flag, assuring her at the same time, that he shall ever entertain a grateful sense of this mark of her benevolence." The "Old Fox" was not to be taken in so easily. To have accepted the articles would have opened the Washingtons to criticism in the tory and patriot press for having accepted favors from the enemy. (Fitzpatrick, *Writings*, 22:250.) Most of the original correspondence is in the British Headquarters Papers at the William L. Clements Library, University of Michigan.

From John Parke Custis

Camp Before York, October 12th, 1781[1]

My Dear & Hond Madam,

I have the pleasure to inform you that I find Myself much better since I left Mt Vernon, notwithstanding the change in my Lodging &c, and that the General tho in constant Fatigue looks very well; I staid a night with my Uncle[2] in my way down, and had the pleasure to find him and Family in good Health, likewise of seeing my Grandmother,[3] I think She looks very well, but discovers her great Age more than when I last saw Her. She now lives with my Uncle. My Aunt Henley lives where she formerly lived.[4] They are very desirous of seeing you, My Grandmother wishes you to bring down both Bet and Pat,[5] but I told Her it would be too inconvenient for you to bring down both. My Uncle has suffered very much by the Enemy; They are all very desirous of seeing you, and if the General has no Objection, I think you might come down;[6] as he is writing to you I shall refer you to him for advise on this matter, as well as for News.

I am dear Madam with the
sincerest affection
Your very dutiful son
J.P.Custis

P.S. please to inform Mr. Washington[7] that I have made every possible Enquiry after his Negroes, but have not seen any belonging to him, the General or myself, I have heard that Ned is in York a pioneer, old Joe Rachier is in the Neighborhood tho I have not been able to see him. His Wife is dead, and I fear that most who left Us are not existing,[8] the mortality that has taken place among the Wretches is really incredible. I have seen numbers lying dead in the Woods, and many so exhausted that they cannot walk. I should be glad to hear from Mr. Wn. whether he has sold any of my horses, they are not high price in comparison to what they sell for here.

J.P.C.

ALS, ViMtV.

1. John Parke Custis joined the General during the seige at Yorktown and acted as a civilian aide. While there he contracted "camp fever" (probably typhoid fever). Seriously ill, he was taken to Eltham, the home of his uncle and aunt, the Burwell Bassetts. His mother and wife, residing at Mount Vernon, were sent for. Following the surrender at Yorktown, General Washington left the peninsula on November 5th and arrived at Eltham the following day, in time to witness the death of young Custis. He was buried in the family burial plot at Eltham.

2. Bartholomew Dandridge.

3. Frances Jones Dandridge. She resided with her son, Bartholomew Dandridge at "Pamocra," New Kent County.

4. Elizabeth Dandridge Aylett Henley.

5. Elizabeth (Eliza) Parke Custis and Martha (Pat) Parke Custis.

6. Mrs. Washington did not come to Eltham until notified of the serious illness of her son.

7. Lund Washington, still acting as manager at Mount Vernon.

8. Slaves who had run away from Mount Vernon.

Note:

Madame Washington begged me to write for her to M le Comte de Custine, whose regiment was at Colchester that day to invite him and all the officers of his corps to do her the favor to dine with her the next day. Von Closen Journal, July 19, 1782. 10 W (3) 230. Jean Christopher Louis Frederic Ignace, Baron de Closen-Haydenbourg, Captain of the Regiment Royal Deux-Ponts and aide-de-camp to General Rochambeau. Adam Philippe le Comte de Custine (1740-1793) was quartermaster-general of the French forces in America from 1778 until 1783. He was present at the Yorktown campaign. He returned to France in 1783 and was guillotined in 1793.

From George Washington

My dearest   Verplanks point 1st Oct 82

If this letter should ever reach your hands, it will be presented by Mr Brown, - son to a Gentlman of that name in Rhode Island,[1] from whom I have received civilities, & to whom, or his connections I could wish to make returns. - As he has thoughts of going into Virginia I recommend him to your notice & attention

I am most sincerely &
affectionately - Yrs
G°: Washington

(Address leaf)
To Lund Washington[2]
at Mount Vernon
Virginia

ALS, RHi.

1. James Brown was one of the six children of John and Sarah Smith Brown. John Brown (1736-1803), one of the well known merchant family of Providence, R.I. has been considered the leader of the expedition that burned the Gaspee in 1772. In 1778 he presented a butt of wine for use at headquarters at White Plains. He was agent for the purchase of tent cloth, munitions, and supplies. *DAB*, 3:128; *Writings*, 8:64; 12:246.

2. General Washington addressed the cover to Lund Washington, in the event Mrs.

Washington was absent. The verso of the letter has the following notation: "James Brown Son of John & Sarah his wife received this letter at Verplanks Point on the river Hudson about 40 miles distant from N York City in October 1782 being then on this way to the South, on a jaunt of Pleasure, or a visit to the world of which he knew but little at that time having never before been in any other City except Boston. But as this Journey to the South extended at that Setting out no further than Baltimore this introductory letter from George Washington was never delivered - Afterwards in 1786 during the month of December He stopped at M. Vernon the immortal Man and his very kind & hospitable Lady were there, and the attention he recd while there from all the family made an impresssion so strong and so agreeable, that it never can be erased from the Tablet of Memory - Bushrod Washington with whom he was well acquainted in Philada in 1783 was on the first visit to his uncle with his new married Lady. This circumstance made the residence of some days in that interesting mansion still more interesting." This is the third known letter of George Washington to Martha Washington.

To -

(Newburgh February 7, 1783)

Yesterday there was an interesting scene at Headquarters. Over fifty soldiers, thinly clad, and with pale but happy faces, whom the General had pardoned in the morning for various crimes, came to express their gratitude for his mercy and kindness to them

They had come in a body. One of them was spokesman for the rest. My heart was touched and my eyes were filled with tears. I gave the speaker some money to divide among them all, and bade them "go, and sin no more." The poor fellow kissed my hand and said "God bless Lady Washington." Poor fellows.[1]

Location unknown

1. From Lossing, *Mary and Martha*, p. 220. Lossing does not give his source, although he states it was written to Mrs. Washington's sister, Anna Maria Bassett. This is obviously incorrect, since Mrs. Bassett died in 1777. If based on an authentic letter, it has been substantially edited. In the General Orders of February 6, 1783, General Washington granted "a full and free pardon to all military prisoners now in confinement." *Writings*, 26:102-03.

To Major General Henry Knox

(Newburgh March 6, 1783)

Mrs Washington presents her compliments to General Knox[1] and begs his acceptance of two Hair netts.[2] They would have been sent long ago but for want of tape, which was necessary to finish them and which was not obtained till yesterday.

newburgh March the 6th 1783

ALS (third person) MWi:W-C.

1. Henry Knox (1750-1806), Major-general in the Continental Army and chief of artillery. His first great achievement was to bring the captured cannon from Ticonderoga to Cambridge in the dead of winter of 1775, a distance of 300 miles. He was a skilled commander of this branch of Washington's army as well as an efficient administrator. After the war he

became Secretary of War under the Confederation and later in the Washington administration.

2. A loosely woven bag used to support the queue. General Washington wore a black one
on occasions. See, Decatur, *The Private Affairs of George Washington*, p. 97, 327, Boston, 1933.
Hereafter referred to as *Private Affairs*.

From Major General Henry Knox

(West Point March 8, 1783)

General Knox has the honor to present his most respectful compliments to Mrs Washington and to assure her he is deeply impressed with
the sense of her goodness, in the favor of the hair nets for which he begs
her to accept of his sincere thanks.

West point 8th March '83

ALS (third person) MWi:W-C.

On two occasions Mrs. Washington was requested to make copies of letters for the General.
The first was a copy of a letter from George Washington to Alexander Hamilton, Newburgh,
New York, March 31, 1783. The two-page folio letter is entirely in the handwriting of Mrs.
Washington. The postscript and docketing is in the handwriting of General Washington. The
second copy, also of a letter to Alexander Hamilton, Newburgh, New York, April 22, 1783,
is three pages folio. The last sentence, initialed signature, and docketing are in the
handwriting of General Washington. Both copies of these very significant letters are in
DLC:GW.

IV

Return to Mount Vernon:
The Period of Peace,
1784–1788

Subject: Frances (Fanny) Bassett, age 18. Artist: Robert Edge Pine, 1785. Medium: Oil on canvas. *Credit*: Mount Vernon Ladies' Association.

To Hannah Stockton Boudinot

My Dear Madam[1]   Mount vernon 15th Jan 84

Your polite and affectionate congratulatory Letter on the termination of our trobles, and the return of the General to domestic life would, under any circumstances; have been highly pleasing to me; but the value of it was particularly enhanced by the friendly terms in which you have conveyed them to us.

In return, permit me to offer you my sincere compliments on your restoration to your own House, after an exile of seven years[2]- and on Miss Boudinots better state of health;[3] which with much pleasure I learnt from the General was considerably amended, if he might be allowed to form a judgment of it from her improved looks.- The difficulties, and distresses to which we have been exposed during the war must now be forgotten.- we must endevor to let our ways be the way of pleasentness and all our paths Peace.

It would give infinite pleasure to see you Mr and Miss Boudinot at this place without which I almost despair of ever enjoying that happyness, as my frequent long Journeys have not only left me without inclination to undertake another, but almost disqualified me from doing it, as I find the fatiegue is too much for me to bear.

My little family are all with me; and have been very well till with in these few days, that they have been taken with the measles. - the worst I hope is over, and that I shall soon have them prattling about me again. - with best respects to Mr. Boudenot, and love to Miss Susan and yourself - in which the General joins I am my dear madam with much esteem

Your most affectionate
Friend
Martha Washington

ALS In the private collection of Dr. Walter Ostromecki, Jr.

1. Hannah Stockton Boudinot (1738-1808) was the sister of Richard Stockton, New Jersey Signer of the Declaration of Independence. She married Elias Boudinot in 1762. Boudinot was an early supporter of the revolutionary cause, a member of the New Jersey Provincial Congress, the Continental Congress, and served latter as president. His work as a commissary-general of prisoners during the war was commendable. *DAB*, 2:477.

2. At the outbreak of the war the Boudinots were living in Elizabeth Town, New Jersey. Nearby hostilities drove them to a farm near Basking Ridge. During the winter of 1777-78 Boudinot was with the army at Valley Forge. See, Bill, *A House Called Morven*, p. 47, Princeton, 1954. Hereafter referred to as *Morven*.

3. Susan Vergereau Boudinot (1764-1854) married William Bradford (1755-1794), a colonel in the Continental army. Later he became attorney-general and chief justice of Pennsylvania, and attorney-general of the United States. See Butterfield, *Letters of Benjamin Rush*, 1:306, Princeton, 1951. Hereafter referred to as *Rush*.

To Hannah Bushrod Washington

My Dear Madam[1]-   Mount Vernon June 22d 1784

After a very long passage the Cotton arrived safe, - I was much concerned that I should have given Mr B. Washington[2] the troble, - He thought it would be a very easy thing to procure, - it was to add to some thread I have had spun several years in the House, - I thank you for the Cotton, and should be very unhappy if you have disfirnished yourself by spairing it out of your own stock, - it would have been noe inconvenience to me, to have stayed another year, for to have my piece of Cloth finishd, - my spinners had just spun up all the wool and had little to doe, was the reason I thought of spinning cotton - and I could not get any in this part of the country - the West Indea cotton not being brought to Alexandria in the shops -

It would give me much pleasure to come to Bushfield[3] to visit you and will when it is conveniant to the General to leve home on a visit; he has so much business of his one and the publicks to gather that I fear he will never find lazure to goe see his friends; I would with pleasure have sent you the weeping willow but the man told me he was not going down derectly, - if he had, it was two late to plant it this summer, at the proper time for planting it, you may have as much as you please as it would give me pleasure to send you anything of that sort that is worth sending to you from here.

I am happy to hear Mrs Washington[4] has incresed her family and is well I wish she could make it convenient to come to see us.

The General joins me in love and good wishes to you and all with you

> I am Dear Madam
> Your affectionate
> sister and friend
> Martha Washington

Mrs. Washington, Bushfield

ALS, ViMtV.

1. Hannah Bushrod Washington, daughter of John Bushrod of "Bushfield," Westmoreland County, Va. She married John Augustine Washington (1736-1787), brother of George Washington.

2. Bushrod Washington (1762-1829), son of John Augustine and Hannah Washington. By the terms of George Washington's will, he inherited Mount Vernon following the death of Martha Washington. He was named an associate justice of the United States Supreme Court by President John Adams.

3. Bushfield was the home of John Augustine and Hannah Bushrod Washington. It consisted of 1500 acres on Nomini Creek, Westmoreland County.

4. This might be Mrs. Mildred Washington, first wife of Thornton Washington. Thornton Washington was the son of George Washington's younger bother, Samuel. Mrs. Thornton Washington's second child was John T. A. Washington, born in 1783.

To Frances Bassett

My dear Fanny -   Mount Vernon August the 7th 1784

Tho' I have never been alone since you left this, - yet I cannot say but I have missed your company very much - The General is still determined to set out the first of next month, over the mountains[1] I have not heard anything from my Brother,[2] whether he will be up before the General goes or not I expect to come down to see him sometime in September - I shall not fix the time till I hear from you or him -

Mrs Stuart is getting better[3] your stays and other things came from Annapolis the Sunday after you left this - I have payed Mrs Charles Stuart[4] the money she payed, the mantua maker: £ 3.2.6 I will keep them or bring down as you think you may want them - I think Miss Ramsay[5] was married before you left this - we have nothing new that I hear off.

My little Nelly[6] is getting well and Tub[7] is the same clever boy you left him - He sometimes says why don't you send for Cousin - you know he never makes himself unhappy about absent friends.

Remember me to all Friends with you, the General had a letter from your pappa[8] by the last post that never mentioned you or any other person. The letter was dated at Richmond I should have been glad to have heard where you was -

If you should see my Brother[9] Remember me to him and family, my love to your Brothers[10] - My compliments to your pappa in which the General joins me -

I am my dear Fanny your most affectionate

Martha Washington

ALS, ViMtV.

1. On September 1, 1784 George Washington set out on visit to his "landed property west of the Apalachian Mountains." He was accompanied by Dr. James Craik, his son William, Bushrod Washington, and the servants. *Diaries*, 4:1.

2. Bartholomew Dandridge

3. Eleanor Calvert Custis Stuart, the widow of John Parke Custis. She married Dr. David Stuart (1753-1814) late in 1783. They continued to live at Abingdon until 1789, when they moved to Hope Park and later to Ossian Hall, both in Fairfax County. *Diaries,* 4:72 n.

4. Elizabeth Calvert Steuart, a sister of Eleanor Calvert Custis Stuart. She married Charles Steuart of Annapolis. *Diaries,* 3:155 n.

5. This may be Ann Ramsay, daughter of William Ramsay. She was married to Robert Allison, an Alexandria merchant. *Diaries,* 4:164.

6. Eleanor Parke Custis, (1779-1852), Martha Washington's granddaughter.

7. George Washington Parke Custis (1781-1857), Martha Washington's grandson. He was usually called "Washington," but occasionally "Wash" and "Tub."

8. Burwell Bassett, I.

9. Bartholomew Dandridge

10. Burwell Bassett, II (1764-1841) and John Bassett (1765-1822).

To Mercy Otis Warren

My dear Madam   Mount Vernon June the 9th 1785

I had the pleasure to receive your obliging Letter of the 14th of April by Mrs Macauly Graham[1] - the kind expression of which, added to the Recollection of those days in which you honored me with your friendship, fill me with agreeable sensations; and will ever be dear to my remembrance, -

I thank you for introducing a Lady so well known in the literary world as Mrs Macauly Graham, whose agreeable company we have had the pleasure of a few days - she now returns to make happy those whome she left.

The friendship which subsisted between General Warren and Mr Washington will never be forgotten by the latter. it was among the first formed, and most lasting at Cambridge.- and with equel pleasure would be renewed by him - why it has slept the general cannot tell.- he recollects writing a long letter to Genl Warren in the year 1779, when the enemy were cantoned on the Rariton near Boundbrook in the Jerseys.- since which, all intercourse by letter has ceased: tho friendship is the same, -

He joins me in every good wish for you and General Warrin, and begs me to add the strongest asurances of the sincear esteem and regard he has for you both.- with sentiments of friendship and affection - I am Dear Madam your obed and obliged

M Washington

(Docket)
Mrs Washington
Mount Vernon
June 9th 1785

ALS, MHi.

1. Catherine Sawbridge Macaulay Graham (1731-1799), celebrated English woman of letters. One of her principal works was a history of England. She and her husband, William

Graham, visited Mount Vernon from June 4-14, 1785. While there she perused Washington's military correspondence and discussed the shortcomings of the government under the Articles of Confederation. After the ratification of the Federal Constitution she and the General carried on a correspondence in which he attempted to enlighten her on its provisions.

To Colonel and Mrs. Thomas Blackburn

Monday October 10, 1785

Genl and Mrs. Washington present their compliments to Colo and Mrs Blackburn[1]; are much obliged to them for their kind invitation to the Wedding[2] on Thursday. They would attend with pleasure, but for the indisposition of the latter; and the particular engagements of the former which confine him at home this week, and oblige him to attend the Board of Directors at Georgetown, the Great Falls, &c the beginning of next. The Genl and Mrs Washington will always be happy to see the young couple at Mount Vernon.

ALS (Third person) DLC:GW.

1. Colonel Thomas Blackburn (c.1740-1807) and his wife, Christian Scott Blackburn. They resided at Rippon Lodge, near Dumfries, Prince William County. They were frequent visitors at Mount Vernon. The Washingtons often stayed at Rippon Lodge. Their granddaughter married John Augustine Washington (1792-1832), grand nephew of GW. He later inherited Mount Vernon from his uncle, Bushrod Washington.

2. Bushrod Washington (1762-1829) was the son of GW's younger brother, John Augustine Washington (1736-1787) and his wife, Hannah Bushrod Washington. His bride was Julia Ann Blackburn (1768-1829). See supra. Bushrod Washington later became an associate justice of the Supreme Court. Under the terms of GW's will, he inherited Mount Vernon.

To Dr. David Stuart

Dear Sir   Mount Vernon November 6th 1786

I have had two letters from a Gentleman in Ireland, - He calls himself John Custis - says he is of the same Family of the Custis s in virginia - and thinks he is a Brother's son to my childrens grand Father, - The Hon John Custis that died in Williamsburg in the year - 1750. - If you should meet with any gentleman from the Eastern shore that is acquainted with the family, - and will be so obliging as to give me a geneological account of it, - It would be taken exceedingly kind - I am anxious to know them myself too - and shall be glad to inform the Gentleman that has written to me. The General has had a letter sometime agoe from Brussels from a Mr. Charles Custis - is of the same family as he says -[1]

> I am with Esteem sir
> your most obt sert
> M Washington

Dr. Stuart

ALS, ICHi.

1. The first Custis of record is John Custis of Rotterdam. He and his wife, Joanne, came to Virginia prior to 1640 and probably settled on the Eastern Shore. In Rotterdam he had been an innkeeper and well known among the English travelers. In his narrative of a voyage to Virginia in 1649, Colonel Norwood states he met Custis and that he "kept a victualling house in that town (Rotterdam), liv'd in good repute, and was the general host of our nation there." He had six sons and one daughter: John Custis II, a major-general of militia during Bacon's rebellion; William and Joseph who settled on the Eastern Shore; Thomas, who settled in Baltimore, County Cork, Ireland; Edmund, who resided in London; Robert, who remained in Rotterdam; Ann, who married Col. Argall Yardley of Northampton County, son of Governor Yardley. Major-general John Custis had one son, John Custis III of Wilsonia. By his wife, Margaret Michael, he had a son, John Custis IV, who was the father-in-law of Martha Dandridge Custis Washington. It was Major-general John Custis who provided the English education for his grandson, John Custis, IV. See, *VMHB*, 3:320-321; *Virginia Historical Register and Literary Advertiser*, v. II, no. III, July, 1849, p. 121-137.

From Elizabeth Willing Powel

Dear Madam   (November 31, 1787)

I fear I have suffered in your Esteem on the score of both gratitude & Politeness, from having so long delayed to return you Thanks for your Civilities & attention to me while I was under your hospitable Roof;[1] but a Desire to accompany my Letter with the Collars for the young Ladies, has alone prevented an earlier Acknowledgement of my Sense of the elegant Hospitality exercised at Mount Vernon, where the good Order of the Master's Mind, seconded by your excellent abilities, pervades every Thing around you, & renders it a most delightful Residence to your Friends. I should have been happy to have prolonged our Visit had I not been sensible that the Depression of Spirits under wch I then was, rendered me a totally unfit Companion for ye cheerful & happy. My recent Separation from my favorite Sister and her Family,[2] with the probability of never seeing her again, the Reflection of having left her encircled with Difficulties almost too great for a Man to cope with, unconnected & unprotected by any Friend, able or willing, To serve her, almost broke my Heart. She is a disinterested amiable Woman. The Settlement made on her in lieu of Dower, is amply sufficient during her life, for all ye purposes of comfortable & excellent living. Her genius is penetrative, her abilities uncommon. More moderate abilities serve our Purposes better on some Occasions. Indeed, I am clearly of the Sentiment that our Sex were never intended for the great Affairs of Life. They have happy Talents for suggesting & can see the ends of the chain, but it requires masculine Powers to discern the intermediate Links & connect them with Propriety. A Hope of being able to serve the Heirs of Colo Byrd, wh ye interests of her own Children were involved, & a Desire to comply with his Will, induced her to undertake ye management of his Estate.[3] This has obliged her to prosecute claims which many find it inconvenient to comply with. A Love of Justice or a Sense of Gratitude are but weak Incentives with ye great bulk of Mankind to do what is right-when it clashes with private Interest; & not contented with evading what is just they too generally become ye Enemies of those they have injured. What a dismal Reverse did I find from what I had been a Witness to three and twenty years ago. For tho Colo Byrds Estate was then involved, he lived in such a Scale as to be sought after & apparently respected. But so passeth away the Vanities of this World; & happily for us, we shall soon pass from all temporal Concerns. I flatter myself your own good heart will plead my apology for speaking on a Subject no ways interesting to you, but so far as it relates to the cause of Humanity, which can never be indifferent to a benevolent Mind.

I hope the collars will meet your Approbation. The cost runs three dollars. You have paid something more for theyre being made in Phila; but the english ones were too long for your Purpose. Those I have sent may be raised by means of the Screw. I have made a little Ornament of Ribband, which may be worn over them as a Disguise when ye young Ladies are dressed or go without a Vandike. It is a Pity that a fine Form should be spoiled by a childs not holding herself erect. Indeed I think it is so essential to Health as to Beauty, to hold up the Head & throw back the shoulders. It expands the chest & prevents those ridiculous Distortions of the Face & Eyes which girls, at a certain age, frequently fall into from a foolish Bashfulness, or so the French call it a mauvaise haute. There are collars with Backs for the Shoulders; but this is so like putting them in Harness that I reprobate them, as I do all Ligatures on the human Form. Native grace is superior to all that Art can do; and it is so natural to hold up the Head, and open the chest, as to lollop the Head in the Bosom & raise the Shoulders to the Ears. I found that the guinea you gave me for the Collars was sufficient to pay for the Ribband, and to add Sashes of the same I have therefore taken ye the Liberty, without orders, to send them.

I have sent our little Favorite, Master Custis the Work I promised him. I wished to have got it in small Volumes, such as I had sent to a little Friend, and better adapted to his Size, but they were not to be had, and this, such as it is, I think he will be pleased with. I shall distrust my Skill if he is not a Child of Penetration & Genius. He has sweet conciliating manners like your charming little Eleanor. When I was with you, you were so civil as to express your Approbation of a Morocco Thread Case that I was using. On my return I met with one of the same Kind, which I must beg your Acceptance of as a small Testimony of my Recollection & Esteem.

Be pleased to present me affectionately to the General, Master Custis, & the young Ladies. My best compliments & good Wishes attend Major & Mrs Washington.[4] I hope she is returned perfectly reinstated in her

Health. There was something so pleasing in her Appearance & Manner that even a Stranger could not see her without being interested in her Welfare. If I can render her or you any Services in Phila you will be so obliging as to command them.

I have the Honor to be with affectionate Regards dear Madam

> Your most obt & obliged
> Servt.
> Eliza Powel

November 30, 1787
Mrs Washington

ALS, ViMtV.

1. Elizabeth Willing Powel was one of the seven daughters of Charles Willing, mayor of Philadelphia, and his wife, Ann Shippen. She married Samuel Powel in 1766. Her sister, Mary (1740-1814), married William Byrd III in 1761. See Tinling, *The Correspondence of the Three William Byrds of Westover, Virginia 1684-1776*, 2:835, Charlottesville, 1977. Hereafter referred to as *Byrd*.

2. Plagued by debts incurred by gambling and high living; involved in a dispute with his mother and the four children by his first wife, Elizabeth Carter Byrd, over the estate of his father, William Byrd II; condemned for his Loyalist sympathies at the outbreak of the Revolution, he committed suicide on January 1, 1777. For an excellent resume of his life see, *Byrd*, 2:603-14.

3. William Byrd III and his second wife, Mary Willing Byrd, had ten children. *Byrd*, 2:829-30.

4. Major George Augustine Washington (1763-1793) was the son of Charles Washington, younger brother of the General. During the early part of the Revolution he served as a lieutenant in Lee's Partisan Light Dragoons. In 1780 he became an ensign and then lieutenant in the 2nd Virginia Regiment. Early in 1781 he became an aide to General Lafayette and served with him through the Virginia campaign that terminated with the surrender of Yorktown. At the termination of hostilities he came to Mount Vernon where he met Frances Bassett, Mrs. Washington's niece. In 1784, suffering from ill health- probably tuberculosis - General Washington sent him to the West Indies and South Carolina to regain his health. He returned to Mount Vernon, very little improved. He and Fanny Bassett were married at Mount Vernon on October 15, 1785. Later that year he succeeded Lund Washington as manager at Mount Vernon. The Washingtons had three children, Maria, Charles, and Lafayette. His health gradually deteriorating, he died at Eltham, February 5, 1793.

To Mrs. Elizabeth Powel

Dear Madam   Mount Vernon January the 18 1788

I have now to thank you for the very polite and affectionate letter of December the 7th - we were exceedingly happy to hear by it and by the two Mr Morris's[1] that you reached Philadelphia without accident, and without fright in crossing the Bay and that you had the happiness to find all your friends there well. The circumstances will be an inducement to you I hope, to visit your friends to the southward more frequently. I am my dear madam much obliged for your kind attention in getting the collars for the girls. They suite very well, for I prefer them to those with Backs; - and am well pleased that you laid out the remainder of the money in ribbon and sashes for them. My pretty boy is so pleased with the Book you sent him that he had read it over and over and over and says he will write to Mrs. Powel and thank her himself, for her kind remembrance of him.

Fanny returned much better of the cough, and a good deal better in health than when she went over the mountains; but not perfectly recovered. She left this about ten days agoe - with a design to lay in at her fathers. She expects sometime in March next;[2] in her way down she called at a Mr. McCartys to see her Brother married to the daughter of that gentleman, which will make it sometime before I shall hear from her.[3] She is a child to me, and I am very lonesome when she is absent. Her ill luck with her first child is the only reason of her wishing to change the place of her lying inn this time.[4] If her child lives, it will be sometime in May before she can come up - and the distance is too farr for me to goe down to see her.

The moroco thread case you was so obliging as to send me, came safe with the other things, for which please to accept my thanks. I can assure you, my dear madam, that we were much mortified at not being able to prevail on you to stay longer with us as you returned - whilst you were on the road we thought of you often and as you find the ways tolerable, and the commencement (that is the preparation for a journey) nearly half the execution of it, we shall flatter ourselves with hopes of seeing you again in this state; change of air is always conducive to health; and tho we are not as gay as you are at philadelphia, yet in this peaceful retreat you will find friendship and cordiallity; which no one who does not go fully into all the gaities of the city, will I flatter myself, be quite as agreeable.

I do most truly sympathize with you on your sisters disappointments in life. These now come, in a greater or less degree, are what all of us experience. She is blessed however with a charming family of children, and providence has been bountiful in giving her resolution and strength of Body and mind to be able to undertake the care that have developed upon her. There are few women that would not sink under the load; to the entire ruin of their families.

Mrs Stuart has lately lost her father Mr Calvert which has distressed her exceedingly. She is now with her mother, the girls are with me.[5] Miss & Miss Patty Custis say that I would thank you in their names for the collars. They will ware them with pleasure as you was so good as to take the trouble of providing them. My little Nelly is very well, and often asks when Mrs. Powel will come to see us again. Many thanks for your kind offer in rendering Fanny and myself service. Should I have occation, I will with much freedom, accept your kind offer

My warm wishes and affectionate regards attend you and Mr Powel, in which the General begs to be included - and believe me to be with

> great esteem dr Madam
> your affectionate Friend
> and Hble Servant
> M. Washington

ALS, ViMtV.

1. Robert Morris and Gouvernor Morris arrived at Mount Vernon on November 19, 1787 and departed on November 21st. They came to Virginia on a business mission.

2. Frances (Fanny) Bassett Washington delivered a daughter, Anna Maria Washington (1788-1814), on April 3, at Eltham. She was usually called Maria. Fanny's cough may have been one of the overt manifestations of tuberculosis, probably contracted from her ailing husband.

3. Burwell Bassett, Jr. (1764-1841) was married to Elizabeth McCarty, daughter of Daniel McCarty of Pope's Creek, Westmoreland County on January 10, 1788.

4. Fanny Bassett Washington had delivered a male infant on April 10, 1787. The infant died on April 25, 1787, after an illness of four days. *Diaries*, 5:131, 142.

5. Benedict Calvert died at Mount Airy, Prince George County Maryland, January 9, 1788. The Washington carriage was sent to bring Elizabeth and Martha from Abingdon to Mount Vernon.

From John Dandridge

My Dr. Madam -   Pamocra[1] Jany 18. 1788

It is a long time indeed since I wrote to you last; and was I not assured that you have had information from your Friends in this county, by other sufficient communications in the interval, I should blame myself more than I now do, for neglecting it on my part - I have in fact of late lost all relish for correspondence, for whenever I write, my letters are so tinctured with my uneasiness of spirit, that they must excite an unhappy sympathy on my Friend, without any alleviation to myself - This will be somewhat the case at present: but connected with me in the double tie of Friendship & relationship, you will bear with me while I address you on one subject of my uneasiness & beg your assistance therein

My Father,[2] particularly attached to his property in Negroes, by his will devised them specifically to his children,[3] & gave almost all his lands to his executors to sell & apply to the discharge of his Debts - This deprived his exectrs of the power to sell any of the Negroes (tho' it might have been done to great advantage to the Children) until they had first sold the land and applied the whole profit thereof to the payment of his Debts - Anxious as his exetrs & immediate representative to settle & satisfy all demands against his estate, I have used every endeavor to sell the lands & get the money - but such has been the state of public affairs since his death, that I have been able to do it but in part-He was indebted considerably more than he was aware of-particularly by some late speculation & securitiships:

The burning of his papers in his house also occasioned me to lose most of his outstanding Debts: And property has now so fallen in its current price, that all his Negroes would not at present, if sold for cash, satisfy the amount. I have been obliged to sell land on considerable credit sometimes, to get anything near the value, & the creditors not agreeing to wait 'till I can get in the money have sued, & will issue executions against the Negroes as soon as they get judgt - Had I been at liberty, under my Father's will, I should have sold at least one half of them towards satisfying the creditors: as we have not land to work them, & there is a great proportion of women & children, many of them are a charge to my Mother,[4] & the money arising from the sale of lands on credit would have been better for the children at interest: For all the negroes are given to my Mother & grandmother[5] for their lives, & they may if they choose it keep them for the children when grown up - It is necessary, however, for my Mother to have some negroes to support her in the education of the young Children - When I wrote to you about the Genls[6] Debt you informed me, he wished me not to sell anything on his acct. immediately; but as the negroes will be sold by somebody, before I can raise money from the land, he is better intitled to them than almost any other creditors. If however he can wait longer with us for the money, & does not see any impropriety in the measure, I would request him to send the bonds immediately to B. Bassett[7] as his attorney, & let me give him a judgt. at March court next: Directing it to be levied on the Negroes, including such as (among which I can have included such as my Mother is particularly attached to) & have them purchased for him. They may then remain his & subject to his claim till I can raise money enough from the lands to sell & Debts due the Estate, to satisfy him - As in time there will be enough to satisfy all the creditors - After this I mean to let Doctr Stuart[8] sell as many of the remaining negroes as will satisfy his immediate demand for money - I intend not thus by any means to defraud any creditor of his just Debt; for if there shall not be enough after paying the Genl, to satisfy the balance I will sell the negroes secured under his Judgt. & all my own individual property, to do it - But this will not be the case -

I make this request thro' you, my Dr Madam & not directly to the Genl, that if you see any impropriety in it, you will stop it & pardon my weakness: Because I would suffer anything rather than propose what may bear the appearance of dishonesty; even in a case like the present, where I am not personally interested but in the welfare of my Mother & her younger children - My own interest in the personal estate I have long since sacrificed to the benefit of the creditors, by selling my share of the negroe, which my mother delivered to me, & paying them the amount - If what I request can be done, I shall get time to sell the remainder of the land (which I have as exetr.) to advantage; to collect the money for what has been sold & get in some other Debts: and whilst relieved from the continual distress of such, judgts. & executions, be better enabled to do general justice to all the creditors -

My mother (on whose account principally I have written the above) desires to be remembered to you affectionately: and has only waited a convenient passage to embrace your invitation to patsy[9] - She has grown a great girl & resembles her grandfather's[10] picture, I think very much - She continues to stay with Sister Claiborne[11] yet, & is, as well as the other children, remarkbly healthy - Julious[12] is in very good business & reputation with Mr. Alexander[13] still - Bat[14] lives with Mr. Wm. Dandridge[15] who has commenced Merchant in this County - My Aunt Henley[16] continues another year at the Whitehouse & is just about having another child - we are all well here, except my Grandmother[17] who has been ill this winter; & have moved into our new house, tho' it is not finished -

You will be so good as to make my respectful complts. to the Genl., & send me an answer before March - Immediately if you please -

Believe me my Dr. Aunt, that, tho' the accident or indisposition to it may prevent my continual protestations, I shall not cease to be with less affection & sense of Duty.

Your Nephew
J: Dandridge[18]

Mrs. Washington
From
Jno Dandridge Esqr
to Mrs. Washington
respectg Bonds
18th. Jan: 1788[19]

1. "Pamocra" was the New Kent County home of the Burbidges and Dandridges. It was named in the will of Mann Page in 1730 and purchased in 1744 from Mann Page, Jr. by Julius King Burbidge. Bartholomew Dandridge, Sr. and his wife, Mary Burbidge, daughter of Julius King Burbidge, made their home with Mrs. Burbidge. His mother, Frances Dandridge, the widow of John Dandridge, Sr. and mother of MW, also resided at "Pamocra" after 1768. Both Bartholomew, Sr. and his mother are buried there. His son, John Dandridge, lived there until his death in 1799, his mother having deeded him nine hundred acre tract by 1789. *Harris*, 1:62-64, 82-84.

2. Bartholomew Dandridge (1737-1785) was the brother of MW. He was the son of Colonel John Dandridge (1700-1756) and his wife, Frances Jones (1710-1785).

3. The children of Bartholomew and Mary Burbidge Dandridge were: John, Bartholomew (Bat), William, Judith, Mary Burbidge, Frances Lucy, Julius, and Anne. 5 W (1) 36; See Aylett-Henley Bible, photostat 21245, VSL.

4. Mary Burbidge Dandridge (? - 1804), daughter of Julius King Burbidge. *Diaries*, 6:274; *Harris*, 1:63.

5. This must be his maternal grandmother, Mrs. Julius King Burbidge, since his paternal grandmother, Frances Dandridge, died nine days after her son, Bartholomew Dandridge, Sr., in 1785. *Harris*, 1:63.

6. GW.

7. Burwell Bassett, Jr. (1764-1841), son of Burwell Bassett of Eltham (1734-1793) and Anna Maria Dandridge Bassett (1739-1777), a younger sister of MW. *Diaries*, 5:158.

8. Dr. David Stuart (1753-c.1814), the second husband of Eleanor Calvert Custis Stuart. He was executor of the estate of her first husband, John Parke Custis, following the death of Bartholomew Dandridge, Sr. *Diaires*, 5:291.

9. Martha Washington Dandridge, daughter of Bartholomew Dandridge, Sr. *Diaires*, 6:362. She married Dr. William Halyburton of Haddington, England. *Diaires*, 6:362; 5W (1) 36.

10. He likely refers to a painting of his grandfather, John Dandridge, Sr. V, 3:8.

11. Anne, daughter of Bartholomew Dandridge, Sr., and his first wife, Elizabeth Macon. She married William Dandridge Claiborne. 14 W (1) 265-7; 6 W (1) 251; 12 W (1) 126-7; V 25:434.

12. Julius Dandridge, son of Bartholomew Dandridge, Sr. See supra, n. 3.

13. A Benjamin, Elisha, Thomas, and John Alexander all had taxable lands in Kew Kent County in 1782. *Harris*, 1:553.

14. Bartholomew Dandridge, Jr. (d. 1802), brother of John Dandridge, Jr. He was secretary to GW during the presidency, secretary to the legation at the Court of St. James, and consul to San Domingo. He died there, unmarried, in 1802. *Diaries*, 6:236.

15. Because of a plethora of William Dandridges, he has not been identified.

16. Elizabeth Dandridge Henley (1749-1799), youngest sister of MW. At this time she was pregnant with her eighth child, Bartholomew Henley, born March 14, 1788. She later had two additional children. At this time her husband, Leonard Henley, was overseer at White House, New Kent County. Aylett-Henley Family Bible Photostat 21245, VSL.

17. This must be Mrs. Julius King Burbidge (Lucy), mother of Mary Burbidge Dandridge, since his paternal grandmother, Frances Jones Dandridge, died in 1785. 6 W (1) 251.

18. John Dandridge (d. 1799), the eldest son of Bartholomew Dandridge, Sr., practiced law in New Kent County. His wife was Rebecca Jones Minges. *Diaries*, 5:101.

19. The docketing is in the handwriting of GW. See GW to Burwell Bassett, Jr., Febraury 3, 1788. *Writings*, 29:398.

To Fanny Bassett Washington

My Dear Fanny   Mount Vernon February 25th 1788

I was very happy to hear by the Major[1] that you arrived at Eltham without accident and that he left you very well with your friends. I hope you have continued to be so since he came away - as you know that Business is the cause of his leving you. I trust that you will endeavor to reconcile your self to his absence, as you are very sencible that if he does not attend to his affairs he will get nothing done & if his people does not make bread how will he be able to pay the taxes if nothing else is wanting he is very well and we all think he is growing fatt - we have not a single article of news but pollitick which I do not conscern myself about - I wish you could see the papers that comes hear every week as you are fond of reading them - I wrote a long letter to you before the arrival of the Major hear - indeed I was sorry to hear by him that it had not come to your hands- as I think I had written it long enough for it to have got to you before he come away -

Mr Porter and Miss Ramsay was marred on shrove tuesday - and Mr Lear says she looked handsomer the next morning than ever he see her [2] Mrs Jenifer wrote to Mr Stuart some days after that she looked charmingly[3] I have not been to see her, or Mrs West yet but intend to goe to see them as soon as I can get out we have had a remarkable cold winter hear - the snow has never been off the ground since you left us - besides the very cool winds has made it very disagreeable to goe out. Doctor Crack[4] was hear today I asked him how Mrs West was he said very well - but a little sick at times with a smile Mrs Jenifer has not been to see me since you went away - Major Wagener[5] has been ill which was a means to carry her home from the new marred folks sooner than she intended to leve them -

My Dear little children have all been very well, till today my pritty little Dear Boy complains of a pain in his stomach. I hope it proceeds from cold as he is much better than he was some months agoe and a good nights sleep I trust will carry of his complaints altogether - I cannot say but it makes me miserable if ever he complains let the cause be ever to trifeling - I hope the almighty will spare him to me -

The General did not goe up the river as he intended he got a bad cold and the dismal weather togather prevented - tho he set out satterday with an intention to reach Mr Fairfaxes that night but some disapointment in fixing the day caused him to turn back and the Colo seemed to bear his disapointment with tolerable patience - and often said he thought himself quite as well by the fire side at Mt Vernon as he should be at the Shenandoah.[6]

The General is very well - as to myself I am as usal - neither sick or well - the major talked of leveing this about the tenth of march you have just time enough to consider if you should want any thing that I have I can assure my Dear Fanny that it would give me great pleasure to send her anything that would add to her pleasure or happyness

Our compliments and love are offered to your father and all Friends with you

> and believe me my Dear
> Fanny your most
> affectionate
> M Washington

(docketed)
From Mrs M.Washington
Feb ry 1788

ALS Formerly ViWF, present location unkown.

1. Fanny's husband, Major George Augustine Washington. See supra.

2. Thomas Porter was married to Sarah Ramsay, daughter of William and Ann McCarty Ramsay, on February 5, 1788. *Diaries*, 5:273.

3. Sarah Craik Jenifer, daughter of Dr. James Craik of Alexandria.

4. Dr. James Craik (1731-1814) was born in Scotland, studied medicine in Edinburgh, and

came to America in 1751. He served with Colonel Washington at the Great Meadows, the Braddock expedition, and at the taking of Fort Duquesne. During the Revolution he served in various medical capacities. On several occasions he and GW traveled to the west. Craik was often called to treat the Washington family, slaves, and servants. He was the first physician called upon to treat GW in his final illness. He was one of the General's most intimate friends.

5. Peter Wagener (1742-1798) was a county lieutenant of Fairfax County.

6. On Saturday, January 12th, Washington, accompanied by Colonel David Humphreys (1752-1818), set out for the Falls of the Shenandoah for a meeting of the directors of the Potomack Company. They returned to Mount Vernon the same day when informed the meeting was postponed. *Diaries*, 5:264.

From John Dandridge

Mr Dr Madam   Pamocra[1] February 29th 1788

I received your answer to my Letter of the 25th of last month, in due time & safely.[2] I have to thank you for its kind contents in behalf of my Mother & Family[3] - The Genl's Letter inclosing the Bonds I have not delivered to B Bassett[4] yet: He has not been in New Kent since his marriage,[5] but is expected now daily -. I suppose the Genl has informed him that when judgment is obtained & an execution levied on the negroes of my Fathers Estate, he or myself may purchase on the Genl's acct -

My grandmother[6] whom I informed you was recovering, has relapsed & is now very ill - My mother is well & just returned from visiting my Sister Claiborn.[7] who has been almost dead, but has got better - Mr. Claibornes mother died a few days since, after a long illness -

My compliments to the Major[8] & tell him that his Fanny[9] was well two days ago.

If I can spare the time & raise the money, I wish to go to Kentucky in the spring or fall, in which case I shall call to see you, otherwise I do not know when I shall have the satisfaction of paying my duty to you - My whole attention for three years past has been applied to my Father's[10] affairs & to the care of my Mother & the children: And I must now endeavor to do something for myself; it shall never be in way by which I must remit my care & attention to them -

The bearer hereof is a Mr. Thos. Allison[11] who has brought home a runaway belonging to us, that had rambled as far as your neighborhood. He promises to have this delivered to you immediately. -

You will make my respectful compts to the Genl. - Give my love to Wash[12] & Nelly[13] and believe me your ever dutiful & Affectionate

Nephew
J: Dandridge[14]

From
John Dandridge Esq

to Mrs. Washington -res
pecting Bonds
29th Feby 1788[15]
Mrs: Washington
Mount Vernon
Favor'd by
Mr. Thos. Allison

1. See supra, John Dandridge to MW, January 18, 1788, n. 1.

2. Apparently John Dandridge wrote an earlier letter to MW on January 25. Neither this letter nor MW's letter has survived.

3. See supra, John Dandridge to MW, January 18, 1788, n. 3, 4.

4. See supra, n. 19.

5. Burwell Bassett, Jr. married Eliza McCarty, daughter of Daniel McCarty (d. 1795) of Pope's Creek, Westmoreland County, January 10, 1788. *Harris*:48; 15 W (1) 187.

6. See supra, n. 5.

7. See supra, n. 11.

8. George Augustine Washington (1763-1793), nephew of GW and son of Charles Washington, his younger brother. He was aide-de-camp to General Lafayette. After the Revolution he was manager at Mount Vernon until illness forced his retirement.

9. Frances Bassett Washington (1767-1796) was a niece of MW, the daughter of her sister Anna Dandridge Bassett (1739-1777) and Colonel Burwell Bassett of Eltham (1734-1793). She married (1) George Augustine Washington, and (2) Tobias Lear.

10. See supra, n. 2.

11. Thomas Allison lived in the Accotink Creek area, near GW's mill.

12. George Washington Parke Custis (1781-1857) was MW's grandson, the only son of John Parke Custis.

13. Eleanor Parke Custis (1779-1852), MW's granddaughter and the third daughter of John Parke Custis. She and her brother, George Washington Parke Custis, were the "adopted" children of GW and MW.

14. See supra, n. 14.

15. The docketing is in the hand of GW. *Writings*, 29:266, 398-99, 440. The bonds were sent to GW. After judgment was rendered in the suit, he then requested John Dandridge to purchase whatever slaves he desired from him and the money then realized was to be turned over to Dandridge's mother. In 1785 Bartholomew Dandridge, Sr. was shown with 103 taxable slaves. Personal communication of Dr. Malcolm Harris and G.H.S. King, February 16, 1959.

To Mrs. Ann Welsh

Madam   Mount Vernon, Decr 8th 1788
You may readily conceive that I felt sensible for your situation - and that were it as much in my power as it is my desire I would contribute effectually to your relief - after having said this, I need only add, that as the general possesses the same good disposition towards you, - and writes on the subject himself, it is unnecessary for me to say more than that my best wishes attend you, - and that I am madam[1]

> Your most obed servt
> M Washington

Mrs. Welsh
Mrs. Martha Washingtons Letter

ALS, MiU-C.

1. Mrs. Ann Welsh, a resident of Connecticut, wrote General Washington requesting his aid in obtaining the commutation notes due her as a result of the loss of her husband and brother during the Revolution. Both were officers and were her sole support. See: Ann Welsh to GW, November 12, 1788; GW to Ann Welsh, December 8, 1788. DLC:GW.

V

The Presidential Era, 1789–1797

To John Dandridge

My Dear John[1]   Mount Vernon. April the 20th 1789
    I am truly sorry to tell that the General is gone to New York, - Mr Charles Thompson came express to him, on the 14th - when, or wheather he will ever come home again god only knows, - I think it was much too late for him to go in to publick life again, but it was not to be avoided, our family will be deranged as I must soon follow him[2]
    I am greved at parting, and sorry to part with your sister as well as with the rest of the family, - I expect to set out the middle of may and have it not my power to send Patty home;[3] I shall be very glad to see you hear before I goe and wish you could make it convenient to come up for Patty - as it is out of my power to send her down - the same Horses that carred the General is to return for me to carry me to New York -
    My love and good wishes to your mother grandmother Brothers and sisters and believe me Dear

> John your most
> affectionate
> Aunt
> M Washington

ALS, DLC:GW.

1. John Dandridge was a nephew of Mrs. Washington, the son of her brother Bartholomew Dandridge. He practiced law in New Kent County.

2. Due to a lack of quorum, the new Federal Congress was not able to count the electoral votes for the presidency until April 6, 1789. It was almost certain that Washington would be elected. John Langdon, president pro-tem of the Senate, dispatched Charles Thomson, long time secretary of the Continental Congress, to Mount Vernon to inform Washington of his election. Thomson left New York April 7th and arrived at Mount Vernon on the 14th. Washington immediately dispatched a letter of acceptance to Langdon. Accompanied by

Thomson and Colonel David Humphreys, he set out for New York on the 16th, arriving there about 2:00 P.M. on the 25th. He was sworn into office on April 30th. The President's coach then returned to Mount Vernon in order to carry Mrs. Washington and her party to New York. She was accompanied by her nephew, Robert Lewis (1769-1829) and her two grandchildren. They arrived in New York on May 28th. Lewis was the son of The President's only sister, Betty Washington Lewis. The President usually called him "Bob." See, *Private Affairs*, p. 23. For an interesting account of Mrs. Washington's journey, see Robert Lewis's journal in the archives of the Mount Vernon Ladies' Association of the Union.

3. Martha Washington Dandridge, sister of John Dandridge. She was called Patcy by the family. She arrived at Mount Vernon on July 17, 1788 for an extended visit.

From Col. Clement Biddle

Madam

I waited on you with Mrs. Biddle but not finding you within, beg leave to offer you our Services if we can be of any use while you are in town and if you should choose to direct any persons to me for payment I have money of the Presidents in my hands.

> With great respect
> I am
> Madam yr. mo. obedt. Ser
> C.B.[1]

Sunday May 24 1789
The Doctor say
Billy will
be able to be sent
forwarded some
day this week[2]

Text taken from *Pennsylvania Magazine of History and Biography*, 43:64. Hereafter referred to PMHR.

1. Clement Biddle (1740-1814), a Philadelphia merchant, was active in the revolutionary cause. He was deputy quartermaster-general for the New Jersey and Pennsylvania militia, with the rank of colonel, and had participated in the battle of Trenton, Brandywine, Germantown, and Monmouth. Later he was one of General Greene's aid-de-camps. Following the war he resumed his mercantile business and was the President's factor in Philadelphia. Mrs. Washington was enroute from Mount Vernon to join the President there. She arrived in New York on May 28th, accompanied by Mrs. Robert Morris, who had joined her in Philadelphia.

2. Billy (William Lee) was the President's body servant and favorite slave. See, supra, MW to Mrs. John Parke Custis, May 15, 1779, n. 3. Billy Lee had fractured one knee cap in 1785 and the other one in 1788, and as a result encountered considerable pain and disability on the journey. He was left in Philadelphia for treatment. The President discouraged his taking up residence in New York, since it would entail climbing three flights of stairs, however, Billy persisted and the President acquiesced. See, *Private Affairs*, p.4.

To Fanny Bassett Washington

My dear Fanny   (June 8, 1789)

   I have the pleasure to tell you, that we had a very agreable journey, - I arrived in philadelphia on fryday after I left you without the least accident to distress us,[1] were met by the President of the state[2] with the city troop of Horse and conducted safe to Grays ferry, where a number of Ladies and Gentlemen came to meet me, - and after a cold colation we proceed to town, - I went to Mr. Morrises[3] - the children was very well and chearfull all the way, Nelly[4] complained a very little of being sick - as soon as I could I sent for the stay maker and gave him your measure and directed him to send the stays to Colo Biddle, when done to be sent to you, - also two pair of shoes of a new fashioned kind those with Low Heels are for you, those with the high heels is for Mrs. Stuart,[5] with a pr apiece for the two dear little girls[6] - all which I hope has come to your hands before this

   I set out on Monday with Mrs Morris and her two Daughters[7] and was met on wednesday morning by the President Mr. Morris and Colo H[8] at Elizabethtown point with the fine Barge you have seen so much said of in the papers with the same oars men that carried the P. to New York - dear little Washington[9] seemed to be lost in a mase at the great parade that was made for us all the way we come - The Governor of the state[10] meet me as soon as we landed, and led me up to the House, the paper will tell you how I was complimented on my landing - I thank god the Prdt is very well, and the Gentlemen with him are all very well, - the House he is in is a very good one and is handsomely furnished all new for the General - I have been so much engaged since I came hear that I have never opened your Box or directions but shall soon have time as most of the visits are at an end - I have not had one half hour to myself since the day of my arrival, - my first care was to get the children to a good school, which they are boath very much pleased at ... as no other kind of cushing are worne hear but the crape cushing, or the Hair draped like one I did not send one for you - all the genteel people say Crape cushing is not proper to send to you - but I think in the country where you cannot have a hair dresser they will do very well - My Hair is set and dressed every day - and I have put on white muslin Habits for the summer - you would I fear think me a good deal in the fashion if you could but see me - My dear Fanny send me by some safe convance my Black lace apron and handkerchief they are in one of my drawers in the chest of drawers in my chamber and some thread lace or joining nett it is in one of the Baskets on the shelf in my closet they were fine net Handkerchiefs which I intended to make cap boarders off - I think I shewed it to you and told you I intended to make a border of them - if my Black Handkerchief is not in the drawer Charlot[11] knows where it is to be found - I should think that there could not be any impropriety in Hariot's[12] going to see her cousin whenever she desires it - Remember me to all and believe me your most affectionate -

M Washington

give my love to
Harriot and send
me the measure of
her foot

ALS. Text from Decatur: *Private Affairs*, p. 20-21, 28.

    1. Robert Lewis would hardly have agreed with his aunt. See his "Journal" in the Mount Vernon archives, in which he recounts the harrowing experiences of the journey as far as Baltimore.

    2. Thomas Mifflin (1744-1800), aide-de-camp to the General, major-general and quartermaster-general of the Continental Army. He participated in the seige before Boston, the battles of Trenton and Princeton, and in the cabal against the General in 1777. Serving in the Continental Congress, he became its president for a brief period, during which time it fell his duty to accept the return of General Washington's commission at Annapolis, December 23, 1783. Mifflin was a member of the Constitutional Convention and signed the document. He served three terms as governor of Pennsylvania. He has been accused of being petulant, slipshod, jealous, and inefficient. *DAB*, 12:606.

    3. Robert and Mary White Morris.

    4. Eleanor Parke Custis.

    5. Eleanor Calvert Custis Stuart.

    6. Elizabeth Parke Custis and Martha Parke Custis.

    7. Mary White Morris (1748-1827) was the daughter of Thomas and Esther Hewlings White. She was a sister of William White, the first Episcopal bishop in the United States. Her daughters were Hetty and Maria. See, Young, *Forgotten Patriot: Robert Morris*, p. 194, 245, 255, N.Y. 1950.

    8. Colonel David Humphreys.

    9. George Washington Parke Custis.

    10. George Clinton (1739-1812), brigadier-general during the Revolution and seven times governor of New York. He was twice elected vice-president of the United States, serving under Presidents Jefferson and Madison.

    11. A dower negress who seems to have acted as head housekeeper and personal maid to Mrs. Washington.

    12. Harriott Washington (1776-1822), daughter of George Washington's brother, Samuel, and his wife, Ann Steptoe Washington. At her father's death in 1781, she and her brothers, George Steptoe and Lawrence Augustine Washington, were almost destitute. The General provided a home for Harriott and support and education for the boys. Harriott later married Andrew Parks. See, *Private Affairs*, p. 179-80.

To Fanny Bassett Washington

(July 1789)

......I wish you to take a prayer book yourself and give one to Hariot the other two to be given to Betty & Patty Custis -

I am pleased to hear that the domestic concerns goe on well - sickness is to be expected and Charlot will lay herself up for as little as any one will - it was right to give them more thread if I did not put enough in each bundle - I am truly sorry to hear of another death in the family so soon[1]-

I shall think myself much obliged to Mrs Bassett[2] for any particular notice she may take of Patty Dandridge - I have a great regard for her and wish her to do well - When you write to your Brother remember me affectionately to them - I was very sorry that I was obliged to leave home so soon after they came to Mount Vernon - My dear Fanny remember me to all enquiring friends to Mr & Mrs L. Washington -[3] the Major and give sweet little Maria a thousand kisses for me - I often think of the dear little engaging child - and wish her with me to hear her little prattle - we shall get the letters for her before she will want them.

ALS. Text from *Private Affairs*, p. 41-42.

1. Probably the death of one of the slaves. The Washingtons often referred to their slaves and servants as part of the Mount Vernon "family."

2. Mrs. Burwell Bassett, II, Elizabeth, the daughter of Daniel McCarty of Pope's Creek, Westmoreland County.

3. Lund and Elizabeth Foote Washington of "Hayfield," Fairfax County.

To Fanny Bassett Washington

(Summer 1789)

Nelly shall begin Musick next week[1] - she has made two or three attempts to write you; but has never finished a letter - she is a little wild creature and spends her time at the window looking at carriages &c passing by which is new to her and very common for children to do.

ALS. Text from *Private Affairs*, p. 20.

1. See, accounts kept by Tobias Lear, October 16, 1789: By Cont'g't Exps. pd Mr. Reinagle for teaching Miss Custis Music & furnishing books 17-0-0; May 15, 1792 "Contingt Expenses pd A. Reinagle for four months tuition of Miss Custis & for Music for her 62 - 20." *Private Affairs*, 33, 76-77, 259. During the second year of his marriage, GW purchased a spinet for Patcy (Martha Parke Custis). After her death in 1774 it apparently remained at Mount Vernon. Many years later it may have been used by her niece, Eleanor Parke Custis. By 1793 she had become proficient enough that the President felt warranted in purchasing a harpsichord for her. It was moved from Philadelphia to Mount Vernon at the termination of his presidency. Ultimately it was taken to Woodlawn Plantation after her marriage to Lawrence Lewis. It was later returned to Mount Vernon by one of her descendants, where it remains. Mrs. Washington was a strict disciplinarian with regard to "practice time," and insisted on four or five hours of practice each day. Nelly rebelled and cried bitterly, but to no avail. See, infra, Martha Washington to Eleanor Parke Custis, February 25, 1797.

To Elizabeth Schuyler Hamilton

August 30, 1789
Monday noon

Mrs Washington presents her compliments to Mrs. Hamilton[1] and if she is disengaged this Evening will do herself the pleasure to visit her

LB, ViMtV.

1. Elizabeth Schuyler Hamilton, daughter of Major-general Philip Schuyler and wife of Alexander Hamilton, Secretary of the Treasury and a member of the President's cabinet.

From Mrs. Ann Willis

Mrs Willis[1] presents her most respectfull complements to the President an Lady and begs there acceptance of four glasses of Virgia honey. She has not a doubt of that article being plenty in the State of New York but perhaps not wrought in the same manner and of course not so pure. She flatters herself if it has no other recommendation than being sent by an acquaintance from a place near that of his Nativity they will be induced to taste it and will be happy to hear of the welfare of the family and that they have made an agreeable breakfast on it.

Fredericksburg[2]
Septr 18 1789

ALS (Third person), DLC:GW.

1. Mrs. Ann Willis was the second wife of GW's cousin, Lewis Willis (1734-1813). He was the son of GW's aunt, Mildred Washington Gregory Willis (1696-c.1745) and her third husband, Colonel Henry Willis. See page ?? for draft of GW's reply.

2. The Willis's resided at Willis Hill, near Fredericksburg.

To Dr. David Stuart

Dear Sir   New York, September 21, 1789

Your letter of the 12th instt. came duly to hand. I have given the subject of it every consideration that time and my situation would enable me to do. The result is, that if Mr. Alexander, upon your recovery of the land for which the price, and mode of payment is disputed, and paying rent for it during the time it has been out of his possession (the latter to be fixed by men of judgment and impartiality) is disposed to accomodate the Suit which is pending between you, as administrator of John Parke Custis Esqr. deceased, and himself, that it would, all circumstances considered, be most advisable to accede to it. My reasons for this are many.

It is unnecessary I conceive to detail them if I had leisure, which in truth is not the case. I am - Dear Sir[1]

> Your Most Obedt. Hble
> Servt
> G°: Washington

My opinion coincides with the above, and I advise the adoption of the measure accordingly.

> Martha Washington

ALS, ViMtV.

1. John Parke Custis had purchased the Abingdon tract from Robert Alexander in 1778 at a price the General considered excessive. After Custis's death in 1781, his uncle, Bartholomew Dandridge, became executor of the estate. At Dandridge's death in 1785, Dr. David Stuart, who had married Custis's widow, Eleanor, was named executor. After several years of negotiations over the remuneration to Alexander, a compromise was reached. Alexander would take back the land in return for a fair rent for the years it had been out of his possession. During these years the Custis-Stuarts had been living at Abingdon. After repossession by Alexander they moved to Hope Park, about five miles from Fairfax Courthouse.

To Mrs. Abigail Smith Adams

(October 1789)
Mrs Washington presents her compliments to Mrs Adams and family and requests the pleasure of their company today to dinner & if agreeable will in the evening accompany her to the concert.[1]

LB ViMtV.

1. A heavily corrected draft, superimposed upon the draft of the letter from Robert Lewis, the President's nephew and secretary, to Mrs. Ann Willis of Willis Hall, Fredericksburg, Virginia, thanking her for the honey sent the Washingtons. See supra, Ann Willis to the Washingtons, September 18, 1789. Lewis wrote the acknowledgment in the absence of the President, who had just left New York on his New England tour, October 15, 1789. See *Diaries*, 5:340.

To Fanny Bassett Washington

My dear Fanny   New York October the 23d 1789
I have by Mrs Sims[1] sent you a watch it is one of the cargoe that I have so long mentioned to you, that was expected, I hope is such a one as will please you - it is of the newest fashon, if that has any influence on your tast - The chain is of Mr Lears[2] choosing and such as Mrs Adams the vice Presidents[3] Lady and those in the polite circle wares. It will last as long as the fashon - and by that time you can get another of a fashonable kind - I send to dear Maria[4] a piece of Chino to make her a frock - the piece of muslin I hope is long enough for an apron for you, and in exchange

for it, I beg you will give me the worked muslin apron you have like my gown that I made just before I left home of worked muslin as I wish to make a petticoat of the two aprons - for my gown - Mrs Sims will give you a better account of the fashons than I can - I live a very dull life hear and know nothing that passes in the town - I never goe to the publick place - indeed I think I am more like a state prisoner than anything else, there is certain bounds set for me which I must not depart from - and as I can not doe as I like I am obstinate and stay at home a great deal -

The President set out this day week on a tour to the eastward Mr Lear and Major Jackson[5] attended him - my dear children has had very bad colds but thank god they are getting better My love and good wishes attend you and all with you - remember me to Mr & Mrs L Wn[6] how is the poor child - kiss Maria I send her two little handkerchiefs to wipe her nose

> Adieu
> I am my dear Fanny yours
> most affectionately
> M Washington

Mrs F Washington
Mount Vernon
Favored by
Mrs. Sims

ALS, PHi.

1. Probably Nancy Douglas Simms, wife of Colonel Charles Simms of Alexandria. *Diaries*, 6:313.

2. Tobias Lear (1762-1816), a native of New Hampshire, was recommended to Washington as a private secretary and tutor to the Custis children. He arrived at Mount Vernon on May 29, 1786. For the next seven years he lived at Mount Vernon as one of the family and became confidante, loyal friend and devoted employee. During the presidential years he accompanied the President to New York and then to Philadelphia. On the presidential tour of New England in 1789, Lear accompanied the President. In 1790 Lear married Mary (Polly) Long of Portsmouth, New Hampshire. They had one son, Benjamin Lincoln Lear. Mary Lear died in 1793, as did Major George Augustine Washington, the husband of Fanny Bassett Washington. It would not have been unusual, being family members at Mount Vernon and with youthful passions, that Fanny and Lear should fall in love. They were married in August, 1975. But, in late March Fanny died, probably of the consumption that had killed her first husband. Lear had left the employ of the President and spent the years of 1793-94 in Europe. When war with France became imminent in 1798, Washington, then in retirement, was called back to lead the American army. He appointed Lear as his military secretary, with the rank of colonel. He was present during Washington's final illness and death. In 1802 he took as his third wife, Frances Dandridge Henley, another niece of Mrs. Washington, a first cousin of Fanny, his second wife. During the years 1801 and 1802 he remained at Mount Vernon, acting as secretary advisor to Mrs. Washington, devastated by the death of her husband. After her death in May of 1802, he left Mount Vernon and from then until his death he was in the employ of the United States Government, assistant consul-general to San Domingo and Algiers. As the architect of and unfavorable treaty with the Dey of Algiers, he was recalled to Washington and given a position as an accountant in the War Department. He committed suicide on October 11, 1816. See, *DAB*, 11:76-77; Brighton, *The Checkered Career*

of Tobias Lear, Portsmouth, 1985.

3. Abigail Adams (1744-1818), wife of John Adams (1742-1826). She was the daughter of Reverend William Smith and his wife, Elizabeth Quincy. Always of delicate health, she became noted as a woman of letters. Following the Treaty of Peace in 1783, she spent almost four years in Paris and London. The following twelve years were spent as the wife of the Vice-President and President. After 1801 her life was spent at her home in Quincy, Massachusetts where she continued as housewife, mother, and correspondent.

4. Anna Maria Washington (1788-1814) was also called Maria. She was the youngest child of Fanny Bassett Washington and Major George Augustine Washington. Left without parents at an early age, she had a difficult childhood. She seems to have been shunted from one relative to another. Maria was a great favorite of Mrs. Washington and in spite of her erratic behavior as a child, she became a gracious lady, married Reuben Thornton, bore two children and died at the age of twenty six.

5. William Jackson (1759-1828), was born in England and reared in South Carolina. During the Revolution he served on General Benjamin Lincoln's staff in the Southern Department. Later Jackson was instrumental in obtaining supplies for the army in Europe. Following the war he remained in Philadelphia and embarked on a successful mercantile career. In 1787 he applied to General Washington for the position of secretary to the Constitutional Convention and was accepted. Upon taking office, Washington appointed him one of his secretaries. Jackson accompanied the President on his New England tour in 1789 and the Southern tour in 1790. He resigned his position of secretary in 1791. In 1795, when Bartholomew Dandridge resigned as one of the secretaries, Jackson again volunteered his services, but was appointed surveyor of customs at Philadelphia. For the last twenty-eight years of his life he served as Secretary of the Society of the Cincinnatti. See, *DAB*, 9:559-61.

6. Lund and Elizabeth Foote Washington.

To Abigail Smith Adams

My Dear Madam   (November 4, 1789)

I should have been very happy to have seen you yesterday. - and am truly sorry the bad day disappointed me of the plesure, your servant brought you kind favor faver yesterday while I was at dinner. he could not stay and the evening was so bad, - I have the plesure to ask you, how yourself Mrs Smith[1] Miss Smith[2] and the little ones[3] are today, I intended yesterday after the sermon to bring the children out with me on a visit to you, but the weather prevented me -

I will my dear Madam - doe myself the pleasure to dine with you on satterday with my family and shall be very happy with General Knox[4] and the Laides, - mentioned or any others you plese

> I am dear Madam with
> esteem your
> your affectionate Friend
> and Hble Svt
> M Washington[5]

Wednesday Morn
4 November
Our best wishes to
Mrs Smith & ca

(Address)
Mrs Adams[6]
(Docketed)
Mrs Washington
Nov br 4 1789

ALS, MHi.

1. Abigail Adams Smith, Daughter of John and Abigail Smith Adams. She married William Stephen Smith.

2. Sarah Smith, sister of William Stephen Smith. She resided with the Adamses in New York and Philadelphia. She married Charles Adams, the alcoholic son of John and Abigail Adams. *Diaries*, 5:456-57.

3. William Steuben Smith (b. 1787) and John Adams Smith (b. 1788). Whitney, *Abigail Adams*, Boston, 1947, p. 99, 213, 222.

4. Secretary of War, General Henry Knox. See supra, Martha Washington to General Henry Knox, March 6, 1783, n. 1.

5. The President left New York for his New England tour, Thursday, October 15, 1789 and returned on Friday, November 13th. During his absence Mrs. Washington remained in New York. *Diaries*, 5:460, 498.

6. At this time the Adamses were living in a mansion on Richmond Hill, at the corner of Varick and Van Dam Streets. See, Bowen, *History of the Centennial Celebration of the Inauguration of George Washington as First President of the United States*, New York, 1892, p. 18.

To Mercy Otis Warren

My Dear Madam   New York December the 26th 1789
　　Your very friendly letter of the 27th of last month has afforded me much more satisfaction than all the formal compliments and emty ceremonies of mear etiquette could possably have done. - I am not apt to forget the feelings that have been inspired by my former society with good acquaintances, nor to be insensible to thair expressions of gratitude to the President of the United States; for you know me well enough to do me the justice to beleive that I am only fond of what comes from the heart. - Under a conviction that the demonstrations of respect and affection which have been made to the President originate from that source I cannot deny that I have taken some interest and pleasure in them. - The difficulties which presented themselves to view upon his first entering upon the Presidency, seem thus to be in some measure surmounted: it is owing to this kindness of our numerous friends in all quarters that my new and unwished for situation is not indeed a burden to me. When I was much younger I should , probably, have enjoyed the inoscent gayeties of life as much as most my age; - but I had long since placed all the prospects of my future worldly happyness in the still enjoyments of the fireside at Mount Vernon -
　　I little thought when the war was finished, that any circumstances could possible have happened which would call the General into public life again. I had anticipated, that from this moment we should have been left to grow old in solitude and tranquility togather: that was, my Dear madam, the first and dearest wish of my heart; - but in *that* I have been disapointed; I will not, however, contemplate with too much regret disapointments that were enevitable, though the generals feelings and my own were perfectly in unison with respect to our predilictions for privet life, yet I cannot blame him for having acted according to his ideas of duty in obaying the voice of his country. The consciousness of having attempted to do all the good in his power, and the pleasure of finding his fellow citizens so well satisfied with the disintrestedness of his conduct, will, doubtless, be some compensation for the great sacrifices which I know he has made; indeed in his journeys from Mount Vernon - to this place; in his late Tour through the eastern states, by every public and by every privet information which has come to him, I am persuaded that he has experienced nothing to make him repent his having acted from what he concieved to be alone a sense of indespensable duty: on the contrary, all his sensibility has been awakened in receiving such repeated and unaquivocal proofs of sincear regards from all his country men. with respect to myself, I sometimes think the arrangement is not quite as it ought to have been, that I, who had much rather be at home should

occupy a place with which a great many younger and gayer women would be prodigiously pleased. - As my grand children and domestic connections made a great portion of the felicity which I looked for in this world. - I shall hardly be able to find any substitute that would indemnify me for the Loss of a part of such endearing society. I do not say this because I feel dissatisfied with my present station - no, God forbid: - for everybody and everything conspire to make me as contented as possable in it; yet I have too much of the vanity of human affairs to expect felicity from the splendid scenes of public life. - I am still determined to be cheerful and to be happy in whatever situation I may be, for I have also learnt from experianence that the greater part of our happiness or misary depends upon our dispositions, and not upon our circumstances; we carry the seeds of the one, or the other about with us, in our minds, wherever we go.

I have two of my grand children with me who enjoy advantages in point of education, and who, I trust by the goodness of providence, will continue to be a great blessing to me, my other two grand children are with thair mother in virginia. -

The Presidents health is quite reestablished by his late journey[1] - mine is much better than it used to be - I am sorry to hear that General Warren has been ill: hope before this time that he may be entirely recovered - we should rejoice to see you both, I wish the best of Heavens blessings, and am my dear madam with esteem and

> regard your friend and Hble
> Sert
> M Washington

Mrs Warren

ALS, MeHi.

1. About the middle of June, 1789, the President developed a fever, followed by tenderness over the left thigh. Swelling and inflammation soon followed. Dr. Bard and two other consultants were unable to make a diagnosis. Consideration was given to the fact that the President might have contracted anthrax. As the swelling progressed, so did the discomfort until at last he was in excruciating pain. Cherry Street, in front of his home, was roped off to prevent the noisy wagons and carts from disturbing his rest. By the 20th the swelling "pointed" into an abscess or carbuncle. It was lanced and drained, whereupon the fever began to subside. For about three weeks it was difficult for him to move about or sit without discomfort. His condition gradually improved, but still continued to drain during September. See, *Freeman,* 5:214-19.

To Fanny Bassett Washington

My Dear Fanny   (March 22, 1790)
    I wrote to you yesterday but forgot to ask you, to look in my old
trunk in the garret, - and you will find a silver seal with my father's arms,
it will be more convenient to make a good impression than to send the
seal, - you may do as you think best, I wish to have it as soon as you can
send it to me, - there was a white necklace in the paper with the pins please
to send that and some small mother of pearl beads that is in one of the
drawers in my cabinet - if you seal them secure in a paper they will come
to me very safe, - you must have them directed to the President, - my love
and good wishes attend you and all with you Remember me to all
enquiring friends - and believe me your most affectionate

                                            M Washington

ALS, ViMtV.

To Robert Morris

                                            (March 27, 1790)
    The President and Mrs. W - Compliments and thanks to Mr. Morris
for his politeness. - They have nothing to charge Mr. Morris with but their
affectionate regards for Mrs Morris and the family; and to wish him a
pleasanter journey than the state of the Roads promise, and a safe return
to this City[1] when his business in Philadelphia shall be accomplished

                                            Saturday 27th March 1790

Al, third person, by GW. Feinstone Collection, David Library of the American Revolution,
Washington Crossing, Pennsylvania. On loan to the American Philosophical Society,
Philadelphia, PA.
    1. New York City, at that time the seat of government.

To Mercy Otis Warren

My Dear Madam,   New York, June the 12th 1790
    I ought to apologize for the interval that has passed between a
receipt and acknowledgment of your obliging letter written in March last;
but I hardly know what apology will be sufficient to excuse the apparent,
though unintentional neglect. I believe the truth is always the best ground
for an apology on such occasions.- Though I may not have a great deal
of business of consequence to do; yet I have a great many avocations of
one kind or another which imperceptibly consume my time - and I know
not whether one's reluctance to writing much does increase with one's

years. The sevear illness with which the President was attacked some weeks ago absorbed every other consideration, in my care and anxiety for him - These reasons, I trust, will have their due weight in your candid mind.-During the President sickness, the kindness which everybody manifested, and the interest which was universally taken in his fate, were really very affecting to me. He seemed less concerned himself as to te event, than peraps almost any other person in ye united states.[1] Happily he is now perfectly recovered and I am restored to my ordinary state of tranquillity, and usually good flow of spirits. - For my part I continue to be as hapy hear as I could be at any place except Mount Vernon. In truth I should be very ungreatfull if I did not acknowledge that everything has been done, which politness, hospitality or friendship could suggest, to make my situation as satisfactory and agreeable as possible. My grand-children have likewise good opportunitieas for acquiring a useful and accomplished education. In their happiness, my own is, in a great measure, involved. But for the ties of affection which attract me so strongly to my near connection and worthy friends, I should feel myself indeed much weaned from all enjoyments of this transitory life.

If congress should have a recess this summer (as it is expected will be the case) I hope to go home to Mount Vernon for a few months: and from that expectation I already derive much comfort. Especially as, I believe, the exercise, relaxation and amusement to be expected from such a journey, will tend vey much to confirm the President's health. This is also the opinion of all his Physicians.

In passing down the vale of time, and in journeying through such a mutable world as that in which we are placed, we must expect to meet with a great and continual mixture of afflictions and blessings. This a mingled cup which an overruling providence undoubtedly dispences to us for the wises and best purposes. - and as you justly observe, shall we shortsighted mortals dare to arraign the decrees of eternal wisdom - that you and yours may always be under the kind protection and guardianship of that providence is the sincre wish of

> Dear Madam
> your affectionate friend
> and humble Servant
> M Washington

ALS. Feinstone Collection, David Library of the American Revolution, Washington Crossing, Pennsylvania. On loan to the American Philosophical Society, Philadelphia, PA.

1. On May 10, 1790, The President complained of "a bad cold." The cold increased in severity within the next two days. He then developed symptoms of pneumonia and for the next several days his physical condition rapidly deteriorated. Four physicians were called into attendance. They despaired of his life, and it became widely known throughout the city that he was dangerously ill, that he might not survive. On the morning of May 15th his breathing became labored. Those nearest him felt the end was near. Suddenly about

4:00 P.M.his fever suddenly dropped and he developed profuse perspiration. His condition improved rapidly and by the 20th of May he was considered out of danger. His convalescence continued for a period of six weeks. *Diaires*, 6:76-77. *Freeman*, 6:259-61; *Staff Meetings of the Mayo Clinic*, February 18, 1942, p. 111.

To Elizabeth Schuyler Hamilton

Wednesday 7th July 1790

Mrs Washington presents her compliments to Mrs Hamilton, and requests she will have the goodness to transmit her best thanks to Mrs Church[2] for the token of remembrance so elegantly wrought by the hands of the amiable donor, Mrs Washington wishes that her acknowledgements may be expressed in such true and forceable language as to render them particularly acceptable to Mrs Church.[1]

ALS (Third person), MHi.

1. Unidentified. Appended to the note is the following: "This note presented to Mrs. G. Lee by Mrs. Alexander Hamilton." It was in a scrap-book made by Mrs. George Gardner Lee (1780-1865).

From John Lamb

Honored Madam, New York 10th Dec. 1790

I have to beg your acceptance of three Barrells Apples, one Jar preserved Ginger, & Kit of Soused Salmon which are on board the Sloop Union, William Watson Master; enclosed, is a receipt for the same - you will be pleased to present my most respectful compliments to his Excellency the President & permit me to subscribe myself with sentiments of the highest respect.

Honored Madam
Your most obedient
& very humble servant
John Lamb[1]

Copy[2] DLC:GW.

1. John Lamb (1735-1800), Colonel and later Brigadier-general in the Continental Army. His service was almost entirely limited to the artillery. Lamb was present at the attack on St. John's, Quebec, and served with distinction at Yorktown. Following the war he was customs collector at New York from 1784-1797.

2. The text is taken from a copy made by Rev. William Buell Sprague (1795-1876). Sprague graduated from Yale College in 1815. The following year he was employed as a tutor for the children of Lawrence and Eleanor Parke Custis Lewis, at Woodlawn Plantation. Sprague, who was one of the first autograph collectors in the United States, ingratiated himself to Justice Bushrod Washington. Justice Washington had inherited Mount Vernon and all the papers of George Washington. He naively gave permission for young Sprague to remove whatever portions of the Washington correspondence he wished, provided he would leave copies. See, Draper, *An Essay on the Autographic Collections of the Signers of the Declaration of Independence and of the Constitution*, (New York, 1889), p. 14; Eaton (ed.), *Index to the George Washington Papers*, Library of Congress, p. x, Washington, 1964.

To Colonel Clement Biddle

Mrs. Washingtons compliments to Colo Biddle - will be glad to know, if he had got the knives and fork, - and wine, if it is very good and what quantity she will be very glad to see the list of the things when he has collected them altogether she beggs to know if he has remembered the ginn and liquers the General desires to have them sent and that they may be of the best kind - MW begs he will let Mr Powel know when the vessel goes that the Chariot and coach Harness may go round with the other things they will be packed up ready for to be put on board[1]-

Sunday one oclock

(Address)
Colo Biddle

ALS (Third person), PHi.
1. The letter concerns supplies for the presidential household in New York. Colonel Biddle was the President's factor in Philadelphia, where goods were more available than in New York.

To Colonel Clement Biddle

We are much in want of perfumes such as orrange flower water & for cooking

....

Will you be so good as to get for me the Beauties of Milton Thompson Young and Harvey

M W - n

....

We are much in want of mops and clamps for scouring Brushes - will you get 6 of each and two Cloths Baskets 1 larger than the other

....

Pickled walnuts
India Mangoes
Thompson's Seasons
Guthries Geography
Art of Speaking
6 mops or sweeping brushes
6 Clamp scrubbing brushes
2 Cloths Baskets
Orange flower Water
perfumes for Cooking.[1]

AN, PHi.
1. The first three notes are in the handwriting of Mrs. Washington. The last list of items is in an unknown hand.

To Abigail Adams

Mrs Washington, presents her compliments to Mrs Adams, - if it is agreable to her, to Let Miss Smith[1] come to dance with Nelly & Washington, the Master attends Mondays Wednesdays and Frydays at five oclock in the evenings.

Mrs Washington will be very happy to see Miss Smith

Tuesday morning
January 25 (1791)[2]

ALS, ViMtV-W.
1. Miss Smith was the granddaughter of Vice President John Adams and his wife, Abigail Adams.
2. In his diary for January 1790, GW identifies the 25th as Monday. The year 1790 not being a leap year, January 25, 1791 would occur on a Tuesday.

To Janet Livingston Montgomery

Dear Madam[1]   Philadelphia January the 29th 1791
I must trust to your goodness to receive the apology I shall offer for this late acknowledgement of your letter of the 26th of October, - I received it but a few days before I left Mount Vernon, and you will redily conceive that my time and my mind were so fully occupied with and about my friends there as to afford me little oppertunity for writing; and since my arrived in this place the business of settling in a new habitation receiving and returning visits have left me no time for myself while in health;[2] and for some weeks past a very severe cold has rendered me incapable of doing anything - I am thank god now recovering.

Having offered the reasons for this delay in answering your letter permit me madam to congratulate you upon your safe arrival in your native country and to the arms of your friends, none but those who have been as long absent as you have, and at so great a distance from their friends can conceive of the sensations which are experienced upon meeting them again; I dare say your feelings on that occasion were not to be described - and that you returned from Europe with all your prejudices in favor of America I have no doubt; for I think our country affords every thing that can give pleasure or satisfaction to a rational mind, I never apprehended that your good sence would be so far overcome by the splendour and hurry which you might see abroad as to make a return to your native Country unpleasant -

I beg you will be asured that I have a greatful sence of the affectionate terms in which you express your regret at not finding us in New York - I have been so long accustomed to conform to events which are governed by the public voice that I hardly dare indulge any personal wishes which cannot yield to that - But whare ever I may be my friends may always relay upon a greatful and affectionate remembrance; and and altho I will not give up the expectation of seeing you again; yet in any event you will be remembered with friendship and will have my best wishes

I beg you will present my kind regards to your mother and sisters[3] - the President writes with me in congratulations on your return and presents his complements to you

> with very great regard
> I have the honor to be
> Dr. Madam your
> most obdt Hble
> M Washington

ALS, MB.

1. Janet Livingston Montgomery (1743-1828), was the eldest daughter of Judge Robert R. Livingston of Clermont (1718-1775) and Margaret Beekman (1724-1800). She was the widow of Brigadier-general Richard Montgomery (1736-1775), killed at the siege of Quebec.

2. The Washingtons left Philadelphia on Monday, September 6, 1790, and arrived at Mount Vernon, Saturday, September 11th. They returned to Philadelphia on Saturday November 27th, and took up residence in a house on Market Street, belonging to Robert Morris. During their stay at Mount Vernon the Philadelphia house was vacated by the Morrises, remodeled and redecorated. See, Baker, *Washington After the Revolution*, Philadelphia, 1898, p. 196-200. Hereafter referred to as *Baker*.

3. Mrs. Montgomery's mother was Margaret Beekman Livingston (1724-1800). Her sisters were Margaret, Catharine, Gertrude, Joanna, and Alida. They all married men of prominence and would have been known to the Washingtons. See, Livingston, *The Livingstons of Livingston Manor*, (New York, 1910), p. 555-57.

To Fanny Bassett Washington

My dear Fanny   Philadelphia April the 19th 1791

By Austin[1] who is come home to see his friends - I have the pleasure to tell you we are all tolerable well - I have never heard from the President since he left Mount Vernon - nor from you, - some day last week I wrote to you and inclosed some muslin borders for Charlot to hem - when they are done be so god as to send them back to me by Austin when he comes as his stay will be short indeed I could but illy spare him at this time but to fulfill my promise to his wife - the children join me in love to you the Major and children - you must let me know if you are in a certain way and when the event will happen,[2] as it must be very inconvenient to you for us to come home about the time - our stay will be short and I wish to have all well if possible, at this time - I expect to be coming home some time about the first of August - how are your Brothers,[3] is B. Lewis married[4]

> adue my dear Fanny &
> believe me your
> most affectionate
> M Washington[5]

ALS, ViMtV.

1. Austin, a dower negro slave who had been with the Washingtons in New York and Philadelphia, was returned to Mount Vernon to visit his wife and friends. It is likely the reason for returning him to Virginia was to prevent his possible emancipation. According to Pennsylvania law, when a slave owner took up citizenship in that state, his slaves, providing they were of age, would become emancipated at the end of six months. While Washington was not a citizen of Pennsylvania and was thereby excluded from the law, he nevertheless did not wish to assume the risk. All but three of the servants were dower slaves, and did not wish to lose them, and thus be required to re-imburse Mrs. Washington's estate for them. See *Private Affairs*, 223-26.

2. Fanny was indeed pregnant. She delivered her fourth child, Charles Augustine Washington early in the summer of 1791. See, *Private Affairs*, p. 226.

3. Burwell Bassett, II, of Eltham (1764-1841), and John Bassett (1765-1822), of "Farmington," Hanover County.

4. This might be Betty Lewis (1772-1836), grand niece of the President and daughter of Captain Fielding Lewis, Jr. (1751-1803), who was his nephew. She married Alexander Spottswood c. 1790.

5. See *Private Affairs*, p. 226.

To Fanny Bassett Washington

My dear Fanny   Philadelphia June the 5th 1791
      Your letter of the 29th of May, did not reach my hands till yesterday - I was then very sick having got cold by the change of weather; - or I would have got and sent by Hercules[1] the silk and & - I will as soon as I am well enough to go out make the best collection I can and send it by a safe hand. I believe they are to be had in this city. As to fine muslin I have never been able to find a yard of fine Jaconet muslin in this place. nor is the Book fine - I will lay the money out in the best way I can. - I sent by Hercules some rufles for my little Boys bosom which I beg you will make Charlot hem - and ship them ready to sew on and send me six at a time as his old ruffles are worne to raggs - Hercules comes home to be ready for his master - I have got several things for kitchen use but - the vessel will not sail in time to be there as soon as he will - I also send some East India sugar - it seems to be clean and while I was in hopes it would have arrived in time to preserve and dry cherreys - I have had letters from the President from savanna - and expect he will be with you by this day week.[2] I should be very happy to come on to see you and meet him but that is out of my power, I am not well enough to bear the journey - and

if I was - I could not come so long a way without a gentleman - and Mr. Lear could not leave this to come with me - if you can get timothy for half a crown in town it is much cheaper than it can be had hear - the last India vessels has brought nothing but tea and nankeens and the very coarse set kind of callacos - and such muslin that sells for four and five shillings a yard - I was thinking to get some of the coarse cotton to make her under coats she must have them of some kind or other - it would be well for the major to mention it to the General - I sent to Betty Custis[3] a pr. of stays which Mrs. Stuart[4] says will fit her and she sent them to Mr. Snow to return to me if they will suite Miss Harriet[5] she may as well keep them - as to have a pair made for her - I have seen no timothy hear sold for less than four & six pence and that but one piece[6] - I got what was left and sent it to the girls.

Batt Dandridge[7] arrived hear yesterday he is as yellow as a mulato, - he is inoculated this day for the small pox - Mr. Lear's child[8] has got quite well, and grows finely - the children are both well - and so is all our family except myself - and god only knows wheather - I shall ever be in tolerable health again -I am sorry to hear that your little Boy[9] is not in good health - worms is the cause of all complaints in children - I have sent three Butter printers send one of the larger ones to Mrs. Stuart and - keep the others until I come. - my love to the major - kiss the children. - and believe me my dear Fanny.

Your most affectionate
M Washington

ALS, CPc0.

1. Hercules was a Mount Vernon slave who accompanied the Washingtons to Philadelphia as a cook. He was affectionately called "Uncle Harkless." See, *Private Affairs*, p. 214.

2. Mrs. Washington was correct in her schedule. The President arrived at Mount Vernon on June 12th.

3. Elizabeth (Eliza) Park Custis (1776-1832).

4. Eleanor Calvert Custis Stuart, mother of the above.

5. Harriet Washington, (1776-1822), daughter of Samuel Washington, the President's younger brother.

6. Unidentified material. This might mean dimmity, a cotton cloth, alternately woven with coarse threads.

7. Bartholomew Dandridge, Jr. (d. 1802), a nephew of Mrs. Washington and one of the President's secretaries.

8. Benjamin Lincoln Lear, (1791-1832), son of Tobias Lear and his first wife, Mary (Polly) Long. He was born in the President's house in Philadelphia, March 11, 1791. *Private Affairs*, p. 129.

9. George Fayette Washington (1790-1867).

To Fanny Bassett Washington

My dear Fanny -   Philadelphia August the 29th 1791
        Your letter of the 25th is come to hand with the ruffles - I wish you'd
had them whiped - it was but little more trouble for Charlot, they cannot
be sewed on the wristbands till they are whiped - she is so indolent that
she will doe nothing but what she is told she knows how work should be
done, - I cannot find how it is possible for her and Caroline to be
althogether taken up in making the peoples cloths - if you suffer them to
goe on so idele they will in a little time doe nothing but work for
themselves - I am sorry for pore Giles[1] - & fear he never will be well again
- I am glad to hear that you and the children are well again and that the
Major was getting better - the President talks of living this place about the
20th of September to come to Mount Vernon - I hope you will be all well
- as it is the greatest pleasure I have to come home to see you and Mrs
Stuart and the dear girls - I shall send Hercules home when I leve this and
will have some porter put up to send by a vessel that will sail for
Alexandria some time this week - as you know my dear Fanny that it is
probable that we shall have company all the time we stay - it will be
necessary to make some provision for us - we shall not stay longer at home
than the 17th of October - we bring so many with us that it requires some
preparation and I have been so much indisposed my self that I shall leve
the House keeping altogether to you - I shall not conscern in the matter
at all, - but leve it to you, - make Nathan clean his kitchen and every thing
in it and about it very well - I shall bring work for Charlot to doe for me
so that she must endeavor to get your family business done as fast as they
can, - I hope Mrs. Stuart will come to meet us at Mount Vernon. I shall
let her know the time I expect to be there - have they got a Carriage or
Horses yet - The General has got the better of all his complaints - dear little
Wash is quite well and has a very good apetite and gains flesh and
strength every day he is now well enough to go to school - I hope the
Major will be better for his trip over the mountains let us know how he
is when you hear from him - my love to the children - and all friends -

                                   I am my dear Fanny your
                                   most affectionate
                                   M Washington

(Docket)
From Mrs M Washington
August 1790 (sic)
(Address)
Mrs F Washington

ALS, ViMtV.
    1. Giles was one of the Washington slaves and a coach driver and postillion.

From John Dandridge

My Dr. Aunt   Pamocra[1] Septr. 6, 91

　　I was very sorry to hear of Washington illness sometime ago, by a letter from Bart,[2] as well (for your account as on my) - I hope he is well by this time & that you are enjoying the pleasure of his recovery -

　　I expected to have heard (illegible) Bart (illegible) in the presidents' Family, from you before this & I now request you to afford me your information on that subject - Bart is very well pleased with his situation I find by his letters, & I hope he will endeavor to please every body he acts for - I trust you will exercise your authority as a relation as well as your advisor to inforce on him a proper sense of his Duty, & to guard him from being led astray by the temptation to idleness & extravagance which surround him -

　　I now find I shall not be able to raise out of my fathers[3] estate enough to pay all in Debt - The property I had to sell has depreciated in value below any suspicisions, & I have not collected anything due to him in his life, as he kept but four regular accounts & vouchers & those few were burnt in his house - worth £550- paid as security to one (Quarter?) I have also lost as the president perhaps expected that my Mother[4] would be able to pay for the negroes he had lent her hitherto, I have thought it necessary to undeceive him, & I have accordingly write to on the subject[5] - the loan of so many negroes is too much for her to expect, & as she must be reduced to it sometime or other, she had better begin to accomodate herself to the want of them at once - I really thought that I should have been able to buy some of them for her, or I should not have written to you as I did in 1788 - I fear the president may suspect that I meant to deceive him by exciting expectations of payment, which I knew were not well founded: however I assure you, I have till lately been mistaken in my opinion of my Fathers Estate, & I take this early opportunity of informing you & him of it - I would give every farthing I have to my Mother & work myself for the support of her & her little children sooner than I would practise such a Deceit knowingly on any one much less on a benefactor[6] -

　　We are well except my mother who has still a hectic disorder - The Family join in sending their Love & duty to you the Children Th(?)

　　　　　　　　　　　　　　　　　　I am My Dear aunt yrs.
　　　　　　　　　　　　　　　　　　dutifully & affcty
　　　　　　　　　　　　　　　　　　J Dandridge

Let me hear from you
shortly

Df, ViMtV.

1. "Pamocra," New Kent County, was the home of Bartholomew Dandridge, Sr., brother of Martha Washington.

2. Bartholomew Dandridge, Jr., son of the above. He was one of the President's secretaries.

3. Bartholomew Dandridge, Sr. had died at "Pamocra" in 1787.

4. Mary Burbidge Dandridge, widow of the above.

5. John Dandridge, son of Bartholomew Dandridge, Sr., was a lawyer and practiced law in New Kent County. He wrote his uncle, the President, on September 6, concerning his mother's inability to pay for the negroes out of his father's estate and denying any attempt to deceive him.

6. In a letter to John Dandridge, October 2, 1791, the President denied any feeling of misrepresentation on the part of the Dandridges, would permit Mrs. Dandridge the use of the slaves until such time as he would require them, and would give her "timely notice." See, *Writings*, 31:378.

From Anonymous

Mrs. Washington,
Madam,

I am induced from your well known generosity of heart, and charitable disposition, to intrude for a moment on your patience - the object of these lives is to crave a Boon which the writer hopes your benevolence of Soul (manifest on every occasion of this nature) will not refuse to grant to a person whose necessities compell him to make this uncommon request - a request which Madam, is as distressing to his feelings as it may appear to you extra-ordinary, for an Anonymous Signature to make -

A young man of genteel connections in this city, from unforseen circumstances, is likely to be involved in difficulties which if not speedily prevented will be greatly to his disadvantage - if not his utter ruin, his case is of so delicate a nature that he would sooner suffer death, than make it known to the circle of his Friends - 30 Dollars would relieve him from the most inconceivable distress - & to you Mrs Washington as the patroness of distress'd merit he submits his case presuming on that beneficence of mind which is the greatest ornament of human nature & with which Madam, you are so eminently endowed to extricate him from a Scene of (ruin) that will inevitably ensue unless your friendly hand will be pleased to administer that relief which he now humbly sollicits. -

I am Madam
Yr Most Obedt & hum Sert
Anonymous

Philad a 2 Feby 1792

ALS, DLC:GW.

From Anonymous

Mrs. Washington,

    A few nights since I had the honour of leaving a few lines for your perusal signed Anonymous - I now request you will be pleased to give an answer thereto -

    I hope Madam that pity will direct your heart to grant the Boon I have ask'd & I shall, as in deity bound ever pray

Yr. Mo. Obedt Sert
Anonymous

Philada 7 Feby, 1792.

ALS, DLC:GW.

From John Lamb

Honored Madam,   New York 22nd March 1792

    Enclosed is a receipt for two Barrells of Newtown Pippins which I have shipped on board the Sloop New York Packet, and I have to beg your acceptance of them, when they arrive. Mrs. Lamb presents her most respectful compliments to yourself, and his Excellency, the President, to whom you will be pleased to make my best wishes acceptable - and permit me to subscribe myself.

With sentiments of
the highest respect
Honored Madam
Your most obedient
and very humble Servant
John Lamb

The Honorable Mrs. Washington
(Address)
Tobias Lear
Secretary to the President
Philadelphia
(Docket)
Genl Lamb
22 March 1792

ALS, DLC:GW.

To Fanny Bassett Washington

My dear Fanny   Philadelphia April the 22 1792

I am happy to find by your last Letter that your dear little Babes are all well, so young as they are it is quite as well, if they do not take the Hooping cough at this time - the season is favorable and it is provable they would have the complaint very light - yet it is not desirable that they should have it while they are so small - I wish you would let me know in your next which you will reather have chocolate in cakes or the shells I should suppose the expence of boath is the same and I will send that you like best and everything that we shall want, how are your stock of spices nutts are so dear hear that we must do with the indian wallnutt if Frank[1] has taken care to put up a good many of them, sugar is also very high - as is every thing else is it was a very careless trick in Mrs Stuarts maid, to let the children break the Looking glass if one is necessary you can get it in Alexandria as cheap as hear, and as I have no choice get such a glass as you like yourself as it is a matter of indefference to me what kind of glass it is - I am sorry my dear Fanny - you should feel a moments uneasiness for the rose water - I know it was not wanted with you and there is a great deal got hear to use in the way of cooking, and sent for it the mint water - I want myself (as I) have often of late had the cholick and pepper mint water is not to be had hear, I beg you will when the season comes to still mint have some desilled in time when the pepper is in blume and have it duble desilled for me - I have been unwell for some weeks with chollick complaints - I dont say by - yet I am not well - I think it would be well to have the cotton for the table cloths wove as soon as you can as they will be wanting for servants when we come home - The President talks of coming to Mount Vernon about the middle of next month - it would give me pleasure to come with him - but as he is to return in a few days - I must let it alone till the vacation of the schools when I can bring the children with me - I should be truly unhappy to leve Washington least the fever he had last summer should (retur)n again. I am sorry to find (in) your letter that the Major is indisposed I wonder he is not more cautious when he so often suffer by neglect of himself[2] - my love to him & Harriot - kiss the little ones for me and believe me my Dear

Fanny your
most affectionate
M W (ashington)

Mrs Harrison has
just heard of her brother
Adams death which has
affected her very much

238 *July* 1792

(Address)
Mrs Washington
(Docketed)
From Mrs. M Washington
April 1792

ALS. Feinstone Collection, David Library of the American Revolution, Washington Crossing, Pennsylvania. On loan to the American Philosophical Society, Philadelphia, PA.
1. "Frank" was a slave whose occupation was that of waiter.
2. Major George Augustine Washington's physical condition was rapidly declining.

From Elizabeth Willing Powel

The Speaker of the Senate of Pennsylvania will have the Honor to wait on the President of the United States and Mrs Washington on Thursday next.

Mrs. Powel has the Pleasure to present her respectful Compliments to them and to express her Regrets that she cannot have the Honor of dining with them upon that Day.
Friday 8 June 1792

ALS (Third person), ViMtV.

To Fanny Bassett Washington

My Dear Fanny -   Philadelphia July the 1st 1792
I am happy to hear of your letter of June the 25th that you and the children are well - and truly sorry you had not better accounts from the Major when you last heard from him[1]- I hope in god that you have since had more favorable accounts from him - The President has fixed on the 12th to leave this place for Mount Vernon if nothing happens to prevent us[2] - wish my dear Fanny that you would make Frank clanse the House from the garret to the sellers - have all the Beds aird and mended and the Bed cloths of every kind made very clean the Bed steads also well scalded - and the low bed steads put up to be ready to carry out of one room into another as you know they are often wanted. I have not a doubt but we shall have company all the time we are at home - I wish you to have all the chinia looked over, the closet clened and the glasses all washed and every thing in the closet as clean as can be than they will be ready when wanted with much less troable than to have them to look for when ever in hurry they may be wanted.
I do not wish to have the clouded cotten made into chear covers - nor the chares stuffed, or done anything to, till I come home as it is probable that the old covers will last as long as I shall stay home by a vessel

that will live this in a day or two - I shall send several articles - that could not be had when we sent the last things round - I hope the major will not hurry him self back if he finds benefit from the mountain air it is of the greatest concequince that his health should be established and I hope he will be very careful in doing as the Doctors directs him - I shall be sorry not to see dear Little Maria if the jaunt is for her good - I must be content. I am glad that Fayette is recovered and hope I shall find you and the children quite well - impress it on the gardener to have every thing in his garden that will be nessary in the House keeping way as vegetable is the best part of our living in the country - I dare say you have made the table cloths as well as they can be done - as to the window curtain and bed curtain they may as well be put up - I shall send a carpit for our parlor so that it will be ready by the time I get there if the vessel lives this on tuesday as we expect

The President has given miss Harriot a guitarr - I have inclosed the key it is sent in the vessel with several other things - I shall be glad to have the little caps made and sent before I live this as I wish to give them to the ladie as soon as done we are all well - Mr & Mrs Lear intend a trip to the eastward when we set out for the southward - the weather is extremely warm hear and has been so for some days past - all hear join me in love to you and children - and believe me my dear

> Fanny your most
> affectionately
> M Washington

(Docket)
From Mrs. M Washington
July 1st - 1792

ALS, IKB.

1. The text of the letter would indicate George Augustine Washington had gone to the mountains, most likely Berkeley Springs, for rest, fresh air and altitude, all three of which were recommended for tuberculosis at that time. Nowhere is there a direct reference to this, however.

2. The Washingtons left Philadelphia on Wednesday, July 11th and arrived at Mount Vernon on July 18th. They remained at Mount Vernon until Monday October 8th. They arrived in Philadelphia on Saturday October 13th.

From Giuseppe Ceracchi

Madame

Besides the generality of gentilmen all the Ladyes on Oland are ravished at the sight of my model that rappresent General Washington, what dignity they sais what (illegible) shows in his mind. happy must be the Lady that possesses his heart.

In this occassion Madame, I feel the graet advantage of indolging myself, informe the Ladyes of the high end Eminent perfact Estine end Respects

> Madame
> Your Most Obb end
> most Humb Serv
> J: Ceracchi[1]

Amsterdam 16 july
1792
(Docket)
From M. Caracchi
to
Mrs Washington
16 July 1792

ALS, DLC:GW.

1. Giuseppe Ceracchi (1760-1802) a native of Corsica and pupil of Canova, the noted sculptor, came to America in 1791 in order to persuade Congress to erect a colossal monument to commemorate the American Revolution. Washington's likeness was to play a prominent part in the design. The idea, while laudable, was abandoned because of the expense. Ceracchi made several busts of Washington. One was purchased by Congress, but was destroyed in the fire that consumed the Library of Congress in 1851. Another was presented to the Spanish ambassador and eventually found its way to America. It is now in the Corcoran Gallery in Washington. Another was retained by the artist, to be used as a model. This might have been the one offered to Mrs. Washington. See n. infra. Ceracchi returned to Europe and was a conspirator in a plot to assassinate Napoleon in 1801. He was guillotined in 1802. See, Johnson, *Original Portraits of Washington*, p. 170-71, (Boston, 1882).

From John Lamb

Honored Madam,   New York 30th November 1792
Enclosed is William Watson, receipt, for the delivery of two Barrels Apples, and one Barrel Nuts, - which, I have put on board the Schooner Dolphin; and I have to beg your acceptance, of the same. - Be pleased, to make my best wishes acceptable, to his Excellency, the President. and permit me to subscribe myself.

> With the highest respect,
> Honored Madam
> Your most obedient
> and very humble Servant
> John Lamb

The Honorable
Mrs. Washington
(Docket)

From
Genl Lamb
Mrs. Washington
30 Nov. 1792

ALS, DLC:GW.

To Fanny Bassett Washington

My Dear Fanny   Philadelphia December the 3d 1792
    Your letter of the 23d of November came to my hands yesterday -
I am truly glad that the Major has had some little relief, and I trust ere this
he has found ease from pain in his breast and side,[1] I beg my dear Fanny
to write one day in every week and then we shall know when to expect
her letters - we are very anxious when the southern post comes to hear
from you, I write to you by every Monday Post, your Letters comes to us
on Satterday.-I hope you will pay some attention to your own health as
I feared you were in a very delicate situation when I left you at Mount
Vernon[2]-Thank god we are all tolerable well hear tho I know you are with
your friends that is ready to give you every assisstance and kindness - yet
if there is any thing hear that you cannot get whare you are that you may
want - I beg you will let us know and it will give us pleasure to supply
you with it -
    I am happy to hear that your dear little Babes keep well -
    Our compliments to Mr. Bassett - my love and good wishes to
yourself and the Major - your brothers and sisters - kiss the children for
me -

> I am my dear Fanny
> Your most affectionate
> M Washington

(Address)
Mrs Frans Washington
Eltham
From Mrs M Washington
December 3d, 1792

ALS, MWi:W-C.

1. There was a marked deterioration in Major Washington's health in the summer and fall of 1792. He developed numerous and prolonged episodes of hemoptysis and lung hemorrhages, at times unable to speak. The President, greatly attached to him, was very upset by his failing condition. Even Secretary of War Henry Knox sent medications from Philadelphia. During August and September he was bed-ridden and unable to walk for six weeks, "a shadow of what he was." The decision was made to take him to Eltham, a warmer climate, so that he would not be subjected to the colder weather of Mount Vernon. Too weak

to ride in a carriage, he and Fanny left by boat on October 9th. *Writings*, 32:55, 100, 115, 142, 156, 163, 173.

   2. In a letter of the President to Tobias Lear, October 1, 1792, "His fate is unquestionably fixed, & Fanny's from prest. appearances, is very unpromisg. probably terminating in the same disorder." *Writings*, 32:172.

From George Bateman

Madam   (December 1792)
   The tender feelings of humanity which generally governs people of your Rank in life, has lead me to apply to you on behalf of the Bearer (my wife). She lived for several years as attendant to the Countess of Orkney & Inchiquin (deceased). I have been bred to the Land Surveying Business, am a perfect Accomplant, and have a Letter of Thomas Lea, Esqr recommendatory - We are from Europe several months - have sufficient Vouchers of our Proper conduct there. I have endeavoured to secure myself employment in Philadelphia, but am disappointed in every Application. I humbly Sollicit yr Excellency to interest yourself in behalf of yr Addressers by getting me any small employment to enable me to keep her from distress. I am with the most profound Respect

                              Yr Excellency's most Hble
                              Obedt Servt
                              George Bateman

ALS, DLC:GW.

To Fanny Bassett Washington

My Dear Fanny   Philadelphia February the 3d 1793
   The southern post not getting in this week, I have not had the pleasure to hear from you, - we are all tolerable well, the winter has been remarkable warm - which occations the season to be very sickly - I hope you and the children are well, Mr Blair[1] is arrived hear and tells his friends that a great number of our acquantances are dead below - the winter has been so warm hear that the farmers have been plowing all winter - and we are in fear that there will not be Ice to fill the Ice Houses in the city - which will be a great disappointment to us in the warm season Ice is the most agreable thing we can have hear - I hear from Mrs Stuart and the girls often, she tells me that she has not seen Mr Fairfax,[2] since he was at Hope Park with me - but does not say where he is, wheather he is got to England or not - Mrs Harrison[3] is well she very often enquires very kindly after you - Mrs Mercer[4] is in town but she is so often sick that I do not see

her but very seldom - my love to the Major - I hope are this that he has got the better of the spitting Blood you mention in your last -

My love to your Brothers and sisters in which the President joins kiss your dear little Babes for me and Believe me my dear

> Fanny your most
> affectionate
> M Washington

(Address)
Mrs Frans Washington
(Docket)
From Mrs. M Washington
February 8th 1793

ALS, ViMtV (on loan).

1. John Blair (1732-1800) Signer of the Federal Constitution, Associate-Justice of the United States Supreme Court. He was the son of John Blair, member of the Council and Acting Governor of the Colony of Virginia.

2. Reverend Bryan Fairfax (1736-1802), lifelong friend of the President and son of Colonel William Fairfax of Belvoir. He was a half-brother of George William Fairfax. Fairfax took Holy Orders in 1789 and in 1793 became the eighth Lord Fairfax, Baron Cameron.

3. Probably Anne Craik Harrison, daughter of the President's friend and physician, Dr. James Craik. She was the wife of Richard Harrison, a Maryland merchant who later settled in Alexandria. He served as auditor of the United States Treasury from 1791 till 1836. *Diaries,* 3:209.

4. Probably Sophia Sprigg Mercer, wife of Colonel John Francis Mercer, congressman from Maryland.

To Fanny Bassett Washington

My dear Fanny   Philadelphia February the 10th 1793

Since my last, your letter of the 25th January is come to hand. - I am sincearly sorry to hear that the pore majors complaints continue, - the alwise disposer of events only can relive him and I trust he will in his good time delver him from his great distress and difficulties - I am sorry dear Little Charles is not well-the season of the year is bad for all complaints the weather being so very warm - it is happy for you that Maria and Fayette keep well[1]- indeed My Dear Fanny I am very glad to hear from you and I am pleased that kind providence has enabled you to support yourself under your great afflictions. I can with the greatest truth assure you that the President and myself feel very sincearly for you in your heavy afflictions and will take pleasure in doing every thing we can to make your trobles as light to you as we can - thank god we are tolarable well - if Patty Dandridge can be useful to you I hope she will stay with you -

I will my dear Fanny, have you a bonnit and cloak made and sent by the first oppertunity at this time thare is no vessel hear from Richmon but I expect thare soon will be, as the river is free from Ice which is a very uncommon thing at this season of the year, - my love the major and kiss the children in which the President joins me, - my love to your Brothers and sisters and to Patty Dandridge tell her that her Brother[2] is very well Nelly and Washington send thair love to you and children - and that you may be enabled to keep your health - is the prayers of your most affectionate

> M Washington
> The post yesterday has not
> come in

ALS, ViMtV.

1. Anna Maria, George Fayette, and Charles Augustine were the children of Fanny and Major George Augustine Washington. They were great favorites of Mrs. Washington and she was always very solicitous of their health and welfare.

2. Bartholomew Dandridge, Jr., one of the President's secretaries.

To Fanny Bassett Washington

My Dear Fanny   Philadelphia February the 18th 1793
    Your Brothers Letter of the 5th came to my hands some days after I wrote to you last. - Tho we were prepared to expect the event by every letter from you, - yet we were much shocked to hear that our dear Friend was no more.[1] - I hope you will now look forward and consider how necessary it is for you to attend to your own health for the sake of your dear little Babes - you have, my dear Fanny, received a very heavy affliction; but while it pleases god to spare the President he will be a friend to you and to the children: he would have written to you by this post but is so pressed at this moment by public business that it is not in his power to do it, but will try by the next[2] - we are all tolarable well; the President joins me in love and sincere condolence to you and your children, -
    My love to your brothers and sisters, Mr. Dandridge, Nelly and Washington send their love to you and children and Friends

> I am my Dear Fanny your
> truly affectionate
> M Washington

Mrs Frans Washington
Eltham
From Mrs M Washington
Feb. 18th, 1793

ALS, formerly ViWF. Present location unknown.

1. Major George Augustine Washington died at Eltham on February 5, 1793 and was buried there in the family burial ground in the garden close to the house. The President was also saddened by the death of one of his closest friends, Colonel Burwell Bassett of Eltham.

He was the father of Fanny Bassett Washington. On his way to Mount Vernon in early September, Bassett was stricken with "gout." *Writings,* 32:142. The description of his ailment by Washington leaves little doubt he suffered a cerebro-vascular accident. His death occurred January 4, 1793, following a fall from his horse. *Washington Papers,* DLC:GW, Governor Henry Lee to George Washington, January 6, 1793. The President and Mrs. Washington arrived at Mount Vernon, April 2, 1793. Funeral obsequies were held at Mount Vernon for a few friends and relatives. Reverend Bryan Fairfax officiated at the service. *Writings,* 32:413-14.

2. The President wrote to Fanny Washington on February 24th, sending his condolences, "love, friendship, and disposition to serve you." He suggested she make Mount Vernon her home. *Writings,* 32:354.

To Elizabeth Willing Powel

(21 February 1793)

The President and Mrs. Washington offer the comliments of the day to Mrs. Powell (sic). -[1] They sincerely wish her the return of many anniversaries of it. - that with each her happiness may increase - & the satisfaction of her friends thereby promoted.

The President and Mrs. Washington would, with pleasure have been of Mrs. Powell's party on the present occasion, this evening, had it not been for the late event which has happened in their family. -[2]

Wednesday 21st February
1793

AL (Third person). In the handwriting of George Washington. ViMtV.

1. Mrs. Powel shared her birthday with the President.
2. The Washingtons had gone into mourning following the death of George Augustine Washington.

From John Hewson

A Citizen

Presents to the Consort of our most worthy President; a piece of elegant Chintz, the fabrick of which was imported from India, in an American bottom: and printed by the subscriber in his manufactory at Kensington, adjoining the glass-house. It is presumed if the worthy person here address'd, would honor the manufacture of our own country so far as to wear a dress made of the piece accompanying this; it might be a great means of introducing the like amongst the more affluent of our fellow citizens, and would help remove the prejudice, that at present too much prevails against American manufactures.

The subscriber is willing to risque his reputation on the piece herewith presented, as the best performance ever exhibited on this continent to the present day. The wholesale price is nine shillings Pr. Yd. and upon strict enquery, it will be found that no importer in this city can present a piece of equal fabrick and workmanship, from any part of the world at a less price.

If anything appears improper in the freedom here taken, it is hoped that candor will cast a veil over it.

From Citizen
John Hewson[1]

Kensington - February 27th.: 1793
P.S. The person who delivered this letter with the piece of Chintz will call for an answer on Saturday next. - J.H.

ALS, DLC:GW.

1. John Hewson (1747-), the son of Peter Hewson, a London linen draper, became a cotton spinner and calico printer. He came to the notice of Benjamin Franklin, who encouraged him to immigrate to America. Franklin asssisted him in procurring property for his factory, where he established a linen printing works in 1779. Hewson also served as a soldier during the Revolution. In 1789 he received financial aid for his business from the Pennsylvania Assembly. He was a friend of the Washingtons, with whom he exchanged visits. *PMHB*, 8:298; 37:118-19.

From Elizabeth Willing Powel

Dear Madam   (March 10, 1793)
    The Evening I had the Honor to wait upon you, you were so obliging as to say that you would take Tea with me either on Tuesday or Wednesday next, I fixed on Tuesday as the earliest and, of course conformable to my wishes, without recollecting a previous Engagement I had with Mr. Hill to accompany a few married Ladies to his House as Chaperone I suppose, to a number of little girls what he considers neither as Children or Women but who as he expressed himself to me began to have "little delicate Sensibilities flying about their Hearts." To these Novitiates in Love he proposes giving a Ball which I had entirely forgot, until Mrs. Penn[2] yesterday reminded me of my Engagement.
    If you are disengaged Wednesday next will you do me the Honor to take Tea with us? If you will I must request the Favor of you to mention my Inadvertency to Mrs. Lear and the gentlemen

I am
Dear Madam
With Respect & Esteem
Your affectionate
Eliza Powel
Sunday Mar 10th, 1793
Mrs Washington

ALS, ViMtV.

1. Ann Allen Penn (d. 1835), wife of Lieutenant-governor John Penn (1729-1795), grandson of William Penn.

From Fanny Bassett Washington

My dearest Aunt   Hanover March (1793)

I had the pleasure to receive your favor of the 4th inst. inclosed with the Presidents letter to my Brother Burwell.[1] I feel a great deal of concern that your coming to Virginia is delayed so long. I flatter myself I should have had the pleasure of being some months with you (this) summer & that your society at Mount Vernon woud soften the sorrows I must feel on going there -from this last circumstance I was (it was my understanding that the President woud not stay at home more than a week on his first visit) rather inclined not to go until you came in, but as this is delayd so much longer than I expected & the President also mentions that he shall probably stay at home a fortnight, I have determined to go up at the time he expects to be there The consolaton & direction I shall receive from his kind advice, has greater weight with me than any other circumstances that woud oppose my going. I am very deserous of carrying my children to see their grandpapa & grandmama[2] in Berkely. I thought of deferring it untill the latter end of summer. This however woud interfere with my staying with you all the time you continue (missing) very unwillingly give up & (missing) me to change my plans so frequently, I will, if you think there is impropriety in it, go up to Berkley after the President leaves Mount Vernon & spend a part of the time untill you come home. The President will not I hope think it a material circumstance for me to take Harriet Washington[3] up with me, if I go the Berkley it will be shortly after he leaves Mount Vernon & I wish if agreeable to him to send for her when I return there, it is the first wish of my heart my dear aunt to act with approbation. I cannot thank (illegible)

Df, NNHi.

1. Burwell Bassett, Jr. (1764-1841). See, George Washington to Burwell Bassett, March 4, 1793, concerning the settlement of the estate of George Augustine Washington, *Writings*, 32:373.

2. Charles Washington (1738-1799) and his wife Mildred Thornton. They lived in Berkeley County, Virginia, now Jefferson County, West Virginia.

3. Harriet Washington (1776-1822), the daughter of Samuel Washington, the President's younger brother.

To Abigail Smith Adams

(c. April, 1793)

Mrs Washington, returns her best compliments to Mrs Adams, she has been much indisposed with a cold since fryday last - she is reather better today, - and will with pleasure visit Mrs Izard[1] at any hour Mrs Adams will please to apoint
wednesday. ten oclock

(Docketed)
Mrs Washington
Note

AN (Third person), CSmH.
    1. Alice Delancy Izard, wife of Ralph Izard, Senator from South Carolina.

To Elizabeth Willing Powel

(N.p., N.d.)
    General & Mrs Washington present their compliments to Mr & Mrs Powel, and are very much obliged to them for their kind invitation to a tea party tomorrow - but the General dining out - Mrs Washington engaged (on Wednesday last) Mrs Debert[1] & Miss Reed[2] to take a family Dinner and spend the day with her tomorrow - Expecting to be along - which will put it out of her power to wait upon Mrs Powel as she otherwise would have done with pleasure

(Address)
Mrs Powel

ALS (Third person), ViMtV.
    1. Miss or Mrs Debert. Unidentified.
    2. Miss Reed. Unidentified.

To Mr and Mrs Samuel Powel

    The President and Mrs Washington present their complimts to Mr & Mrs Powell and (agreeably to Mrs Powells request) have the honor to inform them that Mrs Washington is so much indisposed with a cold as to make her fear encreasing it by going to the Circus this afternoon - The President & rest of the family propose to be Spectators at the exhibition of Mr. Rickets[1]

Wednesday
24th Aprl
Mr & Mrs Powell
1793

AL (Third person). In the handwriting of George Washington. ViMtV.
    1. John Bill Ricketts, an English equestrian, first came to Philadelphia in 1792, where he opened the first circus in America. In 1793, at the corner of 12th and Market Streets, he built a large circular wooden building, capped by a conical roof. The building was ninety-seven feet in diameter, contained a center stage and seated 700 people. The performance consisted of tight-rope and slack-wire walking, clowns, and trick equestrian riding. Speight, *A History of the Circus*, London, 1980, p. 112-15.

From The Editors of the Ladies' Magazine

We beg your acceptance of the 1st Vol. of the Ladies Magazine,[1] and request that we may have the pleasure of considering you in future as an incourager and Patron of the Worke- and while we assure you it was not for want of respect or veneration for Your character, that you were not waited on before - but from a misunderstanding or neglect of the persons employed to procure subscriptions - we sanguinely hope that you will overlook any inaccuracies or defects which may appear - By granting us this favor you will confer an obligation on those who will remember it with gratitude. -

The Editors

Phila: May 18, 1793
Mrs Washington
Mrs Washington.
If agreeable you will
favor us with your
name to the within proposal
From The Editors of the
Ladies Magazine to Mrs.
Washington
18th May 1793

ALS, DLC:GW.

1. *The Ladies Magazine,* and repository of entertaining knowledge. V. 1-2; June 1792 - May 1793. Philadelphia, W. Gibbons.

To Fanny Bassett Washington

Sentiments dictated by G.W. in a Letter from Mrs. M Washington, to Mrs Frs Washington 2d June 1793.[1]

"The President says you are already acquainted with his sentiments on the propriety of renting out your lands & negroes in Berkeley. As it seems to be the intention to settle another plantation there, he thinks that the negroes, with such as you may incline to move up from Fairfax, had better be divided between the two places & each rented to some man of character and responsibility, who will be able to give security for the performance of the agreement. This will ease you of much trouble & reduce your income to a certainty, which never will be the case under overseers at a distance, as you seem to experience already. He thinks articles should be drawn up by some professional & skilful person: and every precaution taken to prevent waste of timber, or the cutting down too much thereof - and no abuse of either the Land or Negroes permitted.

As to the term for which you would let the Estate, it must depend upon your own view of the subject, the Will & advice of your friends there, who are much better acquainted with the circumstances attending the Estate & the utility of a longer or shorter term, than he is at this distance."

LB DLC:GW.

1. The text is taken from the letter-book copy in the Washington Papers, Library of Congress. It is in a secretarial hand.

To Fanny Bassett Washington

My Dear Fanny   Philadelphia August the 4th 1793
    I am very happy to hear by your letters that yourself and children are all well - we have had a melloncholy time hear for about a fortnight past Mrs. Lear was taken with a fever - the doctor was called in but to no purpose her illness increased till the eight day she was taken from us. - she never lost her senses till just before she expired - Mr. Lear bares his loss like a philosipher - she is generally lamented by all that knew her she was a pretty spritely woman - and always in very good health.[1]
    I am glad you had your room white washed - I whish you had made austin use everything of the kind while he was about the House - I should think Frank might white wash the Kitchen and his room in the seller - he cannot have much to do if he will only set about it he may very soon get done - my dear Fanny make him clean every part of the House constantly every week sellers and all[2] - that I may have things in tolerable order if I come home which I expect to do some time next month -
    The gold thread I prized for - Mr. Lewis[3] got the silk - I told him I would pay for it but he never brought me the bill so you must pay him for it - I was a good deal surprised to be told By Austin that the Bacon was all of it spoiled in the smoke house will you let me know if it is so - the fine wet summer by bye such necessaries as one wanted about the house - as it will be needless to put up a large quantity for winter. tell Mrs. Washington[4] - I will with pleasure get a muslin for her - I sent the lockets by a gentleman going to alexandra last week the shoes went yesterday on board a vessel directed to Mr. Porter which I hope will get safe to you. I have not as yet got the bills - but will send them in my next.- the President says that the linnin may be got for the House people - having the Cutting out of the winter cloths for the people that Charlot may set about making them - I sent some lose linning last week by Capt Elwood to make Babe clothes - for the negro women - cut shirts and caps and necessary things for them only.
    I am truly sorry to hear of so many deaths - the wet raney season has made it sickly every where - I shall be glad when the frost comes to clear the air - I hope you will get the cloth safe The Capt. had great charge

given about it - I wish you Brother Burwell had come to this part of the country he wuld have met with much more agreeable fair besides seeing more of the United States - a trip to New York and Road Island would have been very pleasant this warm season - of the year

The President myself and children are pretty well thank you and all join in love to you Mrs. W- Mr. Lewis and the children -

> I am my dear Fanny your
> every Honorable
> M Washington

(Docketed)
From
Mrs. M Washington
August 4th 1793

ALS, ViMtV.

1. Mary (Polly) Long Lear, first wife of Tobias Lear. It is possible she died of yellow fever, just then making an early appearance in Philadelphia. She and her husband lived with the Washingtons.

2. Austin and Frank were slaves and house servants. Frank was regarded as especially lazy by most of the family.

3. Robert Lewis, nephew of the President and a son of Betty and Fielding Lewis.

4. Probably Mrs. Lund Washington.

From Elizabeth Willing Powel

My dear Friend & very dear Madam   (August 9, 1793)
        Your affectionate & friendly Attention to me, at this awfull Moment[1] filled my Heart with so much Sensibility as rendered me incapable of expressing my Feelings on the Subject of our Conversation, and when my Amiable Friend, the President, renewed his Invitation to me to accompany you to Virginia,[2] I could only say That I would let you know this Evening, the Result of a Conference I meant to have with Mr. Powel. After a long conversation with him, I collected that he saw no Propriety in the Citizens fleeing from the only Spot where Physicians conversant with the Disorder that now prevails could be consulted, nor does he appear to be impressed with the degree of Apprehension that generally pervades the Minds of our Friends - however he wished me to follow my own Inclination and the Dictates of my own Judgement in a Matter that may eventually affect my Life and his Happiness - this has thrown me into a Dilemma the most painful. The Conflict between Duty and Inclination is a severe Trial of my Feelings; but as I believe it is always best to adhere to the line of Duty, I beg to decline the Pleasure I proposed to myself in accompanying you to Virginia at this time. The Possibility of his being ill during my Absence & thereby deprived of the Consolation and Aid, he might derive from my

Attention to him would be to me a lasting Source of Affliction;[3] and God knows, I need not voluntarily add to the List of Sorrows. My Life has been sufficiently embittered to make me now very little anxious about protracting or prerserving it. Death has robbed me of many Friends, and Time has abated the Ardor of others, so that life in my latter Years has been little more than a Sieve to let thro some Joy or some Blessing. Mr. Powel, who is highly sensible of your Friendship to us, desires to unite in every good Wish to you and yours.

That God may preserve and bless you both, and that you may safely return in a short Time, is the unfeigned Prayers of your

> sincere affectionate
> Eliza Powel

Mr Powel would have done himself the Pleasure of waiting upon you before your Departure, had he not apprehended that a Visit in the Moment of Preparation for a Journey would have been ill timed.
Monday August 9th, 1793
The President and Mrs Washington
(Docketed by G.W.)
Mrs. Eliza Powel
9th Sep (sic) 1793

ALS, DLC:GW.

1. Yellow fever struck Philadelphia early in July, 1793, apparently introduced by infected French refugees from San Domingo, fleeing to escape the slave revolution. Sickness and death gradually increased, and by mid-August it became clear a major epidemic was present. By the end of the month approximately one-third of the population had fled the city. The death toll was set at about 5000. The mass exodus from the city brought the federal government to a standstill. Colonel and Mrs. Alexander Hamilton were both stricken, but recovered. The Secretary of State (Jefferson), Secretary of War (Knox), and the Attorney-general (Randolph) left the city. The President was one of the last to leave. For an account of the epidemic, see C.F. Jenkins *Washington in Germantown*, (Philadelphia, 1904).

2. In order to escape the epidemic it was decided Mrs. Washington and the children should return to Mount Vernon. They suggested Mrs. Powel would be welcome to accompany them. However, Mrs. Washington was reluctant to leave the President alone in the midst of the epidemic. Neither did he wish to leave the city until about September 20th. However, he was reluctant to expose her and the children to the disease. He acquiesced and they left Philadelphia on September 10th and arrived at Mount Vernon on the 14th. The President remained at Mount Vernon until October 28th, when he set out for Germantown. Mrs. Washington joined the President at Baltimore and they arrived at Germantown on November 1st. Jenkins, *Germantown*, p. 99.

3. It was most fortunate Mrs. Powel forsook the trip to Virginia. She left the city to visit her brother, Richard Willing. Mr. Powel visited her there. On his return to Philadelphia he stopped at his farm, Powelton, was taken ill, and died of yellow-fever several days later, September 29th. Jenkins *Germantown*, p. 13.

To Elizabeth Schuyler Hamilton

(September 1793)

I am truly glad my Dear Madam to hear Colo Hamilton is better today[1] you have my prayers and warmest wishes for his recovery I hope you take care of yourself as you know it is necessary for your family - we were luckey to have three bottles of the old wine that was carred to the east Indees which is sent with three, of the other kind which is very good and we have a plenty to supply you as often as you please to send for it - of the latter

The President joins me in devoutly wishing Colo Hamilton's recovery[2] - we expect to hear this tomorrow - and beg you will send to Mrs Emerson[3] for any thing that we have that you may want

I am Dear Madam your very affectionate Friend

M Washington[4]

ALS, DLC:GW.

1. Yellow fever struck Philadelphia in July, 1793, and by early August it was epidemic. By early November, with the advent of cooler weather, it had subsided. There were about 5000 fatalities. The Washingtons left Philadelphia on September 10th and arrived at Mount Vernon on the 14th. They returned to Philadelphia about November 25th. See, Baker, *Washington After the Revolution*, Philadelphia, 1889, p. 263-67.

2. Alexander Hamilton developed yellow fever in early September. *Writings*, 33:83. He recovered later in the month. See, GW to Alexander Hamilton, September 25, 1793, *Writings*, 33:102.

3. Mrs. Emerson was the housekeeper for the Washingtons in Philadelphia.

4. There is a printed version of this letter in *Mary and Martha*, p. 302. It is reproduced in A. M. Hamilton, *Life of Alexander Hamilton*, N.Y., 1910, p. 17-18.

To Elizabeth Schuyler Hamilton

Mrs Washington sends her Love to Mrs Hamilton, she intends visiting Mrs Peters[1] this fore noon, if it is (missing) agreable to Mrs H to goe with her she will be happy to have companey, - Mrs H will be so good as to be ready as soon as she can after nine oclock. - will Mrs H come to Market street or shall Mrs W call for her; either way is conveniant to Mrs W

Fryday morning 7 oclock

AL (Third person), MHi.

1. Sarah Robinson Peters, wife of Judge Richard Peters (1744-1828). The Peters were intimate friends of the Washingtons.

From The Countess of Buchan

Dryburgh Abbey January 8th 1794
The Countess of Buchan[1] presents her compliments to Mrs Washington & begs her acceptance of a Medallion Paste of Her Husbands Portrait as a Mark of the Interest she takes in the House & Family of Mount Vernon & in the happiness of Mrs Washington.

AL (Third person), ViMtV.

1. Margaret Fraser, wife and cousin of David Steuart Erskine, 11th Earl of Buchan (1742-1829).

To Fanny Bassett Washington

My Dear Fanny   Philadelphia January the 14 1794
I now set down to thank you for your two Last letters, by the one from Eltham I was very glad to hear that you were safe arrived at yoar jouney end - by Mr Lewis s[1] account of your going to Cole chester I was affraide you would have a very disagreeable journey with your pore little children - and thank god we are all well - and not the least fear of the yellow fever while the weather is cold some people seemes to anticipate its return again in the summer - but I believe they have no cause but that of a glumay dispossion - they have suffered so much that it can not be got over soon by those that was in the city - almost every family has lost some of thair friends - and black seeems to be general dress in the city - the players are not allowed to come hear nor has there been any assembly. Yet the young people wish it and talk of having them soon - I am truly sorry to hear that your Brother John[2] has been ill - I hope he wil soon be well again - what is the matter with Patty Dandridge[3] her Brother told me soon after I came hear that he heard she was sick - I hope she has got well are this I shall be much obliged to you to enquire about my pore sister[4] and let me hear of her from you - I had the pleasure to hear by Mrs Griffin[5] that she was very well just before she left virginia - I have got your stays done and ready to send to you by the first oppertunity - I fear that it will be some time before I shall be able to send them by water to Richmond - the river is so full of Ice that noe vessel can pass -
My dear Fanny as you memorandum mentions one Dozen and half of shears half a dozen to be different from the dozen - would it not be more convenient to have them all alike, - and of what kind of stuff would you chuse to have the Bottoms made off plase to lett me know as soon as you can - as we wish to have your memorandum put into the work mens hands, as they are very tedous in everything they undertake indeed there has been so many of those sort of people taken away by the fever - that it is with much difficulty any kind of work can be done the work men all

complain of the want of hands to carry on every branch of business - The President joins me in love to you and I can with much truth my dear Fanny tell you that it always give us pleasure to hear from you - kiss your dear little children for me - I have sent maria a fashenable sash -

My love to your Bothers and sisters - I think if your Brother Burwell[6] and his wife would try the nothern air it would have a better effect on thair constitution, than the back country has had To come early in the spring and spend the summer in Boston where the heat is not so intense as it is to the southward - he would always have agreable company and good accomodations whare ever he had a mind to stay for a few weeks - the President deseres you will request your Brothers or either of them to get for him as many of the Honey locust seeds as they can, and if there is no oppertunity to send them round by water that they may be sent by the stage to alexandria so as to be in time to be planted this spring dercted for Mr Pearce at mount vernon

My love and best wishes attend you and children in which the president joins me Nelly and Washington send thair love to you and all - as dos Mr Dandridge[7]

> I am my dear Fanny your
> ever affectionate
> M Washington

(Docket)
For Mrs. M Washington
January 14th 1794

ALS, CSmH.

1. One of the sons of Betty Washington and Fielding Lewis of Kenmore, Fredericksburg, Va.

2. John Bassett (1765-1822), of Farmington, Hanover County. He was a brother of Fanny Bassett.

3. Martha Washington Dandridge, also known as "Patcy," and "Patty." She was the daughter of Mrs. Washington's brother, Bartholomew Dandridge. She married Dr. William Halyburton, of Haddington, Scotland. 5W (1) 36.

4. Elizabeth Dandridge Aylett Henley. She was a younger sister of Mrs. Washington. Her second husband, Leonard Henley, was an alcoholic.

5. Probably Betsy Braxton Griffin, wife of Samuel Griffin (1746-1810) of Williamsburg, and daughter of Carter Braxton.

6. Burwell Bassett, Jr., of Eltham. His wife was Anne Claiborne.

7. Bartholomew Dandridge, Jr., son of Mrs. Washington's brother, Bartholomew Dandridge, Sr. He was secretary to the President. 5W (1) 36.

To Fanny Bassett Washington

My Dear Fanny   Philadelphia February the 10 1794
    I am happy to hear by your Letters of the 12 and 26th of January -
that you and your children were all well, - and exceeding sorry that your
Brother Burwell[1] has had a spotting of blood - I hope it was some accidental
complaint that occationed it, and trust he is perfectly recovered before this
thank god we are all tolarable well - I have the cholic some times - and I have
lately had it but am better again - the inhabitants of this city say that
Philadelphia was never more healthy than it has been for some months
past, the weather has been very unsettled - we have had very suddin
changes from heat to violent cold the river has been impassable for several
weeks - it is now snowing fast - tho not cold indeed it thaws as fast as it
falls - all communication by water has been stopt for some time - as soon
as a vessel can get around to Richmond your stays will be sent to the care
of Mrs Julious Dandridge[2] they are already packed up - to be sent -
    I am very glad to hear that my sister[3] is well & will write to her by
the next post I am plased to find Fanny Henly[4] can write so prittyly - will
you tell me in your next her age - I really dont know how old she is -
    I shall give your memorandom to the worke man in order that your
furniture may be ready to send round Early in the spring that you may
not waite for it thare has been such a loss in the class of people that it will
require some time to get work of any kind done.[5]
    The President will give such derections to Mr Pearse[6] as you have
desied - and will at al times be ready to assist you in any thing he can -
by giving derection to Mr Pearse - who I hope will do very well - as we
hear no complaints from him or of him - he was obliged to leve his family
till the spring he lives in the house - himself - and will do so till his Family
arrives wich will be as soon as the ice is gone, we have been very dull hear
all winter, thare has been too assemblys - and it is said that the players
are to be hear soon - if they come and open the new theater I suppose it
will make a very great change - many people seem to wish it in this city
something of that sort seems to be necessary as a great number of the
people in this town is very much at a loss how to spend their time agreably
The gay are always fond of some new seens let it be what it may - I dare
say a very little time will ware of the gloom if gay amusements are
permitted hear
    Kiss you dear little Babes for me give my love to Fanny Henly - my
love to your Brothers and sisters in which the President joins Nelly and
Wash send thair love to you and all with you

                          I am my dear Fanny your
                          most affectionate
                          M Washington

ALS, CSmH.

1. Burwell Bassett, Jr. (1764-1841), eldest brother of Fanny Bassett.

2. Julius Burbidge Dandridge, son of Bartholomew Dandridge and Mrs. Washington's nephew. He was cashier of the United States Bank, Richmond.

3. Elizabeth Dandridge Aylett Henley, younger sister of Mrs. Washington.

4. Frances Dandridge Henley (1779-1856), daughter of the above. She later became the third wife of Tobias Lear.

5. There was a shortage of labor and craftsmen in Philadelphia, due to the yellow fever epidemic that had struck Philadelphia in September, 1793.

6. William Pearce was manager at Mount Vernon from January, 1794 until poor health forced him to resign in December, 1796. He was capable, diligent, and efficient. He and the President carried on an extensive correspondence concerning agricultural matters at Mount Vernon.

To Fanny Bassett Washington

My Dear Fanny   Philadelphia February 15th 1794

I was very much pleased to hear by your Letter of the 31st of January, that you had arrived safe at Eltham without dificulty as the season was late to carry out children and the weather very cold hear, Mrs Peter[1] set out on the same day that you did on Monday and arrived hear fryday night much fatagued - the girls had boath had colds ever since they gott hear Mrs Peter delivered me your letter and (illegible) which I will with much pleasure attend to and have all the articles got according to your derection - and done to be sent by water as soon as the river is navagable as yet we have had no vessels from Alexandria but I expect thair will soon be an oppertunity by water which is a much better way to convoy things than by the stage as they are very apt to get rubed and tumbled if not packed well - I have had a letter from my porre sister[2] by Mrs Blair[3] she tells me she and her children have been all sick and were not well when she wrote she tells me she has lost another of her children a fine Boy she has enough left if she could get into a more healthy part of the country They seem to me to be always sick. I shall be much obliged to you if you will make some inquire into her wants if you can do it in a delicate way as I know she is very unwilling to let me hear that she is in want of any trifle, as I shall be glad to give her any thing that I can or do anything that would contribute to her happyness -

I am glad to hear so favorable an account of my nephew J Dandridge[4] and wish him every happyness This world can give him, - I wish Patty[5] may marry well she is a clever girl and I am the more anxious that she should marry well as I am sure it will be an advantage to her young sister The time is drawing near to the the leaving of the express but when it is (illegible) that the President will have it in his power to come to mount vernon he cannot at this time tell as it depends on so many things as are to happen and to take place before we can fix a time to leve this city for so long a time as it will take him to go home and back, - and in that case we shall be very sorry that you should leve your friends sooner than you intend - particularly as the President will not stay at mount vernon a moment longer than he has looked over his Farms - I look forward to the summer with pleasure - as I hope nothing will happen to prevent our coming down to see you and all friends with you - the girls made a flying trip to New York they were only two days in the city rode around it - and went to church on Thursday - and to a play - they seemed so delighted with the jaunt all togather - they seemed much fatagʊed (illegible) is (illegible) this evening

Your things will all be (illegible) be sent in the course of a week and I will send them directed to the care of Colo Gilpen[6] and if you should think of anything else let me know - and I will with cheerfulness get it for you - My love to your Brothers - and sisters - I shall be glad to see your Brother Burwell[7] hear - wheather he is in Congress or not I should hope a trip to the eastward in summer will be very efecatious as to Mrs Bassetts health[8] - please to give my love to Mrs Lyons and compliments to Mr Lyons[9] and all enquiring friends - my love and good wishes to you and your children in which the president and the girls join me -

> I am my dear Fanny your
> ever affectionate
> M Washington

This letter was to have
been sent last week
From Mrs M Washington
February 1794

ALS. From a copy supplied by ViMtV; the location of the original is unknown.

1. This might be Mrs. Robert Peter. Peter was a prominent merchant of Georgetown and its first mayor. It is possible she escorted Martha Parke Custis and Elizabeth Parke Custis to Philadelphia to visit their grandmother. In 1795 their son, Thomas Peter, married Martha Parke Custis.

2. Elizabeth Dandridge Aylett Henley. See supra.

3. Unidentified.

4. John Dandridge (176?-1799), son of Bartholomew Dandridge, Sr.

5. Martha Washington Dandridge, daughter of Bartholomew Dandridge, Sr. See supra.

6. George Gilpin (1740-1813), a wheat and flour merchant of Alexandria and prominent in the affairs of the Potomac Company. *Diaries*, 4:141.

7. Burwell Bassett, Jr., brother of Fanny Bassett Washington. He was not elected to the national congress until 1805.

8. His wife, who seems to have been in poor health, was Ann Claiborne of King William County.

9. Judith Bassett Lyons and Peter Lyons. She was a sister of Burwell Bassett, Sr. She married attorney and later justice Peter Lyons. *Diaries*, 4:132.

To Mary Ann Aitken

(February 24, 1794)

It is with regret that Mrs. Washington informs Miss Aitken that she cannot accept the beautiful Screen which Miss Aitken has been so polite as to send her. However painful it is to Mrs Washington to deprive Miss Aitken of the pleasure which her acceptance of this present might have given her; yet Mrs Washington feels constrained to do it in conformity to a line of conduct which she has hitherto observed on such occasions. The taste and beautiful execution of the Screen are such as to reflect the highest credit on the talents of Miss Aitken - and the time in which it was executed does no less honour to her industry -

Mrs Washington begs that Miss Aitken will be assured that she has the same sense of Miss Aitkens politeness and respect towards her as if her present had been accepted.

Thursday Feby 24th, 1794
Miss Mary Ann Aitken
Market Street[1]

Df, PHi.
1. The draft is in the handwriting of Tobias Lear. The diction is probably Lear's. See *PMHB*, 26:406.

To Fanny Bassett Washington

My dear Fanny   Philadelphia March the 2nd 1794

I have now to thank you for your favor of the 12th of February and am very happy to hear by it that you and your children enjoy good health, - and that your Brothers and sisters and all your Friends are all well - I think upon the whole this has been a rather unhealthy winter - the changes in the weather has been so very sudden; Nelly has been unwell with a kind of rash, - Washington is as thin as he can be - but thank god is very well and Nelly is getting well - I have had the pleasure to hear that Mrs. Stuart[1] has another son which they seem to be much pleased with she intends to call him Charles Calvert from what I can hear Patty and Mr. Peter[2] is to make a match - The old gentleman[3] will comply with Doctor Stuart's bargain and in the last letter I had from Mrs Stuart she says Patty had given him leve to visit her as a lover - I suppos by that he is agreable to all parties -if it is so I shall be very happy to see her settled with a prospect of being happy - I really believe she is a very derserving girl - I am told that he is clever, - I indeed my dear Fanny I should think that you can spend you time much more agreable to yourself with your Friends than you will up the country till the roads and weather is quite setled - I shall have your furniture sent round as soon as the river is open - but

I fear you have not considered what a number of articles is necessary for to begin housekeeping with - if I was at mount vernon I should be able to assist you with many things - and at this time I can not give the least gess when I shall leave this place - I fear it will be late in the summer as usual.

Thear is a new French minister[4] arrived about ten days agoe - he seems to be a plain grave and good looking man - but can't speak a word of English - he will soon learn if he stays hear, as far as we can judge from his looks, and manners he is a very agreable a man.

After a good deal of writing in the newspapers, the players are come to the city and have acted with very great applause several nights I have not been to a play as yet, - I expect to goe this week - my love to your dear children. I am very glad to hear that they are in good health - kiss them for me - my love and good wishes to your Brothers and sisters in which the President joins me

> I am my dear Fanny you
> ever affectionate
> M Washington

Please to give my love to Patty Dandridge I am very happy to hear she is getting better I thank you my dear Fanny for mentioning my dear sister it gives me real pleasure to hear she is well - and her Family - and know she has a tolerable time at home - where is it that Mr. Henley[5] is going to live is it worth his while to rent a place while he has one of his own - I hope he does not mean to sell the place he has without settling on another of his so that his family may not be distressed if any accident should happen to him.

> I am yours,
> M Wn

ALS, ViMtV.

1. Eleanor Calvert Custis Stuart, the widow of John Parke Custis. She subsequently married Dr. David Stuart. See supra.

2. Patty refers to Martha Parke Custis, daughter of the above, and granddaughter of Mrs. Washington. Thomas Peter (1769-1834) was the son of Robert Peter and his wife Elizabeth Scott. Martha Parke Custis and Thomas Peter were married in 1795.

3. Robert Peter (1726-1806) was a prominent merchant of Georgetown and its first mayor.

4. Jean Antoine Joseph Baron Fauchet was acknowledged as Minister plenipotentiary of the French republic on February 22, 1794. *Journal of the Proceedings of the President*, February 22, 1794. DLC:GW.

5. Leonard Henley, second husband of Mrs. Washington's sister, Elizabeth. They resided in Williamsburg at Pine Grove.

To Fanny Bassett Washington

My Dear Fanny   Philadelphia March the 9th 1794
    I have now to thank you for your agreable favor of the 20th of February I was sorry to find by it that you and your children have had bad colds it has been a general complaint hear - owing to the sudden changes in the weather - it seems to be getting more moderate - and I hope that the fine weather we have had for this last week will continue and restore health to all, in this city - pore Mrs Moylan (who you have seen out at mount vernon some years agoe) is dead with in this week[1] - and has left two little girls to lement her loss - the Congress is up and all the members gon home, the President has not fixed the time for him to goe home - as he has some particular business which will prevent his fixing the time as yet the girls and Mrs Peter has been with me five weeks Betsy thinks of staying with me and let Patty go down without her[2] Mr Peter talks of going from this place about the 16th which will be next Monday the girls have been very well since they came hear except colds they boath got in travelling in the extreme cold weather - we hear often from Mrs Stuart she and her children are all well -
    I am sorry to hear that Mrs Bassett[3] is somewhat indisposed her complaints has been so long that I very much fear the northern air will not have the wished for effect - if she comes on this summer to the eastward so as to escape the violent heat in July nd August it will be her best chance to get well - I am very sorry for Mrs Lyons loss[4] - it is the case with all parents that have many children - they lose them as soon as they rase them generally
    I expected that your Brother John had built himself a good House, and was well settled by this time living in small Houses and being crowded many in a room is a very great cause of thair being so sickly be so good as to give my love to them - I am much obliged to you my Dear Fanny for your attention to my pore sister, Mr Blair[5] was so good as to bring her letter to me - and I shall write to her very soon I realy thought it was one of John Dandridge's jokes when he wrote to his Brother that he was marred[6] - he seemed to doubt it for some time - I am glad he has made an agreable choice - I wish with all my heart that Patty may doe well - it would give me much pleasure to hear that she was well marred - should you get this letter before you live New Kent - be so good as to remember me to all my Relations and friends - and all enquiring friends - the President joins me in love to you and the children - and believe me my Dear Fanny your ever affectionate

                                        M Washington

The girls all send love

to you - Washington begs
his love to you and children
From Mrs. M Washington
March 1794

ALS. Location unknown. Taken from a photocopy at ViMtV.

1. Mary Ricketts Van Horn Moylan, of Phil's Hill, New Jersey. She married Stephen Moylan on September 12, 1778. He had been muster-master general, secretary to General Washington, quarter-master general, and brigadier-general during the Revolution. Washington appointed him Commissioner of Loans in Philadelphia in 1793. The Moylans were visitors at Mount Vernon in 1785. See, *DAB*; *Diaries*, 4:129 ff.

2. Betsy, refers to Elizabeth Parke Custis. Patty, refers to Martha Parke Custis, her sister. Mrs. Peter, refers to Ann Scott Peter. Mr. Peter, refers to Robert Peter, see supra.

3. Ann Claiborne Bassett, wife of Burwell Bassett, Jr., of Eltham.

4. Mrs. Judith Lyons, wife of Judge Peter Lyons.

5. John Blair, Associate-justice of the United States Supreme Court.

6. John Dandridge (176?-1799) was a nephew of Mrs. Washington and son of her brother, Bartholomew Dandridge. His wife was Rebecca Jones Minge. 5W (1) 36.

To Fanny Bassett Washington

My dear Fanny   Philadelphia March the 16th 1794

I am very happy to hear by your letter of the 26, February that you and your children are all well - and am exceedingly sorry to hear that the small pox has been so fatal in richmond that they have lost so many of the inhabitants I heard Mrs Coles[1] say that more then two hundred had died some time agoe, want of care - I should think, or proper care, must be the reason of it, the season was bad which made against them - I hope you have not lost any of your relations, has Mrs Lyons[2] had the small pox, Mrs Carter Harrison[3] told me some time agoe that Mrs Stith[4] was dead Now Betsy[5] is unfortunate to be left without her mother - I have the pleasure to tell you that we are all well - and that I believe that there has not been the least symptoms of the yellow fever in this city since I came to it, thare has been frequent alarms but the Doctors say thare has not been the least foundation for it, every care is taken to clean and air the Houses and Clean the Streets which I hope will effactually prevent any infection unless it should be again brought in to the ciy by vessel which are constantly coming up to the town from all quarters -

I am glad to hear that Patty Dandridge[6] is in better health, and hope the spring comming on will carry of the effects of the cols.

My love to your Brothers and sisters Be so good my dear Fanny to remember me to Mr & Mrs Lyons and all inquiring friends Kiss your dear children for me - and believe me my dear Fanny

Your ever affectionate
M Washington

The President desires
his love to you and children
Mrs Frances Washington
Eltham
From Mrs. M Washington
March 16th 1794

ALS, NN.

1. Catharine Thompson Coles, wife of Isaac Coles, member of Congress from Halifax County, Virginia.

2. Judith Bassett Lyons, aunt of Fanny Bassett Washington.

3. Jane Byrd Harrison, wife of Carter Harrison. She was the daughter of William Byrd, III. Carter Harrison was the son of Benjamin Harrison, the Signer. His mother was Elizabeth Bassett Harrison, aunt of Fanny Bassett Washington.

4. This may be Mary Townsend Washington Stith, daughter of Lawrence Washington of Chotank, King George County. She married Colonel Robert Stith.

5. Elizabeth Stith, daughter of the above.

6. Martha Washington Dandridge, daughter of Mrs. Washington's brother, Bartholomew Dandridge.

To Guiseppe Ceracchi

(March 17, 1794)

Mrs Washington in presenting her compliments and best wishes to Mr Ceracchi, finds herself at a loss for words to express her sensibility for the marble representation of the President which he sent her; and which she thinks, both in workmanship, and resemblance of the original, does great credit to the masterly hand from which it proceeded -

Mrs Washington will take an opportunity of conversing personally with Mr Ceracchi on the subject of his Bust and will then endeavor to impress him more fully with the sense she entertains of his goodness[1] -

Philadelphia March the 17th 1794

ALS, MHi.

1. The diction resembles that of the President, although the letter is in the handwriting of Mrs. Washington. The Washingtons did not acquire the bust. See supra, G. Ceracchi to Martha Washington, July 16, 1792.

To Fanny Bassett Washington

My dear Fanny   Philadelphia March the 23 1794

I have at last sent you the peiece of muslin I promised - I should have sent it to you sooner but I really could not find a piece that I thought fine enough (missing) since I came hear I (missing) you that we are all well (missing) roads have prevented the post coming in regularly - I hope I shall now hear from you oftener - it seems to be more like april hear than March we have had no wind or bad weather all the month of March

I hope you and your children injoy good health. My love to them and all your friends with you

The President desires his love to you and children

> I am my dear Fanny
> your ever affectionate
> M Washington

ALS, CSmH.

To Don José de Jáudenes

The Compliments of the President of the U. States & Mrs W, are presented to Don Josef de Jaudenes[1] - Informing him that they will with pleasure receive the introduction of Dona Matilda Shoughton de Jaudenes his lady at 12 o'clock tomorrow

Friday the
11th of Apl. 1794

Df by GW. Feinstone Collection, David Library of the American Revolution, Washington Crossing, Pennsylvania. On loan to the American Philosophical Society, Philadelphia, PA.

1. Jaudenes was the Spanish charges d'affaires. He was presented to the Washingtons, July 19, 1791. President Washington ultimately considered him "arrogant and inconsistent." *Writings,* 34:258.

To Fanny Bassett Washington

My dear Fanny   Philadelphia April the 13 1794

I am very sorry to find by your letter of the 19th of March that you were indesposed sore eyes has been a very general complaint in this town all winter; in some cases they have been very bad

Mr Pearce tells the President that he is seeing about the repairs of the House in alexandria for you - your furniture is done and will go round in a vessel this week to alexandria I hope it will get safe - I fear that we shall not be able to see mount vernon this summer from the present apearance of things - as soon as congress rises the President will go home for a short time unless he can stay some time I shall not goe with him - at this time I dont think that thare will be room for the servants that we should be obliged to carry Mr Pearces family lives in the servants Hall - and he lodges in the House which would make it very inconveniant for us to be there any length of time - you may my dear Fanny take the little bed sted and bed that Nelly & Washington used to sleep on when you goe to house keeping - I do most devoutly wish I could have been at home

- at the time of your coming up and setling in your House; - I have the
pleasure to tell you that we are all very well - it is said by the inhabitants
hear that Philadelphia was never more healthyer than it is at this time -
I trust that there will be no return of yellow fever this summer - thare never
has been any symptom of it since I came to the city -

if you should be with Mrs Lyons when this reaches your Hands -
remember me affectionately to her and Mr Lyons -

My love to your Brothers and sisters and all friends - kiss your
children for me, the President desires to be remembered to all friends

My love and good wishes attend you and believe me my dear

> Fanny
> your most affectionate
> M Washington

ALS (formerly ViWF). Feinstone Collection, David Library of the American Revolution,
Washington Crossing, Pennsylvania. On loan to the American Philosophical Society,
Philadelphia, PA.

To Mr. Whitelock

April 14, 1974

Mrs Washington will be much obliged to Mr Whitelock to make for
her a set of teeth - to make them something bigger and thicker in the front
and a small matter longer She will be very glad if he will do them as those
she has is almost broak -

To
Mr Whitelock

AN (Third person). The Reynolds historical Library, The University of Alabama at
Birmingham.

To Fanny Bassett Washington

My Dear Fanny   Philadelphia May the 25th 1794

I have now to thank you for two letter I did not write to you at the
usual time - I hope this will find you safe arrived thair with your children[1]
I do not know whether the House is ready for you in Alexandria - to go
into - the President has requested Mr Pearce to get it done so as to be ready
against you came up[2] - he tells him it is about (done) but complains much
of the Idle set of Thomas Green and his people[3] - town is a place for them
to idle away time and I am affraid he has but little influance of the negroes
under him - not enough to keep them to their worke - I should my dear
Fanny be very glad is I could have come home this summer - to see you
and assist in fixing you in Housekeeping but the President tells me the

Publick business will keep him in this town all the summer - to goe and return as he does - I could not deal it - so I must endevour to content my self as well as I can Hear - thank god we are tolerable well hear - Mr Julious Dandridge has been in this city 3 weeks or more he talks of leaving it in the (?) of next week he has or he pretends to have a great deal of Business - I seldom see him tho I often press him to come and see me - and to take dinner with us.[4] Batt Dandridge[5] seems to be in bad health he has never been well since he came up in the fall with the President - I wish he may not be Inclined to a Consumption he looks very thin and has a bad cough at this time.

I hope Miss Lyons[6] has made a good choice in the man she married when (sic) are they to live - it would be hard to her to live all (sic) her friends - to come to the north ward with her Husband - is he a man of fortune - what could be her inducements to marry a stanger - I expect that the President will set out to Mount Vernon soon after the Congress rises - To make a very short stay there. my love and good wishes attend you kiss the children for me the President sends his love to you and children Nelly and Washington[7] join in love to you and all with you I am my dear Fanny your most affectionate

M Washington

ALS. Feinstone Collection, David Library of the American Revolution, Washington Crossing, Pennsylvania. On loan to the American Philosophical Society, Philadelphia, PA.

1. Fanny Bassett Washington's husband, George Augustine Washington (1763-1793), died after an illness of almost ten years. Following his death she and her three children moved to *Happy retreat*, Berkeley County, near Charles Town (now in Jefferson County, West Virginia). This was the home of Charles and Mildred Thornton Washington, the parents of George Augustine Washington. Charles Washington was a younger brother of GW. See, Wayland, *The Washington and Their Homes*, Staunton, 1944, p. 168.

2. Following the death of George Augustine Washington, his uncle, GW, offered one of his Alexandria houses to his widow, Fanny. He directed his Mount Vernon manager, William Pearce, to oversee the repairs and modernization of the house to fit Fanny's needs. *Diaries*, 4:249.

3. Thomas Green was overseer of the plantation carpenters. He and his crew were taken to Alexandria to repair and remodel the President's house there, in preparation for its use by FBW and her children. Greeen was an incompetent alcoholic. About this time he absconded, leaving his wife, Sally, and their children destitute. She was the daughter of Thomas Bishop, GW's old servant during the French and Indian War. *Diaries*, 4:249.

4. Julious Dandridge, son of MW's brother, Bartholomew Dandridge, Sr. and his wife Mary Burbidge Dandridge. Later he becaome cashier of the United States Bank in Richmond. He died, unmarried.

5. Batt (Bartholomew, Jr.) Dandridge was also a son of MW's brother Bartholomew Dandridge, Sr. In 1793 he became secretary to his uncle, the President, Succeeding Tobias Lear. He later became secretary to William Vans Murray, Minister to The Hague, secretary to the legation at the Court of St. James, and Consul to San Domingo. He died there, unmarried. 5W(1) 36, *Diaries*, 6:179, 236.

6. Not positively identified. She might be Lucy Lyons, daughter of Peter Lyons and Judith Bassett Lyons, who married John Hopkins, a merchant of Richmond, and later U.S. Commissioner of Loans. Lucy was a counsin of Fanny Bassett Washington.

7. Eleanor Parke Custis and George Washington Parke Custis, MW's grandchildren.

To Fanny Bassett Washington

My dear Fanny   Philadelphia June the 2d 1794
        I am very glad to find by your letter of the 27th that you had got safe to your journeys end, and happy to hear that your children are all well - I wrote to you last week and the President inclosed it in his letter to Mr Pearce - which must be with you are this - it would my dear Fanny be perticularly pleasing to me to come home this summer if it was conveniant the President thinks that the public business will keep him in this place all summer - and it would not be agreable to me to stay at mount Vernon without him - Mr Pearce living in the family would make it very inconveniant, - as we should be obliged to bring servants with us we could not find room for them when the servants Hall is occupied with alarge family if I could bear the journey I should like to make you a flying visit - but that you know I cannot (illegible) as I am always so much fatagued after I get home for several days - that I could not think of setting out again for some time - I do not know what keys you have - it is highly necessary that the beds andbed cloths of all kind should be aired if you have the keys I beg you will make Caroline put all the things of every kind out to air and Brush and Clean all the places and rooms that they were in - the President has hopes of seeing mount vernon soon he cannot fix the time till after the Congress is up they talk of rising in the course of this week but I dont know wheather it is certain or not - the members going off every day - the house is I believe pretty thin at this time - when the President comes down I beg you will get the key of my closet if you have not get it and send me the two bags that has my worked chear Bottoms in, as I intend to have them made into something if they are not spoiled and Eaten up with the moth if you have the key - I shall be obliged to you to send them in the first vessel that comes hear I have never got the rose water and mint water that was sent to Alexandria to come round hear to me. will you make an enquire about it and have sent hear - I often want it. My love and good wishes attend you and children in which the President and Nelly and Wash joins - I am my dear

                              Fanny your most
                              affectionate
                              M Washington

Mrs F Washington

ALS, ViMtV.

From Fanny Bassett Washington

(June 1794)

as I expected the happiness of seeing the President shortly I did not in my last mention one or two things which I thought of proposing to him respecting the repairs he is so good as to have done for me in Alexandria. I trust he will forgive the appearance of importunity which any request from me might have to him, who has already shown me so much kindness & benevolence, which I wished to propose is that he will be so good as to allow Mr Pearce to have one end of the stable laid with plank floor, for without it I shall be much at a loss to accomodate the servants I am obliged to carry with me. to have a small inclosure made on the lot as a place of security for my wood as I have no wagg(on) (missing) & must endeavour to have enough (missing) to last some time, & the ravages of wicked or (missing)[1]

Df ViMtV. Contained on the verso of the letter of Martha Washington to Fanny Bassett Washington, June 2, 1794.

1. Following the death of her husband, Fanny Bassett, given her choice, preferred to occupy one of the President's houses in Alexandria. He gave explicit orders, from time to time, to Mr. Pearce to put the house and yard in good repair and ready for occupancy by May, 1794. As requested by Fanny, he directed the stable be floored and a safe place for wood storage be provided. Both brick hearths were to be replaced with stone and that he would send wallpaper from Philadelphia. *Writings*, 33:196, 200, 242, 267-68, 368, 400, 427.

To Fanny Bassett Washington

My Dear Fanny   Philadelphia June the 15th 1794

I am sorry to hear of your Letter of the tenth that your little girl has been so ill[1] - I hope she has got quite well before this - I have not a doubt but worms is the principle cause of her complaints Children that eat everything as they like and feed as heartely as yours does must be full of worms - indeed my dear Fanny I never saw children stuffed as yours was when I was down and reather wondered that they were able to be tolarable with such lodes as they used to put into thair little stomachs - I am sure thare is nothing so pernisious as over charging the stomach of a child-with every kind of food that they will take - expearance will convince you of the impropriety if nothing else will -

I can with much truth say that I am really sorry that - I cannot come down to M Vernon this summer particularly on your account - the president says he cannot make a longer stay than a few days - which would make it very inconveniant to me to be thare without him - besides I should not like to have any thing to do with Mr Pearces Family in the House The President will bring two white men with him - one of them may sleep in Whitings room the other in the Garet - let thare be a bed put in the Garret-room - and one for the other man as they may be ready - the President tells of living this on tuesday morn- and I suppose he will make all the dispach he can as he does not expect to be gon long from hear-[2]

I sent to Mr Palmer[3] as soon as your letter came to my hands - he is out of town and his work men knows nothing of your measure it will be as well for you to send one of your old shoes when the President returns, and then you will be scertain that your shoes will fitt - and I will have them done as soon as I can it is difficult to get anything done hear - the trades people suffered very much in the yellow fever - the shoe makers complain of the want of journeymen - I hope it will be better now the Congress is gon - every man must have some thing either to send or carry home - which constantly imployed the trades people in this city

My dear Fanny if Mrs Herberts[4] spinnett is not sent home - I beg you will have it carefully (sent) up in the Boat when your things (missing) with many thanks to her for the lone of it - I hope it is not got any injury staying in our house this winter - I charged Frank to have it sent up directly but I fear thare is not much dependance on him - my love and good wishes attend you and children and believe me my

> Dear Fanny your
> most affectionate
> M Washington

(Address)
Mrs Frans Washington
Mount Vernon

(Docket)
From Mrs M Washington
June 15th - 1794

ALS. PPRF.

1. Anna Maria Washington (1788-1814).

2. The President left Philadelphia on June 17th and arrived at Mount Vernon on June 20th. He left Mount Vernon on July 3rd and arrived in Philadelphia on Monday July 7th. *Writings*, 33:405, 422 n.

3. Unidentified, but apparently a master shoemaker in Philadelphia.

4. Sarah Carlyle Herbert, daughter of John Carlyle of Alexandria, and wife of William Herbert, an Alexandria merchant and importer. The Herberts were frequent visitors at Mount Vernon.

To Fanny Bassett Washington

My Dear Fanny   Philadelphia June 30th 1794

I am very glad to hear by your letter of the 23d that your children were all well - we have had rain almost every day these ten days, - The damp is very great hear Many people are complaining of tooth acks and swilled faces and violent colds Thank god we are tolarable well - Nelly has had the tooth ack which she is very subject to She has got better but it will return when she gets cold - She will not be perswaded to take care of herself - she is a pore thoughtless child -

I have been so unhappy about the Presidt that I did not know what to do with myself -he tells me in his letter of Wednesday that he is better,[1]- I hope in god that he is so - if I could have come down with any conveniance - I should have set out the very hour I got the letter I hope and trust he is better and that he will soon be able to return hear again if he is not getting better my dear Fanny dont let me be deceved let me know his case and not say he is getting better if he is not - it would make me exceeding unhappy to be told or made to believe he is getting better if he is not - I besech you to let me now how he is as soon as you can and often, - if he is likely to be confined at mount vernon longer than was expected I will get into the stage or get stage horses and come down emidately to you, - I very sincearly wish you may find the House in town as agreable as you wish - in every stage of our life we find trouble wheather you will find more in house keeping than living in any other way must be left to time as you cannot judge befour you try which will be the most agreable to you - Maria and Fayette are boath old enough to go to school[2] - my love to the children in which Nelly and Washington join me that you may enjoy every happyness is the sincear wish of you ever affectionate

M Washington

ALS. Courtesy of Forest Lawn Memorial - Park and Mortuary, Glendale, California.

1. While riding horseback to the falls and locks of the Potomac on Sunday, June 22nd, his horse stumbled on the rocks. To avoid a fall of the horse and himself onto the rocks, he suffered a severe strain of the muscles of his back. GW to Henry Knox, June 25, 1794. *Writings*, 33:411.

2. Anna Maria Washington and her brother, George Fayette Washington. They were the children of Fanny Bassett Washington and her deceased husband, George Augustine Washington.

From Fanny Bassett Washington

the little experience I have had, my Dear Aunt, has taught me not to look for happiness in this world - on the contrary I must acknowledge myself sometimes deprest at the task that is before me, but I endeavor to banish every murmering reflection & trust to the Providence that has hitherto conducted me through life, for assistance in the discharge of duties which his will has evidently lain on me.[1]

Df. Courtesy of Forest Lawn Memorial - Park and Mortuary, Glendale, California.

1. Df in the handwriting of Fanny Bassett Washington, written on the back of one page of the letter from Martha Washington to Fanny Bassett Washington, June 30, 1794.

To Fanny Bassett Washington

My Dear Fanny   Philadelphia July the 14th 1794

The President arrived hear on monday a good deal fatagued with his ride - I fear he got some cold, it rained all day on satterday and he rode in the rain and was wet[1] I dont think he is better now than he was when he come home,- I very much fear that it will be a troublesom complaint to him for some time or perhaps as long as he lives he will feel it at times

I am glad to hear that you and the children are well - it would have given me a great deal of pleasure to have been with you if I could - I have noe prospect at this time of seeing you this fall - if the President is not a good deal better he could not undertake so long a journey -

I received your silk - and the shoes - which Mr Palmer has got to make - but said he could not get them done till a fort night - as soon as they are done and an oppertunity offers by water - I will send them your silk I will get dyed as soon as it can be done and send them altogether - if they can be done soon - I dont recolect wheather I put the needles that I worked the cross stitch with in the bag with the chare covers if they are not I dont know whare to derect you to find them - if they are to be found I beg you to send them to me in a letter will be as ready as any way - I dont believe any needles of the kind is to be got hear and I shall want them - I intend to set about my chear and get them done if these that are worked is good for any thing I shall soon have them done -

I am glad to find that the President is so well plased with Mr Peares management he will not I hope be so anxious about his plantation Business as he has confidence in Mr Pears - I am sorry to hear that his daughter is so ill - from the account I hear of her there can be no hope that she can ever recover - and when that is the case it must be a releaf to her and her friends when it is plase god to take her -

I am pleased with your putting out such things as is necessary for the use of the House - and should like that Mr Pearse should have anything for his sick child that he can want that is in the House

I think that thair is two barrells of chocolate shells in the store room if you think to have it take as much of it as you please or anthing else that is thare, in the way of house keeping - tea I beleive thare is not much in the room; but a little will serve to begen with - I wish you may be happy in keeping House - your children will always be companey for you when they are not in school I have the pleasure to tell you that I am well myself and the children tolarabl well - my love and best wishes attend you and children in which the President and children join me I am dear Fanny your ever affectionate

M Washington

Mrs F Washington
From Mrs M Washington
July 14th 1794

ALS, CSmH.

1. The President arrived in Philadelphia on Monday, July 7th. For an account of his journey see, GW to William Pearce, July 13, 1794. *Writings*, 33:424.

To Fanny Bassett Washington

My Dear Fanny   Germantown August the 3d 1794[1]

Your favor of the 28th - July is come to my hands I am happy to hear by it that you and your children are all well, and hope they will continue so, pore Mrs Craik[2] I am truly sorry for her - I am told that her son was a very amiable youth, as she has several good children left she should endevour to reconcile herself to the loss of one however hard it may be, to her, to part plase to remember me to the Doctor and Mrs Craik - Mrs Harrison[3] and boath her children has been sick she came to this fine airy place and have all got well again she means to stay hear while the hot weather lasts I have got your silk done Mr Palmer has not brought your shoes home yet I hope to have them all done and sent with the mattress by the Packet that brought the bacon and other things sent from mount vernon The President says you may have either the broad or the narrow borders put on as you like best - he thinks he thinks any of them will suite and answer very well - do then as you like the best - The President is getting better fast[4] - and he has had Doctor Tate[5] to look at the spot on his face he makes light of the thing - I hope in god that he will very soon be well of it, the medicine that is given has not the last effect that can be perceived except that the spot is a little sore at times - I trust in god that it will soon be perfectly well - Nelly is returned very much pleased with her jaunt thank god we are all tolarable well - Mr Dandridge[6] has been so unlucky as to sprain his shoulder with his other complaints make him look very badly - I wish he may not be in bad health he has been a good while complaining - indeed my only motive for coming to this place was the hopes of its being servisable to the President, the children, and him,- my love and good wishes attend you and the children in which the President and the children joins me

> I am my Dear Fanny your
> ever affectionate
> M Washington

ALS, ViMtV.

1. The Washingtons and their staff moved from Philadelphia on July 30th to escape the summer heat. They returned to the city on September 20th. GW to William Pearce, August 3, 1794, *Writings*, 33:452; September 21, 1794, 33:502.

2. Merrianne Ewell Craik, wife of Dr. James Craik (1730-1814) was a cousin of the President and daughter of Charles Ewell of Belle Air, Prince William County. Her four sons were, James, Jr., William, George Washington, and Adam. Apparently it was Adam who had died. *Diaries*, 4:189-90.

3. Mrs. Robert Hanson Harrison, daughter of George Johnston of Belvale. Her two daughters were Sarah and Dorothy. *Diaires*, 4:121.

4. Dr. James Tate was a Philadelphia physician. He had been a surgeon on the 3rd Pennsylvania Regiment of the Continental Army. *Writings*, 33:4

5. Bartholomew Dandridge, one of the President's secretaries, was a nephew of Martha Washington.

To Mary Stillson Lear

> German Town August the 24th 1794
> a small village near the City of
> Philadelphia

Dear Madam[1]

I now set down to thank you for your two kind letters - and to answer you that it gives me real pleasure to hear from you - and my dear little Lincoln.[2] I often think of the dear child and wish the distance was not as great between us - if it was not I should have asked you to let him come to see me - but I know how inconvenient it would be for a child of his age to be carried so long a journey - The President has heard lately of Mr Lear in a letter from Mr Jay[3] - he mentions that Mr Lear was gone to Liverpool in order to imbark for america, - I hope it will not be long before we see him hear - be so good my dear Madam as to tell dear Lincoln that I send my love to him and am very glad to hear he is a god Boy - The President sends his love to the child - he loves him dearly and we are all anxious to see the dear little creature - I often think whether I should know the child if I ever see it again - it must be a good deal grown since it left us - my grand-children are very much grown Nelly is a woman in size - and Washington begins to be a sturdy Boy - my children often talk of dear little Lincoln and wish they had him with them - if I live to see Mr Lear bring the child into this part of the world - tho I love him and wish to see him, - I shall feel a good deal for your anxiety for the babe if it is taken from you as I suppose Mr Lear as a fond father will wish to have his child with him.

We all join in love to the dear little child and compliments and good wishes for you and hope we shall see Mr Lear soon -

> I am with esteem and affec-
> Dear Madam your Hble
> servant
> M Washington

ALS. From Decatur, *The Private Affairs of George Washington*, p. 206.

1. Mary Stillson Lear (1739-1829), mother of Tobias Lear.

2. Benjamin Lincoln Lear (1791-1829) was the son of Tobias Lear (1762-1816) and Mary (Polly) Long Lear (d. 1793). He was named for his father's benefactor, General Benjamin Lincoln. Following the death of his mother he was taken by his grandmother, Mary Stillson Lear, to Portsmouth, N.H., where he lived, during his father's extensive travels abroad.

3. John Jay (1745-1829). In 1794 the President appointed him special envoy to Great Britain, with whom relations were strained almost to the breaking point. The culmination of his mission was the Jay Treaty, which smoothed the differences and probably prevented war between the two nations.

To Fanny Bassett Washington

My Dear Fanny   German Town September the 15 1794
    I am sorry to hear by your letter of the 10th that Fayette has been sick - as you were giving him the bark I hope he is now perfectly well - this is a season for children to have complaints of different kinds and as you let your children eat as much fomites[1] or any thing else as they will - I am not surprised that a delicate child like Fayette is sick for certain it is that children should not eat every thing that they will - expearance is the only thing that will covince a fond mother that her child should be in some instance controlled in thair diet I hope it will be soon that you will see it or that child will suffer very much in his health -

I am glad your things are arrived safe - and that your silk is done as you like, and that you got it all safe - I had not time to count the peices when it was brought home, - I have often lamented my dear Fanny that you are so far removed from all your connections as they would ad greatly to your felicity - but you are not now so young but you must have got experiance in the world and if you consider, if your friends was about you - you would be obliged to attend to your own concerns as thare are few people that can manage more than their own business - I very sinceary wish you would exert your self so as to keep all your matters in order your self without depending upon others as that is the only way to be happy to have all your business in your own hands without trusting to others that will promise and perhaps never think of doing it till they see you - I woud rouse myself and not trouble any mortal - your concerns are not so large but you might with proper attention have them all ways kept in good order - I hope my dear Fanny you will look upon this advice in the friendly way it is ment - as I wish you to be as independent as your circumstances will admit and to be so, is to exert yourself in the management of your estate if you do not no one elce will - a dependence is I think a wrached state and you have enough if you will mannage it right.

I am glad to hear Maria and Charles are boath well The season is now so far advanced that I hope you will have no more ague and fever

thank god we are all well and shall move back to the city[2] there are frequent alarms that the yellow fever is in town but I believe it has all been without foundation - the president Mr Dandridge Nelly and Washington all join me in love and good wishes for you and your children - I wish you had mentioned how Mrs Calvert[3] was when you wrote to me

> I am my Dear Fanny your
> most
> affectionate
> M Washington

ALS, CSmH.

1. Fomites, plural of fomes (rare), any porous substance capable of absorbing and retaining contagious effluvia. (OED).

2. The Washingtons returned to Philadelphia from Germantown on September 21st.

3. Elizabeth Calvert Calvert (1730-1798), daughter of Charles Calvert, colonial governor of Maryland. She was the wife of Benedict Calvert (1724-1788) and the mother of Eleanor Calvert Custis Stuart (1754-1811).

To Elizabeth Dandridge Henley

My Dear Sister[1]   Mount Vernon September the 24, 1794

Mr Maddison[2] called on the President which affords me an opportunity to send the enclosed for you, and your daughter[3] and to tell you that I am greatly disappointed at not seeing you as I had promised myself that pleasure, and looked for ward for the time of your coming with impatience. I dare say Betty you have good reasons for not coming. I hope you have recovered your health. I shall be glad to hear from you. I expect to leave this for Philadelphia about the 13th of October. As it is probably that we shall never meet in this world You have my prayers for this worlds blessing. All here join me in love and good wishes to you and all with you. Mr. Maddison is waiting, so I must bid you farewell - farewell my dear Betty, and believe me your ever affectionate,

> M Washington[4]

ALS, CCamarSJ.

1. Elizabeth Dandridge Aylett Henley, younger sister of MW. She was the wife of Leonard Henley of Pine Grove, James City County. At this time she was living at Pine Grove.

2. It is difficult to accept the "Mr Maddison" referred to as James Madison, the congressman and future 4th President of the United States. Madison was not in Philadelphia at this time. He was married to Dolly Payne Todd on September 15th, 1794, at Harewood, Berkeley County, the home of Dolly's sister, Mrs. Samuel Washington. Four or five days after the wedding they journeyed to Winchester and then returned to Harewood. On October 5th he wrote his father as follows, "In eight or ten days we expect to set out for Philadelphia." Brant, *James Madison, Father of the Constitution*, Indianapolis, 1950, p. 410-11.

3. Frances Henley, daughter of Elizabeth Dandridge Henley and Leonard Henley. She later married Tobias Lear as had her first cousin, Fanny Bassett Washington, previously.

4. Text taken from the catalogue of the W. W. Cohen Sale, American Art Association, February 5-6, 1929. It is identical with the copy furnished by CCamarSJ.

To Fanny Bassett Washington

My Dear Fanny   Philadelphia September the 29th 1794

I am sorry to find by your letter of the 29th that your children are still complaining and hope the cool weather and change of air - if you take them up to Berkley - will perfect their cure. The weather has been uncommonly hot hear, which has made it very sickly in the Town and neighbourhood, - it has several times been reported that the yellow fever is in the city - one Doctor says it is in Town - and another says it is not - several people have dide with different complaints, - I hope the cool weather will carry of fevors of every kind; sore throats among the children has been fatal in many cases, many have died with that complaint.[1]

The President desired me to tell you he has not been unmindful of his promise to take Fayette - he only waits till he is old enough to be put to a good school in this city, Thare are no schools but College, and that is a very indifferent one for big boys - little ones are not attended to at all, - as you find by Doctor Stuarts complaints of my grandson[2] he attends as constant as the day comes- but he does not learn as much as he might if the Master took proper care to make the children attentive to thair books. -

My dear Fanny, I wish I could give you unerring advise in regard to the request contained in your last letter; I really dont know what to say to you on the subject; you must be governd by your own judgement, and I trust providence will derect you for the best; it is a matter more interesting to yourself than any other The person contemplated[3] is a worthy man, and esteemed by every one that is aquainted with him; he has , it is concieved, fair prospects before him; - is, I belive, very industri(ous) and will, I have not a doubt, make sumthing handsome for himself.- as to the President, he never has, nor never will, as you have often heard him say, inter meddle in matrimonial concerns. he joins with me however in wishing you every happyness this world can give. - you have had a long acquaintance with Mr Lear, and must know him as well as I do. - he always appeared very attentive to his wife and child, as farr as ever I have seen; he is I believe, a man of strict honor and probity; and one with whom you would have as good a prospect of happyness as with any one I know; but beg you will not let anything I say influence you either way. The President has a very high opinion of and friendship for Mr. Lear; and has not the least objection to your forming the connection but, no more than myself, would wish to influence your judgement, either way - yours and the childrens good being among the first wishes of my heart -

The insurgents in the back country has carried matters so high that the President has been obliged to send a larg body of men to settle the matter - and is to go himself tomorrow to to Carlyle to meet the troops:[4] god knows when he will return again. - I shall be left quite alone with the children. - should you go to Berkley be so good as to send the keys you have of our House to Mr Pearce; in case the President should take Mount Vernon in his way back to this place. - my love and good wishes attend you in which the President joins me, with love to the children - adu my dear Fanny and believe me with sincere wishes for your happyness your ever affectionate

M Washington

From Mrs Washington
Septr 29th 1794

ALS, NNPM.

1. Probably diptheria.

2. George Washington Parke Custis. He was as dilatory as his father, John Parke Custis had been as a student. Dr. David Stuart was his step-father.

3. After being closely associated with Fanny Bassett Washington, as a member of the Washington household for six years and following the deaths of their respective spouses, Lear proposed marriage. Fanny had requested advice from the Washingtons in a letter of August 29th. The letter is missing.

4. The President left Philadelphia on September 30th for western Pennsylvania, to accompany the militia, sent to quell the whiskey insurrection. He returned on October 28th.

To Fanny Bassett Washington

My Dear Fanny   Philadelphia October the 18th 1794

I had the pleasure to recieve your kind favor some time in the last week and have put your letter so secure as not to be able to find it today. I am very glad to hear you are tolerable well your self and your children better, your happyness my dear Fanny is I assure you, very dear to the President and myself, I have not a doubt but you have considered well what you are about to undertake - and I hope that the same providence that has heatherto taken care of you will still be your gardien angel to protect and derect you in all your undertakings, you have my fervent prayers for your happyness[1]

Mrs Izard[2] a ladie of my acquantance since I have been hear is settng out on a journey to her seat in charlestown - south carolina - Mr Izard has been in congress ever since the president has - after serving his six years he means to retire and his family goes on this fall, they will come to alexandria and wish much to visit mount vernon if it is not very inconvenient to you I shall be much obliged to you to goe down to mount vernon with Mrs Izard and her family as they would be glad to rest thair a day it would be well to let Mr Pearce know it - the Ladies intend to set out on wednesday - next - thair present intention is to go by lancaster and little York town - and come from thance to the Federal City - I would wish you to be very kind to them and put up a supply of good bread or any thing else that they may want - I shall give Mrs Izard a letter for you which she will send to you as soon as she gets to Alexandria Mrs Mannagold[3] is her daughter and will I expect go all together to mount vernon - I will when I write next week give you all the information I can as to the time they expect to get to Georgetown Mr Lear is very well acquanted with the Ladys and gentleman if he will be so good as to let you know when they arrive at the city and go down with them it would be the more agreable to them as he would be able to walk about with them -

My love and good wishes attend you and children. I have not heard of the President since he left carlyle - I am my dear Fanny your ever affectionate

M Washington

From Mrs. M Washington
Octr 1794

ALS. Text from a photocopy copy. Location of original unknown. An edited version is printed in *Wharton*, p. 247-49.

1. Fanny had apparently accepted Lear's proposal of marriage.

2. Alice Delancey Izard, wife of Ralph Izard (1741/42-1804), senator from South Carolina. She was a niece of Governor Delancey, colonial governor of New York.

3. Margaret Izard Manigault (1768-1824) married Gabriel Manigault of Charleston, South Carolina.

To Fanny Bassett Washington

My Dear Fanny   Philadelphia October the 22d 1794
I expect that this letter will be handed to you by Mrs Izard the Lady that I mentioned to you in my letter of the 19th of this month, - who has a desire to see mount vernon - if you could make it convenient to your self, I shall be much obliged to you to go down with the Ladys to mount vernon, as I wish every thing thair to be made as agreable to them as

possible as the notice is short, Mrs Izard is a very agreable Lady and her family amiable - we have been acquanted ever since I went up to new york - I should be very much gratified to hear that the Ladis of Alexandria shews to Ladis sevility - if they should be obliged to make any stay thair - you will find them all very agreable, Miss Izard[1] has been long a friend of Nellys - do my dear Fanny have every thing as good as you can for them and put up any little thing that may be necessary for the children on the road - I send you a fashonable cap caul and Border - if you will scollop or over cast the borders it will add to their beauty -

My love and good wishes attend you and the children - I am my dear Fanny your ever affectionate

M Washington

October I have not heard
from the President since
the eleventh.[2]
From Mrs. M Washington
Octr 1794

ALS, PHi.

1. One of the eight daughters of Senator Ralph Izard and his wife, Alice Delancey Izard.

2. On the 11th of October the President was in Carlisle, Pennsylvania, on his return to Philadelphia. *Writings*, 34:1.

To Fanny Bassett Washington

My Dear Fanny   Philadelphia November the 11th 1794

I am happy to hear by your letter of the 21st of october - that you were well and your children better except Maria and I hope the jaunt over the mountains has cured of her complaints - I do not know how my letter miscarred - I was very anxious that it should get to your hands - Mrs Izard a lady of my acquantance was going down to the federal city - and wished to see Mount Vernon in that letter I beged you to go down with them to our House - I am sorry you were out of the way as it was particularly unlucky for them - as at the time they got to mount vernon the President expected Mr Pearce was gone to the Eastern Shore - so that there was no person there that could get things for thair accomodations as I realy esteem the Laides and wished them to have every thing there as agreable as it could be -

The President returned from the westward very well - and I am in hopes that the spot that was on his face is quite gone There is not the least appearance of it to be seen now - I thank god that we are all very well - Mr Dandridge looks much the better for his trip - and is in better health than he has been for some time past - poore Billy Dandridge how does he like to be bound out - I hope and trust it is for his good yet I cannot say but I am sorry to have him taken from his friends - such a distance - his Brothers - I am sure think it is the best that they can do for him - and I hope he will turn out well -[1]

Since I wrote the above - Mr Izard has called in to tell me he has heard from Mrs Izard she was at mount vernon but was so unlucky as not to find any person at home - she speaks much of Franks politeness and kindness to them she thought Mr Lear had promised to go down with her, and she set out in expectation of his following of them but he never arrived at m vernon they left it early the next day - I am truly sorry you was out of the way when the good Laides was in virginia - I am sure you would have been highly pleased with their company - my love and good wishes to you and children in which the President joins me I am my dear Fanny your most affectionate

M Washington

I have at last my dear Fanny sent a little bundle which I promised to Maria - by Capt Elwood[2] if you will send her measure I will have a pritty pair of shoes made for her-
From Mrs M Washington
Novr 1794
July 1st 1 dozn
          1 do
          1 do
          1 do
          8 bottles 82

ALS, CSmH.

   1. William Dandridge, nephew of MW and son of Bartholomew Dandridge, Sr. (1737-1785 and his wife Mary Burbidge Dandridge (d. 1809).

   2. Captain John Ellwood, Jr., skipper of the sloop, Harmony, plying between Philadelphia and the Potomac ports.*Writings*, 34:143, 372.

To Fanny Bassett Washington

My Dear Fanny   Philadelphia November the 22d 1794
   I recieved your kind favor of the 18th yesterday and am very glad to hear that you are all well yourself, and your children getting better, I hope the weather is so cold that it will carry off all complaints of the ague and fever I sent the chocolate for you by Capt Mitchel[1] which I hope you will get soon - Mr Lear sets of this morning, and I have been a good deal ingaged, I shall only tell you in this that we are all very well I will get the shoes for Maria as soon as I can and send them to you - I am sorry to hear that the schools are in such bad repute it seems to be the case everywhere

- in this city every one complains of the difficulty to get their children educated my dear Little Washington is not doing half so well as I could wish he is at the college hear[2] - and we are mortified that we cannot do better for him, my love and good wishes attend you in which the President and the children joins me

> I am my dear Fanny your
> ever affectionate
> M Washington

I see your cousin Carter Harrison[3] yesterday he enquires very kindly after you - he said he loved you very much but was unluckey enough never to meet with you he has brought his family hear to spend the winter they are all very sick - his children are in the small pox
Mrs F Washington
By Favor of Mr Lear
(Docket)
From Mrs M Washington
November 1794

ALS, ViMtV.
1. Probably the captain of a ship plying between Philadelphia and the Potomac River ports.
2. The College of Philadelphia, later the University of Pennsylvania.
3. Carter Harrison's mother was Elizabeth Bassett, sister of Fanny's father, Burwell Bassett.

To Fanny Bassett Washington

My Dear Fanny   Philadelphia November the 30th 1794
    Not having received any letter from you since my letter to you by Mr Lear - I have only to tell you that we are all well - and hope when I next hear from you, that I shall have the pleasure to hear that your children are quite well, - I am my dear Fanny, glad you brought the keys of our House home with you and desire you will keep them, - the President seemed a good deal surprised - at the quantity of wine that you have given out, as it never was his intention to give wine or goe to any Expence to entertain people that came to Mount vernon out of curiosity to see the place; if it is continued - we shall have but very little for ourselves if we should come home - rum may always be had - and I beg you will not give out another Bottle out of the vault - I make not the least doubt but Frank drinks as much wine as he gives to the visitors - and rum boath, - and wish you not to give more out unless the President should order it - my love and good wishes for you and the children in which the President

joins me I am my dear Fanny your ever affectionate

M Washington

Mr & Mrs West[1] arrived hear last week - by them I hope to get th shoes for maria -

ALS, ViMtV.

1. This is possibly Roger West (d.1801), son of John West, Jr., and his second wife, Marianne Craik West, daughter of Dr. James Craik. His sister was Nancy Craik, wife of Richard Harrison, auditor of the United States Treasury from 1791-1836. The latter would be living in Philadelphia at this time.

To Fanny Bassett Washington

My Dear Fanny   Philadelphia December the 15th 1794
    Your letter of the forth has given me great pleasure to hear by it that you and your children are in much better health - that the fall complaints are far off - and I trust that the children will enjoy good health this winter - I have been extreemly anxious and uneasy - on hearing that Doctor Stuart[1] was so very ill, in a Letter from Mrs Stuart she tells me he is so well as to be able to go down to Mr L. Washingtons. I hope he is recovered - I dont know what his poore family would doe without him if it should please god to take him from them - I trust he will be spared to them - I sent the shoes for Maria By Mrs West[2] - who made a flying visit to her sister hear I hope they will fitt the child -
    Thank god we are all very well, I dont think Nelly so much grown as Mr Lear describes he can see the alteration more than I can the very same clothes fitts her as she had made at Alexandria last fall - Wash has out grown his cloths that was made since - Thank god they are boath very well - and I hope when Nelly has a little more Gravatie she will be a good girl - at present she is I fear half crasey - my love and good wishes to you and the children in which the President joins me Nelly Wash and Mr Dandridge send thair love to you and children

I am my dear Fanny your
ever affectionate
M Washington

From Mrs M Washington
Decr 1794

ALS, ViMtV.

1. The nature of his illness is not known. He had recovered before February 1796. GW to Dr. David Stuart, February 7, 1796. *Writings*, 34:452.

2. See supra, n. 1.

From R. G. C. Clifford

Mrs Washington   March 30th 1795
    Madam
    Your Humble Servant that addresses you is a Mr R G C Clifford, who thro' some little misadventure in Life, threw himself on the Stage - which threws himself entirely on your kind patronage to assist him in the Nomination of even Midshipman on board the new *Frigate* of *Philadelphia* already on the stocks[1] It is Clifford with Submission that Sung Washingtons *Council forever* while on *the* Stage, but whither to better himself in which he has been accustomed to - Your kind answer to General Jackson[2] of Boston or at the Theater by interceding for me will greatly Oblige as a Stranger One that is with every Dutiful respect

                              Your most Humble Servant
                              faithful to Commands
                              R.G.C.Clifford

The Honble Lady Washington
of General George Washington
Philadelphia
From R G C Clifford
30 Mar. 95
Solicitg a Birth on board
a frigate Midship man

ALS, DLC:GW.
    1. He is apparently referring to one of three 44 gun frigates under construction. The frigate under construction in Joshua Humphrey's shipyard in Philadelphia was the *United States*. It was launched May 10, 1797. H. I. Chapelle, *The History of the American Sailing Navy*, New York, 1949, p. 128-29.
    2. The reference here is to either Brigadier-general Henry Jackson (1747-1807), or Brigadier-general Michael Jackson (1734-1821). The former served throughout the Revolution and afterwards commanded the Massachusetts militia. The latter served during the French and Indian War and throughout the Revolution. Both commanded Massachusetts regiments.

To Fanny Bassett Washington

My Dear Fanny   Philadelphia April the 6th 1795
    I was exceedingly pleased to hear by Mr Lear that you was arrived safe at home - the roads are not so bad down the country as they are hear - if they had been any thing like the roads in this part of the country it would been very difficult for you to have got on - I am sorry to find by your letter of the 21st of March - that your Brother[1] is disapointed - in his election - I see by the Richmond paper that Mr. Clopton[2] is the

representative - I am sorry to hear that Mrs B Bassett[3] enjoys such bad health and she can have very little pleasure if her life to be always indisposed - they have tryed the sweet springs - wish they would try a northern trip - as they might then be able so to judge which air would be best for them young folks will have thair own way -

I had all your things done and put on bord of a vessel with several things of Mrs Peters - and am surprised that you have not got them - as Mr Lear told me that the vessel was arrived - your two boxes were directed to the care of Colo Gilpin[4] - I hope you have got them by this time - I was anxious to have them done by the time you came up - I hope your gowns will fitt and made as you like - there was no silk to be got nearer the colour that you mentioned than the one sent - I thought it a very pritty one -

I am very much greved to hear that my pore sister[5] is in such a wreched situation it is impossible that things can go one tolerably if Mr Henley is always drinking brandy - everything he has must suffer - be sides the strain it must give to his family - I fear he has but little affection for them - or he would devote this time to take care of them reather than to be always drinking - pore Dear Betsy has had a hard lot in this world I hope her children will be a comfort to her as they grow up - and not follow in thair unhappy Fathers bad example - I often think of her with the greatest concern - I should be very glad if it could so happen that she would come up to see me when I go home - she is in such distress that I fear she will never have resolution to leve her children to come so long a journey - I shall let her know when I am coming home - if she can come your Brother B promised to let her have a man servant to bring her up -

It gave me pleasure my dear Fanny to hear that your children are well and think it very proper that Maria and Fayette are put to school as they wil learn much better at school than at home if the teacher is tolerable good - Mr Lear arrived hear on thursday and intends to set out tomorrow to the eastward -

Betsy Custis[6] told me, she wished to stay with me, and I wrote to her mother for her permission which she redily gave, - She seemed to be very grave I was in hope that being in the gay world would have a good effect on her, but she seems to wish to be at home - and very much by herself - she takes no delight to goe out to visit - she would not go with Nelly and myself to the assembly last week she dont like to go to church every sunday thinks it too fatiguing - to be always to be indisposed she often complains of not being well - she took ill when she first came here - but is much better and looks better tho she does not like to be told so - the girls have lived so long in solatude that they do not know how to get the better of it - Betsy seems so reconciled to be alone - the girls are to go to Miss Morris[7] wedding on thursday next - she is to be marred to one of our country men Mr James Marshall

Colo Humphrey[7] has made us a short trip he has taken leve of us to return to Portigal again - thank god we are all well - the President expects to set out on Monday the 14th to visit mount vernon.[9]

The girls send thair love to you - the President joins me in love to you and your cildren

> I am my dear Fanny your
> ever affectionate
> M Washington

From Mrs M Washington
April 1795

ALS, ViMtV.

1. John Bassett (1765-1822), one of the two sons of Burwell Bassett and Anna Maria Dandridge Bassett and a nephew of MW. He was an attorney and had attended William and Mary. His residence was at Farmington, Hanover County, and later at Eltham, New Kent County. *Harris*, p. 48.

2. Judge John Clopton (1756-1816) of "Rosyln," New Kent County. He attended William and Mary and later the University of Pennsylvania. Clopton was a first lieutenant of artillery in the Revolution, member of the General Assembly from 1785-1789, elected a member of Congress in 1795 and served until his death in 1816. *Harris*, p. 229-30.

3. Philadelphia Anne Claiborne Bassett, second wife of Burwell Bassett, Jr., and daughter of William Dandridge Claiborne of "Liberty Hall," King William County. *Harris*, p. 48.

4. Colonel George Gilpin (1740-1813) a Maryland native who settled in Alexandria before the Revolution and set up a mercantile business. He was colonel of the Fairfax militia and became very active in the affairs of the Potomac Company. Gilpin was a frequent visitor at Mount Vernon. *Diaries*, 4:141.

5. Elizabeth Dandridge Aylett Henley, youngest sister of MW and wife of Leonard Henley.

6. Elizabeth Parke Custis (1776-1832), eldest child of John Parke Custis and Eleanor Calvert Custis, and MW's eldest grandchild.

7. Hetty Morris, daughter of Robert Morris (1734-1806) and his wife, Mary Willing Morris. She married James Marshall, younger brother of Chief-justice John Marshall.

8. David Humphreys (1752-1818), long-time secretary to GW, was appointed Minister to Portugal in August, 1790. He became deeply involved in attempts to free the American citizens held hostage by the Algerians. He returned to the United States, February 2, 1795, to consult with the President and the Secretary of State, concerning the Algerian dispute. He sailed from the United States on April 8, 1795, arriving at Lisbon, via Paris, on November 5th. F. L. Humphreys, *Life and Times of David Humphreys*, (New York, 1917), 2:222-36.

9. The President left Philadelphia on April 14th and arrived at Mount Vernon on the 19th. He left Mount Vernon on April 26th and reached Philadelphia on May 2nd.

To Fanny Bassett Washington

My Dear Fanny   Philadelphia May the 10th (1795)

I thank you for your two kind letters and am very glad to find by them that you, and your children are all well, - I will get the silk dyed - and bring it down when I come, which I hope will be some time towards the latter end of July - the Letter you sent to my care - I delivered it today to Mr Leare he arrived in this city late last night and came in to breakfast with us this morning The President arrived safe hear on satterday week he had a more agreabl journey back the roads are mending as the summer adva(n)ce[1] the cold weather and rains that we have had hear has been the cause of the peoples being very sickly in general - I hope the city will be helhther as the warm weather is coming on and the weather setled - thank god we are all well - Betsy you know is often complaining - I dont think she has much cause of complaint as she looks much better than she did when she came up to this place - I have often told her that you expected she would write to you - but I believe she has never thought about it as yet - nor never will the girls boath complain that they have no time to work or do any thing that they should do - but can stand at the window all day to look at what is doing in the street Betsy does not take much pleasure in going out to visit - she has had a great many visits to see her -

My Dear Fanny the President mentioned to me - that you told him, Mr Pearces House Keeper was going to leve him, - if you think she is carefull and industress - I shall be much obliged to you if you will desire Mr Pearce to engage her to keep house for me while I am at Mt Vernon as I am at a very great loss for a person in that time - and wish to get one to superintend the care of the servants if she will only stay while I am at home it will serve my purpose - The President the girls and Washington join me in love to you and the children I am my dear Fanny your ever affectionat

M Washington

Mrs F Washington
From Mrs M Washington
May 10th 1795

ALS, CSmH.

1. The President arrived in Philadelphia from Mount Vernon on Saturday, May 2nd. *Diaries*, 6:200.

From Ruthey Jones

Dear Madam   Belfast May the 12 1795

It is not without some timidity, that I have taken up my pen - with a humble request that you will accept of these little matters which I hope will go safe to you, and I flatter myself you will use them with as much Pleasure as I made them, I have long wisht for a safe opportunity and this I hope will prove so - as I have sent this little box to the particular care of Mrs Footman[1] who is an only Daughter to the Laidy I live with - I have requested it as a singular favour of her, to send it to you by some safe hand, which I hope she will do - I now begg leave to wish you, and the Best of men, your Worthy Husband, all the happiness this world can offerd, and the best of Blessings here after

I now remain Dear Madm; with the greatest respect

Ruthey Jones[2]

Mrs. Wshington
in Philadelphia
Honord by Mr. R. Samuel Footman
Ruthey Jones
May 12th 1795

ALS, DLC:GW.
    1. Unidentified.
    2. In a letter to GW, of the same date, Mrs. Jones states she had a grand uncle, James Washington, of Virginia. She states she was informed that GW was a son or grandson of this same James Washington. There were no James Washingtons in the ancestry of George Washington. DLC:GW.

To Fanny Bassett Washington

My Dear Fanny   Philadelphia May the 24th 1795
    Your affectionate favor of the 20th is come to my hands - I am very glad to hear by it that your children are well - and yourself - I am truly sorry that any thing should happen in your family to give you pain Black children are liable to so many accidents and complaints that one is heardly sure of keeping them[1] I hope you will not find in him much loss the Blacks are so bad in thair nature that they have not the least gratatude for the kindness that may be shewed to them -
    from what I have heard of Mr Pearces House Keeper[2] I wished very much to have her engaged to stay at mount vernon while I was at home - so goe into the sellers meat house and look into the milk and butter Kitty has had it so long under her care - that I think she should be looked too to give a better account of it - we shall bring white servants with us - which will make it necessary that I should have a person to see to thair having what is proper,done for them, and have thair vituals alwas in proper order - I think it is really necessary to have a person such a one as Mrs Skinner is in our family while I am thare besids that of looking after the women that work they always idle half their time away about thair one business and wash so bad that the cloths are not fitt to use - if she will come only to stay while I am thair I shall be very much pleased to have her - I do expect we shall have a good deal of company many hear talk of coming to see the Federal city and will take that oppertunity to come to Mt Vernon while we are there
    I am my Dear Fanny very sencible of your goodness and attention in having everything done for me as you can - but it always gave me pain

to see you have so much trouble while I was at home - if Mrs Skinner will come I shall be much happyer to have her to do the drudgry - and then I shall have the plasure to have more of your company - and shall see my friends with chearfullness - which could not be the case if I have not a person whose bussness it is to attend to all the wants and cares about the house -

I am very much obliged to you my dear Fanny for offering to preserve strawberry for me - I dont think it will be worth while - to do any - I wish to live in a plain stile while I am at home - and we shall always have greene fruit which can be preserved at the time it is wanted which will be better for use- should thair be any goosberry I should wish to have some bottled and some of the morelly cherrys dried - I should think old Doll cannot have forgot how to do them if she has Mrs Skinner may come to the hous as soon as she will - and she may have all the Beds and Bed Cloths air and clened the Bedsteads all taken down and cleand and well rubbed - so that thair may be nothing of that kind to do when I come home - and to have every part of the House cleaned from the garrets to the sellers as I wish to have every thing done that can be done before I come home -

Thank god we are all well - the President has been very well since his return

The girls and Washington are well - and join the President and me in love to you and children we have not heard this week neither from Mrs Stuart nor Mrs Peter - I wish the House was done for when I go to house keeping I am affraid Patty will get leasey if she has not some thing to do soon -

I am with love and affection my dear Fanny your sincear well wisher

M Washington

From Mrs M Washington
May 1795

ALS, CSmH.

1. Apparently one of the negro slave children, belonging to Fanny, had died.

2. Mrs. Skinner was probably the housekeeper for Mr. William Pearce, GW's resident manager at Mount Vernon. She is not further identified.

To Eleanor Parke Custis

My Dearest Nelly   Philadelphia January the 3d 1796
      Your letter of the 20th December came to my hands on Thursday last - I am exceeding glad to find by it that your sister Nancy[1] was getting better - I was truly sorry to hear that your Mamma[2] was in so much trouble and hope are this reaches you that your sisters and brother[3] will be all perfectly recovered - the wet open winter it is to be feared will make it

a very sickly winter and spring - I was very sorry my dear child to hear that you had been sick, and had the tooth ack you should be very carefull how you go out in the cold to keep your feet dry and take care of your teeth to clean them every day - I sent you Brushes and tooth powder in case you should want it - by Mrs Nichols[4] - and hope you have got the things safe - I am much plesed my dear with the cap your Lasey sister[5] has not done the one she had and I am much in want of it, to finish and put the finishings I had made altogether so as to have them ready to be sent when an oppertunity offers to George town.

The President and my self are much obliged to you my dear for your good wishes to us - we have spent our Christmas at home as we always have done - I intended to have gon to the assembly last Thursday but it rained so hard in the afternoon that it prevented our going out your friends make many enquires after you - Mrs and Miss Bordly[6] was hear New Years day - Mrs Bordly has been very much indisposed Mr Bordly[7] told me that Miss Bordly had writen to you lately - I desired him to tell her that if she would send her letters for you to me I would take care of them and send them to you - the letter of Miss Morris s[8] came after our letter was sent to the post office is the reason of its being so long delayed - we had a very large companey hear on fryday and Fryday evening. Miss Temple[9] is still in town - she is not grown so much as you would expect she is short and fat and not pritty

I was in hopes my dear child to have had a picture drawn of me for you before this I have set several times[10] - the picture is not yet done nor do I know when it will be ready to send to you as the painter beged I would not hurry him - and as I know the only value of a picture is the likeness it bears to the person it is taken for - I shall wait till he brings it to me I met with a prity book which I send you with the pretiest gold chain that I could find which I hope will get safe to you and soon - I have also sent your conkshell clasp and six small buttons that I think you asked me for - Kiss Master (_____) for me and tell him when I come to Mount Vernon I will bring him a pritty thing for his goodness to you - our compliments to Doctor Stuart our love to your Mamma and children - your Brother is run out and says he will write to you next sunday - you know how difficult it is to get him to write Thank god he is very well and getting fat again - I hope my dear that this will be a happy year to you and that it will plese god to make you good and Bless you is the sincear prayer of your ever affectionate

M Washington

The President sends his love and good wishes to you and all with you - I will send your Pin cushing as soon as I can it is too big to send in a letter it is an indifferent thing - I have got for you the Iron to make the filigree and will try to get some paper if there is any in this city -

ALS, ViMtV.

1. Ann Calvert Stuart (1784-) was the eldest child of Dr. David Stuart and Eleanor Calvert Custis Stuart. She was a half sister of Eleanor Parke Custis.

2. Eleanor Calvert Custis Stuart (1754-1811), was the eldest daughter of Benedict (Swingate) Calvert of Mount Airy, Prince George County Maryland, the illegitimate son of Charles Calvert, fifth Lord Baltimore. Benedict Calvert married Elizabeth Calvert, daughter of Charles Calvert, colonial governor of Maryland. Their daughter, Eleanor Calvert, married John Parke Custis on February 3, 1774. Widowed in 1781, she married Dr. David Stuart late in 1783.

3. Eliza Parke Custis (1776-1832), married Thomas Law, a native of England and nephew of Lord Ellenborough. They separated after several years of marriage. Martha Parke Custis (1777-1854), married Thomas Peter of Georgetown. George Washington Parke Custis (1781-1857), married Mary Lee Fitzhugh. They resided at "Arlington."

4. Probably Mary Nichols, wife of James Bruce Nichols of Fairfax County. They were frequent dinner guests at Mount Vernon after the Revolution. *Diaries*, 6:249, 263, 287-88, 317, 336.

5. Probably Eliza Parke Custis.

6. Mary Chew Bordley, wife of John Beale Bordley, see infra. Elizabeth Bordley, daughter of John Beale and Elizabeth Chew Bordley. She was a friend and confidante of Eleanor Parke Custis. Their extensive correspondence is preserved at Mount Vernon. She later married James Gibson.

7. John Beale Bordley (1727-1804) of Baltimore and Wye Island, Maryland. He was a lawyer and jurist and noteworthy as an experimental agriculturist. He had an abiding interest in all things concerning agriculture, which brought him into friendly contact with GW. *Diaries*, 3:307; 5:390. *Writings*; 30:47-52.

8. Probably Maria Morris (1779-1852), daughter of Robert Morris and his wife, Mary White Morris. *Diaires*; 5:326.

9. Elizabeth Temple, daughter of Sir William Temple and his wife, who was the daughter of Governor James Bowdoin of Massachusetts. Temple was a native of Boston and was the British Consul-General. He had inherited his title from his great-grandfather. Elizabeth Temple lived with the Bowdoins during the Revolution. There she met Franklin, Lafayette, Chastellux, and other distinguished personages. Chastellux described her as, "an angel in the guise of a young girl," which differs somewhat from MW's impression. R. W. Griswold, *The Republican Court or American Society in the Days of Washington*, (New York, 1856), p. 9-10, 94.

10. The drawing has not been identified.

To Eleanor Parke Custis

Mr Dear Child   January the 14th 1796

hearing of an oppertunity late Last night - to send the trunk to your sister Peter I have put into it everything that you have asked for, and every thing I promised you, when I send the Picture which I hope to have ready to send by Mrs Bassett[1] with two pocket handkerchiefs which will make six - I sent four with the paper - for you and cannot help reminding you that it is necessary for you to be carefull of all your cloths - and have them kept togather and often look over them - the President and your Brother are well and send love to you - I am my Dear Nelly your ever affectionate

M Washington

(Address)
Miss Nelly Custis

ALS, ViMtV.

1. This might be Philadelphia Anne Claiborne Bassett, wife of Burwell Bassett, Jr., or Elizabeth Carter Bassett, wife of John Bassett. Both Bassetts were nephews of MW.

To Thomas Law

The text of the letter of George Washington and Martha Washington to Thomas Law, March 28, 1796, is not available.

In a letter of March 30th to Elizabeth Parke Custis Law, GW wrote as follows: My compliments to Mr. Law. In a joint letter, written a few days ago to him, by your Grandmamma and myself, we offered you both our congratulations on your union. and I repeat them again, with sincerity being Your Affectionate

G°: Washington

Writings, 45:1.

To Tobias Lear

My dear Sir   Philadelphia 30th Mar; 1796
    Your former letters prepared us for the stroke, which that of the 25th instant announced;[1] But it has fallen heavily notwithstanding -
    It is the nature of humanity to mourn for the loss of our friends; and the more we loved them, the more poignant is our grief. - It is part of the precepts of religion and Philosophy, to consider the Dispensations of Providence as wise, immutable, uncontroulable; of course, that it is our duty to submit with as little repining, as the sensibility of our nature is capable of, to all its decrees. - But nature will, nothwithstanding, endulge, for a while, its sorrows. -
    To say how much we loved, and esteemed our departed friend, is unnecessary - She is now no more! - but she must be happy, because her virtue has a claim to it
    As you talked of coming to this place on business, let us press you to do so. - The same room that serves Mr Dandridge & Washington is large enough to receive a Bed also for you; and it is needless to add, we shall be glad of your company. - The change may be serviceable to you; and if our wishes were of any avail they would induce you to make your stay here as long as your convenience would permit. -[2]
    At all times, and under all circumstances, we are, and ever shall remain, your sincere and affectionate friends

G°: Washington
M Washington[2]

Mr. Tobias Lear

ALS, NNPM

1. In letters to GW on March 21st and 23rd, Lear informed the Washingtons of the precarious state of Fannie's health. The letter of the 25th announced her death. All three letters are in DLC:GW. At the time of Fannie's death the Lears were living in Washington, the new Federal City. The President had suggested to Lear that he be a Commissioner of the Federal City but had refused the appointment. Instead he preferred to live there where he could better promote the affairs of T. Lear and Company, his commercial enterprise, as well as those of the Potomac Company, of which he was a director.

> Afflicted as I am I have thought it my duty to write the enclosed which will communicate an event that must be distressing to you, my dear friend, as well as myself. The Partner of my life is no more!

> and I am too much distressed at this moment to add more than to assure you that tho my life is now not worth preserving, yet as it is, it is most Sincerely & devotedly yours

Tobias Lear
March 25, 1796.

The Washingtons had also been informed of Fanny's death by a letter from Eliza Parke Custis Law, written March 25. *Writings*, 35:1.

2. The letter is in the handwriting of GW and signed by him and MW.

NOTE: In a letter of April 1, 1796, Andrew Parks sought the permission of the President to court his niece, Harriot Washington (1776-1822), daughter of his deceased younger brother, Samuel Washington. Since her father's death, GW had acted as her guardian and had provided for her financially. She had spent considerable time at Mount Vernon, during which time GW had become fond of her. On April 7th GW answered Parks's letter. The retained file copy was written by MW. A photographic copy is at ViMtV.

From John Trumbull

Madam   London October 7th 1796

I have desired Mr. Anthony[1] to present to you a proof print engraved from the whole length Portrait of the President, which you remember I painted in Philadelphia.[2] I beg you will do me the Honor to accept it Madam, not as a fine likeness, or in itself a valuable work, but, as an acknowledgement of the Grateful Respect with which I have the Honor to be

Madam
Your very much obliged
and Humble servant
Jno Trumbull[3]

Mrs. Washington
From John Trumbull
7th Oct. 1796

ALS, DLC:GW.

1. Joseph Anthony, Jr. (1762-1814), a Philadelphia jeweler, silversmith and goldsmith. He mounted miniatures, made mourning rings and lockets, and "set devices in Hair." The Washington household account books show a number of payments to him for items purchased by Mrs. Washington. *PMHB*; 53:210; 31:57, 79, 83.

2. In his autobiography Trumbull states, "In 1792 I was again in Philadelphia, and there painted the portrait of General Washington which is now placed in the gallery at New Haven, the best certainly of those which I painted, and the best, in my estimation, which exists, in his heroic military character." W. S. Baker, *The Engraved Portraits of Washington*, (Philadelphia, 1880), p. 89. The engraving sent MW is probably that, "Engraved by T Cheesman. London Published by A. C. Depogge No 91 New Bond Street June 1796." Baker, p. 91.

3. John Trumbull (1756-1843) was the son of Governor Jonathan Trumbull of Connecticut. Receiving his art education in England and France, he was a pupil of Benjamin West and John Singleton Copley. Trumbull was an officer during the Revolution, having served as aide to General Washington at Cambridge. During the Revolution he sailed for England to pursue his art. For a time he was severely persecuted there for the part he had played in the conflict. He excelled as a portraitist, miniaturist, and as a painter of historical subjects.

To Mary Stillson Lear

My Dear Madam[1]   (Philadelphia, November 4, 1796)

Your letter of the 30th of October did not reach my hands till yesterday or you should have had an answer sooner - as soon as we came to town the President sent Mr Dandridge to enquire of the Minister of the Moravian church - if he could get Maria into the school at Bethlehem[2] - I am sorry to tell you that his answer was that the school was full - so that it would be some time before she could be taken in - The President says he will wright to Bethlehem and endeavor if it is possible to get her in - if not - Mr Lear I think would do well to send her to her uncle[3] till some thing better could be done for her - we cannot take the child in hear our family is large - and I could not pay the attention to Maria as I think would be necessary to such a child as she is - I have been told that there is a very good bording school in Georgetown - if Maria was put to bord with Mrs Smith[4] she might mannage her if she was put under her particular care and stayed with her altogether which the President and myself think would be very much to the childs advantage.

I was extremely sorry to be told after Maria went from Mr Laws[5] - how ill she had behaved to you had I known it before I should have reprimanded her very seriously - she has always been a spoiled child - as indeed they were all - the Boys[6] are more in Mr Lear's way to manage than a girl - I wish something may be done with her for her advantage - I loved the childs mother and I love her it gives me pain to think that a child as circumstansed as she is should not have a disposion to make herself friends - her youth will plead for her.

I have the pleasure to tell you that we had a very agreable journey hear the weather was fine all the way, we arrived on Monday[7] - take our compliments to Mr Lear - and love to the Children - Nelly joins me in love and good wishes for you

I am dear Madam with esteem and affection

your Friend & Hble servant
M Washington

Text from *Private Affairs*, p. 385.

1. Mary Stillson Lear (1739-1829), mother of Tobias Lear.

2. After the death of Fanny Bassett Washington Lear, Tobias Lear appealed to his mother for assistance in caring for Fanny's three children. She and Lear's young son, Lincoln, arrived in Philadelphia on May 31st and left on June 2nd. They arrived at Washington City on June 5th. GW to Tobias Lear, June 3, 1796, *Writings*, 35:74. Bartholomew Dandridge, secretary to the President, inquired of Rev. Medor, a member of the Moravian clergy in Philadelphia, concerning admission of Maria into the Moravian School at Bethlehem, Pennsylvania. He was informed there were no vacancies. The President then applied directly to the principal, Rev. Jacob Van Vleck. GW to Tobias Lear, November 16, 1796, *Writings*, 35:284. The President's intercession was successful, for Van Vleck agreed to accept Maria and her cousin, Mildred Ball, as students. GW to Tobias Lear, January 13, 1797, *Writings*, 35:366. The President was forced to cancel their attendance due to the illness of, "Maria Washington . . . . is in very declining health (in short that she is in a consumption) and therefore adjudged by her Aunt, with whom she lives, to be unfit for the change which had been contemplated." GW to Rev. Jacob Van Vleck, June 14, 1797, *Writings*, 35:466. Maria recovered (temporarily), grew to adulthood, married Reuben Thornton, and died in 1815, at the age of twenty seven, survived by two small children.

3. Burwell Bassett, Jr. Maria was living, at this time with her aunt, Mildred Washington Hammond. GW to Burwell Bassett, April 24, 1796, *Writings*, 35:27.

4. Unidentified.

5. Elizabeth Parke Custis Law and her husband, Thomas Law. They were living in the Federal City.

6. George Fayette Washington (1790-1867) and Charles Augustine Washington (1791- ?).

7. The Washingtons left Philadelphia on September 19th and returned on Monday, October 31. GW to Alexander Hamilton, November 2, 1796, *Writings*, 35:251.

From Elizabeth Willing Powel

My dear Madam (Philadelphia, December 7, 1796)

The last time I had the Pleasure of seeing you at my House you mentioned that you had taken Noyan[1] as a Medicine to cure the Colick; but that you did not think it was as pure as that you then tasted, knowing that the true Martinique Noyan is not to be purchased at this Time, I have taken the Liberty to send you a Bottle, tho I hope you will not have Occasion to use it as a Remedy for any Complaint half so distressing as the Colick - tho I think it would not be amiss if my good Friend the President will take a glass on his return from the Congress I know his Sensibility, Diffidence, and Delicacy too well not to believe that his Spirits will be not a little agitated on the Solemn & I fear last Occasion that he will take of addressing his fellow Citizens.[2] He appears to have an invincible Diffidence of his own Abilities,- the only Subject on which he has the Timerity to differ with the Virtuous Penetrating and Wise Part of Mankind - Present me affectionately to him & be assured I am

Dear Madam
Respectfully &
Affectionately yours
Eliza Powel

Wednesday December 7th '96
Mrs Washington

ALS, ViMtV.

1. Noyau, "a liqueur made of brandy and flavored with the kernels of certain fruits." *OED*.
2. The eighth annual address to the Congress, December 7, 1796, *Writings*, 35:310-20.

From S. St. Mary

Madam,   Philadelphia Dbre the 18th 1796
When public charity is requested I think no one is more obliged to contribute but those who are making their fortune by the Public.

This induced me to have my Elephant exhibited for the benefit of the suffering by the late fire at Savanah.[1] to succeed in my End, it is necessary to have Some Patrons; I could not look upon any one more qualified than you, Madam, known as you are every where by those qualities of humanity which makes the only difference amongst Mankind.

You will, I make no doubt excuse the liberty I take of sending you a few tickets for the persons of your circle & acquaintance.

I will be very proud to raise a good subscription for those unhappy Sufferers & more so if it is with your recommendation.

I am with respect
Madam
Your most obedt
humble Servt
S. St. Mary[2]
331 Market Street

Mrs. Washington
Philadelphia
From
Mr. St. Mary
17 Decemer 1796

ALS, DLC:GW.

1. The conflagration occurred on November 26, 1796. Two hundred twenty nine buildings, except outhouses, were destroyed. Lee and Agnew, *Historical Record of the City of Savannah*, (Savannah, 1869), p. 73.

2. Unidentified. Several entries for charges to view an elephant are in the "Washington Household Account Book," published in *PMHB*, viz: June 24, 1796, "pd for President for to see Elephant ---1.75;" November 16, 1796, "Conting't Exp's - p'd for family to see the Elephants---3.50."

To Eleanor Parke Custis

My Dear Nelly Miss Greene[1] played this hymn for me and I thought the prettest set I have ever herd She was so obliging as to write it for you and send it and beg you will set it in one of your books - so as may have it to play for me if I live to see you[2]

AN, ViMtV.

1. Probably one of the three daughters of the late Major-general Nathanael Greene and his wife, Catherine Ray Greene. They were: Martha Washington Greene (Patty), Cornelia, and Louisa.

2. The composition has been identified as "La Marsellaise."

To John Trumbull

Sir   Philadelphia the 12 January 1797
     From the hands of Mr Anthony,[1] I received a proof print engraved from the whole length Portrait of the President. I received it, Sir, as a mark of your esteem and polite attention, and shall set great store by it accordingly. -

A few weeks now, will place me in the shades of mount vernon, under our own vines and fig trees; whare with very sincere assurances I may add we should be always extreemly happy to see you. - for the numberless instances of you politeness to me, I pray you to accept my thanks; and to be persuaded of the great esteem and regard

> you most obedant
> and obliged Hble servant
> M Washington[2]

The President has enjoined
it upon me to tender you
his sincear regards

John Trumbull Esqr
(Address)
Mrs Washington
Phila
12th January 1797 - Recd
25th March
Ansd April 25th

ALS, CSmH.

1. Joseph Anthony, Jr. (1762-1814) was a Philadelphia gold and silversmith and he mounted miniatures and set various devices in hair mourning rings and lockets. The Washington household account books reveal a number of payments to him for sundries for Mrs. Washington. *PMHB*, 53:210; 31:79, 183.

2. The letter was drafted by GW. The draft, in a secretarial hand, is in DLC:GW. The recipient's copy, in MW's handwriting, is at CSmH.

To Catherine Littlefield Greene Miller

My Dear Madam[1]   Philadelphia 3d March 1797
    Your favor of the 3d of december came safe to hand, and gave us the
pleasure of hearing that you and the family were all well.[2] - That you may
remain so, is my sincear wish.-
    We were much indebted to your politeness for the orranges you had
the goodness to ship for us: but the severity of the frost preventing the
vessel from getting into this River, and forcing it to new york, we had not
the oppertunity of *eating your health* -
    My love and thanks to Miss Greene[3] for her intention to finish the
goddess of liberty: as a reward for which, the President (who you know
is always expressing his best wishes that girls may be provided for in that
way) hopes in her marrage, and that soon, she may find a god like man.-
    The winter has been very sevear hear, and upon the whole; but is
now moderating and drawing to a close, with which the curtain will fall
on our public life, and place us on a more tranquil theater - The president
and Nelly Custis (Washington is at Princeton college) unite with me in
wishing you and all who are dear to you, every possable happyness

> I am my dear madam your
> affectionate Friend and Hble
> servant
> M Washington[4]

ALS, CtY.
    1. Catherine Littlefield Greene Miller (1753-1814), the widow of General Nathanael
Greene (1742-1786) They were married July 20, 1774. After the Revolution Greene retired to
his home, Mulberry Grove, their plantation near Savannah, where he died suddenly of
"sunstroke." Mrs. Greene continued to live there. She married Phineas Miller in 1796. Mrs.
Greene was one of the General's favorite dancing partners, since Mrs. Washington did not
dance. The Miller's were married in Philadelphia the last part of May. The marriage was
witnessed by the Washingtons. Mrs. Greene-Miller was noted for her beauty and
vivaciousness.
    2. The letter has disappeared.
    3. The Greenes had three daughters: Martha (b. March 1777), Cornelia (October 1778),
and Catherine (b. 1780). The reference is to Martha, who married Peyton Skipwith in 1801,
since Cornelia had married John Nightingale in 1794.
    4. The diction of the letter is that of the President.

From John Trumbull

Madam   29 Birners Street London April 25th 1797
    Permit me to return you my thanks for the Letter which you did me
the Honour to write to me on the 12th January,[1] and which came to my
hands some days ago. - I am only to regret that it has not been in my power
to offer any more estimable acknowledgment of the continued civilities

which for many years I have had the honor to receive from the President and yourself - from the time when the very inadequate talents of a Boy illy fitted me for the situation in which I had first the honor to be near the General at Cambridge to the present moment. I have viewed with that gratitude which is due to him from all his Countrymen, the great and continued service which he has not ceased to render to America and have admired in common with the World, that great Example which his Life has offered to Mankind. I earnestly hope that He and you Madam may long enjoy in Health and Tranquility, the delightful contemplation of that expression of human Happiness to which his Labors have so highly contributed:[2]

Df, ViMtV.

1. See supra, MW to John Trumbull, January 12, 1797.

2. Draft written on the verso of a signed draft of a letter by Trumbull to GW, April 25, 1797.

To Catherine Meade Fitzsimons

Dear Madam[1]

Your very polite and obliging letter of the 29th of March has been duly received, and I pray you to accept my best thanks for the Bale of Moko coffee. - Until Mr Lear arrived (which was long after the date of it) I was unacquainted with the obligation you had laid me under; for I supposed the coffee was part of the Stores Mr Dandridge had been directed to lay purchase for the use of our family. - I wish my dear Madam this kindness of yours may not have disfurnished your own stores.

Mr. Washington is very grateful for your kind recollection of him; and desires me to present his best respects to you and at the same time shall be sensibly (illegible) for your kind intentions. Nelly Custis wants no other token of your remembrance of her than your kind wishes - we all unite in compliments to you and Mr. Fitzsimons[2] and am

> Dr Madam Yr obed Servt
> M. Washington

To Mrs Fitzsimons
30th April 1797

Df in handwriting of GW. ViMtV.

1. Catherine Meade Fitzsimons, daughter of Robert Meade, Philadelphia merchant. She married Thomas Fitzsimons in 1761.

2. Thomas Fitzsimons (1741-1811) served during the Revolution. His mercantile firm gave financial aid during the war. He was a member of the Continental Congress. Fitzsimons was a delegate to the Federal Constitutional Convention and signed the Constitution. He became a congressman and was a firm supporter of the President.

VI

Under Our Own Vine and Fig Tree, 1797–1799

To Mrs Elizabeth Powel

My Dear Madam -   Mount Vernon May the 1st 1797

Mr Craiks[1] return to Philadelphia (to accompany his sister Mrs Harrison,[2] to Alexandria) affords me an oppertunity of offering our respects to you; and, if you will be so good as to allow me, to ask at the same time, if the man who lived with Mr T Francis[3] and was recommended to us, is to be found in philadelphia; and could be induced, if there, to come to us as a steward, or cook. -

The person we brought from thence is totally inadequate to the purpose for which he was imployed. - He posseses, it is true, some valuable properties, for I believe he is thoroughly honest, sober and carefull, is obliging in the extreem, but he knows nothing of cooking - arranging a table - or servants; nor will he assume any authority over them. - Indeed he cannot understand them, nor they him; it may readily be conceived then that much confusion ensued[4] -

Will you be so obliging my Dear Mrs Powell as to let me hear from you on the above subject, and if the person Here mentioned is unattainable, wheather it is probable any other competent character could be obtained; - when; - and on what terms: for the inconvenience I am put to since the loss of my cook is very great, and rendered still more sevear for want of a steward, who is acquainted with the management of such like matters. -

We hope you have not relinquished the thoughts of visiting your friends in this state, and giving us the pleasure of seeing you at Mt Vernon: The General unites with me in a tender of every good wish, and Nelly and Washington would, I am sure do the same, if they were at home, boath are in the Federal City, with thair sister -

I am dear Madam with esteem and affetion your most obdiant Hble Ser[t]

M Washington[5]

P.S. my principle want is a well disposed cook and if the characters of steward and cook cannot be blended in the same person, I would prefer the latter.

ALS, Location unknown.

1. George Washington Craik (1774-1808), youngest son of Dr. James Craik, GW's physician. GW helped finance his education. He became a secretary to GW on April 12, 1796, and held the post for about a year. He studied law and for a time practiced in Alexandria. Young Craik was a frequent visitor at Mount Vernon. In 1799 he became a lieutenant of light dragoons and served until 1800. *Diaries*, 4:188; 6:222, 265.

2. Anne (Nancy) Craik Harrison, was the wife of Richard Harrison, a Maryland merchant who later settled in Alexandria. He served as auditor for the United States Treasury from 1791-1836. *Diaries*, 2: 226, 209-10; 4:121, 343.

3. T. Francis, Jr. (1730-1800), was an uncle of Colonel Tench Tilghman, one of GW's aides during the Revolution. He was a resident of Philadelphia and was the first cashier of the Bank of North America. *Diaries*, 5: 163-64.

4. Unidentified. He may have been a native of France.

5. The letter was drafted by GW and copied by MW. Except for minor variations they are identical.

To Mrs Elizabeth Powel

My Dear Madam   Mount Vernon 20th May 1797

Your polite and affectionate letter of the 9th instant[1] I have been duly honoured with, and thank you sincearly for the assurances you have given me of continuing your enquires for such a servant as you conceive will answer my purposes. -

The qualities you enumerate and discribe, are exactly such as would answer these purposes; and fortunate indeed should I think myself if they could be obtained -

Drudgery duties either in the Kitchen or house would not be required of him - To superintend boath and make others perform the duties allotted them is all that would be asked of him unless unusual occations should call for particular exertions (which is not likely to happen) -

There are always two persons, a man and woman, in the Kitchen; and servants enough in the house for all needful purposes - These require Instructions in some cases, and looking after in all. - To be trust worthy - careful of what is committed to him - sober and attentive, are essential requisits in any large family, but more so among blacks - many of whom will impose when they can do it.

We learn with regret that your journey hitherwards is postponed until autumn. - For the purpose of a purchase in the Federal City that period will not, I dare venture to say, be too late; although we are told by one of the commissions the other day that the Public buildings were going on with great activity. - It is possable however, that some of the best situated lots may be disposed of in the interim: - but even of this nothing can be said with certainty. -

Mr Fitzhugh[2] has not removed to Alexandria, nor is it expected he will do so untill the Fall -

It was long before I got rid of my cold but at present am as well as usual - The General and Nelly Custis enjoy perfect health; and unite with me in wishing you, not only the continuance of that blessing, but of every other this world affords - with great esteem, and affectionate regard

> I remain my dear Madam
> your obliged Humble
> Sert
> M Washington[3]

ALS, ViMtV (copy).

1. The letter has disappeared.

2. This might be Nicholas Fitzhugh (1764-1814), son of Henry Fitzhugh (1723-1783) of Bedford, and his wife, Sarah Battaile Fitzhugh (1731-1783). His wife was Sarah Ashton, daughter of Burdett Ashton and Ann Washington Ashton, daughter of GW's elder brother, Augustine.

3. The letter was copied by MW from an original draft by GW. The two are almost identical.

To Lucy Flucker Knox

I cannot tell you, My dear friend,[1] how much I enjoy home after having been deprived of one so long, for our dwelling in New York and Philadelphia was not home, only a sojourning. The General and I feel like children just released from school or from a hard taskmaster, and we believe that nothing can tempt us to leave the sacred roof-tree again, except on private business or pleasure. We are so penurious with our enjoyment that we are loath to share it with any one but dear friends, yet almost every day some stranger claims a portion of it, and we cannot refuse.

Nelly and I are companions. Washington is yet at Princeton and doing well. Mrs. Law[2] and Mrs. Peter[3] are often with us, and my dear niece Fanny Washington, who is a widow lives in Alexandria, only a few miles from us.[4] Our furniture and other things sent to us from Philadelphia arrived safely; our plate we brought with us in the carriage.[5] How many dear friends I have left behind. They fill my memory with sweet thoughts. Shall I ever see them again? Not likely, unless they shall come to me here, for the twilight is gathering around our lives. I am again fairly settled down to the pleasant duties of an old fashioned Virginia house-keeper, steady as a clock, busy as a bee, and as cheerful as a cricket.[6]

Text taken from *Mary and Martha*, p. 313-14.

1. Lucy Flucker Knox, wife of Major-general Henry Knox, the General's chief of artillery during the Revolution and Secretary of War in his cabinet.

2. Elizabeth Parke Custis Law, wife of Thomas Law. *Diaries*, 6:239.

3. Martha Parke Custis Peter, wife of Thomas Peter of Georgetown. *Diaries*, 6:239.

4. Fanny Bassett Washington Lear had been dead for almost a year.

5. The Washingtons arrived at Mount Vernon on Wednesday, March 15, 1797. W. S. Baker, *Washington After the Revolution*, (Philadelphia, 1898), p. 347. *Diaries*, 6:239.

6. The diction is not that of MW. There are parts of the letter that resembles the style of GW. Factual portions of the letter are plausible. However, if based on an authentic letter, it has been extensively edited and embellished. The reference to Fanny Bassett Washington Lear casts serious doubts as to its authenticity.

To David Humphreys

Dear Sir[1]   Mount Vernon June 26th 1797
    Your Polite & obliging letter of the 18th of Feby came safe to my hands as did the Gold Chain which you have had the kindness to present me with as a token of your remembrance.

    I wanted nothing to remind me of the pleasure we have had in your company at this place; but shall receive the chain, nevertheless as an emblem of your friendship, & shall value it accordingly, - about the middle of March we once more (and I am very sure never to quit it again) got seated under our own Roof, more like new beginners than old established residenters, as we found every thing in a deranged (sic), & all the buildings in a decaying state.[2]

    Poor Mrs Stuart has had very ill health for the last 6 or 8 months but is better now - Her two oldest daughters as you know, or have heard, are both married & each have a daughter[3] - Nelly lives as usual with us - to all of whom I have presented you in the terms you required, and all reciprocate your kind wishes in an affectionate manner

    - Mr Lear who often visits us, has lost his second wife more than a year ago;[4] Mr Lund Washington died in August last.[5]

    - Our circle of friends of course is contracted without any disposition on our part to enter into new friendships, though we have an abundance of acquaintances and a variety of visitors. - Doctr Craik[6] is well and enjoying tolerably good health, but Mrs Craik declines fast[7] - they have lately lost their second daughter, Mrs. West,[8] who has left five young children -

    Perceiving by your letter to Mr W - that you were - on the eve of an important change I wish you every possible happiness in it.[9] - With very great esteem & regard

I am Dear Sir
Yr obedt Hble Servt

Colo Humphreys
From - Mrs. Washington
To Colo Humphreys
26th June 1797

Df, in the handwriting of GW. DLC:GW.

1. Colonel David Humphreys (1752-1818), longtime aide and secretary to GW during the Revolution and personal secretary during the presidency as well as in private life. He was a close companion and friend.

2. The Washingtons arrived at Mount Vernon on Wednesday March 15, 1797. Eleanor Parke Custis to Mrs. Oliver Wolcott, Jr., March 18, 1797. Baker, *Washington After the Revolution*, (Philadelphia, 1898), p. 347.

3. Martha Eliza Eleanor Peter (1796-1800) and Eliza Law (1797-1832). She married Lloyd Nicholas Rogers on April 5, 1817.

4. Fanny Bassett Washington Lear died the latter part of March, 1796.

5. Lund Washington, born in 1737, died in August, 1796. He was the son of Townsend Washington and Elizabeth Lund Washington of Chotank. His great-grandfather, Lawrence, was brother to GW's great-grandfather, John. Lund Washington was manager at Mount Vernon during the Revolution as well as at other times during the absence of GW.

6. Dr. James Craik (1731-1814) was GW's personal physician, comrade in arms through two wars, confidante, and close friend.

7. Mariamne Ewell Craik (1740-1814) was the daughter of James Ewell and Sarah Ball Ewell. The latter was a second cousin of GW. The Craiks were married in 1760. *Diaries*, 2:226.

8. Meriamne Craik West, one of the three daughters of Dr. and Mrs. James Craik. She was the second wife of Roger West, son of Colonel John West. They lived at West Grove, near the mouth of Hunting Creek.

9. The President had apparently extended an invitation to Humphreys to share his retirement with him at Mount Vernon. In a letter from Lisbon, January 1, 1797, Humphreys informed the President he could not accept, "your most cordial & affecting invitation." His reasons were: a duty to his country to continue his career in public service; his impending marriage. Humphreys married Ann Francis Bulkeley, daughter of John Bulkeley, head of a banking and mercantile firm in London. F. L. Humphreys, *Life and Times of David Humphreys*, (New York, 1917), 2:250-54.

To Elizabeth Willing Powel

My Dear Madam   Mount Vernon 14th July 1797

Your obliging favors of the 25 of June and 8th instant have been duly received and are entitled to my particular acknowledgments[1]

The objections (indeed a third, unacquainted with blacks) occur to employing the French man mentioned in the letter. - first the want of a character from those whom we know, and secondly his wages: sixteen dollars is the most we have ever given to a servant, except to Mr Kitt[2] and the other stewards of the family; who had three times the trouble that any one in that line could have in this family, where every thing would be provided to His hands, instead of marketing for it himself; by doing which, if he applies the means honestly that is put into his hands, he cannot gain, but might loose if he is not very correct in keeping his accounts. -

Finding there is no prospect of engaging a suitable character in Philadelphia without giving extravagant wages - I must take the chance of getting one hear; but for your kind endevours to serve me in this business - I pray you to accept my grateful thanks. -

As you have said nothing respecting Mrs Hair[3] in your last lettr, we hope and expect that her health is perfectly restored.

Upon slight foundations it some times happens that large super-structures are erected; but how to do it without any foundation at all, is difficult to devine: such is the case relative to the report of Nelly Custis's overturn, for no such event ever happened; nor has she even received the least hurt by any other accident; but she is as well as she ever was at any period in her life. - The report respecting the General's having a serious attack of the ague and fever is equally groundless. In a hot day in May he threw off his flannel; and a sudden change in the weather at night gave him a cold, which disordered but never confined him. This is all the foundation for that report.

It is with extreme regret we hear of Mr Morris's situation and confine-ment;[4] and none wishes his relief from it more sincerly than we do. -

We had the pleasure of a visit from your friend Mrs Fitzhugh a few days ago - they expect to be living in Alexandria in October, but not fixed thair before November

The General and Nelly Custis unite with me in every good wish for you, and I am with the most affectionate regards

> My Dear Madam
> Your most obedt and
> obliged Hble servant
> M Washington[6]

ALS, ViMtV.

1. The letters have disappeared. Mrs. Powel had apparently located a French cook in response to the Washington's appeal for aid. Hercules, their slave cook ran away the day the Washingtons left Philadelphia to return to Mount Vernon.

2. Frederick Kitt was the household stewart in the presidential household in Philadelphia. His aid was also solicited to locate a cook for the Mount Vernon household. On several occasions GW appealed for his help in locating Hercules, his fugitive slave. Affectionately called "Uncle Harkless" by the family, he was a "dandy" who could not accept the quiet life of Mount Vernon after living for so many years in the big city.

3. Margaret Willing Hare, wife of Robert Hare and sister of Elizabeth Willing Powel. Hare came from England in 1773. He became a brewer, prominent business man of Philadelphia, Speaker of the Pennsylvania Senate, and Trustee of the University of Pennsylvania.

4. Caught up in the financial morass brought about by his extensive land speculation and huge unpaid loans, Morris was confined to the Prune Street Jail, the prison for debtors, for three years, six months, and ten days. He was released by the passage of the federal bankruptcy act. MW's remarks on his confinement must have been based on rumor or speculation on the part of Mrs. Powel, since he was not incarcerated until February, 1798.

5. See supra, MW to Eliza Powel, May 20, 1797, n. 2.

6. There can little doubt GW drafted the letter for MW.

To Elizabeth Dandridge Henley

My Dear Sister[1]   Mount Vernon August the 20th 1797

I have the pleasure to tell you that our dear Fanny came safe to mount vernon she got to Mrs Washington early in the day that her Father left her - she is very well and did not complain of fatague[2] - I should have written to you last week but companey prevented - am obliged to be my one Houskeeper which takes up the greatest part of my time, - our cook Hercules[3] went away so that I am as much at a loss for a cook as for a house keeper. - altogether I am sadly plaiged - I am sorry to hear that the ague and fevor has attacked you so soon - I was in great hopes that you would have moved to a healther place before this Fanny tells me you are better in health then you generally are at this season of the year it is sickly hear fluxes and many other complaints - but not dangerous that I hear of - Nelly has been indisposed but has got well again - Washington Custis is at school at Princeton College he was sent thare as soon as we went back to Philadelphia in November last he is very well and is much gown since you see him - My grand Daughters are boath well in the city They have each a child a little girl[4]

The General and myself enjoy tolerable health - he joins me in love and good wishes for you and all with you - nelly sends love to you - I hope the time will come when it may be conveniat for you to make a trip to see us as it is the first wish of my heat to see you often Fanny is I hope very happy hear she and Nelly is to go soon to the city to see Mrs Law and Mrs Peter - adue my dear sister

> and bleive me your ever
> affectionate
> (M Washington)[5]

AL, ViMtV.

1. Elizabeth Dandridge Aylett Henley, youngest sister of MW.

2. Frances Henley, daughter of Elizabeth Henley, and niece of MW. She was a first cousin of Fanny Bassett Washington Lear, who had died in March, 1796. She became Tobias Lear's third wife.

3. Hercules (affectionately called Uncle Harkless by the family) was a slave and cook for the presidential household in Philadelphia. He was a "dandy," who liked nothing better than to outfit himself in his finery and strut up and down the streets of Philadelphia in the evenings. On the day the Washingtons left Philadelphia, at the close of the second term, Hercules disappeared, rather than return to the quiet life of Mount Vernon. In spite of GW's attempts to apprehend him, he apparently was never found. See supra, MW to Mrs. Eliza Powel, July 14, 1797, n. 2; *Private Affairs*, p. 296.

4. See Supra, MW to David Humphreys, June 26, 1797, n. 3.

5. The letter is not signed.

To Elizabeth Dandridge Henley

My dear Sister   November the 22d 1797

Mr. B Bassetts[1] coming up has afforded a favorable oppertunity for Fanny[2] to get down to you we are sorry to part with her indeed nothing but yours and her Fathers desire that she should come with Mr Bassett would have induced me to part with her this winter It is reather too late and the weath(er) is bad but he cannot stay I wished him to stay till Monday but he says he cannot so my dear Fanny sets out with him he has promised to take great care of her and I think she will go better with him than any other person - we all part with Fanny with great reluctance and nothing but the commands of a Father and mother would have prevaled with us to let her go at this cold season of the year - I hope my dear sister if I live till the summer you will let Fanny spend the sickly months with us she has been perfectly well ever since she came hear as you will see by her looks, being hear a summer or too will carry off all her various complaints that she has been so long subject to - I should my Dear sister been very glad if you could have made it convenient to have come to see us this summer I hope if I live till next the next you may find time to come hear - as it is the first wish of my Heart to see you hear - It gives me great pleasure to hear that you have enjoyed better health this summer than usual - I hope in god that you will get the better of all your complaints, and as you grow older enjoy better health - I shall be anxious till I hear that Fanny is safe with you I trust she will not take cold in the stage - The General and myself are well - Nelly Custis is complaining a good deal with the tooth ack - other ways she is well - Washington is with us he will spend this winter hear with us He is in good health - my Dear sister we hardly know how to part with my dear Fanny but the commands of Parents must be obayed I hope she will get home so well that you will be enduced to let her come hear again to stay with us - pore Nelly is all most broken hearted at parting with her cousin - and I am very sorry I hope you will find getting hear not so great an undertaking - as I trust she will get home well Mr Bassett seems to be very careful - and has promised to see her safe to you - my love and good wishes to you and all with you concludes me my dear sister your ever affectionate

                                                  M Washington

The general desires to
be affectionately remembered to you
and all with you
Alex 9 Jany Free
Mrs Elizabeth Henley
near
Williamsburg

Recmd to
the care of the
Postmaster there
Free
G: Washington

ALS, MdAN.

1. Burwell Bassett, Jr., of Eltham. Nephew of MW and son of Burwell Bassett and Anna Maria Dandridge Bassett, sister of MW.

2. Frances Henley, MW's niece and daughter of Leonard Henley and Elizabeth Dandridge Aylett Henley, sister of MW.

To Elizabeth Willing Powel

My Dear Madam   Mount Vernon 18th Decr 1797

It is unnecessary, I persuade myself to assure you, that with whatsoever pleasure your letters may be received, the sattisfaction to be derived from them, will fall far short of that which your company would give: but as stern winter (which has commenced with uncommon severity) has closed all expectation of the latter, I can only offer my thanks for your kind remembrance of us in your letter of the 24th of November; while I add, as our hopes, that when all things will be blooming hear in the spring, except the withering proprietors of the mansion, that you will carry into effect the long promised visit to this retreat; and make it your head quarters during your stay in Virginia.

It was indeed with sympathetic concern we heard of the late calamitous situation of Philadelphia; and of the death and indisposition of some of your friends - These occurences, however are inflicted by an invisible hand as trials of our Philosophy, resignation, and patience, all of which it becomes us to excercise.[1]

Dear Mrs Morris![2] I feel much for her situation, and earnestly pray that Mr Morris may, and soon, work through all his difficulties; in which I am persuaded that all who knew him heartily joins me; as they do that their ease, quiet and domestic enjoyments, may be perfectly restored. - Mrs Marshalls'[3] arrival must be a comfort to them all, how ever disapointed she may be, in the apparent reverse of their situation, since she embarked for Europe: - we hear with concern too of the declining state of Mrs Whites[4] health, and to her, Mrs Morris, and the rest of our Phila acquaintances, we would thank you, when occation offers, to present our best and sincerest regards -

Mrs Fitzhugh[5] and famaly have within the last fortnight become residents of Alexandria, and we should 'ere this have made them a congratulatory visit on the occasion, but the bad weather in which they travelled has indisposed Mrs Fitzhugh so much, as to confine her to her room with an inflamation more troublesome than dangerous. -

I am now, by desire of the General, to add a few words on his behalf, which he desires may be expressed in the terms following, that is to say, - that disparing of hearing what may be said of him, if he should really go off in an apoplectic or any other fit (for he thinks all fits that issue in death are worse than a love fit, or a fit of laughter, and many other kinds which he could name) he is glad to hear before hand, what will be said of him on that occasion conceiving that nothing extra will happen between this and then, to make a change in his character - for better, or for worse - and besides as he has entered into an engagement with Mr Morris and several other Gentlemen not to quit the theatre of this world before the year 1800, it may be relied upon, that no breach of contract shall be laid to him on that account, unless dire necessity should bring it about maugre[6] all his exertions to the contrary. - In that case, he shall hope they would do by him, as he would by them, excuse it: - at present there seems to be no danger of his giving them the slip, as neither his health, nor his spirits were ever in greater flow, nothwithstanding he adds, he is disending, and has almost reached the bottom of the hill; - or in other words, the shades below. -

For your particular good wishes on this occasion, he charges me to say that he feels highly obliged, and that he reciprocats them with great cordiallity.- Nelly Custis (who has been a little indisposed with a swelling in her face) offers her thanks for the kind expressions of your letter in her behalf, and joins the General and myself in every good wish for your health and happyness -

> I am my Dear Madam with
> the greatest esteem your
> most affectionate
> M Washington

ALS, ViMtV.

Note: There is a draft of the above letter from MW to Mrs. Eliza Powel, December 17, 1797, in the handwriting of GW. It is almost identical to the recipients copy. The draft is in the Rosenbach Museum and Library, Philadelphia. See, *The History of America in Documents*, The Rosenbach Company, Philadelphia, 1950, Part Two, p. 64.

1. Yellow fever again ravaged Philadelphia during the summer and fall of 1797.

2. Mary White Morris, wife of Robert Morris. It was during this period that Morris's financial empire was collapsing, due to over-extended land speculation, large loans that he was unable to repay, and a world-wide economic and political upheaval. It culminated in his incarceration in debtors prison the following February.

3. Hetty Morris Marshall, wife of James Marshall, brother of John Marshall. In 1795 the Marshalls sailed for Europe to seek loans and investment capital to save the Morris financial empire from ruin. They returned to America in 1797.

4. Mary Harrison White, wife of Bishop William White, first Protestant Episcopal Bishop in America. He was the brother of Mrs. Robert Morris.

5. See supra, MW to Eliza Powel, May 20, 1797, n. 3.

6. Archaic, meaning, "in spite of, or notwithstanding."

To Mrs. Bryan Fairfax

Mrs Washington returns compliments and many thanks to Mrs Fairfax,[1] for her polite attention in procuring the patterns of Lutestrings[2] - Mrs Washington does not recollect which of them resembles most Mrs Peter's dress; she will therefore defer getting either until Mrs P. comes to Mount Vernon; she is expected the last of the ensuing week. -

Mrs. Washington and Miss Custis unite in compliments to the Ladies at Mount Eagle[3] -

Mount Vernon

Df, in the hand of a secretary. Location unknown. Copy furnished by ViMtV.

1. Jane (Jenny) Dennison (sometimes appears as Donaldson) Fairfax (d. 1805) was the second wife of Bryan Fairfax (1737-1802). His first wife was Elizabeth Cary Fairfax. He was the son of Colonel William Fairfax of Belvoir, cousin and agent of Lord Thomas Fairfax, 6th Baron Cameron. Bryan Fairfax was ordained an Episcopalian clergyman in 1788. The House of Lords confirmed him 8th Lord Fairfax in 1800. He was a close friend and companion of GW and was a frequent visitor at Mount Vernon. Fairfax and several others were the last visitors at Mount Vernon prior to GW's death. *Diaries*, 6:387.

2. Lutestring - a variation of lustring, a type of glossy silk fabric used as dressmaking material and ribbon. (OED)

3. Mount Eagle was the Fairfax County residence of Bryan Lord Fairfax. GW visited here seven days prior to his death. *Diaries*, 6:378.

From Elizabeth Willing Powel

My dear Madam   Phila. January the 7th 1798

It is said by the experienced that good habits have a powerful influence on the conduct of life, my present sensations evince the truth of the observation. I have for some time past been in the habit of paying my compliments to you at the commencement of a New Year; and I now feel a propensity too strong to be resisted, to present to you, and the General my best wishes that the present and succeeding Years, may bring an accession of every blessing that can render the remnant of your lives happy.

I had the pleasure of receiving your Letter of the 18th of last December, on Christmas Day, and I availed myself of the presence of the greatest part of my family (who celebrate the day at my House) to present your good wishes to your Phila Acquaintances; they sincerely reciprocate them as does the good Bishops family.[1] Poor Mrs. White has at length paid the last tribute to suffering humanity.[2] Mrs. Morris I have not seen for some Weeks, yet I too well know that her Situation is truly deplorable.[3]

I thank you my dear Madam for your gracious, and friendly invitation to Mount Vernon in the Spring; But I suspect that my vanity will admonish me not to contrast myself with all the bloom that will pervade that delightful Spot at a Season when all nature is bursting into beauty. As to the withered Proprietor as you take the liberty to call your Husband, he has a donceaur (should I admit the Epithet to be appropriate) and his vanity may perhaps, be satisfyed with the dowry that succeeding Generations will bestow, by making his fame bloom as long as gratitude and the Empire of reason are respected by Mankind. When I visit you I suspect it will be late in the Autumn. I think your Winters are charming; and indeed I enjoy life, and society with higher glee in cold weather than in any other Season.

In answer to that part of your Letter that you say was dictated by the General, and expressed in his own words. I can only observe that I am greatly surprised, that with his well known penetration, and knowledge of human Nature, that he should pretend not to know what will be said of him after he is dead. Sureley he well knows that Mankind are generally disposed to do justice when the Object of envy is removed; and especially when they have every excitement to truth, from a sense of benefits unrewarded by any deductions from their Store, and National pride gratifyed by having produced a Character that concentrated all that was valiant, just, and wise; with a disposition to apply those virtues and talents to their benefit. He says that he had given his promise to Mr. Morris and several Gentlemen, that he will not die before the Year 1800. If the fulfilment of his promise depended on an act of volition he would not be pardoned for a breach of his contract even by me who am disposed to view his conduct on all occations through the medium of friendship. "He says that he thinks that all Fits that issue in death are of the worst sort." With submission to his better judgement, I think he should have defined the kind of death that is so objectionable, as there are various deaths, nay it is sometimes necessary to die that we may live again, for instance I have known a fainting Fit essential to the preservation of life, and fainting is certainly a cessation of all the animal functions. A laughing Fit may be painful when carried to excess - a love Fit frequently terminated in the destruction of the happiness of the most sensible Mind. a Fit of despare may shatter the finest, and firmed understanding - a fit of disappointment may break the Heart; but of all fits that which you have at present the greatest objection to after this long Letter, must be a fit of prolixity. I will therefore no longer put your patience to the test, - than to request that you will present me most affectionately to my good friend the General, and your Grand-Daughters.

> With sentiments of esteem
> I am dear Madam
> Yrs - affy
> Eliza. Powel

January 7th 1798

P.S.

My much valued friend the Revd. Mr Duche' has taken his departure for the Regions of eternal bliss.[4] I am induced to mention the death of this (?) Gentleman to you, from the recollection that you had considerably mitigated his anguish under the most acute disease incident to humanity, by the valuable Prescripton that you sent to him in 73, and for which he frequently mentioned you with gratitude to his friends

E.P.

Mrs. Washington

ALS, ViMtV.

1. Bishop William White (1748-1836) was the first Protestant Episcopal bishop of the Diocese of Pennsylvania. He succeeded Rev. Jacob Duche' as rector of Christ Church, Philadelphia, when Duche' defected to the British in 1777. 20 *DAB* 121; see infra.

2. Mary Harrison White (d. 1797), wife of Bishop William White. 20 *DAB* 121.

3. Mary White Morris (1749-1827), sister of Bishop William White. She was married to Robert Morris, March 2, 1769. For many years they were intimate friends of the Washingtons. His financial genius during the Revolution did much to assure its success. Burdened with debt, engendered by land speculation, he became insolvent. Morris was confined to the Prune Street debtor's prison in Philadelphia on February 28, 1798. The passage of the bankruptcy act in April, 1800, resulted in his release on August 26, 1801. He died May 8, 1806. On September 21, 1799, during Morris's imprisonment, the Washingtons invited Mrs. Morris to stay at Mount Vernon "for as long a stay as you shall find convenient." See infra; Young, *Forgotten Patriot Robert Morris*, (New York, 1950), p. 25, 238-259.

4. Rev. Jacob Duche' (1737-1798), rector of Christ Church, Philadelphia and chaplain to the Continental Congress. Following the Declaration of Independence and the military reverses of 1776-1777 he lost his zeal for the patriot cause. When Sir William Howe took Philadelphia he was incarcerated for a time. After his defection to the British he wrote a fourteen page letter to GW, October 8, 1777, urging him to repudiate the Declaration of Independence and to use his influence with Congress to negotiate for peace. GW immediately turned the letter over to the Continental Congress. Duche' was immediately regarded as a treacherous enemy and his property confiscated. He sailed for England in December, 1777. He was not allowed to return to America until 1792. He called upon GW to explain his actions and was properly received. Duche's letter to GW and GW's letter of transmittal are in The Papers of the Continental Congress, Library of Congress. Copies by Colonels Alexander Hamilton and Tench Tilghman are in the Washington Papers, Library of Congress. 5 *DAB* 476.

To Henrietta Merchant Liston

Dear Madam,[1]   Mount Vernon 22d Feby 1798

Before I had the honor to receive your favor of the 12th Inst from Phila we were informed (by Mr Patten)[2] of your having passed through Alexandria on your return from Charleston; and of the accidents which you had met with on the journey. - on your happy escape from which we sincerely congratulate you. -

It is unnecessary, I trust, to assure you of the pleasure we should have felt in seeing you on your return to Philadelphia, and which we shall feel, at all times, when it may be convenient, & agreeable to you to visit us in our Retreat.

Your Voyage from hence to Norfolk was of a length hardly ever known before; This accompanied by bad weather, & a short allowance of Provisions; of which we could have no conception from the provident care we supposed Mr Patten had taken to lay in a store, must have rendered your situation very unpleasant; & have given you an unfovourable idea of the Navigation of Potomac. -

Mr Washington begs to be respectfully presented to Mr. Liston & yourself. - Nelly Custis would do so likewise was she at home, but she is, at present, with her Sister Peter in the Federal City. - Washington Custis is thankful for your kind remmbrance of him, & With Compts to Mr Liston I am - Dr Madm

> Yr. Most Obt Hble Servt
> M.W.

To
Mrs. Liston
from Mrs. Washington
22d Feby, 1798

Df, (in handwriting of G.W.) DLC:GW.
   1. Henrietta Merchant Liston, wife of Robert Liston (1743-1836), British Minister to the United States from 1796-1802. In February 1796 he married Henrietta Merchant, daughter of Nathaniel Merchant of Antigua. Mrs. Liston's letter of February 12th has not survived. *Diaries*, 6:268.
   2. Unidentified.

To Sally Cary Fairfax

My Dear Mrs Fairfax[1]   Mount Vernon May the 17th 1798

Whether you are indebted to me, or I to you a letter, I shall not (because it would not comportt with that friendship I have always professed, and still feel for you) enquire; but shall proceed, having so good an opportunity as is offered by Mr Fairfax s[2] voyage to England, to assure you that although many years have elapsed since I have either received or written one to you that that my affection and regard for you, have under gone no diminuation, and that it is among my greatest regrets now I am again fixed (I hope for life) at this place, at not having you as a neighbour and companion. - This loss was not so sensibly felt by me while I was a kind of perambulator during eight or nine years which I resided at the seat of the general government, occupied in scenes more busied, tho not more happy than in the tranquil employment of rural life, with which my days will close. -

The changes which have taken place in this county since you left it (and it is pretty much the case in all other parts of this state) are, in one word, total - In Alexandria I do not believe there lives at this day a single family with whom you had the smallest acquaintance. - In our neighborhood, Colo Mason,[3] Colo McCarty and wife,[4] Mr Chichester,[5] Mr Lund Washington[6] and all the Wageners[7] have left the stage of human life: and our visitors on the Maryland side are gon, and going likewise -

These, it is true, are succeeded by another generation; among whom your niece Mrs Herbert[8] has a numerous off spring; - and as she, Mrs Washington of Fairfield,[9] and your nephews Thomas[10] and Ferdinand Fairfax[11] are as I am informed) among your correspondents, it would perhaps be but an imperfect repetition of what you receive more correctly in detail from them, to relate matters which more immediately concern themselves. - I shall briefly add, however, that Mrs Washington[12] has just lost another daughter;[13] who lately marred Mr Thomas Faifax, and is the second wife he has lost; both very fine women[14] -

With respect to my own family, it will not, I presume, be new to you to hear that my son died in the Fall of 1781.[15] - He left four fine children; three Daughters and a son, a fine promising youth now. - The two eldest of the girls are marred and have children; the second, Patty,[16] marred before her elder sister; she has two fine children boath girls.[17] - the eldest, Elizabeth marred Mr Law a man of fortune from the East Indies and Brother to the Bishop of Carlyle - she has a daughter:[18] Martha marred Mr Thomas Peter son of Robert Peter of Georgetown, who is also very wealthy. - boath live in the Federal City. - the youngest daughter Eleanor[19] is yet single, and lives with me, having done so from an infant, as has my grandson George Washington[20] - now turned of seventeen - except when at college; to three of which he has been - viz - Philadelphia, New Jersey and Annapolis at the last of which he now is

> I am Dear Madam with
> great esteem
> and regard your affectionate
> Friend
> M Washington[21]

ALS, C-S.

1. Sarah (Sally) Cary Fairfax (c. 1730-1811), eldest of the four daughters of Wilson Cary (1703-1772) of Ceelys and Richneck, and his wife, Sarah Pate Cary. On December 17, 1748 she married George William Fairfax (1724-1787), the eldest son of Colonel William Fairfax (1691-1757) of Belvoir, and his first wife, Sarah Walker Fairfax. They made their home at Belvoir, the next plantation down river from Mount Vernon, until 1773, when they left America for England, never to return. During the years at Belvoir they were close friends of the Washingtons, frequent visits being exchanged. GW's admiration for her during his early years, "has given rise to persistent legends of a romantic infatuation." *Diaries*, 1:4.

2. Reverend Bryan Fairfax (1737-1802), eighth Baron Fairfax of Cameron, was the son of Colonel William Fairfax of Belvoir and his second wife Deborah Clarke Fairfax. He was a half brother of George William Fairfax (see supra, n. 1). He married (1) Elizabeth Cary, sister of Sarah Cary Fairfax (see supra, n. 1). His second wife was Jane Dennison (sometimes called Donaldson). He became a deacon of the church in 1786 and was ordained in 1788. His voyage

to England was to claim the title, vacated by the death of Robert, 7th Lord Fairfax. His title was confirmed by the House of Lords in May, 1800. He was a close friend and companion of GW for a half century, even as he passively supported the Loyalist cause during the Revolution.

3. George Mason (1725-1792) of Gunston Hall, planter, statesman and constitutionalist. He was the author of the Non-importation Agreement of 1774, the Fairfa xResolves, The Virginia Declaration of Rights, a major portion of the Virginia Constitution, and was one of the revisors of the Virginia laws. Mason was a member of the Virginia Convention of July 1775, the Mount Vernon meeting of 1785, and the Federal Constitutional Convention, where he was one of the five most frequent speakers. He was a firm believer in the ultimate sovereignty of the Northwest Territory. Out of his Virginia Bill of Rights came the first ten amendments to the Federal Constitution. Mason opposed the ratification of the Federal Constitution, his objections ultimately being proved justified. He was a close friend and collaborator with GW and was a frequent visitor at Mount Vernon.

4. Col. Daniel McCarty (d. 1791) and his wife, Sinah Ball McCarty (d. 1798). Both were distant relatives of GW through his mother, Mary Ball Washington. Their residence was Mount Airy, several miles down the Potomac from Mount Vernon. He served on the vestry of Truro Parish with GW and the families exchanged frequent visits. *Diaries*, 1:248.

5. Richard Chichester (c. 1736-1796) was a distant relative of GW through the Ball family. His second wife was Sarah McCarty. GW was godfather to his second son, Daniel McCarty Chichester. The family settled on Accotink Creek, Fairfax County.

6. Lund Washington (1737-1796) of Hayfield was the faithful and capable manager at Mount Vernon before and during the Revolution. His great grandfather, Lawrence, and GW's great grandfather, John, were brothers.

7. Peter Wagener (1742-1798), was county lieutenant of Fairfax County during the Revolution. He married Sinah McCarty, daughter of Daniel McCarty. They were frequent guests at Mount Vernon.

8. Sarah Carlyle Herbert, eldest daughter of Colonel John Carlyle and his first wife Sarah Fairfax Carlyle. She was a niece of Sally Cary Fairfax. She married William Herbert (1743-1818), an Alexandria merchant.

9. Hannah Fairfax Washington, of Fairfield, the wife of Warner Washington. She was also a daughter of Col. William Fairfax of Belvoir. Warner Washington was the son of John Washington, brother of Augustine Washington, GW's father. He was therefore a first cousin of GW.

10. Thomas Fairfax (1762-1846) of Vaucluse and Ash Grove, was the eldest son of Rev. Bryan Fairfax, and a nephew of Sally Cary Fairfax. He became the ninth Baron Fairfax of Cameron upon the death of his father. He refused to claim his title and never allowed it to be used in his presence, being an ardent Republican. He was a Swedenborgian, freed all his slaves and then spent much time and money attempting to make them self sufficient. His efforts were in vain, since they all returned, begging to be taken back under his care. He was a man of many talents, which included scientific experimentation and the manufacture of lightning rods, which he forged himself. His grandson became the tenth Baron Fairfax of Cameron. 7W(2)87-89.

11. Ferdinando Fairfax (1769-1820), third surviving son of Rev. Bryan Fairfax and his wife, Elizabeth Cary. He inherited Belvoir from his uncle, George William Fairfax. GW was his godfather.

12. Mrs. Hannah Washington, wife of Warner Washington of Fairfield. See supra, n. 9.

13. Thomas Fairfax (see supra, n. 10) married Louisa Washington, daughter of Warner Washington and Hannah Fairfax Washington, at Winchester, January 18, 1798. She died April 28, 1798.

14. Thomas Fairfax's first wife was Mary Aylett, whom he married in November, 1795. She died April 30, 1796. His third wife, whom he married in January, 1800, was Margaret Herbert, his second cousin, daughter of William Herbert and Sarah Carlyle Herbert. See supra, n. 8; *Tyler's Quarterly*, 2:284; 18 W (1) 280, 283. *Burke's Peerage*, (London, 1976), p. 977.

15. John Parke Custis (1755-1781) married Eleanor Calvert Custis of Mount Airy,

Maryland. He died about one week following the Battle of Yorktown, where he contracted "camp fever," while acting as civilian aide to his stepfather, GW.

16. Martha Parke Custis Peter (1777-1854).

17. Martha Eliza Eleanor Peter (1796-1800) and Columbia Washington Peter (1797-1820).

18. Eliza Law (1797-1832) married Lloyd Nicholas Rogers, April 15, 1817.

19. Eleanor Park Custis (1779-1852) later married Lawrence Lewis, nephew of GW on February 22, 1799. Their home was Woodlawn, near Mount Vernon.

20. George Washington Parke Custis (1781-1857). He married Mary Fitzhugh. Their home was Arlington.

From Reverend William DuBourg

Madam   Georgetown July 20th 1798

Yet uncertain whether the pressing calls of his country will or not deprive us of the presence of the General,[1] at the exhibition we are preparing for the evening of the 30th instant: I take the liberty of praying both you Madam, & the accomplished Miss Custis, either to complete our happiness by accompanying him, if he resolve to come, or if not, to console us for his absence by gracing with your own attendance the first essay of our juvenile stage. Having made bold enough to (?) ourselves into the (?) of seeing it encouraged by the presence of the eminent man, on whom all eyes are so disemidly fixed, our disappointment in not obtaining this favor can only be compensated by the satisfaction of beholding his place filled by the two persons who by the lustre they derive, both from their intimate connections with him & their personal virtue possess the next claim after him to the highest reverence of

> Madam
> Your most obt & humble
> Servt.
> Wm DuBourg[2]
> President of GeoTown
> College

Mrs Washington
(Address)
G.Town 19 July
Mrs Washington
Mount Vernon
Revd Mr. DuBourg
Presdt GeoTown College
20th July 1798

Copy of original, by William B. Sprague. DLC:GW.

1. At this time GW had been appointed Lieutenant-general and Commander-in-Chief of the United States Army by President Adams during the quasi war with France.

2. Father Louis Guillaume Valentin DuBourg (1766-1833) was born in San Domingo and educated for the Roman Catholic priesthood in France. He came to the United States in 1794 and in 1796 was appointed president of Georgetown College. Founded in 1789, it was the first Roman Catholic college in the United States. Father Du Bourg was an occasional visitor at Mount Vernon. The letter is a copy made by Dr. William B. Sprague. The two undecipherable words may be Sprague's failed attempt to copy the text.

To Colonel Charles Simms

Sir,[1]   (October 14, 1798)

Agreeably Conformably to my promise, I requested the favour of the Secretary of War (supposing it was more in his line than any other to cause them to be executed properly) to have the colours which I intended myself the honor of presenting to the Company under your Command, to be made and sent to me without delay. -

Some little About a fort night ago they arrived, but in an unfinished state - havg. neither fringe nor Tassels. - Of this Mr McHenry was informed, & requested to supply the deficiency. - To His an answer is just received, that the person who made them, has fallen a victim to the malignant fever which prevails in Phila. - unhappily to the interruption of all kinds of business - but, that he would, as soon as it was practicable remedy the defectives and a question was asked whether defects. - He was asked too, if some mistake had not been made in sending Cavalry, for Infantry Colours & in that case to send forward as much suitable Silk as would accomodate them to the latter purpose - to which no reply has been made. -

Hearing that there is to be a grand parade on Wednesday, send them up as they have been are received - in order, if there be any materials that they may be completed - at my expence - in Alexandria if there be materials or workmen to do it; of which you will be pleased to inform me - that Mr McHenry may be advised accordingly. -

> I am Sir Yr. most Obedt
> Hble Servt
> MW

Colo Simms
or Officer
Comm g the Silver Greys[2]
To
Colonel Simms
from
Mrs Washington
14th Oct. 1798

Df, (in handwriting of GW) DLC:GW.

1. Charles Simms (1755-1819), lieutenant-colonel of the 6th Virginia Regiment during the Revolution. He practiced law in Alexandria, was a member of the Potomac Company, later collector of the port of Alexandria, and mayor. He was a fellow Mason and active pall bearer at GW's funeral. *Diaries*, 6:123.

2. The colors were to be presented to the Alexandria Silver Grays, an Alexandria home guard regiment commanded by Colonel Simms. *Writings*, 36:418.

To Frances Dandridge Henley

My Dear Fanny[1]   (November 30, 1798)
    I see the children of the abbey[2] advertized in a book store in the city, if you can get a set with plaits or cuts - I beg you will get a set for me -
    My love and congratulations to Mr & Mrs Peter[3] and good wishes to the children - I have been a little indisposed for a day or too - but am better today -

                    I pray god to bless you all -
                    M Washington

November the 30 1789[4]
(Address)
Miss Henley

ALS, ViMtV.
    1. Frances Dandridge Henley, niece of MW.
    2. The Mount Vernon mansion library contains a copy of volumes 3 and 4 of Regina Maria Roche's, *The Children of the Abbey, A Tale*, (New York, 1798). It bears the inscription: "Eleanor Parke Custis, February 2, 1799, I E P Custis value this old Novel because my revered & loved grandmother Mrs M Washington read and like it. 1840."
    3. Congratulations upon being pregnant with her third child, John Peter, born in 1799.
    4. This date is in error, MW having transposed the last two digits of the year. The New York edition of the book was not published until 1798. The Peters were not married until 1795.

To Mary Stead Pinckney

My dear Madam,[1]   Mount Vernon 20th April 1799
    I have received with pleasure grateful sensibility, your obliging favours of the 16th & 28th of last month; and thank you for the mellon seeds which you had the goodness to send me & which came safe, & very opportunely.
    It gave me, and all our family much pleasure to hear of your safe arrival, & happy meeting with your friends, in Charleston, after so long & tiresome a journey as you performed in the depth of Winter. - In the weather, however, except the few first days of January, you were much favoured; as it was remarkably fine for the Season here. -

We had only to regret the shortness of your stay at Mount Vernon[2], a place at which we shall always be pleased to see you gratified in seeing General Pinckney[3] yourself or any of the family; - to which let me add a hope, if his Military duties should call him to the State of Virginia, that you will always consider this place as your head quarters during your abidance in it. -

Long 'ere this, I hope the General is safely returned to you from his Military Excursion to Georgia,[4] and no one can unite more heartily with you than I do in wishing that the newly proposed Negociations may (illegible) more serious movements; but from a faithless Nation, whose injustice & ambition know no bounds short of their inability its power to accomplish them little is expected from this Negociation (if the proposion should be acceded to at all by Treaty) by those who wish for a permanent Treaty - arrogance, or deception, as is best calculated to promote the views of the French Directory seem to be the only Rule of the French Government at present - of course nothing (is) to be expected from their domineering spirit when uncontrouled by events - as too many unhappy Nations of Europe and recently the poor Italians have experienced to the entire annihilation of their Government.[5]

By the first fit conveyance, I will with pleasure send you the Profiles of the General & myself, & feel the compliment of their being asked.[6] - They could not go by Post without folding, & consequent injury or they would have accompanied this letter - a small one however, of his, is herewith enclosed requesting your acceptance of it

The General's birthday (22d of Feby) united the fortunes of Mr Lewis (who you saw here) and Nelly Custis.[7] - They are at present, & have been for sometime, at her Mothers or she would most cordially have united with the General & me in reciprocating all the good wishes of yourself & Miss Eliza,[8] & would rejoice to hear of the Happiness of her friend Mrs Harriot Rutledge.[9] With sentiments of perfect esteem & regard

> I am, my dear madam your
> most obedient Hble Ser
> M W--n

Mrs Genl Pinckney
20th April 1799

Df, (in the handwriting of GW) DLC:GW.

1. Mary Stead Pinckney, second wife of General Charles Cotesworth Pinckney. They married in 1786. The first Mrs. Pinckney died in 1784. She was Sarah Middleton, daughter of Henry Middleton, first president of the Continental Congress.

2. General and Mrs. Pinckney and their daughter, Eliza, dined at Mount Vernon on December 25, 1798. They departed from Mount Vernon on December 28th. *Diaries*, 6:327-28.

3. General Pinckney served during the entire Revolution, for the most part as a colonel. He was breveted a brigadier-general in 1783. In 1798 he was appointed major-general, ranking just below GW and Alexander Hamilton.

4. Pinckney was placed in command of the military forces south of Maryland, including those in Kentucky and Tennessee.

5. The reference is to the machinations of the French Directorate and the X-Y-Z Affair. Pinckney had been a principal figure in the negotiations.

6. The Pinckneys had requested silhouettes of the Washingtons. It is likely MW intended to send those cut by Eleanor Parke Custis, but due to their large size were not sent. The silhouette of GW sent to Mrs. Pinckney has not been identified. See, H. and N. Laughon, "Shadow Portraits of George Washington," *Antiques Magazine*, February 1988, p. 402-09.

7. Lawrence Lewis (1767-1839), nephew of GW, married Eleanor Parke Custis (1779-1852), granddaughter of MW. Lewis was the son of Betty Washington Lewis and Fielding Lewis.

8. Eliza Pinckney, one of the daughters of General Pinckney by his first wife, Sarah Middleton Pinckney.

9. Harriet Pinckney Horry married Frederick Rutledge (1768-1821) on October 11, 1797. She was the daughter of Daniel and Harriet Pinckney Horry. *South Carolina Historical and Genealogical Magazine*, 31:93-4.

From T. C. Radcliffe

August 18, 1799

The text of this letter is not available.

To_____

September 18, 1799

At midsummer the General had a dream so deeply impressed on his mind that he could not shake it off for several days. He dreamed that he and I were sitting in the summer house, conversing upon the happy life we had spent, and looking forward to many more years on earth, when suddenly there was a great light all around us, and then an almost invisible figure of a sweet angel stood by my side and whispered in my ear. I suddenly turned pale and then began to vanish from his sight and he was left alone. I had just risen from the bed when he awoke and told me his dream, saying, "you know a contrary result indicated by dreams may be expected. I may soon leave you." I tried to drive from his mind the sadness that had taken possession of it, by laughing at the absurdity of being disturbed by an idle dream, which at the worst, indicated that I would not be taken from him; but I could not, and it was not until after dinner that he recovered any cheerfulness. I found in the library, a few days aftrwards, some scraps of paper which showed that he had been writing a Will, and had copied it.[1] When I was so very sick, lately, I thought of this dream, and concluded my time had come, and that I should be taken first.[2]

1. George Washington's will was signed on July 9, 1799. A contemporary copy, made by Albin Rawlins, one of his secretaries, also bears the same date. See, Prussing, *The Estate of George Washington, Deceased*, (Boston, 1927), p. 36, 40.

2. Martha Washington was ill during this period. Her illness necessitated visits by Dr. James Craik on September 1st and the 6th. *Diaries*, 6:363, 366. The text is taken from Lossing,

Mary and Martha, p. 324-26. Lossing states the letter was sent to "a kinswoman in New Kent," and that he obtained the text from the letter at Arlington House. The letter seems consistent with the facts.

To Mary White Morris

Septr 21st 1799
Mount Vernon

Our Dear Madam,[1]

We never learnt with certainty, until we had the pleasure of seeing Mr. White[2] (since his return from Frederick) that you were in Winchester.

We hope it is unnecessary to repeat in this place, how happy we should be to see you and Miss Morris under our roof, and for as long a stay as you shall find convenient, before you return to Philadelphia; for be assured we ever have, and still do retain, the most Affectionate regard for you Mr Morris[3] and the family. -

With the highest esteem & regard, and best wishes for the health & happiness of the family you are in we are

Dear Madam
Your Most Obedt and
Very Humble Servants
G°: Washington
Martha Washington

LS. (Letter in the handwriting of GW) NhD.

1. Mary White Morris, wife of Robert Morris. See supra.

2. Alexander White (1738-1804), lawyer, member of the Virginia House of Burgesses and the Virginia General Assembly. He was a staunch Federalist and supported ratification of the Constitution. Under the new government he served in the 1st and 2nd Congress. From 1795-1802 he was on the commission to lay out the City of Washington. White was a native of Frederick County and lived near Winchester. He was a frequent visitor at Mount Vernon. He was present on September 21st and left on September 23rd. *Diaries*, 6:366.

3. Robert Morris, financier of the Revolution, and now in serious financial straits due to excessive speculation.

VII

Alas, Alone: Widow Washington, 1799–1802

From Maria S. Ross

December 24, 1799

The text and location of this letter is unknown.

From Elizabeth Willing Powel

My Dear Madam

To tell you that I most sincerely sympathize with on the late melancholy Event,[1] but faintly expresses my sensibilities on the afflictive Subject, and tho the Season is far advanced, and the Roads bad, I would most certainly pay a Visit to your House of Mourning, could I afford to you the smallest consolation under this seemingly hard dispensation of Providence; but I too well know that no consolation can be affected by human Agency. The healing Hand of Time, and pious resignation to the inscrutable decrees of God can alone tranquilize your Soul, not that I believe that one Trace of the amiable Qualities of your departed Friend will during your life be obliterated from your mind; but the Wounds of affliction admit only the involuntary shrinkings of nature under the heavy pressure of Affliction will never surely be imputed to no as criminal. You have lost the man of your choice the protector and support of your declining years; but he is removed to regions of bliss, and his departed Spirit may still be permitted to hover round you, and those Friends that justly appreciate his merit. I am told that he ended his glorious well spent Life by a painful tho hasty death that he retained the faculties of his mind to the last moment, and died as he had lived like a man and christian, and I sincerely hope that you may be enabled to support the severe Trial with fortitude and resignation. I presume your Grand children are with you, and doubt not that they will afford you every consolation that existing circumstances will admit. Present me affectionately and sympathetically to them they also have lost a protecting affectionate connection and I have lost a much valued Friend.

It will give me great satisfaction to hear that your Health is perfectly reinstated, sorry indeed I was to find by your good Friend Judge Washington[2] in October last that you had been ill.

Adieu my dear Madam and believe me truly and sincerely

> Your affectionate
> Sympathizing Friend
> Eliza Powel

Phila - December the 24th 1799
Mrs Washington
(Docket)
From Mrs Elizh Powel 24 Dec. 1799

ALS, ViMtV.

1. General George Washington died on December 14, 1799 between the hours of eleven and twelve o'clock, P.M., after a short illness of about fifty hours, aged 67 years, 10 months and 22 days.

2. Bushrod Washington (1762-1829, newphew of GW, son of John Augustine Washington (1736-1787) and his wife, Hannah Bushrod Washington. President John Adams appointed him an Associate Justice of the Supreme Court on December 20, 1798.

From Abigail Smith Adams

December 24, 1799

The text of this letter is not available.

From Mary Stead Pinckney

December 26, 1799

The text and location of this letter is unknown.

From Mary White Morris

Philadelphia, Decr 27th 1799

Permit me my dear Madam to pour into your afflicted Bosom the sympathetic feelings of sincere affection and friendship as some small consolation in the hour of distress, few very among the numerous admirers of our deceased friend had opportunities of contemplating his virtues, - and I believe there is not one on whom they have made stronger impressions - they are such as can never be effaced whilst memory exists reverencing and esteeming Him as you know I did you will admit me to mingle tears and share your sorrow, you have lost the friend of your heart the sharer of former bliss the dispenser of happy hours, I feel the loss of one who in paying me respectful attentions gratified the sensibilities of a mind strongly attached by having witnessed the frequent exhibition of most excellent qualities in a systematic conduct that commanded respect and esteem from all - But what are the sacrifices of friendship as compared with the deprivation which our Country sustains the Public sentiment receives such an universal and lively expression that even grief like yours must subside at times in the contemplation of it, - my attachment to you my dear Mrs Washington being founded upon Intamacy that has led to the knowledge of your merits, - is most sincere and my present wishes is that I could be with you to manifest the truth there - of by such attentions as might assist in leading your mind to the possession of such peace and comfort as is left Mr.Morris to whom I have shown what I have writen sayd He most sincerely unites with me in every word and request, that you will accept at my hand these as his as well as my sentiments - He intended writing to you also but as you will probably have too many calls upon your feelings he hopes that the expression of his affectionate regard through my Pen will be accepted and he joins me in assuring you that if any circumstance should occur in the course of our lives which we or either of us can manifest our regard it will be seized with avidity - should future events draw either of us to the southeard we will not fail to pay you our Personal respects.

Accept dear Madam the best wishes of your truly affectionate

Mary Morris

Mrs Washington
Mount Vernon
(Address leaf bears the free frank of John Marshall)
Mrs Washington
Mount Vernon
From Mrs Maria Morris
Decr 27, 1799

ALS, ViMtV.

From John Adams

Madam   Philadelphia, December 27. 1799

In conformity with the desire of Congress, I do myself the honor to inclose, by Mr William Smith Shaw my Secretary, a copy of their resolutions, passed the twenty fourth instant occasioned by the decease of your late Consort, General George Washington, assuring you of the profound respect Congress will ever bear, to your person and Character, and of their condolence on this afflicting dispensation of Providence. In persuance of the same desire, I entreat your assent to the interment of the remains of the General under the marble monument to be erected in the capitol, at the City of Washington to commemorate the great events of his military and political life.

Renewing to you Madam, my expressions of condolence on this melancboly occasion, and assuring you of the profound respect which I personally entertain for your Person and character, I remain with great Esteem

> Madam your faithful and
> obedient Servant
> John Adams

Mrs Washington (Docket)
The President of the United States
Decr 27. 1799.
Enclosing a Resolution of Congress

ALS, DTP.

1. Following the death of General Washington the Congress of the United States passed the above mentioned resolution, that a marble sarcophagus be erected in the capitol building and that, subject to the approval of Mrs. Washington, he be interred therein. Mrs. Wshington acceded. When Mrs. Washington died in May, 1802, her body was placed in the "old tomb" at Mount Vernon, beside that of her husband. In 1816 the Virginia Assembly directed Governor Wilson Cary Nicholas to request of Judge Bushrod Washington that the remains of General Washington be "removed from the family vault at Mount Vernon and interred near the Capitol of Virginia, beneath a monument to be erected at public expense, and to serve as a memorial to future ages of the love of a grateful people." Judge Washington felt compelled to deny the request, since it was the General's express wish that he be laid to rest at his beloved Mount Vernon. Again in 1832, Congress directed President Jackson to request John Augustine Washington, the owner of Mount Vernon, that the remains of the General be transferred to the Capitol. At the same time a request was made of George Washington Parke Custis that his grandmother's remains also be moved to the Capitol. Custis agreed, but John Augustine Washington adamantly refused. The sarcophagus beneath the dome of the capitol remains unoccupied. See, Jones, "The Translation of Washington", *Virginia Cavalcade*, 14:28-37, n. 3.

From Bushrod Washington

The Will should be proved at the first Fairfax Court, and this can be easily done by Mr Lewis[1] carrying it up and presenting it to the Court for probate, the whole of it being in the Testator's own hand writing and that well known by most of the members of the Court.

An Inventory of the whole estate (except Land) of whatever nature and to whoever given should be immediately made out, specifying each

& every article by its proper name, except as to the Stock of horses which may be taken previous to proving the will.

When the will is proved such of the executors as happen to be present ought to qualify thereto and then obtain an order appointing Commissioners to appraise the property mentioned in the inventory. When every thing is prepared so as to diminish as much as possible the trouble of the appraisers, they may be sent for and the property produced to them - I think it will be proper to appraise every thing, since the nature of an Executor's oath requires it.

The next thing to be done is to provide the means of paying all the debts and legacies. The executors has a power to dispose of any part of the personal estate for these purposes, but it will be as much our duty, as I trust it will be inclinations to select such of the property as my aunt thinks she can best spare and such as from its nature can produce her no profit. - Of this description I consider the Jacks (except the Knight of Malta)[2] and Jennies the Stud horse, and other horses & Mares which Mr Anderson[3] may consider as unprofitable & useless to the estate - The sooner these are sold the better after the consent of the other executors can be obtained and due notice in one of the Alexa, Freds & Richmond papers is given. The next article for sale will be the flour & wheat on hand, if the latter can be ground up and the whole kept till the spring a good price may be obtained, and this I think ought to be done if possible. But if demands of a pressing nature are made, I think we ought to prepare for their discharge without regarding sacrifices.

Should my Aunt pursue the plan I have recommended of getting clear of her negroes & of plantation cares & troubles, there will be horses, Mules, cattle, sheep, hogs & plantation utensils for sale to a considerable amount; but as she will keep the estate this year in its present situation these sales will not be in time to meet the demands against the estate. It will be better therefore for Mr. Anderson to make out a schedule of such parts of the property mentioned in this clause as he thinks can be spared without injury & they I think should be sold in the spring.

There are many other articles which properly may be spared, some of which (such as the riding horse, watch &c &c) which having been particularly attached to the general's person ought not I think to be exposed to public Sale. A Just valuation may perhaps be placed upon them by the agreement of the Legatees and taken by them at such price. As to these articles I allude to such only as my Aunt may not please to keep in her own possession during her life.

The specific Legatees ought to be informed of the bequests to them as soon as the will is proved and they should also be informed that such legacies will be delivered on demand.

The houses in the City of Washington ought I think to be finished as expeditiously as possible, and the General's contract relative thereto ought to be performed by his Executors with punctuality. To do this it will probably be necessary to hasten the sales of such parts of the estate as can be spared, as much as circumstances will admit. The property when rented will I hope afford my Aunt not only a handsome income but one which can easily be collected.[4]

As to the property rented to Welch, some confidential person should be sent to the premises in order to distrain for the rents now due. It is not probable that a sufficiency of property for the payment of the rents can be found, yet this step is necessary before any regular measures for recovering possession of the property can be pursued.[5]

> Bushrod Washington
> Mount Vernon
> December 27, 1799

I think it would be best for my Aunt to let Mr. Lewis have the hogs at the distillery at the appraisment price or at such valuation as Colo Lear & Mr. Anderson may put on them, the interest of which she will receive from Mr. Lewis during her life.

B.W.

ALS, ViMtV.

1. Lawrence Lewis (1767-1839), nephew of GW and husband of Eleanor Parke Custis Lewis. He was named by GW as one of the executors of his will. The other executors were: Martha Washington (wife), William Augustine Washington, Bushrod Washington, George Steptoe Washington, Samuel Washington (nephews) and George Washington Parke Custis, when he reached the age of twenty (step grandson).

2. "Knight of Malta": was the jack ass sent as a gift by the Marquis de Lafayette in November, 1786. Accompanying him were two jennets. All were spirited out of Malta by Lafayette. Somewhat previous to the arrival of the Maltese asses, GW had received a jack ass as a gift from Charles III, King of Spain. He was named "Royal Gift." J. H. Powell, *General Washington and the Jack Ass*, South Brunswick, 1969, p. 176-190. *Writings*, 28:359-362; 29:74.

3. James Anderson, a native of Fife Scotland. He succeeded William Pearce as manager at Mount Vernon in 1797. He continued at Mount Vernon for several years after the death of GW. Sometime prior to 1806 he became manager of the White House tract in New Kent County. He had a thorough understanding of agricultural practices and husbandry.

4. GW had purchased two lots on what was to become "Capitol Hill" in the City of Washington. The legal description was "Lots 6 and 16 in Square 634," comprising 54 feet-8 inches on the west side of Capitol Street, between B and C Streets. The price was $964.10. Dr. William Thornton drew up plans for the two houses. Construction was under way and Thornton had been paid $7000, on account, on November 27, 1799. In less than three weeks GW was dead. The houses were completed under Thornton's direction in 1800. They were occupied by General Henry Dearborn, Secretary of War during the Jefferson and Madison administrations, and destroyed by fire during the British invasion of 1814. They were rebuilt and enlarged in 1817. In 1910 they were demolished when the land was acquired by the federal government. *Prussing*, p. 245-251.

5. James Welch approached GW in 1797 with a proposal to lease 23,000 acres of GW's land on the Great Kanawha River. The lease was to stand for 125 years at 6% interest, payable on each January first. He also had an option to purchase the tract for $200,000. Welch gave 100,000 acres of land in Roanoke County as collateral. Unfortunately Welch defaulted on his

first payment, whereupon GW wrote him several letters demanding payment in no uncertain terms. He never received payment of any kind. GW's executors collected nothing and no suit was ever instituted. Welch seems to have been released from the transaction and his collateral refunded. The lands were finally distributed to the devises as provided in GW's will. *Diaries*, 6:270, 272, 274, 319, 346-47; *Prussing*, p. 119-21, 464-75.

From Jonathan Trumbull

Lebanon, Dec. 30, 1799

Among the number of those who will approach you with their expressioins of Condolence, on the afflicting event of the much to be lamented Death of your most respected & Honorable Consort, there is no one who will do it with more tender, sincere & affectionate regard on this solemn & distressing occasion, than the writer of this letter.[1]

You know too well Madam, the high respect, & affectionate regard, which I ever entertained for the illustrious Deceased to need any assurances of the deep affliction & sympathy which I felt on this very mournful Event. A second Father, as he has been, in many respects to me, - his Death has opened afresh the deeply impressed Wound, which the Loss of my first venerable parent had formerly occasioned.[2] But he is gone and our Duty, however hard it may be at the first instance, is to Bow submissive to the Divine Will --- His own words, written to me on a similar occasion (the Death of my Father) are so peculiarly consolatory at the moment, and are also so particularly consolatory at this moment, and are also so particularly applicable to my subject as well as to himself that I am impelled to give them to you without apology, etc.

ALS. Location unknown.

Letter sold in the Hale Hunter Sale, Anderson Galleries, Sale No. 1270, January 25-26, 1917, item 371.

1. Jonathan Trumbull, Jr. (1740-1809) was the son of Jonathan Trumbull (1709-1784) and Faith Robinson Trumbull. He held various appointments in the Continental Army and was named secretary to General Washington in 1781. He was a staunch Federalist. In the new government under the Constitution Trumbull served in the First, Second, and Third Congresses and was Speaker of the House of Representatives. He served as governor of Connecticut from 1797 until 1809.

2. Jonathan Trumbull (1710-1785) was a leading patriot of the Revolution. He served as governor of Connecticut from 1769-1784. He was also the father of John Trumbull, the artist. *Writings*, 28:283.

From Jedidiah Huntington

New London, 31st December 1799

(answd Jany 15 1800 by T. Lear)

Accept, dear Madam, my Condolence for the Loss of the best of Men - although the Part I take, in this sore and extensive Calamity, will appear like a small Stream, compared with the unbounded Sea of your Grief, yet my Sorrow has a quality, in the sincerity of my Esteem Respect and Affection, for the deceased, which is peculiarly suited to unite with yours --the Experiences of a solid Piety have, I am persuaded, anticipated my devout prayers that you may derive all that support and consolation which the religion of the Gospel, and a well-founded Hope, are calculated to afford - Mrs Huntington presents with her best Love, her tenderest Sympathy[1] - that you may long enjoy consoling alleviations, in your affliction, from the affection and Endearments of your surviving Family & Connections, the fervent wish of, dear Madam your very respectful Friend & Servant

Jedidiah Huntington[2]

Mrs. Washington
(Address)
Mrs. Washington
Mount Vernon
(Docket)
From Genl Jedidiah Huntington to Mrs. Washington
Huntington
Decr. 31st, 1799

ALS, ViMtV.
1. Ann Moore Huntington, second wife of General Huntington.
2. Jedidiah Huntington (1743-1818) was a member of the politically and socially prominent Huntington family of Connecticut. He served in the Continental Army throughout the Revolutioin. He was appointed Brigadier-general in May 1777, and breveted Major-general in 1783. Huntington was appointed collector of customs at New London, Connecticut, by President Washington and served in that capacity for twenty-six years.

To John Adams

Sir   Mount Vernon, December 31, 1799
    While I feel with keenest anquish the late Disposition of Divine Providence I cannot be insensible to the mournful tributes of respect and veneration which are paid to the memory of my dear deceased Husband - and as his best services and most anxious wishes were always devoted to the welfare and happiness of his country - to know that they were truly appreciated and greatfully remembered affords no inconsiderable consolation. Taught by the great example which I have so long had before me never to oppose my private wishes to the public will - I must consent to the request made by congress - which you have had the goodness to transmit to me - and in doing this I need not - I cannot say what a sacrifice of individual feeling I make to a sense of public duty.[1]

With greatful acknowledgement and unfeigned thanks for the personal respect and evidences of condolence expressed by congress and yourself.

> I remain, very respectfully
> Sir
> Your most obedient &
> Humble servant
> Martha Washington

ALS, DLC.

1. There are four copies of the letter, viz: a preliminary draft written by Tobias Lear, furnished by Stephen Decatur, Jr.; a final draft written by Tobias Lear, in the collection at Tudor Place; a copy in an unknown hand in the National Archives (RG 233 Records of the United States House of Representatives, 6 Congress: 1 Session); holograph letter, signed by MW, in the Library of Congress.

To Abigail Smith Adams

December 31, 1799

The text and location of this letter is unknown. There is a signed holograph letter from MW to Abigail Adams, dated January 1, 1800, in the Pierpont Morgan Library. The letter of December 31, 1799 may be a draft by Tobias Lear. It is likely the texts are similar. Under the circumstances it is unlikely MW would write two different letters to the same individual on successive days. See infra for letter of January 1, 1800.

To Abigail Smith Adams

My dear Madam   Mount Vernon, January the 1st 1800
Accept the thanks of a heart opprest with sorrow but greatfull for your friendly sympathising letter.

To that almighty power who alone can heal the wounds he inflicts I look for consolation and fortitude.

May you long very long enjoy the happiness you now possess and never know affliction like mine

with prayers for your happiness

> I remain your sincear
> Friend
> Martha Washington

ALS, NNPM.

From Colonel William Stephens Smith

Union Brigade New Jersey, Jany 1. 1800

Most respected Madam.

Permit me to present to you a model of that monument, which myself and the officers of the Brigade I have the honor to Command, consisting of the 11th. 12th. & 13th Regt. of Infantry, have determined to erect at this Cantonment to the memory of our much lamented Commander in Chief

If the attempt I have made in the Composition and the design of the monument, will not minutely bear the Eye of Critisism, I must solicit indulgence; as it is the first and only thing of the kind I ever attempted

And considering my former situation in the last War with your departed friend, I hope I shall stand excused in presuming, to attempt, to contribute, with the Corps I Command, to the respect paid to his memory, in Common with my Countrymen at large -

By you Madam, I hope it will be received as a pledge of my deepest Sorrow, for my Countrys' Loss, and your particular distress - may that Power whose penetrating Eye, must have always looked with satisfaction on your Glaring Virtues, preserve you from future ills, and arm your soul with the resignation to the dispensations of His Providence - with the most perfect reverence and respect, I have ye honor to be - Madam

Your Most Obedt
Humble Servt
W.S.Smith[1]

(Docket by Tobias Lear)
From Colo. Wm. S Smith
January 1, 1800
Answd by T. Lear
Jany. 11. 99 (sic)

ALS, ViMtV.

1. Colonel William Stephens Smith (1755-1816) was a former aide to GW, from 1781-1783. He married Abigail Amelia Adams, only daughter of John and Abigail Adams. GW appointed him marshall of the district of New York and later surveyor of the port of New York. He sat in Congress, 1813-15.

From Elias Boudinot

January 2, 1800

The text of this letter is not available.

From Alexander Hamilton

January 2, 1800

The text of this letter is not available.

From Elizabeth Spottswood

My Dear Madam   New Post, January 2ᵈ. 1800
Under your present affliction you have the Sincere Sympathy of this Family. Remember my Dear Madam soon after we came into the world we were taught to know that we were not to Live forever & that sooner or Later the Dearest Friends must Part & altho those Tender Feelings early engrafted in us by the Almighty puts it out of our power on the Loss of a Dear Friend, to Suppress the first Effusions of grief, yet when that subsides, (altho impossible to forget) it is our duty to bear up against our misfortune, & not repine at the will of the most High.

Remember my Dear Madam, altho it has Pleased God to take from you (from all of us) the Greatest, best, & most Virtuous of men, whose memory will be revered all over the world, yet his Goodness has left you still many Comforts - which Comforts, I hope you will Live to Enjoy many, many, years in Health.

I pray you my Dear Madam to be resigned, & believe me when I assure you, that I shall seek for many opportunities to testify to you, with how much Sincerity, I am Dear Madam

Your Affectionate
Elizabeth Spotswood[1]

PS the Family desires there best regards, to you, Mr., & Mrs. Lewis, in which I Unite so soon as the spring sets in - Mr. Spotswood, my Self, & the Girls, will come & spend a week with you alone
(Address)
Mrs. Martha Washington of Mt Vernon Near Alexandria
From Mrs. Elizh Spotswood
2 January 1800.

ALS, DTp.

1. Elizabeth Washington Spottswood (1750-1814) was the eldest daughter of GW's elder half brother, Augustine Washington and his wife, Anne Aylett Washington. She was the wife of Alexander Spottswood (1751-1818), grandson of colonial governor, Alexander Spottswood (1676-1740), one of the Knights of the Golden Horseshoe. They lived in Spottsylvania County.

From _____ Huntington

January 4, 1800

The text and location of this letter is unknown.

From Bushrod Washington

Walnut Farm, Jany 4. 1800 (FN)

Dear Aunt   Recd. Jany 30 - 1800[1]

Upon my return to Westmoreland I found the price of corn so encreased that it could not be purchased in any quantity for less than fifteen shillings per barrel. Colo Washington is the only considerable corn maker in this County upon the Potamack, and has agreed to let you have 600 barrels at the above price and to wait for the mony until the 1st of May. Being well satisfied that the price of this article will rise before the spring, I thought it prudent ot confirm the bargain with him, after discovering not only that he could obtain it from others, but that it would be difficult for you to get the quantity you want from any one person in this part of the country & upon the same length of credit.

Colo. Washington thinks it would be imprudent in you to have so large a quantity of Corn beaten out & put into bulk at this season of the year, being apprehensive that it would heat & spoil; he thinks it best that you should get or procure as much as may suffice for two months & to take the balance in March. In this I am of opinion you will be a gainer, independent of the risk of heating which you will thereby avoid.

After this full statement of the business, I beg you my dear Aunt to write me by the first post your pleasure, or to get some of the family to do so. It will be well I think that you should previously consult with Mr Anderson' but I trust you to write without delay, as I shall leave home by the 15th Inst

I am with very sincere
esteem & regard

Your Affect Nephew & friend
B Washington

(Address)
Templemans X Roads
12 Jany
Mrs. Washington at Mount Vernon Fairfax County
From the Honble Judge Washington to Mrs Washington
Jany 4. 1800

ALS, DLC:GW.
    1. Notation by Tobias Lear.

To Maria S. Ross

January 10, 1800

The letter was probably written for Martha Washington by Tobias Lear, in answer to the letters of Maria Rose to M.W., Dec 24, 1799. See supra. The text is not available.

To Colonel William Stephens Smith

Dear Sir,   Mount Vernon, January 10, 1800

Mrs. Washington has received your letter of the 1st instant, enclosing a model of the monument proposed to be erected by yourself and the Officers of the Union Brigade to the memory of your much lamented Commander in Chief, and has requested me to express the Grateful Sensibility with which she views this tribute of respect and veneration paid by yourself and the Corps under your command, to the memory of her beloved Husband; and at the same time to assure you of her sincere acknowledgements for the fervent wishes which you express for her consolation under the late afflicting dispensations of Providence.[1]

> With great Respt & esteem
> I am dr Sr
> Yr Mo Ob st
> Colo. W.S. Smith

To Colo. Wm S. Smith
Jany 11. 1800

Df, ViMtV.

1. See supra, Col. William Stephens Smith, to MW, January 1, 1800. The letter was written for MW by Tobias Lear.

From The Grand Lodge of Massachusetts

Madam   (Boston) January 11th 1800

The Grand Lodge of the Commonwealth of Massachusetts, have deeply participated in the general grief of their Fellow Citizens, on the melancholy occassion of the death of their beloved Washington. As Americans, they have lamented the loss of the Chief, who had led their armies to victory, and their country to glory; but as masons, they have wept the dissolution of that endearing relation, by which they were enabled to call him their friend and their brother They presume not to offer those consolations which might alleviate the weight of common Sorrow, for they are themselves inconsolable. The object of this address is, not to interrupt the sacred offices of grief like yours; but, whilst they are mingling tears with each other on the common calamity, to console with you on the irreparable misfortune which you have individually experienced To their expressions of Sympathy on this solemn dispensation, The Grand Lodge have subjoined an order that a golden Urn be prepared as a deposit for a lock of hair, an invaluable relique of the Hero and the Patriot whom our wishes would immortalize, and t(hat) it be preserved with the jewell and r(eliques) of the society Should this favour be granted, Madam, it will be cherished as the most precious jewell in the cabinet ofthe Lodge, as the memory of his virtues will be forever be, in the hearts of its members We have the honour to be with the highest respect

> your most obedient Servants
> John Warren[1]
> Paul Revere[2]
> Josiah Bartlett 3

At a Meeting of the Grand Lodge of Massachusetts, at Boston
January 11, 1800

AL 5800.

Noted That John Warren Esqr Paul Revere Esqr & Josiah Bartlett Esqr Past Grand Masters, be a Committee, to write a letter to the Widow of our deceased Br George Washington, in behalf of this Grand Lodge, condoling with her on the heavy affliction, she had experienced; and to request of her, a lock of her deceased husband's hair, to be preserved in a golden Urn, with the jewels and Regalia of the Grand Lodge.

> A true Copy of Record
> Daniel Oliver[4]

Grand Secretary (Address) Madam Washington Mount Vernon(Docket)[5]
From The Grand Lodge Massachusetts
Jany 11th 1800

LS, DTP.

1. John Warren (1753-1815), physician, surgeon, anatomist, veteran of the Continental Army during the Revolution.

2. Paul Revere (1735-1818), goldsmith, silversmith, coppersmith, and engraver. He was a messenger of the Massachusetts committee of safety and a lieutenant colonel during the Revolution. Revere was a prominent member of the Sons of Liberty and a participant in the Boston Tea Party. As master of the Grand Lodge of the Masons, he laid the cornerstone of the new Massachusetts state house in 1795.

3. Josiah Bartlett (1759-1820) was a native of Charlestown, Mass., the son of George Bartlett, a sea captain. Bartlett studied medicine in the military hospitals and served as surgeons mate during the Revolution. After the Revolution he practiced medicine in Charlestown, was elected Representative, Senator to the State Legislature, and became a member of the Executive Council. He served as Grand Master of the Grand Lodge of

Freemasons. Levi Bartlett, *Sketches* of the Bartlett Family in England and America , *Lawrence Massachusetts.* 1876, pp. 92,

4. Daniel Oliver was the Grand Secretary of the Grand Lodge of Massachusetts from 1794 until his resignation in 1801. He was a member of the Rising Sun Lodge and received his degree as Master Mason in 1794. His occupation was designated as "merchant."Abstracts of Proceedings of the Grand Lodge of Massachusetts for the Year #5800 (1800), p. 74, 157-164. Personal communication, The Museum Of Our National Heritage, Lexington, Mass.

From Reverend Samuel Miller

January 14, 1800

Text and location of letter not available. Reverend Samuel Miller (1769-1850) was a prominent Presbyterian clergyman and the author of numberous religious treatises. For his sermon on the death of GW, see infra, Tobias Lear to Rev. Samuel Miller, January 27, 1800.

To Jonathan Trumbull

Dear Sir   Mount Vernon, January 15, 1800

When the mind is deeply affected by those irreparable losses which are incident to humanity the good Christian will submit without repining to the Dispensations of Divine Providence and look for consolation to that Being who alone can pour balm into the bleeding Heart and who has promised to be the widows god - But in the severest trials we find some alleviation to our grief in the sympathy of sincear friends - and I should not do justice to my sensibility was I not to acknowledge that your kind letter of condolence of the 30th of December was greatfull to my feeling.

I well knew the affectionate regard which my dear deceased husband always entertained for you and therefore conceive how afflicting his death must have been to you - the quotation which you have given of what was written to you on a former melancholy occasion is truly applicable to this - the loss is ours the gain is his.[1]

For myself I have only to bow with humble submission to the will of that God who giveth and who taketh away looking forward with faith and hope to the moment when I shall be again united with the Partner of my life But while I continue on Earth my prayers will be offered up for the welfare and Happiness of my Friends among whom you will always be numbered being

Dear Sir
your sincear and
afflicted Friend
Martha Washington[2]

His Excellence Governor Trumbull New London Lebanon Connecticut N. London forwd.
(Docket) Mount Vernoon 15th Jany 1800 from Mrs Washington reply to mine on the death of her husband

ALS, PHi. A copy is also at DTP.
    1. See supra, Jonathan Trumbull, Jr., to MW, December 30, 1799.
    2. A draft by Tobias Lear is at DTP.

To Jedidiah Huntington

Sir   Mt. Vernon, Jany 15, 1800
    At the request of Mrs. Washington I have the honor to acknowledge the receipt of your letter to her of the 31 of Decr.[1] and to assure you that she receives with grateful sensibility, the (?) condolence of yourself & Mrs. Huntington on her late afflicting & irreparable loss.- and while she looks to that Divine Being alone, for consolation to whose Dispensations her Christian Duty teaches her to know, with humble submission, she feels as she ought, the tender sympathy of her friends, as an alleviation to her grief in this heart-rending affliction.- She begs Mrs. Huntington & yourself to accept her grateful acknowledgements for your kind wishes, and to assure you that you will always have her prayers for your health & happiness.

                        With very great respect
                        I have the honor to be Sr

Yr mo. ob Svt
Tobias Lear Genl Jedediah Huntington
To Genl. Jedh. Huntington Jany 15. 1800

Df, ViMtV.
    1. See supra, General Jedidiah Huntington to MW, December 31, 1799.

From Stephen Williamson

                                January 16, 1800
The text and location of the letter is unknown.

From Henry Knox

                                January 17, 1800
The text of this letter is unavailable.

From Samuel Bayard

Philadelphia, 18 Jany 1800
(Recd 30 Jany, 1800)
Dear Madam (Answd by T Lear 5 Feby, 1980)

Excuse the liberty I take in forwarding you the enclosed testimony, of profound veneration for the merits - & of unfeigned sorrow for the departure of your late dear & invaluable husband.[1] It would be presumption to offer consolation on so afflective an event - yet could universal sympathy afford you any aleviation, never could sorrow be so assuaged as yours - You have the sympathy of millions & the affectionate regrets not of America alone but of the wise and good throughout the world

May Heaven enable you to improve this melancholy bereavement: & while the streams of earthly comfort are dry'd up - may you derive the richest consolations from the favour & love of the Creator & Redeemer of the world -

With the highest respect & esteem
I remain Dear Madam - your obdt servt.
Sam Bayard[2]

(Address)
Mrs Washington Mount Vernon.
(Docket)[3] From Mr. Saml Bayard 18 Jany 1800 To Mrs Washington Ansr Feby 5

ALS, ViMtV.

1. A Funeral Oration, Occasioned by the Death of Gen. George Washington, and delivered on the First of January, 1800, In the Episcopal Church; at New Rochelle, in the State of New York. By Samuel Bayard, Esq. New Brunswick. Printed by Abraham Blauvelt, 1800. 8:24.

2. Samuel Bayard (1767-1840), lawyer, clerk of the United States Supreme Court. After the ratification of the Jay Treaty in 1794, GW appointed him agent to prosecute the American claims before the British admiralty courts. He was one of the founders of the American Bible Society and the New-York Historical Society. He was the author of numerous legal and religious treatises.

3. By Tobias Lear.

To Elias Boudinot

(January 18, 1800)
The letter was written for MW by Tobias Lear. See supra, Elias Boudinot to MW, January 2, 1800. The text of the letter is not available.

To Alexander Hamilton

(January 23, 1800)
The letter was written for MW by Tobias Lear. See supra, Alexander
Hamilton to MW, January 2, 1800. The text of this letter is not available.

From Joseph Scott

Madam   Philada, Jan. 25th 1800
In consideration of the elevated rank of your departed husband,
whose extraordinary atchievements place him among the first of heroes,
I have been urged to issue proposals for publishing his life. The enclosed
is a copy. I pray you do Justice to my principles, and believe me sincerely
devoted to the love of truth With sentiments of great respect

> I have the honor to be
> Madam,
> your most obt. Sert.
> Joseph Scott[1]

(Address) Mrs Washington Mount Vernon
(Docket by Tobias Lear) From Mr. Josh Scott Jany 25. 1800 To Mrs.
Washington.

ALS, DTP.
   1. Unidentified. The "copy" is unknown.

From Bushrod Washington

My dear Aunt
The improved Lot in Alexandria; the household furniture including
(as I concieve in that description) the pictures & plate; the kitchen
furniture; the liquors, groceries & dead victuals laid in at the time of the
General's death belong absolutely to you & may be disposed of by you,
when & how you please.
The Specific legatees are entitled immediately to recieve & enjoy the
legacies bequeathed to them - Those Legacies I concieve it would be
unecessary to enumerate as they can be at once distinguished by reference
to the will. You have a right I think, to retain the possession of the residue
of the estate of every kind from Land down to a penknife and to recieve
& enjoy the profits & interest of such parts thereof as yield profit during
your life. But as you, or your representatives after your death, will be liable
to account for all the personal estate delivered into your hands according
to the inventory thereof, (except for such articles as may perish or be
consumed in the ordinary support of the family) you will readily percieve,

that you have no power to dispose of any article mentioned in the inventory (unless such as are given to you absolutely & forever) or even such as may be omitted, for a longer period than during your life, in which case, your representatives will be accountable for the forthcoming of such property, unless it should have been decayed, or been destroyed, as mentioned above.

But it must be understood, that your right to the residue of the estate, not specifically given to you, or to others, is subject to the superior claim of the executors, to so much thereof, as may be necessary for the discharge of the debts and mony legacies. For these purposes, the executors, may sell any part of the personal estate not specifically devised to you, or to others, most likely in their opinion to produce the sums required

Unless for the purpose of paying the debts & Legacies, the executors, have no right to sell any part of the estate during your life without your consent, unless it be such as is of a perishable nature, or which may be render'd worse by Keeping.

Should you find it your interest (and I think it certainly will be) to get clear of the unecessary stocks of Cattle, horses &c. as soon as possible, the Executors may with your consent sell them & invest the money in some of the funds, so as to insure the interest thereof to you, during your life; or, if the sales of such property should become necessary for payment of debts & Legacies, the executors may make them whenever they think proper.

The rents of lands and the interest upon the public or bank Stocks due at the time of the General's decease, belong to the estate, and are to be collected by the Executors, to be by them applied to the discharge of the debts & Legacies if necessary; or if not necessary, to be invested in the funds, so as to insure to you the interest thereof during your life.

As to the rents of lands which become due & payable after the General's death, I am inclined to think, that you have a right to recieve them to your own use.

There are some other points of consequence, as to which you ought to be informed, such as 1st, whether you are entitled to the whole of the interest of the public & bank stocks not due at the time of the General's death,or only to a proportion thereof, according to the time the interest had been running? 2dly To what interest upon debts due the estate you are entitled? 3d. Whether the free school is entitled to the accruing interest upon the 20 shares of Alexandria bank stock, but not due at the death of the testator - These are points of considerable difficulty, and I shall consult with Genl Marshall[1] upon them when I go to Philadelphia, and will acquaint you with the result at my return. Should our opinion not coincide with yours, I will state the points for consideration of any other council you may mention.

I need not state I presume, that everything purchased for the house, or for the plantation & negroes since the death of the General, must be at your expense: It is clear, that the executors have nothing to do, but to collect the debts, sell when necessary, & discharge the debts and legacies due from the estate.

You will consider the above, as being merely the opinion of a friend, given without an opportunity of consulting books, or of bestowing as much consideration upon the subjects as they perhaps deserve. I may possibly be mistaking in some of the points; but should I upon further reflection discover any errors in this opinion, I shall lose no time in correcting them. My object is to define the rights which belong to you, so that none of them may be lost to you, & to prevent you so far as possible from committing any mistake which can in any manner embarrass or perplex you.

> Yr Affect Nephew
> B Washington
> Jany 26, 1800

(Address) Mrs Washington of Mount Vernon
(Docket in handwriting of MW) Mr B. Washingtons Letters to M Wn

ALS, ViMtV.

1. John Marshall, serving as secretary of state, was the greatest legal mind in Virginia. At this time he was often referred to as "General Marshall."

To The Grand Lodge of Massachusetts

Gentlemen   Mount Vernon, January 27. 1800
Mrs. Washington has received with Sensibility, your letter of the 11th instant, enclosing a vote of the Grand Lodge of Massachusetts requesting a lock of her deceased Husband's hair to be preserved in a Golden Urn with the Jewels & Regalia of the Grand Lodge. In complying with this request by sending the lock of hair, which you will find enclosed, Mrs. Washington begs me to assure you, that she views with gratitude, the tributes of respect and affection paid to the memory of her dear deceased husband, and receives with a feeling heart, the expressions of sympathy contained in your letter.

> With great respect & esteem
> I have the honor
> Gentle
> Your most Obed, Serv.

Tobias Lear[1]
John Warren
Paul Revere, Esqrs.
Josiah Bartlett

Past Gnd Masters Grand Lodge Massachusetts To John Warren Paul Revere
Josiah Bartlett Past Grand Masters of the Grand Lodge of Massachusetts
Jany 27 1800
Address

Df by Tobias Lear. DTp.
   1. See supra, Grand Lodge of Massachusetts to MW, January 11, 1800.

To Reverend Samuel Miller

Sir,   Mount Vernon, January 27th: 1800 Revd.
    Mrs. Washington has received your letter of the 14th instant,[1] together with the Discourse accompanying it;[2] and in acknowledging the receipt thereof, she requests me to present her best thanks for your goodness in sending her a copy of your performance, which she shall read with great Satisfaction. - And while she sees, with grateful sensibility, the numerous evidences of the warm affection and high veneration in which the dear deceased partner of her heart was held by our nation, she receives, with a feeling heart, the offerings of sympathy made to herself, and looks for consolation to that Divine Source alone, which never fails to grant it, when supplicated with sincerity.

> With very great respect
> I have the honor to be
> Revd Sir
> Your most obedt Servt
> Tobias Lear

The Revnd Samuel Miller

ALS, ViMtV.
   1. See supra, Reverend Samuel Miller to MW, January 14, 1800.
   2. A Sermon Delivered December 29, 1799; occasioned by the Death of General George Washington, late President of the United States....By Samuel Miller, A.M. New-York; Printed by T & J Swords. 1800. 8:39.

From The Earl of Buchan

Madam: Dryburgh Abbey, January 28, 1800
    I have this day received from my Brother[1] at London the afflicting tidings of the death of your admirable Husband - my revered Kinsman and Friend. I am not afraid under this sudden & unexpected stroke of divine providence to give vent to the immediate reflexions exerted by it,

because my attachment to your illustrious Consort was the pure Result of Reason, reflexion and Congeniality of Sentiment.

He was one of those whom the Almighty in successive ages has chosen and raised up to promote the ultimate designs of his goodness and Mercy in the gradual melioration of his creatures and the coming of his Kingdom which is in Heaven. It may be said of that great & good man who has been taken from us what was written by the wise and discerning Tacitus concerning his Father in Law Agricola "That tho' he was snatched away whilst his age was not broken by infirmity or diminished by bodily decay of reason yet that if his life be measued by glory, he attained to a mighty length of days." For every true felicity, namely all such as arise from virtue, he had already enjoyed to the full;as he had likewise held the Supreme Authority of the State with all the confidence and applause of all wise and good men in every part of the World, as well as among those he governed and had enjoyed triumphal honours in a War undertaken for the defense of the unalienable rights of mankind. What more (humanly speaking) could Fortune add to his lustre and renown? After enourmous wealth he sought not, an honorable share he possessed. His course he finished in the peaceful retreat of his own election in the arms of a dutiful & affectionate wife & bedewed with the tears of surrounding relatives and friends with the unspeakably superior advantage to that of the Roman General in the hope afforded by the Gospel of Pardon & Peace (to continue my parallel) may be accounted singularly happy since by dying according to his own christian & humble wish expressed on may occasions whilst his credit was nowise impaired, his Fame in its full splendor, his Relatives & Friends not only in a state of comfort and security but of honour, he was probably to escape many ends inadvert to declining years. Moreover he saw the Governemnt of his Country in hands to our joint wishes & to the safety of the nation & a contingent succession opening not less favourable to the liberties & happiness of the People. Considering my uniform regard for the American States manifested long before their forming a separate nation I may be classed as likewise among their Citizens especially as I am come of a worthy ancestor Lord Andros[2] who found refuge there in the last century & had large property in Carolina where Port Royal now is situated. I hope I will not be thought impertinent or offencing if I recommend to that Country and nation of America at large the constant remembrance of the moral and poltical maxims conveyed to the Citizens by the Father & Founder of the United States in his Farewell address and in that Speech which he made to the Senate and House of Representatives when the last hand was put to the formation of the Federal Constitution and may it be perpetual: It seems to me that such maxims and advices ought to be engraved on every forum or place of common assembly among the people & read by Parents, teachers and Guardians to their children & pupils, so that true Religion & virtue its inseparable attendant may be imbibed by the rising generation to remotest ages "and the Foundation of National Policy be laid & continued in the pure & (?) princip-les of private morality." Since there is no truth more thoroughly established than that there exists in the economy & cause of nature an insoluble union between, Virtue & Happiness, between duty & happiness, between duty & advantage, between the genuine maxims of an honest and magnanimous People and the solid rewards of publick prosperity and felicity. "Since we ought to be no less persuaded that the perpetual smiles of Heaven can never be expected on a Nation that disregards the eternal rules of order and right, which Heaven itself had ordained and since the preservation of the Sacred fire of Liberty and the destiny of the republican model of government are justly considered as deeply perhaps finally staked on the experiment entrusted to the hand of the American People."

Lady Buchan[3] joins with me in the most sincerly respectful good wishes and I must intreat of you Madam in both our names to say every thing that is kind and consolatory to the worthy Mrs. Lewis.[4]

I am Madam: with sincere Esteem

> Your obedient, & faithful
> Humble Servt
> Buchan[5]

Mrs. Washington

ALS, ViWF.

1. Hon. Henry Erskine (DNB)

2. Sir Edmund Andros (1633-1714), Colonial Governor of Massachusetts, New York, and Virginia.

3. Margaret Fraser, Lady Buchan. She was the eldest daughter of William Fraser of Fraserfield, Aberdeenshire. She married Lord Buchan, who was her first cousin, in 1771. She died in 1819. (DNB)

4. Eleanor Parke Custis Lewis, granddaughter of MW.

5. David Steuart Erskine, Lord Cardross, 11th Earl of Buchan (1742-1829), historian, antiquarian, agriculturist, and patron of the arts. He purchased Dryburh Abbey in 1786 and retired there the following year. He was the author of numerous articles on literature, poetry, history and the fine arts. One of his eccentricities was to claim kinship with distinguished persons past and present, "to whom he was in the remotest degree related." In 1792 he sent GW a box made from the oak tree that sheltered William Wallace after the battle of Falkirk, July, 1298. He requested GW to bequeath it to the person in America he considered most worthy to receive it. Not to be "put on the spot," GW bequeathed it back to Buchan, for him to make his own selection. See *DNB*; *Prussing*, p. 57-58; Sparks, *The Writings of Washington*, 10:229-231.

From Richard Varick

January 28, 1800

The text of this letter is not available.[1]

1. Richard Varick (1753-1831), was aide to General Philip Schuyler during the Revolution. In 1780 he became aide to General Benedict Arnold at the time Arnold defected to the British. Convinced of his loyalty to the American cause, and that he had played no part in Arnold's conspiracy, GW appointed him his military secretary, responsible for the transcription of his military correspondence. He later became recorder of the City of New York, a member of the General Assembly, attorney general, and mayor of the City of New York.

From Richard Washington

January 31, 1800

The text of this letter is not available.[1]

1. Richard Washington was a London tobacco merchant with whom GW had corresponded and done business for a number of years. *Diaries*, 3:297-98. Ragsdale, *George Washington, The British Tobacco Trade, and Economic Opportunity in Prerevolutionary Virginia*, VMHB, 97:133-62.

From Theodore Sedgwick

Madam,   Philadelphia, 4. Feby. 1800
I have the honor, thro' the mayor, at the request of the common council of the city of New York, to you the inclosed oration -[1] Permit me, therewith, to present to you my sincere condolence, on the melancholy event which it celebrates, and to assure you that I am, most respectfully,

> Madam,
> your obedt. &
> very huml. Sevt
> Theodore Sedgwick[2]
> Mrs. Washington.

(Docket by Tobias Lear)
From Theodore Sedgwick esq
4 Feby 1800

ALS, DTP.
1. Not in Sabin or Griffith.
2. Theodore Sedgwick (1746-1813), lawyer, Revolutionary officer, member of the Continental Congress, of the Massachusetts ratifying convention, of the United States House of Representatives. He was a United States senator and its president pro tempore in 1797. In 1799 he was again elected to the House of Representatives and was chosen speaker.

Tobias Lear to Samuel Bayard

Sir,   Mount Vernon, Feby 5th 1800
Mrs. Washington requests me to acknowledge the receipt of your letter to her of the 18th ultimo, together with the Oration accompanying it; and at the same time to beg your acceptance of her best thanks and grateful acknowledgements as well for the testimony of respect and veneration paid to the memory of her dear deceased Husband, as for the sentiments of condolence and wishes for her happiness expressed in your letter. -[1]

To the late afflicting dispensation of Divine Providence, Mrs. Washington submits with humble resignation, and altho' she looks only for consolation to that Being from whom only we can receive comfort in the severest trials; Yet she acknowledges, with due sensibility, the alleviation which she receives from the numerous testimonies of sincere grief for the loss, and of profound respect which have been paid to the memory of the partner of her heart; and in placing your performance among the number of those, she begs you will be assured of her best wishes for your happiness.

> With great respect,
> I am Sir,
> Yr. most obt St
> Tobias Lear

Saml Bayard Esq.
To Saml. Bayard Esq. 5 Feby 1800

Df, ViMtV.
1. See, Samuel Bayard to MW, January 18, 1800, and n. 1,

From David Austin, Jr.

February 8, 1800
The text is unavailable. David Austin, Jr. (1760-1831), clergyman in New Jersey and Connecticut. He was the author of numerous religious pamphlets and sermons. He probably transmitted a copy of his address, viz: A Discourse delivered on the occasion of the death of George Washington late president, general and Commander in Chief of the forces of the United States of America, in compliance with the request of the Mayor, aldermen, and Common Council, of the Borough of Elizabeth, December 25, 1799. Also sketches of a running discourse delivered to the Union Brigade, in compliance with a request from Colonel Smith, thee Commanding officer, December 26, 1799, with an address to the throne of grace, offered at the door of the tabernacle of the cantonment on Green

Brook, Feb. 22 the birthday of our national luminary. By David Austin, Jun. New York, Printed by G.F.Hopkins, 1800. 4to pp. 36. It contains an allegorical plate.

To General Henry Knox

February 9, 1900
The text of this letter is not available. It was written for MW by Tobias Lear, in response to General Knox's letter of January 17, 1800.

From Reverend Uzal Ogden

Newark, Feby 11, 1800
Rec.d Feby 15, 1800
Madam   Answd by T Lear Feby 17, 1800
While I most sincerely condole with you in your late very great afflictions, I beg your acceptance of a Pamphlet, containing two Discourses, sent & (?) occasioned by the truly melancholy Event.[1] Your Piety, I doubt not, occasions you to enjoy the Consolations of the Gospel; and it is my fervent Prayer to Almighty God, that he may ever favor you with the Comforts of his Holy Spirit; support you under all the Trials and Vicissitudes of Life, and at last (?) you with the Rewards of Virtue and Piety in his Heavenly Kingdom, with your and Americas' departed Friend!

> With very great Esteem and
> Respect, I am
> Madam
> Your most obedient and
> very humble Servant
> Uzal Ogden[2]

Mrs. Martha Washington
(Address) Mrs Martha Washington Mount Vernon
(Docket by Tobias Lear)
From The Revd Uzal Ogden 11th Feby. 1800

ALS, ViMtV.

1. Two Discourses, Occasioned by the Death of General George Washington,... December 14, 1799. By the Rev. Uzal Ogden, D.D. Rector of Trinity Church, Newark. in ... New Jersey. Delivered in that Church, and in the Church in union with it, at Belleville, December 29th, and January 5, 1800, ... Newark: Printed...by Matthias Day MDCCC. 8:46.

2. Uzal Ogden (c1744-1822), Episcopal clergyman of New Jersey. He was elected Bishop of New Jersey in 1798 but was refused consecration because of irreconcilable differences with his parish. He thereafter became a Presbyterian and continued on in a missionary capacity.

To Mrs. Martha Laurens Ramsay

Madam,[1]   Mount Vernon, February 13th: 1800

I have duly received your kind letter of the 27 of January, and the excellent Oration which accompanied it; for which, as well as for the prayers and wishes for my health and happiness expressed in your letter, I beg your acceptance of my sincere thanks.[2]

If the tears of sympathizing Friends - if numerous tributes of respectful veneration - if evidences of the sincere mourning of a grateful Country - or if universal grief for the loss of departed worth and excellence could give consolation to my breast, I should receive it in the highest degree. - These testimonies I see and acknowledge with grateful sensibility; and so far as human efforts can alleviate afflictions of this kind, they have their effect; - but knowing that no Earthly Power can retrieve my loss, I bow, with humble submission to the Dispensation of the Most High, and to him only do I look for comfort and consolation With my best wishes for the health and happiness of yourself and those who are dear to you I remain, Madam, very respectfully

Your obliged & obedt Servt

Mrs Martha Laurens Ramsay

Df by Tobias Lear. ViMtV.

1. Martha Laurens Ramsay (1759-1811), daughter of Henry Laurens (1724-1792) and his wife, Eleanor Ball Laurens (17?-1770). She was the third wife of Dr. David Ramsay, surgeon and militant patriot during the Revolution. Ramsay was a prolific writer on medical subjects and the Revolutionary War. His *Life of Washington* was published in 1807. Mrs. Ramsay's memoirs and diary was published by her husband in 1812.

2. Undoubtedly Mrs. Ramsay forwarded a copy of her husband's oration on the death of GW. An Oration on the Death of Lieutenant-General George Washington. Delivered in St. Michael's Church, January 15, 1800, at the request of the Inabitants of Charleston, South Carolina; and published by their desire. By David Ramsay, M.D. Charleston: Printed by W. P. Young MDCCC. 8:30.

From A Society of Females

Mrs Washington,   Providence, Feby 14th 1800

Conscious of the presumption this address implies, we offer it with trembling diffidence, and while we sympathize we respect your sorrows: Pardon however this intrusion on them, and suffer us to name the motives for it -- Our Fathers fought with Washington! they taught our Infant lispings to repeat His name and since have shewed to us the vast volume of His worth. He defended our Mothers from the Tomahawk of Savage barbarity and warded from their Breasts the polished (?) of more refined cruelty. Gratitude struggles for utterance, but the attempt is vain and to the feeling heart we leave it to conceive it. Such an one we are now addressing, and while the memory of Washington shall ever remain in our hearts (?) we wish also for some external remembrance of the Man "first in War, first in Peace and first in the hearts of his Country". Could we Madam receive from you a lock, (however small) of his invaluable hair, while life remained we would wear it as a charm to deter us from ill and while gazing on it, think on the bright perfections of its former owner, till by degrees we engrafted them on our own Nature's. Do not Madam term this the language of presumption, we wait your award with humble respect and should our sanguine hopes be crushed by a refusal we will receive it as the just punishment of our rashness, but should smiling assent deign to reach us we will preserve the precious present till age has "On our temples shed The blossoms of the grave."

We will then bequeath to our Children the sacred talisman of virtue - With sentiments of the most profound respect and prayers for your happiness

> We remain Madam
> ever yours
> Julia Bowen[1]
> Mary B. Howell[2]
> Sarah Halsey[3]
> Abby Chace[4]

P.S. Would it not be ( ) in presumption we would also (in behalf of a society of Females) request a lock of your hair. altho we have not the happiness of being personally acquainted with you Madam, yet the chosen Friend of Washington, will ever be dear to our Hearts.

ALS, ViMtV.

1. Julia Bowen (1779-1805), daughter of Ephraim Bowen of Pawtuxent, R.I. She married John D. Martin. H. J. Martin, *Notices: Genealogical and Historical of the Martin Family of New England---* Boston, 1880, p. 126.

2. Mary B. Howell, married Mason Shaw in 1806. Personal communication from Ms. Maureen Tayloe, Rhode Island Historical Society.

3. Sarah Halsey (1779-1864) was the daughter of Thomas Lloyd Halsey and the aunt of Julia Bowen, above. Chapin, *Thomas Lloyd Halsey*, Providence, R.I., 1912.

4. Abby Chace (1834), daughter of Amos Chace, married Philip Peck of Providence, R.I. in 1807. Peck, *Genealogical History of the Descendants of Joseph Peck---* Boston, 1868, p. 160.

To Theodore Sedgwick

Sir,   Mount Vernon, Feby 15. 1800

Mrs. Washington requests me to acknowledge the receipt of your letter to her of the 4th instant - and to beg your acceptance of her best thanks for your goodness in forwarding the Oration to her, at the request of the Common Council of the City of New York, and for your sincere

Condolence on the late melancholy event.[1] - At the same time she requests the favor of your forwarding the enclosed to the Mayor of the City of New York.[2]

> With very great respect
> I have the honor to be
> Sir,
> Yr. Mo Ob, St.
> Tobias Lear

The Hona. Theodore Sedgwick

Df by Tobias Lear. DTP.

1. This is probably, *An Oration upon the Death of General Washington, by Gouverneur Morris. Delivered at the request of the Corporation of the City of New York, on the 31st day of December, 1799 and published by their Request. New York, 1800.* See, Hough, F. B., *Washingtoniama*, 2:137-50, Roxbury, 1865.

2. The letter has not survived.

To Richard Varick

(February 15, 1800)
The text of this letter is not available. It was probably written for MW by Tobias Lear in response to Varick's letter of January 28, 1800.

From Theodore Sedgwick

Madam: Philadelphia, 17 Feby, 1800

As the inclosed is of better execution than the first edition of General Lee's oration, I have ventured to hope that it would not be unacceptable to you[1] I pray you, with it, to receive an assurance of my most sincere wishes for your support and consolation.

> With much esteem & regard
> I have the honor to be
> Madam
> Your most obedt. & most
> humble svt.
> Theodore Sedgwick[2]

Mrs. Washington

1. The first edition was entitled, Funeral Oration, (n.p.n.d.) 8:17. *The second edition was: A Funeral Oration in Honor of the Memory of George Washington Late General of the Armies of the U. States; Prepared and Delivered at the Request of Congress, at the German Lutheran Church, Philadelphia, on Thursday, the 26th of December. By Major Gen. Henry Lee; One of the Representatives from the State of Virginia. Brooklyn: Printed by Thomas Kirk 1800.* 8:16 (Probably the first book printed in Brooklyn).

2. The location is unknown. The text is from a typescript in DLC.

To Uzal Ogden

Revnd Sir,   Mount Vernon, Feby 17th, 1800
    Your letter of the 11th instant, to Mrs. Washington, and the Pamphlet therein mentioned, have been duly received, for which she begs your acceptance of her most grateful acknowledgements. And requests me to assure you, that while her great consolation, in the late melancholy Event, is drawn from the precepts of our Holy Religion; Yet she is truly sensible of the sincere sympathy of her friends, and highly grateful for their kind efforts to alleviate her grief. Your discourses will be read with much satisfaction, and your prayers that she may receive the Consolations of the Gospel will be remembered with gratitude.

> With very great Respect
> I have the honor to be
> Revd Sir
> Your mo ob st
> Tobias Lear

The Revd Uzal Ogden
To The Revd. Uzal Ogden 17th Feby 1800

Df by Tobias Lear. ViMtV.
    1. See supra, Uzal Ogden to MW, February 11, 1800.

From Colonel David Humphreys

Dear and Respected Madam: Madrid, February 22, 1800
    Too long was I an inmate of your hospitable family, and too intimately connected with the late illustrious head of it, not to share in the poignancy of your distress for the death of the best of husbands. The loss of the most distinguished man of the age is an event which has produced an extensive mourning in Europe as well as in America. On the return of this day, which was signalized by his birth and which was accustomed to be celebrated with heartfelt festivity throughout the United States, what mingled ideas crowd upon the recollection! Grief more genuine or more universal was never manifested in any age or in any nation. While a grateful country offers to you the joint tribute of sympathetic tears, I am encouraged to hope that the solitary condolences of an absent friend will not be unseasonable or unacceptable. Accept, then that pledge of my sincere affection and respect for you. In the season of severe afflictions, I know you were ever exposed to listen to the voice of friendship, reason, and religion. When, nearly nineteen years ago, you were bereaved by death of a dear, an only son, after having mentioned the superior motives for a resignation to the dispensations of the Deity, I attempted to

adminster some consolaton, by showing that the lenient hand of time might mitigate the severity of grief, and that you had still the prospect of enjoying many good days on earth in the society of the best of friends, as well as in beholding your grandchildren happily established in life, as a comfort for your more advanced years. Highly favoured have you been by Providence, in the uninterrupted fruition of those felicities, until the late fatal stroke, which has removed, all you held most dear forever from this world. Having lived long enough for himself, and long enough for glory, he has gone before us from these mutable scenes of trouble to the mansions of eternal rest.

We too, are hastening to follow him "to that undiscovered country from whose Bourne no traveller returns." The only difference is, whether we shall commence our journey a few days sooner or later. In either case the idea of meeting our dear departed friends will serve, in some degree, to cheer the gloomy passage. To those who have already passed into the vale of declining life, it is true everything here below ought to appear too transitory and too shortlived to allow them to calculate on permanent enjoyments. If the consolation which was once naturally drawn from the expectation of still seeing many good days on this earth, be diminished, the resources of reason and religion are everlasting as they are inexhaust-ible. The noble sentiments and principles of your departed husband remain for your support. Your long alliance with that exalted character cannot fail to elevate your mind above the pressure of immoderate sorrow; we are apt to assimilate ourselves, as far as we are able, to the character, and, as it were, to identify our own with the destinies of those we love. Your hope of happiness is with him on high. but without suffering your intellectual view to be diverted from the higher contem-plation, may you not experience some soothing sensations in contem-plating a whole people weeping over the tomb of your beloved; in seeing them strive to bestow unequalled honours on his memory, and in knowing that they wish to alleviate your sorrow by a participation of it? And may you not derive some rational comfort from the recollection that the great and good man whom we now mourn as having been subject to the lot of mortality, has faithfully discharged every duty in life; from a belief that he has now entered upon a glorious immortality; and from a conviction that, after having rendered to his country more important services than any other human character ever performed, his example will continue to be a blessing to mankind so long as this globe shall exist as a theater for human action?

Since the fatal news reached me, I have found my heart so much oppresed as not to be able to give vent to those effusions which can alone afford me some relief. I wish to express my sensations, but feel myself incapable of the effort; so true is the observations of the author of the pathetic elegy on Mr. Addison:

"What mourner ever felt poetic fires!
Slow comes the verse that real woe inspires;
Grief unaffected suits but ill with art,
Or flowing numbers with a bleeding heart."

When my own grief shall become a little moderated, I propose to indulge my melancholy meditations in endeavouring to delineate such features of the deceased father of his country, and such events of his interesting life, as have left the most indelible impressions on my mind. I shall thus procure the double advantage, first for myself, of holding a kind of spiritual intercourse with him; and, next, of exhibiting for others an admirable model for imitation. Could I flatter myself with the expectation of being able to express (in any adequate proportion) what I know and what I feel on a subject which will employ the pens of innumerable writers, I might then hope to do not less justice to his public and private virtues than others. For, conscious I am that few have had opportunities of knowing him better and that none could appreciate more justly his morals and his merits. If the task which gratitude, affection and duty impose shall not be executed in a manner too unworthy of the subject, even in my own judgment, I shall ask your acceptance of the production when finished.[1] In the meantime, may you receive while here on earth, every species of consolation of which an afflicted virtuous mind is susceptible: and may the choicest of heaven's benedictions attend you through the whole period of your existence. Such is the fervent prayer of

Your most affectionate and most obliged friend and servant,

David Humphreys

P.S. I request you will present my most affectionate regards to Mrs. Stuart and family, to all your amiable grandchildren, to Mr. Lear, Dr. Craig and family, and in general, all my ancient friends in your neighbourhood. Mrs. Humphreys, although she has not the honour of being personally known to you, cannot but take a deep interest in your affliction. She requests me to tender the homage of her best respects to you.[2]

Reprinted from Humphreys, *Life and Times of David Humphreys*, New York, 1917, Vol. 2, pp. 266-69. See also Humphreys. *Miscellaneous Works of David Humphreys*.

1. A Poem on the Death of General Washington Pronounced at the House of the American Legation on the 4th day of July, 1800, being the Twenty-fourth Anniversary of the Independence of the United States of America; Miscellaneous Works of David Humphreys, late Minister Plenipotentiary from the United States of America to the Court of Madrid, New York, 1804.

2. Mrs. Ann Frances Bulkeley Humphreys, daughter of John Bulkeley, head of the banking and mercantile establishment of London. The Humphreys were married in 1797. Afte the death of Colonel Humphreys in 1818, she remained a widow until December, 1829, when she married Count Etienne Walewski, a veteran of the Napoleonic wars. She died in Paris in 1832. See: Humphreys, *Life and Times of David Humphreys*, v. II, p. 151, 266-69, 434-35. New York, 1917.

From Catherine Garretson

My dear Madam: (February 27, 1800)

Your late Afflictive loss, calls for every exercise of Friendship to console you under the presence of so trying a Calamity - But What My dear Madam, shall we say. God is Wise - and He does all things Well - Submission to his Will, and a Gracious improvement of his dispensations is all he will require.

If the Grief, and sympathy of thousands could lessen the tyde of prostrate sorrow; this in an eminent degree Madam, is reserved for you - But I have no doubt you can Cry out with afflicted *Job*, Miserable comfortor are you all. You have doubtless long since experienced the World is a broken Reed which will pierce the side of him who leans upon it for support. Will you then my dearest Madam in this time of trial,and distress,admit the Council of one that loves you of one who is touched with sorrow at your loss; and would point you to the only true Consolation, that remains for you to enjoy on this side of Eternity.

Religion Pure and undefiled Religion Holds out to you a happiness far beyond anythng this vain World can either give or refuse. I speak now from the experiece of upwards of 12 years. And I Recommend to you that *Jewel*which I found at a Moment when the Whole Creation was to me a dreary void, from which I turned with disgust. In that moment I fell helpless at the Feet of Jesus The Friend of the distresed And I found him a Savious in (?). Ah My dear Madam: What did I then partake of - A new Creation of Love, Peace, and Joy were opened in my Soul.- I found myself united to God -I felt I had entered into the fold by the Only *Door*that could admit me into the number of Christ's Flock. I found in my Breast a Witness that I was a Child of God; an Heir of Glory: and gratitude was continually urging to (?), and thanksgiving. I spent this Winter With my Mother Alone, in the Country, and I do aver it was the happiest Winter I had ever seen.......New Sources of pleasure were opened, of which before I had only faint Consceptions, My highest enjoyments were in pouring out my soul to God, and receiving from him foretastes of that Felicity his Word has promised and taught me to expect in the World above. Am earnest fever and desire for the universal Salvation of Mankind assured me law of love was written by the finger of God, in this new heart he had given me.

It was now first I began to live - The past Appeared like a vain Dream, on which I would scarcely alow myself to think a Moment. A line of separation appeared to be drawn between me, and all my former pleasures and pursuits - I found that tho' in the World, I was not of the World. And I bless God, from that time, to the present, I am not weary of his Service; Who has called me to take my Cross and follow him through good and evil report. I find myself amply repaid for every sacrifice: and all beyond the Grave is smiling peace.

Tis not, my much Esteemed Mrs Washington, any desire to exalt myself in your estimation, that has lead to this account, of God's gracious dealings with my soul. Tis with far other views. I want you to give Credit to my Assertions, that you may be induced to make the same surrender, and be as blessed in the event - Rest assured there is a real power in Religion to change the heart, and make it capable of obedience to the Laws of God. There is such a thing as delighting in God; and receiving communications of his love and favor. Rev: 22d. 17. The Spirit and the Bride say Come. and let him that heareth say come. And let him that is a thirst come. and whover will , let him take the Water of life freely.

Let me, my dear Madam, Join the invitation of Friendship, with that of the Spirit , and the Church, and say, come. Oh Come with me, and I will shew thee good. Come Buy Wine, and Milk, without Money and without price.

Thro' the tender mercies of a Good God my Mother still enjoys a very tolerable share of Health, and the unimpaired use of her (?) and most of her senses . She now wholly resides in the Country, all her children but one settled in the Country around her. When I had the honor of seeing you, I expected to have paid my respects once more, but I was soon after confined, which continued, till a day or two before I left Philadelphia It is now not probable we shall ever meet again in this World: But it is my earnest Wish to meet you at the Right Hand of the Judge of all the Earth. With a Palm of Victory in your Hand, and your Robes Washed in the Blood of the Lamb. God bless, Comfort, sustain, and enrich you with every Grace of his Holy Spirit, bring you safely through the pangs of the New birth hereafter, crown you with Glory everlasting, in the bright region of eternal day. I am in Sincerity with Esteem and Friendship

> Your Obedient
> Servant
> Catherine Garretson[1]

Rhinebeck Febr. 17 1800
(Address)
Mrs. Martha Washington Mount Vernon Virginia

ALS, DTP.

1. Catherine Livingston Garretson (1752-1849), daughter of Robert R. Livingston of Clermont (1718-1775), and his wife, Margaret Beekman Livingston (1724-1800). She was a younger sister of Janet Livingston Montgomery. See, MW to Janet Livingston Montgomery, January 29, 1791; Janet Livingston Montgomery to MW, March 10, 1800. She married Reverend Freeborn Garretson, a prominent Methodist clergyman and missionary, in 1793. E. B. Livingston, *The Livingstons of Livingston Manor*, N.Y. 1910, pp. 555-56.

To Theodore Sedgwick

February 27, 1800
The text of this letter is unavailable. It was written for MW by Tobias Lear. Undoubtedly it is a letter of appreciation for the copy of the second edition of General Henry Lee's oration, sent by Sedgwick to MW, February 17, 1800. See supra.

From Marie Jean Paul Joseph Roche Yves Gilbert du Motier, Marquis de Lafayette

(February 28, 1800)
The text of this letter is unavailable.

From Monsieur A. Belin

March 5, 1800
The text of this letter is unavailable.It may be from the Secretary of the French Masonic Lodge. See, Sidney Hayden, *Washington and His Masonic Compeers*, New York, 1905, p. 215: "There existed in Philadelphia at that time, under a warrant from the Grand Lodge of Pennsylvania, a French Lodge of Ancient York Masons, known as 'L'Amenite', No. 71.' On the following week (January 1, 1800), a *sorrow lodge* was held by these brethren, which was attended by the officers of the Grand Lodge and a great number of the Fraternity of that city. After the concluson of ceremonies peculiar to such a lodge, an oration was delivered by its orator, SIMON CHAUDRON. in the French language, which was followed by an address in English by the Master, JOSEPH DE LA GRANGE. This oration was published in both the French and English languages, and copies were sent to the President and Vice-president of the United States, to the Governor of Pennsylvania, and to Mrs. WASHINGTON at Mount Vernon. They all acknowledged their receipt by letter; and Mrs. Washington's by the hand of the private secretary of her late husband,...." See, infra, Tobias Lear to Mon. A. Belin, May 15, 1800.

From Reverend D. Rogers

March 6, 1800
The text of this letter is not available. The sender has not been identified.

From Reverend Mason Locke Weems

(March 8, 1800)

The honor of Mrs Washingtons Acceptance of this little book is requested.

By her Sincere Wellwisher
Mason L. Weems[2]

March 8. 1800
Dumfries
(Address)
Mrs Martha Washington
(Docket by Tobias Lear)
From The Revd Mr. Weems 8 March 1800

ALS, DTP.

1. Mason Locke Weems (1759-1825), Episcopal clergyman, bookseller, and author, was a native of Maryland. He was ordained in England in 1784 and then returned to America where he served several churches in Maryland. He began writing and publishing books about 1791. Thereafter bookselling interests dominated his life. In 1794 he became an agent for Mathew Cary, the young Philadelphia publisher. He traveled tirelessly up and down the country, peddling books. In the meantime he found time to write biographies of Frankllin, Francis Marion, and William Penn, as well as other moralizing religious publications. He would probably be unremembered today except for his *Life and Memorable Actions of George Washington*, c. 1800. From 1800 until 1927 it passed through some seventy editions. Additional ones have found their way into print since then. Most of his life, when not traveling, was spent at Dumfries, King William County, Virginia. See, Cunliffe (ed), *The Life of Washington By Mason L. Weems*, Cambridge, 1962, pp. ix-xiii. As early as June 1799 Weems had begun preparing a small pamphlet entitled *The Beauties of Washington*. On June 24, 1799, six months before the death of Washington, he wrote Mathew Cary, the Philadelphia publisher, offering it to him for publication. GW's death, notwithstanding, Cary did not respond. On January 12, 1800 Weems again wrote to Cary, revealing his plan for a Washington biography, and again Cary waas unresponsive. Weems then wrote to Cary for the third time, on February 2, stating he had sent him an excerpt from "The History of Washington." Not obtaining a response, had a small number printed at his own expense. This was the first edition, a pamphlet consisting of eighty pages, and published anonymously by George Keating, a Baltimore printer. This was probably the edition sent to MW. The seond edition followed shortly after and was published by Breen & English, of Georgetown. It was dedicated to MW and bore the authorship of Weems. The third edition was published by John Bioren of Philadelphia, in the spring of 1800. It was also dedicated to MW. See E. E. F. Skeel, (ed) *Mason Locke Weems His Works and Ways*, N.Y. 1929, 1:1-13.

From Janet Livingston Montgomery

Madam

Will you accept (for it is all I have to offer) the tears of a fellow suffer; and a fellow Mourner; I will make no attempts to comfort you? I well know how vain the project: twenty four years are gon away since I lost my husband - And still my tears flow and my heart sighs. - and my tongue repeats his name, in anguish -[1]

Need I remind you my dear Madam of my falling tears on that day of general festivity at West Point - when you, with all the Ladies present had their Husbands at their sides - these had all, weathered the storms of War. and I alone stood formost in woe? And the woe of a widow? -[2] This you now know but to know it in its fullest extent you must have suffered as long as I have done-In any distress we are apt to look at the darkest side - it is they say from contrast that comfort is taken - how much may you derive in a comparison with me whilst the hope of this - leads me to open wounds very imperfectly closed - all the time I have Mourn'd for my lost soldier you held yours in your arms - Then what a consolation were you allowed! how favor'd to be allowed to offer every suport to him- to kneel at his bedside to clasp his hand to catch his last words - to close his eyes - to gaze at a loved face to you so dear and last of all to watch over his hearse and see him confined to the grave of his fathers Whilst she who writes to give you comfort Who shall console? for a Husband bleeding dieing, on the inclement field of Abraham far from help? far from friends -[3]

Dear Madam forgive the rest as wild immagination permits me to persist no further My Mother offers you her best wishes & regrets that the distance between us does not allow her to hope ye shall meet she says we are all going on towards our journeys end - and immagins we shall know and meet in happier worlds where we shall part no more - There is certainly a consolation in this Idea which is very flattering to poor mortality - may it sooth you under your great loss - and induce you to support life & every blessing still held out to you

With sincerest wishes and highest consideration for your happiness I remain

> Yours to command
> Janet Montgomery

March 10th 1800
Rhinbeck house Dutchess County
Mrs Washington
answered Apl 5 1800
(Docket)
From Janet Montgomery 10 March 1800

ALS, ViMtV.

1. The letter is remarkable for the bitterness it betrays. Janet Livingston Montgomery (1743-1828) was the eldest daughter of Judge Robert R. Livingston of Clermont and his wife, Margaret Beekman. She was the widow of Brigadier-general Richard Montgomery (1738-1775). They were married July 24, 1773. Montgomery, a native of Ireland, had held a captain's commission in the British army. He had served in America during the Seven Year's War. Realizing a limited future in the army, he sold his commission in 1772, moved to America, and purchased a farm near King's Bridge, New York. He was appointed a brigadier by the Continental Congress on June 21, 1775.

The strategy for the capture of Canada involved a two-pronged attack on Quebec. One force, under Major-general Philip Schuyler, was to proceed north through the lake regions and the St. Lawrence corridor, taking Montreal, and then on the Quebec. The other force, under the command of Colonel Benedict Arnold, was to proceed from Fort Augusta, by way of the Kennebec River, the Dead River, across the Heights of Land, then to the Chaudier River and up the St Lawrence River to Quebec. The two expeditions would then join forces and take the city by assault. Schuyler fell ill and was succeeded by Montgomery, his second in command. Arnold, in spite of insufficient supplies, bitter cold weather, desertions, and difficult wilderness terrain, arrived first, and crossed the St. Lawrence on the night of November 13, 1775. Montgomery, moving north, took Fort St. John, Chambly, and Montreal. He joined forces with Arnold on December 2nd. The assault began on December 31, 1775.

Both Arnold's and Montgomery's forces were decimated. Montgomery was killed instantly. Arnold, severely wounded, lived to fight another day. For further biographical details see Randolph Adams' sketch in DAB. Also, E. B. Livingston, *The Livingstons of Livingston Manor*, N.Y. 1910, p 555. For the best account of the Canadian expedition, see Allen French, *The First Year of the American Revolution*, New York, 1934, Chapters XXVII, XXXV.

2. The allusion is to the celebration commemorating the Birth of the Dauphin of France, held at West Point, May 31, 1782. G.W. first announced the birth to the army on May 22, and directed "such demonstrations of joy as are thougt proper for the occasions." A feu de joye was ordered for May 30, and the attendance of all officers not detained by duty was requested. The celebration was postponed one day. There were no general orders or communications issued from headquarters on the 31st, unusual in itself. An interesting description of the elaborate preparations for the event was noted by Thacher, p. 309-12. See also, 5 Freeman, p. 416.

3. Mrs. Montgomery speaks figuratively when she mentions the Plains of Abraham, a favorite dying place of heroes, as the place where her husband fell. He was killed in a narrow passageway along the edge of the declivity of the Citadel. See French's *First Year*, pp. 614-15, supra.

To Mr. Stewart

(March 10, 1800)

The text is not available. It was written for MW by Tobias Lear. On a list once made available to ViMtV, a portion of the address leaf bears the word, "Painter." It is conceivable the "Mr Stewart" referred to is Gilbert Stuart, the portraitist of GW and MW.

From Francis Adrian van der Kemp

Madam

Permit mine condolence to interrupt your grief. Words are here inadequate to the task. We must apply our thoughts to the virtues of that excellent Man : and then we may find strength of mind enough to adore Providence and imitate your example in obliging your Countrymen by a new most affectionate sacrifice.

Your Politeness which I experienced after I crossed the Atlantic, will find an excuse for this intrusion.

May the choice of Heavens blessings, peace of mind and Serenity of Soul, be your constant Share till that moment you return to your Maker, is the ardent wish of him who remains with the highest considerations of admiration and respect.

> Madam
> Your most obt. and most
> obedient Servant
> Franc: Adr. van der Kemp[1]

Recd March 10, 1800
Answd by T. Lear March 13 1800

ALS, DTP.

1. Francis Adrian van der Kemp (1752-1829) was a Dutch soldier and Mennonite clergyman. He was a leader of the Patriot Party in the Netherlands attempting to limit the powers of the House of Orange and the Stadtsholder. Their ultimate goal was the recovery of the "ancient rights" of the Dutch people. Following a military uprising in Utrecht he was taken prisoner and incarcerated for about six months. Upon payment of a £7500 levy he was released. To him asylum in American seemed the only recourse. He arrived in America in March, 1788 with a letter of introduction from the Marquis de la Fayette to GW. He had previously made the acquaintance of John Adams in the Netherlands. He visited Mount Vernon on July 29 and 30, 1788. He took up resident in up-state New York, became an American citizen, and pursued agricultural, literary, and scholarly pursuits. 5 *Diaries*, 369-70; 29 *Writings* 504-6; 30 *Writings*, 103; *The Papers of Thoms Jefferson*, 16:285, Princeton, 1961. See also *DAB*, 19:179.

To Julia Bowen, Mary B. Howell, Abby Chace, and Sally Halsey

Ladies   Mount Vernon, March 12, 1800

In granting the request contained in your sympathetic letter of the 24th of February, I beg you to be assured of the grateful sensibility with which I receive your expressions of condolence and kind wishes for my happiness. If innumerable testimonies of respect and veneration paid to the memory of my dear departed Husband, or if universal sympathy in my afflicting loss could afford consolation, mine would be complete. But while I see and acknowledge these with a grateful heart I find consolation only in the bosom of that Being by whose dispensation I have been afflicted.

That your Virtues may be exemplary - that your passage through life may be marked with the Blessings of Heaven and that happiness hereafter may be your portion prays

> Your friend & obedt Servt[1]

Misses Julia Bowen
Mary B. Howell
Abby Chace
Sally Halsey

1. Four copies of this letter are known. The above copy is from the collection at Tudor Foundation and is the only one in the hand of Tobias Lear. Another, dated March 12, 1800, is from the collections of the Rhode Island Historical Society and was accompanied by a lock of Washington's hair. A third copy was once in the possession of Miss Emilie M. Rivinus. Miss Rivinus found the letter among the papers of her great great grandmother, Mrs. Samuel Galloway of Tulip Hill, Anne Arundel County, Maryland. The request mentioned in the first line of the letters was for a lock of General Washington's hair. The text of the remaining copy was obtained from the *Florida Times Union*, Jacksonville, Florida, March 18, 1908. All the texts, except that of Miss Rivinus, bear the date, March 12, 1800. Miss Rivinus's copy is dated March 18, 1800 and was personally communicated to the editor.

To Catherine Livingston Garretson

Mount Vernon, March 15t, 1800

The kind sympathy which you express for my afflictive loss - and your fervent prayers for my present comfort and future happiness, impress my mind with gratitude. The precepts of our holy Religion have long since taught me, that in the severe and trying scenes of life, our only sure Rock of comfort and consolation is the Divine Being who orders and directs all things for our good.

Bowing with humble submission, to the dispensations of his Providence, and relying upon that support which he has promised to those who put their trust in him, I hope I have borne my late irreparable loss with Christian fortitude. - To a feeling heart, the sympathy of friends, and the evidences of universal respect paid to the memory of the deceased, - are truly grateful. - But while these aleviate our grief, we find that the only sense of comfort is from above.

It gives me great pleasure to hear that your good Mother yet retains her health and faculties unimpaired, - and that you experience those comforts which the Scriptures promise to those who obey the Laws of God. - That you may continue to enjoy the blessings of this life - and receive hereafter the portion of the Just is the prayer of your sincere friend & obt Servt.[1]

Df by Tobias Lear. DTP.
1. See supra, Catherine Livingston Garretson to MW, February 27, 1800.

From Timothy Pickering

Madam,

Mr. Ames desires me to forward the enclosed oration to you "as a testimony of his very great respect."[1] Permit me to embrace the occasion to assure you of mine.

Timothy Pickering[2]

Philadelphia March 17, 1800
Mrs. Washington

from Colo. Pickering
17th March 1800

ALS, ViMtV.

1. Fisher Ames (1758-1808), a native of Massachusetts, was a brilliant intellectual and as an orator comparable to Patrick Henry and Henry Clay. He worked diligently for ratification of the Federal Constitution in Masssachusetts and was a member of the first four Congresses. As a militant Federalist he was a staunch supporter of Hamilton and his policies. His speech before Congress in support of the Jay Treaty remains one of the greatest ever delivered before that body. The oration referred to was: *An Oration on the Sublime Virtues of General George Washington, pronounced at the Old South Meeting House in Boston, Before His Honor the Lieutenant Governor, the Council, and the Two Branches of the Legislature of Massachusetts, At Their Request, ----8th of February, 1800, By Fisher Ames. Boston: 1800.*

2. Timothy Pickering (1745-1829) served in the Continental Army. He rose to the rank of adjutant-general and later quartermaster-general. During the Washington administration he served a brief term as postmaster-general and in 1795 became secretary of war. Later in the year he succeeded Edmund Randolph as secretary of state. As an ardent Federalist he was an admirer of Washington, a loyal supporter of Hamilton, but became a political enemy of John Adams.

From Theodore Foster

Much respected Madam   Philadelphia, March 18t 1800

In condoling with you sincerely on account of the Death of the great and excellent General Washington, the Boast and the Glory of our Country, I do no more than is done by every just Citizen, and by the World at large. - Silence therefore, expressive, on this very mournful Occasion, would have best become Me, had not my Friend Doct William Rogers[1] requested Me to forward the inclosed Pamphlet, containing a Copy of the Religious Exercises, at the Time of the Eulogy, at the German reformd Church, in this City[2] on the 22d Ulto. - The Universal Condolence of the Nation, so sincerely felt and manifested, indicates the highest public Esteem and Gratitude for your late Husband, who reigned in the Hearts, and possessed in a Manner unparellelled the Affections of a great and numerous People. The public Testimonials of Respect for his Memory, and the general Solicitude for the Happiness of yourself and Connexions must afford you some Consolation in the Scene of Affliction you experience, especially when it is considered that this Respect for him and his immediate Connexion, is not a Temporary thing, - That it will go down the long Stream of Time, with increasing Veneration, to the latest Ages of Posterity. For he was so universally belovd that his Eulogy is now and will continue to be a delightful Theme, for the good, the Sentimental and the ingenious in all future Time. That Almighty God may preserve you, in Health, console you by the Supporting Influence of his Spirit, and bestow on you all possible Happiness is the sincere Prayer of

Madam,
Your respectful and

Obedient Servt
Theodore Foster[3]

ALS, DTP.

1. Theodore Foster (1752-1828), held a number of political offices in Rhode Island. He was United States senator from Rhode Island from 1790 until 1803.

2. The German Reformed Church in Philadelphia, dating from 1747, was located on Race Street, near Fourth.

3. *A Prayer, delivered on Saturday the 22nd of February 1800, in the German Reformed Church, in Philadelphia, before the Pennsylvania Society of the Cincinnati. By William Rogers, D.D. one of the Members of said Society, and Professor of English and Belles Lettres, in the University of Pennsylvania. Published by particular request. Philadelphia: printed by John Ormrod. 1800, 8:12.*

From Charles Humphrey Atherton

(March 23, 1800)

The text of this letter is not available. It is likely a letter of condolence in which Atherton's eulogy was enclosed.[1]

1. Charles Humphrey Atherton (1773-1853) was native and resident of Amherst, N.H. After graduating from Harvard he studied law and practiced in Amherst. He served in the New Hampshire state legislature and in the national Congress during the session of 1815-17.

Eulogy on Gen. George Washington; delivered at Amherst, N.H. before the Inhabitants of the Town of Amherst, the inhabitants of the Town of Milford, and the Benevolent Lodge, on the 22d day of February, 1800, at the Request of the Committee of the Selectmen and other respectable Citizens of the Town of Amherst, to which was superadded the request of the Committee of the Benevolent Lodge. By Charles Humphrey Atherton. From the Press of Samuel Preston, Amherst. 1800, 8:23.

From George Washington Lafayette[1]

(March 24, 1800)

The text of this letter is not available.

1. George Washington Lafayette (1779-1849) was the only son of General Marie Joseph Paul Yves Roch Gilbert du Motier, Marquis de Lafayette. Arrested by the Austrians, then at war with France, he was imprisoned in Prussia and in dungeon at Olmutz, from 1792-97. In 1795 young Lafayette and his tutor, Felix Frestal, escaped to America. His arrival proved a great embarrassment to GW. His great desire was to take the only son of his old friend into his household. But, he was on the "horns of a dilemma." As president of the United States he did not wish to offend the French government, who had proscribed General Lafayette. Neither did he wish to inflame the pro-French faction who favored France and were anti-British since the passage of the Jay treaty. "Voila!" He would arrange to have the young men reside in New York, at the home of Colonel Louis Sainte Ange Morel, under the family name of Motier. Morel had been an aide-de-camp to General Lafayette during the American and French Revolution. In April, 1796, GW threw precaution to the winds and, despite advice to the contrary, took the two young men into his Philadelphia household. They remained a part of the family in Philadelphia as well as at Mount Vernon, following the presidency. Hearing that his father might be released from Olmutz, young Lafayette and Frestal departed from New York on October 26, 1797 and arrived at Lehmkuhlen in February, 1798. He rejoined his family at Witmold-Holstein. Young Lafayette served in the French army from 1800-08 and was a member of the Chamber of Deputies in 1822. In 1824 he accompanied his father on his triumphal tour of the United States. On his return to France he again was a member of the Chamber of Deputies from 1827-48. See, 6 *Diaries*, 236-67, 161; Gottscalk, *The Letters of Lafayette To Washington, 1777-99*, N.Y. 1944, pp. xxi-xxiv, 369-72.

From Bishop James Madison

Bishop Madison presents his best Respect to Mrs Washington, & begs her Acceptance of the Discourse herewith forwarded, as a small Testimony of the Sincerity of his Condolence.[1]

March 24th 1800
Williamsburg

ALS, DTP.

1. James Madison, president of the College of William and Mary and first bishop of the Protestant Episcopal Church in Virginia. Madison served as president of the college from 1777 until his death. During a portion of this time G.W. served as chancellor. Largely through his efforts the college was brought through the upheavals caused by the revolution. He was also as devoted to the cause of reorganization of the Episcopal Church in Virginia.

A Discourse, on the Death of General Washington; delivered on the 22d of February, 1800, in the Church in Williamsburg. By James Madison, D.D. Bishop of the Protestant Episcopal Church in Virginia, and President of William and Mary College. Richmond: printed by T. Nicolson. 1800. 8:25. A second edition was printed in New York and a third edition in Philadelphia.

From Reverend James Kemp

March 26, 1800

The text and location is unknown. It probably concerns the transmission of condolences and a copy of Reverend Kemp's oration on the death of General Washington,[1] viz: *A Sermon, Delivered ...in Cambridge, in Maryland; On the Twenty-second of February, 1800, Being the Day of Mourning, appointed by Congress for the Death of General George Washington ... By James Kemp, A.M. Rector of Great Choptank Parish, Easton: Printed by James Cowan 1800. 8v0,*

James Kemp (1764-1827), a native of Scotland, came to America in 1787 and settled in Maryland where he became a tutor. He studied theology and was ordained an Episcopal priest in 1789. In August, 1790, he became rector of Great Choptank parish on the eastern shore. He served there for over twenty years. In 1814 he was consecrated suffragan bishop of Maryland and bishop in 1816. In 1815 he was named provost of the University of Maryland.

To Theodore Foster

Sir,   Mount Vernon, March 28, 1800

Mrs. Washington has requested me to communicate to you her acknowledgements and best thanks for the expressions of condolence contained in your letter to her of the 18h instant, and for your polite attention in forwarding the Pamphlet,[1] containing a copy of the Religious Exercises performed at the German Reformed Church, on the 22d of

February.

While these evidences of respect and veneration paid to the memory of our illustrious Chief, make the most grateful impression on the heart of Mrs. Washington, she finds that the only source of Consolation is from that Divine Being who sends Comfort to the Afflicted, and has promised to be the Widow's God. Your prayers for her health and happiness are received with gratitude, and reciprocated with sincerity.

Be assured, Sir, of the great respect and esteem with which I have the honor to be

> Your most obedt Sert
> Tobias Lear

Theodore Foster Esq.

Df by Tobias Lear. DTP.

1. The text is taken from *Life in Letters*, Vol. III, No. 5, February, 1940, American Autograph Shop, Merion, Pa. See supra, Theodore Foster to MW, March 18, 1800.

To Reverend William Rogers

Revrd Sir   Mount Vernon, March 28th, 1800

Your kind attention in sending to Mrs. Washington a copy of the Religious Exercises, at the time of the Eulogy in the German Reformed Church, on the 22nd of February demands her grateful acknowledgements, which she begs you to accept, with her best wishes for your health and happiness.

> With great respext
> Your most obedt servt
> Tobias Lear

The Revd Dr. Rogers

ALS, Location unknown.[1]

1. The text is taken from *Life in Letters*, Vol. III, No. 5, February, 1940, American Autograph Shop, Merion, Pa. See, Reverend William Rogers to MW, March 6, 1800.

From Peleg Wadsworth

(March 28, 1800)

The text of this letter is unavailable.

1. Peleg Wadsworth (1748-1829), graduate of Harvard. He entered the Revolutionary army and served as aide to General Artemas Ward. He was present at the battle for Long Island in 1776. Twice during the Revolution he was taken prisoner by the British, the last time making his escape. He served in the Massachusetts senate and in the national congress from 1793-1807. He was the grandfather of Henry Wadsworth Longfellow.

To Timothy Pickering

Sir,   Mount Vernon, March 28, 1800
   While Mrs. Washington returns you her best Thanks for your goodness in forwarding Mr. Ames' Oration, she begs you will be pleased to assure that Gentleman of the gratitude with which she receives this testimony of respect and that her best wishes will always attend him.[1]

> With very great respect & regard
> I have the honor to be Sir
> Your most obedt Servt
> Tobias Lear

Colo. Timothy Pickering

Df by Tobias Lear. ViMtV.
   1. See Timothy Pickering to MW, March 17, 1800.

From Julia Bowen, Mary B. Howell, Abby Chace, & Sarah Halsey

Mrs. Washington Madam.   Providence, April 2d 1800
   Pardon this second intrusion on your goodness. We felt it a duty incumbent on us to acknowledge the receipt of your respected letter, and its invaluable contents. Our hearts are bursting with gratitude, while our pen is unable to express our feelings. but the generosity with which you received our request, shall be recorded as one of the most important events of our existence. with the most ardent prayers, Madam, for your happiness, we remain with respect and esteem, ever yours,[1]

> Julia Bowen
> Mary B. Howells (sic)
> Abba Chace (sic)
> Sarah Halsey

Mrs. Martha Washington Mount Vernon

ALS, DTP.
   1. See footnotes to letter from A Society of Females to MW, Febraury 14, 1800.

From William Cunningham, Jr.

                                          Lunenburg, near Worcester, April 2, 1800
Dear Madam.   ansd by T. Lear May 15, 1800
   I take leave to enclose my Eulogy on the Life of your late Illustrious Consort, which I beg you to accept as expressive of my respect for his

Memory, and sincere condolence in the dispensation of Providence, so afflictive to his Country - so distressing to his Companion and Friends.

With the address my mind renews the pleasure of a day, which with Mrs Cunningham, I passed at Mount-Vernon in the summer of 1796, and Mrs C. joins sincerely in respect and sympathy.

> I remain, with perfect
> respect
> Dear Madam
> Your most obt sert.

Mrs Martha Washington
Wm. Cunningham[1]
Mrs. Mrtha Washington Mount Vernon Mail
From Mr. William Cunningham, Jr. April 2d. 1800

ALS, ViMtV.

1. *An Eulogy delivered at Lunenburg, on --- the 22d of February 1800. The Day recommended by Congress to commemorate the --- Services of Gen George Washington --- By WIlliam Cunningham, Jun --- Worcester: Isaiah Thomas, Jr. 1800* vol. 8, p.78.

From Clement Biddle

Philadelphia, 5 April 1800

Madam   Ansd by T. Lear Apl 20 1800
    I did not hear of Judge Washingtons going until it was too late to send the shoes and Gloves by him, but have sent them by a Gentleman to Mr. Carleton postmaster at Georgetown -the amount is at foot - could not get the Gloves exactly to order.

I shall shortly write to Mr. Lewis[1] with the amount which I cannot close until I get an accot. of some Duties on wine from the Custom house
Mrs. Biddle[2] begs to be most respectfully remembered to you

> I am Madam
> Your mo Obed.
> & very Huml Sert
> Clement Biddle

Mr. Fenton[4]

2 pr Shoes	4.94
4 pairs long Gloves	75cts 3-
2 pairs short do	50 -1
	8.94

Mr. Carleton will forward them
(Address) Mrs. Washington Mount Vernon
(Docket) From Col. Clement Biddle April 5. 1800

ALS, DTP.
1. Lawrence Lewis (1767-1839), nephew of GW and husband of Eleanor Park Custis Lewis, granddaughter of MW.
2. Rebekah Cornell Biddle, second wife of Clement Biddle.

From John D. Blair

April 5, 1800

The text of this letter is unavailable.

To Bishop James Madison

Mrs. Washington begs Bishop Madison's acceptance of her most grateful acknowledgements for his excellent Discourse while he has been so good as to send her, and which she receives as a valuable Testimony of his sincere condolence in her late afflictive Loss.[1]

Mount Vernon, April 5, 1800
To Bishop Madison 5 April 1800

AL. DTP.
1. The letter was written for MW by Tobias Lear. See p. Bishop James Madison to MW, March 24, 1800, supra.

To Janet Livingston Montgomery

My dear Madam,   Mount Vernon, April 5th 1800
    I have received with deep sensability your sympathizing letter of the 10th of March - To those only who have experienced losses like ours can our distresses be known - words are inadequate to convey an idea of them - and the silent sympathy of Friends who have felt the like dispensation speaks a language better known to the heart than the most expressive eloquance can communicate - your affliction I have often marked and as often have keenly felt for you but my own experience has taught me that griefs like these can not be removed by the condolence of friends however sincere - If the mingling tears of numerus friends - if the sympathy of a Nation and every testimoney of respect of veneration paid to the memory of the partners of our hearts could afford consolation you and myself would experience it in the highest degree but we know that there is but one source from whence comfort can be derived under afflictions like ours To this we must look with pious resignation and with that pure confidence which our holy releigion inspires
    I pray you to offer my best wishes to your good mother and assure her of my affectionate remembrance - That we shall not meet again in this

world is almost certain but as you justly observe it is certainly a consolation and flattering to poor mortality to believe that we shall meet here after in a better place.

With sincere thanks for your good wishes and prayers for your happyness I remain

> My Dear madam yours
> sincerely
> Martha Washington[1]

(Docket) 1800 Martha Washington

ALS, MB.

1. Df copy, by Tobias Lear is at ViMtV. See supra, Janet Livingston Montgomery to MW, March 10, 1800; Catherine Garretson to MW, February 27, 1800.

To Peleg Wadsworth

Sir,   Mount Vernon, April 5: 1800

Mrs. Washington has duly received your letter of the 26th ultimo, enclosing one from your daughter, expressing an earnest wish to have a scrap of General Washington's handwriting: or a lock of his hair, to keep as a memorial of veneration for his Character. - The ardent wish expressed by your daughter - and the earnest desire for its gratification which the feelings of a parent naturally suggest, have induced Mrs. Washington to comply with the request by sending the lock of hair, which I have now the honor to enclose: and at the same time to assure you that Mrs. Washington receives your expressions of condolence with due sensibility.

I return your Daughter's charming letter and have the honor to be

> very respectfully,
> Sir,
> Your most Obedt. Servt.
> Tobias Lear

The Honle
Peleg Wadsworth Esq.
(To)
The Honble   Free
Peleg Wadsworth Esqr.
Member of Congress.
Philadelphia

ALS of Tobias Lear for Martha Washington. MeHi.

From Timothy Pickering

Department of State: Philadelphia,
7 April 1800

Madam (Answd by T. Lear Apl 8 1800)
I have the honor to enclose a copy of an Act of Congress, extending
to you the privilege of franking letters and packages, and to be

With great respect
Your most obed. Servt.
Timothy Pickering.[1]

Mrs. Martha Washington Mount Vernon

(Docket) From Colo. Pickering April 7, 1800

ALS, DTP.

AN ACT to extend the privilege of franking letters and packages to Martha Washington. BE
IT ENACTED by the Senate and House of Representatives of the United States of America,
in Congress assembled, That all letters and packages to and from Martha Washington relict
of the late General George Washington, shall be received and conveyed by post free of
postage for and during her life. Thodore Sedgwick Speaker of the House of Representatives.
Th: Jefferson Vice President of the United States, and President of the Senate.
Approved April 3d 1800
John Adams
President of the United States

DS, DTP.

1. Timothy Pickering served as secretary of state from August 20, 1795 until May 12, 1800.
See Adams, R. B., *A History of the Foreign Policy of the United States*, States, p. 445, New York,
1924.

From Gouverneur Morris

New York, 7 April 1800
(answd by T. Lear Apl 23. 1800)
Permit me my dear Madam to offer and pray your acceptance of the
enclosed Copy of an Oration pronounced on our deceased friend.[1] I
should earlier have taken this Liberty but I thought it most fitting to wait
untill Time had in some Degree Soothed your deep affliction fearful lest
even this slight memorial might excite too strong Emotion.

Believe me no person has felt a greater individual share in the public
grief or sympathized more sincerely with you in this heaviest Loss.

With sincere and respectful attachment I am

my dear Madam
Your obedient Servant
Gouv Morris[2]

Mrs. Washington
From Gouvr. Morris Esqr April 7 - 1800

ALS, ViMtV.

1. *An Oration, upon the Death of General Washington, by Gouverneur Morris. Delivered at the request of the Corporation of the City of New York, on the 31st day of December, 1799. And published by their Request.* New-York, printed by John Furman. 1800. 24 pp. 8vo.

2. Gouverneur Morris (1752-1816), member of the Continental Congress (1777-1779), member of the Federal Constitutional Convention, appointed minister to France (1792-1794) by GW, and elected United States senator. GW and Morris carried on an extensive correspondence. He was a frequent visitor to the Washingtons during the Revolution and at their residences in New York, Philadelphia, and Mount Vernon.

To Charles H. Atherton

April 7, 1800

The text of this letter is unavailable. It was probably written in answer to Atherton's letter to MW, March 23, 1800. See supra and n. 1.

From Henry Lee

Madam   Pha, 10th April 1800
As soon as we understood that the postage of letters to you had become immoderate, a bill was introduced extendg to you the right of franking

In this new testimonial of respect to yourself I am happy in communicating the unanimous assent of Congress - Permit me to avail myself of this opportunity in repeating my unceasing disposition to contribute by every means in my power to yr happiness or convenience - with the highest respect & most sincere regard I have the honor to be Madam

Yr most ob: h: ser
Henry Lee[1]

Mrs. Washington
From Genl. H. Lee April 10, 1800

ALS, ViMtV.

1. Henry (Light Horse Harry) Lee (1756-1818), Revolutionary War cavalry officer and long-time friend of GW. Lee was a member of the Continental Congress (1785-88), and of the Virginia ratifying Convention. He served as Governor of Virginia from 1792 till 1795. In 1799 he was elected to Congress and was the first to describe GW as "first in war, first in peace, and first in the hearts of his countrymen." Lee remains one of the great cavalry officers in American history. He was the father of Robert E. Lee.

From William Griffith

(April 14, 1800)

The text of this letter is unavailable. It relates to the transmittal of a copy of Griffith's oration on the death of General Washington, viz: An Oration, delivered To the Citizens of Burlington, *on the 22d of February, 1800, in Commemoration of Gen. George Washington, ... By Wm Griffith, Esq. To which is added A Prayer on the same occasion By Charles H. Wharton, D.D. ...* Trenton; Printed by G. Craft MDCCC. Griffith (1766-1826), a native of New Jersey, was a prominent lawyer and noted for his legal and historical writings.

From John Dexter

Providence, April 15th, 1800

Madam   (Answd by T. Lear May 6)

The Standing Committee of the Society of Cincinnati in the State of Rhode Island having directed that a copy of Doctor Hitchcock's discourse on the Death of Your late beloved Partner and their revered President General be presented to You, I have now the honour of inclosing one to You and of assuring You,[1]

> I am, with great
> consideration
> Madam
> Your Obedient Servant
> Jno Dexter[2]

Mrs. Martha Washington
From John Dexter Esqr April 15, 1800

ALS, ViMtV.

1. Enos Hitchcock, D.D. (1744-1803), Congregational clergyman, was ordained in 1771. He served as chaplain in the Revolutionary Army and was present at Ticonderoga, Saratoga, and witnessed the execution of Andre. On several occasions he preached sermons in the presence of G.W. He was a prominent member of the Society of the Cincinnati in Rhode Island. See biographical sketch in D.A.B. His discourse, sent to M.W., is entitled: *A Discourse on the Dignity and Excellence of the Human Character; Illustrated in the Life of General George Washington* _____ *Delivered February 22, 1800, in the Benevolent Congregational Church in Providence and Published by Request of that Society, Providence, 1800.*

2. John S. Dexter served as a captain in a Rhode Island regiment during the revolution. He was appointed assistant to the adjutant-general by G.W. on May 24, 1779, and promoted to major in August, 1781. He served until November, 1783. G.W. appointed him supervisor of the Connecticut district for the collection of duties on distilled spirits. See *Writings*, 15:137; *Writings*, 31:234.

From Theodore Sedgwick

(April 15, 1800)

The text of this letter is unavailable.

From Joseph Willard

Harvard University Cambridge, April 16. 1800
recd June 3ᵈ, 1800
Madam,   Ansᵈ by T lear june 6, 1800
All who belong to the University, both Governors and Pupils, have shared largely in the heart-felt grief which has pervaded our Nation, upon the death of General Washington, the tender Father and disinterested Friend of his Country, and your affectionate and excellent Husband.

Inclination as well as duty induced the Government of the University to have public notice taken in the Society of the very painful event. - A part of the performance has been printed; and the College begs your acceptance of one Copy for yourself, one to be presented to the Academy in Alexandria, of which he was a Patron and liberal Supporter, and one to be reserved for the National University, for the founding and establishing of which he has made so generous and noble bequest,[1]

> I beg leave to subscribe,
> with the most sympathetic
> feelings,
> and with the highest esteem
> and respect,
> Madam,
> your most humble &
> obedient servant
> Joseph Willard[2]

Mrs Washington
(Address) Mrs Washington
Mount Vernon Virginia
From The Revd Joseph Willard April 16. 1800.

ALS, DTP.

1. *An Address in Latin, by Joseph Willard ... and a discourse in English, by David Tappan ... and delivered before the University in Cambridge, Feb 21, 1800, in solemn commemoration of Gen. George Washington. (Charlestown, Mass) E. typis Samuel Etheridge. 1800* 4 to pp. 31.

2. Joseph Willard (1738-1804) graduated from Harvard in 1765. He became pastor at Beverly, Massachusetts in 1772. During the Revolution Willard supported the patriot cause. In 1780 he became one of the founders of the American Academy of Arts and Sciences and was its long-time secretary. In 1781 he became president of Harvard. He was regarded one of the leading American scientists and was well known for his knowledge of mathematics

and astronomy. Politically he was an ardent Federalist. During his presidency Willard rehabilitated the university following the ravages of the war and greatly improved its facilities and broadened the fields of instruction.

From John Gadsby

Mrs. Washington Dr
　To Beef 7/6 To N 7 Beef 9/ To (?)
　Recd the above

John Gadsby[1]

ADS, ViMtV.

　1. John Gadsby, an Englishman, leased the old City Tavern in Alexandria in 1794. He continued to operate a tavern there for a number of years.

To Clement Biddle

Dear Sir　　　　　　　　　　　　　Mount Vernon, April 20: 1800
　Mrs. Washington has received your obliging letter of the 5th instant together with the Articles therein mentioned; and requests me to offer her best thanks for your attention to her small commissions. - She also begs you will be so good as to direct Mr. Fenton to make her two pair of black velvet shoes, which you will be so kind as to forward by the first convenient opportunity. As the interest due on the General's public stock, at the time of his death,[1] as well as what have have accrued since belongs to Mrs. Washington, she will thank you to let her know the amount, and also whether the power you now have will enable you to draw it, or whether another shall be furnished, as she wishes payment to be made from this fund for such articles as she may get from Philadelphia. Mrs. Washington requests Mrs. Biddle & yourself to accept her best wishes

I am Dear Sir, very
respectfully
yr. mo. ob. Ser.
Tobias Lear

Colo. Clement Biddle

Dfs, DTp.

　1. At the time of his death General Washington possessed United States (public) stock valued at $6246. He had loaned the United States over $33,000 during the Revolution, for which his estate received $7450, besides interest. See, Prussing, *The Estate of George Washington, Deceased*; Boston, 1927, p. 113-14.

To Reverend James Kemp

(March 26, 1800)

The text is unavailable. It was written for MW by Tobias Lear and likely contains her acknowledgement of the receipt of Kemp's oration on the death of GW, given February 22, 1800. See supra, Reverend James Kemp to MW.

To General Henry Lee

Dear Sir,   Mount Vernon, April 20: 1800

At the request of Mrs. Washington, I have the honor to acknowledge the receipt of your letter to her of the 10th instant - and to convey her best thanks for your friendly attention in communicating the Unanimous assent of Congress for extending to her the right of franking. - This evidence of personal attention, from the Representatives of our Nation, has impressed her mind with grateful sensibility.

For the repeated assurances of your disposition to contribute, by every means in your power, to her happiness or convenience, Mrs. Washington begs you to accept her sincere thanks, - and at the same time to receive her prayers for your health & happiness - in which most cordially unites Dear Sir,

> Your respectful & Obedt sr
> Tobias Lear

Genl. H. Lee
To Genl. H. Lee April 23d. 1800

Dfs, ViMtV.

To Timothy Pickering

Sir,   Mount Vernon, April 20: 1800

At the request of Mrs. Washington, I have the honor to acknowledge the receipt of your letter to her of the 7th instant, enclosing an authenticated Copy of an Act of Congress, extending to her the privelege of franking letters & packages,[1] - and to beg your acceptance of her best thanks for your politeness in transmitting the same.

> With great respect
> I have the Honor to be
> Sir
> Your most Obedt Servt
> Tobias Lear

Colo Pickering

ADfS, DTP.
  1. See supra, Timothy Pickering to MW, April 7, 1800.

To William Griffith

(April 23, 1800)
The text is not available. It was written for MW by Tobias Lear. It probably contains an acknowledgement of the receipt of a copy of Griffith's oration on the death of GW, delivered at Burlington, New Jersey, February 22, 1800. See supra, William Griffith to MW, April 14, 1800.

To Gouverneur Morris

Dear Sir,   Mount Vernon, April 23d 1800
    Mrs Washington has received, with lively sensibility, your friendly and sympathetic letter of the 7th instant, together with the Oration which accompamied it.[1]
    In acknowledging the receipt of these, at her request, she begs me to assure you, that your public testimony of respect & veneration for your deceased friend, and the expressions of sympathy for her irreparable loss, are received with a grateful heart, while the delicate apology, for not having sooner offered these to her view, enhances their value, as it evinces a feeling heart and a sincere grief. - She offers her best wishes for your health and happiness.

> With great respect
> I have the honor to be
> Sir
> Yr. mo. obt St
> Tobias Lear

Gouvr. Morris Esq.
Gouvr. Morris Esq. April 23d. 1800

ADfS, ViMtV.
  1. See supra, Gouverneur Morris to MW, April 7, 1800.

From A. Gray

Madam,   New Kent, April 28th 1800
    Although unknown to you, I have taken the liberty to make use of your name to convey Safely the several package to Miss M.W. Dandridge now an inmate of yours.[1] If I have presumed too much upon your

goodness in so doing, I beg your pardon for it; & in order to prevent any idea of impropriety in my correspondence with her. I think it is my duty to inform you that leave has been granted me by your young friend's respectable Mother,[2] who honours me with a particular regard, & for whom & her family I entertain more than common sentiments of consideration & friendship.

Let me, Madam, avail myself of this opportunity to pay you my compliment of condolence on the irreparable loss you & your country have experienced by the sudden departure of the greatest man this age has produced. Nature had been for many generations, for many ages, moulding a hero; we have to lament that instead of withdrawing him so soon. She has not allowed him to live for as many ages & as many generations. She could not however effectually destroy that inestimable work of her hands; The illustrious Washington has made his exit, but he will successively live in the heart of all his countrymen & of all good men throughout the enlightened world, his virtues his Services, will be transmitted to the remotest posterity. It will be honourable to endeavor to imitate him. His name will add a new lustre to the personal qualities of those who will bear it; You in particular, who have Shared his glory in so distinguished a manner; who perhaps have been the hidden Spring of his great actions, for whose sake perhaps he won so many trophies, you at whose feet he has laid all the laurels he has been so deservedly crowned with, will undoubtedly enjoy forever the love and veneration of the inhabitants of America & with Sincerity of Heart, I beg leave to assure you that I am deeply impressed with these Sentiments, & think it a peculiar advantage in having an opportunity to inscribe myself,

> Madam,
> Your most humble, obedient
> & respectful Servant
> A. Gray

Mrs. Martha Washington Mount Vernon

ALS, DTP.

1. Martha Washington Dandridge, a niece of Mrs. Washington, was the daughter of Mrs. Washington's brother, Bartholomew Dandridge (1737-1785) and his wife Mary Burbidge.

2. Mary Burbidge Dandridge (17?-1809) was the daughter of Julius King Burbidge of Pamocra, New Kent County.

From John Russell and John West

Boston, 28th April 1800

Madam,   Ansd by T. Lear May 12 1800

As a small tribute of our veneration for the memory of your Illustrious, deceased Husband, and respect for your Amiable and dignified Virtues, we have ventured to Dedicate the volume which accompanies this Letter to You - fondly hoping that it will meet the sanction of your approbation, and in some measure prove a Solace to the gloomy hours which Your and the Nation's irreparable Loss, has occasioned.

with the highest Respect,
we are
Madam
your most Obedt Servts
John Russell[1]

Jno West[2]
Mrs. Martha Washington
Mrs. Martha Washington Mount Vernon
From Messrs. John Russell & John West 28 April 1800

ALS, DTP.

1. John Miller Russell was the author of: *A Funeral Oration on General George Washington, By John Miller Russell, Esq. Boston: Printed by John Russell, for Joseph Nancrede, 1800. 8:22.* See Sabin, *Books Relating to America* Vol. XVIII, p. 150. It is likely this is the volume sent to Mrs. Washington.

2. A John West is listed as the proprietor of a bookstore at No. 75 Cornhill, Boston. In 1797 and 1799 West published a cattalogue of books published in America. See Sabin, *Books Relating to America, Vol. XXVIII, p.74.*

To Dr. John Lemoyere

(May 1, 1800)

The text is not available. It was written for MW by Tobias Lear. Dr. Jean Pierre Le Mayeur, a French dentist, came to America during the Revolution. In the summer of 1783 he came to Washington's headquarters and performed dental work for the General. During 1784 he was living near Alexandria and was a frequent visitor and overnight guest at Mt. Vernon. He later settled in Richmond where, surprisingly enough, he advertised his ability to perform dental surgery and transplant teeth. He was a great favorite of George Washington Parke Custis by virtue of a gift of a wooden toy horse. See *Diaries,* 4:193-94. *Writings,* 27:465.

To John Dexter

Sir,   Mount Vernon, May 6: 1800
    Mrs. Washington requests I will communicate to you her best thanks for your polite letter to her of the 15th of April, inclosing (agreeable to the direction of the Standing Committee of the Society of Cincinnati in the State of Rhode Island) a Copy of Doctor Hitchcocks excellent Discourse on an event deeply afflicting to herself and regreted by all, and she begs you will assure the Committee of the sensibility with which she receives this mark of respect & veneration for her late beloved partner.[1]

                        With great consideration
                        I have the honor to be
                        Sir
                        Your most obdt Sert
                        Tobias Lear

John Dexter Esq. Providence, R.I.
To John Dexter Esq May 6, 1800

ADfS. ViMtV.
    1. See supra, from John Dexter to MW, April 15, 1800.

To John Russell and John West

Gentlemen,   Mount Vernon, May 12th. 1800
    Mrs. Washington has duly received your obliging letter of the 28 of April, with the volume accompanying it; and while requesting me to acknowledge the receipt of them, she begs I will assure you of the sensibility with which she receives this mark of attention, particularly as the subject is one nearest to her heart, and which engrosses her most serious reflections. - She prays you will accept her best wishes for your happiness & prosperity.[1]

                        With great respect
                        I am Gemtl
                        Yr mo ob ser
                        Tobias Lear

Messrs John Russell
John West
Boston To Messrs Jno Russell
John West
May 12th 1800

ADfS, DTP.
    1. See supra, John Russell and John West, to MW, April 28, 1800.

To Mons. A. Belin

Sir   Mount Vernon, May 15, 1800

In compliance with Mrs. Washington's request, I have the honor to acknowledge the receipt of your letter to her of the 15th of March, with three copies of the funeral oration which the French Lodge, L'Amenite', in Philadelphia, have consecrated to the memory of her husband.[1]

Impressed with a lively sense of this testimonial of respect and veneration paid to the memory of the partner of her heart, Mrs. Washington begs the lodge will be assured of her grateful acknowledgements; and you will be pleased to accept her best thanks for the obliging manner in which you have communicated their sympathy in her affliction and irreparable loss.

> I am, sir,
> Very respectfully,
> Your obedient servant
> Tobias Lear
> Secretary to the late
> General Washington

1. See note, Monsieur A. Belin to MW, March 5, 1800. Text, see, *Washington and his Masonic Conveyers*, by *Sidney Hayden*.....NY 1905. p. 215-216.

To William Cunningham

Sir,   Mount Vernon, May 15, 1800

Mrs. Washington has duly received your obliging and sympathetic letter of the 2d of April, together with your Eulogy on the life of her late beloved Husband.[1]

While Mrs Washington requests me to acknowledge the receipt of them, she begs you will be assured of the grateful sense which she entertains of this tribute of respect and veneration ( ) to the memory of the Partner of her heart - and desires that you and Mrs. Cunningham will accept her prayers and best wishes for your health and Happiness.

> I am Sir, very respectfully
> Your most obed svt
> Tobias Lear

Mr. William Cunningham Junr Lunenburg,
near Worcester Massachts
To Mr. Wm. Cunnngham Jr. 15 May 1800

ADfS, ViMtV.

1. See supra, William Cunningham to MW, April 2, 1800.

From Bartholomew Dandridge

(May 25, 1800)

The text is unavailable. Bartholomew Dandridge, Jr., was MW's nephew, the son of her brother, Bartholomew Dandridge, Sr. He had been private secretary to GW during the presidency, after which he became secretary to American legation at the Court of St. James. Later he became counsul to San Domingo. He died there, unmarried, in 1802. 5 W (1) 36.

From Sir John Sinclair

Madam:

Permit me to request your acceptance of a work in which, on various accounts, you will naturally feel yourself deeply interested. In the volume herewith transmitted, you will find the letters of one to whom you had been long united by ties of the tenderest nature, & in the course of the communications which I had the honour of receiving from the president of the United States, you will perceive with what pleasure he anticipated the memorable era "when the Scenes of his Political Life should close and leave him in the Shades of retirement," a circumstance on which he could not have dwelt with such peculiar satisfaction had he not found in you an agreeable companion & a faithful friend.

You will also find various particulars in those letters, honourable to the memory of General Washington, both as a man and as a statesman, and at the conclusion of the whole, an attempt, however imperfectly the task is executed, to do justice to the character of this most extra-ordinary personage whose merits cannot be surpassed by those of any individual that either ancient or modern times have produced.

No monument is unquestionably necessary to perpetuate the fame of so great a man, but anxious that nothing of a mean or mercenary nature should be connected with the name of Washington, I resolved to dedicate any emolument that might be derived from the publication to the paying of some tribute of respect to his memory.

These are all the circumstances connected with the work in question with which it is necessary for me to trouble you.

Sincerely wishing that you may long witness the grateful sense which America must necessarily entertain of the merit & virtues of your illustrious husband, I beg to subscribe myself,

> with much respect
> Madam
> Your very Humble &
> most obedient Servant
> John Sinclair[2]

29 Parliament Street,
2d June 1800
Ansd. by T. Lear Feby 23, 1802

Text taken from a typescript in the Library of Congress, furnished them by Eugene E. Prussing. Location of original unknown.

1. The volume sent Mrs. Washington was probably: *Letters from his Excellency George Washington, President of the United States of America, to Sir John Sinclair, Bart. M.P. on agricultural and other intersting Topics. Engraved from the original Letters, so as to be an exact facsimile of the Hand Writing of that celebrated Character. London: the Letter-press by W. Bulmer and Co.; the Letters engraved by S. J. Neale; and the Work Sold, by G. and W. Nicol. 1800.* 57:4 to. See Catalogue of the Washington Collection in the Boston Athenaeum, A.P.C. Griffin and W. C. Lane, Boston, 1897, p. 299.

2. Sir. John Sinclair, Baron Caithness (1754-1835), was educated as a lawyer in the Inns of Court, and was called to the English bar in 1780. He was a member of Parliament from Caithness for thirty years. He was named Baronet in 1782. On many occasions he was a follower of Pitt but on two occasions there was a wide rift between them. Sinclair was the first president of the Board of Agriculture. In 1811 he became commissioner of excise and was forced to relinquish his parliamentary seat. In 1813 he retired as President of the Board of Agriculture and returned to private life in Edinburgh. He died in 1835 and was entombed in Holyrood chapel. He was a voluminous author and correspondent on agriculture, history, literature, and statistical surveys of England and Scotland, and a staunch advocate of rural and financial reform. One of his contemporaries exclaimed Sinclair was "the most indefatigable man in Britain." See *Dictionary of National Biography.*

To Dr. David Stuart

4th June - 1800

Received from D:d Stuart[1] two hundred and twenty five pounds which with the sums formerly received by me is payment in full of my annuity for the year 1800.[2]

Martha Washington

DS. From the collection of Mr. Elmer Glasser, New London, Ohio. Photocopy furnished through the courtesy of ViMtV.

1. Dr. David Stuart (1758-c. 1814) was the son of Reverend William Stuart, Rector of St Paul's Parish, Stafford County. He was a graduate of the College of William and Mary and received his medical degree from the University of Edinburgh. He Married Eleanor Calvert Custis, widow of John Parke Custis, in 1783. They lived first at Abingdon Plantation, north of Four Mile Run, on the Potomac. About 1792 they moved to his Hope Park Farm, and then later to Ossian Hall. All three residences were in Fairfax County. GW appointed him one of the first commissioners of the District of Columbia. *Diaries*, 4:92.

2. In his will, GW stated that having sold his lands in Pennsylvania, a portion of a tract in New York State, the Dismal Swamp tract, lands in Gloucester County, the lands on the Great Kanawha River, and the Difficult Run tract, the money arising when the contracts were paid, was to be invested in "Bank Stock." The dividends from these shares were to be made available to MW during her life. After her death the principal was to "be subject to the general distribution hereafter directed." The annuity mentioned above probably refers to the interest derived from the bank shares. Prussing, *The Estate of George Washington, Deceased*, Boston, 1927, p. 56-57.

To Reverend Mr. Moffatt

Dear Sir,   Mount Vernon, June 6, 1800

Mrs. Washington has received from the President of the University at Cambridge a Copy of the performances at that Seminary,[1] commemorative of the Death of the Father of our Country, with a request that it might be presented to the Academy in Alexandria,[2] of which he was a Patron and Liberal Supporter; and in compliance with her desire I have now the honor to transmit the same to you.

> With great respect & esteem
> I am dear Sir
> Yr. Mo. Ob. Svt
> Tobias Lear
> The Revd. Mr. Moffatt[3]

Dfs, ViMtV.

1. See supra, letter from Joseph Willard, April 16, 1800, n.1.

2. The Alexandria Academy was founded in 1785, through the efforts of a number of Alexandria residents. George Washington was named a trustee in November, 1785. His nephews, George and Lawrence Washington, were enrolled there. Washington bequeathed the Academy 4000 Dollars (20 shares of Bank of Alexandria stock), only the dividends from which was to be used by the trustees. The Bank of Alexandria wound up its affairs in 1832 and the principal disappeared with it. See Prussing, p. 45; Helderman, *George Washington, Patron of Learning*, New York, 1932, p. 176-83.

3. At this time Reverend Moffatt was the master of the Alexandria Academy. General Washington noted in a letter to Dr. David Stuart, February 26, 1798, he doubted Mr. Moffatt would be able to discharge his duties at the Academy and have time to supervise the lackadaisical George Washington Parke Custis. 36 Writings, 170.

To Reverend Joseph Willard

Reverend Sir,   Mount Vernon, June 6, 1800

In compliance with the request of Mrs. Washington, I have the honor to acknowledge the receipt of your letter to her of the 16th of April, together with three Copies of the performances of the University over which you preside, commemorative of the death of her beloved Husband.[1]

This tribute of respectful veneration paid to the memory of the Partner of her Heart, Mrs. Washington receives with grateful sensibility, and while she acknowledges the deep impression made on her mind by the sympathetic feelings expressed in your letter, as well as in the performances, she begs that her best thanks may be made acceptable to yourself and the college; and requests me to assure you that your wishes, with respect to two of these copies, shall be truly fulfilled.[2]

In making this communication, permit me, Revd Sir, to express the profound Respect which I have for the Character who so honorably presides over my Alma Mater.[3]

(Tobias Lear)

Df, ViMtV.

1. See supra, letter of Reverend Joseph Willard, April 16, 1800.

2. Willard directed Mrs. Washington to retain one copy. A second copy was to be presented to Alexandria Academy. The third copy was to be presented to the National University.

3. Tobias Lear graduated from The University at Cambridge in 1783.

To James Anderson

Mount Vernon, June 21st 1800

Recd of James Anderson[1] Twenty two pounds four shillings d 7 1/2. being the Balc th accot recd by him of P. Marsteller[2] for rent of my House & Lot in Alexandria.

£22.4.7 1/2

M Washington

Receipt 21 June 1800 for £22.4.7 1/2 even Dollars $74 - 10

DS, ViMtV.

1. James Anderson, a native of Fife, Scotland, had lived in America for about five years before coming to Mount Vernon. He succeeded William Pearce as manager in 1797. Washington characterized him as "honest, industrious, and judicious," but found him dilatory and supersensitive. He had an excellent knowledge of farming, husbandry, distilling, and milling. Washington felt his desirable attributes far outweighed his undesirable ones. He remained at Mount Vernon for several years after the General's death. Sometime before 1806 he became manager of the White House tract. He died at White House, New Kent County and was buried there. There is an interesting entry in a family Bible, dated November 28, 1806, "Margaret Anderson was united in marriage with Richard Young, Parson Blair officiating. The marriage ceremony was performed in the very room where Washington was married to the charming widow Custis." Margaret was the daughter of James Anderson. See, VMHB, 52:232-33. Personal communication of Dr. Malcolm Harris, September, 1959.

2. Philip Marsteller, an Alexandria merchant, acted as agent for Washington for the purchase of plantation and personal supplies. He was instrumental in obtaining the German immigrant Overdonck family, employed as laborers and craftsmen, for Mount Vernon. Marsteller rented the General's house in Alexandria. The General recommended him for an army commission. See 29 *Writings*, p. 84, 110-12; 30 *Writings*, p. 360. He was the only one of the six honorary pallbearers at GW's funeral that was not a member of the Masonic order. *Freeman*, 7:630 and n. 72.

From David Humphreys

Madrid, July 5th. 1800
recd - Feby 1802

Dear & respected Madam   Answd by T. Lear - March 6,1802

In conformity to the intimation given in my letter dated the 22nd of Feby last, I now dedicate to you a Poem on the death of your late Husband delivered yesterday at the House of the American Legation in this City, in presence of a respectable number of Persons belonging to different nations. Their partiality to the subject led them to listen to it with peculiar indulgence. And from you, I flatter myself, it will meet with no unfavorable reception even if it should not have the desired effect of diminishing the source of your sorrow, as it contains a representation (tho but an imperfect one) of my melancholy sensations and as it is rather the production of the heart than of the head. When I wrote to you on the 22d of Feby last, I was ignorant that day had been set apart as sacred to the memory of Genl Washington...I was inconscious that the voice of mourning was raised at that moment throughout every district in the United States for your & their irreparable loss. Yet, on a day which had been rendered forever memorable by his birth, it was so natural for the feelings of the nation to be in sympathy, that I could not fail of participating in the mournful solemnity which I afterwards found had been recommended by the President to the People of the Union.

The Anniversary of Independence produces, in some sort, a renovation of the same sentiments. For who can separate the idea of our Washington from that of our Independence? Who can avoid renewing their lamentations that he, who contributed so largely to the establishment of it, is now no more? That he was raised up by Heaven to be more instrumental than any other mortal in obtaining the acknowledgement of our right to be an independent nation & in securing the enjoyment of our civil liberty under a good form of Government, no one has ever pretended to deny. For the accomplishment of this glorious destiny, it was indispensably necessary that he should have been born just so long before the Revolution, as to have acquired all the quality of body & mind adequate to the performance of the important part he was called upon to act. This observation has probably often occurred & been expressed. But I beg leave to mention another which has not to my knowledge, hitherto been made. It seems not unreasonable to suppose (from the wonderful change of sentiments which has since taken place in France) that his death was ordained by Providence to happen exactly at the point of time, when the salutary influence of his example would be more extensively felt than it could have been at any other period. So that it may be said of him, with peculiar propriety, that his whole existence was of a piece & that he died as he lived, for the good of mankind. Perhaps the efficacy of his example could not be so much needed at any moment hereafter, as it is at present, to recommend systems of morals & manners calculated to promote the public felicity. Had he died when the Directory governed France; it cannot be doubted that his name, if not loaded with (?) would at least have been treated with contempt in that country and so far as it was possible consigned to oblivion, the circumstances are now greatly changed, & the Good & the Brave in that, as in every other nation, consider themselves as having lost in him the ornament & glory of the Age. In the British Dominions, distinguished honours have been paid to his memory. In France itself, a public mourning has been decreed for his death. There, those descriptions of Men just now mentioned have given utterance to their generous feelings, and the cry of grief & admiration has resounded in the very place, where the howling of rage & malediction was but lately heard. In the funeral Eulogium pronounced by Fontanes,[1] at the command of the French Government (of which I have made & enclosed a translation for your perusal) you will find many correct, useful & sublime ideas. The men who now possess the Supreme Power have ordered the Models of public Virtue (if I may so express myself) personified at different Epoches, to be placed before them. The bust of Genl Washington is associated with those of the greatest human Characters that have ever existed. This is a happy presage of better intentions & better times; for Ambition & Selfishness, shrinking from his presence, could ill support the mute reproaches of that awful marble.

In either extremity of life so immediately does the lot of Genl Washington appear to have been the charge of Heaven. Since the *mortal* as well as the natal hour if unchangeably fixed, it becomes our duty to acquiesce in the wise dispensation of the Deity. The illustrious father of his Country was long since prepared for that event. You will remember, when his life was despaired of at New York, he addressed these words to me: "I know it is very doubtful whether ever I shall arise from this bed and God knows it is perfectly indifferent to me whether I do or not." --Amidst all the successes & all the honours of this world he knew "that no man is to be accounted happy until after death."

Happy is it that the seal of immortality is set on the character of his, whose counsels, as well as his actions were calculated to encrease the sum of human happiness. The counsels are now the more likely to be spontaneously obeyed, since his career has been successfully finished, and since it is every where fashionable to speak of his talents & services in terms of the highest applause. In fine, the world is disposed in this instance to do justice to the most *unsullied worth* it has perhaps ever witnessed. While Heroes & Statesmen & Nations contemplate with complacency his public life as a perfect model for a public character; it remains for those who knew him in the calm station of retirement, to demonstrate how dearly they prized his amiable disposition & domestic virtues, by imitating his conduct in private life. To be great is the lot of few --- to be good , is within the lot of all. What are the inestimable consolations of a good Conscience, in the hour of affliction, no one knows better than yourself; and it ought not to be indifferent to you that Posterity too will know, that, in all your social relations & in discharging all the duties of your sex, the whole tenour of your conduct has been highly exemplary and worthy of the most unreserved approbation; Indeed, that it has been worthy of the wife of Genl Washington.

With such consolatory reflections I bid you an affectionate adieu, in renewing the assurances of the great regard & esteem, with which

> I have the honour to be
> Dear & respected Madam
> Your Sincere friend &
> humble Servant
> D. Humphreys[2]

Mrs Washington &c &c &c Mount Vernon
P.S. I request my best respects may be offered to all my friends with you & in your vicinity. The poem alluded to is prepared for publication in America.
From Colo. Humphrey July 5. 1800

ALS, ViMtV.

1. Eloge funebre de Washington. Prounce dans le temple de Mars, par Louis Fontanes, de 20 pluviose an 8 (Feb. 8, 1800) Paris; de l'Imprimerie de H. Agasse, 1800.

2. David Humphreys (1752-1818), a native of Connecticut , graduated from Yale, and shortly after joined the Revolutionary Army. He had a brilliant military, career rising to the rank of Lieutenant-colonel and Aide-de-camp to Washington. Following the war his diplomatic career was as brilliant as his military one. He was abruptly called home by his political enemy, Jefferson. He then then turned to raising thoroughbred merino sheep and founded a successful company for the manufacture of cloth. Throughout his adult life he wrote considerable poetry. He had a life-long devotion to General Washington, which was reciprocated. He was without a doubt Washington's favorite aide and confidante. His close friend, John Trumbull, penned a poetic eulogy which ended, "here Humphreys rests - belov'd of Washington." See, *Humphreys*, 2:439-41.

Thomas Peter to Lawrence Lewis

(July 5, 1800)
Recd. July 5, 1800 of Mr J. Carlton, Clerke of the Potomack Company Four hundred and forty one dollars, sixty nine cents by power of an order drawn in favor of Mrs Martha Washington by Law Lewis[1] acting Executor of Genl George Washington and by me applyd to the use of Mrs Washington agreeable to her instructions.[2]

> Thomas Peter[3]

(Duplicate)
Mr. Lawrence Lewis
Woodlawn Virginia

Receipt
Thomas Peter
$441.69
July 5 1800

ADS, NjMH.

1. Lawrence Lewis was a nephew of General Washington, and the husband of Mrs. Washington's granddaughter, Eleanor Parke Custis Lewis. He was one of the executors of General Washington's estate.

2. According to General Washington's will, each of the legatees was allowed to take one share of his stock in the Potomack Company. See, *The Last Will and Testament of George Washington*, Mount Vernon, Va., 6th Edition, 1992, pp. 26, 48

3. Thomas Peter was the husband of Mrs. Washington's granddaughter, Martha Parke Custis Peter. He was one of the executors of Mrs. Washington's estate.

From James Anderson

Madam   Ferry, 21 July 1800

Ever since I had a Management of this Estate (I am sorry to say) it has been very unproductive.

This spring past, the prospect was a little flattering. But from the attacks of the Fly, and Rust, the crop of wheat will be very poor, and that crop is all the Dependence And as will appear by the inclosed Note £ 362 - 10 will be requisite to pay Hires on the Estate, Exclusive of finding those persons to whom those Hires are payable. After this the other expences of the Farms Such as Iron, Leather for Shoes, backbands, & ca, Linen for the Negroes Shirts Taxes Doctors Bill the incidental expence which can neither be forseen nor yet avoided. Of all these a copy is inclosed.

And being fully convinced that the sales (after rendering to the House at Mount Vernon the articles wanted for consumption there) will not nearly Ballance the expence that I must confess I feel hurt. And think it my Duty to resign. And do hereby beg leave to inform that on the last of December next, I shall retire from the management of this Estate of Mount Vernon - Meantime any arrangement which you may think right to make, respecting the Farms - my services are at your command untill the time mentioned[1]

And I beg leave to offer my sincere thanks for the many favors bestowed on my Family & me. And with much esteem I am

> Madam
> Your most obed &
> Humble Svt
> Jas Anderson

From a photostat in the Manuscript Division, Library of Congress.

1. The letter illustrates Anderson's sensitive nature that Washington found annoying. On the whole, Anderson was a capable manager. Someone, possibly Lawrence Lewis, prevailed upon him to remain, for he later managed the White House tract in New Kent County. See supra, MW to James Anderson, June 21, 1800, n.1.

From David Hale

District of Maine Portland, July 24th 1800

Madam,   (answd Oct 31 1800)

Having been summoned on a late occasion by the voice of my fellow citizens of this town & vicinity, to contribute my mite, however small, towards perpetuating the remembrance of that important era in the annals of our country, which is justly celebrated as the birthday of her Independence; I seize the opportunity, by presenting you a copy of what was exhibited on that occasion, to testify to you the veneration with which I have been accustomed to contemplate the virtues & talents of your deceased lord, who bore so distinguished a part in the establishment of that Independence - to assure you of the deep sense, which I entertain, of the extent of the calamity occasioned by his decease, both as it respects your individual, and as it respects the public, loss - and to offer you the sincerest condolence, which a heart, penetrated with ye magnitude of its country's woe, & overwhelmed with grief excited by the decease of amiable, an affectionate wife, is capable of bestowing.

> I have the honour to be
> Madam,
> Your obedient servant
> David Hale[1]

Mrs. Martha Washington
Mrs. Martha Washington Mount Vernon Virginia
From David Hale July 24, 1800

ALS, ViMtV.
1. An Oration...Portland...July 4, 1800...by David Hale...Portland...E.A.Jenks. 1800.

From Charles Lee

Madam   Alexandria, 19th September 1800

I have the honor to enclose a draft of an instrument which I have prepared for your last Will agreeable to the ideas contained in the Instructions given to me under your hand which are now also returned to you that you may be better enabled to consider the same.

Permit me to observe that it appeared proper to limit your legacy relative to the Glebe to a reasonable period for buying it, least your intended bounty to the Court should be locked up in the hands of your executors an unreasonable length of time.

I have left a blank to be filled up by yourself as to the *number* of prints that your grandson is empowered to choose.

The Saver (sic) China being of a nature difficult of division among many and having signified your preference they should be sold if their value should be nearly obtainable, I thought it best to prevent disagreements that the sale should be devised without condition. Any of the family may then buy any part that shall be most desirable. Instead of Bank Stock I think on every account *account funded* stock is to be preferred for your purposes.

These matters I have stated that you may not suppose I have negliently deviated from your intentions: on the contrary it has been endeavour to fulfill them in the most convenient perfect and advantageous manner.

It is to be regretted that accidently the instrument is soiled by a drop or two of ink. This will not however affect its validity when duly executed.

There should be two or more disinterested Witnesses who should subscribe as witnesses in your presence, and it will be prudent to put your signature to the bottom of each page and in their presence who should so attest.

With sentiments of profound respect I have the honor to be Madam your most obedient humble servant

Charles Lee[1]

Copy in a clerks hand, contained in a bound manuscript: "Inventory and Settlement of the Estate of Martha Washington." Arlington County Court House, Arlington, Virginia.

1. Charles Lee (1758-1815), the elder brother of Henry (Lighthorse Harry) Lee. He was a graduate of the College of New Jersey in 1775 and received his legal training from Jared Ingersoll in Philadelphia. From 1777 until 1789 he was Naval Officer of the South Potomac. Lee was also a delegate to the Continental Congress and the Virginia Assembly. He worked diligently for ratification of the Federal Constitution by the Virginia Convention. In 1795 Lee was appointed Attorney-general by President Washington, serving until 1801. He was a staunch supporter of GW's policies and an anti-Jeffersonian Federalist.

To David Hale

Sir, Mount Vernon, Octr 31 1800

Mrs Washington requests me to acknowledge the receipt of your letter to her, under date of the 24th of July, together with the Oration which accompanied it, and to offer her grateful thanks for your expressions of sympathy on her afflicting loss, and to beg you will be assured

that she receives with warm sensibility, the public tribute of respect &
veneration which you have paid to the memory of her dear departed
Husband[1]

> With great respect
> I am Sir
> Your most Obed Servt
> Tobias Lear

Mr. David Hale
To David Hale Esq Octr. 31st. 1800

ADfS, ViMtV.
   1. See supra, David Hale to MW, July 24, 1800.

To Mary Stillson Lear

My Dear Madam   Mount Vernon, November 11th 1800
   I received your kind letter of september the 8th a few days ago - it
gives me pleasure to find by it, that you were in good health - we have
had an uncommon sickly autumn; all my family whites, and Blacks, have
been very sick, many of ill - thank god they have all recovered again and
I was so fortunate as not to loose any of them As to myself - I have always
one complaint or another - I never expect to be well as long as I live in
this world Mr Lear is tolerable well and for the present talks of setting
himself down at his farm[1] he comes often to see me
   The Boys are very well,[2] I am told lincoln is a very cleaver Boy and
learns his book very well - the three Boy live in Charles town they are
borded thair and have a very good school and master school Mr Lear
thinks, the Boys has had very good health ever since they went into that
back country - Maria[3] is with her aunt Hammond[4] - who is a second
mother to her - I am told that she is a very fine child - I have not seen her
since she first went up the country - I have long wished to see her but it
has been thought improper to take her from school I with much pleasure
send you the hair you so obliging desired[5] and shall be always ready to
give you any information I can that will contribute to your happyness
   with much esteem and regard I am dr madam your affectionate
Friend

> Martha Washington

Text taken from the facsimile published in Decatur, *Private Affairs of George
Washington*, p. 306. Boston, 1933.

ALS.
   1. At the marriage of Fanny Bassett Washington and Tobias Lear in 1795, the President
presented them a life lease, rent free interest in a 360 acre tract of land as a wedding present.

The tract was called Walnut Tree Farm and was a section of the Clifton Neck portion of Mount Vernon. It later became known as "Wellington". It still stands. In his will GW confirmed the lease for the lifetime of Lear.

2. George Fayette Washington, (1790-1865). He married Maria Frame. Charles Augustine Washington, (ca 1790 - ?). He was unmarried. The date of his death is unknown. He is said to have died in Cadiz, Spain. Benjamin Lincoln Lear, (1791-1832). He was the only son of Tobias Lear and his first wife, Polly Long.

3. Anna Maria Washington, (1788-1814). She was the oldest child of George Augustine Washington and Fanny Bassett Washington. She married Reuben Thornton.

4. Mildred Washington Hammond, (1777-1804), was the daughter of General Washington's brother, Charles and therefore a sister of George Augustine Washington. She married Thomas Hammond and was the recipient of a 1/23 share of the estate of GW.

5. Mary Stillson Lear, the mother of Tobias Lear, had apparently requested a lock of the General's hair.

From Robert Lewis

Dear Aunt, (Ca. 1801?)

I am notified thro' my Brother Lawrence[1] of your inclination for a settlement of my Rental a/c. for the last year - Had I been prepared, I assure you, it wou'd have superceded the necessity of a summons, as it has ever been a rule with me never to retain money in my hands which was intended for or belonged to another person - I have at present near one hundred dollars of your money which has been the Collectors for State & Continental taxes - The balance (shou'd there be any) together with what I may collect from the Sheriff when the executions shall be return'd satisfied, will be remitted as early as possible-Tomorrow, I sett out by appointment to receive from the Sheriff, if the Sales of property has taken place, the whole or such part of the money as he may have recd. on a/c of the distresses - when I return, you shall hear more fully from me - I must now request, as I have often thought to do, that you will not pay any act. which may be presented to you by any publick officer on account of that part of the Estate which I have the management of- You have not been apprised, I judge, of the valuation of the property by the assistant assessors, if not, you will most assuredly be taken in - There is also claims against the Estate of Geo: Mercer which have been frequently & artfully blended in the Generals a/cs

Of this circumstance, I am the only person acquainted - you will, therefore, shou'd application be made, please to refer them to me.

I am sorry to hear of your indisposition , and hope ere this arrives, that you may have perfectly recover/d - A little excursion up the Country, probably as far as Doctr. Stuarts[2] might be attended with beneficial consequences. - I remain, with great respect, your very affectionate nephew

Robt: Lewis -[3]

ADfS, ViMtV.

1. Lawrence Lewis (1767-1839) was the son of Fielding Lewis (1725-1781) and his second wife, Betty Washington Lewis (sister of GW - 1733-1797). This nephew of GW married Eleanor Parke Custis, granddaughter of MW and "adopted daughter" of the Washingtons. They were married February 22, 1799 at Mount Vernon. At the time of this letter they were still residing at Mount Vernon.

2. Dr. David Stuart (1753- c.1814) married Eleanor Calvert Custis, widow of John Parke Custis, in 1783. He was the son of Rev. William Stuart of St. Paul's Parish, Stafford County. Stuart was a graduate of William and Mary; in medicine, from the University of Edinburgh. He was a member of the Virginia Assembly, the Virginia ratifying convention, and one of the first commissioners for the District of Columbia. 4 *Diaries* 72.

3. Robert Lewis (1769-1829), son of Fielding Lewis and his wife Betty Washiington Lewis. See supra. MW did not leave Mount Vernon for New York until May, 1789. Robert was instructed by his uncle to accompany her to New York. For a detailed account of this interesting journey by Robert, see "A Journey from Fredericksburg Virginia to New York," in the Mount Vernon archives. He remained in New York as secretary to the President until 1791. He acted as agent for the management of GW's western lands and continued in that capacity after GW's death.

5 *Diaries* 448.

To Martha Washington Dandridge

My dear Patty[1]   Mount Vernon, February 12th 1801
     I send this letter for you to your Brother Julious[2] by Mr David Randolph[3] as a safe convenience. I wished it to get to your hands soon - in it I send three Hundred dollars one hundred dollars to your sister Polly[4] one hundred dollars to Fanny[5] and one hundred dollars for yourself - in six fifty dollar bills - it is the entrest of Mr L Lewis[6] Bond that I gave to you and them I thank you my dear patty for your affectionate letter I have been and am at this time very much indisposed Nelly has been very unwell and Washington ill[7] thank god he is getting better Fanny went to the city with Mrs Law[8] soon after Christmas and has not returned yet - it will always give me pleasure to see you or either of your sisters here - I have often lemented the great distance I am from you
     My love and good wishes to your mother sisters & Brother[9] and believe me your ever affectionate

M Washington

ALS, NN.

1. Martha Washington Dandridge, daughter of MW's brother Bartholomew Dandridge and his wife, Mary Burbidge. She married Dr. William Halyburton, a native of Haddington, Scotland.

2. Julius Burbidge Dandridge, son of Bartholomew and Mary Dandridge, d. unmarried. He was cashier of the United States Bank, Richmond.

3. David Randolph (1760-1830), was a captain of dragoons in the Revolution. GW appointed him United States Marshall for Virginia. He was the son of Richard Randolph of "Curles" and his wife, Anne Meade Randolph. He married Mary Randolph of "Tuckahoe." See Henderson, *Washington's Southern Tour*, p. 59. Boston, 1923.

4. Mary Dandridge, m. John Willison.

5. Francis Dandridge, m. George William Hunt Minge.

6. Major Lawrence Lewis (1767-1839), the son of Fielding Lewis of Kenmore, and his wife, Betty Washington Lewis, sister of GW. He was manager at Mount Vernon and married Eleanor Parke Custis (Nelly).

7. Nelly (Eleanor Parke Custis) and Washington (George Washington Parke Custis), grandchildren of MW.

8. Elizabeth Parke Custis Law was the wife of Thomas Law, and a granddaughter of MW.

9. Mary Burbidge Dandridge (d. 1802) was the daughter of Julius King Burbidge and his wife, Lucy. They lived at "Pamocra", New Kent County. The sisters are mentioned above. The brother referred to is probably Julius, although there were three others, one of which was Bartholomew, Jr., one of GW's private secretaries.

To Colonel Lloyd Nicholas Rogers

Sir[1]   Mount Vernon, Sept 10, 1801

I have received your polite letter of the 10th ult. and it gives me pleasure to comply with your request. The only miniature I have of myself was painted by Mr. Robison[2] in 93, Mr Peter[3] will carry it to the city and endeavour to procure an early opportunity of sending it to you in Baltimore. The lock of hair you requested I enclose in this letter, mine is with the picture.

The regard I have ever felt for you and Mrs. Rogers[4] added to the esteem my Beloved and lamented Friend, allways expressed for you, renders this opportunity of gratifying your wishes peculiarly pleasing - The talents of your daughter I have heard highly spoken of, and have no doubt that her performances are worthy of him from whom she inherits her abilities. Mrs. Rogers and yourself will accept my regards and wishes for your health and happiness.

With great esteem
I am yr obt Srvt
M Washington

Copy of letter is in an unknown hand-in the collections of Smith-Harrison Museum, Washington-Custis Artifacts, Columbiana, Alabama.

1. Lloyd Nicholas Rogers (1753-1822), son of Nicholas Rogers, a Baltimore merchant, was educated in Europe. At the outbreak of the Revolution he returned to America. He became Aide to Major-general Charles Jean Baptiste Tronson du Coudray and later to Baron Kalb, attaining the rank of colonel.

2. Archibald Robertson (1765-1835) was educated as an artist in Edinburgh and the Royal Academy. Learning that he was immigrating to America, David Erskine, Lord Buchan, commissioned him to paint a portrait of GW, which was to be sent to him at Dryburgh Abbey. Robertson was well received at Mount Vernon. In addition to the portrait he painted miniatures of the family. He was an accomplished miniaturist, architect, and linguist.

3. Thomas Peter (1769-1834) was the son of Robert Peter, a prosperous merchant of Georgetown. In 1795 he married Martha Parke Custis, the granddaughter of MW.

4. Eleanor Buchanan Rogers (1757-1812), married her first cousin, Colonel Nicholas Rogers.

To Robert Lewis

(Mount Vernon)

Received September 15th 1801 of Robert Lewis[1] (on account of the collection of my rents) four hundred and eight dollars.

M Washington

DS, NN.

1. Robert Lewis (1769-1829) was the son of Fielding Lewis and Elizabeth(Betty) Washington Lewis, sister of GW. He was born at "Millbank," later called "Kenmore". The President hired him as a secretary upon taking office in 1789. He remained with his uncle until 1791, when he returned to Virginia. Robert accompanied MW from Mount Vernon to New York, several weeks after GW's inauguration. (Robert Lewis's diary, "Journey from Fredericksburg Virginia to New York, May 13-20, 1789, VIMV). After his return to Virginia Robert acted as his uncle's agent and manager. He was a frequent and welcome visitor at Mount Vernon.

To Colonel Richard Varick

Sir,[1]   Mount Vernon, December 15th 1801

Your several favours of Nov. 20th 28th & December 2nd I have received and beg you will accept my sincerest acknowledgement for them and the excellent apples you have been so good as to send me. The first barrel have came safe to hand and your friends here have feasted on the fine Spitzenburghs - The Peppins are also extremely good, and I have only to regret, that you have not added to the obligation by forwarding the bill for them.

Will you oblige me by informing the cost of those apples & the remaining three barrells you have been so good as to select for me, & how I shall convey the money to you - Mrs Varick[2] & yourself will accept my best thanks for the trouble you have taken in wrapping and packing the apples, which will last very well I have no doubt Also for the enquiries you have made respecting my old Cook Hercules,[3] since I had the pleasure of seeing you I have beem so fortunate as to engage a white cook who answers very well. I have thought it therefore better to decline taking Hercules back again.

Your friends here are very happy to hear of yours and Mrs Varick health and remember with pleasure your kind visit to M Vn, we hope you will be induced to repeat it the next summer - when Mr & Mrs Lewis[4] will also be sincerely pleased to see you in their dwelling - Mr & Mrs Law[5] are well and with Mr & Mrs Lewis, my nieces & grandson unite in respectful & affectionate regards to you & Mrs Varick, with acknowledgements for your kind remembrance of them.

My regards and best wishes attend Mrs Varick & yourself.

> Beleive me your obliged
> Hble servant
> M Washington[6]

Free[7] Coll Richard Varick New York M Washington
Dec.15. 1801 From Mrs. Washington Bal. 28d

The letter was written and signed for MW by Tobias Lear. There is a franking signature of MW on the cover. Photocopy supplied by Mrs. Frank Hollowbush, Allenhurst, New Jersey, a previous owner. Present location unknown. Parke-Bernet Galleries, Sale No. 1385, item 389, November 25, 1952.

1. Richard Varick (1753-1831), a native of New Jersey, became a captain in a New York regiment in 1775. Later he became military secretary to Major-general Philip Schuyler, and then deputy quarter master-general of the Northern department, with the rank of lieutenant-colonel. When Arnold took command at West Point in August, 1780, Varick became his aide. At the discovery of Arnold's defection he was devastated with grief. Feeling he was being looked upon with suspicion, he asked GW to appoint a court of inquiry. He was acquited of all responsibility and complicity. Later GW selected him to act as his recording secretary. His duties consisted of classifying, copying and arranging GW's war-time correspondence. His work in this capacity was monumental and he received the appreciation and accolades of GW. The forty-four volumes of this work, still in use, are called The Varick Transcripts (DLC-Washington Papers). Varick became speaker of the New York assembly, attorney-general, and mayor of New York. He was an ardent Federalist.

2. Maria Roosevelt Varick, daughter of Isaac and Cornelia Hoffman Roosevelt.

3. Hercules, affectionately called "Uncle Harkless," was slave and cook at Mount Vernon. During the presidential years he was taken to New York and Philadelphia. Periodically he was returned to Mount Vernon with the Washingtons, since he was needed as a cook. This also served the purpose of averting the Pennsylvania statute that gave slaves their freedom after a continuous residence of six months. Hercules was something of a "dandy," dressing every evening in the height of fashion, cane in hand, strutting the streets of New York and Philadelphia, to the admiration of his fellow blacks. At various times special clothing was bought for him, which may have contributed to his vanity. Upon the return of the Washingtons to Mount Vernon in 1797, Hercules, apparently missing the delights of the city, departed. The Washingtons, much indisposed by the loss of their favorite cook, made frequent attempts to locate him during the winter of 1798. They seemed reasonably certain he had gone to Philadelphia. In letters to Frederick Kitt, of January 10th and 29th, 1798, GW even suggested hiring a "private" eye to search for him in his usual haunts. This experience brought about GW's resolve never to purchase another slave. Hercules was never found. See, *Decatur*, pp.169, 173, 190, 214, 224, 239, 277, 296; 36 *Writings*, 70, 123, 148.

4. Lawrence Lewis and Eleanor Park Custis Lewis. He was a nephew of GW and she, a granddaughter of MW.

5. Thomas Law and Elizabeth Parke Custis Law, she a sister of Eleanor Parke Custis Lewis.

6. The letter and signature is in the hand of Tobias Lear.

7. This is the only free frank of MW that is known. The reason for the twenty eight cent charge is unknown.

To George Washington Parke Custis

March 4th, 1802[1]

I give to my grand son, George Washington Parke Custis my Mulato man Elish[2] that I bougt of Mr Butler Washington[3] to him and his heirs forever

M Washington[4]

ADS, ICHi.

1. This copy of the codicil to the will of MW, dated March 4, 1802 is in the Gunther Collection, Chicago Historical Society. It is not on paper of the period, shows evidences of having been traced or deliberately forged, and probably dates from the late nineteenth century.

2. Here MW refers to Elijah, who was probably a dower slave, since MW was transferring ownership to her grandson. She would not have done so had Elijah been a Washington slave. See *Prussing*, p. 392.

3. Butler Washington (d. 1817) was the son of John Washington and Catherine Washington Washington. They were "Chotank Washingtons" from King George County.

4. As in the authentic will, there are "signatures" of Martha Peter and two of MW.

To Winthrop Sargent

Sir[1]   Mount Vernon, March 30th 1802

Your very polite favour of January 27th I have just received, and request you will accept my sincere acknowledgments for the expressions of respect contained in it. Nothing can be more soothing to my mind than *those* testimonies of respect and veneration paid to my deceased and ever regretted Friend, particularly by those who knew him well, and whom he considered with esteem and regard -

Permit me to offer my best wishes for the welfare of Mrs Sargent,[2] and to express my hopes, that your expectations in regard to a son may be realized.

My family unite in sincere wishes for the happiness of Yourself and Mrs. Sargent

Please to accept the esteem
and regard of
Your ob't Serv't
M. Washington[3]

Colo Winthrop Sargent The Grove near Natchez.

Df, MHi.

1. Winthrop Sargent (1753-1820), a member of a prominent Massachusetts family, Harvard graduate, and brevet major in the Continental Army. Following the war he became one of the organizers and developers of the Ohio Company. Sargent played an important part, politically and militarily, in the development of the Northwest Territory. He became General Arthur St. Clair's adjutant-general in the ill-fated expedition against the Indians in

1791 and was wounded twice. Resigning his secretaryship of the Northwest Territory in 1798, he became the first governor of the Mississippi Territory. His ardent federalism and conscientious administration led to frequent criticism by the frontier republican faction. Jefferson refused to appoint him in 1801 and he returned to his plantation near Natchez. Sargent was a member of the American Philosophical Society and other learned societies because of his interest in scientific subjects.

2. Mary Mc Intosh Williams Sargent, second wife of Winthrop Sargent.

3. Draft in the handwriting of Tobias Lear.

To Edward Stabler

Mount Vernon, April 22nd - 1802

Mrs. Washington desires Mr. Stabler[1] will send by the bearer, a quart bottle of the best Castor Oil and bill for it.-[2]

(Address) Mr. Stabler Alexandria

AN, Alexandria Landmarks Society. Original has disappeared.

1. Edward Stabler, a young Quaker from Petersburg. He opened a pharmacy at Fairfax and King Streets in 1792. The pharmacy is now a museum and is operation by the Alexandria Landmarks Society.

2. Written for MW by an unidentified person.

To Elizabeth Willing Powel

Dear Madam   (n.d., Philadelphia)

I am much obliged to you for your kind enquiries - I am today much better - I have had a very violent cough which has prevented my taking rest - I hope and trust the cold is now better - and that I shall in a few days be able to see my friends

I am truly sorry to hear that you are unwell - colds are so general at this season of the year - Doctor Jones[1] tells me that a great many are complaining in this town

The President joins me in good wishes that you may speedyly get well of the Head ack

believe me Dr Madam most
affectionate Friend & M
Washington January 17

ALS, ViMtV.

1. Dr. John Jones (1729-1791), a native of Wales, received his medical degree at the University of Rheims, and praticed medicine and surgery in Philadelphia. In 1775 he published a treatise on wounds and fractures. During the Revolution he served as a surgeon for the American army. He taught surgery and obstetrics in Philadelphia and was a member of the Philadelphia Agricultural Society. Jones was the personal physician of Benjamin Franklin and an occasional one to GW. Dr. Jones was sent for, from Philadelphia, as a consultant during GW's near fatal illness of May, 1790.

To -

Dear Madam   (n.p., n.d.)
Tom brings you 37 lb of butter which is all that could be put into the
pots we intended to come see you this week but Jack told us you woud
come some day but did not say what day prevented our visiting you as
we shoud have done had we not expected you every day, as the weather
was so fine we shall expect to you soon - Thair is a cask of apples hear
for you Mr Wan woud have sent them but he had no barrel that the
malloges[1] coud be put in or shoud sent them boath to you. I am with my
compliments yours very sincerely

                                                      Martha Washington

ALS, ViMtV.
    1. Unidentified.

To Mrs. John Beale Bordley

                                                            (n.p., n.y.)
    Mrs Washington's affectionate compliments to Mrs. Bordley and if
she wishes to go to the play tonight - it will be agreeable to Mrs W - to
drink tea with Mrs Bordley any evening next week -[1] June 25

Df (secretary) ViMtV.
    1. Sarah Fishbourne Mifflin Bordley ws the second wife of John Beale Bordley (1727-1804).
Bordley was a native of Annapolis, where he studied law and later became a jurist. He had
an avid interest in farming, crop rotation and experimental agriculture. He published a
number of tracts on agricultural subjects. The Bordleys moved to Philadelphia in 1791. For
a number of years they were welcome visitors at Mount Vernon and they were frequent
guests of the Washingtons in Philadelphia. Their daughter, Elizabeth, was a friend and
correspondant of Eleanor Parke Custis Lewis.

To Mr. Foster

                                                            (n.p., n.d.)
    Mrs Washingtons compts to Mr Foster[1] and sends a little book of his
with "John Gilpin"[2] in it which Mrs Crawford[3] had to look at some time
ago - Mrs W. thought it had long since been returned - but should Mr.
Foster think he cannot readily dispose of it, she will either send it to Mrs
C or take it herself. Compliments to Mrs Foster
    (Address leaf) Mr Foster Please sir let my servant have a brush for
cleaning a house

AN (unknown hand) ViWF.

1. Foster is said to have been the operator of a country store near Alexandria. See note 1., infra.

2. "John Gilpin's Ride," by William Cowper.

3. This might be the Mrs. Crawford who, in May of 1786, was on the point of having her negroes sold to satisfy a debt of her deceased husband. GW offered to settle the account for her to prevent the sale. See, 28 *Writings*, 415.

To Mr. Foster

(n.p., n.d.)

Mrs Washington will thank Mr. Foster[1] to let her know what he sells needles at by the thousand, and to answer the enquiries contained in her note of Saturday.

AN by Tobias Lear.

ViMtV.

1. Accompanying the above is the following note: The "Mr Foster" to whom this note of Mrs Washington is addressed, is said to have been "a large country store keeper" in Alexandria Va. between the years 1790 & 1800- The person who sent me the above, said he "had several such strips of Mrs W's they are all gone but the one I send you - June 1863 - D.D." The writer of this note remains unidentified.

To Elizabeth Willing Powel

(n.p., n.d.)

General & Mrs Washington present their compliments to Mr & Mrs Powel, and are very much obliged to them for their kind invitation to a tea party tomorrow but the General dining out - Mrs Washington engaged (on wednesday last) Mrs Debert[1] & Miss Reed[2] to take a family Dinner and spend the day with her tomorrow - Expecting to be alone - which will put it out of her power to wait upon Mrs Powel as she otherwise would have done with pleasure

(Address) Mrs Powel

ALS, (Third person). ViMtV.

1. Possibly the wife of Dennis DeBerdt. He was the brother of Esther DeBerdt Reed, wife of Colonel Joseph Reed, friend, confidante, and aide to General Wshington, Member of the Continental Congress, and President of the Supreme Executive Council of Pennsylvania. See, *The Life of Esther DeBerdt, Afterwards Esther Reed of Pennsylvania*, Philadelphia, 1853, p. 18-27. 2. This may be Martha Reed (1771-1821), the invalid daughter of Col. Joseph Reed and Esther DeBerdt Reed, *Ibid*, p. 166-67.

To Eleanor Park Custis

My Dear Nelly   (N.P., N.D.)

I expect to get your things every moment to put up - a servant of Mrs Easterns[1] is going to Alexandria the Box will be put under her care for you I cannot get a pair of white tassles in the city - I think your chemese will look much better with a handkerchief than without - I have sent you one of mine in case you should not have one of your own - I have put up every thing that I could think you could want - ask your cousin[2] to assist in dressing you when you go to the ball - I wish you to look as neat as possable - and let all of your things be of a peice my love to you & wish you may have as much pleasure as you expect - going to these places one always expects more pleasure than they realize after the matter is over

Wednesday morning My Dear child - after hurring Mrs Waight[3] and getting your things put up and sent to the place they were to go from - the person was not ready to go and the stage is gone without it - I shall have it put under the care of the stage master and send it tomorrow - I hope you will get it early on Monday - The feathers are the only tolerable ones to be had They have been picked so often that they are (illegible) left that was handsome give my love to your sister & the President joins me in love to you and wishing you every happyness - I am my dear your ever

affectionate
M Washington

as I told you before you must not depend altogether on the dress that is going in the stage[4] give my love to your cousin
Miss Nelly Custis

ALS, ViMtV.
    1. Unidentified.
    2. Unidentified.
    3. Unidentified.
    4. The letter was possibly written from Philadelphia about 1795, since MW refers to "the President." Prior to this Eleanor would not be of sufficient age to attend a ball. She was probably at Mount Vernon. The stage leaving on Thursday and arriving on Monday would be consistent with the usual five day journey from Philadelphia to Alexandria.

To Mrs. George Clinton

(N.P., N.D.)

Mrs Washington presents her Compliments to Mrs Clinton,[1] and find that Congress will contrary to their usual practice on saturdays assemble tomorrow, proposes to Mrs Clinton to visit the federal Building at six O'Clock tomorrow afternoon, if it should be convenient to her.

Friday afternoon[2]

AN. By an unidentified secretary. NHi.

1. Cornelia Tappan Clinton, wife of Governor George Clinton

2. The note was undoubtedly written during the period when New York City served as the capitol city (1789-1790). Mrs. Washington took up residence there in May, 1789 and continued her residence until she and the President left for Philadelphia on August 30, 1790.

From Mrs. George Clinton

(n.p., n.d.)

Mrs Clinton presents her respectful Compliments to Mrs Washington - It will be equally covenient - to her to visit the Federal Building this afternoon & she will accordingly be ready to wait upon Mrs Washington for that purpose at Six O Clock.

Satturday monring

Df by Governor George Clinton.[1] NHi.

1. George Clinton (1739-1812) served in the French and Indian War. He was trained as a lawyer and early became a prominent member of the minority revolutionary party in New York. Clinton was elected to the New York Assembly and in 1775 was elected to the Second Continental Congress. During the revolution he served as a brigadier-general of militia as well as in the Continental Army. He was elected seven times as governor of New York. As a young man and thereafter till his death he was a political power in New York. He twice served as vice-president of the United States and was once a candidate for president.

To Jane Donaldson Fairfax

(Mount Vernon, n.d.)

Mrs Washington returns compliments and many thanks to Mrs Fairfax,[1] for her polite attention in procuring the patterns of Lutestrings,[2] - Mrs Washington does not recollect which of them resembles most Mrs Peter's dress, she will therefore defer getting either until Mrs P. comes to Mount Vernon; she is expected the last of the ensuing week.-

Mrs. Washington and Miss Custis unite in compliments to the Ladies at Mount Eagle -

Mount Vernon

AN. (Third person). Copy furnished by ViMtV. Location of original unknown.

1. Lutestring - var. of lustring; a kind of glossy silk fabric; a dress or ribbon of this material. (OED).

2. Jane "Donaldson" Fairfax ("Jenny" Dennison), second wife of Rev. Bryan, eight Lord Fairfax. They lived at "Monteagle," Fairfax County. She died in 1805.

Recipe

Recipe Take the wild or Indian Turnip when it is in blossom or has the fruit on it, wash and cut it in thin slices Run a thread thro it, and hang it in the chimney corner to dry quickly but do not let the fire come to it - when it is very dry power it in a mortar - the potion to take as much as will lay on the point of a knife when the difficulty of breathing or coughing come on make it in to a bolus with honey - it may be repeated as often as the stomack will bear till it gives ease.

AN, MHi.

The Will of Martha Washington

In the name of GOD Amen I Martha Washington of Mount Vernon in the County of Fairfax being of sound mind and capable of disposing of my Worldly Estate do make Ordain and declare this to be my last will and Testament hereby revoking all other Wills and Testaments by me heretofore Made IMPRIMIS, It is my desire that all my Just Debts may be punctually paid, and that as speedily as the same can be done.

ITEM. I give and devise to my Nephew Bartholomew Dandridge[1] and his Heirs my lot in the town of Alexandria situate on Pitt and Cameron Streets devised to me by my late Husband George Washington deceased

ITEM. I give and bequeath to my four Nieces Martha W. Dandridge,[2] Mary Dandridge,[3] Frances Lucy Dandridge[4] and Francis Henly the debt of Two Thousand pounds due from Lawrence Lewis[6] and secured by his bond, to be equally divided between them or such of them as shall be alive at my death and to be paid to them respectively on the days of their respective marriage or Arrival at the age of Twenty One Years whichsoever shall first happen together with all the Interest on said Debt remaining unpaid at the time of my death, and in case the whole or any part of the said principal sum of Two Thousand pounds shall be paid to me during my life then it is my Will that so much Money be raised out of my Estate as shall be equal to what I shall have received of the said principal debt and distribute among my four Nieces aforesaid, as herein has been bequeathed and it is my meaning that the interest accruing after my death on the said sum of Two thousand pounds shall belong to my said Nieces and be equally divided between them or such of them as shall be alive at the time of my death, and be paid annually for their respective uses until they receive their share of the principal.

ITEM. I give and bequeath to my Grand-son, George Washington Parke Custis all the Silver plate of every kind of which I shall die possessed, together with the two large plated Coolers, the four small plated Coolers with the Bottle Castors, and a pipe of Wine if there be one in the house at the time of my death - also the Set of Cincinnati tea and table China, the bowl that has a stop in it, the fine Old China Jars which usually Stand on the Chimney piece in the New Room also - all the family pictures of every Sort, and the pictures painted By his sister,[7] and two small skreens worked one by his sister and the other a present from Miss Kitty Brown[8] - also his Choice of - prints - Also the two Girandoles and Lustres that stand on them - also the new bed stead which I caused to be made in Philadelphia toegther with the bed, mattrass, boulsters and pillows and white dimity Curtains belonging thereto; also the two other beds with bolsters and pillows and the white dimity Curtains in the New Room also the Iron Chest and the desk in my Closet which belonged to my first Husband; also all my books of Every Kind except the Large Bible, and the Prayer Book, also the set of tea China that was given me by W Vanbram[9] every piece having M W on it

ITEM. I give and bequeath to my Grand Daughter Elizabeth Parke Law, the dressing Table and Glass that stands in the Chamber called the Yellow Room, and General Washingtons Picture printed by Trumbull.

ITEM. I give and bequeath to my Grand Daughter Martha Peter my writing table and the seat to it standing in my Chamber, also the print of General Washinigton that hangs in the passage

ITEM. I give and bequeath to my Grand Daughter Eleanor Parke Lewis the large looking glass in the front parlour, and any other looking glass which she may choose - also One of the New side board Tables in the New Room also twelve Chairs with Green Bottoms to be selected by herself also the marble table in the Garret also the two prints of the dead soldier, a print of the Washington Family in a box in the Garret and the Great Chair standing in my Chamber; all the plated Ware not hereinbefore Otherwise bequeathed, also all the sheets table linen, Napkins towels pillow cases remaining in the House at my death, also three beds and bedsteads Curtains Bolsters and pillows, for each bed such as she shall choose and not herein particularly otherwise bequeathed, together with counter-pains and a pair of blankets for each bed, also all the Wine Glasses and decanters of every kind, and all the blue and white China in Common use.

ITEM it is my will and desire that all the Wine in Bottles in the Vaults to be equally divided between my Grand-Daughters and Grandson, to each of whom I bequeath Ten Guineas to buy a ring for each.

ITEM it is my will and Desire that Anna Maria Washington[10] the daughter of my Niece be put into handsome Mourning at my death at the Expence of my Estate and I bequeath to her Ten Guineas to buy a ring.

ITEM. I give and bequeath to my Neighbor Mrs. Elizabeth Washington[11] five Guineas to get something in remembrance of me

ITEM I give and bequeath to Mrs. David Stuart[12] five Guineas to buy her a ring

ITEM I give and bequeath to Benjamin Lincoln Lear[13] one hundred pounds Specie to be vested in funded Stock of the United States immediately after my decease and to stand in his Name as his property which investment my Executors are to cause to be made.

ITEM When the Vestry of Truro parish shall buy a Glebe I devise Will and bequeath that my Executors shall pay one hundred pounds to them to aid of the purchase, provided the said purchase be made in my life-time or Within three years after my decease

ITEM It is my Will and desire that all the rest and residue of my Estate of whatsoever kind and description not herein specifically devised or bequeathed shall be sold by the Executors of this my last Will for ready money as soon after my decease as the same can be done and that the proceeds of thereof together with all the Money in the House and the debts due to me (the debts due from Me and the legacies herein bequeath being first satisfied) shall be Invested by my Executors in Eight p. Cent stock of the funds of the United States and shall stand on the books in the Name of my Executors in their Character of Executors of my Will and it is my desire that the Interest thereof shall be applied to the proper Education of Bartholomew Henly[14] and Samuel Henly[15] the two youngest sons of my Sister Henly,[16] and also to the Education of John Dandridge,[17] son of my deceased Nephew John Dandridge[18] so that they may be severally fitted and accomplished in some useful trade and to each of them who shall have lived to finish his Education or to reach the age of Twenty-one years, I give and bequeath one Hundred pounds to set him up in trade

ITEM My debts and legacies being paid and the Education of Bartholomew Henly, Samuel Henly and John Dandridge aforesaid being completed, or they being all dead before the completion thereof it is my will and desire that all my Estate and Interests in whatever form Existing whether in money funded stock or any other species of property shall be equally divided among all persons herein-after mentioned who shall be living at the time that the interest of the funded stock shall cease to be applicable in pursuance of my Will hereinbefore Expressed to the Education of my Nephews Bartholomew Henley, Samuel Henley and John Dandridge, namely among Anna Maria Washington[17] daughter of my Niece and John Dandridge son of my Nephew and all my Great Grandchildren living at the time that the interest of the said funded stock shall cease to be applicable to the education of the said B. Henley, S. Henley and John Dandridge and the same shall cease to be so applied when all of them shall die before they arrive to the age of Twenty One Years, or those living shall have finished their Eduction or have arrived to the age of twenty one Years, and so long as any one of the three lives, who has not finished his Education or Arrived to the age of Twenty One years, the Division of the said Residuum is to be defined and no longer -

Lastly I nominate and appoint my grandson George Washington Parke Custis, my Nephew Julius B. Dandridge,[19] and Bartholomew Dandridge[20] and my son in law, Thomas Peter[21] Executors of my last will and testament. In witness whereof, I have hereunto set my hand and seal this Twenty-Second day of September, in the year eighteen hundred.

Martha Washington

Sealed, signed acknowledged and Delivered as her last Will and Testament in the presence of the Subscribing witnesses who have been requested to subscribe the same as such in her presence -
Roger Farrell.[22]
William Spence.[23]
Lawrence Lewis.
Martha Peter.
March 4th 1802.
I give to my Grand Son George Washington Parke Custis my Mullatto Man Elijah,[24] that I bought of W. Butler Washington[25] to him and his Heirs forever -

M. Washington

AT A COURT held for Fairfax County the 21st day of June 1802 This last Will and Testament of Martha Washington deceased was presented in Court by George Washington Parke Custis and Thomas Peter, two of the Executors therein named, who made oath thereto, and the same being proved by the oaths of Roger Farrell, William Spence, and Lawrence Lewis three of the subscribing witnesses thereto is together with a codicil or Memorandum endorsed, ordered to be recorded - and the said Executors having performed what the law requries, a certificate is Granted them for obtaining a probate thereof in due form Teste,[26]

Wm Moore, C.C.

DS. Fairfax County Courthouse, Fairfax, Va.

1. Bartholomew Dandridge, son of Bartholomew Dandridge (1737-1785), brother of MW and his wife, Mary Burbidge Dandridge. He was secretary to GW, Secretary of the Legation to the Court of St. James, and Consul to San Domingo. He died there, unmarried, in 1802. 5 W (1)36.

2. Martha Washington Dandridge, also known as "Patcy." She was the daughter of MW's brother, Bartholomew Dandridge. She married Dr. William Halyburton, of Haddington, Scotland. 5 W (1)36.

3. Mary Burbidge Dandridge, also called "Polly," was a daughter of Bartholomew Dandridge, Sr. She married John Willison, August 26, 1805. 5 W (1)36.

4. Frances Lucy Dandridge, daughter of Bartholomew Dandridge, Sr. She married George William Hunt Minge. 5 W (1)36.

5. Frances Henly (sic). Frances Dandridge Henley (1779-1856) was the daughter of Leonard Henley and Elizabeth Dandridge Aylett Henley. The latter was a sister of MW. Frances was the third wife of Tobias Lear.

6. Lawrence Lewis (1767-1839) was the son of GW's sister, Betty Washington Lewis and her husband, Fielding Lewis. Lawrence was manager of the Mount Vernon estates for several years, prior to the death of GW. He married MW's granddaughter, Eleanor Parke Custis, February 22, 1799. He was an executor of GW's will.

7. Refers to Eleanor Parke Custis Lewis. See supra (6).

8. This may be the "Miss Brown" who visited Mount Vernon on July 8, 1798. 6 *Diaries*, p. 306.

9. Andreas Everardus van Braam Hockgeest (1739-1801) had been director of Canton operations for the Dutch East India Company. He became an American citizen in 1784. In 1796 van Braam presented a set of tea china to MW. Each piece bore her initials surrounded by a chain configuration. Within each link was the name of one of the fifteen stats. Detweiler and Meadows, *George Washington's Chinaware*. New York, 1982, p. 151.

10. Anna Maria Washington (1788-1814), daughter of Major George Augustine Washington and his wife, Frances Bassett Washington. She married Reuben Thornton. Her father was a nephew of GW and her mother a neice of MW.

11. Elizabeth Foote Washington, the widow of Lund Washington. During the Revolution they resided at Mount Vernon, when Lund managed the Mount Vernon farms. In 1783 they moved several miles away to a new home, Hayfield. 4 *Diaries*, p.80.

12. Elenor Calvert Custis Stuart. She married John Parke Custis, only surviving child of MW, February 3, 1774. Young Custis died shortly after GW's victory at Yorktown in October, 1781. She married Dr. David Stuart late in 1783.

13. Benjamin Lincoln Lear (1791-1832), son of Tobias Lear by his first wife, Mary Long Lear. Young Lear was a great favorite of the Washingtons and lived in the household on several occasions. He was born in the President's house in Philadelphia, March 11, 1791. Decatur, p. 129.

14. Bartholomew Henly (sic), son of Leonard Henley and his wife, Elizabeth Dandridge Aylett Henley, a sister of MW. He was a student at The College of William and Mary. See 8 W (1) 220, concerning a threatened duel with Armistead T. Mason, son of General Stevens T. Mason, in 1806. The duet was thwarted by Bishop James Madison.

15. Samuel Henly (sic) (1792-1825), brother of the above, was a lieutenant in the United States Navy. He died at Vera Cruz, July 14, 1825, unmarried.

16. Elizabeth Dandridge Aylett Henley (1749-18-), was a younger sister of MW. Her first husband was John Aylett.

17. This John Dandridge was a grand nephew of MW. He was the son of John Dandridge, nephew of MW.

18. John Dandridge (176?-1799), son of Bartholomew Dandridge, (1737-1786), brother of MW. His wife was Rebecca Jones Minge. 5 W (1)36.

19. Julius Burbidge Dandridge, son of Bartholomew Dandridge. He was cashier of the United States Bank in Richmond. He died, unmarried.

20. Bartholomew Dandridge (Bat), newphew of MW.

21. Thomas Peter, son of Robert Peter, a prosperous merchant of Georgetown and its first mayor. In January, 1795 he married Martha Parke Custis, granddaughter of MW.

22. Unidentified.

23. Unidentified.

24. Elijah was probably a dower slave, since MW was transferring ownership to her grandson. She would hardly have done so had Elijah been a Washington slave. See *Prussing*, p. 392.

25. W. Butler Washington (- 1817), son of John and Catherine Washington of King George County. 22:329-30.

26. The will was drawn by Charles Lee and is in the handwriting of Eleanor Parke Custis Lewis.

Account of Sales of the Personal Estate of Martha Washington (not specifically devised late of Mount Vernon deceased - as rendered to me by Thomas Peter the Executor.

----

1 Bag of Feathers,	Mrs Timmerman	$ 6.50
1 painting	George Deneale	101.00
2 prints	ditto	30.00
6 ditto	ditto	6.00
1 Paint Louis 16th	Judge Washington	20.00
2 ditto Trumbulls	ditto	30.00
2 Scupture paintings	ditto	40.00
2 China Jars	ditto	41.00
3 Images	ditto	16.00
1 Print of Fayette	ditto	15.00
1 Carpet	ditto	50.00
1 Copper Kettle	ditto	6.00
3 gross bottles	ditto	24.00
Bust of Washington	ditto	250.00
Bust of Paul Jones and Necker	ditto	80.00
4 Bronze Images	ditto	10.00
1 Press and Table	ditto	10.00
1 Fan chair	John Mason	7.0
1 painting	Capt. Geo. Washington	105.00
1 print of America	ditto	6.00
4 prints do	David Peter	10.00
1 Lamp	Wm Fitzhugh	8.00
2 prints Trumbull	Geo Calvert	16.00
2 ditto „	ditto	20.00
4 ditto „	ditto	68.00
1 Print	Jno C. Herbert	9.00
1 ditto	ditto	8.00
4 ditto	Adam Lynn	26.00
3 ditto	ditto	3.15
1 ditto	Jacob Hoffman	8.00
2 Candle Stands	Doct Thornton	18.00
1 piece of sheeting	Wm Carroll	22.00
1 Close Stool	Rob Peter Sr	3.80
1 Mattress	ditto	5.50
1 Side Board	ditto	67.00
1 Iron shovel	Thos. Digges	5.50
1 ditto	ditto	2.00
7 chairs	ditto	14.00
1 looking glass	ditto	5.00
4 Counterpanes	ditto	27.00
1 ditto	ditto	6.00
1 Cooler	ditto	8.50
3 Flower pots	ditto	1.00

1 lot sundries	ditto	5.00
1 Water Jug	ditto	1.00
1 Desk	Roger Farrell	4.50
2 Knife cases	Doctr Weems	10.75
12 Chairs	ditto	60.00
	Amount Carried forward	$ 1300.20
	Amount Brot: forward	1300.20
2 Cases Knives and forks	Francis Roger	20.00
Oval glass	ditto	7.00
2 Gerendoles	ditto	16.00
3 White Jars	ditto	.25
4 demijohns	ditto	3.00
1 steel fender	ditto	.50
1 lot pewter	ditto	2.30
1 Griddle	ditto	1.25
1 lot stone pots	ditto	.75
2 Gerendoles	James Patton	16.00
1 Set Camp Curt	ditto	6.50
2 prints	ditto	29.00
1 Trunk	ditto	1.25
1 pot and fish kettle	ditto	1.50
2 prints	Rob Patton	6.00
1 looking glass	E.P.Law	13.00
1 Chair	ditto	20.00
1 old tea table	ditto	2.50
1 trunk	ditto	1.00
1 Bracket	ditto	1.00
1 marble slater	ditto	2.00
2 Counterpanes	ditto	14.50
1/2 mat	ditto	16.00
1/3 set China	ditto	12.67
1 Bed	M Hodgson	10.00
1 ditto	ditto	17.50
1 print	ditto	10.50
1 Bed	Howell Lewis	35.00
1 ditto	ditto	39.50
1 ditto	T. Preston	29.50
3 prints	ditto	2.
12 chairs	Jno. Coffer	20.00
And Irons and shovel	Drm Steuart	3.20
ditto	ditto	1.25
1 dressing glass	ditto	2.
1 mattrass	ditto	8.
1 glass	ditto	5.
1 mattrass	ditto	10.50
1 Counterpane	ditto	7.50

2 pair blankets	ditto	25.00
1 Carpet	ditto	3.50
2 Trunks	ditto	4.20
14 Chairs	ditto	14.00
1 piece sheeting	ditto	29.00
1 C Kettle	ditto	6.
2 Fenders	ditto	.30
1 lot Copper	ditto	1.25
	Amount carried over	1820.07
	Amount brought over	1820.07
1 Cadet Bedstead	Lawrence Lewis	.55
1 ditto	ditto	.50
4 Bedsteads	ditto	5.25
1 Cooler	ditto	1.50
1 Mattrass	ditto	9.00
1 ditto	ditto	8.
1 Moonlight painting	ditto	113.
1 Chicken coop	ditto	3.
1 pair blankets	ditto	4.50
Waiter bowl & glass	ditto	26.
1 large Kettle	ditto	20.
Chaffin dish	ditto	3.
1/3 Set China	ditto	12.67
4 Flat Irons	ditto	1.20
3 Soap Jars	ditto	6.00
1 Greem bottom chair	ditto	10.
1 White arm ditto	ditto	2.50
Lot of glass	ditto	21.
2 Cases Knives & forks	G.W.P.Custis	26.00
1 pair looking glasses	ditto	45.
1 Mattrass	ditto	6.
4 Nolts	ditto	4.
2 paintings	ditto	120.
1 Set Curtains	ditto	20.
2 pair blankets	ditto	21.
Shovel tongs and fender	ditto	13.
2 Carpets	ditto	46.
2 prints	ditto	22.00
2 ditto	ditto	22.
2 ditto	ditto	34.
1 Side board	ditto	10.
12 Chairs	ditto	36.
1 lot baskets	ditto	1.
1 Bureau	ditto	6.
1 Breakfast table	ditto	2.50
2 Window Blinds	ditto	5.00

1 leather couch	ditto	16.
1 Settee bedstead	ditto	30.
1 pr. andirons	ditto	3.25
1 table	ditto	15.
2 trunks	ditto	5.
3 ditto	ditto	4.35
2 dining tables	ditto	15.
1 old chair	ditto	7.25
Saddle and Bridle	ditto	5.
6 Water plates	ditto	5.
Bake oven	ditto	2.
Thermometre	ditto	7.
1 doz. Camp seats	ditto	3.50
Wooden scales and weights ditto	8.25	
Seine & Ropes	ditto	78.00
Table	ditto	3.00
2 Cowes	ditto	32.32
	Amount carried up	2788.96
	Amount brought up	2788.96
2 Trunks	Thomas Peter	7.40
1 Safe	ditto	5.00
1 Clothes Horse	ditto	.60
2 Setts quilting frames	ditto	1.20
1 Bedstead	ditto	3.
1 Cooler	ditto	1.50
1 Set fire Utensils	ditto	16.
12 Chairs	ditto	33.60
1 looking glass	ditto	10.25
1 Tea Caddy	ditto	3.25
5 Mattrasses	ditto	107.50
2 Carpets	ditto	11.00
1 Chest drawers	ditto	30.50
2 Counterpanes	ditto	14.50
3 Sets bed curtains	ditto	45.00
1 Pair Blankets	ditto	11.50
1 Stand	ditto	1.
1/2 Matt	ditto	16.00
1 Carpet	ditto	5.50
1 looking glass	ditto	5.00
3 Lots Baskets	ditto	7.00
1 looking glass	ditto	19.50
3 Jugs and Bason	ditto	3.00
Bowl glass and Waiter	ditto	33.00
1/3 Set China	ditto	12.67
4 Cracked Bowls	ditto	2.00
2 Brackets & Girendoles	ditto	17.50

1 Warming pan	ditto	2.00
Small pieces of Carpeting	ditto	6.50
1 old Case	ditto	1.
Lot sundries	ditto	29.00
Lot ditto	ditto	1.
6 Water plates	ditto	7.
Thermometre (broken	ditto	1.
1/2 doz: Camp seats	ditto	1.50
3 Tubs	ditto	4.25
Griddle	ditto	1.60
Fire pan	ditto	1.00
1 large looking glass	ditto	100.
1 Wax work	ditto	10.
7 Cowes & five Calves and some kitchen furniture	ditto	162.62
1 Time piece	Charles Carter	60.00
	Sales for Cash	189.95
		$ 3735.25

A. Moore
M.C.

The Estate of Martha Washington

Dr. Rental to the Estate of Martha Washington decd.

		Acres Land	Rent	Agregate Amot		
1800	Berkley County Tenants					
Decr.	John Ariss decd	700	£ 60: 0: 0	£	S	D
25th	George Stubblefield Do	200	60: 0: 0			
	Thomas T. Greenfield	183	10: 0: 0			
	John Dimmett	200	6: 0: 0			
	John Bryan	200	6: 0: 0			
	Thomas Griggs	200	6: 0: 0			
	George Riely	200	6: 0: 0			
	Evans Marsh Berkley ditto	1883	154: 0: 0	154	0	0
1800	Benjamin Kercheval	113	4: 0: 0			
Decr	John Bowley	113	20: 0: 0			
25	James Shirley	225 1/2	6:15: 0			
		451 1/2	30:15: 0	30	15	0
	Frederick County Tenants					
	Ewel Skip	216	35: 0: 0			
	William Clayton	174 1/2	35: 0: 0			
	William Kercheval	174 1/2	45: 0: 0			
		565	115: 0: 0	115	0	0
1800	Fauquier & Loudon County					

Decr	included in one Survey					
25	Gerrard McDonald junr	120	2: 8: 0			
	William Collings	260	15: 0: 0			
	Abel Morgan	100	4:10: 0			
	Deel Clyman	160	5: 0: 0			
	William Carrel	150	7: 0: 0			
	Elias Porter	230	9: 0: 0			
	Henry Shover	100	5: 0: 0	75	18	0
	John McDonald	120	10: 0: 0			
	John Keas	100	5: 0: 0			
	William Grant	106	4: 0: 0			
	David Hoge	106	4: 0: 0			
	Daniel Harris	113 1/2	5: 0: 0			
	Aggregate Amots card. up	1665 1/2	75:18: 0	375	18	0
1800	Aggregate Amounts brot	Acres Land				
Decr	forward	1665 1/2	75:18: 0	375	18	0
25	Jesse Harris	110	4:10: 0			
	John Porter	113 1/2	5: 0: 0			
	Thomas Read	100	6: 0: 0	35	10	0
	Robert McWhorter	100	5: 0: 0			
	William Deerman	100	5: 0: 0			
	Gerrard McDonald Senr.	140	10: 0: 0			
			35:10: 0			
			75:18: 0			
			£ 111: 8: 0			
1800	Goose Creek Tenants	Acres				
Decr	William F.R.Davis	196	11: 0: 0			
25	Benjamin Rust	206	15: 0: 0			
	Philip Grose	133 1/2	6: 0: 0			
	Daniel Brown	200	15: 0: 0			
	Jesse Hitt	200	10: 0: 0			
	Daniel Flowree	133 1/2	6: 0: 0	63	0	0
			63: 0: 0			
1800	Winchester Lotts	Acres				
Decr	Doctr Robert Mackey	1/2	3: 0: 0			
25	Philip Bush junr.	4	2: 0: 0			
		4 1/2	5: 0: 0	5	0	0
	Aggregate Amot of Rental			£ 479	3	0
	Carried over					

Dr. Rental to Mrs. Martha Washington's Estate Continued

1800	To amount brought over	£ 479: 0: 0
1801	To ditto for 1801	479: 0: 0
		£ 958: 6: 0

Contra   Cr.

1800

22 Septr By cash paid to the Collector of	£ 15: 8: 9
Direct taxes	

1801
22d Octr By ditto   111: 0: 0
21st Feby By ditto   63: 0: 0
1802
Feby 9 By ditto   120: 0: 0
1801   By ditto unreceipted   120: 0: 0
Septr 15 By ditto   120: 0: 0
                        By taxes for 1800 & 1801   6: 0: 0

(Docket) Rental in 1800

AD, NNHi.

Appendixes

Appendix I

The Marriage of Martha Dandridge and Daniel Parke Curtis

The Parke, Custis, Jones, and Dandridge Families

There is no existing record of the first meeting of Martha Dandridge and Daniel Parke Custis. As a young girl it is likely she saw him at Saint Peter's Church or at neighborhood social functions, since their respective homes were only a few miles apart. The twenty year disparity in their ages would certainly discourage any interested thoughts on the part of either until Martha's physical maturity was attained. Such a time must have arrived about 1748 or 1749. Daniel, then a thirty-eight-year-old bachelor, was living at White House, one of his father's plantations, on the south side of the Pamunkey River in New Kent County. Martha, the eighteen-year-old eldest daughter of John Dandridge, was living at her home, Chestnut Grove, somewhat closer to New Kent Courthouse than White House.

Custis was the only son of the eccentric and wealthy John Custis, one of the largest land holders in the colony. He held large tracts of land on the Eastern Shore, Smith's and Mockhorn Islands off the coast, York County, New Kent County, King and Queen County, King William County, and smaller parcels of property in Williamsburg, James City, and Hanover Counties. He was the fourth of his name in Virginia.

The first John Custis and his wife, Joanne Powell, were inn-keepers in Rotterdam, where they "kept a victualling house in that town, liv'd in good repute, and was the general host of our nation there."[1] It is thought they came to the Eastern Shore prior to 1640, although there are no substantiating records. Of their six sons and one daughter, four remained in Virginia. John, William, and Joseph settled on the Eastern Shore. Daughter Anne married Colonel Argall Yeardley, son of the royal governor, Sir George Yeardley.[2] John II was named Sheriff of Northampton County in 1664. During Bacon's Rebellion in 1676 he served as major-general of the local militia. He was also a member of the council. His first wife was Elizabeth Robinson.[3] Their son, John (III) of Wilsonia (1653-1713), married Margaret Michael. Proof of his prominence and importance was his appointment to the Council in 1693.[4]

Their only son, John Custis IV (1678-1749), by virtue of astute management, the sagacious patenting of lands, inheritance, and a fortuitous marriage, increased the family wealth. Along with success came a tragic marriage, bad temper, eccentricities, and contentiousness. It was most unfortunate that he chose to successfully woo Frances Parke, one of the two daughters of the controversial Colonel Daniel Parke.

William Parke (-1633), an Englishman, was the first of the Parke family in Virginia. The surname of Sarah, his wife, is not known.[6] Their son, Daniel Parke I (1628-1679), married Rebecca Evelyn (-1672), daughter of George Evelyn and widow of Bartholomew Knipe, about 1658. Daniel Parke died eleven years later in 1679. This first Daniel was an extensive land owner and became Secretary and Treasurer of the Colony and a member of the Council.[7]

Daniel Parke II, one of their three children, made the Parke name famous and notorious. Born in 1669, he was married at the age of seventeen to Jane Ludwell, the daughter of Philip Ludwell, one of the most influential and powerful men in Virginia.[8] Within a few years son-in-law Parke became embroiled in the political disputes between Lord Effingham, the Royal Governor, and his Ludwell father-in-law. In 1688, at the age of nineteen, he was elected Burgess. Probably for political reasons he made a voyage to England in 1691. The following year saw him back in Virginia, accompanied by a Mrs. Berry, whom he preferred to call "Cousin Brown." Accompanying them was "Cousin Brown's" infant son, Julius Caesar Parke, more than likely the natural son of Parke, and who he referred to as his "godson." During the next five years he experienced a meteoric rise to prominence - Burgess, Vestryman for Bruton Parish Church, Councillor, Naval Officer and Collector, and one of the Governors of the College. Apparently there was also time to be merchant, planter, ship builder, and brickmaker.[10] By 1697, he again, became ensnarled in another political feud - the quarrel between Governor Sir Edmund Andros, who was Parke's patron, and Francis Nicholson. Disillusionment with the political scene, whereby Nicholson was to replace Andros as Royal Governor, restlessness, and escape from a boring marriage, determined him to leave Virginia and return to England about

1697. He packed up "Cousin Brown" and set sail, never to return to Virginia, but conveniently leaving his illegitimate son, Julius Caesar Parke, to the care of his abandoned wife. Setting himself up in Hampshire and under the patronage of the Earl of Peterborough, he was elected to Parliament. In 1702 he was accused of election bribery by the Tory majority, and was expelled from Parliament. Having previously become the friend of John Churchill, first Duke of Marlborough, he participated in the Flanders campaign against the French under the command of Lord Arran. Shortly he was appointed aide-de-camp to the Duke of Marlborough, with the rank of colonel.[11] After the Battle of Blenheim, August 13, 1704, Colonel Parke was designated by the Duke to carry the news of the victory to his Duchess, and then carry the good news to Queen Anne. So pleased was the Queen that she rewarded Parke with a gift of 1000 guineas and a diamond encrusted miniature of her royal self.[12] Later that year there was serious talk in London of his being named Virginia's Royal Governor, succeeding his old enemy, Governor Francis Nicholson. If so, he would be the first native Virginian to be named governor. The rumor died when the Earl of Orkney received the royal nod.[13] However, in March, 1705, he received the appointment as Governor General of the four Leeward Islands, his residence, Antigua.[14]

His abandoned wife, Jane, and their two daughters, Frances and Lucy, continued to live at Greensprings, James City County, with her brother, Philip Ludwell. There was little communication between the Parkes until July 12, 1705, when she wrote him a long and pitiful letter complaining of the cruel treatment and wanton neglect to which he had subjected her. She asked to be relieved of the sole responsibility of raising their daughters into womanhood and also asked to be relieved of the task of rearing his "godson," Julius Caesar Parke. She complained bitterly of having the care of him for eight years, during which he had attended the College. Apparently it had not benefitted him and he had become a serious disciplinary problem. He had become an ignorant indolent dolt. At some period thereafter he was packed off to England, where he continued to run up debts against Governor Parke.

At about this time John Custis IV had become romantically attracted to Frances Parke, eldest daughter of Governor Parke and his wife.[16] In a letter from London, August 25, 1705, Governor Parke chided John Custis of Wilsonia, and his suitor son, for not sending him "an account of his real and personal effects." Parke was quick to point out he did not know "your young gentleman," that his daughter would inherit all his lands in Virginia; 7000 acres in New Kent County, to say nothing of the extensive holdings in York and James City Counties. He further agreed if their marriage was finalized he would present the bride "half as much as he (Custis) can make appear he's worth."[17] The twenty-seven-year-old John

married eighteen-year-old Frances the latter part of 1705. Shortly thereafter Frances' sister, Lucy, became the first wife of William Byrd II, of
Westover.

Within five years Governor Parke's administration in the Leeward
Islands had become so morally and politically corrupt that on December
9, 1710 he was overthrown in a violent uprising and was killed by the
insurrectionists.[18] It seems Parke had taken as his mistress, one Catherine
Chester, the wife of a local unsavory character. It was alleged her daughter
Lucy, had been fathered by the Governor. In the looting of his residence,
following his murder, incriminating letters and documents were found
apparently linking the Governor to improper intimacies with other wives
and daughters of the citizens.[19]

Governor Parke's will, drawn January 29, 1709 was proved May 15,
1711 in Antigua.[20] He bequeathed all his property in the Leeward Islands
to his illegitimate daughter, Lucy Chester, regardless of the name her
mother might bestow upon her. Should Lucy die before reaching the age
of twenty-one, the estate would pass to her mother, for the duration of
her life. At her demise it would then pass to Julius Caesar Parke in
England. If Lucy married, the will provided that she, her husband, and
any progeny must adopt the surname, Parke, and use the Parke coat of
arms, in order to inherit the property. If Lucy, her husband, or any of her
progeny refused the name of Parke or to use the Parke arms, it would
revert to Julius Caesar Parke. If Parke should die without legal heirs the
property in the Leeward Islands would then pass to Frances Custis and
her heirs at law, failing in which it would pass to Lucy Byrd and her heirs
at law, providing they take the surname, Parke, and use the Parke arms.

The will also stipulated that Frances Custis was to inherit the estate
in England and Virginia. Should Frances have no direct heirs the estate
would pass to her sister, Lucy, to be then followed by Lucy Chester, and
then by Julius Caesar Parke. In case of a failure of heirs the estate was to
be liquidated for the benefit of the poor of Whitechurch, Hampshire.
Frances was directed to pay her sister Lucy £1000, the amount Colonel
Parke had settled upon with Colonel Byrd, at the time of his marriage to
Lucy, and which Parke had never paid. Frances was also directed to pay
£50 annually to Julius Caesar Parke; to each of his sisters and their
children, £50 for rings; to the English executors, £20 each.

Another disturbing stipulation was the clause: "my will is that my
daughter Frances Custis pay out of my estate in Virginia and Hampshire
all my legal debts and bequests." Did that mean the Virginia heirs were
responsible for the huge debts Parke had accumulated in the Leeward
Islands and England? Or did it mean the Leeward Island heirs were
responsible for Parke's debts there, and Frances liable for the £1000 owed
her sister, Lucy, and the English debts? From England came a hint of
another "son" bearing the name of Parke.

Separate executors were named for the Leeward Island Estates, England, and for Virginia. As Douglas Southall Freeman has so aptly put it, it was "as if there had been two Daniel Parkes, whose lives and fortunes were not to be mingled unless there were a failure of direct heirs.....he seemed to be pursued by an ambition to have his name perpetuated by all who were of his blood, whether by lawful or by wayward descent."[21]

For almost forty years the sexual profligacies of Colonel Parke arose to periodically haunt John Custis's peace of mind. Lucy Chester lived to marry Thomas Dunbar, also of Antigua. They immediately took the name of Parke, in order to qualify for the inheritance, and he thereafter went by the name of Dunbar Parke. The legal jousting continued on, always with the threat that the legitimate heirs might be required to pay all the debts accumulated by Colonel Parke in England, The Leeward Islands, and Virginia. If this be so, then it might wipe out the value of the whole estate in England and Virginia.[22] Over the years deaths of the principals and their legal representatives postponed a final decision. Dunbar Parke continued to insist on reimbursement for the Parke debts that he had paid or that were still outstanding. Death too claimed him prior to Febraury, 1735. However, the legal struggle was continued by Charles Dunbar, the beligerent brother of Dunbar Parke, on behalf of himself and his deceased brother's children. The chancery suits continued all during the lifetime of John Custis, his son, Daniel, and during Martha's widowhood. It ultimately involved George Washington as well, since Martha's half of the estate became his property under Virginia law. Sixty years after the death of Colonel Parke, Colonel Washington was still contending with Parke's amorous associations. His tactics were different than those of old John Custis. The latter preferred to settle the matter in an aggressive manner. Washington preferred to play a waiting game, in the hopes the suit would wither and die on the vine. His method proved to be the correct one since we hear nothing more of it after about 1772.

Julius Caesar Parke disappeared early from the scene. In 1711 Micajah Perry, London agent for John Custis and one of the English executors of the Parke will, informed Custis that "Julius Caesar was thought to be in prison and there let him be."[23] Nothing more was heard of the "godson" of Parke, out of "Cousin Brown."

The prenuptual ardour of John and Frances Custis soon cooled and it was not long until they were in violent disagreement over matters of importance, as well as trivialties. Acquisitiveness, pride, ambition, violent temper, and contentiousness on the part of both, made the marriage a shambles. The relationship deteriorated to such a remarkable degree that friends and relatives convinced them to draw up a marriage agreement, delineating rules of conduct for both husband and wife, and to file it with the Northampton County Court. The Eastern Shore was rife with the amusing stories of their tumultuous relationship.[24]

John Custis's abilities had been efficient enough to encourage his father-in-law into offering him a fifth of the profits derived from his Virginia estates if Custis would consent to move from the Eastern Shore and manage the mainland estates. At first reluctant to do so, he finally acquiesced and they took up residence on Queens Creek, York County.

The mutual antipathies of the Custises did not prevent the production of an offspring. Frances Parke Custis was born September 13, 1710 at Arlington, on the Eastern Shore. The Reverend William Dunn, Mrs. Dunn, and the parents stood as Godparents.[25] The following year, October 15, 1711, Daniel Parke Custis was born at Queens Creek. Governor Spottswood, William Byrd, II, and Mrs. Hannah Ludwell were the Godparents.[26] Previously a son and daughter had been interred beside Major-General John Custis at Arlington.

The conciliatory agreement of June, 1714 between John and Frances Custis came to naught. Frances died of smallpox March 13, 1714/15 and was buried at Queens Creek.[28] Undoubtedly Custis was relieved to be rid of his quarrelsome, contentious wife. He continued to live at Queens Creek and at his house in Williamsburg, several miles away.[29] He managed his plantations efficiently, and long hours were spent cultivating the gardens at his Williamsburg home. He corresponded with botanists and fellow gardners in England and America, sending botanical specimens and seed and propagating those he received in return.[30] He took great pride in his children, of whom he said, "My children are all the comfort I have in the world, for whose sake I have kept myself single, and am determined so to do as long as it shall please God to continue them to me."[31] His first loathful marital experience made him reluctant to enter into another that might end similarly. The one unfortunate marriage of his daughter, Frances, and the tragic marriage of his mother-in-law must have further influenced him to remain unmarried.[32] He was contentious, impatient, short-tempered, acquisitive, and irrascible. However, he also had a redeeming side to him; ambitious, gregarious, friendly, overly generous with friends and acquaintances, a keen observer, well-educated, the possessor of a keen scientific mind, and an inquisitiveness for knowledge. His public duties included long service as a member of the House of Burgesses, representing Northampton County and after 1718, the College of William and Mary. He received his appointment to the Council in 1727 and served until shortly before his death in 1749. For a very short time he was acting governor following the departure of Governor Gooch and the death of John Robinson.

All the while, young Daniel remained under the control of his domineering father. He seemed determined that his only son not repeat the marital misadventures of his grandfather, grandmother, sister, and himself. For a number of years he was not entrusted with the management of any of his father's plantations. Eventually, however, he was allowed to take up residence at the White House tract on the Pamunkey River in New Kent County. The land had been acquired from the Lightfoot family about 1736. Daniel served as caretaker, overseer, owner, and eventually lived out his life there.[33]

Daniel was anxious for a wife.[34] The legendary beautiful Evelyn Byrd, daughter of William Byrd as well as Daniel's first cousin, was a likely prospect as was her sister, Anne. However, Colonel Custis could not be brought to terms concerning the financial arrangements and Colonel Byrd broke off the affair, refusing to deal with the vacillations of Colonel Custis.[35] A London relative, Mrs. Parke Pepper, also brought up the subject of the marriage of her daughter to Daniel in a letter to Colonel Custis in 1731. The father, however, discouraged the match, citing distance and consanguinity as a deterrent.[36] At twenty he was also courting a "Miss Betty." Just who "Miss Betty" was, remains unknown. As late as 1741 Daniel was wooing "Annie" Byrd, daughter of William Byrd II.[37]

Sometime in 1748, at the age of thirty-seven, he took notice of Martha Dandridge, the seventeen-year-old daughter of John and Frances Dandridge of Chestnut Grove. Love resulted! It was definitely not a parentally arranged match. She was petite, just under five feet tall, pretty, and as charming as any eighteenth-century girl could be. Both occupied a place of prominence in the community. They usually worshipped at Saint Peter's Church, where father and suitor were vestrymen. Daniel had the additional honor of being churchwarden.[38] What had shortly before been a gangling adolescent, romping around the churchyard, and hiding behind the tombstones, now had suddenly matured into an attractive woman. She quickly caught Daniel's eye. How could John and Frances Dandridge ever object to such a match for their eldest child? But the father of the suitor was another matter.

The Dandridges were comparative late-comers to Virginia. The first to arrive was William Dandridge. Under what circumstances he first set eyes upon the Virginia capes is uncertain. He may have been a young immigrant Englishman seeking opportunity in America. It is possible he may have been a young officer aboard an English merchantman. Probably his younger brother, John, accompanied him. They came of a large family - fourteen children of the two marriages of their father.

Early records place the Dandridges in Oxfordshire in the 16th century.[39] Bartholomew Dandridge, born not later than 1580, was a yeoman farmer in Drayton St. Leonard, a dozen miles southeast of Oxford. He was a landed freeholder, just beneath the social status of "gentleman." In 1604 he married Agnes Wilder, who gave him eight children.[40] Of particular interest are William, born Janaury 30, 1613, and Francis, born in 1619.[41] Following the death of their father in 1638, they continued on as yeoman farmers in their home locality. During the Civil Wars, William and Francis supported the Royalist cause.[42] The names of their wives are not known. William and his wife had three sons. William, Francis and John. Francis, the brother of the elder William had five children by his wife, Anne, the two eldest also named Francis and John. The elder sons of the two brothers, (William and Francis) were sent to the grammer school of Sir John Fettiplace, at Dorchester on Thames, in order that their sons might have better opportunities than a rural English countryside could provide.[45] William apprenticed his youngest son, John, age thirteen, to Thomas Postlethwaite, a master painter-stainer, of London, in October, 1668. About the same time, the elder Francis apprenticed his sons, Francis and John to the apothecaries.

By 1676, John had become a journeyman painter-stainer. As a member of his guild he painted, stained, drafted and designed coats of arms, signs, heraldic devices, as well as other ornamental objects. Shortly after becoming a journeyman, John married Bridget Dugdale at St. Mary Magdalen Church in Fish Street. The following year they had a son, John, but the mother did not survive.[44] John, the elder, soon rose to the top of his guild and was elected master of the Painter-Stainer Company. He next married Anne, surname unknown. His first son, John was also apprenticed to his father's guild, but died in 1695. William, his oldest son by Anne, was born December 29, 1689, followed by Bartholomew in 1691, Mary in 1693, Francis in 1697. Another John was born July 14, 1700. By 1711 Anne had presented him with thirteen children, seven of whom grew to adulthood.[45]

John, the Master Painter-Stainer, never lost social contact with his apothecary cousins. They had become prosperous residents of the Covent Garden neighborhood. One of them, Francis, died unmarried in 1714, leaving a considerable estate. Money was bequeathed to the poor of his native town, £2500 to various relations, and to Cousin John went all his extensive London properties.[46]

Twenty-six-year-old William and fifteen-year-old John immigrated to Virginia, about 1715. Bartholomew, educated at St. Paul's School, was destined to become one of the foremost portraiturists of his day. Francis eventually succeeded his father as the master of the guild. The Dandridges had come a long way since their fathers and grandfathers had been farm boys in Oxfordshire.[47]

William and John Dandridge first established themselves in Elizabeth City County as merchants and landowners.[48] Apparently their rise was rapid. By December 14, 1727, William was sworn in as a member of the Council.[49] The following year, he, along with William Byrd and Richard Fitzwilliam, were selected as Virginia commissioners to survey the boundry dispute between Virginia and North Carolina.[50] He also served as a colonel of militia and for a number of years was a captain in the Royal Navy.[51] His principal residence was Elsing Green, on the north bank of the Pamunkey River in King William County where he died in 1743.[52]

John Dandridge, his younger brother, owned property in Hampton in 1722.[53] By 1727 he had acquired land on the South Anna River, in Hanover County.[54] In 1730 he purchased approximately 500 acres from the Burnell estate, on the south bank of the Pamunkey River in New Kent County and built Chestnut Grove.[55] On July 22, 1730 he married Frances Jones.[56] Frances Jones, born August 6, 1710, was the daughter of Orlando Jones (1681-1719) and Martha Macon Jones.[57] Orlando was the son of the Reverend Rowland Jones (1644-1688), who had been educated at Merton College, Oxford, and had become pastor at Little Kimble, Buckinghamshire. Immigrating to Virginia he became the first rector of the new parish of Bruton in 1664, formed by the union of Middletown, Harop, and Marston Parishes.[58] At the organization of the new church he made a substantial contribution.[59] He served there as rector until his death in 1688.[60] His father, also named Rowland, received his B.A. from Christ Church, Oxford, and then served as rector of several churches in Buckinghamshire. We know little of him other than that he also served as a clerk.[61]

Martha Macon Jones was one of the four children of Gideon Macon (1650-1703) the first of his family in Virginia. He is said to have been a Huguenot from the Auvergne region of France. He was listed as an inhabitant of York County from 1672 and as attorney there in 1675, of James City County in 1678, and of New Kent County from 1682 until his death.[62] He served as a Burgess from New Kent County in 1693 and 1698.[63] Macon was on the quit rent rolls of New Kent County for the Parishes of St. Peter and St. Paul, for 270 acres in 1704.[64] His name was on the vestry list of Bruton Parish Church, ending in 1679[65] In 1690 Macon served as churchwarden for the "new upper church" of Blissland Parish.[66] Macon's home was at Mount Pleasant, New Kent County, where he is buried. His widow was the daughter of William Woodward, the Indian interpreter.[67]

Orlando Jones attended William and Mary in 1698 where, with three other students, he signed a memorial thanking the Speaker of the House of Burgesses for their patronage and encouragement and begging them for their continued approbation.[67] Next we find him sitting as a Burgess for King William County in 1714 and 1718.[68] At his death in June 1719, he willed to his daughter, Frances and her heirs forever, his next best feather bed and furniture, the trunk that was her mother's and all its contents; all the land joining John's Creek in King William County. Orlando died at his Queens Creek plantation, near Timson's Neck on the York River.[69]

John Dandridge and Frances Jones were married July 22, 1730.[70] He was then serving as deputy clerk of New Kent County, and had recently purchased Chestnut Grove. That same year, on the death of the clerk,

Colonel John Thornton, he became county clerk. Their eldest, Martha, was born June 2, 1731, between 12 and 1 o'clock in a room at the east end of the house.[72] Dandridge was able to manage his modest plantation of about 500 acres and still continue his duties as clerk. But at age 56, while on a visit to his niece, Mary Spottswood, at Fredericksburg, he had a cerebral hemorrhage and died suddenly, August 21, 1756. We have no records concerning the childhood of Martha Dandridge. The education she received was probably from her parents, an itinerant tutor or an indentured servant. Her father who had sufficient education to success-fully conduct the office of Clerk of New Kent County for twenty five years, would certainly be capable of instructing his children. It is also fair to assume her mother had been exposed to some education, being the daughter of a graduate of the College who possessed a library much larger than the average Virginia gentleman.[73]

In addition to reading and writing, she certainly received instruc-tions from her mother in the womanly art of housekeeping, management, cooking, and needlework, for she excelled in these all through her adult life. In the social graces she grew to have no peer. She may also have received some musical instruction. Her compassion, empathy, generosity, kindness, and thoughtfulness for those about her would indicate she was well indoctrinated in good Christian principles, the foundations of which must have begun in early childhood. As a child she was certainly taken to St. Peter's Church for regular services. Her father was a vestryman and there she undoubtedly saw another vestryman, Daniel Parke Custis. In these early years she certainly paid him little heed.

That Daniel was eager to marry is evident from a letter written to him in 1744 by his close friend, John Blair.[74]

> "And my Dear Friend I will not yet despair to see you blest in a sweet Companion for life with all the Endearments that attend the State when most happy. But patience yet awhile."[75]

No young lady was acceptable to the eccentric and perverse father, that is unless she came with a huge monetary settlement or its equivalent. Certainly Miss Dandridge did not qualify. Daniel seemed unable to please the old gentleman, who went into a rage at the least provocation, real or imaginary. He seemed obsessed with the belief that no member of the fair sex was worthy of marriage to his son, unless they had a fortune commensurate with the one his son would someday inherit.

Custis, possibly for reasons of spite, had become greatly attached to a little slave boy, Jack, the son of "my slave Alice."[76] It was said that following an outburst occasioned by Daniel's request for shoes for his father's slaves at White House, he made a will leaving everything to Jack and nothing to Daniel, and had the will recorded. Later through the remonstrances of friends, and better judgement, he rescinded the will.[77]

However, he could not bring himself to capitulate completely and to save face he manumitted Jack.[78] Apparently Daniel had not confessed his affection for Martha to his father, fearing another tantrum. Nevertheless the head of the family had heard the news of the courtship from others. A difficult situation was made worse. Living in constant fear, anxiety and uncertainty, who could blame the son?

For a number of years the irascible father had given away valuable possessions to neighbors and friends. To four individuals he had given fifteen young negroes, varying in age from two to twenty years. To several others he gave sizable tracts of land.[80] The most flagrant presentations were those to his neighbors, Matthew and Anne Moody.[81] Included were: a dozen black walnut chairs, a walnut table, bed and furniture, a dozen pewter plates, two skillets, a roan horse and chair harness, numerous pieces of silver plate (one of which bore the Custis crest), silver buttons and rings, a silver tankard, and gold shoe buckles for Anne, upon which was engraved, "in Memory of John Custis."[82] As if to heap further insult upon his son, he allegedly appointed Matthew Moody trustee for a tract of land presented to his negro boy, Jack. When Anne Moody remonstrated with him over the gifts and suggested he should give them to his son, he grew vehement and stated, "he would dispose of his property as he pleased," that she was an old fool; that if she refused them, "he would throw them into the street for any body to pick up that had a mind for them." The tirade continued:

> "That he had rather this Defendt. should have them than any Dandridge's Daughter or any Dandridge that ever wore a head he said he had not been at Work all his Life time for Dandridges Daughter alluding as this Deft. understood to be a Daughter of Mr John Dandridge of New Kent County to whom the complainant as this Deft. heard about that Time was making his address by way of Courtship for which Match this Deft. had at several Times heard the sd: John Custis express a very great Dislike imagining as the Defent. had understood that the sd: Mr Dandridge's Daughter was much inferior to his Son the Complaint. in point of fortune."[83]

It was a thoroughly disagreeable courtship and an unfortunate family situation.

Daniel was not easily discouraged. In the spring of 1749, not wishing to subject himself to the wrath of his father, he applied to his old friend, John Blair, for assistance with his troubled romantic endeavors.[84] Blair, in turn, sought the aid of Colonel Thomas Lee, who happened to be visiting Blair when Daniel's letter arrived.[85] Lee was an old and trusted friend of John Custis and a fellow member of the Council. Aside from that, he already had some insight into the difficulties of the romance. He was of the opinion that the difficulty laid with Daniel for not letting his father know of his intentions concerning Miss Dandridge. He recommended Daniel inform his father of his affection for the young lady in a forthright manner. He also added he would do what he could to help the romance along to a happy conclusion. Blair upheld Colonel Lee's recommendations.[86]

Daniel continued to procrastinate. In a letter from Blair, somewhat later, Thomas Lee was critical of Daniel's delay and was of the opinion the old man was in a receptive mood. In the same letter Blair divulged that he spent the night with Custis, found him in a surly mood brought on by a difference of opinion concerning plantation management at White House. However, the father did acknowledge his son's admirable character and sobriety, that he, Custis, had "done enough, since all he did would be only for Jack D-D-ge." Both Blair and Lee advised Daniel to marry without his father's approbation and that he would, when it was all over, be reconciled to it. But Daniel was still reluctant to take such a gamble, fearing his father's wrath and reprisal in the form of a disinheritance in favor of Jack.

Shortly thereafter Daniel sought the aid of his close friend and attorney, James Power.[88] Power called on Colonel Custis in Williamsburg and found him in an unusually peaceful frame of mind. He inveigled an overnight invitation from Custis. Power turned out to be the consummate negotiator. Working on Custis's infatuation with Jack, he made the young boy, in the name of Daniel, a gift of his own son's horse, saddle, and bridle, and came away with the old gentleman's approval of the marriage, as well as his high esteem for Martha. He immediately sat down and penned the good news to Daniel.

> Dear Sir:
> This comes at last to bring you the news
> that I believe will be the most agreeable to you of any
> you have ever heard - that you may not be long in
> suspense I shall tell you at once - I am empowered
> by your father to let you know that he heartily and
> willingly consents to your marriage with Miss Dandridge
> that he has so good a character of her, that he had
> rather you should have her than any lady in Virginia
> nay, if possible, he is as much enamored with her
> character as you are with her person, and this is
> owing chiefly to a prudent speech of her own. Hurry
> down immediately for fear he should change the strong
> inclination he has to your marrying directly. I stayed
> with him all night, and presented Jack with my Jack's
> horse, bridle , and Saddle, in your name, which was
> taken as a singular favor. I shall say no more, as I
> expect to see you soon tomorrow, but conclude what I
> really am,
> Your most obliged and affectionate humble servant
> J. Power[89]

Coincidentally Custis's health began to deteriorate. On May 11, 1749 Governor Gooch gave his farewell address to the General Assembly and prepared to return to England because of ill health. Until a new Royal Governor arrived, the senior member of the Council would become the Acting Governor. The three senior members of the Council, in order of seniority, were the elder John Robinson, John Custis, and Thomas Lee. John Robinson died shortly before Governor Gooch set sail from York-town. Colonel Custis, too infirm and incompetent to serve, asked to be relieved of his duties as a member of the Council on August 25, 1749.[90] His request was granted and his friend, Thomas Lee assumed the office of acting Governor.

Realizing his life might be drawing to a close, Custis drew up a new will on November 14, 1749. Its purpose was served when he died on November 22, 1749.[91] His will, witnessed by Thomas Dawson, George Gilmer, and John Blair, Jr., was proved April 9, 1750.

The will was as unique as the testator. It provided amply for Jack's welfare and comfort and reaffirmed his manumission; supplied him with riding and work horses; to live under the supervision of Daniel until age 20; during that time he was to be handsomely maintained. To Anne Moody he gave £20 annually, together with Jack's portrait. His "dear friend," Thomas Lee, was to receive £200. His "esteemed friend," John Blair, was to receive £100. Mrs. Blair was to receive five guineas for the purchase of a mourning ring. For the many services he had rendered, John Cavendish was given the house and lot where he lived, rent free, for his natural life. All other lands were left in fee simple to Daniel. One of the unusual stipulations provided for his "real body" to be taken to Arlington on the Eastern Shore and buried beside hs grandfather, Major-General Custis, "who had provided me with an English education as a young man." He further directed his tombstone be brought from England, that it bear the Custis crest, and that it contain the following inscription:

> Under this Marble Tomb Lies the Body
> of the Hon. John Custis, Esq.,
> of The City of Williamsburg
> And Parish of Bruton,
> Formerly of Hungars Parish On The
> Eastern Shore
> Of Virginia, and County of Northampton,
> Age 71 Years and Yet Lived But Seven Years,
> Which was the Space of Time He Kept
> A Bachelor's Home At Arlington
> On The Eastern Shore Of Virginia
> This Inscription Put on His Tomb Was By
> His Own Positive Orders

The will directed that should the tombstone be lost, the executor was to order another, and if he refused to carry out the bequest he was to be disinherited and given one shilling sterling. As usual, Daniel followed his father's orders. The monument stands today, as ordered.

Daniel Parke Custis and Martha Dandridge were married at Chestnut Grove, the home of the bride on May 15, 1750.[93] From there he took his young nineteen year old bride to White House. With the aid of overseers, he managed his plantations in New Kent, King William, King and Queen, York, Northampton, and other smaller tracts throughout the colony. In all they were in excess of 17,000 acres.[94] His principal crop on the Eastern Shore was grain, while tobacco was the mainstay on the western side of the bay. Three English mercantile firms, Robert Cary and Company, John Hanbury and Company, and James Gildart continued to receive his shipments, much as they had during his father's lifetime. Following the sale of his tobacco, whatever credit balance remained, was used to purchase plantation and household supplies, and personal items for the family.

Daniel's predicament was identical with the rest of the Virginia and Maryland planters. They were the victims of a two-edged sword: sell at a depressed price and purchase at an inflated price. In 1660 Parliament had passed a Navigation Act in response to a need for money to maintain employment at home, to curtail the trade and expansionist policies of the Dutch, and maintain a naval superiority in ships, sailors, and naval stores. The Act of 1660 was an augmentation of a previous act of 1651, which was the beginning of a philosophy of economic imperialism that was to endure for almost three hundred years. No foreign ships were permitted to engage in trade with the English colonies, nor were they allowed to import colonial products into Great Britain. Neither were foreign merchants permitted to trade directly with the colonies. Certain commodities were "enumerated" and could be sent only to England, Ireland, or Wales, and after the Act of Union, to Scotland. It further stipulated that the enumerated items were to be transported in English ships, manned by a specified percentage of English sailors. Among the enumerated items of greatest importance to the southern colonies were tobacco, sugar, cotton, and indigo.

To further tighten the vise, Parliament passed the Staple Act in 1663, prohibiting the direct importation of all goods from Europe into the American colonies. Goods must first be carried to England. After duties and various handling charges were paid, they could then be reshipped to America. All such extra charges were, of course, ultimately borne by the American purchasers. Thus, the Acts required the colonist to send his raw materials to England to be made into finished goods, where it might be sold anywhere in the world, or sold back to the colonials, with the result that the English merchant and manufacturer could dictate the price of what America sold and bought.

Tobacco, in particular, was funneled through Great Britain and then trans-shipped to the continent. As an example, in the course of a year, of 96,000 hogsheads of tobacco shipped from Maryland and Virginia, 82,000 hogsheads were re-exported to the continent. Freight rates and insurance fees were high, often set by the English factor who also owned the ship and wrote the insurance. A high import duty was then levied at the English port of arrival. Tobacco re-exported to the continent incurred additional freight charges, insurance fees, commissions, and other handling charges. The secondary re-shipment charges were borne by the producer and not by the British merchant or the continental consumer. Of course there was also the possibility a shipment would never arrive, falling prey to natural forces or a hostile enemy. The English factor constantly complained of the poor quality of the tobacco, in spite of rigid inspections made before leaving the American ports. Few letters from them were laudatory, and yet they continually begged and fawned for the planter's tobacco. Fraudulent acts were also perpetrated, which further decreased the planter's income.[95] Ever increasing prices and a decreasing quality of finished goods became a constant source of irritation to Daniel. He was vociferous in his complaints and was not above sending instructions to English firms on the proper method of making axes, hoes, and scythes more durable. They could not have cared less.[96]

By the standards of his day we can conclude Daniel was a capable planter. In a letter to Robert Cary and Company he stated, "If every one would take the same Pains with their Tobacco and Fling away as much as I do there would not be such complaints of the Inspectors as there are."[97] In order to prevent bruising of the leaves, he recommended the unstemmed tobacco leaves should be placed in layers in the hogsheads, rather than tying them in bundles.[98] They were assured that if his purchases were of good quality he would increase his tobacco shipments as well as his orders for additional goods.[99] Increasing his tobacco shipments meant converting grain production to tobacco on the Eastern Shore.[100] At the same time he contracted with Edward Lovely to drain his Claiborne Marsh land in King William County, "dry enough to grow corn and other grains."[101]

Orders were placed annually for linens, brocades, callico, silk, tabby, and other dress-making materials.[102] When the materials were pleasing to Martha, her husband so informed the agents.[103] Martha was fond of clothes, judging from the frequency, length, and diversity of the orders that went to London. Married to one of the most affluent and generous Virginia planters, she must have been one of the best dressed matrons in the colony.

The Dunbar suit continued to disturb Daniel, just as it had his father. His old friend, James Power, and the aggressive John Mercer continued to serve as attorneys. The outcome did not look favorable for the Custises, and there was the distinct possibility they might lose everything in order to cover the debts the late Colonel Parke had incurred in England and the Islands. Mercer, however, maintained an attitude of cautious optimism, but seemed pessimistic over a rapid termination of the suit. At the same time he appealed to Daniel for a loan of £1000 to ease his own dire financial straights.[104] Another annoyance was the bequest of £20 Sterling to be paid annually to Matthew and Anne Moody.[105] Perhaps more aggravating were the gifts of family plate, furniture, jewelry, a horse, and other miscellaneous items Custis had given to the Moodys in a fit of temper. In an attempt to have the property returned, Daniel took the dispute to court. The Moody's defense was based upon the allegation that Custis had been adamant in his insistence they be accepted as gifts. Apparently there were witnesses to his largess. As for the £20 bequest, there was nothing for Daniel to do but pay.[106] The irritation engendered by his father's bequests to Jack did not remain long. The young negro boy died after a brief illness.

The Custises lost little time in acquiring a family. By April, 1751, Martha knew she was pregnant. Daniel Parke Custis II was born on November 1751. James Power, his daughter Molly, and John Dandridge and his wife Frances (Martha's parents) were Godparents. On April 12, 1753, when Daniel was fourteen months old, Martha presented him with a sister, Frances Parke Custis. The Godparents were Martha's sister, Anna Maria (Nancy) Dandridge, and the little girl's parents. Another sister, Martha Parke Custis, followed in 1754. The following year brought a much desired son, John Parke Custis.[108]

Suddenly a succession of sadnesses swept the White House family. Young Daniel died February 19, 1754, and was buried close to his grandmother, Frances Parke Custis, at Queens Creek Plantation. A tombstone was ordered from the Cary firm. Later the father complained that he "wanted a genteel Tomb and not a great deal of money to be spent on it...too great for such a young child." At the same time he ordered three dozen bottles of "Genuine Red Port Wine-such as Old Mr Robt Cary used to drink himself."[109] About September 2, news came from Fredericksburg, that Martha's father, John Dandridge, had died of apoplexy, August 31, while visiting his niece, Mary Spottswood. Due to the extreme heat, he was promptly interred there in St. George's churchyard.[110] June brought additional sadness. Three-year-old Frances died, and again the sad procession made its way toward Williamsburg and to the old Queens Creek Plantation, where she was laid to rest beside her brother and grandmother.[111]

Making his way south, on a journey that would take him through Maryland, Virginia, the Carolinas, and ultimately to the Bahamas, was an itinerant English painter, John Wollaston. His meanderings from one plantation to another, where he sought commissions to paint the aristocracy and their progeny, brought him to White House, shortly after the death of little Frances. How long he stayed is not known, but it was long enough for him to begin three portraits, one each of Martha and Daniel, and another of young John Parke Custis (Jacky), together with his younger sister, Martha Parke Custis (Patcy).[112]

The grief was fresh in Martha's heart when Jacky was taken ill about June 12, 1757. Dr. James Carter, a Williamsburg physician, sent several medicines to White House. But about July 4th something far more serious arose. Daniel, the father, was suddenly taken ill. Remedies were again sent by Dr. Carter. After several days without improvement, Dr. Carter made the twenty-five- mile trip and arrived on July 7th, accompanied by a veritable armamentarium of medicines. It was all in vain. Daniel died on July 8, aged 46.[113] Dr. Carter remained an additional three days, treating Jacky, who recovered. The usual funeral arrangements were made: a lined walnut coffin was made; clothes were altered and additional mourning clothes were ordered.[114] The little family and a few friends and relatives accompanied Daniel's remains to Queens Creek Plantation, where burial was beside his mother and two children.[115]

At the age of twenty-six, Martha was a widow with two young children, probably the wealthiest widow in Virginia. One month after Daniel's death, Dr. Carter was called again to White House to attend the widow, Martha. The illness was serious enough for him to remain three days.[116] In a period of three-and-one-half years, death had claimed Martha's father, husband, and two children. Due to Daniel's sudden death, he had died intestate. It was a crushing burden that she was ill prepared to meet. Suddenly she was alone - the owner of a substantial fortune in cash reserves, over 17,000 acres of widely separated land,the guardianship of two children, the owner of several hundred slaves, for which she was responsible, bills to be paid, money to be collected, overseers to be supervised, correspondence to be continued with the English agents, as well as the responsibilities of executrix of her husband's estate. If all that was not enough, the spector of the Dunbar suit was again rearing its ugly head. It was an awesome task for someone without a pence worth of experience in managing such complicated affairs.[117] It was a time of sadness, but there was also much work to be done. Fortunately, there were those upon whom she could rely for advice and assistance in the management of her day-to-day affairs and in the settlement of Daniel's estate. She could rely on such men as Robert Carter Nicholas, Benjamin Waller, John Mercer, John Robinson, James Power, Peter Lyon, John Blair, her brother, Bartholomew Dandridge, and the reliable overseer, Joseph Valentine. In an era of sudden death and short widowhood, perhaps another husband might arrive to help solve some of her dilemmas.

1. The first Custis of record was Edmund Custis of Cirencester, Gloucester County, England, the father of John Custis I, of Rotterdam. See "Colonel Norwood's Voyage to

Virginia in 1649," *V.H.R.*, v. 2, no. 3, July, 1849.

  2. 58 *V* 402.

  3. 24 *V* 195-208, 195-208.

  4. 52 *V* 28.

  5. *Ibid.*

  6. 13 *V* 192.

  7. 2 *W* (1) 256; 20 *V* 25, 140, 237.

  8. 54 *V* 307-15.

  9. 54 *V* 308-09.

  10. *Ibid* 309.

  11. *Ibid* 309-10.

  12. Coxe, W.C., *Memoirs of John Duke of Marlborough*, London, 1820, I, 231-32; 2 *Freeman*, 280, 285 (facing).

  13. 54 V 311.

  14. *Ibid.*

  15. 54 *V* 312-15. The original is in the Custis Papers, ViHi.

  16. John Custis to Frances Parke, February 4, 1705, *Recollections*, 16 n.

  17. Daniel Parke to John Custis, August 25, 1705, *Recollections*, 16 n.

  18. 20 *V* 378-89. In all fairness, it must be stated the previous government in the islands had been lax and inefficient. There were apparently many rebellious, lawless characters who resented Parke's attempts at reform. See, George French, *The History of Colonel Parke's Administration*, London, 1717; George French, *An Answer to a Scurrilous Libel*, London, 1719.

  19. *Recollections*, p. 24-26; P.R.O., C.O., 152:42, No. 54, Thomas Morris, February 27, 1711; P.R.O., C.O. 153: No. 11, p. 312. 2 *Freeman*, 282.

  20. 20 *V* 372-73.

  21. 2 *Freeman* 283. For the best summary of the legal entanglements generated by the will of Daniel Parke, see 2 *Freeman*, p. 276-91.

  22. Circa 1724 the amount of indebtedness in the Leeward Island stood at about £10,000. A legal opinion, in an unknown hand, now located at ViMtV, written about 1724, states, "that if ye Estate in England and Virginia be not only liable to ye debts in Virginia and England, but allso to those in ye Leward Island; then Frances Custis, Nor her sister Lucy Burd, will take anything by the said Will because all ye debts will amount to a much greater value, than the whole estate in Virginia and England is worth, wch cant possible be ye intent and meanning of the Testator."

  23. *Byrd Title Book*, 208, ViHi.

  24. One legend concerns a ride they took in their small chariot. As Custis drove the horse toward the edge of the shore, his wife said, "where are you going, Mr. Custis?" His reply was, "to Hell Mrs. Custis!" She rejoined, "Drive on Mr. Custis. Anything is better than living at Arlington with you."

  25. Custis-Lee Family Bible. G.W.P. Custis gives the year of her birth as 1710. *Recollections*, 18.

  26. Custis-Lee Family Bible. Byrd was the uncle of the infant and Hannah Ludwell was a great-aunt.

  27. *Brothers*, p. 13.

  28. 32 *V* 239 n. Her sister, Lucy, the wife of William Byrd II, also died of smallpox in London, November 21, 1716. William Byrd II to John Custis, December 13, 1716, *Recollections*, p. 32. Byrd stated his wife, Lucy died of smallpox, "the very same cruel distemper that destroyed her sister."

  29. Later known as "Six Chimney House". It stood at what is now the south east corner of Francis and Nassau Streets, Williamsburg, Va.

  30. Swem, *Brothers of the Spade*. Correspondence of Peter Collinson of London and of John Custis of Williamsburg, Virginia (1734-1746), *Barre*, 1957.

31. John Custis to Mrs. Parke Pepper, ca. 1731. *Recollections*, p. 18.

32. 2 *Freeman* 291; 15 *V* 302; *Recollections*, 18: for the two marriages of Francis Parke Custis, see also, 1 *Harris* 78-80; 2 *Harris* 606-7. Her first marriage to William Winch lasted only a few months when her husband deserted and returned to London, ostensibly due to the failure of her father to pay the £1000 promised him prenuptually.

33. John Custis acquired the White House tract sometime between 1730-35. For a more detailed history of the tract, see, 1 *Harris* 120-25.

34. John Blair to Daniel Parke Custis, March 13, 1744. *Etting Collection*, PHi.

35. *Recollections*, p. 18-19.

36. *Ibid.*

37. *Secret Diary*, p. 175.

38. Meade, *Old Churches, Ministers and Families of Virginia*, Philadelphia, 1:387.

39. *Genealogists Magazine*, v. 15, No. 14, p. 608.

40. *Ibid.*, 608.

41. *Ibid.*, 609.

42. *Ibid.*, 609.

43. *Ibid.*, 609.

44. *Ibid.*, 612.

45. *Ibid.*, 612.

46. *Ibid.*, 608-13.

47. *Ibid.*, 613.

48. 32 *V* 376, 399-400.

49. 32 *V* 238.

50. *Ibid.*

51. 14 *V* 117.

52. 32 *V* 238; 14 *V* 117.

53. 32 *V* 399-400.

54. 32 *V* 376.

55. 1 *Harris*, p. 82-86.

56. *Dandridge Family Bible*, see, 1 *Harris*, p. 82-83.

57. 8 *V* 261.

58. 3 *W* (1) 172.

59. *Ibid.*

60. 2 *W* (1) 150.

61. *Ibid.*

62. 58 *V* 136; 1 *T* 269, 275.

63. 15 *V* 439-441.

64. 31 *V* 224.

65. 3 *W* (1) 180.

66. 53 *V* 249.

67. 21 *V* 75.

68. 2 *V* 7; 8 *V* 261.

69. 8 *W* (1) 126; 2 *V* 438.

70. *Henly Family Bible*, copy at ViMtV; a *Harris*, 85

71. 1 *Harris*, 82-83

72. *Henly Bible*, 1 *Harris*, 83-86. The house was a two-story frame dwelling with end chimneys and a hip roof. It was destroyed by fire in 1926.

73. 3 *W* (1) 246-47; 17 *V* 150.

74. John Blair (1687-1771) Member of House of Burgesses (1734-1740); Auditor-general (1728-1771); Member of the Council (1745-1771); one-time Acting-governor.

75. John Blair to Daniel Parke Custis, March 13, 1744. *Etting Collection*, PHi.

76. "Old Alice" is listed among the Custis slaves. *Custis Papers*, ViHi.

77. Among them was Mrs. Thomas Lee. See, *Recollections*, p. 20, n.

78. 6 *York Records*, 63, February 15, 1747/48.

79. Notation in the handwriting of D.P.C., *Custis Papers*, ViHi.

80. *Ibid.*

81. The Moodys were inn-keepers at Queen Mary's Port, on the west side of the road near Capitol Landing on Queens Creek, two miles north of Williamsburg. Their inn was close to the Queens Creek Plantation of John Custis.

82. See Moody's answer to D.P.C.'s bill of complaint, n.d. *Custis Papers*, ViHi.

83. Following the death of John Custis, Daniel entered suit against the Moodys for the return of the property. For Moody's answer, see supra, n. 82.

84. See, supra, n. 74.

85. Thomas Lee of Stratford (1690-1750), Member of the Council.

86. John Blair to D.P.C., April 9, 1749, *Etting Collection*, PHi.

87. John Blair to D.P.D., portion of letter, date missing, *Etting Collection*, PHi.

88. James Power, an attorney, is believed to have been a native of Ireland. He was a burgess from King William and New Kent County, Power sat on numerous committees of the House of Burgesses concerning defenses against the Indians on the western frontier.

89. James Power to D.P.C., n.d., *Recollections*, p. 20; 2 *Freeman*298-304; 23 *V*369.

90. 5 *E* /288, 312.

91. 2 *Freeman* 294.

92. *Custis Papers*, ViHi.

93. It has long been held the marriage took place prior to the death of John Custis in November of 1749. G.W.P. Custis and all others have given the year as 1749. Freeman also states the year as 1749, but does not give the exact date. See, *Recollections*, p. 496; 2 *Freeman*, 249. The Custis-Lee Bible states as follows: "Daniel & Martha Custis was by the Reverend Thacker married on Tuesday ye 15th of May 1750." Written on the flyleaf of the Bible is the following notation: "This was the Bible which my great grandmother Mrs Washington always read during morning devotions (Signed) Mary A R Lee 1838." Dr. Malcom Harris gives the date as June 15, 1750, a discrepancy of one month from the Custis-Lee Bible. He does not give his source. 2 *Harris*. Since it was the custom for marriages to be performed at the home of the bride, it is virtually certain the ceremony took place at Chestnut Grove. Reverend Chichely Corbin Thacker (1704-ca 1761), a graduate of Oriel College, Oxford, was the minister of the "upper Church" of Blissland Parish, also called Warreneye Church, from 1729 until 1758. 1 *Harris* 89. Reverend David Mossom was the rector of St. Peter's, the church both families attended. Why he was not chosen is not known. Illness or the closer proximity of Reverend Thacker may have been reasons.

94. Freeman's total of 17,438 acres is based on John Blair's receipt for payment of £22/10/5 in gold for quit-rents, dated May 8, 1758. The acreage actually exceeded this amount. The Custis lands were located in the counties of Northampton, York, King William, New Kent, Hanover, James City, and the City of Williamsburg. The Arlington tract in Northampton County consisted of 536 acres; Smith's Island, Northampton County, 4038 acres (4 *Lee* 388); Mockhorn Island, Northampton County, 4000 acres (*Brothers* 150); White House in New Kent County, 3000 acres according to Swem (*Brothers* 121) and 4000 according to Freeman (4 *Lee*386); Claiborn's, later known as "Romancoke," King William County, 4000 acres (4 *Lee* 386); Queens Creek, York County, 3330 acres (*Brothers* 121); Hanover County, a relatively small tract whose acreage is not known (5 *Writings* 331); James City County, small tracts; City of Williamsburg, approximately 3 acres (13 *Writings* 56). The total would be a bit in excess of 19,600 acres.

95. *The Case of the Planters of Tobacco in Virginia*, London, 1733; Bernard Knollenberg, *Origin*

of the American Revolution, N.Y., 1960, p. 138-84; John C. Miller, *Origins of the American Revolution*, Boston, 1943, p. 4-7.

96. D.P.C. to Coleburns, June 15, 1756, *Etting Collection*, PHi. In a letter of May 5, 1755 to John Hanbury and Company, Daniel complained of wood planes unfit for use, nails brittle that "scarce bear driving," *Etting Collection*, PHi. To Robert Cary and Company, June 16, 1756, he complained of being charged for two-dozen felt hats, but receiving twenty-one. In the same letter are complaints concerning the quality of iron hoes, *Etting Collection*, PHi.

97. D.P.C. to Robert Cary and Company, May 5, 1755, *Etting Collection*, PHi.

98. D.P.C. to Robert Cary, June 16, 1756; D.P.C. to James Gildart, June 13, 1756, *Etting Collection*, PHi.

99. *Ibid.*

100. *Ibid.*

101. D.P.C.'s contract with Edward Lovely, May 3, 1756, *Etting Collection*, PHi.

102. A list of twenty-eight dress-making items were purchased from Jane.

103. D.P.C. to Robert Cary and Company, May 5, 1755, *Custis Papers*, ViHi.

104. John Mercer to D.P.C., April 17, 1754, October 30, 1754, *Custis Papers*, ViHi. 105.

105. The Moodys operated an inn at Queen Mary's Port, near Capitol Landing. The location was close to Custis's Queens Creek plantation, where it would have been necessary for him to pass on his way to and from Williamsburg. In 1759 twelve of Moody's lots on the west side of the road leading to Capitol Landing were taken into the City of Williamsburg, 16 W (1)21.

106. A copy of Moody's deposition is in the *Custis Papers*, ViHi. There are no documents that reveal the outcome of the suit. It is doubtful, under the circumstances, that the Moodys returned the property. There is a receipt for a payment of £15 to the Moodys, June 8, 1751 in the *Custis Papers*, ViHi. Freeman was of the opinion this was the "last payment." This refers to the last current payment, since the editor has, in his collection, a receipt dated, February 13, 1755, for £15. See n. 82, supra. No other details concerning further payments of the bequest are known.

107. The Diary of John Blair, 7 W (1) 152, "ab 1 or 2 in ye morng. Col. Custis's Favourite Boy Jack died in abt 21 hours illness being take ill a little before day the 18th wth a Pain in the back of his Neck for wch he was blooded." The cause of death may have been meningitis.

108. *Brothers*, p. 117-19; James Power to D.P.C., April 8, 1753, *Custis Papers*, ViHi; 1 *Harris*, 116. The Custis children were all born at White House.

109. D.P.C. to Robert Cary and Company, June 16, 1756, *Etting Collection*, PHi.

110. 32 V 400. The maintenance of the tomb of John Dandridge was of concern to G.W. See G. W. to Charles Carter, June 28, 1788, 30 *Writings* 8.

111. *Brothers*, p. 119.

112. John Wollaston (ca 1710 - died after 1776) was an English portrait painter who came to America in the 1740's. He painted portraits in New York, Philadelphia, Maryland, Virginia, the Carolinas, and the Bahamas at various periods. See pages 11, 96 for a receipt of October 21, 1757, for a payment of 56 pistoles for painting three pictures. It is unlikely Wollaston arrived prior to the death of Frances, in June, since her portrait is not included. Whatever sittings Daniel had were before the onset of his final illness on July 4th. It is doubtful Martha would have sat after Daniel's death, as her portrait gives no hint of mourning attire. It is possible he remained at White House following Daniel's death on July 8, to finish the three portraits, and then received his fee on October 21st. Or, he may have gone elsewhere in the neighborhood and returned for his fee. The portraits are now at Washington and Lee University.

113. The suddeness of onset, in a previously healthy man of 46, would indicate death was caused by a cardiac condition. Freeman and his consultants were of this opinion. This editor, after reviewing the medications used, the acute onset, and the rapidly fatal termination, concurs. See audit of Dr. Carter's account with the Custis estate, November 28, 1757, *Custis Papers*, ViHi; 2 *Freeman*, 299.

114. See charges of Charles Crump, for making and lining a coffin, March 6, 1758; invoice

from Elizabeth Vaughan, for altering clothing, August 31, 1757, *Custis Papers*, ViHi.

115. The approximate location of the Queens Creek plantation house is known. Its distance north and somewhat west of where the present Capitol Landing Road lies on Camp Peary property, a short distance north of Interstate 64 and west of the entrance to Camp Peary. There are no visible remains. The buildings appear on the 1782 map by Colonel Desandrouins, General Rochambeau's chief engineer (Carte des Environs de Williamsburg in Virginie ou les Armees Francaise et Americaine out Campe's en Septembre 1781). It appears on the map as, "Mr Custis." The family cemetery was probably close to the main house. The tombstones of the Custis children, and of their father and grandmother, were removed in 1895 by Magruder-Ewell Camp of the Confederate Veterans of Williamsburg, and placed in Bruton Parish churchyard, along the north wall of the church. They may be seen there at the present time. Dr. Earl G. Swem visited the site of the Queens Creek plantation prior to 1957 and stated no surface indications of the buildings or cemetery were visible. The Custis mill, located a short distance southwest of the plantations buildings, became the property of Colonel Waller and then became known as Waller's Mill. This area is now a part of Waller Mill Park, administered by the City of Williamsburg. Dr. Lyon G. Tyler was of the opinion the Custis family burial ground was on the site of the original Marston Church, one of the three parishes that were amalgamated to form Bruton Parish. *Brothers*, 119-20; 4 W (1) 66.

116. Dr. James Carter's account, the estate of D.P.C., November 28, 1757, *Custis Papers*, ViHi.

117. The estate was appraised at £23,632. See Summary of the Account of D.P.Custis, 1857, in the handwriting of John Mercer, *Custis Papers*, ViHi.

Appendix II
The Marriage of Martha Dandridge Custis and George Washington

Early in August, 1757, while on military duty as commander of the Virgina forces at Winchester, Colonel Washington began experiencing mild dysentery. Initially the condition did not limit his activities or his ability to carry out his duties.[1] During that month he spent approximately ten days at Alexandria and Mount Vernon, conferring with George Lee concerning the settlement of the estate of his brother, Lawrence.[2] The following month he again made the trip to Belvoir and Mount Vernon to attend the funeral observance of his close friend and mentor, Colonel William Fairfax. His return to Winchester was prompt.[3] Nearby Indian depredations prompted him to write Governor Dinwiddie, urging a major offensive that would drive the French and Indians from the Ohio valley.[4]

The governor replied he would be returning to England in November. Because of Dinwiddie's impending departure, Washington, in a letter of October 5th, requested permission to return to Williamsburg in order to settle his accounts with the Governor and the committee of the House of Burgesses.[6] The unfinished state of the fort at Winchester (Fort Loudon) and the constant threat of attack by marauding French and Indians prompted Dinwiddie to refuse his request.[7]

Washington's physical condition continued to deteriorate during the fall of 1757 and his dysentery, then called "bloody flux," became worse. Debility, fever, violent chest pain, an inability to walk, sit, or write letters forced him to seek medical advice. Dr. James Craik, the military surgeon, bled him twice and then insisted, over George's protestations, that he avail himself of "changing his air...going some place where he can be kept quiet." His command was left in the hands of Captain Robert Stewart, who was instructed to notify the governor and Colonel John Stanwix of his illness and of his decision to return to Mount Vernon. Always uppermost in his mind was the thought that he might be developing the consumption that had carried off his brother, Lawrence, five years before.[9]

On his arrival at Alexandria he consulted Dr. Charles Green, the rector of Pohick Church, who, prior to taking holy orders, had been a practicing physician.[10] During the month of December and of January, 1758, his condition was one of alternating remission and regression. At the end of January he set out for Williamsburg to settle his accounts with the committee of the House of Burgesses and report to President Blair on the "state of the frontier settlements." He progressed as far south as Colonel Baylor's residence, Traveler's Rest, when the dysentery, fever, and pain returned, forcing his return to Mount Vernon.[11]

His condition continued grave. In a letter to Colonel Stanwix he was apprehensive of an "approaching decay, being visited with several symptoms of such a disease." He was obviously much depressed, as evidenced by his thoughts of resigning his commission, retiring from all business, and turning over his command to someone who would be more successful than he had been.[12]

He again departed from Mount Vernon on March 5th, stopping for a few days at Ferry Farm to visit his mother. From there he proceeded down the northern neck on the north side of the Rappahannock, crossing the river at Hobb's Hole.[13] From there he proceeded to King and Queen County, and stopped at Pleasant Hill, the residence of Speaker John Robinson.[14] There he probably delivered his accounts for audit to the speaker, for he was also treasurer of the colony. From there he crossed the Mattapony River into King William County and rejoined the main road to Williamsburg. Crossing the Pamunkey River either at Claiborne's or Eltham, he passed close to Eltham, the home of the Bassett's, where in later years he was to spend so many pleasant as well as sad days.[15] From there the road passed Warreneye Church, Doncastle's ordinary and Chiswells ordinary.[16] The following day he reached Williamsburg and promptly consulted Dr. John Amson, one of the colony's most capable physicians. Amson assured him his condition was not terminal and that an early recovery was to be expected.[17]

Leaving Williamsburg, Washington retraced his steps, passing Chiswell's and Doncatle's, and on to Barhamsville. There he took the left fork of the road to New Kent Court House and proceeded on to Poplar Grove, the residence of Richard Chamberlayne.[18] There he may have met the young widow, Martha Custis, a neighbor of the Chamberlayne's, on or about March 16, 1758. He apparently stayed a day or day and a half at the Chamberlayne's, for he was back in Williamsburg on March 18th.[20] One week later, March 25th, found him again at the widow Custis's door.[21] Following this second visit Washington returned to Williamsburg, completed his affairs there, and returned by his usual route to Fredericksburg and Mount Vernon, arriving on or about April 1st.[22] From there he rode to Winchester and rejoined his regiment. In two short visits with Martha Custis he had possibly proposed marriage and been accepted. They both liked what they saw. She, a charming and attractive young woman with a large fortune, thousands of fertile acres, and two young children. He, a tall handsome young man, already at the age of twenty-six, a military hero whose reputation was assured. He could be capable of managing the tangled and complicated affairs of her late husband's estate, and might be a suitable guardian for her two young children.

A departure from the usual and time honored account of the circumstances surrounding the courtship of Washington and Mrs. Custis seems necessary. All historians and biographers, except Freeman, have followed G.W.P. Custis's account, which places their first meeting at the time of Washington's crossing of the Pamunkey River on his way south to consult Dr. Amson at Williamsburg.[23] Briefly, Custis's account states Washington crossed the Pamunkey, going *south*, at Williams Ferry, landing at Chamberlayne's wharf, on his way to Williamsburg to conduct business with the governor. Chamberlayne is said to have urged him to remain for dinner. Washington protested, pleading urgency to attend his business. However, Chamberlayne continued to insist and at last overcame Washington's reluctance by informing him he would introduce him to "a young and charming widow, then beneath his roof." Washington agreed on condition that he be allowed to remain only for dinner, after which he would proceed to Williamsburg. So enamored was he with what he saw that he spent the night at Chamberlayne's, leaving about noon of the following day. Riding on to Williamsburg, he completed his business and returned to White House where the engagement was agreed upon and preparations for the marriage begun.

This account, if true, had to be one of the most rapid romances in all of recorded history. The account is a flowery narrative, typical of the 19th century and of G.W.P. Custis. It is illogical and contains a number of inaccuracies and omissions. Washington had been ill for seven months and was on his way to consult a physician, noted for his expertise in treating "bloody flux." This was his *second* attempt to reach Williamsburg. It was possible he might receive a poor prognosis for recovery from Dr. Amson. Custis made no mention of this, and states the purpose of the journey was to carry "important communications to the governor, etc." This is only a partial truth. Custis's grandmother, Mrs. Washington, being the source of his information, might not have remembered the circumstances of some thirty-five or forty years before. We must also remember that Custis was a romanticist. It is doubtful Washington, ill as he was, would have ridden an additional nineteen needless miles from Speaker Robinson's in order to cross Williams' Ferry, or to court the Widow Custis. He was too ill for such a detour or to consider taking a wife under such circumstances. Even had he been previously acquainted with Martha, it is doubtful he would have stopped for a social call under the circumstances. The records indicate Washington, on this occasion, met Martha coming *from* Williamsburg and not on the way *to* Williamsburg.

It seems plausible that Washington, relieved of anxiety over his illness, and knowing of Martha's eligibility, decided to pay his respects to her, with possible romantic intentions in mind. His return to Williamsburg twice after his initial visit to Dr. Amson would indicate his business there was not yet completed and that perhaps his visit to Richard Chamberlayne's home was planned with some objective in mind.[24] Otherwise he would have remained in Williamsburg, completed his business and then returned to his military duties at Winchester.

The circumstances of the introduction of Washington and Martha Custis, as related by her grandson, G.W.P. Custis, might have been told him by his grandmother, thirty-five or forty years after its occurence.[25] Custis did not publish his recollections of it until 1833 - seventy-five years after its occurrence. Such a long period of time does detract from the accuracy of the story. However there are some verifiable facts in his published version. Washington did journey to Williamsburg early in 1758; there was a Williams Ferry that crossed the Pamunkey River, terminating at Richard Chamberlayne's wharf; Chamberlayne did live about a mile from White House, Mrs. Custis's residence.[26]

It is quite possible Colonel Washington and Mrs. Custis had met prior to their two meetings in March, 1758. White House was approximately thirty-three miles from Williamsburg - the commercial, political, and social capitol of the colony - reason enough for the Custis's to have journeyed there. Their Williamsburg home, inherited from Daniel's father, still furnished and maintained, was a commodious and comfortable place for them to lodge. It is doubtful the Custises, both in the prime of life, would have spent all their time sequestered at White House, entirely removed from the center of colonial society. Considering the frequency with which Washington visited the colonial capitol, it would be strange indeed if they had *not* previously met. It was a closed society; a time of sudden death and rapid remarriage. News traveled fast. By the end of 1755 Washington's name was a household word in Virginia, by virtue of his military exploits. He was one of their own kin and kind. During the previous two years he had carried Governor Dinwiddie's message to the French commandant, demanding he vacate the Ohio valley of French troops and their Indian allies; had intercepted and destroyed a French force attempting to infiltrate the frontier; he had acquitted himself well at the Great Meadows battle, even though defeated; by the time of Daniel Custis's death he had accumulated additional laurels by protecting the western frontier of the colony against Indian depredations, in spite of insufficient men, money, and materiel. Through no fault of his he was not always successful. He had played an heroic part in the ill-fated Braddock campaign, a military catastrophe that would have been worse had it not been for his leadership at a crucial time. Undoubtedly, Colonel Washington, the highest ranking colonial officer, was well known among the gentry, if not personally, but certainly by reputation. About his courage and bravery there was no doubt. Undoubtedly, Mrs. Custis knew of him.

Daniel Parke Custis's death and Martha's inheritance of the large estate would certainly have been a topic of conversation in the ordinaries and plantations that Washington frequented on his travel from Williamsburg to the frontier. It could scarcely have escaped his notice that Martha was eligible, attainable, and desirable, for he was on friendly terms with men who knew her and were advising her in the settlement of her late husband's estate.[27] Conversely, she was probably familiar with his military attainments, his character, and appearance.

It is unlikely, deliberate as he was, never acting in a precipitous manner, and giving careful consideration to all important decisions, that he would have acted impetuously on one of the most important steps in his life. As stated previously, it would have been strange indeed if they had not met on some previous occasion, and stranger still if either had acted impulsively on such an important decision, following a supposedly casual and hurried meeting. Martha's stakes were high, for under Virginia law her property became her husband's, and that meant one-third of all the Custis holdings.[28]

Colonel Washington arrived at Winchester on April 5th. In the vicinity he found a large contingent of Cherokee Indians, recruited to fight the French and their Indian allies. The Indians had always been vacillating and unpredictable and it was a situation he would again have to cope with, for he was not without experience in handling their whims.[29] During his absence there had also been a change in the British command. Colonel John Forbes, promoted to brigadier-general, was named to command the expedition to capture Fort Duquesne. During the spring 1758 session of the House of Burgesses a bill was passed to increase the Virginia forces to 2000 men. This provided for an additional regiment and was to be under the command of Colonel William Byrd, III, although when acting together with Washington's First Brigade, the latter was to have over-all command.[30] Preparations were begun throughout the provincial and regular command to move west and assault Fort Duquesne. It was imperative that the campaign be completed by December 1, since the enlistments of the additional regiment expired on that date.

Sir John St. Clair, the British quartermaster-general, directed Washington to return to Williamsburg for consultation with President John Blair, concerning pay for the troops,. additional equipment and ammunition, and to "settle the Affairs of the two Virginia Regiments."[31] Washington left Fort Loudoun (Winchester) on May 24th and arrived in Williamsburg on May 28th.[32] He laid twelve written propositions before President Blair, "to represent in the fullest manner the posture of our affairs at Winchester."[33] He probably remained in Williamsburg for a week, discussing the issues at stake in the propositions with Blair, the Council, and the committees of the House of Burgesses. At this time he probably stayed at the Williamsburg residence of Burwell Bassett.[34] At the conclusion of his consultations, he rode to the Pamunkey River on June 5th, where he paid a call on Martha. At that time she possibly gave her consent to marry or perhaps discussed their upcoming marriage plans.[35] Leaving White House that same day, he crossed the Pamunkey River at Claiborne's Ferry and headed north toward Winchester, arriving there on June 9th.[36] On the day of his arrival Washington received orders from St. Clair to march his 1st Virginia Regiment to Fort Cumberland on June 24th.[37] After a slow and arduous march, they arrived at their destination on July 2nd, a distance of about sixty miles.[38]

After what seemed to Washington undue and prolonged deliberation, General Forbes determined to proceed toward Fort Duquesne by a new route.[39] It would push over Allegheney Mountain, Laurel Hill, and Chestnut Ridge, rather than by way of the old Braddock Road of 1755. Forbes had not reached this decision on his own. He had sought the opinion of Colonels Bouquet, St. Clair, Washington, and others on his staff. The new approach was favored since it was more direct and would avoid some of the obstacles that had been such a nemesis to Braddock.[40] Washington and the Virginia officers, many of whom had been on the Braddock campaign, favored the old route, since it was already established and would require less time in which to reach the forts of the Ohio.

Time was of the essence, for the campaign had to be completed before winter. Besides, the Virginia enlistments were to expire on December 1st. Forbes' choice was over the protestations of Washington.[41] In spite of his persistent and emphatic arguments, Forbes remained adamant, and when the Colonel continued to belabor the point, Forbes became incensed and resentful of the interference and considered Washington "impertinent."[42]

While at Fort Cumberland Washington stood for election as a Burgess from Frederick County. He had previously been defeated in 1755, after being entered as a candidate just prior to the polling.[43] This time, with the support and electioneering of his friends and former comrades, he was successful, and led the poll by a wide margin, even though he was an absent candidate.[44] However, it cost him £39/6 for 60 gallons of liquid refreshments for his constituents.[45]

On September 12th, while still at Fort Cumberland, Washington wrote to Mrs. George William Fairfax, the wife of one of his closest friends, and confessed his friendship for her and the hopelessness of his affection for her because of her already happy state, and of the prospects he had in possessing Mrs. Custis.[46]

Chafing under the delays, Washington at last received orders from Colonel Bouquet to move his troops, wagons, and supplies west.[47] They arrive at Raystown (Bedford, Pa.) on September 21st.[48] Seven days before, an advance reconnaisance party of 750 men and officers, under the command of Major James Grant, had penetrated almost to the gates of Fort Duquesne. Discovered, the French and Indians had cut the force to pieces with heavy losses of regulars and Virginians. Grant had apparently acted rashly and irresponsibly.[49]

Washington and his 1st Virginia Regiment left Raystown on October 13th. Pressing over roads indescribably bad, made so by incessant rains, he ascended the south-east side of Laurel Ridge on October 21st, reached the opposite side of the ridge, and arrived at Loyal Hannon (Ligonier, Pa.) on October 23rd.[50] For months General Forbes had been seriously ill with the "bloody flux." By now, so debilitated he was unable to ride, he was transported on a swinging horse litter.[51] However in spite of his progressive physical deterioration, he was able to command, and arrived at Loyal Hannon on November 5th with the main body of his troops and artillery.[52]

The silence of the forest was shattered on November 12th when an outpost west of Loyal Hannon reported an approaching enemy force. Forbes ordered Washington and 500 of his force to intercept them. About three miles from the camp a skirmish ensued, in which two Indians and a white man were captured. Later in the confusion of darkness, Virginians fired on Virginians. One lieutenant and thirteen men were killed. It was an embarassment for the regimental commander.[53] But, there was a bright side to the disaster. The captured British subject had been a member of the garrison at Fort Duquesne. Under pressure of death he revealed the French forces were small and that many of the Indians had returned home. Armed with this intelligence, and by reports that the Indian chiefs, meeting at Easton with Pennsylvania officials, had signed a treaty, whereby some of the Indians would desert the French and join the British, Forbes determined to mount an all-out attack on the fort with a mobile force. Time was running out. He had two weeks until the enlistments of Colonel Byrd's 2nd Virginia Regiment would expire, and then Washington's 1st Virginia Regiment would have to be pulled back into Virginia to protect the frontier.[54] The British would then, of necessity, be required to spend a winter in the mountains.

Forbes divided his army into three brigades, each with a specific task. Colonel Bouquet and Colonel Montgomerie were each to command a brigade. Washington, now a brigadier, was to have command of the third brigade, consisting of his Virginia regiment, together with the Maryland, North Carolina, and Delaware troops.[55] His principal task was to prepare and build the road across Chestnut Ridge, the last major impediment before reaching Fort Duquesne. The ridge was reached on November 15th.[56] Orders followed for him to push on to Turtle Creek, marking the road and felling trees. Montgomerie's troops were left behind to open the road for passage.[57] The main army at last crossed Turtle Creek on November 22nd.[58] They were drawing close to their objective, but no one actually knew the number of miles.

The following day, November 23rd, Colonel Montgomerie's force of Highlanders opened the road, the artillery being escorted by Washington's troops.[59] By evening they were from twelve to fifteen miles from the fort. Patrols were sent out to scout the woods and determine if the French suspected their proximity. In everyone's mind there seemed to be a recollection of the Braddock massacre. The stillness was awesome - almost a portent of doom. The men were instructed on the procedures to follow should a sudden attack occur.[60] No white men were to be allowed to reconnoitre to Fort Duquesne itself. That task was assigned to a small party of Indian scouts.

Forbes wisely kept his force in camp on the 24th, to await the intelligence it was hoped the Indians would bring back. Only seven days remained before his colonial force might be dissipated. To Forbes and his staff it must have been a long, cold, bleak day and night of waiting - not knowing whether a full-scale battle awaited them or whether the loss of the entire colonial force would necessitate the regulars remaining in the forest over winter. Perhaps a victory might be at their fingertips. For Washington, would tomorrow end in another debacle such as he had experienced at the Monongahela three- and- one- half years before? Would tomorrow be the culmination of all his efforts of the past five years to mount an offensive that would drive the French back to Canada? One Indian scout and then another filtered back through the dark shadows of the forest. They had looked toward the fort and saw smoke billowing into the sky. A closer look revealed it had been consumed by flames, a smoldering ruin. The French were gone. The light horse set out immediately to inspect the site and quench the fires if possible. The main army followed the next day, the 25th, and reached the forks of the river in the early evening. It was as the Indians had said - a charred, blackened ruin.[61] The only inhabitants were a group of Indians on one of the river islands and a few in and about the remains of the fort, anxious to make peace with the English. The British learned from them that the French had loaded their cannons, men and supplies and had gone down the Ohio to the

Illinois country.

It was a hollow victory There was no surrender ceremony, no booty, no spoils of war. But, the expedition was a success, for it had accomplished its purpose. The Fork of the Ohio was in English hands and the French were driven out, never to return. On November 28th Washington sent the news to Governor Fauquier, "The possession of this fort has been a matter of great surprise to the whole army and we cannot attribute it to more probable causes than those of weakness, want of provision, and desertion of their Indians."[62] It was also a tribute to the abilities of Forbes, Bouquet, St. Clair, Washington, Halkett, and many of the other officers and soldiers who participated in the long, difficult, arduous struggle. Most of all it was the genius of Forbes who, though seriously ill, planned and executed the campaign. It is possible that without the expertise for which he was noted, their fate might have been similar to Braddock's.

A small holding force was left at Fort Duquesne, now renamed Fort Pitt. The Virginia troops marched back to Winchester, Washington's regiment being in an especially wretched condition due to extreme fatigue, want of warm clothing, food, and shelter.[63] Washington had already resolved to resign his commission, once the Forts were in English hands. His accounts had to be settled with the Governor, which necessitated a return to Williamsburg. He arrived at Winchester on December 8th.[64] The following day he was at Belvoir.[65] By the 22nd he was at Colonel John Baylor's and Todd's Ordinary.[66] Three days later, Christmas, he stopped at Chiswell's Ordinary.[67] His arrival in Williamsburg was on the 25th or 26th, Chiswell's being only ten miles away. On January 1, 1759 he wrote to his former commanding officer, General Forbes, "I should be extremely glad to hear of your safe arrival at head-quarters, after a fatiguing campaign, and that a perfect return of good health has contributed to crown your success."[68]

About the 5th of January he received *The Humble Address of the Officers of The Virginia Regiment*, in which they expressed their appreciation for his services to them: "---we beg Leave to assure you, that as you have hitherto been the actuating Soul of the whole Corps, we shall at all times pay the most invariable Regard to your will and Pleasure, and will always be happy to demonstrate by our Actions, with how much Respect and Esteem we are...." It was signed by twenty-seven of his fellow officers.[69]

We know nothing of Washington's activities during the first few days of January, 1759. There is no written record to substantiate it, but logically he must have spent part of this time at White House. The marriage ceremony was set for January 6th.

Martha was truly marrying a man of destiny. Toward the end of December, 1754, on his way south from his meeting with the French commandant at Fort Le Boeuf, he was fired upon by an Indian. The shot, fired at "fifteen steps," missed.[70] On May 28th of that year, in his first skirmish with an organized enemy force, his party was subjected to hostile fire. To his brother, Jack, he wrote, "---the right wing where I stood, was exposed to and received the enemy's fire --- I heard the bullets whistle, and, believe me, there is something charming in the sound." He was unscathed although one man beside him was killed and two others wounded.[71] Approximately five weeks later, July 3rd, he survived the French siege at Great Meadows.[72] On July 9, 1755, while serving as a volunteer aide to Major-general Braddock, he took a prominent part in the battle at the Monongahela, which ended in defeat for the British forces seeking to capture Fort Duquesne. Even though ill, he served with reckless bravery, attempting to rally and return order to the regulars and provincials from a situation of chaos. In another letter to Jack, written from Fort Cumberland, July 18th, "As I have heard since my arriv'l at this place, a circumstantial acct. of my death and dying speech, I take this early oppertunity of contradicting both, and of assuring you that I now exist and appear in the land of the living by the miraculous care of Providence, that protected me beyond all human expectation; I had 4 Bullets through my Coat and two Horses shot under me, and yet escaped unhurt."[73] Of 1459 men in the force, a total of 977 were killed or wounded.[74]

During George's tour of the frontier in 1756, he was marked for assassination by an Indian who held his fire. In his autobiography, written years later in 1786, he had this to say, "I passed and escaped almt. certain destruction for the weather was raining and the few Carbines unfit for use if we but escaped the first fire."[75] And lastly, on November 12, 1758, when Virginians fired upon Virginians in the darkness, Colonel Washington thrust himself between the combatants, striking the muskets upward with his sword to deflect the fire.[76] Spared again! This was the man Martha was about to take as her husband - a military hero, already known to some of the crowned heads of Europe, well known throughout America, as well as being a Virginia burgess.

For a century-and-a-half there has been considerable controversy concerning the location of the marriage ceremony of George Washington and Martha Custis. There is no known contemporary documentation as to its location. The early biographies of Washington by John Marshall,[77] Dr. David Ramsay,[78] and Jared Sparks,[79] make no mention of the site of the marriage. The first printed mention was probably that published in 1835 in the *National Portrait Gallery of Distinguished Americans*, written by Martha's grandson, George Washington Parke Custis. Custis stated he was unable to find any record of the marriage in the vestry book of St. Peter's Church and made no statement concerning the location of the ceremony.

The *Alexandria Gazette* of September 30, 1848 carried a news item stating: "a distinguished artist of New York," J. B. Stearns had been visiting Arlington House, the home of G.W.P. Custis, the purpose of which was to copy the early portraits of the Washingtons and to use them in a rendition of the Washington's marriage. The background of the painting depicted the interior of a church, which of course left one with the impression the ceremony was performed at St. Peter's, the parish church of the bride. Some have surmised that Stearns must have discussed the iconography and historical background with Custis and that the painting reflected Custis' belief. And well it might. However, nowhere is there a record of Stearns having discussed the subject with Custis.

Custis's biographical sketch was reprinted in *Recollections and Private Memoirs of Washington*, published by his daughter, Mrs. Robert E. Lee, in 1859. The book was a compilation of the many articles her father had written for the *National Intelligencer* over a period of years. Again, no mention was made of the location of the marriage.

In 1859 that indefatigable popular historian, Benson J. Lossing published his book, *Washington and Mount Vernon*, in which he stated the marriage rite occurred at White House.[80] Unfortunately, he did not state his source. However seventeen years later, in his book, *Mary and Martha Washington*, he stated the marriage took place at St. Peter's.[81] In this latter publication he recounts his many visits to Arlington House, between the years 1848 and 1861. It has been maintained that Lossing must have received different information from Custis that prompted him to change his opinion concerning the location of the ceremony. This seems an unlikely explanation since Custis died in 1857, two years before Lossing's first account appeared in print. Nowhere does Custis say the marriage took place at St. Peter's *or* White House. He merely states he was unable to find the date of the marriage in the vestry book. Neither is there mention in the *Alexandria Gazette* that Custis informed Stearns the marriage was performed at St. Peter's. It is possible Custis may have done so. It is equally possible Stearns preferred to exercise his artistic license and paint the heroic scene in an ecclesiastical setting, which would be far more appealing to the mid-nineteenth century mind than if portrayed in a domestic background.

General Robert E. Lee has unfortunately become involved in the controversy. In a letter written to Miss Virginia Ritchie of Brandon, October 23, 1869, he said, "There are three or four churches in Virginia in which I take peculiar interest. Grace Church in Lexington and St. Peter's in New Kent are two of them and both I think have claims upon the regard of the community--the second for its association with the recollections of General Washington, his marriage and early history."[82] Nowhere does General Lee state the Washingtons were married at St. Peter's. The "association" he speaks of may refer to the time of their "honeymoon" at White House, at which time they possibly would have attended services at St. Peter's, it being the most convenient place of worship and the church which Mrs. Washington had been most closely associated since her childhood.[3] "Association" may also refer to the rector, Reverend David Mossom, who performed the ceremony. Biographers have repeated the writings and opinions of their predecessors with regard to the choice of sites, even repeating the fanciful.[84]

Douglas Southall Freeman and Dr. Malcolm H. Harris have been diligent in their efforts to resolve the dispute. Freeman states, "The marriage ceremony was performed January 6, 1759 at the White House...[85] He gives four reasons: "First, it would have been inconvenient and uncomfortable to have the nuptials solemnized in mid winter at a church to which participants and guests would have been compelled to ride or drive over at least three miles of heavy roads."[86] "Second, at the time of death of Mrs. Margaret Anderson Young, age 95 in 1882, it was stated she had been married in 1806 in the same room at the White House in which the Washingtons had been married.[87] An entry in the family Bible, dated November 28, 1806, states, "Margaret Anderson was united in marriage with Richard Young, Parson Blair officiating. The marriage ceremony was performed in the very room where Washington was married to the charming widow Custis."[88] Mrs. Young's father, James Anderson, was manager at Mount Vernon from December, 1796 until January, 1801.[89] He tendered his resignation but was persuaded to become manager of the White House tract. He lived in White House, died there, and was buried close to the house. "Third, Mrs. Martwell Macon, who resided near White House and lived to a great age, often told her grandchildren that she remembered an aunt who had attended the wedding at White House."[90] "Fourth, Mrs. Clarence G. Burton, of Belona, Powhatan County, Virginia, direct descendant of Parson Mossom, stated in 1948 that her family tradition always was the the ceremony had been at the home of the bride." Mrs. Burton was a great great granddaughter of Reverend Mossom. In a letter to the Virginia Historical Society, Mrs. Burton stated her grandfather had told her father the wedding ceremony was performed at White House.[91]

There are a number of additional reasons that carry considerable weight in favor of White House. First: There is testimony of a descendant of Mrs. Washington who was reared at Tudor Place by her grandmother, Britannia Wellington Peter Kennon, herself a great granddaughter of Mrs. Washington. Mrs. Kennon was born in 1815 at Tudor Place and died there in 1911. The granddaughter writes that her grandmother Kennon stated the ceremony was performed at White House and that it was a tradition in the family that *all* marriages were performed at home.[92]

Second: Reverend E. C. McGuire, an Episcopal clergyman, in his book, *Religious Opinions and Character of George Washington*, states in his introduction, the marriage was performed at White House.[93] McGuire was a son-in-law of Robert Lewis, nephew and former secretary to his uncle, Prseident Washington. Lewis travelled with both the President and Mrs.

Washington, lived with them on several occasions, and was a confidante of both. McGuire's family connection and the period during which he wrote should give his word considerable weight.

Third: Dr. George Bolling Lee, General Lee's grandson, states the family tradition since General Lee's time has been the wedding was performed at White House, notwithstanding his father, Robert E. Lee, Jr., who stated the marriage was solemnized at St. Peter's.[94] Dr. Lee stated, in his opinion, "the wedding ceremony and the following festivities, including the supper were celebrated at the White House proper. Tradition in my family since General Lee's time, has always been such as I have stated above..."[95]

Fourth: Bishop William Meade, long time President Bishop of the Episcopal Church of Virginia, first stated the ceremony took place at St. Peter's Church.[96] However he later stated the marriage took place at White House.[97]

Fifth: The late Dr. Malcolm H. Harris, of West Point, Virginia, an authority on the history of New Kent, King William, and King and Queen Counties, was of the opinion the ceremony took place at White House. He also cited the marriage of Margaret Anderson Young, mentioned above. Dr. Harris pointed out that in 1759 there were few weddings in churches and it was not customary for widows to marry in the church; that it would be unlikely they would journey through the cold, mud, and mire to a cold and unheated church and then return to White House for the festivities.[98]

Sixth: Maude Welder Goodwin in her book, *The Colonial Cavalier*, states they "insisted on holding their marriage ceremonies at home rather than a church, and no minister could move their determination."[99]

Seventh: In 1771, William Eddis wrote, "In this country the marriage ceremony is universally performed in the dwelling house of the parties." His reference, "this country," refers to the inhabitants of the southern colonies.[100]

Eighth: Reverend Hugh Jones, writing in 1724, says, "Ministers are often obliged to bury in Orchards, and preach Funeral Sermons in Houes, where they also generally marry and christen; and as for weddings, there is no Regard to the Time of Day nor the Season of the Year; and in North Carolina, the Justices Marry."[101]

Ninth: Reverend Jonathan Boucher, told of his marriage to Miss Addison of Prince George County, Maryland. "We were married on the second of June 1772 and at her mother's house (as is the custom in that country)." At this time he was writing in England.[102]

As Malcolm Harris so aptly states, "While there is no doubt in the minds of many persons that the marriage did take place at White House, there is no record known to prove it. History is not dead facts lying in a manuscript but the ever reappearing lives of the people who made history while living."[103]

It is probable the Washingtons spent a portion of their honeymoon at White House. However a legend exists that a part of it was spent at a "honeymoon cottage" on the Rickahock Plantation property in New Kent County, then owned by Bartholomew Dandridge, brother of Mrs. Washington.[104] How long the Washingtons remained at White House is not known. Apparently early in February the Washingtons journeyed north as far as Hubbard's Ordinary in Caroline County, within one day's ride of Fredericksburg, but for what purpose we do not know.[105] At least several days prior to February 22nd they journeyed to Williamsburg in order that the bridgegroom take his seat in the House of Burgesses on that day, his twenty-seventh birthday.[106] It was there that the speaker, Peyton Randolph, gave the new member the thanks of the House for his bravery and services performed for the colony. Undoubtedly the new burgess, his bride, and her two children, Jacky and Patcy, and some of the servants took up residence at the Custis house in Williamsburg.[107] Since the House and Council were in session, they must have entered into the lively social life of the capitol city, noted for its gaiety at such times, for they attended at least one ball during the month of March.[108]

There was a *possible* hint of friction between the newlyweds. In a letter George received from his friend, Governor Fauquier, February 7th, "... I shall always have pleasure in gratifying you, in anything I dare say you will ever ask of me, and in obliging the Gentlemen of the Army ...we all wish you and Mrs. Washington as well as you wish each other in which perhaps you are not now on a par."[109]

Even as the House was still in session the Washington's found it necessary to take up their permanent residence at Mount Vernon.[110] On April 5th he sent a servant on ahead, bearing a letter for John Alton, one of his overseers, giving him explicit instructions on readying the house and furnishings for their arrival.[111] More than likely they left White House on Friday, April 2nd. Usually a four days journey, they took five days, arriving at Mount Vernon not later than April 7th.[112] There they would make their home for the next forty years. Many times during that forty years they would be separated and domiciled elsewhere, but Mount Vernon would always be home to them. No matter how far away they might be in time or miles, there was always the intense anticipation of their return to their "own vine and fig tree."

1. 2. *Hamilton*, 231, 242.

2. Ann Fairfax, daughter of Colonel William Fairfax, of Belvoir, had married George's older half brother, Lawrence, owner of Mount Vernon. Lawrence died in 1752. Their only surviving child, Sarah, died in 1754. Under the terms of Lawrence's will, his widow had only a life interest in Mount Vernon. Since their only child was deceased, Mount Vernon would pass to George at her death. She married George Lee and then died in 1761.

3. He left Winchester before September 27, and left Mount Vernon on September 30. 2 *Hamilton* 205-207; PWC 4:430.

4. 2 *Writings*, 135, 148, 151, 155. He made the same appeal to Colonel John Stanwix, the

British commander in North America. 2 *Writings*, 144.

5. 2 *Dinwiddie*, 703.

6. *PWC* 5:3.

7. *PWC* 5:21.

8. 2 *Hamilton*, 231, 242-43. The surgeon was Dr. James Craik, his old comrade in arms during the campaigns of Fort Necessity and the Monongahela. They were close friends for fifty years. *PWC* 5:64.

9. 2 *Hamilton*, 231.

10. 2 *Writings*, 159. *PWC* 5:51.

11. *Ledger A*, folio 37. *PWC* 5:82,86.

12. *PWC* 5:100-103, n. 5,6.

13. Now Tappahannock, Virginia.

14. *Ledger A*, folio 38.

15. Anna Maria Dandridge Bassett, younger sister of Martha Dandridge Custis Washington. She was married to Colonel Burwell Bassett (1734-1793), May 7, 1757.

16. Doncastle's Ordinary, near the present Barhamsville, Virginia. Chiswell's Ordinary, now Toano, Virginia. *Ledger A*, folio 38.

17. *Ledger A*, folio 38.

18. The Chamberlayne house was then called "Ferry."

19. *Ledger A*, folio 38.

20. 2 *Writings*, 167, n.92.

21. *Ledger A*, folio 38.

22. *PWC* 5:110-111.

23. Between January and March, 1758, G W consulted Dr. John Sutherland of Fredericksburg, Dr. John Amson of Williamsburg, and Dr. Richard Brooke of Prince George, Maryland. *Ledger A*, folio 37-38.

24. Washington's official business consisted of settling his accounts with the committee of the House of Burgesses, and a discussion concerning enlistments, pay, and Indian affairs with them and the Acting Governor. Dinwiddie had returned to England because of poor health. Under these circumstances John Blair, President of the Governor's Council assumed the duties of Governor until a new Governor was appointed by the Crown.

25. The text, having been printed many times, is not reprinted here. See 2 *Freeman*, 401-02; *Recollections*, p. 499-503.

26. 2 *Freeman*, 402-03.

27. Robert Carter Nicholas, John Robinson, James Blair, James Power, Burwell Bassett, John Mercer. See *PWC* 5:92.

28. Daniel Parke Custis died intestate. Under Virginia law the estate was divided into three equal shares; one each for Martha and her two children, John Parke Custis, and Martha Parke Custis. Martha's share if she married, would automatically become the property of her husband.

29. 2 *Writings*, 169, 171. The newly constructed fort at Winchester was named Fort Loudon. It should not be confused with Fort Loudon in Pennsylvania. *PWC* 5:109, 113, 117.

30. *Journal H.B.*, 1752-58, p. 506. *PWC* 5:115.

31. 2 *Writings*, 203. *PWC* 5:191-93.

32. 2 *Writings*, 203-05.

33. *PWC* 5:199-204.

34. *Ledger A*, folio 39. On May 29 he gave Colonel Bassett's servants 12 shillings. There is no other record of where he domiciled in Williamsburg. Bassett was a member of the Council. See n. 15, supra.

35 *Ledger A*, folio 39. He gave, "Mrs Custis's Servants 14/6." There is also an entry, "By a Ring from Phila 16/." It is possible GW had requested Col. John St. Clair to purchase the

ring for him, since St. Clair was in Philadelphia at this time and had returned to Winchester on May 21st. The ring may have been an engagement ring to be presented to MC on or about his visit of June 5th. See *P.M.H.B.*, 66:115, where it states it was a wedding ring, costing £2/16. This amount also included re-imbursement to Dr. James Craik for a newspaper subscription for which Dr. Craik had paid.

36. *Ledger A*, folio 39. GW gave "Mr Clayburns Negro 1/3." See 2 *Writings*, 210. Col. St. Clair, in a letter to Col. Henry Bouquet, June 9, 1758, stated that GW arrived at Winchester on June 9th. *Br. Mus. Add. MS* 21639, p.17. *PWC* 5:204.

37. *PWC* 5:197-99, 235.

38. 2 *Writings*, 242. *PWC* 5:256. A letter purported to have been written by GW to Mrs. Martha Custis, was dated July 20th. See page 477 for text and comment.

39. *PWC* 5:353-60, 364-65; Stevens and Kent, *Bouquet Papers* 2:312-14.

40. Bouquet to Washington, July 27, 1758, *PWC* 5:344-46. Washington to Bouquet, August 2, 1758, *PWC* 5:353-60, *PWC* 5:361, n.2.

41. GW to Bouquet, August 6, 1758, *PWC* 5:376-78.

42. *PWC* 5:360-61. GW to Major Francis Halkett, August 2, 1758, *PWC* 5:369-71; GW to Gov. Francis Fauquier, August 5, 1758, *PWC* 5:377. James, *Writings of General John Forbes*, Menasha, Wisc., 1938, p. 170-71.

43. Col. Adam Stephen to GW, December 25, 1755, 1 *Hamilton*, 158.

44. The election was held July 24th. Charles Smith to GW, *PWC* 5:323, 334-44.

45. Charles Smith to GW, *PWC* 5:331, n.1.

46. GW to Sarah Cary Fairfax, *PWC* 5:10-13. For a fresh approach to the significance of this letter see *Ibid*, n.3.

47. Bouquet to GW, September 4, 1758, *PWC* 6:1.

48. *PWC* 6:31.49.

49. GW to Francis Fauquier, September 25, 1758, *PWC* 6:44-46. 2 *Writings*, 290-91. GW to GW. Fairfax, September 25, 1758, *PWC* 6:38-43.

50. *PWC* 6:89.

51. A litter swung from the rump of the lead horse and attached to the front of the following horse.

52. GW to Francis Fauquier, November 5, 1758, *PWC* 6:113.

53. There is no mention of this engagement in any contemporary letters to or from Washington. Thirty years after the event, in 1786, GW mentioned the event in "Remarks," written for a proposed biography by Col. David Humphreys. See *Forbes*, 255-56; 2 *Freeman*, 357-58; 29 *Writings*, 47.

54. Governor Fauquier summoned the Assembly to meet on November 10th, to consider extending the period the Virginia regiments might remain in the field with His Majesty's forces. The Assembly granted Fauquier permission to keep them active an additional month and allotted £5000 for pay. Word of this did not reach the Virginians until after the fall of Fort Duquesne. *PWC* 6:80-81, 111-12, 154.

55. 2 *Writings*, n. 298; *PWC* 6:125, 129.

56. *PWC* 6:113-14.

57. *Ibid.*, 6:135-37.

58. *Forbes Orderly Book*, Nov. 20, 21, 1758.

59. *Ibid.*, Nov. 23, 1758.

60. *Ibid.*, Nov. 23, 24, 1758.

61. *Ibid.*, Nov. 24, 1758; *PWC* 6:157; James, *Writings of Forbes*, 262-64.

62. *PWC* 6:158-60.

63. *Ibid.*, 165-66.

64. *Ibid.*, 160, n. 5.

65. *Ledger A*, folio 52.

66. *Ledger A*, folio 53. The twelve days between his arrival at West's Ordinary and Belvoir, and his arrival at Baylor's was probably spent at Belvoir and Mount Vernon. It is possible he paid a call on his mother at Fredericksburg.

67. *Ledger A*, folio 53. The distance from Todd's Ordinary to Chiswell's was one full day's ride. It is possible on the way he stopped at the Bassett residence, Eltham, as well as at White House to pay his respects to Martha, since his marriage to her was a mere two weeks away. There is no record of this however.

68. *PWC* 6:184-85. General Forbes had returned to Philadelphia, a debilitated, withered man, although only 48 years old. He died there on March 11, 1759, and was interred beneath the chancel of Christ Church.

69. The address composed by Captain Robert Stewart, delivered to GW at Williamsburg by Captain John McNeill, his companion on the frontier in 1756. *PWC* 6:178-81.

70. *The Journal of Major George Washington*, Williamsburg, 1754, p.21.

71. *PWC* 6:118.

72. Out of a total of 400 men, thirty were killed and seventy wounded. 1 *Freeman*, 403-12.

73. *PWC* 6:343.

74. 2 *Freeman*, 84, 86; 1 *Writings*, 150-53.

75. 29 *Writings*,47.

76. 2 *Freeman*, 357-58. Freeman correctly points out that GW never mentioned the incident in any surviving letter. He did, however, relate the circumstances in some detail in his autobiographical sketch, written in 1786. 29 *Writings*,48.

77. John Marshall, *The Life of George Washington*, London, 1804.

78. David Ramsay, *The Life of George Washington*, New York, 1807.

79. Jared Sparks, *The Writings of George Washington*, Boston, 1837.

80. B. J. Lossing, *Washington and Mount Vernon*, New York, 1859, p.51.

81. Lossing, *Mary and Martha Washington, the Mother and Wife of Washington*, New York, 1886, p. 108.

82. 42 *VMHB*, 231; *Richmond News Leader*, May 14, 1961.

83. 46 *VMHB*,63. It was unlikely the Washingtons worshipped at St. Peter's after moving to Mount Vernon in the spring of 1759. Thereafter their visits were at Eltham Plantation, the home of Martha's sister, Anna Maria, who had married Col. Burwell Bassett. The Washingtons and Bassetts were close friends until death parted them. GW spent more time at Eltham, than any house except Mount Vernon. He and Col. Bassett were hunting and fishing companions and were friends of the Rev. Price Davies, the Rector of Warreneye Church. Located about two miles from Eltham, Washington worshipped there when visiting Eltham. 2 *Diaries*, 59-60.

84. Lossing states that the Reverend Mossom officiated at both of Martha's marriages and states that her father-in law, John Custis, kissed her on both cheeks. Rev. Chickely Gordon Thacker officiated at her *first* marriage. At that time John Custis *had been dead six months*. See: Lossing, *Mary and Martha Washington*, N.Y. 1886, p. 101. For descriptions of her second marriage that are almost pure fiction, see: Rupert Hughes's *George Washington*, 1:445-51; Woodrow Wilson's *George Washington*, N.Y., 1896, p. 102.

85. 3 *Freeman*, 1, n.

86. *Ibid.*

87. *Ibid.*; *Richmond Dispatch*, June 2, 1882, p. 1; 42 *VMHB*, 232.

88. 3 *Freeman*, 1, n.

89. 35 *Writings*, 337. For his resignation, see supra, Anderson to MW, p. //needs a page no.//

90. 3 Freeman, 1, n.; 42 *VMHB*, p. 233.

91. 3 *Freeman*, 1, n.; 46 *VMHB*, p.63.

92. C. C. Wall, then resident director of Mount Vernon, to the *Richmond Times Dispatch*, June 23, 1957. Also, Agnes Peter to C. C. Wall, January 19, 1940, MVLA Archives.

93. Rev. E. C. McGuire, *Religious Opinions and Character of George Washington*, N.Y., 1836, xxvii.

94. Capt. Robert E. Lee, *Recollections and Letters of General Robert E. Lee*, N.Y., 1904, p. 364.

95. 42 *VMHB*, 232.

96. Rev. William Meade, *Journals of the Episcopal Diocese of Virginia*.

97. Meade, *Old Churches, Ministers, and Families of Virginia*, Philadelphia, 1857, p. 386.

98. 1 *Harris*, 119.

99. Goodwin, Maude Welder, *The Colonial Cavalier*, Boston, 1895, p.73.

100. Eddi,s William, *Letters from America, Historical and Descriptive*, London, 1792, Letter IX, p. 114.

101. Jones, Hugh, *The Present State of Virginia*, London, 1724, p. 67-68.

102. Boucher, Rev. Jonathan, *Reminiscences of an American Loyalist, 1738-1789*, Boston, 1925, p.91.

103. 1 *Harris*, 119.

104. 1 *Harris*,61.

105. *Ledger A*, folio 55. "Feby 7 By Exps at Hubbards 31/3."

106. Washington had been elected to the House on July 24, 1758, but was unable to take his seat because of his military duties. See supra, n. 43-45.

107. There is no documentary proof the Washingtons occupied the Custis House, known as Six Chimney House. For reasons in support of it, see 3 *Freeman*, 3, n.5. The house was furnished at this time and was not leased until 1760.

108. *Ledger A*, folio 55. "By tickets for a ball 1."

109. 3 *Hamilton*, p. 154.

110. GW was given permission to be absent from the House for the remainder of the session. *PWC* 6:192, n.1.

111. *PWC* 6:200.

112. *Ledger A*, folio 55. April 7. "By Sundry Expens in my Journey from Williamsburg to Fairfax 19 - 1 1/2."

Appendix III
Preservation and Destruction

When George Washington arrived at Mount Vernon, at the conclusion of his eight years of public service, he found his personal affairs in sad disarray and his property badly deteriorated. Even his mansion house was in need of extensive repair.[1] His entire time was spent in attempting to bring some semblance of order out of a chaotic situation. As a result his correspondence and the care, arrangement and preservation of his papers were, of necessity, neglected.[2]

Late in January, 1798, he received a letter from Albin Rawlins, a young man from Hanover County, soliciting the position of writer and bookkeeper. Realizing he was desperately in need of assistance, Washington answered him immediately, offering Rawlins the position. He assumed his duties in mid March as a secretary, copyist, bookkeeper, and "rider."[3]

In his will, dated July 9, 1799, Washington bequeathed his papers, books, etc., to his nephew, associate supreme court justice, Bushrod Washington, as follows:

> "To my nephew Bushrod Washington, I give and bequeath all the Papers in my possession, which relate to my Civel and Military Administration of the affairs of the Country; - I leave to him also such of my private Papers as are worth preserving: and at the decease of wife, and before, if she is not inclined to retain them, I give and bequeath my library of Books, and Pamphlets of every kind."[4]

Shortly after 4:30 P.M. on December 14, 1799, the last day of GW's life, Tobias Lear took the dying man's hand in his own and heard the words he later entered in his diary: "I find I am going, my breath can not last long. I believed from the first that the disorder would prove fatal. Do you arrange and record all my late military letters and papers. Arrange my accounts and settle my books, as you know more about them than anyone else, and let Mr. Rawlins finish recording my other letters which he has begun."[5] Lear was the first person to examine the papers after Washington's death. His diary for Tuesday, December 24th reads as follows: "Spent the day in looking over and arranging papers in the General's Study."[6] In her excellent *Introduction to the Index of the George Washington Papers*, Dorothy S. Eaton was of the opinion Lear was the first to examine the papers after the General's death.[7]

Jared Sparks is authority for the statement that Lear possessed the papers for eight months before turning them over to Judge Bushrod Washington. The entry in his journal for Thursday, January 17th follows,

> "Conversation in the morning with Chief Justice Marshall and Judge Washington respecting the Washington papers. General Washington's private journal is now in the hands of the judge, who says he will let me have it. It is written in small pamphlets. I inquired respecting the papers which Lear has been charged with taking away. Judge Washington said that no such charge had ever been made by him; but that the papers did not come into his hands until about eight months after the death of the general, and that during that time they were in the hands of Lear. When the judge took possession of them, he found that the private journal for a certain period was missing; he thought about the year 1793; and that suspicion of having withdrawn it fell upon Mr. Lear, yet there was no other evidence of the circumstance; nor had he any reason to suppose that any letters were taken away by Lear."[8]

During the eight month period mentioned, Lear continued to live at Mount Vernon, busily engaged in answering the many letters of tribute and condolence sent to Mrs. Washington. Possibly at this time Lear and Rawlins separated out the personal correspondence between the Washingtons and turned it over to Mrs. Washington. It is far more likely the correspondence had been separated previously, even by the General himself, and that it would never have been entrusted to the prying eyes of strangers.

At the close of his presidency the Washingtons left Philadelphia on March 9, 1797, and arrived at Mount Vernon, March 15th.[9] Shortly thereafter, GW received a letter from their close friend, Eliza Willing Powel of Philadelphia. Mrs. Powel had just recently purchased the large desk GW had used in his official residence.[10] Shortly after taking possession of the desk, Mrs. Powel discovered "a large bundle" of letters written by Mrs. Washington to her husband, in one of the drawers. She requested Lear, then still in Philadelphia, to accept the letters so they might be returned to the Washingtons. In spite of repeated urgings, Lear refused to accept them; she sealed the package and penned the following letter to GW:

"Phila 11th March 1897 My very dear Sir Like a true Woman (as you will think) in the Moment of Exultation, and on the first Impulse (for you know we are never supposed to act Systematically or from attentive Consideration), I take up my Pen to address you, as you have given me a complete Triumph on the Subject of all others on which you have I suppose thought me most deficient, and most opposite to yourself; and what is still more charming - Your Candor shall preside as Judge, - nay you shall pass Sentence on yourself, and I will not appeal from your Decision. Suppose I should prove incontestably - that you have without Design put into my Possession the Love Letters of a lady addressed to you under the most solemn Sanction; & a large Packet too. - What will the Goddess of Prudence and Circumspection say to her favorite Son and Votary for his dereliction of Principles to which he had hitherto made such serious Sacrifices. Was the Taste of your Sex predominant in your Breast; - and did the Love of Variety so preponderate; - that because you had never blundered as President, - was you determined to try its Delights as a private Gentleman; but to keep you no longer in Suspence, tho' I know that your Nerves are not as irritable as a fine Ladies, - yet I will with the Generosoty of my Sex relieve you, by telling you that upon opening one of the Drawers of your writing Desk I found a large Bundle of Letters from Mrs. Washington bound up and labled with your usual Accuracy. Mr- Lear was present, I immediately desired him to take Charge of the Package, - which he declined doing, alleging that he thought it safer in my Hands, at least for some Time, - at first I urged it; but finding him Inflexible as I suppose from Motives of Delicacy I sealed them up, And I trust it is unnecessary for me to add that they will be kept Inviolably until I deliver them to him or to your Order. As Mr-Lear has been connected both with you and Mrs. Washington, and as it is probable that some family Circumstances may have been mingled into her Communications to you, to save his Feelings I have sealed the Package with Three Seals bearing the Impression of my blessed Friends Arms. It is the Seal that I myself use. Should Mrs. Washington appear to have any unpleasant Senations on this Subject you will I am certain remove them by reminding her, that tho' Curiosity is supposed to be a prominent Feature in the female Mind, yet it will ever be powerfully counteracted when opposed by native Delicacy, a sense of Honor, and I trust a pious Education.

I shall give to Mr- Lear a Check for 245 Dollars the first Cost of the writing Desk - In my Estimation its Value is not in the least diminished by your use of it, nor from its having been the Repository of those valuable Documents that originated with you during your wise and peaceful Administration for Eight years. I am sensible many handsome & true Compliments might be paid to you on this Occasion; - but as they have been resounded with Elegance & Sincerity through the Whole Continent, and will be re-echoed by Posterity, as you must be conscious they are just and are not yourself a Man of Vanity I will not in my blundering Way attempt a Theme that I feel myself totally inadequate to, for Blundering would not have to me even the Charm of Novelty to recommend it.

And now my dear Sir let me return you Thanks for your Tribute of Affection. Mr. Lear has sent me in your Name a Pair of Lamps & Brackets with the Appendages; from you they are acceptable, tho from no other Being out of my own Family would I accept a pecuniary Favor, nor did I want any inanimate Memento to bring you to my Recollection. I most sincerely hope to hear that you are all well and safely arrived at Mount Vernon long before you will probably receive this incoherent Scrawl. Be pleased to present me affectionately to Mrs. Washington & Miss Custis and believe me

> Truly & affectionately Sir
> Your most Obedt & Obliged
> Eliza. Powel[11]

Washington answered Mrs. Powel as follows:

"Mount Vernon 26th March, 1797

My dear Madam, A mail of last week brought me the honor of your favor, begun the 11th, and ended the 13th of this instant.

Had it not been for one circumstance, which bye the bye is a pretty material one - viz - that I had no love letters to lose the introductory without the explanatory part of your letter would have caused a serious alarm; and might have tried how far my nerves were able to sustain the shock of having betrayed the confidence of a lady. But although I had nothing to apprehend on that score, I am not less surprized at my having left those of Mrs. Washington' in my writing desk; when, as I supposed I had emptied all the drawers; mistaken in this however. I have to thank you for the delicacy with which they have been treated. But admitting that they had fallen into more inquisitive hands, the correspondence would, I am persuaded, have been found to be more fraught with expressions of friendship, than of enamoured love, and, consequently, if the ideas of the possessor of them, with respect to the latter passion, should have been of the Romantic order to have given them the warmth, which was not inherent, they might have been consigned to the flames....."[12]

No further mention of the incident has been encountered in any existing correspondence, and whether GW ever acknowledged his absent-mindedness to Mrs. Washington is unknown.

It would seem reasonable the correspondence between the Washingtons would be carefully sequestered and preserved by GW in his Mount Vernon Library. Private person that he was, he would not likely allow their private thoughts of forty years of married life to be integrated into his general correspondence. To do so would ultimately expose their intimate thoughts to strangers, for already he was receiving applications for permission to peruse his military papers.

There is authoritative documentation that shortly after the death of her husband, Mrs. Washington burned their correspondence. Again it comes to us from Jared Sparks, who recorded the following in his journal for February 26, 1828:

"I visited Mrs. Peter, of Georgetown, today. She was the granddaughter of Mrs. Washington. My principal object was to ascertain what

became of General Washington's letters to his wife. Mrs. Peter assured
me that, shortly after General Washington's death, Mrs. Washington
burnt all these letters except two which seemed to escape by accident.
Mrs. Washington gave her writing desk to Mrs. Peter, and in this desk
were found two letters from General Washington to her. No others
have ever been found. One of these is exceedingly valuable, being a
letter written by General Washington to his wife communicating the
intelligence of his having been appointed Commander-in-chief,
expressing his entire conviction that he was not adequate to so high
a trust. It has never been printed. Mrs. Peter assured me that General
Washington, although grave and not very communicative, was
uncommonly gentle, mild, and kind in his family, fond of little
children, humane to servants, and mindful of all those little attentions
which multiply endearments, and make so large a portion of the
happiness of intimate social intercourse."[13]

Some believe the Washingtons had a pact: the survivor would
destroy their correspondence. There was precedence for it in their own
family circle. Elizabeth Foote Washington, widow of Lund Washington,
burned GW's correspondence with her husband after Lund's death in
1796. Jared Sparks corroborates the occurrence:

"February 27 (1828). Took a line from Judge Washington to William
H. Foote, Esq., on whom I called. He lives about five miles from
Alexandria, and about as far from Mount Vernon. He is a nephew of
Lund Washington, and my object in visiting him was to procure copies
of the letters received by his uncle from General Washington. Mr.
Foote informed me that before his uncle's death he enjoined it on his
wife to destroy all these letters, which injunction was strictly complied
with, except in a few instances where scraps cut from some of the
letters were preserved. These are unimportant, but Mr. Foote promises to send them to me. The loss of these letters is much to be
deplored, as Lund Washington was a confidential correspondent
during the whole Revolution ...."[14]

It is possible the two surviving letters from General Washington to
Mrs. Washington, mentioned by Martha Parke Custis Peter, at the time of
her visit with Jared Sparks did not "escape by accident," but were
intentionally removed and placed there by Mrs. Washington. Did she
have a sense of history? They were the two letters that told of his affection
for her, his concern for her welfare and safety, his reasons for accepting
the command of the army, and of his apprehensions as to his ability to
successfully carry out the task entrusted to him. Were they the letters she
could not bring herself to destroy, but put quietly away in her little desk,
knowing that someday they would be found by her family? They and the
world would someday know of their devotion to each other as well as to
their country.

   1. GW to Sir Edward Newenham, August 6, 1797, 36 *Writings*, p. 4; GW to Rev. William
Gordon, October 15, 1797, 36 *Writings*, p. 49; GW to Sir John Sinclair, November 6, 1797; 36
Writings, p. 67; GW to Bartholomew Dandridge, December 3, 1797, 36 *Writings*, p. 85; GW

To William Vans Murray, December 3, 1797, 36 *Writings*, p. 87; GW to Sarah Cary Fairfax, May 16, 1798, 36 *Writings*, p. 263.

2. GW to Sir Edward Newenham, August 6, 1797, 36 *Writings*, p. 4.

3. Albin Rawlins to GW, January 26, February 7, 16, 1798, DLC:GW; GW to Albin Rawlins, January 13, 1798, 36 *Writings*, p. 150; GW to Albin Rawlins, February 12, 1798, 36 *Writings*, p. 164.

4. E. L. Prussing, *The Estate of George Washington Deceased*, Boston, 1927, p. 55.

5. *Letters and Recollections of George Washington, Being letters to Tobias Lear and others .... With a diary of Washington's last days, kept by Mr. Lear*, N.Y., 1906, p. 133.

6. *Ibid.*, p. 141.

7. *Index to the George Washington Papers*, Washington, 1964. (Introduction by Dorothy S. Eaton) vii-viii. For the definitive account of the peregrinations of the Washington papers, see same reference.

8. H. B. Adams, *The Life and Writings of Jared Sparks*, Cambridge, 1893, 2:46-47.

9. 34 *Writings*, p. 422 n.

10. President Washington purchased the desk at the sale of the effects of Eleanor Francois Elie, le Comte de Moustier, the French minister to the United States. The purchase price was £98, New York currency. Moustier, who occupied the finest house in New York, returned to France in October, 1789. The Washingtons then occupied the house, located on the west side of Broadway, just below Trinity Church. When the seat of government was moved to Philadelphia in 1790, the desk was transported with the rest of the Washington's belongings. At the close of his presidency in 1797, GW sold the desk to Mrs. Powel for $245.00. The desk descended in Mrs. Powel's family and was presented to the Pennsylvania Historical Society by Mrs. Powel's great grand nephew in 1867. See announcement of the annual meeting of the P.H.S., Friday, January 15, 1871, p. 3-4.

11. Elizabeth Willing Powel to GW, March 11, 1797, ViMtV.

12. GW to Elizabeth Willing Powel, March 26, 1797, ViMtV.

13. H. B. Adams, *The Life and Writings of Jared Sparks*, Cambridge, 1893, 2:47. The two letters found by Martha Custis Peter were: George Washington to Martha Washington, June 18, 1775, June 23, 1775, see supra, pages. Only one other letter from GW to MW is known: GW to MW, October 1, 1782, see supra, page 188.

14. Adams, 2 *Sparks*, p.48. For an example, see portion of a letter from GW to Lund Washington, November 26, 1775, ViMtV.

Appendix IV
The Spurious Letter to Martha Washington

While at Valley Forge in January, 1778, General George Washington was informed, in a letter from Richard Henry Lee, that a group of letters he had allegedly written had been published in pamphlet form.[1] Seven letters had been printed: five to Lund Washington and one each to John Parke Custis and Martha Washington. A London printer, J. Bew, was the source, bearing a publication date of 1777. The author of the pamphlet claimed he had received the letters from a friend who was a member of De Lancey's Loyalist regiment in New York. The friend had received them from a mulatto man, "Billy," who had been captured when Fort Lee fell to the British. "Billy," when questioned at length, confessed he was the servant of GW, and had been left behind because of some temporary infirmity. In addition, "Billy" turned over "a small portmanteau" belonging to GW, containing a few articles of clothing, a portion of his diary, and a packet of letters: "two letters from his lady, one from Mr. Custis, and some pretty long ones from a Mr. Lund Washington," and rough drafts of answers to them.[2] It is these answers that became the basis of the publication.

The pamphlet was received with little credence in England. Both *The Monthly Review* and *The Critical Review* considered them "well written," but spurious. The publication soon found its way to America and was reprinted late in 1777, without publisher or place mentioned. It has been attributed by some to be from Philadelphia, a most likely choice.[3]

In a letter to Richard Henry Lee, from Valley Forge, dated February 15, 1778, GW acknowledged he had seen the handbill, published in New York and Philadelphia. He disavowed writing a single word of it and suggested the remaining letters were "equally genuine."[4] Fitzpatrick attributed the handbill to James Rivington, the New York printer, in advance of the pamphlet. While still at Valley Forge, GW received "the pamphlet of forgeries" from Richard Henry Lee, in a letter dated May 6, 1778. "Tis among the pitiful arts of our enemies to endeavor at sowing dissension among the friends of liberty and their country."[5] The General's response on May 25th labelled every word as false, and stated, "These letters are written with a great deal of art. The intermixture of so many family circumstances (which by the by, want foundation in truth) gives an air of plausibility, which renders the villainy greater; as the whole is a contrivance to answer the most diabolical purposes. Who the author of them is, I know not. From information, or acquaintance, he must have had some knowledge of the component parts of my family, but he has most egregariously mistaken facts in several instances; Tho' the design of his labors is as clear as the sun in its meridian brightness."[6]

On May 30, 1778, GW wrote to his friend, Landon Carter, regretting his inability to send the letter allegedly written to MW, since he had sent it on to her, "to let her see what obliging folks there were in the world." However he did enclose the letter "written for me" to John Parke Custis, and voicing the opinion they were written by someone with some knowledge of the family, but deficient in circumstances and facts that resulted in misrepresentations of both.[7]

The principal purpose of the letters was to undermine public confidence in their Commander-in-Chief, and to insinuate he was lacking in enthusiasm for independence. The letters also contained disparaging remarks he was alleged to have made concerning the New England troops and their popular leader, General Israel Putnam; an effort to cause dissension between north and south. Vituperative criticism of Governor Patrick Henry, was done to cause further dissension between the Lees and the administration of the Governor.

The subject of the spurious letters did not surface again until 1788. At that time the Philadelphia publisher, Mathew Carey, then considering the publication of letters of Washington to the Continental Congress, queried GW concerning the letters. The General assured Carey of their lack of authenticity, that they appeared after several of his letters were intercepted in the mail, and then adulterated. He again expressed his opinion they were manufactured by someone well acquainted with the family's personal and domestic life.[8] The situation remained dormant until about 1795 when, with the rise of political parties and the storm over the Jay Treaty with Great Britain, the letters were brought to public attention, largely through the efforts of Benjamin Franklin Bache[9] and

James Rivington.[10] Their purpose was to undermine and destroy the confidence of the people and to create distrust of Washington and his administration. The letters were printed again in 1795, bearing a Philadelphia imprint, and stating it was republished from an out of print Boston edition. It was a verbatim reprint of the 1777 edition.[11] The following year, 1796, a single volume was published in New York under the auspices of G. Robinson, J. Bull, and James Rivington.[12] It contained the previously published letters, together with numerous letters to and from various British and American military personnel during the Revolution.[13]

During and after the Revolution GW made no public denials concerning the authenticity of the letters, although he did make denials in several personal letters to correspondents. In a letter to Dr. William Gordon, who had written a history of the American Revolution, he stated the letters had been published during the war to destroy the confidence of the people and the army in his political principles and that now being republished by Bache and others to would serve the same purpose. To Washington, Bache was a tool and agent of those determined to destroy the people's confidence in their elected officials.[14] He wrote in much the same vein to Col. Benjamin Walker. By this time he was convinced he was being pressed by this new edition of the letters, because of his previous decision to publicly ignore the attacks, leading the people to believe his silence was proof of their authenticity. He denied Billy Lee[15] was ever captured by the enemy or that any of his baggage had ever fallen into enemy hands during the war. He expressed to Walker a desire to have the author identified and to learn his source of information, that only Rivington knew the answer. He requested Walker, should the opportunity present itself, inform Rivington of his desire to know, but was careful to point out the perpetrators would not be put to any disadvantage because of it.[16]

On the last full day of his presidency he wrote to Timothy Pickering, the Secretary of State, setting down for the first time, his *official* response to the letters. Their purpose during the war was to deprecate the motives and integrity of the Commander-in-Chief at a time of crisis. Since another crisis in American affairs was imminent (the Jay Treaty controversy) the same tactics were being resorted to in order to impugn his character and deceive the people. He again denied the capture of Billy Lee or any portion of his baggage. The President felt it was a duty to himself, his country, and that the truth would be better served if he presented an official record of the circumstances, and made a solemn declaration that he letters were "a base forgery," and that he had never seen nor heard of them until they appeared in print. [17] The alleged letter to Mrs. Washington is as follows:

June 24, 1776.

To Mrs. Washington.

My dearest Life and Love, You have hurt me, I know not how much, by the insinuation in your last, that my letters to you have lately been less frequent, because I have felt less concern for you. The suspicion is most unjust; - may I not add, it is most unkind? Have we lived, now almost a score of years, in the closest and dearest conjugal intimacy to so little purpose that, on an appearance only of inattention to you, and which you might have accounted for in a thousand ways more natural and more probable, you should pitch upon that single motive which alone is injurious to me? I have not, I own, wrote so often to you as I wished, and as I ought:but think of my situation and then ask your heart, if I be WITHOUT EXCUSE. We are not, my dearest, in circumstances the most favourable to our happiness: but let us not, I beseech you, idly make them worse, by indulging suspicions and apprehensions which minds in distress are but too apt to give way to. I never was, as you have often told me, even in my better and more disengaged days, so attentive to the little punctilios of friendship, as, it may be, became me: but my heart tells me, there never was a moment in my life since I first knew you, in which it did not cleave and cling to you with the warmest affection: and it must cease to beat, ere it can cease to wish for your happiness, above any thing on earth.

I congratulate you most cordially on the fair prospect of recovery of your amiable daughter-in-law; nor can I wonder, that this second loss of a little one should affect you; I fear the fatigues of the journey, and the perpetual agitation of a camp, were too much for her. They are, however, both young and healthy, so that there can be little doubt of their soon repairing the loss.

And now will my dearest love permit me, a little more earnestly than I have ever yet done, to press you to consent to that so necessary, so safe and easy, though so dreaded a thing - the being innoculated? It was always advisable; but at this juncture it seems to be almost absolutely necessary.

I am far from sure, that, that restless madman, our quondam Governor, from the mere lust of doing mischief, will not soon betake himself to the carrying on a predatory war in our rivers. And as Potomack will certainly be thought most favourable for his purposes, as affording him scope to keep without the reach of annoyance, I have little reason to flatter myself that it would not be particularly pleasing to him, to vent his spite at my house. Let him it would affect me only as it might affect you; and, for this reason, among others, I wish you out of his reach. Yet I think I would not have you quit your house professedly from an apprehension of a visit from him: An appearance of fearfulness and timidity, even in a woman of my family, might have a bad effect; but I must be something more or less than man, not to wish you out of the way of a danger, which, to say the least, must be disagreeable to you, and could do good to no one. All this makes for your going to Philadelphia, a place of perfect security; and it would be almost worth while to be innoculated, if it were only for the fair pretense it furnishes you with of quitting Virginia, at a time when I could not but be exceedingly uneasy at your remaining in it. But I flatter myself any further arguments will be unnecessary, when I shall add as I now do, that till you have had the small-pox, anxiously as else I should wish for it, I never can think of consenting to your passing the winter here in quarters with me.

I would have Lund Washington immediately remove all the unmarried and suspicious of the slaves, to the quarters in Frederick. The harvesting must be got in by hirelings. Let him not keep any large stock of grain trod out, especially at the mill, or within the reach of water carriage; and in particular, let as little as may be, be left at Clifton's quarters. It will not be too late, even in the first week of July, to sow the additional supply of hemp and flax seed which Mr. Mifflin has procured for me in Philadelphia; and which I hope will be with you before this letter. For obvious reasons, you will not sow kit on the island, nor by the water side. But I hope you will have a good account of your crop on the Ohio. If Bridgey continues refractory and riotous, though I know you can ill spare him, let him by all means be sent off, as I hope Jack Custis's boy Joe already is, for his sauciness at Cambridge.

My attention is this moment called off to discovery or pretended discovery, of a most wild and daring plot. It is impossible, as yet to develope the mystery in which it either is, or is supposed to be involved. Thus much only I can find out with certainty (t)hat it will be a fine field for a war of lies on both sides. No doubt it will make a good deal of noise in the country; and there are those who think it useful to have the minds of the people kept constantly on the fret by rumors of this sort. For my part, I who am said to be the object principally aimed at in it, find myself perfectly at my easy; and I have mentioned it to you only from an apprehension that, hearing it from others and not from me, you might imagine I was in the midst of danger that I knew not of.

The perpetual solicitude of your poor heart about me, is certainly highly flattering to me; yet I should be happy to be able to quiet your fears. Why do you complain about my reserves? or, how could you imagine that I distrusted either your prudence or your fidelity? I have the highest opinion of them both. But why should I teaze you with tedious details of schemes and views which are perpetually varying; and which therefore might, not improbably, mislead, where I meant to inform you? Suffice it to say, what I have often before told you, that, as far as I have the controul of them, all our preparations for war aim only at peace. Neither do I, at this moment, see the least likelihood of there being any considerable military operation this season; and, if not in this season, certainly in no other. It is impossible to suppose, that, in the leisure and quiet of winter quarters, men will not have the virtue to listen to the dictates of plain common sense and somber reason. The only true interest of both sides is reconciliation; nor can there be a point in the world clearer, than that both sides must be losers by war, in a manner which even peace will not compensate for. We must, at last, agree and be friends; for we cannot live without them, and they will not without us; and a bye-stander might well be puzzled to find out, why as good terms cannot be given and taken now, as when we shall have well nigh ruined each other by the mutual madness of cutting one another's throats. For all these reasons, which cannot but be obvious to the English commissioners, and ours, as they are to me,

I am at a loss to imagine how anything can arise to obstruct negociation, and, of consequence, a pacification. You who know my heart, know that there is not a wish nearer to it than this is; but I am prepared for every event one only excepted - I mean a dishonorable peace. Rather than that, let me, though it be with the loss of every thing else I hold dear, continue this horrid trade, and, by the most unlikely means, be the unworthy instrument of preserving political security and happiness to them, as well as to ourselves. - Pity this cannot be accomplished, without fixing on me that sad name, Rebel. I love my king; you know I do: a soldier, a good man cannot but love him. How peculiarly hard then is our fortune to be deemed traitors to so good a king! But, I am not without hopes, that even he will yet see cause to do me justice: posterity, I am sure, will. Mean while, I comfort myself with the reflection, that this has been the fate of the best and the bravest men, even of the barons who obtained Magna Charta, whilst the dispute was depending. This, however, anxiously as I wish for it, it is not mine to command: I see my duty, that of standing up for the liberties of my country; and whatever difficulties and discouragements lie in my way, I dare not shrink from it; and I rely on the being, who has not left to us the choice of duties, that while I conscientiously discharge mine, I shall not finally lose my reward. If I really am not a bad man, I shall not long be so set down.

Assure yourself, I will pay all possible attention to your recommendations. But happy as I am in an opportunity of obliging you, even in the smallest things, take it not amiss, that I use the freedom with you, to whisper in your ear, to be sparing of them. You know how I am circumstanced: hardly the promotion of a subaltern is left to me; and free and independent as I am, I resolve to remain so. I owe the Congress no obligations for any personal favours done to myself; nor will I run in debt to them for favours to others. Besides, I am mortified to have to ask of them, what, in sound policy (if other motives had been wanting) they ought to have granted to me unasked. I cannot describe to you the inconveniences this army suffers, for want of this consequence being given to its commander in chief. But as these might be encreased, were my peculiar situation in this respect generally known, I forbear; only enjoining on you a cautious silence on this head. In a regular army, our Virginia young men, would certainly, in general, make the best officers; but I regret that they have not now put it in my power justly to pay them this compliment. they dislike their northern allies; and this dislike is the source of infinite mischief and vexations to me. In the many disputes and quarrels of this fort which we have had, one thing has particularly struck me. My countrymen are not inferior in understanding; and are certainly superior in that distinguished (s)pirit and high sense of honor which should form the character of an officer. Yet, somehow or other, it forever happens, that in every altercation, they are proved to be in the wrong; and they expect of me attentions and partialities which it is not in my power to shew them.

Let me rely that your answer to this will be dated Philadelphia. If I am not busily engaged, (which I hope may not be the case) perhaps I may find ways and means to pay you a visit of a day or two; but this I rather hint as what I wish, than what I dare bid you expect. If you still think the fragments of the set of greys I bought of Lord Botetourt unequal to the journey, let Lund Washington sell them singly, or otherwise as he can, to the best advantage, and purchase a new set of bays. I could as you desire, get them here, and perhaps on better terms: but I have a notion whether well or ill founded I know not, that they never answer well in Virginia. I beg to be affectionately remembered to all our friends and relations; and that you continue you to believe me to be

> Your most Faithful
> And tender Husband,
> G.W.[18]

Who was the perpetrator? It is not likely the letters were the work of a single individual, but rather a small group working under the supervision of a well informed individual who had been close to the Washingtons. At the time it was felt John Randolph was the culprit behind the plot.[19] During the years prior to the Revolution the families had been close friends. As last Attorney-general of the colony, he had a professional relationship with the Custis family and the affairs of the estate. Randolph's father, Sir John Randolph (1693-1737), also King's attorney for Virginia, Member of the House of Burgesses, and Speaker of the House, had represented John Custis. During sessions of the House of Burgesses and on other occasions when in Williamsburg, Washington often dined with Randolph. In his diary Washington noted the Randolphs visited Mount Vernon on three occasions. In the seven years prior to the Revolution there are nine entries in the diaries for dinners at Tazewell Hall, the Randolph's Williamsburg home. There is no doubt they were the most intimate of friends. Though an ardent Loyalist, his son Edmund Randolph, who supported the American cause, was an aide to GW during the Revolution, sat in the Constitutional Convention, and became GW's Attorney General.

Colonel Tench Tilghman states, "The letters published under General Washington's signatures are not genuine ... He suspects Jack Randolph for the author, as the letters contain a knowledge of his family affairs that none but a Virginian could be acquainted with."[20] Worthington Chauncey Ford also quotes a letter from Colonel John Laurens[21] to his father, Henry Laurens,[22] "The letter said to be the General's is partly genuine and partly spurious. Those who metamorphosed the intercepted original committed an error in point of time, for Mrs. Washington was with the General in New York at the date of it."[23]

William Carmichael, who served in the diplomatic mission under Arthur Lee, Silas Deane, and Benjamin Franklin, in Paris, was well aware of what was transpiring in London, whether it be Fleet Street, Whitehall, or the coffee shops. In a letter to C.F.W. Dumas, as early as June 20, 1777, Carmichael wrote, "A Junto of refugees from various parts of the continent, who meet daily in Pall Mall, London to do this dirtywork of government to earn the pittance but scantilly afforded to each of them. At the head of this junto were (Thomas) Hutchison, (Rev. Myles) Cooper, (John) Chandler, (John) Vassal, and others who would not be named but for their infamy. They have forged letters lately under the name of Gen. Washington, which the good silly souls of Europe will swallow as genuine, unless contracted in different gazettes."[24]

Not the least of the proofs offered comes from the Du Simitriere Collection in Philadelphia: a manuscript note on the Philadelphia leaflet of the letter to MW, in the handwriting of Du Simitriere himself, as follows, "Spurious, written in London by a Mr Randolph of Virginia."[25]

1. Richard Henry Lee (1732-1794), Member and President of the Continental Congress, author of the resolution for independence, and United States Senator. Richard Henry Lee to GW, Chantilly, Virginia, January 2, 1778. Ballagh, *The Letters of Richard Henry Lee*, New York, 1911, 1:371.

2. W. C. Ford, *Writings of Washington*, New York, 1889, 4:371.

3. *Ibid.*, p. 133 n.

4. Fitzpatrick, *Writings*, 11:450.

7. Fitzpatrick, *Writings*, 11:495. Landon Carter, of Sabine Hall, Richmond County, Virginia (1710-1778). He was the son of Robert "King" Carter. He was a Member of the House of Burgesses, a firm supporter of Virginia's efforts to drive the French from the Ohio Valley and for the rights of the colonies against the English Crown. He was a frequent correspondent of GW during the French War, during the Revolution, and until his death in 1788.

8. Mathew Carey (1760-1839), publisher, economist, and Irish patriot. Carey was a native of Ireland and extremely active in the Irish separatist movement. Finding it necessary to escape, he disguised himself as a woman and fled to America, landing in Philadelphia in 1784. He became the publisher of *The Pennsylvania Herald, The Columbian Magazine, The American Museum*, and numerous other tracts and books on a variety of subjects. George Washington to Mathew Carey, October 27, 1788. Fitzpatrict, *Writings*, 30:122. This letter was in answer to Carey's letter of October 20, 1788. This letter has disappeared.

9. Benjamin Franklin Bache (1769-1798) was a grandson of Benjamin Franklin and accompanied his grandfather to Europe. His education was obtained there and later in Philadelphia. While in France he learned the printing trade. In 1790 Bache founded the Philadelphia *General Advertiser*, later known as *The Aurora*. Under his ownership *The Aurora* became the mouthpiece of the Jeffersonian Republicans. Histrionic personal abuse of GW overstepped the bounds of human decency. His most notable "scoop" was his publication of the Jay Treaty on July 1, 1795. On the retirement of GW from office, Bache stated, "if ever there was a period of rejoicing, this is the moment every heart in unison with the freedom and happiness of the people ought to beat high with exultation that the name of Washington from this day ceases to give a currency to political iniquity, and to legalized corruption." He died during the yellow-fever epidemic in Philadelphia, in 1798. *DAB*, 1:462.

10. James Rivington (1724-1802) was a London bookseller, printer and publisher. At one time he was one of the most prominent publishers in England. An extravagant life style there drove him into bankruptcy. He moved to America in 1760, living for the most part in New York, where he again became a prominent bookseller and print dealer. Within a few years he was again bankrupt, but managed to pay off his creditors and recoup his losses. Settling at the foot of Wall Street, he began a newspaper in April, 1773, entitled *Rivington's New York Gazeteer*; or the *Connecticut, New Jersey, Hudson's River, and Quebec Daily Advertiser*. It was an instant success and enjoyed a wide circulation in America and the European continent. By 1775 his editorial and reportorial policies had so infuriated the Sons of Liberty in Connecticut, that his plant was burned and destroyed on two occasions. In January, 1776, he returned to England, purchased new printing equipment and machinery, and returned to America. He was appointed King's Printer to New York, and resumed publication in

October 1777, promoting the Loyalist cause. After the British evacuation of New York in November, 1783, he was allowed to remain in the city, forced to apologize, and required to suspend publication. He also was given a severe beating by a man whom he had harmed by his practices. Eventually he ended in debtor's prison and finally died in poverty. G.W.P. Custis, in his *Memoirs*, states that Rivington, being privy to Sr. Henry Cinton's inner circle, garnered much intelligence information which was passed on to GW's New York and Long Island spies. These notes were not Custis's, but were inserted by B. J. Lossing, who gives additional details in his *Field Book of the Revolution*, 2:590-91. The same details are given by Pennypacker in his, *General Washington's Spies*, New York, 1939, p. 5-8, 12-13, It is barely possible Rivington may have been the double agent of the Revolution. He had great polish, a magnificent dresser, and connoisseur of fine wines.

11. *Letters from General Washington to Several of His Friends in June and July, 1776,* Philadelphia, 1795. In the possession of the editor, ViWF.

12. *Epistles Domestic, Confidential, and Official, from General Washington, Written About the Commencement of the American Contest, When He Entered on the Command of the Army of the United States*, New York, Printed by G. Robinson, J. Bull, and sold by James Rivington, New York, 1796. Copy in the possession of the editor, ViWF.

13. The first seven letters are from the 1777 edition. Many of the latter letters are genuine.

14. Dr. William Gordon (1728-1807) was born in England. He became a dissenting clergyman, supported the colonies in their pre-revolutionary struggles with the Crown, and emigrated to America in 1770. Gordon soon became an ordained Congregational minister in Roxbury, Massachusetts, and was named chaplain of the Massachusetts Provincial Congress. He was the author of *The History of the Rise, Progress, and Establishment of the Independence of the United States of America*, published in 1788. His work was not well received in England or the United States, neither place being ready for the truths as he viewed them. Gordon returned to his birthplace in England and died in poverty. GW to Dr. William Gordon, October 15, 1797. Fitzpatrick *Writings*, 36:49.

15. Billy Lee was GW's "val de chambre" for over thirty years. When hunting, he accompanied GW, riding ahead to flush out foxes. On surveying parties he was a chain carrier. Billy accompanied GW on his trip to the Ohio country in 1770. In 1785, while a member of a surveying party, he fell and fractured his patella, forcing GW to abandon the trip and carry Billy out on a stretcher. Again in 1788 he fractured the other patella when he fell on the steps of the Alexandria post office. Thereafter he was crippled for life and it became very difficult for him to walk. Nevertheless, he insisted on accompanying GW wherever he went. On the journey to New York in 1789, he was left in Philadelphia for treatment to his knees, and in spite of GW's insistence that he return to Mount Vernon, he was allowed to come to New York, arriving on June 15th. GW was indulgent with him, tolerant of his whims and fancies, and was kind to him on all occasions. He was an old and faithful slave and servant who had served GW the whole of the Revolution. Under the terms of GW's will he was manumitted, allowed to live at Mount Vernon for the remainder of his life if he wished, and given an annuity of $30 per year for life. In later years he became an alcoholic.

16. Benjamin Walker (1753-1818) was aide-de-camp to Baron Steuben and military secretary and aide to GW. During the Washington administration he was Naval Officer of New York. He was a member of the House of Representatives from 1801-1803. He became the New York agent for the Earl of Bute. GW to Benjamin Walker, January 12, 1797. Fitzpatrick, *Writings*, 35:363-65.

17. Timothy Pickering (1745-1829). Colonel in the Continental Army, Adjutant-general and Quartermaster-general. In the Washington administration he was Postmaster-general, Attorney-general, and Secretary of State. He was a member of Congress and a United States Senator. GW to Timothy Pickering, March 3, 1797. Fitzpatrick, *Writings*, 35:414-16.

18. See supra, n.1.

19. John Randolph (1727-1784) was the son of Sir John Randolph and brother of Peyton Randolph, President of the Continental Congress. He was Burgess for the College of William and Mary and the last King's Attorney for Virginia. He was an intimate friend of Washington and Jefferson, and a kinsman of the latter. He attempted to reconcile the differences between the Crown and the Colony. After much soul-searching, he forsook the cause of the colony

and became a Loyalist, taking his wife and two daughters to England. Following his death, his daughter brought his remains back to Virginia, where they were interred, by his express wish, in the chapel of the College of William and Mary. He was an accomplished musician, had a fine legal mind, wrote the first book on gardening in the colony, and was an excellent classical scholar.

20. Tench Tilghman (1744-1786) was military secretary to GW. He served during the Revolution, from 1775 until December 23, 1783. He was selected by GW to carry the news of the victory at Yorktown to the Continental Congress, carrying the captured British standards. Tench Tilghman to James Tilghman, Valley Forge, April 24, 1778. Ford, *Writings of Washington*, 4:134.

21. John Laurens (1754-1782) was the son of Henry Laurens (see infra). He was a Lieutenant Colonel and aide to GW. Laurens saw action at Brandywine, Germantown and Monmouth. Thereafter he saw much action in the southern campaigns. During the Yorktown campaign his party captured one of the British redoubts. He was killed at Combahee Ferry, South Carolina, in 1782.

22. Henry Laurens (1724-1792), member of the Continental Congress, and was its President in 1777. He was selected to negotiate a treaty with Holland and to arrange a loan of $10,000,000. When crossing the Atlantic he was captured by the British and his papers confiscated, in spite of his attempts to destroy them by pitching them overboard. He was incarcerated in the Tower of London for fifteen months, until exchanged for Lord Cornwallis. He was a strong supporter of GW. See, John Laurens to Henry Laurens, January 23, 1778, Ford, *Writings of Washington*, 4:181.

23. On this date MW had already been successfully innoculated a month previous. See John Parke Custis to MW, June 9, 1776, n. 1, the details of which will give the lie to the spurious letter from GW to MW.

24. William Carmichael (d. 1795) served in the diplomatic mission to France during the Revolution, serving under Arthur Lee, Silas Deane, and Benjamin Franklin. He was a member of the Continental Congress, 1778-79. He became secretary to John Jay in the latter's attempts to secure a treaty with Spain. Unsuccessful, Jay departed for America in 1782, leaving Carmichael as acting Charge'd Affairs. He was later succeeded by William Short, and died before he could return home. He spent fourteen years in the diplomatic service in Spain, ignored by his government, unpaid, and using his own financial resources to maintain himself - a capable, sincere, and largely forgotten public servant. See, Fitzpatrick, *Writings*, 35:365.

25. Pierre Eugene DuSimitriere (- 1784) was a native of Geneva, Switzerland. He was a portrait painter, designer, and naturalist. He is thought to have been born in the early part of the eighteenth century. After spending about ten years in the West Indies gathering natural history specimens, he came to Philadelphia about 1766. He was a member of the American Philosophical Society. One of his principal accomplishments was the formation of a "Cabinet of Natural History - The American Museum." On his visit to America, Chastellux stated it was "unequalled in America." It antedated Peale's Museum. It is believed Du Simitriere executed the first profile painting of GW. See, G. S. Baker, *The Engraved Portraits of Washington*, Philadelphia, 1880, p. 39-43.

Appendix V

George Washington's "Love Letter" to Martha Dandridge Custis

A letter, purported to have been written by George Washington and sent to Martha Dandridge Custis, has been included in several biographies and collected papers. The letter reads as follows:

> We have begun our march for the Ohio. A courier is starting for Williamsburg, and I embrace the opportunity to send a few words to one whose life is now inseparable from mine. Since that happy hour when we made pledges to each other, my thoughts have been continually going to you as another Self. That an All-powerful Providence may keep us both in safety is the prayer of your ever faithful & ever affectionate Friend.
>
> G. Washington
>
> 20th of July
> Mrs Martha Custis

The letter first appeared in print in Benson J. Lossing's book, *Mary and Martha, the Mother and the Wife of George Washington.*[1] Lossing stated he saw the holograph letter at Arlington House, the home of George Washington Parke Custis, about 1860.[2] The text of the letter, quoted above, was taken from Lossing's book. Lossing took it upon himself to state the letter was written from Fort Cumberland. Worthington Chauncey Ford again quoted the letter in *The Writings of George Washington.*[3] Ford did not state where he had obtained the text or whether he had examined the original document. John C. Fitzpatrick again quoted it in his *Writings of Washington.*[4] Fitzpatrick merely stated, "The text is from Ford." Douglas

Southall Freemen included the text is his monumental work, *George Washington*.[5] He was of the opinion the document was either a forgery or a heavily edited version, so altered that the text is untrustworthy. It should also be pointed out that it may have been another example of the frequent untrustworthiness of Lossing's writings. Freeman gives eight reasons for rejecting the authenticity of the letter. It is worthwhile to give his reasons in a brief form:

1. The letter bears the date but does not state from whence it was wrtten, a departure from his usual habit.

2. It lacks a salutation, an omission not usually occurring in his correspondence with ladies.

3. His first sentence, "We have begun our march for the Ohio," was not factual. At the time, he was occupied in clearing a stretch of Braddock's Road, and was fearful that the push for the Ohio would not begin.

4. The style and diction of the opening sentence is much simpler than that customarily used by him at this time.

5. At this period Washington did not use the word *courier*, but always used the term *express*.

6. At this period Washington habitually mispelled the word *opportunity*, usually spelling it *oppertunity*.

7. The complimentary close is not in the style Washington was accustomed to use.

8. To quote Freeman, "___ the letter is in a style conspicuously unlike Washington's and that it is based on the beginning of a march that had not begun and was not expected to start at an early date. Few and precious as are Washington's letters to Martha, this is not entitled to be counted among them. If ever the 'original' is brought to light, it will be substantially different from Lossing's alleged 'copy.'"[6]

The letter was again included in *The Papers of George Washington*, but has been rejected as to accuracy and/or authenticity.[7]

This editor concurs with Freeman that the letter is not authentic in its present form. However unlikely it may be that the original version may come to light, perhaps stolen during the "rape" of Arlington by Federal soldiers during their occupation of the house during the Cilvil War, it would be substantially different than the document quoted above.

1. Lossing, Benson J., *Mary and Martha, the Mother and the Wife of George Washington*, Harpers & Brothers, New York, 1886, p. 99.

2. Ibid.

3. Ford, Worthington Chauncey, *The Writings of George Washington*, G.P. Putnam, New York, 1889. v. 2, p. 53.

4. Fitzpatrict, John C., *The Writings of Washington*, Washington, D.C., 1931. v. 2, p. 242 and n.

5. Freeman, Douglas Southall, *George Washington*, Scribners, New York, 1948.

6. Freeman, v. 2, p. 405-6.

7. *The Papers of George Washington*, ed. Abbott, et al., Charlottesville, 1988, Colonial, v. 5, p. 301.

Bibliography

Abbot, *PGWC*. William W. Abbot, ed. *The Papers of George Washington, Colonial Series*. Charlottesville, University of Virginia Press, 1988.

Abbot, *PGWR*. William W. Abbot, ed. *The Papers of George Washington, Revolutionary War Series*. Charlottesville, University of Virginia Press, 1988.

Adams, *Foreign Policy*. Randolph G. Adams, *A History of the Foreign Policy of the United States*. New York, 1924.

Adams, *Sparks' Writings*. H. B. Adams, *The Life and Writings of Jared Sparks*.Cambridge, 1893.

A.R. *Annual Reports, Mount Vernon Ladies' Association of the Union*. Mount Vernon, Va.

Baker, *Engraved Portraits*. William S. Baker, *The Engraved Portraits of Washington*. Philadelphia, 1880.

Baker, *Washington After*. William S. Baker, *Washington After the Revolution*. Philadelphia, 1898.

Bill, *Morven*. A. H. Bill, *A House Called Morven*. Princeton, 1954.

Blanton, *Medicine in Virginia*. William Blanton, *Medicine in Virginia in the Eighteenth Century*. Richmond, 1931.

Boucher, *Reminiscences*. Jonathan Boucher, *Reminiscences of an American Loyalist, 1738-1789..* Boston, 1925.

Bowen, *Centennial*. Charence Winthrop Bowen, *History of the Centennial Celebration of George Washington as First President of the United States*. New York, 1892.

Brant, *Madison*. Irving Brant, *James Madison, Father of the Constitution*. Indianapolis, 1950.

Brighton, *Lear*. Ray Brighton, *The Checkered Career of Tobias Lear*. Portsmouth, 1985.

Burke's *Peerage*. London, 1976.

Butterfield, *Rush*. Lyman H. Butterfield, *The Letters of Benjamin Rush*. Princeton, 1951.

The Case of the Planters of Tobacco in Virginia. London. 1733.

Virginia Cavalcade, Virginia State Library. Richmond.

Chapelle, *American Navy*. Howard I. Chapelle, *The History of the American Sailing Navy*. New York, 1949.

The Collector. Walter R. Benjamin Autographs. New York.

Coxe, *Memoirs*. W. C. Coxe, *Memoirs of John, Duke of Marlborough*. London, 1820.

Custis, *Recollections*. George Washington Parke Custis, *Recollections and Private Memoirs of Washington*. New York, 1860.

Decatur, *Private Affairs*. Stephen Decatur, Jr., *The Private Affairs of George Washington*. Boston, 1933.

Detweiler and Meadows, *Washington's Chinaware*. Susan B. Detweiler and Christine Meadows, *George Washington's Chinaware*. New York, 1982.

Draper, *Essay*. Lyman C. Draper. *An Essay on the Autographic Collections of the Declaration of Independence and of the Constitution.* New York, 1889.

Eaton, *Index*. Dorothy Eaton, ed. *Index to the George Washington Papers.* Government Printing Office, Washington, D.C., 1964.

Eckenrode, *Revolution*. Hamilton J. Eckenrode, *The Revolution in Virginia.* Boston, 1916.

Eddis, *Letters*. William Eddis, *Letters from America, Historical and Descriptive.* London, 1892.

Fitzpatrick, *Writings*. John C. Fitzpatrick, ed., *The Writings of Washington.* 39 vols. Government Printing Office, Washington, 1931-1944.

Freeman, *Washington*. Douglas Southall Freeman, *George Washington.* 7 vols. New York, 1948-1957.

French, *Answer*. George French, *An Answer to a Scurrilous Libel.* London, 1719.

French, *History*, George French, *The History of Colonel Parke's Administration.* London, 1717.

The General Assembly of Virginia, 1619-1978. A Bi-centennial Register of Members. Richmond, 1978.

Gottschalk, *Letters*. Louis Gottschalk, *The Letters of Lafayette to Washington.* New York, 1944.

Goodwin, *Cavalier*. Maude Welder Goodwin, *The Colonial Cavalier.* Boston, 1895.

Griswold, *Republican Court*. Rufus W. Griswold, *The Republican Court, or American Society in the Days of Washington.* New York, 1856.

Hamilton, *Letters to Washington*. Stanislaus Murray Hamilton, *Letters to Washington and Accompanying Papers.* 5 vols. Cambridge, 1898.

Hamilton, *Life of Hamilton*. A. M. Hamilton, *Life of Alexander Hamilton.* New York, 1910.

Harris, *Old New Kent*. Malcolm H. Harris. *Old New Kent County, Some Accounts of the Planters, Plantations, and Places in New Kent County.* 2 vols. West Point, 1977.

Helderman, *Patron of Learning*. Leonard C. Helderman, *George Washington, Patron of Learning.* New York, 1932.

Hening, *Statutes*. William Waller Hening, ed. *The Statutues at Large: Being a Collection of all the Laws of Virginia from the First Session of the Legislature in the Year 1619.* 31 vols. New York, Philadelphia, Richmond, 1819-1823.

Henderson, *Southern Tour*. Archibald Henderson, *Washington's Southern Tour, 1791.* Boston, 1923.

Hughes, *George Washington*. Rupert Hughes, *George Washington, 3 vols. New York, 1926-1930.*

Humphreys, *David Humphreys*. Frank Landon Humphreys, *Life and Times of David Humphreys,* 2 vols. New York, 1917.

Jackson and Twohig, *Diaries*. Donald D. Jackson and Dorothy Twohig, eds. *The Diaries of George Washington,* 6 vols. University of Virginia Press, Charlottesville, 1976-1979.

James, *Forbes*. A. F. James, *The Writings of General John Forbes, Relating to His Service in North America*. Menasha, Wisc., 1938.

Jenkins, *Germantown*. Charles Francis Jenkins, *Washinigton in Germantown*. Philadelphia, 1904.

Jones, *Present State*. Hugh Jones, *The Present State of Virginia*. London, 1724.

Knollenberg, *Origins*. Bernard Knollenberg, *Origins of the American Revolution*. New York, 1960.

The Ladies Magazine and Repository of Entertaining Knowledge, 2 vols. Philadelphia, 1792, 1793.

Lear, *Letters and Recollections of George Washington, Being Letters to Tobias Lear and Others ... With a Diary of Washington's Last Days, Kept by Mr. Lear*. Bixby Collection, New York, 1906.

Ledger A. Manuscript Ledger in the George Washington Papers, Library of Congress.

Lee, *Recollections*. Robert E. ee, Jr., *Recollections and Letters of General Robert E. Lee*. New York, 1904.

Life in Letters. American Autograph Company, Merion, Pa., 1940.

Livingston, *Livingstons*. Edward Brockholst Livingston, *The Livingstons of Livingston Manor*. New York, 1910.

Lossing, *Mary and Martha*. Benson J. Lossing, *Mary and Martha, The Mother and the Wife of George Washington*. New York 1886.

Lossing, *Mount Vernon*. Benson J. Lossing, *Mount Vernon and Its Associations*. New York, 1859.

McGuire, *Religious Opinions*. E. C. McGuire, *Religious Opinions and Character of George Washington*. New York, 1836.

Marshall, *George Washington*. John Marshall, *The Life of George Washington*, 6 vols. London, 1804-1807.

Martin, *Genealogical Notices*. S. J. Martin, *Notices: Genealogical and Historical of the Martin Family of New England*. Boston, 1880

Meade, *Journals*. William Meade, *Journals of the Episcopal Diocese of Virginia*.

Meade, *Old Churches*. William Meade. *Old Churches, Ministers, and Families of Virginia*, 2 vols. Philadelphia, 1852.

Miller, *Parke of Virginia*. Helen Hill Miller, *Colonel Parke of Virginia, The Greatest Hector of the Town*. Chapel Hill, 1989.

Miller, *Origins*. John C. Miller, *Origins of the American Revolution*. Boston, 1943.

Morton, *Colonial Virginia*. Richard L. Morton, *Colonial Virginia*, 2 vols. Chapel Hill, 1960.

O.E.D. *Compact Edition of the Oxford English Dictionary*. Oxford University Press. 1971.

The Papers of Thomas Jefferson, Julian P. Boyd, ed. Princeton University Press, Princeton, N.J., 1950

PMHB. *The Pennsylvania Magazine of History and Biography*, Pennsylvania Historical Society, Philadelphia.

Powel, *Jacks*. J. H. Powel, *General Washington and the Jack Ass*. South Brunswick, N.J., 1969.

Prussing, *Estate*. Eugene E. Prussing, *The Estate of George Washington, Deceased*. Boston, 1927.

Ramsay, *Life*. David Ramsay, *The Life of George Washington*. New York, 1807.

R. M. Roche, *The Children of the Abbey, A Tale*. New York, 1798.

Rosenbach, *Documents*. *The History of America in Documents*, Part Two. The Rosenbach Company, Philadelphia and New York, 1950.

Selby, *Revolution in Virginia*. John Selby, *The Revolution in Virginia*. Williamsburg, 1988.

Sinclair, *Letters*. Sir John Sinclair, *Letters from His Excellency George Washington, President of the United States of America, to Sir John Sinclair*. London, 1800.

Skeel, *Weems*. E. E. F. Skeel, *Mason Locke Weems, His Works, and Ways*, 3 vols. New York, 1929.

Sparks, *Writings of Washington*. Jared Sparks, *The Writings of Washington*, 12 vols. Boston, 1837.

Speaight, *Circus*. George Spaeight, *A History of the Circus*. London, 1980.

Stetson, *Neighbors*. Charles W. Stetson, *Washington and His Neighbors*. Richmond, 1956.

Stevens and Kent, *Papers*. *The Papers of Col. Henry Bouquest*, 25 vols., Sylvester K. Stevens and Donald H. Kent, eds. Pennsylvania Historical Commission, Harrisburg, 1940-43.

Swem, *Brothers*. Earl Gregg Swem, *Brothers of the Spade: The Correspondence of Peter Collinson of London, and of John Custis, of Williamsburg, Virginia, 1734-1746*. Barrie, 1957.

Thacher, *Journal*. James Thacher, *Military Journal of the American Revolution. From the Commencement to the Disbanding of the American Army*. Hartford, 1862.

Tinling, *Byrd*. Marian Tinling, ed. *The Correspondence of the Three William Byrds of Westover, Virginia, 1684-1776*, 2 vols. Charlottesville, 1977. *Virginia Historical Register*, 6 vols. Richmond, 1848.

VMHB. The Virginia Magazine of History and Biography. Virginia Historical Society. Richmond.

Washington, *Journal*. George Washington, *The Journal of Major George Washington*. Williamsburg, 1754.

Weems, *Life*. Mason Locke Weems, *The Life of Washington*, Marcus Cunliffe, ed. Cambridge, 1962.

Wharton, *Martha Washington*. Anne Hollingswroth Wharton, *Martha Washington*. New York, 1897.

W. The William and Mary Quarterly. Institute of Early American History and Culture. Williamsburg, Va. For example, 18 W (2) 122, indicates vol. 18, 2nd series, followed by the page, 122.

Wilson, *Washington*. Woodrow Wilson, *George Washington*. New York, 1896.

Young, *Morris*. Elenor Young, *Forgotten Patriot: Robert Morris*. New York, 1950.

Index

Q

About the Compiler

JOSEPH E. FIELDS is an independent researcher and the author of several articles.